# creative
# after effects 5.0

animation, visual effects and motion graphics production for TV and video

**angie taylor**

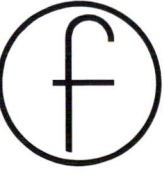

## Focal Press

OXFORD • AUCKLAND • BOSTON • JOHANNESBURG • MELBOURNE • NEW DELHI

Focal Press
An imprint of Butterworth-Heinemann
Linacre House, Jordan Hill, Oxford OX2 8DP
225 Wildwood Avenue, Woburn, MA 01801-2041
A division of Reed Educational and Professional Publishing Ltd

A member of the Reed Elsevier plc group

First published 2001
Reprinted 2001

British Library Cataloguing in Publication Data
A catalogue record for this book is available from the British Library

Library of Congress Cataloguing in Publication Data
A catalogue record for this book is available from the Library of Congress

ISBN 0 240 51622 2

Cover design by Kate Isles. Photography by Angie Taylor

Printed and bound in Italy

For more information on all Focal Press publications please visit our
web site at www.focalpress.com

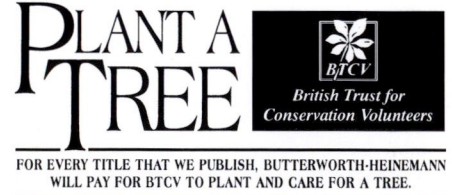

FOR EVERY TITLE THAT WE PUBLISH, BUTTERWORTH-HEINEMANN
WILL PAY FOR BTCV TO PLANT AND CARE FOR A TREE.

# contents

Creative After Effects

# chapter nine – time

# chapter ten – keying

# chapter eleven – effects

# chapter twelve – tracking

# chapter thirteen – parenting

# chapter fourteen – expressions

# chapter fifteen – 3D

# chapter sixteen – type

# Index

To Mum and Dad for all their love and encouragement
and to my brothers and sisters for being there.

To my dogs, Monkey and Stanley for reminding
me that there's more to life than work.

But most of all to Jo, my soulmate, without whose
love and patience this book would never exist.

# acknowledgments

There are so many people that I would like to thank for their help and support in the writing of this book. Big thanks to everyone who knows me for your support and understanding whilst I've been locked in my room, slumped over my desk, grumpily answering phone calls.

To all my clients for understanding my lack of availability over the last year and hopefully for remembering me when I return to full freelancing duties!

I'd like to say a massive thank you to the following peoplewho have helped me with the book;

Marie Hooper and the team at Focal Press for having faith in me
Paul Tuersley for being Mr Fussy and for being a great contributor
Maia Sanders for working extremely hard to get the 3D chapter finished
Fred Lewis for making Parenting seem so easy
Marco Tillman for his 3D wizardry, and the rest of the team at Maxon
The whole After Effects team, nice one guys!
Silke Galloway: my star technical tester who worked really hard
Birgitta Hosea for covering my surplus work whilst I was busy typing!
Carys Edwards at BBC Scotland for her faith in me

The following Adobe (and ex-Adobe) staff, especially:

Steve Kilisky, Erica Schisler, Dave Trescott, Lincoln Lopez, Mark Cokes, Mark Harrison, Rory Duncan, Eve Hatton, Jayne Birch, Stephen Inoue, Alan Hammil, Amacker Bullwinkle, Bruce Bowman, Bruce Bullis and Eric Sanders.

Dave Cockle, Donald Kaye, Simon Harper and Stuart Harris at Apple

Nick Smith and Declan Bemingham at Sony

Julie Hill and the rest of the team at Artbeats Inc.

Kate Isles for all her hard work on the cover and layout

Everyone at:

ICE/Media 100, Artel, Forge Technology, Digieffects, The Foundry, Atomic Power, Cycore, Digital Anarchy, The Toolfarm, Synthetic Aperture, Pinnacle/Puffin, Synthetik Software Inc, Alias Wavefront, Zaxwerks, Maxon, Extensis, Viewercom, Nova Development Ltd, Photodisc/Getty Images, Wacom, AS Music, CLT Multimedia, Groove Tunnel, Crank City Music, Partners in Rhyme, Future Fonts, George Cathro.

Brian Maffit and the guys at Total Training for endlessly inspiring me

Trish and Chris Meyer for their vast amount of generous knowledge

My two best friends, Paul Halliday and Sally Cheyne

and especially to anyone who I have forgotten to mention in my rush to get this off to the publishers, my deepest apologies. I owe you a pint!

# a brief
# **introduction**

I decided to write this book after being persuaded to do so by some of my contemporaries. I have spent the last four years getting to know After Effects; using it for my own creative work as an animator and motion graphics designer for television and new media. I have also been a regular demo artist for Adobe, demonstrating After Effects to delegates at trade shows, exhibitions, press events and seminars around the world.

I have used loads of software applications in my time but none of them compare, in terms of usability, to the creative flexibility and sheer depth of Adobe's After Effects. Originally created by CoSA (The Company of Science and Art) in 1992, it was originally designed as a special effects software program, but it has evolved into so much more than that, as you will discover in the following pages.

Members of the original team are still involved with the program, which is now part of the Adobe stable of top-quality, dynamic media products, ensuring that After Effects remains the leader in desktop Compositing, animation and effects.

Rory Duncan, who was then the European Product Manager of After Effects, introduced me to After Effects in 1995. I was already a keen user of Photoshop, Adobe's industry leading image manipulation tool, and I had an interest in animation and visual effects, stemming from my days as a prop-maker and cartoonist. After Effects was just like Photoshop with wheels! Anything I could do in Photoshop could now be animated over time in After Effects – and more besides.

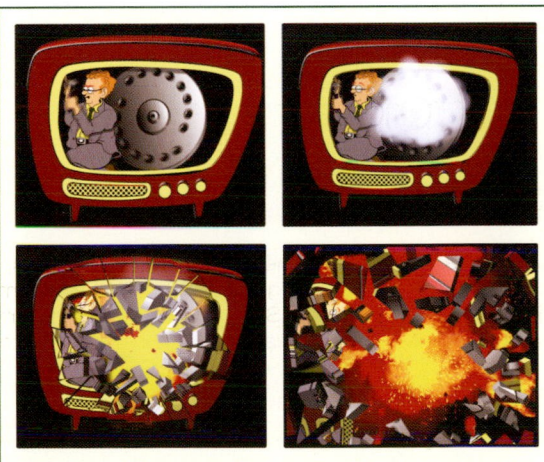

**Still from 'See you, See me – The Inventors', BBC, 1999. Animated Illustrator layers with FE Particles and Evolution Shatter effects.**

In all my years as a designer and demo artist, I don't think there's ever been a time when After Effects has not been able to achieve what has been required of it. Adobe's motto used to be 'If you can dream it, you can do it', with After Effects there should be the adage, 'If you can't do it, you can fake it'. I've seen work which I could have sworn was created in a 3D application but was completely faked using only two dimensions, within After Effects. With the introduction of true 3D compositing in version 5.0, you no longer have to fake it; these days After Effects has no trouble working in both 2D and 3D.

One of After Effects' greatest assets is its support of third-party plug-ins. While After Effects is quite capable of handling most post production tasks, there are a wide range of additional plug-in effects available which integrate seamlessly with the main application. This further extends its already bulging toolbox, providing you with enormous creative flexibility. There are some free filters from some of these plug-in sets on the CD, in the Free Stuff folder, these have been kindly gifted to you by the plug-in companies themselves. There are also demo versions of some of my favorite third party plug-ins in the Demos folder.

After Effects' animation tools are second to none and it remains the tool of choice for compositors, animators and visual effects designers across the creative media industry. It is widely used in television, video production, web broadcast and new media as well as in the film industry. If you've been to see Hollywood movies over the last five years then you're almost guaranteed to have seen special effects created using After Effects.

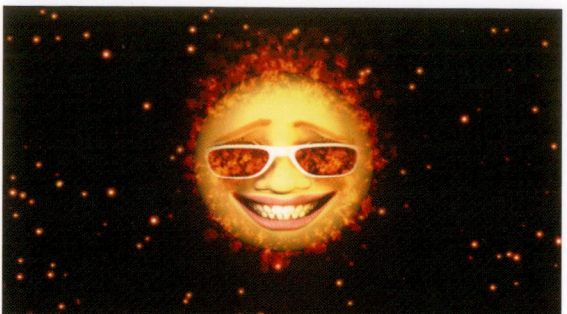

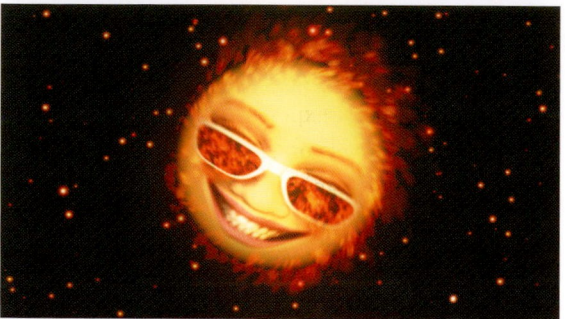

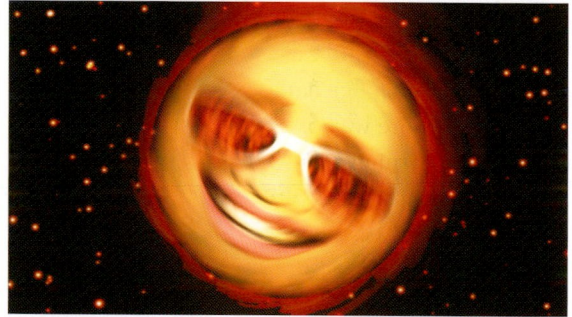

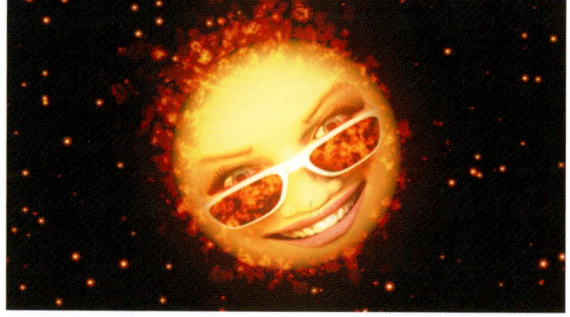

**Animations from 'See, you, See me – The Planets', BBC, 2000. Poser animations were composited onto dancing 2D planets. Stars courtesy of Digieffects Berserk Starfield.**

The After Effects animation system is based upon Keyframes, which you will find out more about later. Included in the software are: Keyframe Assistants to help with every day, repetitive animation tasks; Expressions and Parenting for creating Complex hierarchies and a powerful, yet simple to use, Scripting interface called Motion Math for reproducing complex animations based on real world physics.

After Effects has so much to offer; I have yet to meet anyone who knows the whole application inside out. The most experienced users are still discovering new ways of using the tools; and even the people who designed the software have come to realize that it can do things it was never designed to do in the first place. To me, this is one of the joys of working with After Effects.

In my younger days I wasn't really interested in subjects I felt I couldn't master 100%, learning seemed too much like hard work to me. As I have matured (a polite way of putting it!) I have found pleasure in learning and I can look forward to finding new techniques each time I delve into the application – which can also be a great inspiration for my work.

As time goes by and as web broadcast becomes more popular, I reckon that the television and internet industries will become merged, all being accessible from your domestic TV set. The bandwidth for information will increase until we will all be essentially designing for television. As this happens, more and more designers will be required to know about the laws of TV design.

I would never claim to know absolutely everything about After Effects but I do feel, however, that I have, through working as an animator, designer, demo artist and trainer in After Effects, learned plenty about After Effects to feel qualified to help you understand the software more clearly. I have a background in fine art which I think helps me to experiment with the software in a creative way and this is what I hope to pass on to you in the pages of this book.

I'll warn you now that my methods of using the software are not always the most conventional; I have been told on many occasions that there is madness in my method! I tend to experiment a lot with the software which means I get the job done and also have the added benefit of stumbling over unique ways of achieving certain looks. In my opinion there is no *correct way* or *incorrect way* of achieving your design goals, as long as you do achieve them. This book will give the reader a good understanding of not only how to use the software, but how to use it creatively.

There are a couple of new features in After Effects 5.0 that I am relatively new to myself and am learning more about all the time. As I mentioned earlier, learning is an ongoing experience so I've enlisted the help of three contributors who have helped out in certain areas, simply to ensure that you are getting the best advice possible on these subjects. Please read the following biographies as these give you important information about which chapters they have contributed to. They will also tell you about the wide range of experience that they have to share with you. As well as learning my methods and philosophies, I thought it would be useful for you to also hear from others who use After Effects on a day-to-day basis.

OK, I'll start by telling you a bit about myself. I studied Fine Art at Edinburgh College of Art and left there with an honors degree in Sculpture and Drawing in 1986. I had spells working as a prop-maker, deejay and cartoonist as well as studying music technology and graphic design before buying my first Mac and setting up my own business in 1996. My work involves producing animation and graphics for television and video. Examples of my work can be regularly seen, broadcast on the BBC and Channel 4 in the UK and across Europe. As well as being a regular After Effects demo artist for Adobe Europe, I also provide one-to-one training in After Effects for individuals and companies all over Europe, including some of the top designers at the BBC.

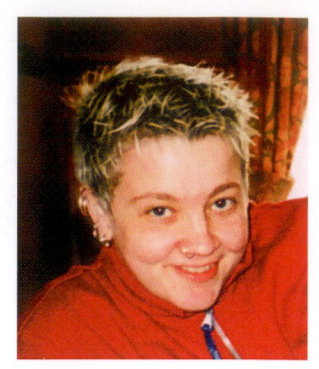

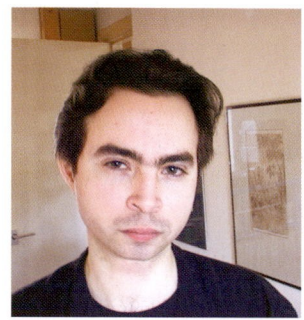

Paul Tuersley is a freelance designer/animator based in London, UK. Graduating from Ravensbourne College of Design & Communication in 1994, he has worked almost exclusively with After Effects since that time. His work includes idents for Carlton and UK Gold, titles for *The South Bank Show* and most recently, the graphics for the documentary *Wingspan*. Paul has contributed greatly to the Expressions and Technical chapters as well as single-handedly producing the fantastic 3D City in the MacDonna project (part of the the 3D chapter). He has also contributed to some of the great little tips, tricks, tutorials and general After Effects jiggery-pokery in the Extras folder on the CD.

Maia Sanders has a MFA in Computer Animation from the Academy of Art College in San Francisco, California, and a BFA in Photography and Painting from Cornish College of the Arts in Seattle, Washington. She is also a member of the Guild of Natural Science Illustrators and is now based in San Jose, California. Maia's influences cross many disciplines: architecture, clothing design, sculpture, cinematography, and social and natural history. Her favorite artistic activity is creating the 'look and feel' of an entire world, designing the ecosystem and social structure of its inhabitants. Maia has written the majority of the 3D chapter and has given great insight into how 3D animators can make use of the new 3D compositing features and filters in After Effects.

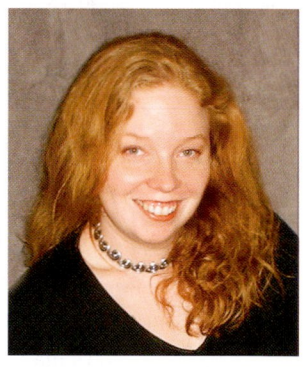

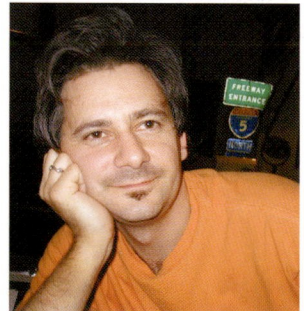

Fred Lewis has been designing and creating animation with or without a computer since the early 1980s. Fred and his wife Thalia Georgopoulos are co-owners of a computer animation company in San Francisco called Moving Media, where, since 1989, they've been designing and creating 2D and 3D computer animations for broadcast, games, interactive presentations, and the web. Fred has a film animation degree from San Francisco State University and also has a variety of experience in related industries. Fred is responsible for the entire Parenting chapter, with the exception of the Graffiti Club tutorials. I invited him to contribute to the chapter after reading his excellent explanations on parenting on various mailing lists.

# chapter one
# mission

## how to use the book

This book is designed as a complete, linear course in After Effects and is intended to benefit people of all abilities, from beginner to advanced. Starting with the basics, it will also cover some fairly advanced techniques. I have found, whilst teaching my advanced After Effects course, that even the most experienced users have skipped learning some of the essential basic functions of the software. Because of this, I recommend that the book be followed from cover to cover by everyone reading it to ensure that nothing is overlooked. You never know; you may stumble upon an easier way of approaching that complicated job! I hope that after reading this book and following the projects within, beginners will build up confidence to go out into the real world and use After Effects on their own. Advanced users may pick up ideas in areas of the program they have never used before.

Everyone approaches After Effects from a different angle. You may not necessarily need to learn the whole application inside out, a small percentage of what's available may be enough for your needs. On the other hand, you may be like me and have an interest in learning about the whole caboodle. Either way you will benefit from seeing the book through from beginning to end.

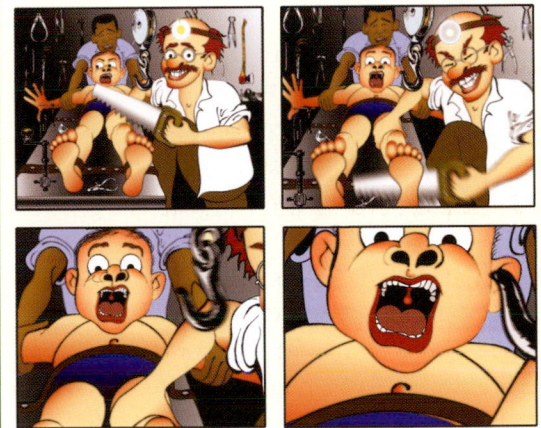

Stills from 'See you, See me – The Inventors', BBC, 1999. Featuring clip-art medical instruments from Art Explosion!

My aim has been to write the book in a free flowing style, using plain and simple English to explain concepts wherever possible. The book has been designed as a project-based course book rather than as a reference book. Each chapter has accompanying tutorials, you'll also work on your own continuing project which you can add to throughout the book. Followed from start to finish, the book provides a comprehensive course in Adobe After Effects 5.0, providing you with a clear understanding of how After Effects works, and with the confidence to explore it in more depth for yourself.

It is important that you keep in mind that this book should be looked upon as your starting point for learning After Effects. It has been designed to give you a good, solid understanding of how to be creative with the software. In these pages I hope to give you the confidence and awareness needed to encourage you to learn more for yourself, developing your own style whilst going through the chapters. There is a bibliography on the accompanying website (http://www.angie.abel.co.uk/book.html) which will provide you with further information. It is worth resourcing these books after finishing this one, as they contain added information about topics covered in this book and, in many cases, go into greater detail about some subjects than I have had space to do here.

Coming from an art college background, I realize how little time students have to prepare original work for degree shows. As a freelance designer I am also aware of the pressure of deadlines. Therefore I have constructed the book in such a way that, if followed from beginning to end, you will complete the course with an original, finished piece of artwork which you can then use as part of your Degree Show or portfolio.

You will start by deciding on a task, creating either a music video or the opening titles for a TV show. Video, audio and still footage is provided on the CD for the purposes of these exercises; you can select which footage you wish to use. You can also bring in your own footage.

After each chapter, you will be expected to take what you have learned and put it into practice on your own experimental projects. After you have finished the book you'll decide which techniques you wish to use on your own personal design project and combine the techniques you have developed throughout the learning process into something original and exciting.

The book has been structured as much as possible to echo the way one would work through a real life project, not only showing you how to use the individual features but also how to combine them to good effect.

Try not to think too hard about your final project, the key to becoming a good artist is to let yourself go and work instinctively; think confident! Your own life experience is a very important part of learning about creativity and design and should not be neglected. It is too easy to put your own life on the back burner by working very long hours in front of a computer; this is *not* good for you, you need to experience life to achieve inspiration.

You may feel inspired by the colors of a landscape in a particular light; by the deep bass line of a song you heard in a nightclub; or from a piece of art you saw in a gallery. It really doesn't matter where it comes from. Remember that everything you see in the world of art and design is derivative in some way. Whether it be inspired by nature, or design, no matter, the talent is in creating something unique which appeals to the human eye. A unique piece of work can still include references to other designs without necessarily copying those designs.

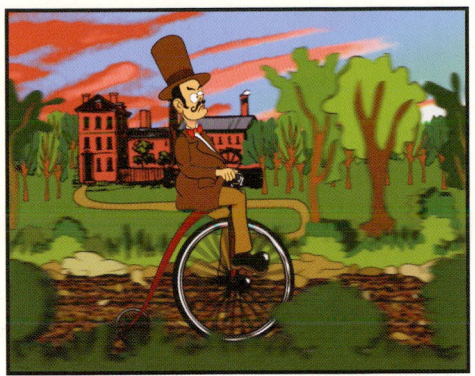

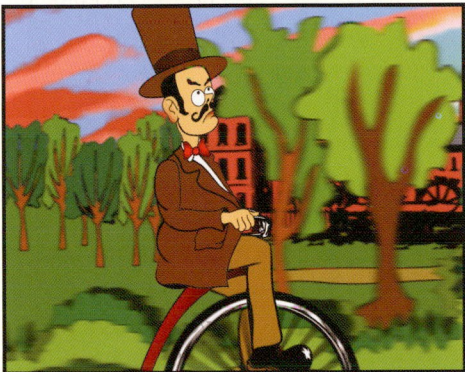

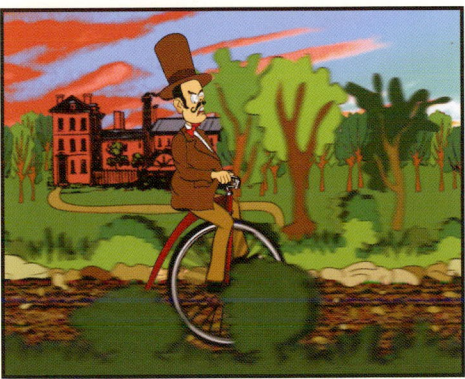

**Animations from 'See, you, See me –
'The Inventors', BBC, 1999. The characters were sketched on paper and then
traced, using a Wacom tablet, into
Illustrator layers. These were than
animated in After Effects using cut out
animation techniques.**

So whilst you read this book and work your way
through the exercises, try not to feel like you are
climbing a mountain, only focusing on reaching the
top. Try to find pleasure in the journey, concentrate
on what's around you and enjoy the scenery, this
way you'll achieve your goals much quicker and
you may stumble upon ways of working that
nobody else has.

As any good designer knows, you have to design
around the limitations of your medium. Television
is no different, there are rules of design, technical
specifications, limitations and techniques that, in
my opinion, it is vital for designers to become
familiar with before embarking on a career in TV
design. We will discuss some of these rules within
the pages of the book. We will also cover some
typography rules, animation rules, color and
composition theories which are equally important
to be aware of as a good designer. You need to learn
the rules first in order to have fun breaking them,
otherwise you won't even realize you're doing it!

There is a technical chapter on the CD, in the
Extras folder (Technical.pdf). This document
contains lots of information on subjects ranging
from pixel aspect ratios and interlacing issues, to
Layer Modes and alpha channels. I recommend
that you read this document to familiarize yourself
with all the things that you need to be aware of
when designing for television.

There will be aspects of the software which are
not covered by this book (it would be virtually
impossible to fit everything in). There are areas
which I would have loved to devote more time and
space to but I have endeavored to cover the areas
which I feel are most important to achieve a good
working knowledge of the application. I have also
avoided covering subjects which are explained
clearly elsewhere and will point you in the right
direction to find these other resources.

Several people have asked me, 'How have you learned so much about After Effects?' Well, like many others, I started by reading the manual (a shock I know!). The After Effects manual is a great resource for anyone learning the application. I don't quite understand why more people don't use it. It is well written, easy to understand and explains all core concepts of the program.

There is also an excellent online help system, which is included in the After Effects installation. This is available from the Help menu and is often more helpful than the manual. If you are unsure about anything whilst working in After Effects, just go to Help > After Effects Help. This will open up the Help system in your web browser, where you can then choose from a list of *Contents*, an *Index* or a great *Search* engine to find the information you need. After Effects will find an answer to your query, it even has illustrations to aid your understanding. This online help system is constantly updated by the After Effects team, providing you with the latest tips and techniques.

There is also a website supporting this book at:

http://www.angie.abel.co.uk/book.html

where you can find out more information and links to other useful resources such as magazines; websites; books; training tapes; software and hardware companies; royalty-free footage companies etc.

It also has lists of recommended hardware and software companies, with links to the suppliers. There are also links to user groups where you can swap tips and tricks and discuss problems with other After Effects users, including some of the most experienced in the industry. The website will also feature any new tutorials, revisions and updates.

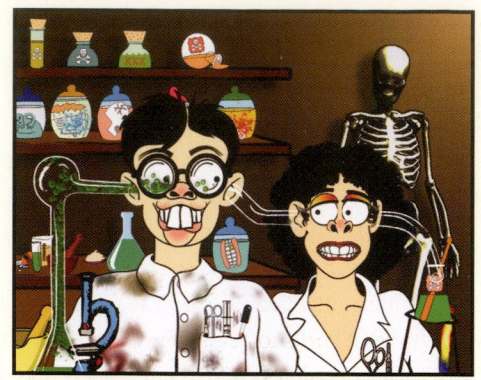

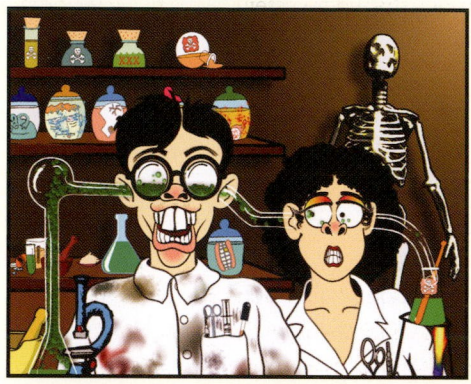

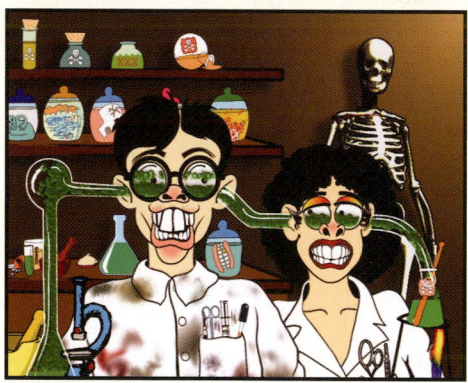

**Animations from 'See, you, See me – The Inventors', BBC, 1999. The flame on the Bunsen burner was created using some royalty-free footage of a blow torch, courtesy of Artbeats Inc. The bubbles inside the test tubes were created using Evolution's Foam.**

# technical specifications

Experience working with desktop computers and a good understanding of your operating system is essential as a prerequisite for using the exercises in this book. It would also help if you have some experience in other graphics or animation packages, although this is not essential. I use an Apple Macintosh Computer for most of my work. I also use a Windows system occasionally. The Mac and Windows versions of After Effects are almost identical. The only real differences are with the keyboard shortcuts. The OpenMeFirst.txt on the CD gives detailed system requirements, please make sure that your system meets these requirements.

I will give the Mac keyboard shortcuts throughout the book, and would just ask that Windows users substitute the Mac's *Command* key with their *Control* key. The *Alt* key is the same on both systems but is also known as the *Option* key to some Mac users. I'll use the term *Alt* as it is common to both platforms. Context-clicking can be done using the *Right Mouse button* on Windows or by *Control-clicking* if you are using a Mac. I am based in Europe and therefore use the PAL broadcast system, I will, where appropriate, include specifications for NTSC.

While it's quite possible to create footage from scratch within After Effects, your work will benefit from a good grounding in Adobe's Photoshop and Illustrator. These two applications complement After Effects superbly and are designed to work seamlessly together. It is also useful to have basic knowledge of an editing program such as Adobe Premiere 6 or Apple Final Cut Pro 2 for capturing and editing footage and printing your movies back to tape. If you don't have access to these applications, you can download demo versions of the Adobe products from the Adobe website (www.adobe.com). These versions are save-disabled but will allow you to follow the exercises provided on the CD. Saved versions of the files used in these exercises will be on the CD for those using the demo versions but I would thoroughly recommend investing in the full versions of these products wherever possible.

There are two versions of After Effects available, the Standard Version and the Production Bundle version. Most of the designers working in TV design use the Production Bundle version. It has high end features and effects which are aimed at broadcast professionals. Some of the exercises in this book cover Production Bundle features but Standard Version users should still be able to follow most of the exercises. Wherever possible, two methods of obtaining the same result will be provided. The tryout version of Adobe After Effects 5.0, provided on the CD is the Standard Version.

Unless you have just installed After Effects fresh from the CD, you will need to reset your preferences file to its default settings. To do this, you simply remove the file and put it in a safe place so that you can replace it after finishing the course. If at any time during the course you wish to restore your original preferences, please make sure that you save a copy of the tutorial preferences file before replacing it. You can then restore them before continuing with the exercises. I have listed below, the locations of the preference files for both Mac and Windows:

If you're running Mac OS 9.1 or earlier versions of the Mac OS, you'll find your *Adobe After Effects 5 Prefs* file in; Macintosh HD > System > Preferences folder.

If you are a Windows user, your Preference file is called *Adobe After Effects 5 Prefs.txt*, and is in the following folders:

Windows 2000
Documents and Settings > [user name] > Application Data > Adobe > After Effects > Prefs

Windows 98 or Millennium Edition (Me)
Windows > Application Data > Adobe > After Effects > Prefs

Windows NT
Winnt > Profiles > [user name] > Application Data > Adobe > After Effects > Prefs

Before moving on I would like you to copy the *Training* folder from the CD on to your hard drive. All the files you will need for the tutorials and projects are in this folder and must be copied to the hard drive before proceeding. Please don't try to use the files directly from the CD as this will impair the performance of the exercises.

You will also need to create a new folder on your hard drive for saving all of your movies and projects into. Please name this folder, *Creative After Effects* and, inside it, create another folder for each chapter title of the book (e.g. 'Animation Chapter', 'Time Chapter' etc.), this will make it much easier to manage your files.

You'll be instructed to save your projects at appropriate points throughout the book, backup versions of the saved projects are on the CD, should you run into difficulty at any point, you'll be asked to open these at the beginning of each new section to ensure that your settings are correct. If at any time during a tutorial, you want to take a break and return to the exercise later, simply save a copy of the current project into your Creative After Effects folder. When you return, you can then pick the project up from where you left off.

Most of the exercises in the book are designed at a much smaller size than they would be for television; this is mainly due to the limited space available on the CD. Reducing the physical size of the source movies allows me to fit more goodies on to the CD for you. The equipment which readers will be using will have varying degrees of sophistication, so I also wanted to make sure that the exercises run smoothly, even on older machines.

These movies are in QuickTime format so you will need to have QuickTime (version 4.1.2 recommended) installed on your system. If you do not have QuickTime installed you can download it from the Apple website at: (http://www.apple.com). Please check out the OpenMeFirst.txt document (on the CD) for further software requirements and installation instructions.

## your task

To begin, I would like you to look through the footage catalogue provided. There are loads of files in the catalogue, courtesy of Artbeats Inc.; Novacorp International; Photodisc; Partners in Rhyme; Groove Tunnel; AS Music; CLT Multimedia and Hand Pict. There are individual folders for each of these companies in both the Free Stuff and Source Images, Sounds and Movies folders. These folders contain information about the companies as well as the clips themselves. The files include QuickTime movies, Picts, Photoshop files, Illustrator files, Sound Effects, Music etc. I have endeavoured to obtain most of the source footage included from a diverse range of footage companies. I did this for the following reasons:

I like to support independent, creative companies like Artbeats who are one of the few footage companies who have remained completely independent, smaller companies tend to be much more accommodating to freelance designers like myself. Some of the files on the CD have been created by freelancers, just like you and me. It is good to support your fellow artists. Having said all of that, the bigger companies tend to own a lot of the classic images and movies and have vast databases of images for you to choose from, they're bound to have something you like. So there are pros and cons when dealing with both large and small companies, shop around and try out lots of different options.

I have included a demo copy of the Portfolio Browser on the CD (in the Software Demos folder), courtesy of Extensis. This is my media browser of choice; it's basically a media database program which allows you to quickly search through previews of image files, movies and sounds without having to open them all up individually. I thoroughly recommend that you install this software immediately. There are Windows and Mac versions of the browser inside the Portfolio folder.

Portfolio is very easy to install, it is also very easy to use. However, if you do have any problems installing or using the software, there are help files along with the software which are there to guide you. Once you have installed Portfolio, double-click on the file named Media.fdb in the Training folder to open the ready-made catalogue. This will allow you to quickly choose the footage you would like to work with.

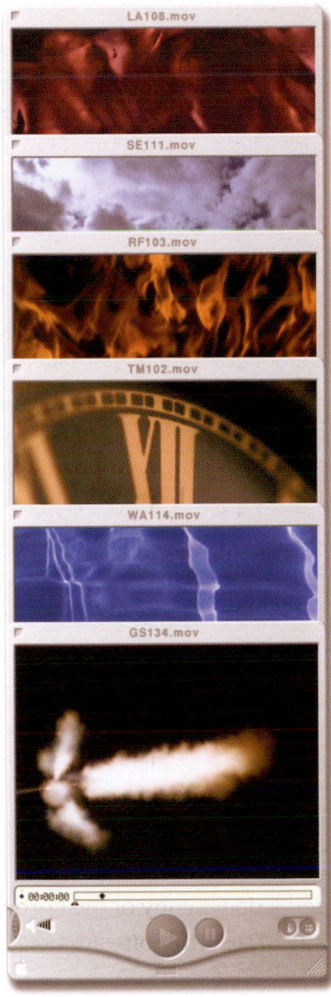

Look and listen for images, movies or sounds that inspire you, they may spark off ideas in your head or you may simply like the look or sound of them.

Your mission is to create one finished movie, using the techniques you have learned whilst working your way through the book. This movie can either be a music video or the opening titles for a TV show. I thought I would give you a choice here, I know this doesn't usually happen in real life situations but I want to give you a little bit more scope for experimentation.

I thought to myself whilst planning the structure of this book, 'Well, I can't ask the readers to do anything I wouldn't be prepared to do myself!' So I have created three examples for you. These are:

- Seattle Evening News – Titles for a news program
- The Graffiti Club – Titles for a kids' program
- The MacDonna video – Pop promo

If you like, you can view these finished movies before we move ahead. There is another Portfolio Browser catalogue file in the Training folder named; ProjMovies.fdb. Double-click this to view the movies which I will be showing you how to build.

In the CD > Extras folder there's an Adobe Acrobat file named 05Elements.pdf. This document has an accompanying project and footage files. This is the start of the opening titles for an Arts program, 'Pop Art: Music & Art of the 1960s'. This project and the others included in the Extras folder are intended to be followed *after* completing the book. I'll be developing this project on the website (http://www.angie.abel.co.uk) so that you can follow its progress.

There is one thing that sets this book apart from others in the same genre. This is the fact that I have broken these projects down into individual tutorials so that I can teach you how to use and combine the techniques to create a finished piece of work. There are a few exceptions to this rule where it was necessary to jump out from the project in order to give a clearer understanding, but most of the exercises in this book are based around these projects.

Once you have decided which project you will be following, get a sketchbook and start to jot down some ideas. Think about the titles and concepts for the show, and the ideas/feelings you need to communicate to the audience. At the end of each chapter, I want you to continue to sketch out ideas, you should also keep a notebook and pen by your side at all times for jotting down ideas and for the odd bit of doodling. It's important to record all of your ideas, even if you don't want to use them right now. You can quickly store up a whole load of ideas for future reference, you never know, what may have seemed like a bad idea six months ago could be developed into something quite brilliant today.

Your ideas may change throughout the course of the book, this is a good thing so don't worry too much about it. It's always a good idea to keep your sketchbook close by, jotting down ideas and sketching layouts as you work; this is generally a lot faster than working things out on the computer. In my flat/studio I have a few sketchbooks and pens dotted around, ensuring that one is always nearby. I even have one next to my bed and another in the loo! You never know when inspiration will hit you! I usually get great ideas in the middle of the night, scribble them down and then wake up in the morning thinking, 'what on earth does that mean?', but don't worry, it usually comes back to me after my morning tea.

We will be working slightly differently from a real life work situation in the way that we will be including techniques learnt within the chapters as we go along. Because of this, you don't want to be too rigid with your ideas, work out lots of rough concepts after each chapter before settling on your final idea at the end of the book.

It is very important not to be too ambitious with your ideas to begin with. Many people who are new users with After Effects see adverts on TV which include special effects and animation that has taken teams of people months to create. Remember, complicated doesn't necessarily mean good. Some of the best designs I've seen are the most simple. You know the ones I mean, where you think 'why didn't I think of that?' Start with well executed, simple ideas, this will also allow you to be more flexible with your projects as they develop.

If you are finding it difficult to come up with any ideas, don't worry, we all have that problem and you are no different. When this happens I usually go off and do something completely different: take my dogs for a walk, go to a gallery or the library, watch some television, listen to music, surf the net, go down the pub (my personal favorite!). You won't achieve anything except lower back pain and eye strain by staring at a blank screen or page (I'm speaking from experience here) so go and inspire yourself by taking your mind off it, even if only for an hour or so.

Perhaps getting to work within After Effects will get your creative juices flowing so let's get right in there and learn the basics, after that, there'll be no stopping you, I can assure you!

# chapter two
# basics

I'd like to start by explaining the User Interface of
After Effects. Several people have said to me,
'I opened up After Effects once, pressed a few
buttons but I couldn't get it to do anything!' This is
a common reaction from people who have never
used a desktop compositing program before.

## the project window

The first time you open After Effects you will be
greeted with an empty Project window named
Project Untitled.aep and a couple of floating
palettes – not the most inspiring start I'll grant
you. Every After Effect movie or animation starts
as a project, you can only open one project at a
time but into this project you can import as many
files as is possible on your system.

The Project window acts as a 'Bin' or folder where
you import and store references to all of your
source files on the hard disk. These source files
can be still images, movies, sound files, image
sequences and even files containing 3D
environment information. You can also import
Photoshop, Illustrator and Premiere files as ready-
made compositions, keeping all their layer
information intact. You can also import other After
Effects projects into your current Project window.
We will have a look at these options later.

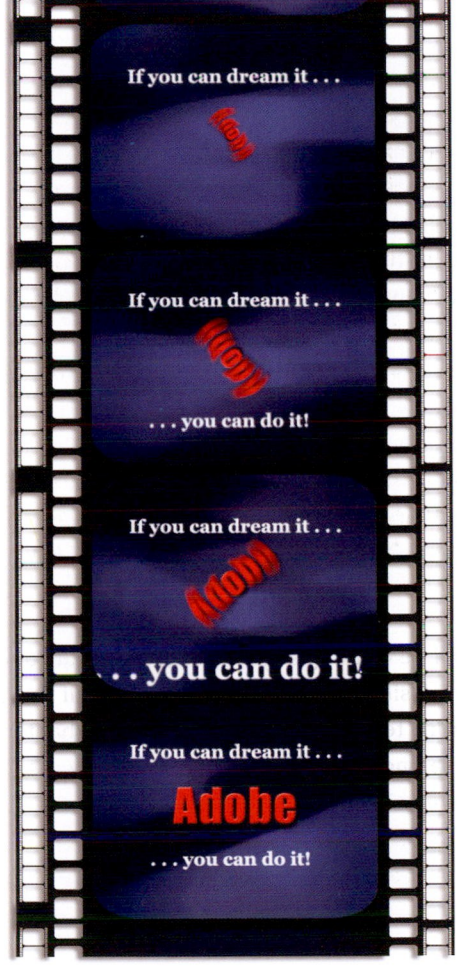

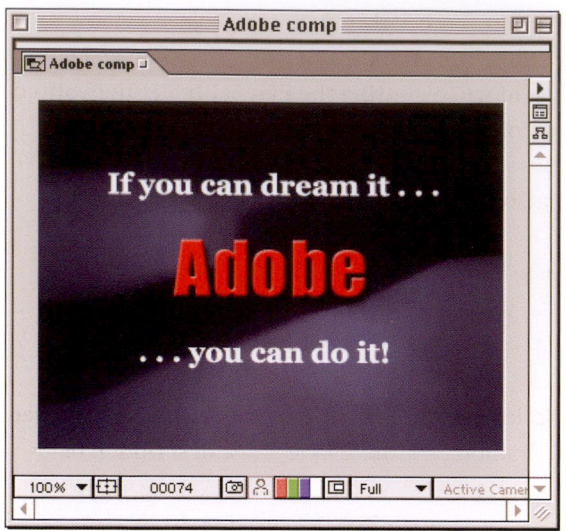

It is important to remember that the references you will see in the Project window are exactly that, references to the original files stored elsewhere on your hard disks. They are not the original files or copies of them. When you save an After Effects project you must ensure that you retain original source files. There is a feature in After Effects 5 called Collect Files which quickly and easily collates all the files pertaining to your project into one folder, ready for saving or sending to a colleague. To find out more about this feature, you can check out the *Collecting Files in One Location* document in the After Effects online help system. To access this document, go to the *Help* menu, and choose *After Effects Help* and then choose the *Search* option to find the document.

Before you start the exercises, you'll need to move your Preference files for After Effects to a safe place. If you haven't done so already, please see page 5, in the Mission chapter for instructions.

Take all of the fonts for your particular platform (Mac *or* PC) from the CD > Free Stuff > Fonts Folder and place them into your system Font folder and then restart your machine. If you are unsure about how to install fonts onto your system, please check your system's help files or user manual for details.

If you don't own a copy of After Effects 5.0 there is a tryout version on the CD in the Software Demos folder, install this before starting. One or two of the exercises make references to Photoshop and Illustrator. If you don't own copies of Photoshop and Illustrator you can download demo versions from the Adobe website at: http://www.adobe.com

## importing footage

**1** Open After Effects. The first thing you will see is the Tip of the Day. I thoroughly recommend leaving the Show at Start-up box checked till you know all of the tips. These are around 200 tips, compiled from the top After Effects users' favorite tips and tricks. There are some real gems in here so make sure that you read them all. Click OK to exit this box.

We will start by importing some files into the Project. When working in After Effects there are several different ways of executing commands, throughout the book I will show you lots of different options, then you will be free to choose your preferred method.

**2** Go to the File menu at the top of your screen and to Import > File.

Notice that keyboard shortcuts are listed next to the commands in the main menus. There's also a Quick Reference Card, listing all keyboard shortcuts included in the After Effects package. I recommend you keep this Quick Reference card nearby your workstation for easy access. There is also a list of all keyboard shortcuts in the Online Help menu within After Effects.

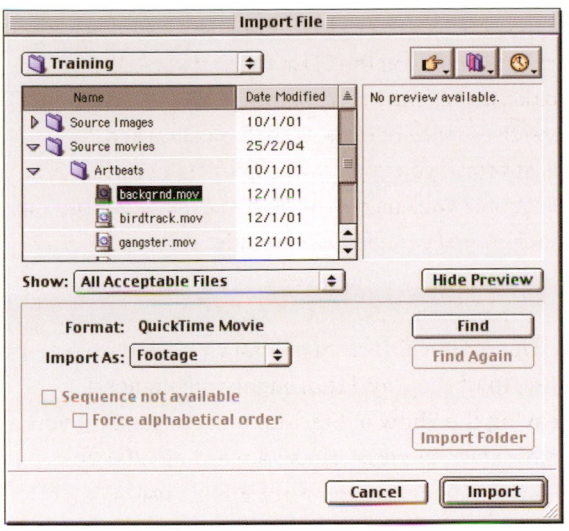

**3** In the Import File dialog box, navigate to the desktop and go to Training folder > Source movies > Artbeats. Double-click on the file named Backgrnd.mov to import it into your project. This is a piece of royalty-free footage from the Liquid Ambience collection courtesy of Artbeats Inc. (ref. no: LA133.mov).

You will notice a reference to this file in your Project window. Notice that under the Type field heading in the Project window it tells you that the file you have imported is a QuickTime Movie.

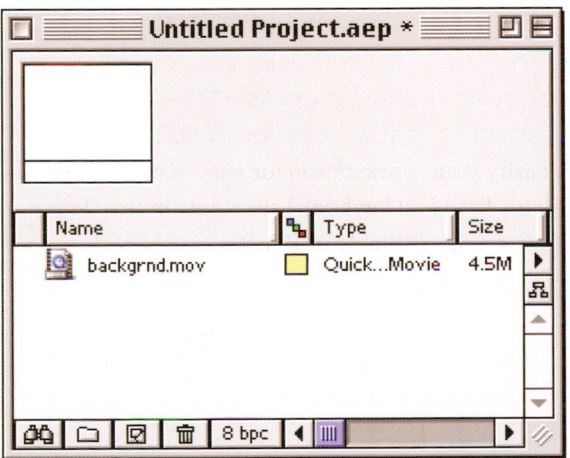

**4** Double-click the file in the Project window to open it up in the default QuickTime Player. Play the movie by hitting the Play button at the bottom left of the QuickTime Player window and then close the QuickTime window when you have finished viewing the movie.

Double-clicking a file in the Project window will playback the movie in its original state before interpretation by After Effects.

Notice that in the Project window you can now see a thumbnail of the movie and a description of its size, length, frame rate and format. We will now use a keyboard shortcut to bring in our next piece of footage.

**5** Hit Command + I to execute the Import Footage file command, an import dialog box will appear.

**6** From Training > Source Images > Angie Images, open the file named Adoblogo.psd. A dialog box with a drop down menu will now appear, click on the drop down menu to look at the options available.

**7** Choose Merged Layers from the drop down menu and then click OK.

When importing a Photoshop file into After Effects you have several choices available to you.

• You can import the file with all layers merged into one, this has a similar effect to flattening the layers of your Photoshop file into one layer before importing it into your project.

• Alternatively you can choose to import individual layers from the Photoshop document. This option will not allow you to retain information about the position of the layer in relation to the other layers in the Photoshop file.

• The final option is to import the Photoshop file as a Composition with all layers intact, retaining all information about position, transparency and order of layers. We will look at this option later in this chapter.

You will now see that the Photoshop file has also appeared in the Project window along with information about its resolution and alpha channel. See the Technical.pdf on the CD > Extras folder for more information about channels.

After Effects sports context-sensitive menus, if you are using a PC or Windows machine for your After Effects work you can use the right mouse button to access these menus by clicking virtually anywhere within the After Effects user interface. If you are using an Apple Macintosh system you can access the context-sensitive menus by Control-clicking on the same areas. The options in these context-sensitive menus will change depending upon where in the interface you click. From this point on, when I want you to access these menus, I will use the term, Context-click, if you are a windows user, simply Right mouse click when you see this, if you are a Mac user, Control-click on the same area.

**8** Context-click in the space underneath your footage items in the Project window to bring up the context-sensitive menu. From the menu, go to Import > Multiple Files (Command + Alt + I).

There are two ways of using this feature. You can either select all the files you wish to import by Shift-clicking them or you can double-click the files one after another.

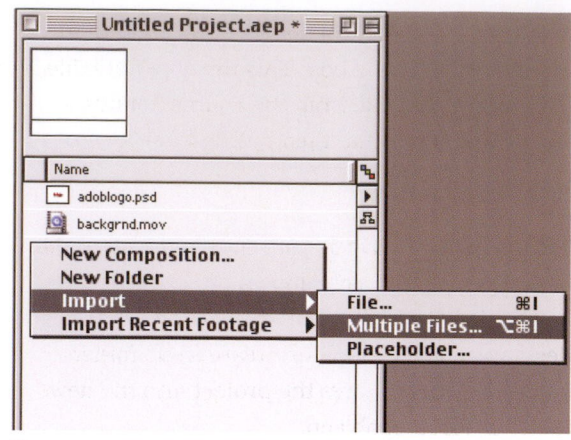

If you use the latter method, After Effects will keep opening the dialog box for you till you have all the files you need and go back to the main interface after you have clicked the Done button.

**9** Select the file named Motto.ai from the Angie Images folder and double-click it to import it into your project. You will then see the drop down menu asking you to choose a layer, select the Dream it layer and then hit the OK button.

**10** You should now be back at the Import Multiple Files dialog box, double-click the Motto.ai layer again but this time, from the drop down menu, select the Do it layer and click OK.

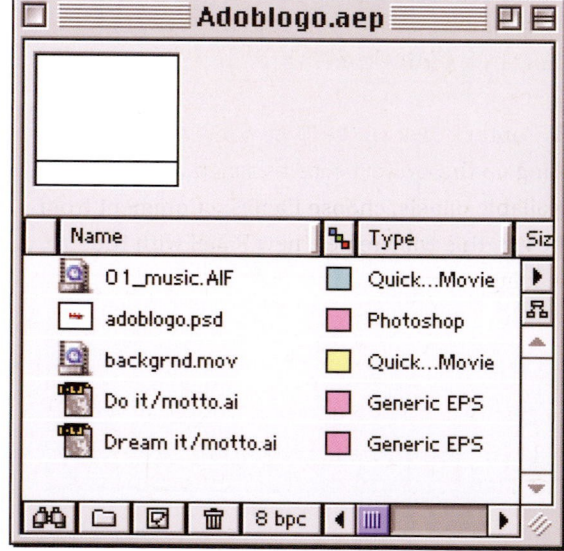

**11** Once again you will be faced with the Import Multiple Files dialog box. This time open the file named 01_music.aif, from the Source Sounds > Crank City folder, and then hit the Done key to close the dialog box.

**12** Go to File > Save as, and then navigate to the desktop; if you haven't already done so, create a new folder called Creative After Effects on the desktop. Inside this folder, create a sub-folder named Basics and save the project into the new folder as Adoblogob.aep.

## managing footage

You will now have five items in your Project window, as a default these items are sorted in alpha-numeric order. You can change the way that footage is sorted by clicking on the different Panel headings in the Project window.

**1** If you do not have a project open, open Adoblogo.aep from Training > Projects > Chapter 02.

**2** If necessary, enlarge the Project window and then click on the Type panel heading to change the order in which the items are displayed. Notice that the items all have colored labels, pink for stills, yellow for movies and blue for sound files. Click on the Size Panel to re-order the footage items by their file size.

**3** Context-click on the Type panel heading to bring up the context-sensitive menu, this lists all available panels, choose Panels > Comment from the list, this will create a new Panel with the heading, Comment.

**4** Stretch the Project window across the screen so that you can see all of the panels. You can reorder the panels by clicking and dragging their headings, you can resize them by clicking and dragging the little handles on the right side of each panel heading. Try this before moving on to the next step.

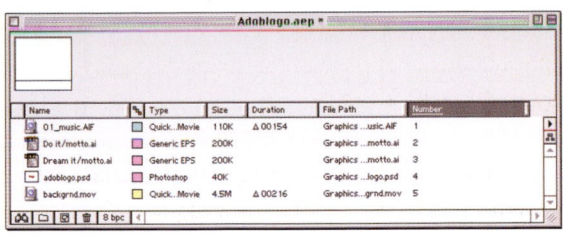

**5** Context-click on the Comment Panel heading and choose *Rename This* from the context-sensitive menu. A dialog box will appear allowing you to enter a new panel heading, type in Number and then click OK to leave the box. Before moving on, check that your footage is currently sorted by file size.

**6** By clicking in the empty fields under the Number panel heading, you can enter your own text. Type in the numbers in the following order, starting from the top (5, 2, 3, 1, 4). We'll use these numbers to resort our footage into a custom order.

**7** Now click the Number panel heading to sort the footage items by their allocated numbers.

**8** Resize the window so that you can only see the Name and Type headers.

**9** Go to File > Save as and, in the Save as dialog box, navigate to your Creative After Effects folder on the desktop and save the project into the Basics folder as Adoblogo1a.aep.

These footage management features are very useful when working on Complex projects with multiple layers and Compositions.

# creating compositions

You now have five items in your project. In order
to put these items together to create a new piece
of footage you need to create what's known as a
composition. Think of the composition as the
place where you compose all of the separate
elements which go together to make up your final
movie. Within one Project you can have several
compositions; each composition can contain
several layers. You can even put compositions
inside other compositions; this process is called
Nesting and we will look at that a bit later, but
first, let's look at how we create these
compositions. There are several methods for
creating compositions.

**1** If you do not have a project open, open
Adoblogo01.aep from Training > Projects >
Chapter 02.

**2** Go to the bottom of the Project
window and you will see five buttons,
click on the center button, which is the New
Composition button. The Composition Settings
dialog box will appear.

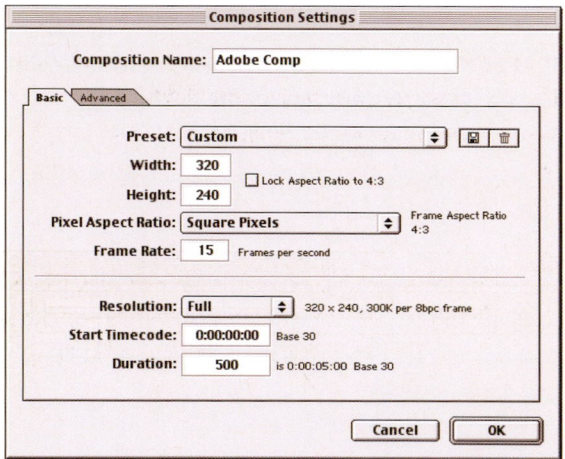

**3** In the Composition Settings dialog box, type
Adobe Composition in the Composition Name field.

It is important to get into the habit of naming your
compositions carefully. When you become more
confident with After Effects and are working with
complicated, multi-layered, nested compositions,
sensible and logical naming conventions can save
you a lot of time, not to mention your sanity!
Remember when using numbers in your naming
convention, use zeros to proceed the numbers,
e.g. 001, 002, 003 etc. This will ensure that your
files will be displayed in the correct alphanumeric
order on your computer.

You will now see the Basic tab of the Composition
Settings box. You can type in custom frame sizes
or select a pre-defined frame size from the drop
down menu.

**4** Look in the Preset drop down menu. You can
see that there are pre-set choices for various
outputs from Small 160 × 120 (ideal for Web
streaming) through to NTSC and PAL settings for
TV and video. There are also settings for
Widescreen and HDTV (High definition television),
as well as Cineon and Film Academy resolutions
for working on feature films.

**5** Choose Medium 320 × 240 from the Frame Size
drop down menu. This setting is commonly used
for CD ROM movies or for web-streaming movies.

**6** Check that the Pixel Aspect Ratio is set to
Square Pixels and change the frame rate to 15
frames per second.

**7** Check that the duration is 5 seconds. To easily change the duration of your composition, select the text in the Duration field and type in 500. There is no need to type full stops, commas or colons, After Effects will convert the number into seconds and frames for you. To the side of the Duration dialog box is a display verifying the new time you have typed in.

Unlike some of the proprietary broadcast systems, After Effects is resolution independent, meaning that it is not restricted to producing output of preset sizes. For example, you can produce something for a television broadcast and then, using the same software, output a copy for the web. You can even type in custom sizes.

The Composition settings or Project Settings can be changed at any time. However, it is usually preferable to create your original composition at the largest size needed for output. For example, if you are creating a movie for Film, TV and the Web, you should create the original composition at the Films resolution and then scale it down for the other output formats. Sizing down comps is not a problem but if you stretch a small comp up to a higher resolution output you can run into image quality problems, we will discuss ways of overcoming these potential problems later.

**8** Click OK to leave this dialog box. You should now have two new windows open.

### the Composition window

The top window is the Composition window, known as the Comp window to its friends. Think of this as a TV monitor. You can see the action taking place in your composition at whatever place in time your Current-Time Marker is.

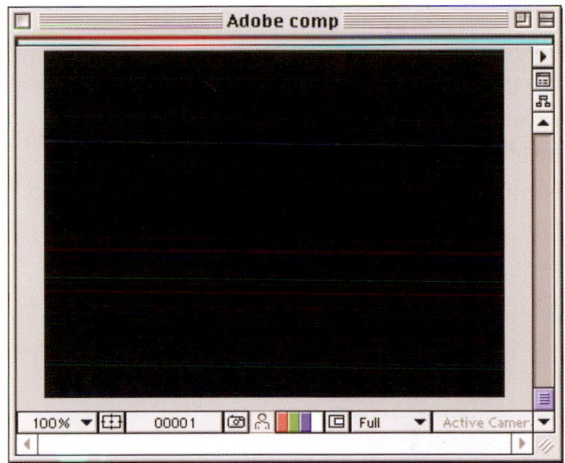

### the timeline

Underneath the Composition window is the Timeline. Think of this as a time ruler, measuring time in a visual, sequential way from left to right. This is where you can move through time and see a global, sequential view of your whole comp from beginning to end. The vertical red line with the blue handle is the Current-Time Marker, you can move through time by clicking on the blue handle and dragging it backwards and forwards along the Timeline.

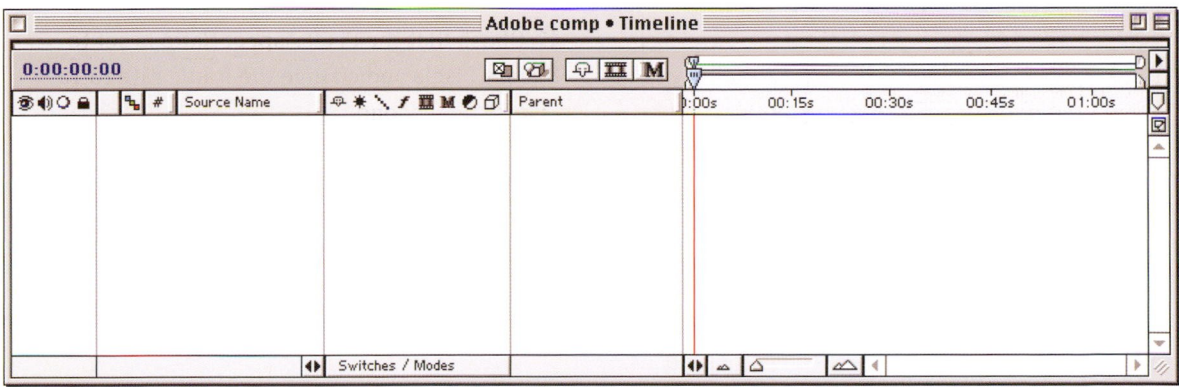

**9** Go to File > Project Settings. You will see the Project Settings dialog box. This is where you change the timecode base and the color depth that After Effects uses for each project.

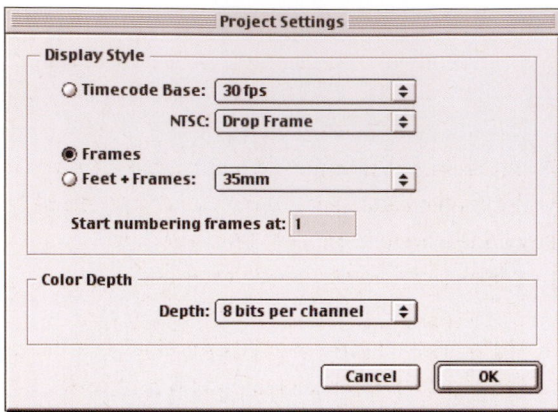

After Effects is using its default timecode Base of 30 frames per second (from now on I will refer to the frame rate using the acronym, fps). This is the Timecode Base for NTSC non drop frame timecode. Timecode issues are discussed in more detail in the Technical.pdf document (which you can find in the CD > Extras folder) but for now we will change the settings so that we are all working in frames. It is largely a personal choice as to how you like your time displayed. People from editing backgrounds tend to prefer to work with timecode. Animators tend to prefer to work in frames. If you are working in Film, you'll probably want to measure in Feet and Frames. To find out more about the pros and cons of using each Timecode Base, more info on this available in CD > Extras > Technical.pdf.

**10** Change the Display Style to Frames and type the number one into the Start Numbering Frames box. I decided to use frames as the Display Style throughout the book because I didn't want to enforce my PAL ways on any of my friends from the USA! I thought this would be a good compromise for all. I personally prefer to start numbering my frames from 1 onwards, I've never been able to get my head round remembering that there's a frame 0!

**11** Go to File > Save as and, in the Save as dialog box, navigate to your Creative After Effects folder on the desktop and save the project into the Basics folder as Adoblogo1b.aep.

The Project Settings dialog box is where you can choose the color depth you wish to work in. A new feature of After Effects 5 is 16-bit-per-channel color support (Production Bundle only). 16-bit images use more colors than 8-bit images (trillions rather than mere millions!) and produce much higher quality output for film and HDTV (High Definition Television).

# adding footage

When you create a new composition it will always be empty. To include a footage file in your comp, you first have to place it in there. There are several methods for doing this.

**1** If you do not have a project open, open Adoblogo02.aep from Training > Projects > Chapter 02.

**2** In the Project window, click once to select the file named Adoblogo.psd. Click and drag the icon over to the Composition window, as you drag the file onto the Comp window you'll see a bounding box with a cross through it which represents your file. As you move the file over the center of the Comp window you will feel it snap to the center of the composition, allow this to happen and then release the mouse to drop the file into your new comp.

**3** You should now see the Adoblogo.psd layer in the center of the Comp window. If you look at the Timeline you will also see a visual representation of the layer there. The pink strip represents the length of the footage. You can see that the footage stretches along the time ruler from frame 1 to frame 76, it fills the length of the comp.

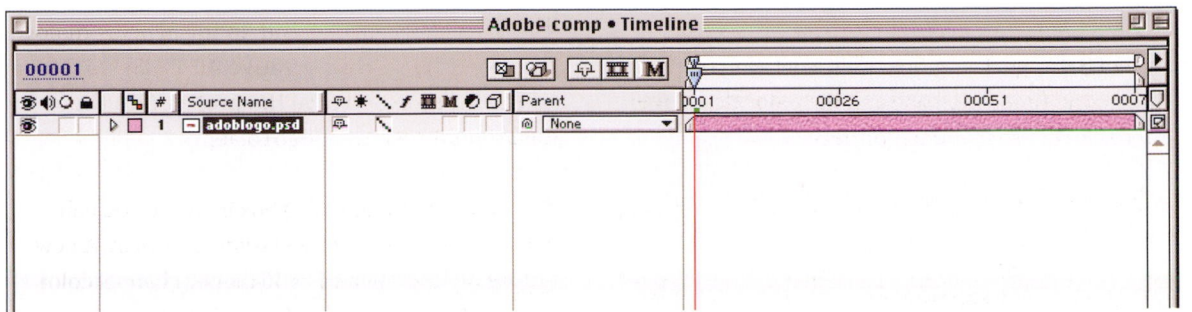

**4** When animating titles I find it easier to have a soundtrack to work to, this is much easier than creating my animation and then trying to match up a sound track to go with it later. Audio is a very important part of any animation. Good audio can make the difference between an acceptable piece of work and a brilliant piece of work.

**5** Go back to the Project window and select the file named Music.aif. This time, drag the icon down to the Timeline and drop it below the Adoblogo.psd layer. As you drag, you will see a black line telling you where in the layer hierarchy the file will be placed. If you did the same with an image or movie file it would be automatically centered in the Composition window.

Notice that the new piece of footage is labeled blue as opposed to pink, this is because it is a sound file and sound files are, as default, labeled blue, images are labeled pink, movies are labeled yellow etc. This makes it easy to differentiate between different footage types.

**6** Make sure that you have audio output from your machine and then hit the Full Stop (Period ) key on the number pad of your keyboard to preview the audio of your composition.

**7** Click once on the audio layer in the Timeline to make sure that it is selected and then hit the L key on the keyboard to bring up the audio level settings. This is where you can set keyframes to animate the levels of the audio, e.g. for fading the volume up or down.

**8** Under the levels you will see the word Waveform, click the little triangle next to this to open up a visual graph of the audio levels. You may need to resize your Timeline to see all layers. You can also access the waveform by double-hitting the L key in quick succession (LL).

**9** Go to File > Save as and, in the Save as dialog box, navigate to your Creative After Effects folder on the desktop and save the project into the Basics folder as Adoblogo02b.aep.

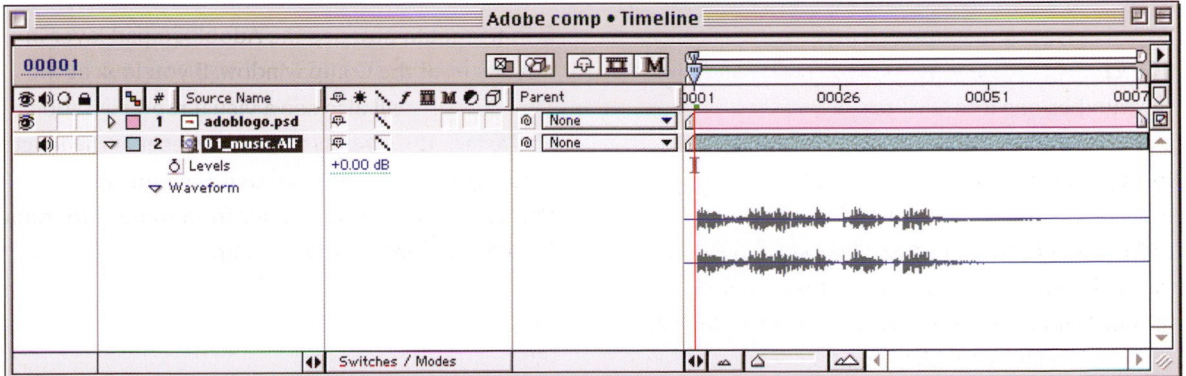

# the timeline

Notice that the audio levels begin right at the start of the composition, this is not usually a good practice to adhere to. Whenever creating compositions, it is a good habit to leave breathing space at each end of your composition for editing purposes, in the same way that you would shoot extra footage at either end when working with video or film cameras. The extra footage will be essential for the editor of the finished program to create transitions into and/or out of the piece. Having the first frame of your animation as the first frame of your composition also has the potential for creating problems in field based editing which we will look at later in the book. I usually leave at least one, usually two or three seconds at either end of my animations.

In the Timeline you will see a vertical red line with a blue handle at the top, this is the Current-Time Marker. This does exactly what the name implies; it marks the current time. So, wherever this marker is (on the time ruler, at the top of the Timeline) will be the current time.

**1** If you do not have a project open, open Adoblogo03.aep from Training > Projects > Chapter 02.

**2** Click on the Blue handle at the top of the Current-Time Marker and drag it until the Current Time Display in the top left of the Timeline reads 15, this will now be the current time of your composition.

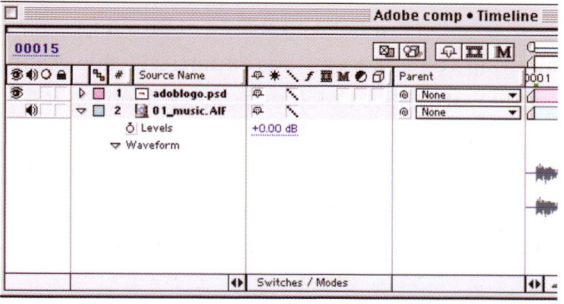

**3** Hit the period key on the number pad again to play the audio from the position of the Current-Time Marker. Notice that the audio loops itself from the position of the Current-Time Marker to the end of the composition. Hit the spacebar to stop playback at any time.

Footage in the Timeline can be moved, trimmed, and altered after it has been brought into the composition. The After Effects Timeline is object based as opposed to layer based, this means that changes made to a single property are not destructive to other properties on the same layer, they can be changed at any time without affecting the other properties. This is what makes After Effects so creatively flexible, you never have to be afraid to make changes because everything is reversible.

We shall now move the audio so that it comes in at the fifteen-frame (one second) mark.

**4** To move the footage in time simply click on the colored part of the audio layer and drag it to the right. Hold down the Shift key as you drag to snap the In-point of the layer to the Current-Time Marker. The audio will now start from the one-second mark. This is now the point at which we will begin our animation. Preview the audio again to hear the changes.

OK, now let's take a look at the properties of this layer.

**5** Select the Adoblogo.psd layer in the Timeline to make it active. Click the little, disclosure triangle next to the layer label in the Timeline to uncollapse the layer and access all of its animatable properties. Under the Layer name you will see three property group labels, Masks, Effects and Transform, these are the three basic groups of animatable properties in After Effects.

## animating properties

When you make changes to a layer's properties, they will be applied in the order in which they appear in the Timeline, Masks are applied first, then Effects and finally Transformations. We are going to work backwards, starting by looking at the Transform properties.

**1** Open up the Transform properties by clicking the disclosure triangle next to the word Transform. You may need to resize your window to see all of your Transform properties. Under here you will see the five basic properties which affect any visible layer. Any or all of these properties can be animated over time in After Effects using keyframes.

The term Keyframe comes from traditional animation. We'll use Walt Disney as an example. Imagine that Walt wants to create a simple animation of a ball bouncing on the floor. He would make three drawings: the ball at its starting point, the ball as it hits the floor and the ball at its end point. All points where major changes occur in the animation. These would be the most important, or *key* moments of the animation, hence the term *keyframes*. He would then hand these keyframes to his assistant animator who would then fill in all the frames *in-between* the keyframes, hence the term *tweening*.

When you are using After Effects *you* are Walt Disney, setting the most important parts, or *keyframes* of the animation (the white balls in the diagram). These are usually where major changes occur. After Effects is your assistant animator or 'tweener', filling in (or *interpolating*) all the frames between (the blue balls in the diagram).

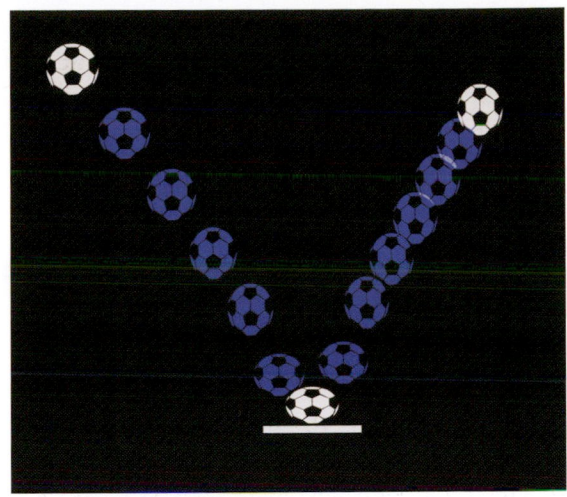

When working in After Effects you start by setting the first keyframe for any property manually; by doing this you are telling After Effects to lock the specified property at the current value, and at the current time. Think of it like tying a knot in the value to prevent it from changing.

**2** With the Current-Time Marker still at fifteen frames, click on the little Stopwatch next to the word Rotation in the Timeline. As you do this, three things will happen.

▷ ⏱ Rotation

**3** A little diamond shaped icon will appear in the Timeline at the position of the Current-Time Marker; this is a default, linear keyframe.

**4** The stopwatch icon will have changed and a little triangle will have appeared at its side, allowing you to access the properties' value graph (don't worry about that for now, we'll look at it later in the book).

**5** A checkbox with a tick inside it will appear in the column at the far left of the Timeline; this checkbox is there to tell you that a property has been keyframed. If the box has a tick in it, this tells us that the Current-Time Marker is currently parked over a keyframe for that property.

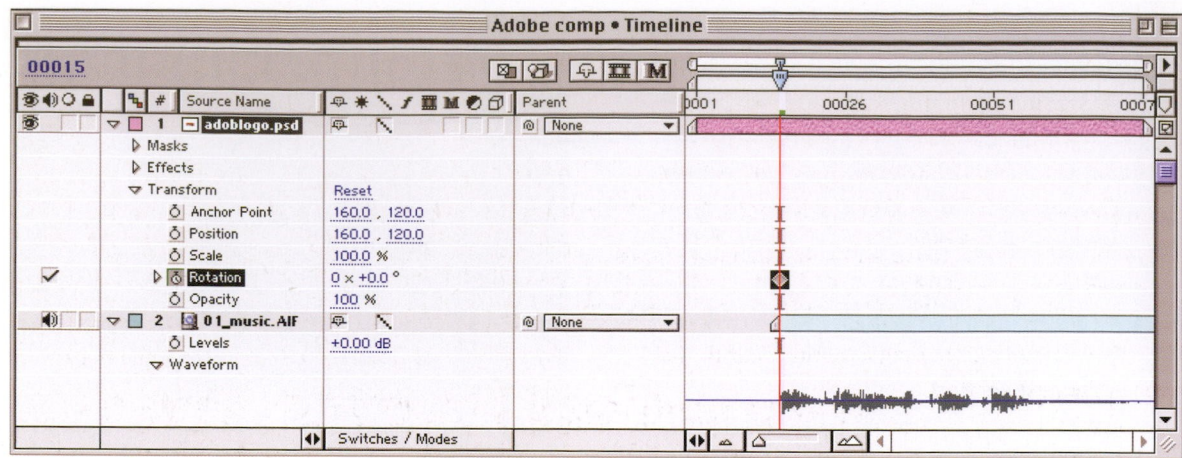

**6** Try toggling the stopwatch on and off, noticing all the things that change when a keyframe is added. Make sure that you finish with the stopwatch switched on.

**7** Another way to move the Current-Time Marker is to click on any part of the gray Time Ruler at the top of the Timeline, the Current-Time Marker will then jump to that position.

**8** Click anywhere on the time ruler to make the Current-Time Marker jump to that position.

Another way to move the Current-Time Marker is to click on the Current Time display at the top, left corner of the Timeline.

**9** Click on the Current Time display; the Go To Time dialog box will appear allowing you to enter a new Current Time. Type in 55 and then click OK. The Current-Time Marker should jump to its new position. You can also hit Command-G to bring up the Go To Time dialog box.

By creating a first keyframe for your animation, you are telling After Effects that you wish to animate that property. Now that you have set the first keyframe, After Effects will automatically set a new keyframe for the property whenever a change occurs.

There are several ways of adjusting values of properties in After Effects. We will start by adjusting the values numerically.

**10** Notice that there are two values for the Rotation property; the first value is for specifying the amount in revolutions, the second is for the amount in degrees. With your mouse, click once on the first Rotation value, which currently reads 0, doing this highlights the text and makes it live so that you can enter a new value. Type in 18 and hit Enter. Doing this will enter a value of eighteen Complete revolutions.

Notice that a new keyframe has automatically been created where the value has changed. After Effects will also have worked out all the frames in-between these two keyframes.

**11** Hit the Home key on the keyboard to move the Current-Time Marker back to the beginning of your composition and then hit the spacebar to preview your animation. The Play button in the Time Controls palette does the same job as hitting the spacebar.

The rotation looks a bit odd at the moment, it looks as if the text is flipping as well as rotating. We will solve this problem by adding a Motion Blur to the layer in the next section.

**12** Go to File > Save as and, in the Save as dialog box, navigate to your Creative After Effects folder on the desktop and save the project into the Basics folder as Adoblogo03b.aep.

Hitting the spacebar will preview the action without the audio. After Effects will play back the frames from your hard disk as fast as it can, sometimes this will be faster than real time, sometimes slower, depending on your machine specifications and on the complexity of your project. Notice the green line that has appeared between the keyframes, this indicates the frames that After Effects has had to render, where changes to the original footage have occurred. These frames are stored in the After Effects RAM Cache which we will discuss later.

# layer switches

The text rotates but looks a bit odd, we will add an automatic motion blur to the text to make it look more realistic. After Effect's Motion Blur is an intelligent motion blur, it looks at the speed and direction your layer is moving and blurs it accordingly. Adjusting the Shutter Angle and Shutter Phase settings in the Advanced tab of the Composition Settings can control the amount of motion blur applied to the layer; we will take a look at those options later.

Layer switches are used to apply Motion Blur to each layer individually. There is also a global *Enable Motion Blur* switch for the composition, allowing you to toggle Motion Blur on and off to speed up previews.

**1** If you do not have a project open, open Adoblogo04.aep from Training > Projects > Chapter 02.

**2** To the right of the Source Name panel heading you will see the Modes Panel. You can togggle the Switches/Modes button at the bottom of this panel to toggle between the Switches and the Modes panel. Make sure that you can see the Layer Switches panel; it is the panel with various little icons running along the top of it. You can also use the F4 key to toggle between these panels.

**3** The M icon represents the Layer Motion Blur switch. Go to the empty checkbox under the M for the Adoblogo.psd layer and click in the checkbox to make a tick, this will activate Motion Blur for this layer. As well as activating Motion Blur for the layer, we also have to enable it for the whole comp.

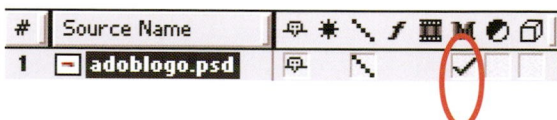

**4** At the top and to the right of the Switches column you will see several large buttons, click the button with the large letter **M** on it, this is the Enable Motion Blur button. Motion Blur takes a bit of time to render, this button allows you to toggle it on when you need to see the results, and off when you wish to speed up your previews. With both of these switches activated you will have a nice, realistic motion blur applied to your animation.

**5** Preview once again by hitting the spacebar. As if by magic, we can see the rotational blur on our layer. Notice that the layer is less blurred in the center and more blurred towards the outside where there is more movement.

# RAM Previews

If you want to preview your animation in real time, along with the audio, After Effects allows you to do this by giving you a RAM Preview option. When you use the RAM Preview option, rather than playing the frames back from the hard disk (which can be slow) After Effects renders the frames into RAM which is a much faster memory than hard disk memory. You can then view your rendered composition at the same frame rate as your composition or as fast as your system will allow, complete with audio. The number of frames that you can load into RAM depends on the amount of RAM that you have on your system. On the Mac, it is also dependent on the amount of RAM you have allocated to After Effects (see CD > Extras > Technical.pdf for details).

**1** To do a real time RAM Preview of your composition, make sure that either the Composition window or Timeline are active and then hit the 0 key on the number pad of your keyboard to start the process. This does the same as clicking the RAM Preview button in the Time Controls palette (see the following diagram for details). After Effects will load all the frames into RAM and then play the result back to you in real time.

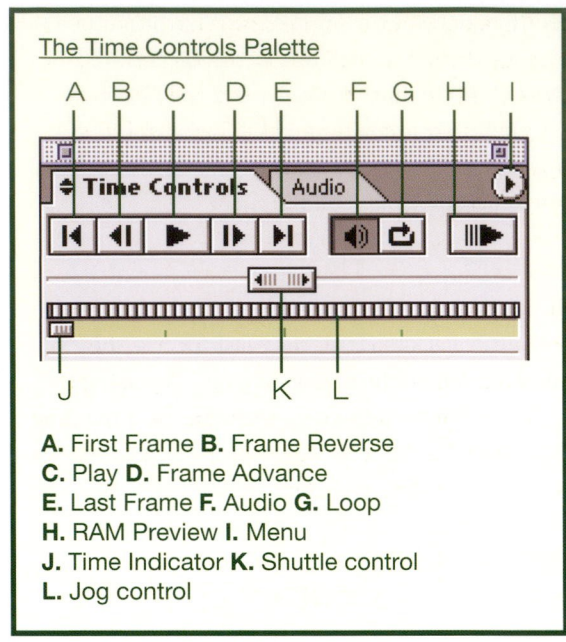

The Time Controls Palette

A. First Frame **B.** Frame Reverse
**C.** Play **D.** Frame Advance
**E.** Last Frame **F.** Audio **G.** Loop
**H.** RAM Preview **I.** Menu
**J.** Time Indicator **K.** Shuttle control
**L.** Jog control

**2** When the frames are being rendered into RAM, a green line runs across the Time Ruler in the Timeline showing you the progress. You can also see the progress in the Time Controls Palette, where it tells you how many frames are loaded out of the total number requested. During playback the same display will tell you how many frames are playing and at what speed they are playing. Notice that After Effects is happily playing 15 fps in real time.

Next to the Audio button, in the Time controls palette, you'll see the Loop button. The default setting for the RAM Preview is for it to loop continuously till you either hit a key or click anywhere within the After Effects interface.

**3** Click once on the Loop button to change it to *Standard* mode and then hit the RAM Preview button to preview. The movie will now play continuously forwards and stop when it reaches the end of the composition.

**4** Click once more on the Loop button to change the mode to *Palindrome* and then hit the RAM Preview button. The movie will now play continuously forwards and backwards. Click anywhere on the screen or hit the Spacebar to stop playback. Click on the Loop button once more to return to *Loop* mode.

**5** There are other controls in this palette for moving through your footage which are shown in the diagram on the opposite page. Try using the different controls to move through the animation. The RAM Preview settings can be customized, we will look at this in detail later.

## animating
## multiple properties

OK, so you have now created a basic animation simply by animating one property of a single layer. In each layer, every property has its own keyframes, this defines an object-based animation system. In layer-based animation there is just one keyframe per layer which controls all properties for that layer. In order to animate a second property you would have to go back and reset the existing keyframes. Not so with After Effects, each properties' keyframes behave independently of each other and can be adjusted, moved, copied and pasted without affecting the other properties.

At the moment we are animating our layers in a 2D environment. It is possible to work in three dimensions within After Effects and we will look at that later but let's master the 2D aspects first. There are ways of faking 3D in a 2D environment and After Effects is king of the fakirs! Often it is easier and quicker to fake a 3D effect than to do it for real in a 3D environment; it can often be quicker to render this way. You will now animate the Scale property of the same layer to give the effect of depth in your animation.

**1** The J (forward) and K (back) keys on your keyboard can be used to jump between visible keyframes, use these keys to jump to the first visible keyframe for rotation.

**2** Click the Stopwatch next to the Scale property name to set a keyframe for scale.

**3** Click on the property value and type in 0 and then hit Enter. The text layer will now disappear from view because it has been scaled down to 0%.

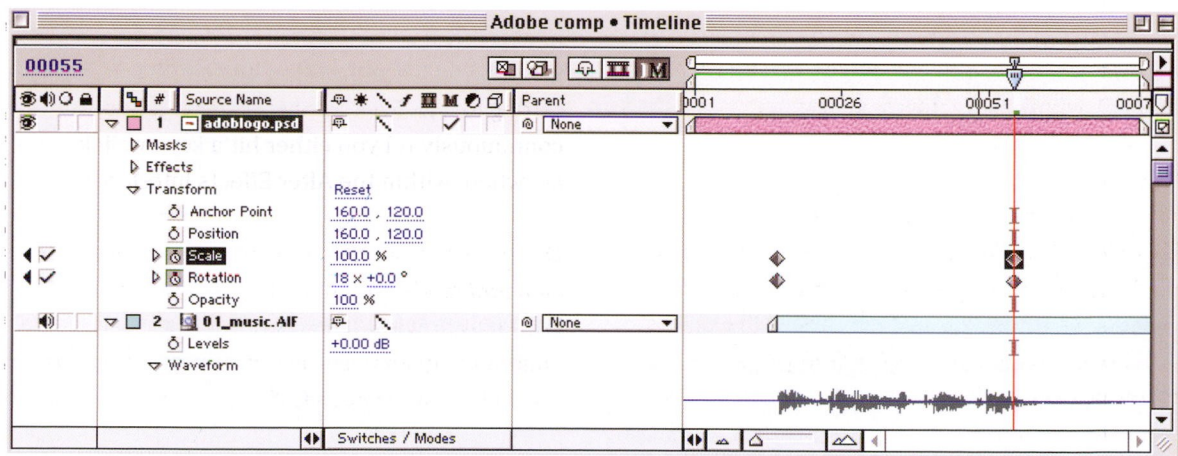

**4** Move to the next visible keyframe by clicking the little black arrow next to the keyframe checkbox for Rotation. These arrows do the same as the J and K keys, allowing you to quickly jump between visible keyframes (these controls only work with keyframes that are visible in the Timeline).

Notice that as you move to the next visible keyframe an arrow appears next to the Scale property checkbox allowing you to jump back to the previous keyframe.

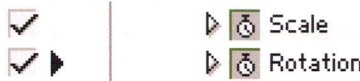

**5** Click once in the Scale text field to make it live, enter a new value of 100 and then hit Enter. A new keyframe will automatically be created for you. RAM Preview your animation by hitting the 0 key. The layer now scales from 0% to 100% whilst rotating, making it appear to spin onto the screen from afar.

**6** Go to File > Save as and, in the Save as dialog box, navigate to your Creative After Effects folder on the desktop and save the project into the Basics folder as Adoblogo04b.aep.

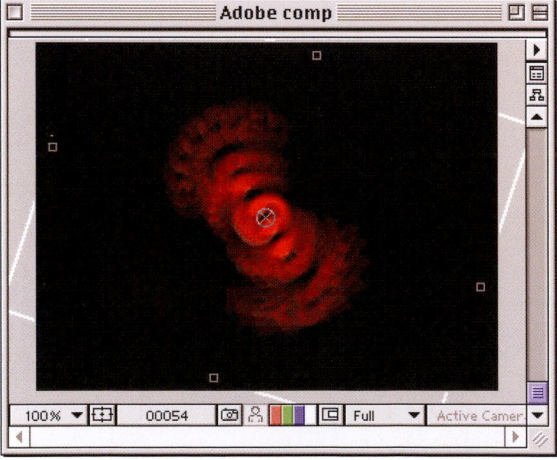

## basic compositing

OK, so you've set keyframes for multiple properties to create a basic animated layer but what about working with more than one layer? Compositing is the term used for the process of composing multiple layers to create one composite image; sort of like a collage. As soon as you place one layer upon another, you have created a composite.

**1** If you do not have a project open, open Adoblogo05.aep from Training > Projects > Chapter 02.

**2** Hit the Home key to go back to the beginning of the composition.

**3** Go up to the Project window and select the file named Do it/Motto.ai.

**4** Hold down the Command key and select Dream it/Motto.ai. You should now have both files selected.

**5** Hit Command + / to bring the files into your composition or go to File > Add Footage to composition. This shortcut for bringing footage into your composition is a very useful one that you will use often. When using this shortcut, footage is centered in the Composition window and the layers are placed at the top of the existing layers. The layer at the top of the Timeline will be the front-most layer in the Composition window.

Now we'll animate the Position properties of these layers over time to make them appear from outside the composition. In many cases it is quicker and easier to animate from the end point of your animation. This is such a case because the text is already in the place where we want it to finish, we can simply set a keyframe to hold it in that position and then move to the start point and make our changes.

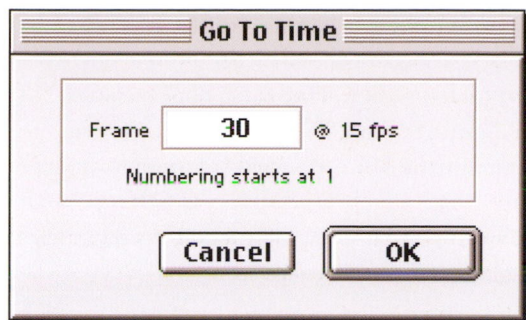

**6** Hit Command + G to bring up the Go To Time dialog box, type in 30 and then click OK (or hit Enter on the keyboard) to move the Current-Time Marker to your new position, two seconds into the animation. This is the point where our text layers will come to rest.

You can imagine that if I have to open up all of my layers to get to their individual properties, that I will very soon run out of screen space. Luckily, After Effects provides you with keyboard shortcuts which allow you to bring up the properties, individually in the Timeline, keeping your screen neater and more manageable.

**7** With the two new layers selected hit the P key on the keyboard to bring up the Position properties for both layers.

If you wanted to bring up Scale you would have hit the S key. For Rotation – the R key. Anchor point – the A key. The only one that is not immediately obvious is the T key for Opacity but if you think of transparency it is quite easy to remember. There are also keyboard shortcuts for setting keyframes for properties.

**8** With both layers still selected hit Alt + P. Doing this will set keyframes for position on both layers (it will also bring up the layer property if it is not already open). Hit the P key on its own to close the layers again.

**9** Close the other two open layers by clicking on the little triangles beside the layer Labels.

There is also a keyboard shortcut to bring up all keyframed properties for selected layers.

**10** Hit Command + A to select all layers and then hit the U key on the keyboard. The U key (also known as the Uber key) will bring up only the properties which have been keyframed for any layers which are selected, this is very useful when working with complex animated compositions and particularly when working with multiple effects.

**11** Go back to the beginning of the composition by hitting the Home key on the keyboard.

As well as being able to adjust values by entering them numerically After Effects allows you to interactively change the values for a layer in the Comp window.

**12** Deselect all of the layers either by clicking in the empty, gray space at the bottom of the Timeline or by hitting Command + Shift + A.

**13** In the bottom left of the Composition window, change the Magnification drop down menu to 50%, so that you can see space at either side of the screen.

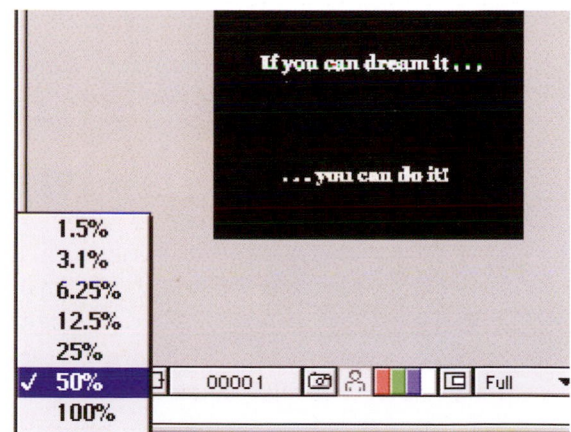

**14** Select the Dream it layer in the Timeline. In the Composition window, you will see eight selection handles and an anchor point, representing the edges, corners and center point of your layer.

**15** In the Composition window, click within the layer and drag the layer off the screen to the right. As you drag, hold down the Shift key to constrain the movement to a horizontal move, make sure that you hold down the Shift key after you have started to drag the layer. The diagram below will help you with positioning your layer. If you make a mistake, don't worry, simply go to Edit > Undo or hit Command + Z and then try again.

**16** Now select the Do it layer in the Timeline. Click on the layer in the Composition window and drag it off the screen to the bottom. Again, hold down Shift after you start to drag the layer to constrain the movement, this time to a vertical move.

**17** Change the magnification back to 100%. Hit the Home key to move the Current-Time Marker back to the beginning and then hit the 0 key to build a RAM Preview of your animation so far.

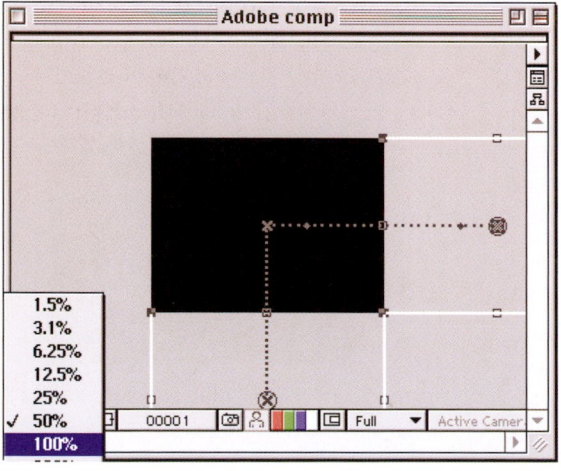

There are a few changes to be made to the animation to make it work. At the moment both layers of text come into the screen at the same time, making it quite difficult to read. We will adjust the existing keyframes to improve the timing of the animation.

**18** Move to frame 45 by using any of the methods that you learned in the previous lesson.

**19** Under the Do it layer, select the second Position keyframe by clicking once on it, the keyframe will be highlighted with a black outline when it is selected.

**20** Drag the keyframe over to the Current-Time Marker; hold down the Shift key as you drag to snap the keyframe to the Current-Time Marker.

**21** RAM Preview your composition and notice that the end point of the Do it layer animation comes in later and fits much better with the music.

The start points of the animation still need some work as they come in too soon.

**22** Move the Current-Time Marker to frame 15 and then drag a selection marquee around the first keyframes for both the Do it and Dream it layers, alternatively you can Shift–select them.

**23** With both keyframes selected, click and drag the first of the two keyframes on to the Current-Time Marker, remember to hold down Shift as you drag to force the keyframes to snap to the Current-Time Marker.

**24** RAM Preview the animation and notice that the text now appears in time with the music, making the animation immediately more dynamic.

**25** Go to File > Save as and, in the Save as dialog box, navigate to your Creative After Effects folder on the desktop and save the project into the Basics folder as Adoblogo05b.aep.

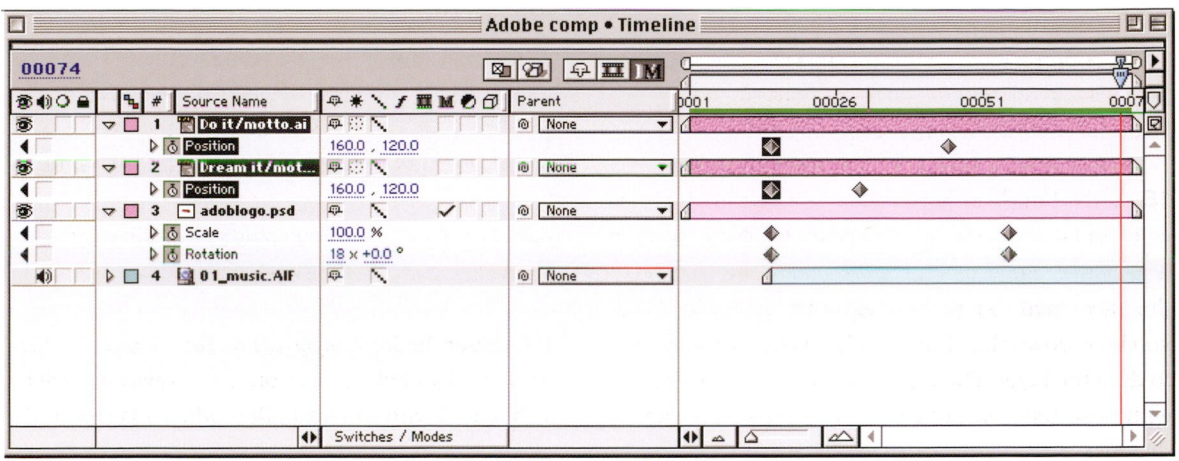

# interpolation

At the moment the temporal (time based)
interpolation between the keyframes is linear,
which means that the speed at which the layer
moves is constant and even. Very few things in
real life move at a constant speed, most things
gradually accelerate or deccelerate; they vary
their speed as they move through time and space.

There are exceptions to this rule. Imagine a car
traveling at a constant speed of say twenty miles
per hour. Suddenly the car crashes into a wall. Up
to the point at which the car is stopped suddenly
by the wall, it is moving linearly through time. In
other words, it moves at a constant speed till the
wall abruptly stops it. It is described as linear
because it is like drawing a straight line between
one point and another.

If the car then reverses away from the wall then
this is no longer a linear move through time and
space, because the car starts off slowly and
gradually accelerates, this would be a curved
interpolation between the two points. It may
still travel between the same two points within
the same space of time but it may start off slowly
and then become much faster, rather than
traveling at a constant speed.

In our example the animation would look
smoother if we gradually slowed the text down
as it approached its end point. You can do this
manually in After Effects but you can also use
pre-built Keyframe Assistants, which will automate
the process for you.

**1** If you do not have a project open, open Adoblogo06.aep from Training > Projects > Chapter 02.

**2** Click on the Motion Blur checkboxes for the Dream it and Do it layers.

After Effects is currently using Draft Quality as its default display setting; this setting does not use anti–aliasing or sub-pixel positioning. In other words, it will position objects to the nearest pixel and will not use any smoothing on edges. This mode is fine for rough work but if you want more precision and/or want to see what your final output will look like you can also look at your layers in Best Quality mode. Previewing in this mode will increase rendering time and therefore slow down the display of your animation. Once loaded into RAM, however, it will play back in real time as it does in Draft mode.

The Quality switches of each layer can be set individually so you can have one layer previewing in Draft mode and another in Best, all within the same composition.

**3** To switch your layers onto Best Quality mode simply click the Quality Switch, for each layer in the Switches column. The switch will currently be represented by a diagonal dotted line. As you click on the switch, the dotted line will change to a solid line.

You can change all Quality switches in one action by clicking the mouse on the first switch and dragging it down across the others.

**4** RAM Preview your animation to see how much better the animation looks when rendered in Best Quality.

**5** Using any of the methods, move the Current-Time Marker to frame 45. Let's animate some more properties.

To make a movement in an animation more dynamic it's a good idea to 'go past the pose'. This is a well known trick used by animators to exaggerate movement. The idea is to push the value slightly above our desired end point, just for a split-second, before finally resting at the end point of the animation. We'll add a little 'scale bounce' to the animation to give it a bit more life.

To show more than one property for a layer without having to uncollapse the whole layer, you can hold down the Shift key whilst hitting the property shortcuts, this will add them to the visible properties already displayed in the Timeline.

**6** Make sure that only the Do it layer is selected in the Timeline and then hit Shift + Alt + S. Holding down Shift whilst hitting the S key will add the Scale property to the Position property, which is already visible. Holding down the Alt key will also set a keyframe for Scale at the current time.

**7** Turn off Motion blur for the composition to improve the speed of your previews by clicking the big M switch at the top of the Timeline, this switch can be activated again when you render the movie, it is not necessary for us to see the blur for now.

**8** Move three frames ahead by hitting the Page Down arrow key on your keyboard three times. Alternatively, use the Next Frame button on the Time Controls Palette to do the same job.

**9** Change the Scale property value to 170% by clicking the Current Value display in the Switches column, entering 170 and then hitting the enter key on the number pad of your keyboard.

**10** Move ahead by another two frames by hitting the Page Down arrow key twice.

As well as being able to drag keyframes around in the Timeline, you can copy and paste them.

**11** Select the first Scale keyframe and then go to Edit > Copy or hit Command + C to copy the keyframe information to the clipboard.

**12** Hit Command + V or got to Edit > Paste to paste the keyframe and its value at the position of the Current-Time Marker.

**13** Jump back to the previous keyframe by hitting the J key on the keyboard. Look at the text and notice that the edges are very fuzzy and pixelated when the layer is pushed past 100%.

This layer is an Illustrator file and they can be stretched to any size within After Effects without losing quality. In order to do this you need to activate what is called Continuous Rasterization. There is an explanation of this process later in the book so for now I'll just show you how to apply it. I don't want to fill your head with too much too soon!

**14** Still watching the text in the Composition window, click on the Continuously Rasterize switch (the one circled in red in the diagram) for the Do it layer. Notice that the text is now much clearer. Do the same for the Dream it layer.

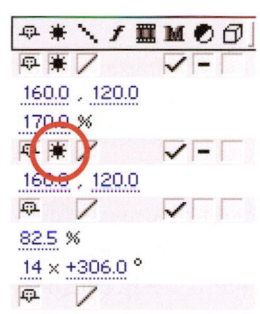

**15** Select both the Do it and the Dream it layers and then go to Composition > Preview > Wireframe Preview, this is a quick way of seeing a real time preview of the animation without having to wait for a RAM Preview to build. It will only preview the layers which are selected in the Timeline, showing them as wireframe outlines, enough to get an idea about the movement of your animation.

Notice that the 'scale bounce' of the Do it layer is very abrupt, I'd like the movement to be a bit softer as it bounces up and down in scale. At the moment the scale is moving linearly.

**16** Make sure that the Current-Time Marker is sitting over the middle keyframe and then drag the Navigator slider, at the bottom of the Timeline all the way to the right to zoom in on the keyframes.

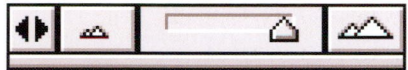

**17** On the Do it layer, click on the disclosure triangle next to the Scale stopwatch to open up the layers value graph. Here you can see a visual display of the animation in graph form. Notice that there is a straight line drawn between each of the keyframes representing a linear move.

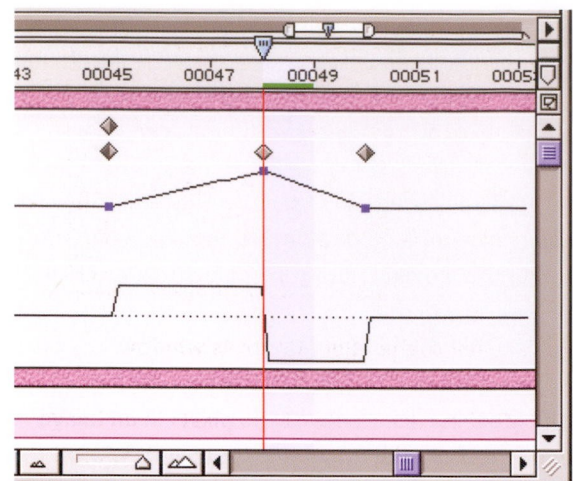

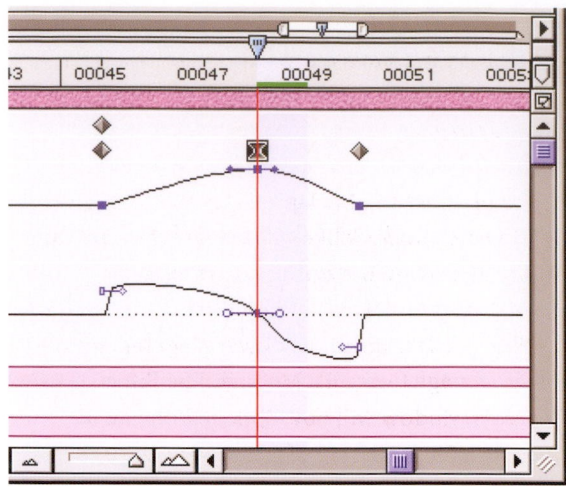

**18** Context-click on the middle Scale keyframe and choose Keyframe Assistant > Easy Ease from the drop down menu to ease the velocity on the way into and out of the keyframe, this will soften the move.

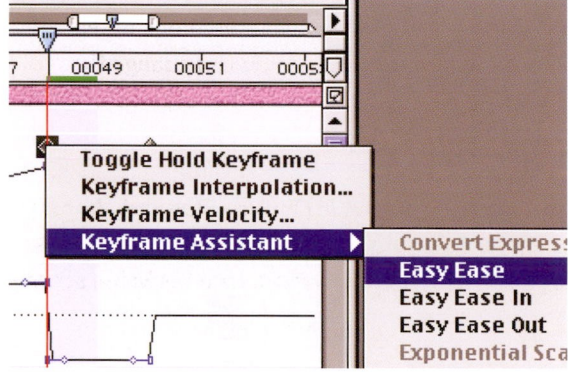

**19** Notice that the value graph has now changed to a nice, smooth curve as it goes through the middle keyframe. Compare the two graphs illustrated at the top of this page. After comparing the graphs, drag the Navigator slider back to the left so that you can see the whole timeline.

**20** Activate the Enable Motion Blur switch again, Context-click on the gray area between the keyframes and choose Preview > RAM Preview from the menu to preview the animation.

**21** Hit the Home key to send the Current-Time Marker back to the beginning of your composition.

**22** Hit Command + A to select all of the layers in your composition and then close all of the layers by clicking the little triangle next to any of the layers names, this will close all selected layers.

**23** In the Composition window, select the file named Background.mov and drag it down to the Timeline. As you drag it on to the Timeline, move it up and down and notice the black line indicating where the layer will be placed. Drag it underneath the other layers and release the mouse button to drop it in as the bottom layer of your composition. Remember that the Top layer in the Timeline represents the front-most layer in the Composition window.

**24** If you dropped it in the wrong place, simply click the name of the movie layer in the Timeline and drag it down the Timeline till it is underneath all other layers, you will see a black highlighted line representing the new position of the layer.

**25** Go to File > Save as, navigate to your Creative After Effects folder on the desktop and save the project into the Basics folder as Adoblogo06b.aep.

# adding effects

**1** If you do not have a project open, then open Adoblogo07.aep from Training > Projects > Chapter 02.

At the moment the background is too literal, I don't want it to look like water, I simply want an abstract, moving background texture.

**2** With the Backgrnd.mov layer selected go to Effect > Image Control > Median. The Effect Controls window will now appear. You can see a diagram of it at the top of the next column.

**3** If you have limited screen space, you may need to hit the Tab key to hide your other palettes in order to see it properly. Hitting the tab key repeatedly will hide and show all open palettes; it's a handy way of hiding them temporarily, I use this shortcut all the time.

You can save custom layouts of your windows and palettes to make managing your screen space easier. It's a good idea to save new configurations for each new layout you devise.

**4** Reposition your windows and palettes so that they make the best use of the space available to you on screen.

**5** Go to Window > Workspace > Save Workspace. Name the new workspace 320 × 240 and click OK.

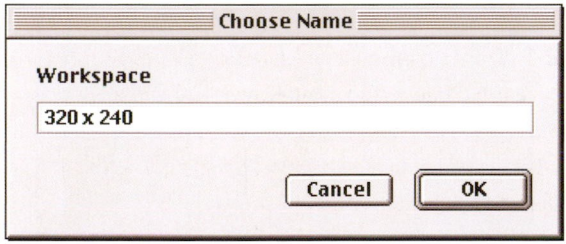

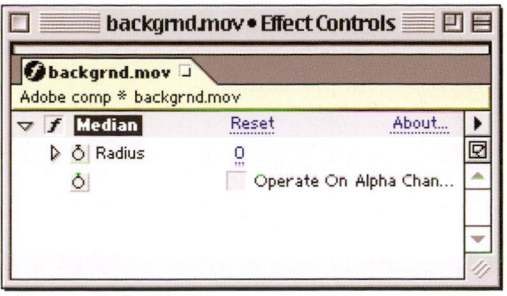

**6** Go back to the Effect Controls window.

The Median effect looks at the pixels in an image and works out the median (or average) color within a selected range. You adjust the range by adjusting the Radius slider in the Effect Controls window. A setting of one will work within a range of one pixel from the center pixel. A radius of ten will work out the average color between pixels in a circle within a radius of ten pixels from the center point. Notice that the slider in the Effect Controls window only allows a maximum radius of ten. If you need a higher setting you can change the slider's minimum and maximum range yourself, I'll show you how.

**7** Context-click on the Radius value and choose Edit Value from the drop down menu, this brings up the Slider control box. Change the Value setting to 35.

Context-clicking on a value will bring up a dialog box where you can find more features to control how a value is adjusted.

**8** Whilst still in the dialog box, change the Maximum Value to 50 and then click OK to leave the dialog box.

**9** Using the slider in the Effect Controls window, change the radius value to 30. To make the slider more accurate, you can hold down the Command/Control key whilst dragging it. To make it scrub faster, hold down Shift key whilst dragging.

The Median effect has softened the background movie to give an effect of movement without the footage being easily recognizable as water. This filter can also be used to get rid of artifacts from badly compressed footage, at a very low setting it can get rid of visual edge noise without having to blur the image.

**10**  Hit the Home key to return to the beginning of your composition and then hit the RAM Preview button or the 0 key on the number pad to preview your movie.

Notice that with multiple layers, effects and motion blur applied, the RAM Preview is becoming slower to load, this is because After Effects is having to calculate (or render) the new frames, working out how the changes you have made will affect the look of your composition. Basically, the more layers, masks, effects, transformations you add to your composition, the slower it will be to render. Keep this in mind when designing your compositions.

**TIP:**  Remember that you can turn off motion blur for your composition to help speed up your previews, it can then be switched on for the checked layers in the Render Settings dialog box before rendering.

**11**  To turn off Motion blur for your composition whilst still leaving the layer switches on, click the big M button at the top of your Composition window.

Switching back to Draft quality will also speed up the preview. You can choose to override these Quality and Motion Blur settings in the Render Settings window when you are ready to render. I normally work in draft quality with motion blur off, I find this is adequate in most situations. I often switch to best quality now and then to check my final output, as you'll see shortly, things can look quite different in Best quality.

There is a quick way to set all layers to Draft quality without having to click the quality switch for each layer.

**12**  Make sure the Timeline is active by clicking its title bar, and then hit Command + A to select all layers in the composition.

**13**  Hit Command + Shift + U or go to Layer > Quality > Draft to change all selected layers to Draft mode.

**14**  RAM Preview your composition in draft quality to see your changes.

Notice that the RAM Preview without motion blur is enough to give you a rough idea of what's happening in your composition. There are other ways of speeding up the preview options when working with complex projects. We'll take a look at them a bit later in the book.

**15**  Go to File > Save as and, in the Save as dialog box, navigate to your Creative After Effects folder on the desktop and save the project into the Basics folder as Adoblogo07b.aep.

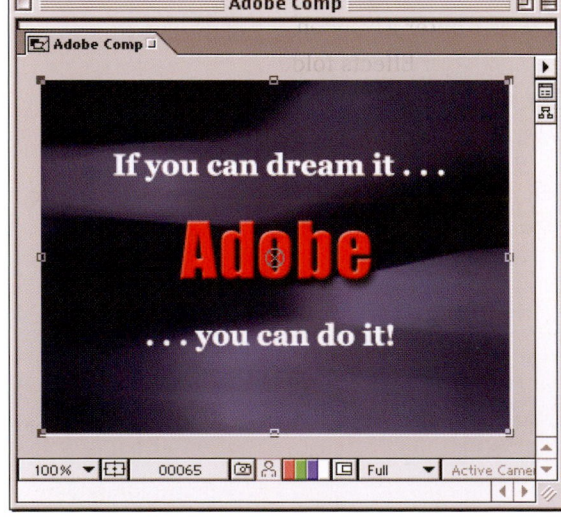

# rendering your movie

OK, you are now ready to render your movie to the hard disk. At the moment references to your source files and information about all the changes you made to them are stored inside the After Effects project. You need to render these changes to a new movie file on your hard disk which can then be used in other applications and even on different systems and platforms. The file that you render from After Effects will be a self-contained movie file, you can still make changes in the original project but to see the changes you would have to re-render the movie file again.

**1** If you do not have a project open, open Adoblogo08.aep from Training > Projects > Chapter 02.

**2** Make sure that either the Composition window or Timeline are selected, then hit Command + M or go to Composition > Make Movie, a save dialog box will appear. As a default, After Effects will name the movie after your composition, if you wanted to change the name of your movie then this would be the time to do it, for now leave it as it is.

**3** Using the dialog box, navigate to the Desktop of your Computer and open your Basics folder, in the Creative After Effects folder.

**4** Click the Save button or hit the Return key on your keyboard to choose to save your movie into the open folder.

You will now see the Render Queue dialog box in front of you. This is where you determine the Render Settings and Output Module settings for your movies. If you look at the Render Settings, next to the drop down menu icon it currently says Current Settings. This means that, if you went ahead and rendered now, After Effects would use the settings that you have set up in your comp i.e. Motion Blur would be off for the composition and all layers would be rendered in Draft Quality. We'll adjust the settings to bypass the settings used in your comp.

**5** Click the drop down menu icon next to Render Settings, notice the choices available to you. These are predetermined settings, which have been saved as templates for you. You can also make up your own templates with your own preferred settings. I'll show you how to do this later in the book.

**6** Choose Custom from the drop down menu and the Render Settings dialog box will appear.

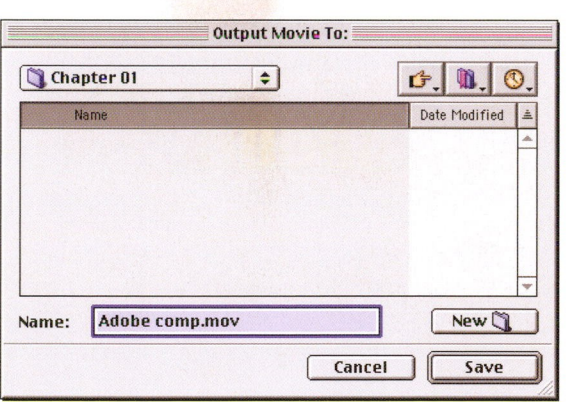

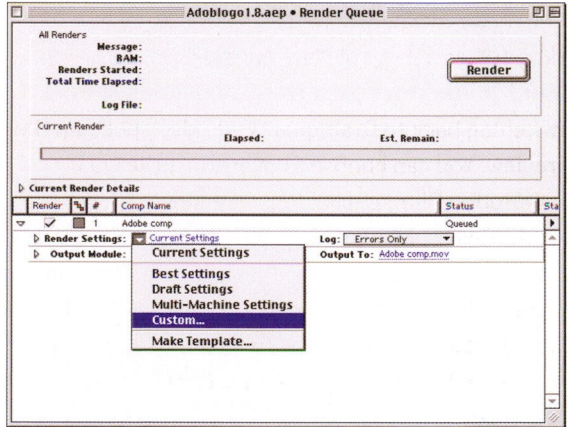

This dialog box may look complicated to you but don't worry, by the time you finish this book you'll know it pretty well. In the top left corner is the Quality drop down menu, this is where you can override the quality settings in your composition.

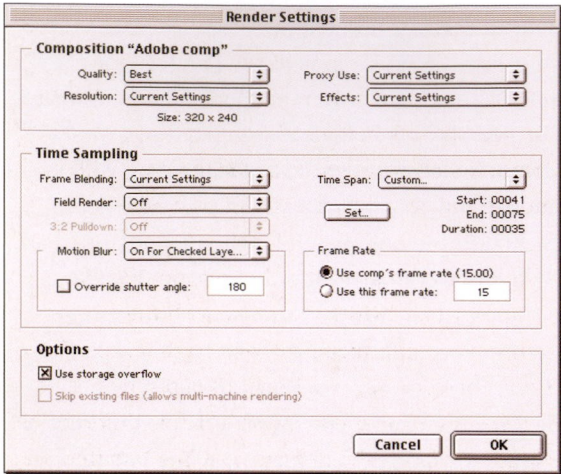

**7** From the drop down menu, choose Best, this will switch all layers in your composition to best quality regardless of the switch settings in the original composition.

Underneath the Quality menu is the Resolution menu, this is where you can override the resolution settings for your composition. You haven't altered the resolution of your comp (we'll take a look at that option later) so the existing settings should be fine.

**TIP:** If you are ever in doubt about this setting, click the drop down menu and choose Full from the menu to render out your movie at full resolution.

**8** Move down to the Time Sampling section and to the Motion Blur menu, which is now set to Current Settings. Look in the drop down menu, at the options available and choose On for Checked Layers, this will turn Motion Blur on for all the layers that we checked in our composition using the Layer Motion Blur switch. This will override the current state of the Enable Motion Blur switch in the composition.

We will leave some of the other menus in here till later, I don't want to bombard you with too much to learn for now but don't worry we'll be back here again, regularly!

**9** Click the OK button or hit the Return key on the keyboard to return to the Render Queue window.

**10** Click on the Output Module drop down menu and look at the templates available for you to use in there. This is where you determine the format of your output file, which channels are output, color depth, codecs used. You can also choose to output audio here as well as crop or stretch your movie file.

**11** Choose Custom from the drop down menu and the Output Module Settings dialog will appear.

**12** Click on the drop down menu for Format, which currently reads Quick Time movie. Notice the huge choice of formats that can be output from After Effects. The format is also sometimes known as the architecture of your file.

As well as being able to output incredibly versatile QuickTime movies and AVI movies which can be read by most computer applications, you can output to various kinds of image sequence (e.g. Pict, Targa, Tiff, SGI) for outputting to proprietary systems such as Quantel's excellent post production and editing systems.

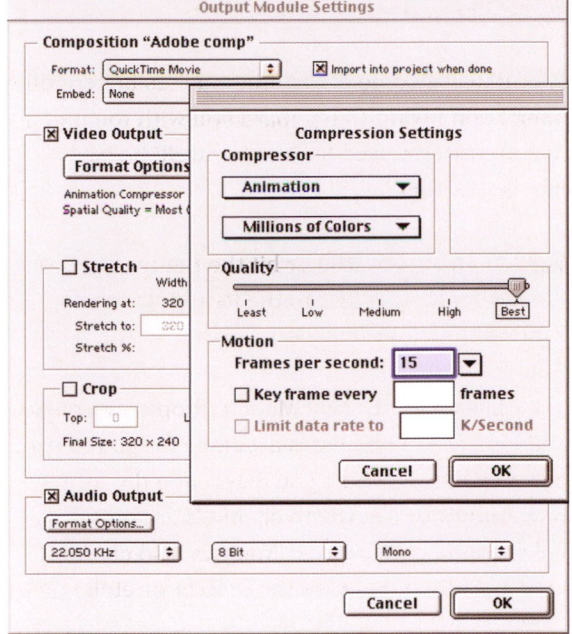

You can even choose to output Cineon sequences for feature film production. At the other end of the spectrum, you can choose to output animated Gifs for inclusion in your web page designs. After Effects even gives you the option to output your movies in Macromedia Flash's SWF format. As well as the comprehensive list of output formats available here, there are plug-ins available to allow you to output to other formats not listed here.

**13** Choose QuickTime movie from the list and then check the box next to the drop down menu, which reads Import into Project When Done. With this box checked, After Effects will import a reference to the finished movie into your current project so that you can view the finished movie without leaving the application.

**14** In the Video Output section, click on the Format Options button to bring up the Compression Settings, this is where you will choose the codec to use for your movie.

A codec compresses your footage so that the Computer bandwidth can cope with the information and decompresses so that it can be played back on screen. Depending on the hardware setup you have you will use different codecs to optimize your footage. You can find out more about codecs and compression issues in the Technical.pdf document in the CD > Extras folder.

**15** Go back to the Compression Settings dialog box and click and hold the top drop down menu. In there you will see a list of available codecs for you to choose from.

The list of codecs available is the codecs that were installed during the installation of QuickTime or Video For Windows. If you have a video card installed on your system you may have some extra codecs showing in this list. Most video cards come with their own codecs that are installed when you install the driver for your video card. Once installed, the codec will be included in the default list of codecs available to you in the After Effects Compressor Settings window.

You can also install other codecs onto your System; the new codecs will then appear in this list the next time you restart your machine. An example of when this can be useful is when preparing footage to be used on an Avid system. You can download the Avid codec from the Avid website and drop it into your System. You can then render directly out from After Effects, using the Avid codec. This movie will then be easily imported into the Avid system in its native format.

**16** From the list of available codecs, choose Animation.

**17** Leave the quality set to Best and check that the frame rate is set to 15 Frames per second. Leave the other options for now, we will look at them later. Click OK.

**18** Go to the Audio Output section at the bottom of the screen and check the checkbox to activate it.

**19** Change the settings to 22.050 kHz, 8 Bit, and Mono and then click OK to leave the Output Module Settings dialog box.

**20** Before hitting the Render button, put the Caps Lock key down (on your keyboard). When you have Caps lock down, After Effects locks the preview in the Composition window and stops it from refreshing on every frame. Doing this will speed up your render time.

**21** Click the little triangle next to Current Render Details. When you start to render, this will show you details of the estimated final file size, free disk space available etc. It will also tell you how long each frame is taking to render each effect or transformation, this is very useful for learning which effects and processes are processor and memory intensive.

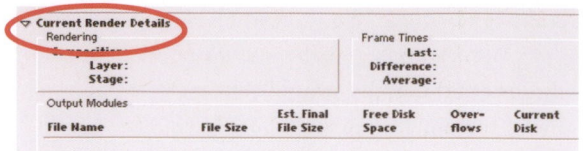

**22** Hit the Render button and watch the frames crunch away! Notice, in the Render details, that the Median effect is taking longer than anything else is to process.

**23** When the movie has finished rendering you will hear the much loved (and hated by some!) After Effects prrring!! This tells you that your movie is ready.

**24** Close the Render Queue window and go to the Project window. In there you will find the movie which has just been rendered (Adobe Logo movie). Double-click the file to open it up in the QuickTime player and hit the Spacebar, on your keyboard to start playback, hit it again to pause the playback.

**25** Go to File > Save as and, in the Save as dialog box, navigate to your Creative After Effects folder on the desktop and save the project into the Basics folder as Adoblogo08b.aep.

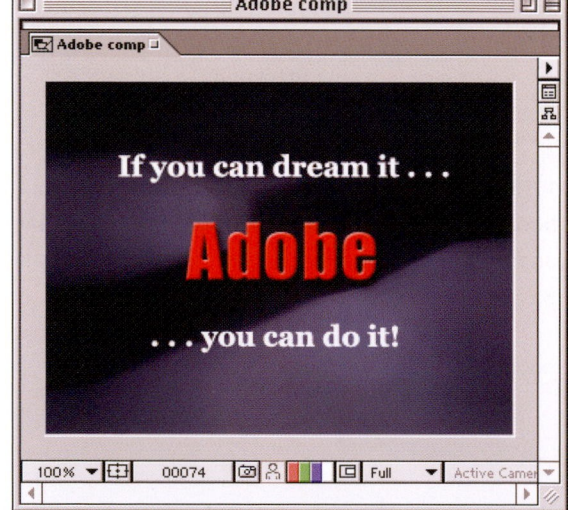

## recap

Congratulations, you have completed the first
chapter of the book! You have learned how to
create a composition within an After Effects
project; import files into the project; add the
footage files to your composition; apply effects to
the layers; animate the properties of the layers
and output the finished animation as a QuickTime
movie. You have also learned a little bit about
Codecs, Keyframes and the different file formats
you can use within After Effects as well as the
fundamental workings of the software.

Now that you've learned enough to get you up and
running, you can start to play with what you've
learned. On the CD there is a folder named *Free
stuff* containing other folders full of plug-ins and
sample files, donated by several excellent plug-in
companies and Royalty-free footage companies.
Make sure to read the License agreements
accompanying these files before using any of them
for commercial work, some are unrestricted but
some have been provided purely for non-
commercial use. Details on how you can buy full
resolution versions of this footage and see the full
collections is in the individual footage company's
folders on the CD, I thoroughly recommend taking
a look at these.

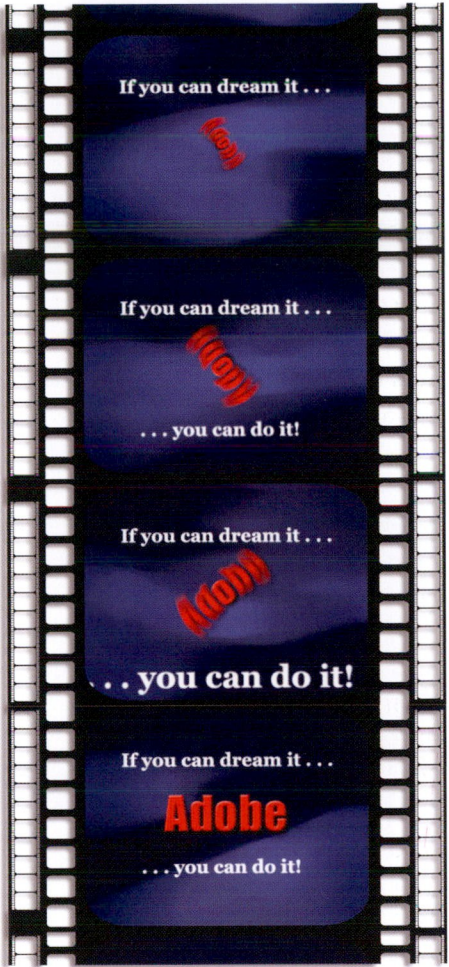

There's also more footage available for you to use
in the Source Movies, Source Sounds and Source
Images folders, within the Training folder. These
folders contain all the other footage used in the
book's tutorials. These also contain conditions of
use documents which you must read carefully.
Remember that you can also use your own
footage, sounds or images too.

In the Training folder is a Portfolio Browser
file called Media.fdb. This allows you to search
through a catalogue of all of these files, showing
you previews and providing you with search
functions, it's like a searchable, multimedia
database. Don't try to work directly with the files
on the CD, make sure they are copied to your hard
drive before using them within After Effects. Using
them from the CD can impair performance.

If you haven't yet installed the free demo version of Extensis Portfolio from the Demos folder, do it now and then open the Media.fdb catalogue file. Portfolio is a great piece of software for managing your footage. With the full version you can create your own libraries of footage (see the Free Stuff > Extensis Portfolio folder for more information about upgrading). As well as these free files, you can use any of the files from the exercise that you have just completed.

I recommend that you choose three or four files to begin with. The secret to learning is to take one step at a time, don't try to be too ambitious by working with too many files, you'll just get flustered and frustrated. Remember, some of the best work seen in the history of design is the simplest.

I would recommend choosing one QuickTime movie file, two or three image files and an audio file to begin with. Create another ten-second animation using the techniques you have just learned. Look upon this exercise as a practice session to help you feel comfortable with the software, don't be too precious about it, it's just a bit of fun.

Keep your final project in mind and if you happen upon something that you would like to use in your final project, great! Simply save any finished projects or movies into your Creative After Effects > Basics folder, you'll probably find uses for any QuickTime movies or projects that you work on later in the book. If you don't come up with anything useful save it anyway and most of all, don't worry, there's plenty of time to develop ideas before the end of the book.

I hope that some of these suggestions will help your creative flow. When I began writing this book, I decided that I wanted it to be a book which would inspire creative thoughts as well as teaching software techniques. During the process of writing I have chatted a lot to other creative people to ask them how they deal with the demands of their work and how they keep coming up with new ideas. I've decided to share a few of these tips and tricks with you. They come from some of the best designers I know, in fields ranging from web and new media design to more traditional skills such as ceramic design and performance art. I also asked them how they go about combatting creative blocks.

These tips have been interspersed throughout the book. The following two suggestions are from Steve Caplin, a very talented graphic designer and author friend of mine. You can view his online portfolio at: http://www.stevecaplin.com

• If you're on a tight deadline, I find the adrenaline rush usually does the trick on its own. It may be the increased oxygen, but outdoor thinking always proves profitable. If possible, think in your own garden - if you hang around parks gazing blankly into space you're likely to be arrested.

• Think obliquely. Often the most obvious idea isn't the one that will work best in practice, and presenting ideas visually is a different matter to explaining concepts verbally. Start by exploring common metaphors and see where they take you.

OK, hopefully you have some ideas which you can start to work with, if not, still no need to worry, perhaps going through the following chapters will help inspire you; in situations where you have an creative block, learning some new techniques can be just the tonic you need. Well, I think that's enough rabbiting from me, time for you to roll up your sleeves and get in there – Happy keyframing!

# chapter three
# the brief

OK, so you've learned the basics about how After Effects works, you should now feel comfortable enough to begin thinking about the more creative side of things. You may have some ideas from the practice session that you've just completed but how can you formulate these ideas into a cohesive working project?

As I told you in the Mission chapter, we will be working on three preconceived projects as we progress throughout the book, you'll also be developing your own personal project as your knowledge progresses.

Most real life projects begin with a brief, given to you by your client. A brief is a set of requirements for a specific project. It can include information about: target audiences, preferred color schemes, information about the program itself and any identities or moods that the program-makers wish to convey. I find that it also helps, when trying to develop new ideas, to make up an imaginary brief for yourself.

The following pages explain the briefs and ideas that I set out for the main projects in this book (and the 60s project, of which there are some elements included on the CD). Read through these briefs carefully and then either use one of the existing briefs or put together an imaginary brief for your own unique project.

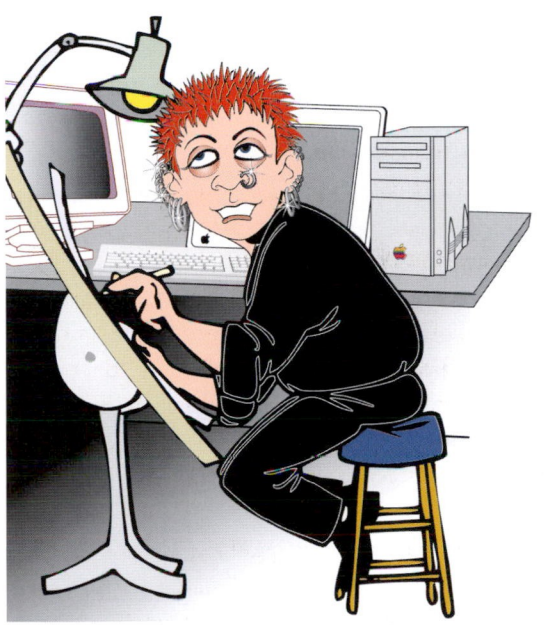

## graffiti club
### the brief

The client in this instance has asked for some animated titles for a Saturday morning TV program. Aimed at children between the ages of 8 and 14, the title for the program is 'The Graffiti Club'. It is an art and music program designed to inspire children to become creative. The show is introduced by two teenagers, Annie and Ellis, who demonstrate to the audience various ways of creating their own; artwork, music, models, clothes etc. using materials easily found at home, in their rubbish bins or from local resources in their areas.

The producer is keen to feature the presenters in the title sequence in some sort of animated form. They have mentioned a desire for rough, hand drawn animation but their budget is pretty low, leaving us less than five days to design and produce this forty-five second animation.

## the design process

OK, time to think about the pros and cons of this job. Let's start with the cons, we have a tight budget, which means a tight deadline. It's very important, when in a real working environment, to stick to schedules. It's all very well thinking to yourself, 'Well, I'll just do a couple of extra hours on it here and there', but if you do that with all your jobs, you'll run yourself ragged and be too tired to produce any quality work.

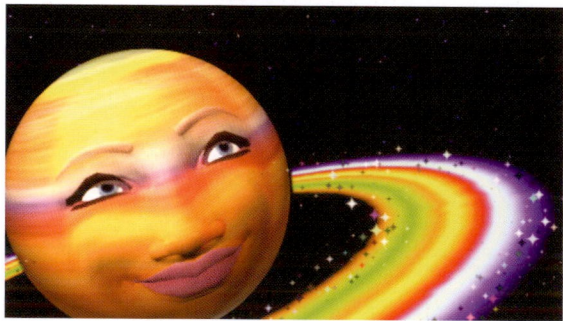

Remember that you need to have some time to inspire yourself, away from the studio. The obvious place to start is to watch some kids' TV on a Saturday morning! Research what's already out there and take notes of things that you think work or don't work. Have a look at kids' magazines, books, movies. Listen to some chart music; basically, try and get in to the 'mood' of the brief. I always allow myself a little bit of time within the schedule for research. Even if the schedule is very tight, an hour or so looking through a book or a website can just help to clear your mind and spark off some good ideas. Don't be afraid to let the pressure take a back seat for an hour or two.

> **Pictured here are more stills from BBC's 'See You, See Me – The Planets' © 2000**

Sometimes having a tight deadline can be a good thing because it forces you to be decisive. A good way to cope is to set yourself a timetable, it'll only take you two minutes and it's a good feeling to have it to refer to when you're feeling under pressure. For a five day job, I'd give myself half a day for research, a day for sketching out ideas and meeting with the client. That leaves three days to complete the job and half a day for last minute changes etc. This may seem like a lot of time to you for producing a forty-five second animation but remember that you must include design time as well as permitting time for trail and error if you are developing a new technique. You'll also look much more impressive to the client if you get your work in early rather than late, they'll definitely come back for more if you come in slightly under budget.

OK, so I've decided that it would be pushing it to do two, good, hand drawn character animations within this time-scale so I need to think of a different solution. The whole feel of the show is one of salvage and creativity. The set is bright and colorful, made from old tires, scaffolding poles and painted corrugated iron. The producers want to introduce this atmosphere in the title sequence. This could work to our advantage: the animation does not require a highly polished, photo-real look, we can be quite rough and ready with the drawing and animation. I did some 'South Park' type animation last year for a BBC job, I'm sure we could use a similar technique to animate the figures. We can then apply some filters to the finished result to make it look more hand drawn. This way, the producer will get the look that she wants within the time-scale.

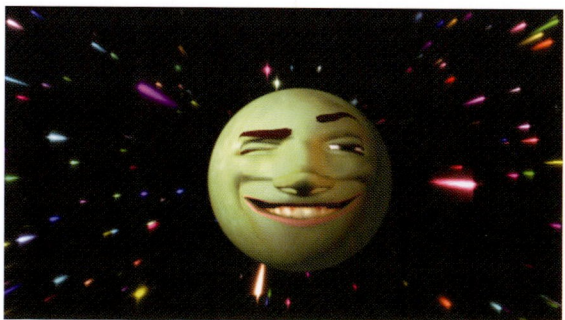

For the background, we can do some salvaging ourselves by reusing some Royalty free photography of graffiti. If you don't have any stock photos to use, you can quite often find some royalty free images on the web or on cover-mounted CDs. Just make sure to check in the license information that it's OK to use them for the purpose you are intending. If you have a camera and a scanner, or a camcorder and video input on your computer, you can always shoot some footage yourself, that way, you're guaranteed to have original footage. If you are really stuck, you could create your own graffiti using the air brush tool and some brick textures in Photoshop.

## the storyboard

Now we've got some ideas, it's time to start playing with them. This is the point where I would go off and sketch my storyboard. I simply divide an A3 sheet of paper in to 12, 4:3 rectangles, with space above, underneath and between each one for comments. I have provided you with an A4 storyboard template on the CD. You can find this in Training > Source Images > Angie Images, the image is named, Storyboard01.ai. This is an illustrator file so you can re-size it to whatever dimensions you like without losing resolution. Print out a copy so that you can develop your own storyboard for the project of your choice. It will be interesting to compare your ideas with the ideas that I have come up with.

The storyboard does not need to be a work of art, the one illustrated below is pretty basic, using only four frames to tell the whole story; sometimes this is all that is needed. Stick figures are there to represent the characters. In this instance I would accompany the storyboard with my hand drawn sketches of the main characters so that the producers can get a clearer idea of what they will look like. This storyboard is really only for working out timing and camera moves.

## seattle evening news
### the brief

The client in this job is a national cable TV station. They want a new identity for their regional news programs which are broadcast simultaneously across the country. Their requirements are for the titles to be attention grabbing, showing current news items in an innovative way. The client also wants to be able to easily update the titles with footage from the different regions. The key is to design one sequence that can be customized for each region, but keeping the same look and feel throughout. The client has also asked for the titles to be relatively simple and clean yet visually exciting.

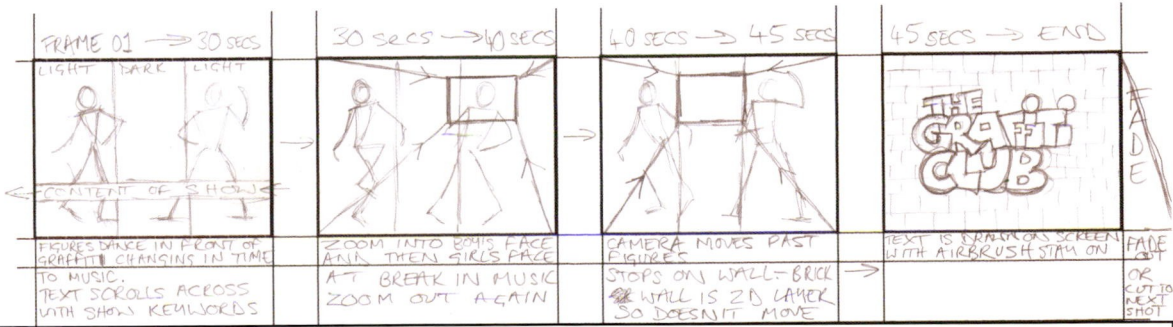

This is an example of a very simple storyboard. Notice that the timing of the animation is written along the top of each drawing, direction notes are underneath and transitions marked between the frames. In frame number two, see how a zoom into the screen is represented by direction lines running between the frame edges and a smaller frame, which is targeting the zoomed area.

## the design process

The producers at the TV station have commissioned some music for the titles which you can listen to; it is in the AS Music folder, in the Source sounds folder within the Training folder and is called 'Newsound.mov'; open it up and listen to it now. The music was designed by the guys at AS Music who specialize in designing music and sounds for TV and film.

As you can hear, the music is quite punchy, ideal for a news program. When listening to music for a piece of work, try to listen for the most distinctive features of the music, it will create good impact if you can time the visuals to coincide with the appropriate parts. In this instance I like the radar-like sound that carries throughout the whole sequence; this conveys the idea of a message being sent across the airways, very appropriate for a newsy feel.

I'd like to emphasize this idea by matching the sounds with a visual reference to radars. It's quite important not to be too literal with this, an image of a radar is a bit too clichéd for my liking; as a designer you must learn to suggest things to the viewer without them actually seeing them. In order to convey the notion of a radar I have decided to use simple concentric circles animating in and out from the center of the screen.

Part of my inspiration for this was taken from graphics which were broadcast on Channel 4 television in the UK in 2001. The graphics consist of a series of vertical strips which move randomly across each other horizontally. Each strip combines with the others to create different shapes as they pass over each other and this is superimposed over footage pertaining to the following program. I'd like to use a similar technique with undulating concentric circles.

The trouble with having to use news footage is that it all tends to be shot in different locations, by different camera operators and is quite often shot using various different formats. You may be given clips from an interview with the Prime Minister shot on digibeta; which are to be edited in with live, hand held action, shot on DVCAM. Without treatment the footage will look disparate and will distract the viewer's eye.

To bring the footage together and give it a unified look I've decided to use one basic color to colorize the news footage, this has the added advantage of keeping the design simple. By combining the single color with some chrome text we will achieve a very lucid design which also looks like it means business.

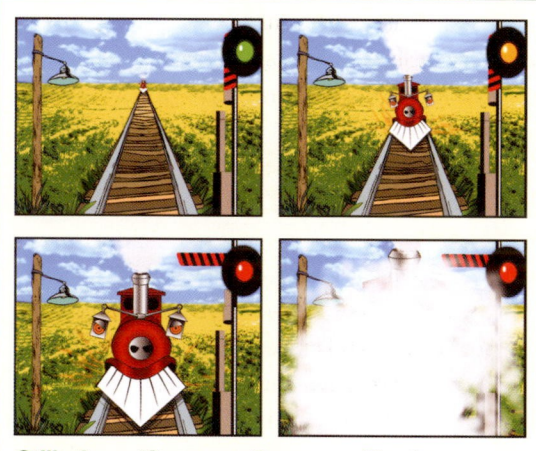

**Stills from 'See you, See me – The Inventors' BBC, 1999. Traditional animation techniques with added special effects.**

## the storyboard

Storyboards have been essential tools used in the production of some of the greatest films and animations of all time. All the great directors have used them including: Hitchcock, Orson Welles, Ridley Scott, Tim Burton and Walt Disney. They allow the director and the designers to work together, finalizing the design before moving into production.

A storyboard can be changed easily to accommodate new ideas without costing the team vast amounts of time and money, leaving the production time devoted to perfecting the techniques needed to tell the story. It's important to remember a few things when drawing your storyboard. As I said before, you don't want to spend too long deliberating over your storyboard, it is supposed to be a rough series of ideas which can be easily adjusted to suit your client's needs so don't be too precious about it.

However, you may find that a lot of producers and directors will not be able to visualize your designs in the way that you can. This can cause problems when the producer dismisses a rough sketch because he/she cannot imagine it in its finished state. To overcome this problem, I often provide two or three stills which are set up to approximate the colors, textures and overall quality of the finished piece. This can be done very easily by mocking up a few layers in After Effects, Photoshop or Illustrator.

## pop art – design and music from the 1960s
### the brief

This program title is pretty self-explanatory, a series of documentaries about design and music from the swinging sixties. In this case clichés are exactly what's needed. In the previous example we were asked to design something new and innovative, this time we are being asked to design something which looks like it could have been produced in the sixties. Of course we will give the sequence a modern twist but essentially it should look of the period.

This time the producers have no music so I have been left the job of sourcing some appropriate music for the piece. I get a lot of my inspiration from music. I always try to get the music right first as it is an integral component of any good opening title sequence.

I called on fellow Scot and extremely talented musician, Rod Spark, for this piece of music. There is a folder within the Source Sounds folder called Groove Tunnel, this contains several excellent snippets of music, all created by Rod. Open the file named, 'TheGroov.mov' and listen to the music to get a real feel of the sixties.

The reason I chose Rod for this job is that every piece of music I have heard from the Groove Tunnel stable sounds genuine, whichever genre it belongs to; Rod has a unique talent for mimicking any style of music you could possibly name. The beauty of working with people like Rod is that he will customize the music exactly how I want it, I can talk directly to the composer without having to settle for something which is not quite right. I also know that I'm not going to hear the same music anywhere else.

### the design process

When I think of the sixties I think of Mary Quants' stark black and white designs; beatniks dancing in seedy nightclubs and classic film titles like the brilliant Bond movie titles. I also think of Saul Bass and Pablo Ferros' fantastic film titles; Blue Note cover art; Andy Wharhol; the Pink Panther animations; Austin Powers and of course the Hippy culture. Now that's quite a lot of inspiration to fit into a minute of graphics. This is one of those situations where your job as a designer is to figure out which are the most important elements from these influences. You then have to figure out how to re-combine them to build something new and exciting – not an easy job but that's why we love our work, it's a challenge.

OK, well from the Bond titles I'd like to use the idea of the circles moving onto the screen one after the other, this will be the starting point of the titles. It is such a classically familiar film title that the viewer will immediately feel like they have been transported back to the sixties. I'd like to continue the circle theme throughout the animation, this will be what pulls the whole design together.

I'll incorporate dancing silhouettes inside the circles; transforming them into psychedelic spirals; play Saul Bass-like tricks by moving from 2D space to 3D space and then eventually end the titles with one of the circles falling to form the letter 'o' in the word 'Pop', perhaps from the lips of a Andy Wharhol-esque image of a girl.

This is the sort of project I relish, loads of inspiration with very few restraints. I've decided that this title will look its best with a widescreen aspect ratio which should be letterboxed for 4:3 transmission, this will be in keeping with the look and feel of film titles from this period.

## the storyboard

It is good practice to look at comic books for ideas of how to put together storyboards; they illustrate a sequence of events in the same way that we want our storyboards to do. Comics can give you some excellent ideas for camera angles and unusual Compositions, the Marvel comics in particular use some fantastic perspective in their frames and should be studied. I also keep a scrapbook of images that appeal to me, these include:

• Interior and exterior shots from home and garden-type magazines. These help me to work out perspectives and give me ideas for layout and Composition of elements within space.

• Figures and faces of all different shapes, sizes and poses. These give me inspiration when developing characters and their poses in my animations.

• Color schemes that appeal to me. If I see a combination of colors in print that work for me, I'll cut out a sample and stick it in my scrapbook, you never know when you will need inspiration, this ensures that you won't forget.

Basically, keep anything that appeals to you, it can be a nice piece of typography, a shape that appeals

to you or a texture that you like. If you can carry a camera with you this can also be very useful, you can get so much inspiration from the world around you if you are observant. Notice everything and photograph what appeals to you, this way you'll build up your own unique library of pure inspiration.

This storyboard needs to be a little more detailed than the last one. It needs to illustrate clearly how one shot leads into another. On the following page you can see a few example frames from the Pop Art storyboard. Notice on frame three and frame eight I have drawn direction arrows to demonstrate the movement happening at this point in the animation.

You can use any materials for your storyboard: markers, charcoal, paint, crayons. I tend to use a good propeller pencil and an eraser as this allows me to easily make changes to my drawings. I also use a chinagraph pencil for filling in large areas of black. It also comes in handy to have a compass, ruler, set square and french curves nearby to help you with your shape drawing.

This brief, unlike the other three has not yet been developed into a finished project but there are some elements that I (and Paul Tuersley) have put together for you to get started with. These projects and tutorials are in the Extras folder on the CD. Feel free to develop these into finished projects, Paul and I will also be developing this brief further and posting the resulting tutorials on the website at:
http://www.angie.abel.co.uk/book.html

The two storyboards you've seen so far have been very rough and hand drawn but there are times when precise geometric shapes are preferable.

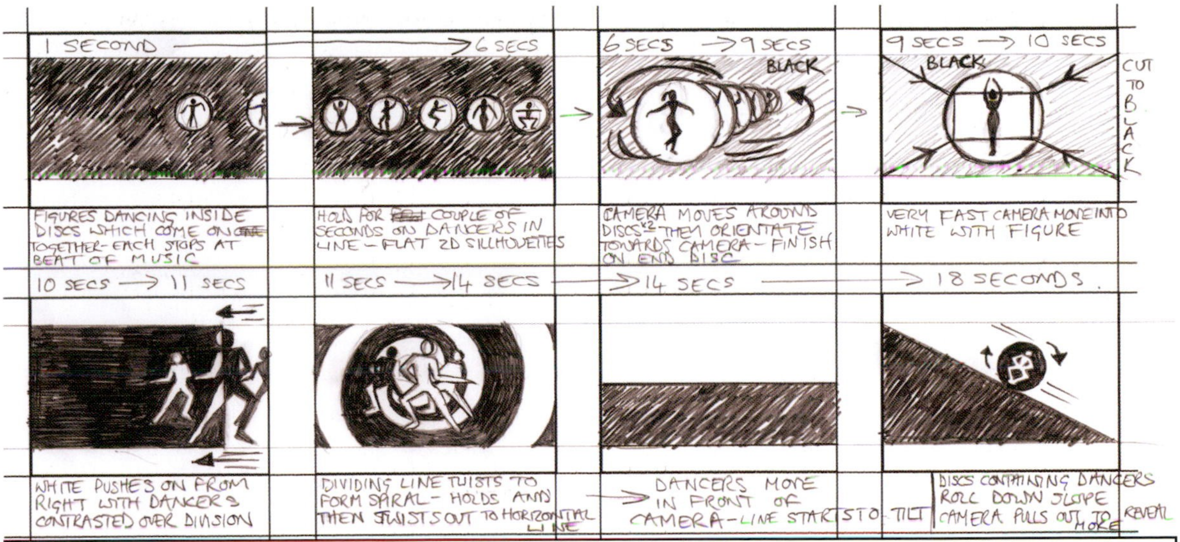
1 SECOND → 6 SECS
6 SECS → 9 SECS
BLACK
9 SECS → 10 SECS
BLACK
CUT TO BLACK
FIGURES DANCING INSIDE DISCS WHICH COME ON TOGETHER - EACH STOPS AT BEAT OF MUSIC
HOLD FOR COUPLE OF SECONDS ON DANCERS IN LINE - FLAT 2D SILLHOUETTES
CAMERA MOVES AROUND DISCS THEN ORIENTATE TOWARDS CAMERA - FINISH ON END DISC
VERY FAST CAMERA MOVE INTO WHITE WITH FIGURE
10 SECS → 11 SECS
11 SECS → 14 SECS
→ 14 SECS → 18 SECONDS
WHITE PUSHES ON FROM RIGHT WITH DANCERS CONTRASTED OVER DIVISION
DIVIDING LINE TWISTS TO FORM SPIRAL - HOLDS AND THEN TWISTS OUT TO HORIZONTAL LINE
DANCERS MOVE IN FRONT OF CAMERA - LINE STARTS TO TILT
DISCS CONTAINING DANCERS ROLL DOWN SLOPE CAMERA PULLS OUT TO REVEAL MORE

**This is an example of a very simple storyboard. Notice that the timing of the animation is written along the top of each drawing, direction notes are underneath and transitions marked between the frames. In frame number two, see how a zoom into the screen is represented by direction lines running between the frame edges and a smaller frame, which is targeting the zoomed area.**

# MacDonna video

## the brief

The final project is a bit of light-hearted relief. I wanted to include a pop promo in the projects because it is such an open art form, giving you the freedom to experiment and express yourself in any way you wish. There are several pieces of music in the source sounds folder and in the Free Media folder which you can choose from for your music video. You can use any style you wish, using live action, stills, animation, whatever, as long as the video relates to the music and enhances the musical experience for the viewer.

A good music video can help to sell copies of otherwise average music in the same way as a good piece of music can bring an average animation to life. Luckily, we have some excellent music for you to experiment with so we should have an excellent piece of animation to accompany it.

This may be the most challenging project because there are no definite guidelines to follow here, you have a completely free reign to come up with an idea for this which can sometimes make things more difficult. In this sort of situation you have to be very decisive, sketch out a few rough ideas and then decide which one you are going to go for. You may be able to combine ideas from different areas of the book in to one finished masterpiece but in order to get started you will need a rough storyline for the sequence. Don't begin with a too rigid idea as you may want to incorporate new ideas as you progress throughout the chapters.

## the design process

The video that I have designed is a bit tongue in cheek. I decided I would make the last project a bit more light-hearted than the others. I've tried to include lots of techniques used in music videos, although I obviously haven't spent as many man hours on this as would normally be spent on a finished music video. The effects in it are pretty quick and dirty, just enough to show you the techniques so that you can then go off and experiment with them.

I decided that I would use live action for this video as most of the others are built from animated elements. I'm a big fan of time-based effects and wanted to feature a few of them in this video so I needed a lot of footage to play with. Each day for a week I went out after work and shot footage in and around Edinburgh, where I currently live. As my budget was low I enlisted my friends to help out as actors, lighting operators, camera people and general dogs bodies – they were stars, the lot of them! I also decided to take the lead role myself so it's ended up as a parody of music videos and a fantasy for myself.

I don't want to say too much more before moving ahead with this project except to encourage you to include some of your own footage in there at some point, whether it be your own music, photographs, drawings or video footage. The only stipulation is that the footage must be copyright free if you want it to be shown on our website. I hope you enjoy it as much as I did making mine.

> **Here are some frames from my MacDonna storyboard. Notice that the drawings have a little more detail but are still fairly rough.**

## the storyboard

I've decided to make a very fast moving video with very quick edits so I need to make sure that my storyboard is detailed enough, incorporating all the important scenes. The other storyboards have focused on camera moves and edits, this sequence will be much more narrative than the others, telling a definite story from beginning to end. We must make sure that the sequence of events can be understood from the storyboard before we go ahead with the project.

The figures will have to be more detailed in this example and the faces need to have expressions. The whole video will be much more focused on people than the last two, which were more abstract. I find that the easiest way to begin is to sketch out rough Compositions, using cylinders and cubes to represent the shapes that make up the Composition. You can draw virtually anything using this technique. Next time you're out and about, look at some every day objects and imagine building them from these primitive shapes, this will help you form a good understanding of shape, form and the underlying construction of objects.

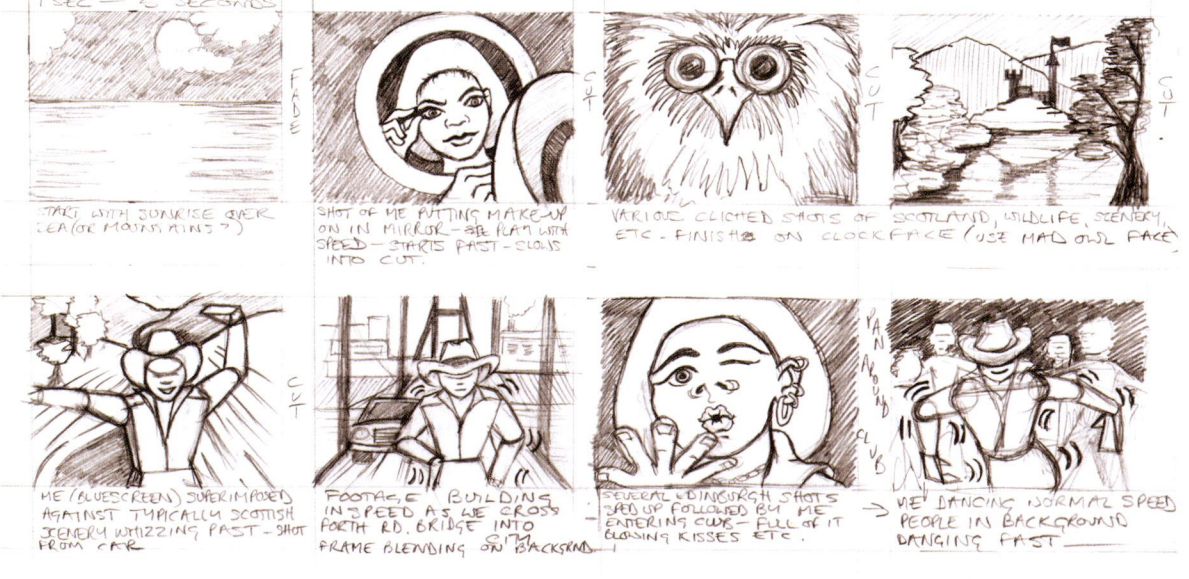

## recap

So, now you know the processes involved in creating a storyboard, I want you to go off, with a sketchbook, pencil, pens, eraser and whatever else you feel you might need to create your own storyboard, based on any of the four briefs you have just read.

If you're beginning to panic and perhaps feel that you 'can't draw', don't worry, nobody else but you will see this. It's only a tool to help you visualize your project. If you have to use stick figures and geometric shapes, that's fine. The more practice you get, the better you'll become. Here are a few tips to help you form your ideas and learn how to visualize and materialize them onto paper and eventually, the big screen!

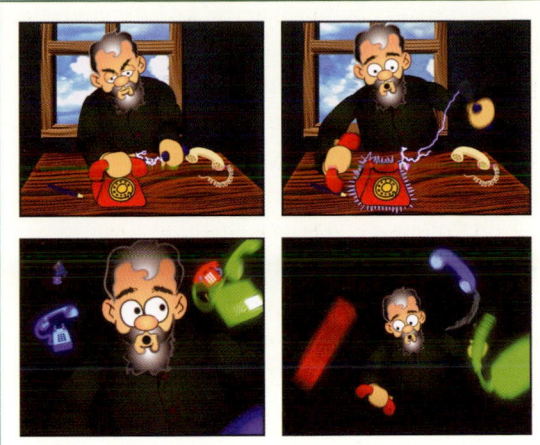

**Stills from 'See you, See me – The Inventors', BBC, 1999. Influences from 'Hobson's choice', the *drunk scene*.**

• If you can't think of any ideas, try looking around your environment for shapes, color combinations and movements that appeal to you. Nature and the world around you are full of inspiration.
• Look at the structure of buildings or machinery, they are full of shapes which interlock to create even more interesting forms.
• Look at the way that a bird swoops, perhaps you want to mimic that movement in your animations? Look at the color of the grass contrasted with the sky or the colors of neon lights against the night sky.
• Cut out some images you like from magazines and papers then play with them on a table or board, shifting them around to make different patterns, textures and collages.

• Just look around you for things that please you or make you feel good. If you have any objects which you love to look at or touch, try to define what it is about that object that makes it so pleasing to you. If you like it so much, then it's likely that other people will also be able to relate to it.
• Design is nothing complicated, it's just a matter of recognizing what appeals to you and then figuring out a way to realize it into your own work.
• If, at first, your ideas are not turning out the way that you want them to, don't give up! It's much easier to think that you are no good at something than it is to feel that you are a success. It takes hard work and courage to persevere with your dreams but if you really want it, you'll succeed.

• If you do panic and feel that you are getting nowhere fast, try deep breathing, I know it sounds ridiculous, I, too, was a scornful sceptic before I was persuaded to try this but it really works. Push all negative thoughts out of your mind each time you breathe out and think positive thoughts each time you inhale.

• If all else fails and you are still staring at a blank piece of paper, try doodling whilst you are watching the television, eating or out drinking in the pub. Sometimes ideas which are deeply buried in your sub-conscious thoughts can come out in doodles when you are half-concentrating on something else.

• You are the only one who has the power to stop your ideas from materializing, don't beat yourself up about it, relax and enjoy!

Right! Enough from me, go and put together some ideas based on the four project briefs I have provided you with. If you have a fantastic, burning ambition to work on any other ideas you have, then feel free, but at some point, try to follow one of the briefs set out in this chapter. It'll be good practice for when you're out in the real world, dealing with awkward clients who won't budge an inch on their own ideas!

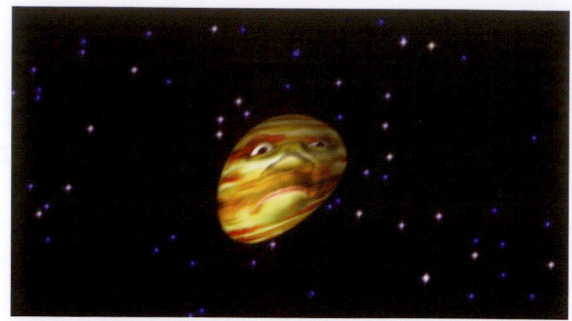

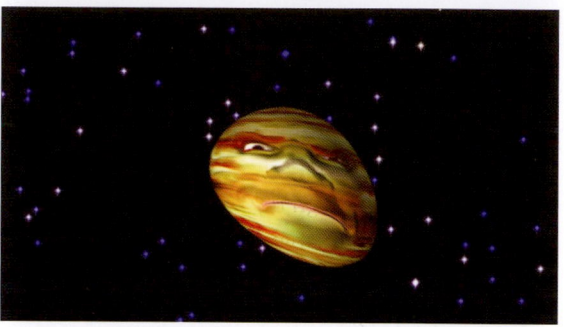

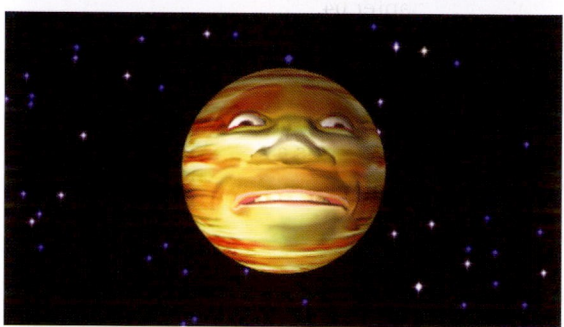

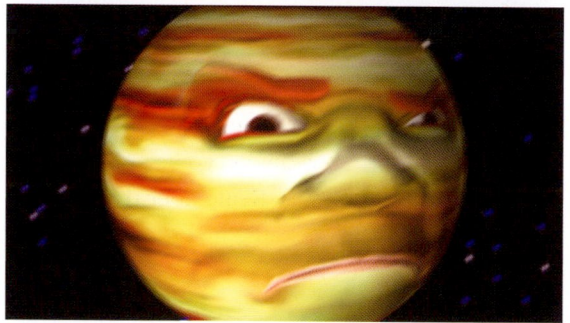

**Animations from 'See, you, See me – The Planets', BBC, 2000. Jupiter's walk was animated using Forge's Freeform plug-in, (demo version included on the CD for you)**

# chapter four
# preferences

Before we go any further with our exercises, I'd like to take you through the Preferences for After Effects. Preferences allow you to customize the software to perform just how you like it. Open up the Prefs.aep project from Training folder > Projects > Chapter 04.

Start by going to Edit > Preferences > General. You will now see the main After Effects preferences dialog box. In the box is a drop down menu, which allows you to access all the individual preferences screens from the one dialog box. We will start by looking at the General Preferences.

## general

### the undo-able actions box

This is where you can set the amount of Undo-able actions possible. Depending on the amount of RAM allocated to After Effects, you can retrace your steps up to 99 times. Remember that your undos are held in RAM so the higher this number, the less RAM you will have available for previews.

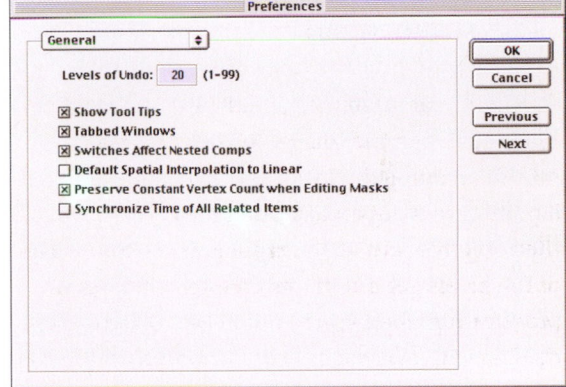

A setting of around 20 should be OK for most situations but you may want to increase this number to about 50 whilst you are learning the software. The checkboxes below allow you to turn on and off some of the interface features of After Effects 5.0.

### show tool tips

**1** If you are new to After Effects then it is a good idea to leave the Show Tool Tips box checked until you get to know the program. With this option selected, each time you hold the cursor over a tool button, switch etc. a tip will appear telling you the name and possible keyboard shortcut for that item.

**2** Click OK to leave the Preferences dialog box and then hold your cursor over any tool from the Tool Palette, make sure that you keep the cursor completely still for two or three seconds. A little, yellow tip will appear, telling you the name of the tool and the keyboard shortcut for it. As soon as you feel comfortable with the tools I recommend that this option be turned off.

**3** Go back to Preferences > General or hit Command + Alt + ; to open up the dialog box. The next checkbox is for Tabbed Windows, a useful feature that you may have seen in other Adobe products.

With this feature enabled, all new comps will open up in the same window but with separate tabs, allowing you to manage your palettes by stacking them together – a great space saver for people with only one monitor. The tabs can be dragged apart at any time in order to compare comps. There are times, especially when working with nested comps, that it is useful to turn this feature off, making it easier to understand the relationship between the nested comps.

**4** Turn this option off for now so that you can see what differences it makes when we go back to the main interface.

**switches affect nested compositions**
When this option is *checked* certain switch settings are carried through into nested comps. With this *unchecked*, the switches will only affect the current comp. Switches affected by this preference are the Enable Motion Blur and Enable Frame Blending switches (these are the buttons which activate Motion Blur and Frame Blending for the whole comp) and Draft 3D. It also affects the Quality switches for your layers. In the next few steps I'll show you how this works.

**1** Make sure that the checkbox is checked and then click OK to leave the Preferences dialog box. Double click the 01_3D ball comp and preview it. This comp consists of an EPS file (the football) which is a 3D layer. The layer has a light shining on it to make it look more three-dimensional. The ball has been selected as the light's parent so that the light follows the ball as it approaches the viewer. Notice that when the layer scales past 100% that the ball looks very pixelated.

**2** Open the 01_Spinning ball comp by double-clicking it in the Project window.

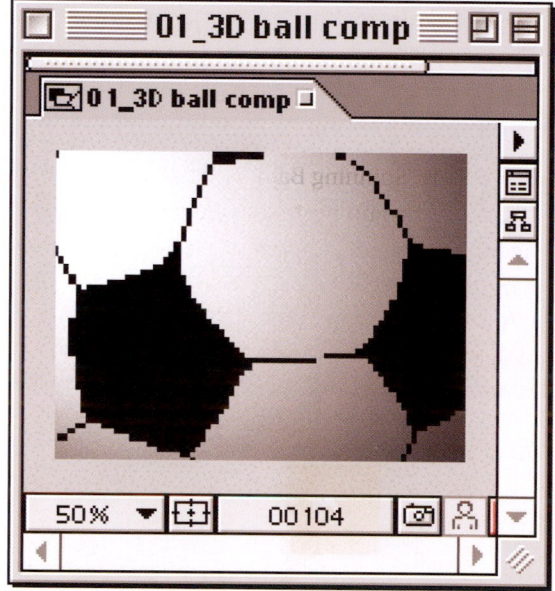

**3** In this comp I've rotated the layer so that the ball, with its light source attached is rotating towards the screen. (The light source should not normally rotate with the ball but we will allow this for the purposes of this exercise!)

**4** Click on the Continuously Rasterize switch to force After Effects to re-rasterize the image on each frame. This will make the image sharper in both windows because whatever happens in the first Comp will be updated in the second Comp.

You can find out more information about Continuous Rasterization in the Technical.pdf in the CD > Extras folder.

Continuously Rasterize on

Continuously Rasterize off

**5**  Open the 02_Spinning Ball comp. Notice that the new comp opens up with its own separate Composition and Timeline windows. This is because we switched off the Preference for tabbed windows. Move the Composition windows and Timeline windows so that you can see all of the windows open side by side. Sometimes it is useful to be able to see both comps at the same time, especially whilst learning the application.

**6**  Preview 02_Spinning Ball comp. This comp has the 01_3D ball comp nested inside it as a layer. Notice three things: the layer is rotating, the Layer Quality switch is set on Draft, and that neither the layer's Motion Blur switch nor the comp's Enable Motion Blur switch are activated.

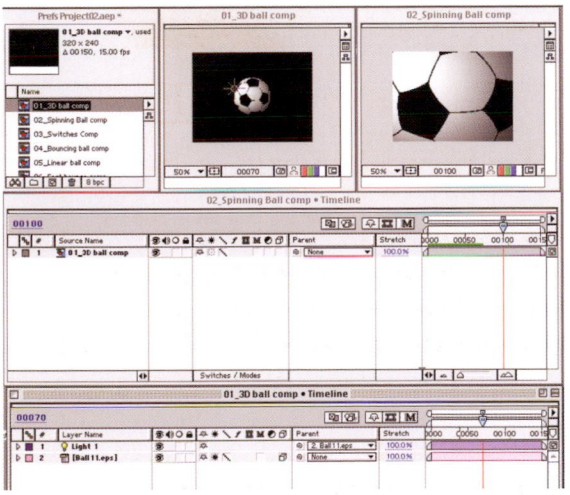

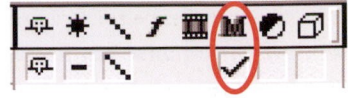

**7**  Click on the Layer Motion Blur switch for the ball layers in each of the open comps. No motion blur will be applied until we activate motion blur for the comps.

**8**  Open up 03_Switches comp. This comp consists of one layer, the 02_Spinning ball comp which has been nested into this new comp. Reposition the windows so that you can see all three Comp windows and all three Timeline windows simultaneously. You may need to drop the magnification in the windows to be able to do this.

**9**  In the 03_Switches comp, click on the Layer Quality switch on the Spinning ball layer and watch the Layer Quality switches in both of the other comps. Because we have the Switches Affect Nested Compositions preference checked, all three comps will simultaneously update.

**10**  Repeat this process with the 03_Switches comp's Enable Motion Blur switch and notice that all three comps again update.

**11**  Enable the Draft 3D switch on the third comp and watch as the lights go out on the football. This is because Draft 3D allows you to work in 3D without rendering the processor intensive lights. It will also reduce the detail in the 3D image for faster working.

**12**  Finally, change the Resolution setting for the third comp to Quarter. Do this by clicking on the drop down menu at the bottom of the Composition window. You may need to resize and reposition your window to do this. The resolution will also change in the other comps.

**13** Not all of the switches work in this way. Try toggling the Continuously Rasterize switch on and off in the third comp. Notice that clicking it does not affect the switch settings in the other two comps.

**14** This preference can be temporarily overridden by holding down the Control key on the Macintosh whilst clicking your chosen switch.

## default spatial interpolation to linear

Phew! That's a bit of a mouthful but it describes exactly what it does. After Effects spatial interpolation (the way it draws a motion path between two keyframes) defaults to Auto Bezier which creates a smooth, curved change of direction through a keyframe, as opposed to a sharp angular change which occurs when using Linear interpolation.

**1** Open up the 04_Bouncing ball comp. Select the ball layer so that you can see it's motion path, notice the smooth curve going through the middle keyframe. This is a default Auto Bezier keyframe. RAM Preview the motion.

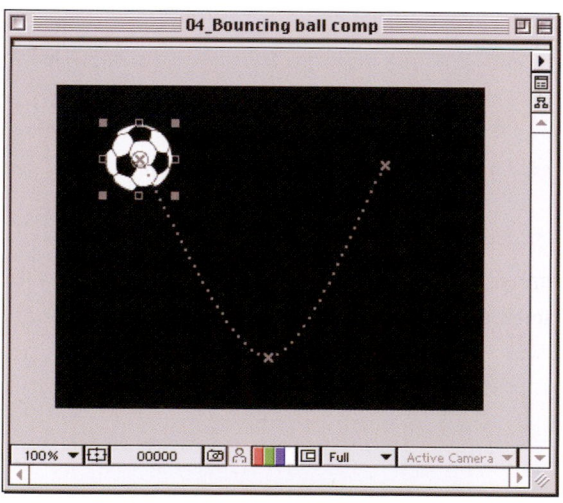

**2** Open up the General Preferences (Edit > Preferences > General), check the Default Spatial Interpolation to Linear checkbox and then click OK to leave the dialog box.

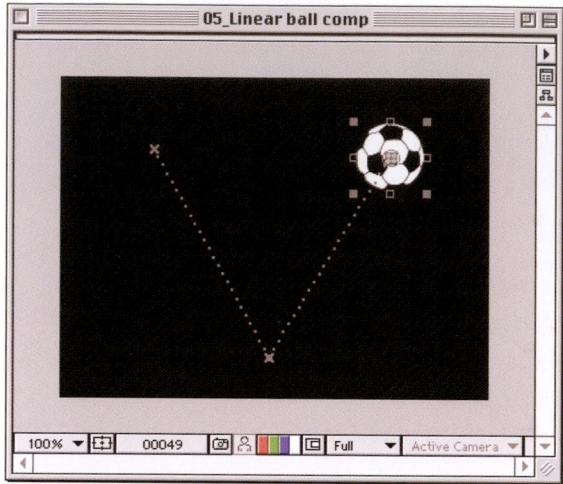

**3** Open up 05_Linear ball comp and select the Ball 11.eps layer. Hit Alt + P to set a keyframe for Position and open up its position values.

**4** Move to the 25 frame mark and drag the ball to the center, bottom of the comp.

**5** Move to the end of the comp and drag the ball up to the top, right of the Composition window.

**6** Preview the results and notice the difference in the motion. The new motion path is sharp and angular.

**7** In my opinion, it is preferable to have this preference set as we have it set now, particularly for beginners. Unexpected results when animating bezier paths can sometimes cause confusion to those who don't fully understand them and it is very easy to use keyboard modifiers to change the way the paths change at any time.

## preserve constant vertex count when editing masks

This is another mouthful! Again, it describes exactly what this preference does. Masks animate more reliably if they have the same number of points throughout an animation. This default preference ensures that if you add/remove points to a mask they will be added/removed from all mask keys so that your mask will always have the same amount of points. We will look more at how masks animate in a later chapter.

## synchronize time of all related items

**1** When checked, this will ensure the Current-Time Marker stays at the same point in time when you move through nested comps.

**2** Make sure that this option is checked and then click OK to leave the dialog box.

**3** Open comps 01, 02 and 03 so that you can see them all on the screen simultaneously. Close any other open comps.

**4** Move the Current-Time Marker around on any of the three comps and watch the Current-Time Markers on the other two comps follow. Having this option checked will ensure that any nested comps will be synchronized and will all be displaying the same frame.

**5** Go back to the Preferences and switch this option off. Repeat the process to see how to make the Current-Time Markers operate independently from each other.

**6** I usually prefer to work with this option turned on but there will be some occasions when you will prefer to have this switched off.

**7** Go back to the Preferences dialog box and turn this option back on by checking the box. Hit the Next button to move to the next Preference panel.

## previews

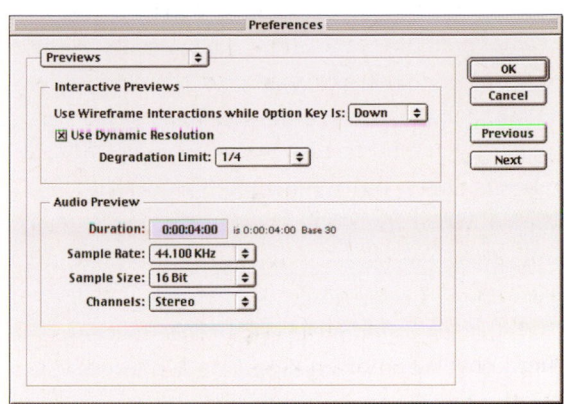

## interactive previews

When you make a change to a layer or when you scrub through the timeline, After Effects will use a dynamic preview to attempt to keep up with the changes. In other words it will drop the resolution in order to maintain a live preview of the changes which you make. If you are working on complex comps and don't want to wait for the screen to update every time you make a change, you can hold down the Alt key to force After Effects to use a wireframe display whilst you make your changes.

**1** Leave the Preferences dialog box.

**2** Close two of the open comps so that only one remains open and move the Current-Time Marker back to the beginning of the open comp by hitting the Home key on the keyboard.

**3** Go to Edit > Purge > Image Caches. This will remove any rendered frames from the image cache, ensuring that we will be seeing a fresh update on screen.

**4** Scrub the Current-Time Marker along the timeline of the open comp. Drag it from the beginning to the point where the football fills the screen. Notice that the resolution (quality) of the image has dropped so that After Effects can render the frames fast enough to keep up with the speed at which you are moving the Current-Time Marker. When you release the mouse, After Effects will update the render to the current settings.

**5** Try doing the same again but this time hold down the Alt key whilst dragging the Current-Time Marker. Notice that you can drag more freely now and that the image on screen does not update till you release the mouse.

**6** The Preferences allow you to reverse this behavior, you can also override the settings by using the wing menu in the Composition window.

**7** Pull out the wing menu and choose Wireframe Interactions. Scrub again and you'll see that the settings have been reversed. You will now see a wireframe representation of your layer which will not update until you release the mouse. If you hold down the Alt key whilst dragging you will see the dynamic update.

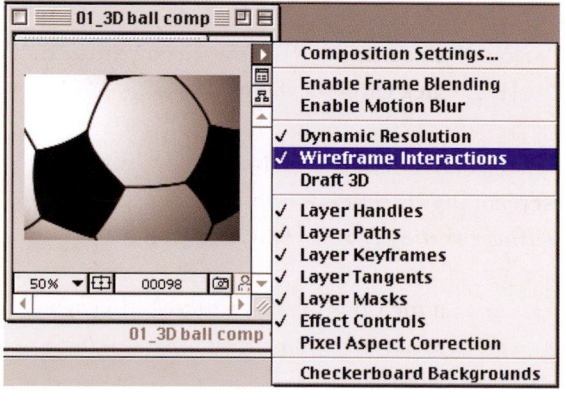

**8** There is also a switch in the Timeline which allows you quick and easy access to this Alt. Click on the this Wireframe Interactions button to deactivate it again.

**9** Go to Edit > Preferences > Previews to go back to the Preferences dialog box.

**10** The first drop down menu in here allows you to change the default setting. I tend to work with the default settings when working on small scale, simple projects but when working on larger, more sophisticated projects I would reverse the default setting.

**11** With Use Dynamic Resolution checked, After Effects will drop the resolution of the image to attempt to redraw the screen as fast as it can. With this unchecked, After Effects will redraw the screen at the current resolution as fast as it can.

**12** The Degradation Limit menu allows you to specify a maximum resolution drop when Dynamic Resolution is used. A setting of 1/4 will drop the image to a maximum of quarter resolution (drawing 1 of every four pixels) in order to gain speed of redraw.

### audio preview

This is where you can tell After Effects how much audio you would like it to load into RAM each time it previews. I find the default setting of four seconds a bit too short for my needs.

**1** Change the Duration setting to 0:00:10:00, do this by highlighting the box and typing in 1000, After Effects will convert this to timecode for you.
If you prefer, you can also type in 10.00 or 10:00 to achieve the same result.

**2** Leave the Sample Rate, Sample Size and Channels settings as they are. These are the settings that After Effects will use when building an audio preview. It is best to have these set at the same settings as the audio you will be working with. This means that After Effects will not have to convert the audio to different settings before previewing, saving you valuable time. If you are mixing audio with different sample rates I recommend leaving the settings at their default.

**3** Click the Next button to move to the next Preference panel.

# display

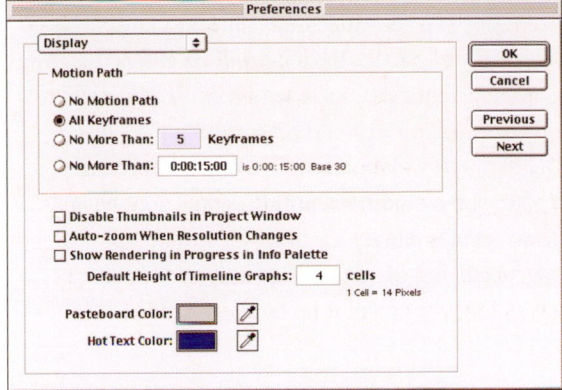

## motion path

These settings determine how the keyframes for your layers are displayed in the Composition window.

**1** Make sure that the All Keyframes radio button is checked and then click OK to leave the Preferences dialog box.

**2** Open the 06_Fast bounce comp and select the Ball layer. Hit the P key on your keyboard to solo the Position value for the layer.

**3** Look at the keyframes for the layer's position value, there are quite a few of them. These keyframes were created using the Gravity Motion Math script which can be used to make the ball bounce around the screen. The Timeline is where you can check the keyframes' position in time.

**4** With the layer still selected, look in the Composition window, here you will see all of the keyframes, each represented by a cross on the screen. The Composition window is where you can check the keyframes' position in space.

**5** Move the Current-Time Marker through the Timeline and watch the ball follow the path created by the keyframes. Move the Current-Time Marker to frame 27 and look at the preview in the Composition window.

**6** It is common practice to edit keyframes within the Composition window. They can be copied, pasted, deleted, added, adjusted and moved interactively in this window. With so many keyframes on the screen it is very difficult to make sense of the path. From the ball's current position it's hard to tell which is the next keyframe and which is the previous one.

**7** Go to Edit > Preferences > Display. Change the Motion Path setting to *No More Than 5 Keyframes* and then click OK to leave the dialog box.

**8** You will now see only five keyframes on the screen; the current one, which the ball will be sitting on, the previous two and the following two.

**9** Click on the Composition window wing menu and choose Layer Handles. This will switch the display of your layer's handles off so that you can see the keyframes more clearly. Try moving through the animation to see the display change to always show the five keyframes closest to the current point in time.

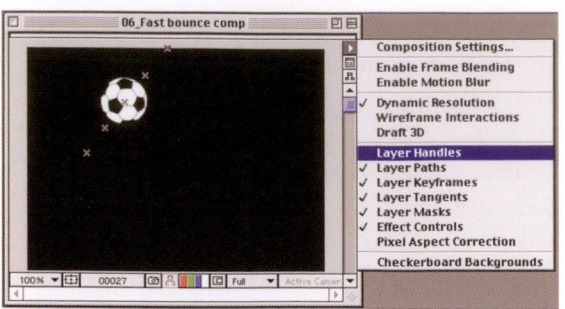

**10** Go back to the Composition window's wing menu and choose Layer Handles again to turn this display Alt back on. Notice that there are other options in the menu for turning on or off other display items such as: Layer Paths, Layer Keyframes, Layer Tangents, Layer Masks and Effect Control points. We will look more closely at these later.

**11** Go back to Edit > Preferences > Display and look at the other choices available to you. Selecting No Motion Path will turn off the Motion Path altogether, whilst the last Alt will allow you to display the amount of keyframes which occur within a particular time range; this works in a similar way to the current setting, distributing the visible keyframes equally before and after the current keyframe.

**12** Change the setting back to show All Keyframes. I think it is best to be able to see all of your keyframes, only making some of them invisible if really needed. This is especially important for new users who may get confused when they think that half of their carefully constructed motion path has disappeared.

## disable thumbnails in project window

Below the Motion Path options are a few more display options. As you saw in the first exercise, when you select a file in the Project window, a small image (or thumbnail) representing that file appears at the top of the Project window. This feature can be useful for reminding yourself what each piece of footage contains, but I find that I generally know what my footage looks like and don't often really need this preview to remind me.

Disable Thumbnails in Project Window allows you to turn off these thumbnails if you deem them unnecessary. This has the added advantage of speeding up your workflow as After Effects does not have to build the thumbnail previews of the files. This is particularly beneficial when selecting Complex, nested comps which After Effects can take some time to build a thumbnail of.

**1** Check the Disable Thumbnails in Project Window checkbox.

## auto-zoom when resolution changes

I find this Alt really useful when working with large Compositions on a small, single monitor. I really recommend the use of two Computer monitors plus one PAL/NTSC monitor when working with After Effects but if you only have one monitor then this preference can be a Godsend for you.

When working in After Effects it is sometimes useful to drop the resolution of a clip to speed up your preview. When you do this After Effects maintains the size of window but renders every second or third pixel which has the effect of dropping the picture quality. With this box checked, After Effects will also drop the window size, giving you a lower resolution without losing picture quality.

**1** Make sure this box is unchecked and then click OK to leave the dialog box.

**2** Open 07_Resolution comp and close all other open comps.

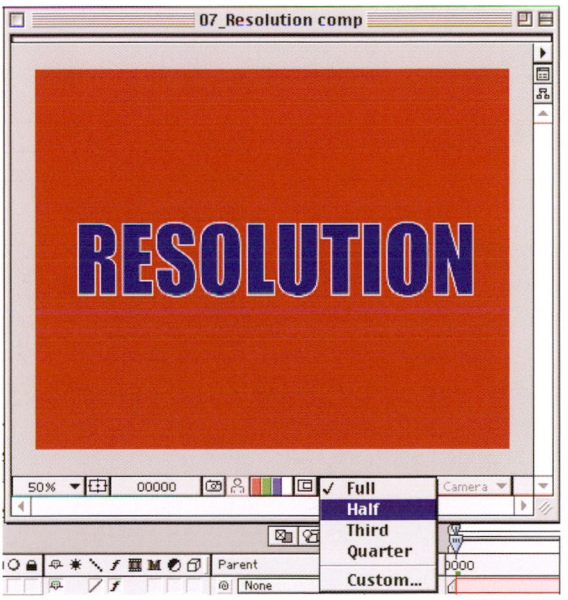

**3** Click on the resolution drop down menu at the bottom of the Composition window. Choose Half from the menu.

**4** The quality of the preview will drop, this is because After Effects is now rendering every second pixel. This has the result of speeding up previews and screen updates of your comp.

**5** The drop down menu gives you a list of preset choices down to one quarter resolution, alternatively you can set your own custom resolution down to a maximum setting, rendering every ninety-ninth pixel. There are separate controls for horizontal and vertical pixels.

As well as being useful for speeding up previews, these can be used creatively. Using this menu is a quick and easy way to create pixelated effects.

**6** From the resolution drop down menu, choose Custom and type in 20 for both Horizontal and Vertical resolution and then click OK. Your footage will now be made up of squares.

**7** Toggle the Quality switch on and off in the Timeline to see the different effects achievable by rendering in draft or anti-aliased quality. Remember that if you like a particular effect better in draft mode, that you can choose to render it in that mode in the Render Settings window.

**8** Change the resolution setting back to half (you can use the keyboard shortcuts: Command + Shift + J to change to Half resolution and Command + J for Full resolution).

**9** Click on the Magnification pop up menu at the bottom left of the Composition window and choose 50% from the list of choices. You can also zoom in by hitting the Period key on your keyboard and zoom out by hitting the Comma key. Holding down Shift whilst doing so will resize the window to fit.

OK, so to recap, we've done two things: we dropped the resolution to Half to decrease rendering time and then we dropped the magnification down to 50% to give us more room on screen.

**10** Use any of the methods to change the display back to Full resolution and 100% magnification.

**11** Go back to Edit > Preferences > Display, check the box next to Auto-Zoom When Resolution Changes and then click OK to leave the Preferences dialog box.

**12** In the Composition window, click on the Resolution drop down menu again and choose Half from the list. Notice that with the Auto-zoom preference checked, the magnification will automatically drop when the resolution drops. This has the effect of keeping maximum picture quality whilst reducing screen clutter and rendering time. After Effects is still only rendering every second pixel but it is rendering the pixels into a comp which is half the size ensuring that picture quality remains.

**13** With the Show Rendering in Progress in Info box checked, After Effects will monitor any effects' rendering times in the info palette, giving you immediate feedback to help you discover which effects are the most processor-intensive. I pretty much always work with this Alt checked.

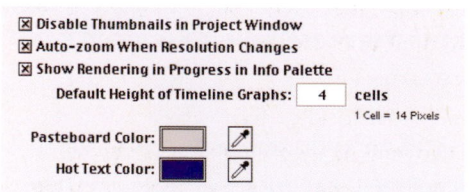

**14** I must say that I have never had the need to change the Default Timeline Graph Height setting. This is what determines the space between your layers when the property graphs are displayed. The default height of four is fine in most circumstances and the graphs can easily be adjusted directly in the Timeline. However, if you do need to change the height of your graph displays then this is where to do it.

**15** Click on the Next button to move on to the Import Preference panel.

# import

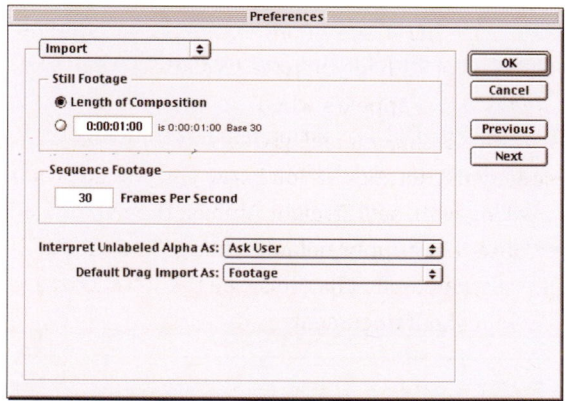

## still footage

The Still Footage preference determines how long a still image will be (in terms of time) when imported into a Project. I usually leave this at the default setting of Length of comp as I can easily trim the footage after importing to suit the individual needs of my comps. Underneath the default settings there is also an Alt available for you to set the length of still images at a user-defined time in hours, minutes, seconds and frames. This Alt is useful if you want to create a sequence of stills of equal length.

## sequence footage

Sequence Footage allows you to specify a frame rate for sequence footage, this depends on what format you are outputting. As I work in PAL, I usually have this set to 25 fps, if you are working to NTSC standard then 30 would be a better choice. As a general rule, this setting should match the frame rate of the comp you are working in.

## interpret unlabeled alpha as

Determines how the Alpha channel of a layer is interpreted when it is imported into After Effects, whether it is straight or premultiplied with a color. There are also options for After Effects to Guess the Alpha information. Just the word 'guess' makes me nervous so I prefer to stick with the Ask User option. When you have this selected a dialogue box appears when you import the file with the Alpha channel, giving you the option to specify the settings. If you know you will always be working with, say, Straight Alphas, then you could choose that as your default setting. To find out more about alpha channels, see the CD > Extras > Technical.pdf document.

## default drag import as

You can simply drag and drop footage files directly into the After Effect Project window from the desktop. If you do this with Photoshop files or Illustrator files, set at its default setting, After Effects will import them as regular footage files, giving you the choice to bring in individual layers or merged layers. If you change this preference to Default Drag Import as Compositions, After Effects will bring in your Photoshop and Illustrator files as ready-made comps with all layers intact. This preference really depends on how you work. If you work with a lot of Photoshop or Illustrator multi-layered comps then you will probably be best to change this. Otherwise, leave it for now.

**1** Hit the Next button to move to the next Preference panel.

## output

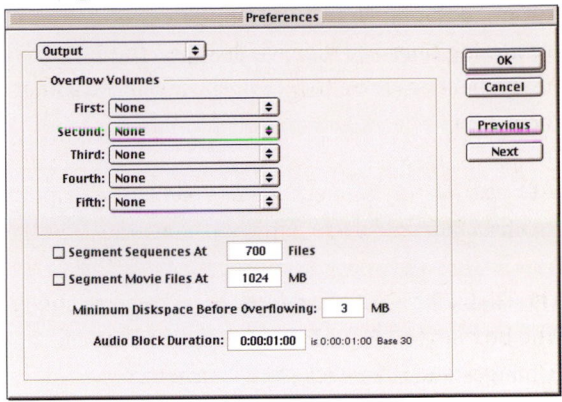

## overflow volumes

If you are working on a very large file and your hard drive is not big enough to cope, After Effects can assign what's called an overflow volume. When the drive you are rendering to is full, After Effects will continue rendering the files to the next drive on the list and so on.

## segment sequences at

You can also tell After Effects to overflow files to new folders when they reach a specified amount of files per folder. Most operating systems have a limit to the amount of files which can be contained in each folder, therefore sequences have to be segmented into different folders to overcome these problems. This Overflow Alt can be activated by clicking in the Segment Sequences At checkbox. The maximum number of files per folder can be entered manually in the text field. Having said all of this, these days the number of files, which can be stored in a folder, is so ridiculously high that it's not something you're likely to have to think about for now.

## segment movie files at

You can also limit movie file sizes by using the Segment Movie Files At preference. Some formats can't handle file sizes over a certain amount. You can set the maximum movie size here, when After Effects reaches the specified limit, it will create a new movie file for the remaining render time.

## minimum disk space before overflowing

Here you can specify how many megabytes will be left in a volume before moving to the next when working with multiple overflow volumes. It is important that you leave enough space for the machine to breathe!

## audio block duration

This feature allows you to specify the block size of your audio files when making movies. When rendering a QuickTime movie, the audio is loaded in blocks. The default setting is 1 second, and, in this case, the rendering pauses once a second to read a chunk of audio, then continues to render. The default setting of 1 second is usually fine but if you are having unexpected synch'ing problems when rendering with audio, this can be fixed by changing the setting so that the audio loads once for every frame. Conversely, if you ever hear 'popping' or clicking noises at regular intervals in your movie, this can be caused by the loading of the audio. The solution is to change this setting to the same length as your movie so that the audio loads in one big chunk.

# grids and guides

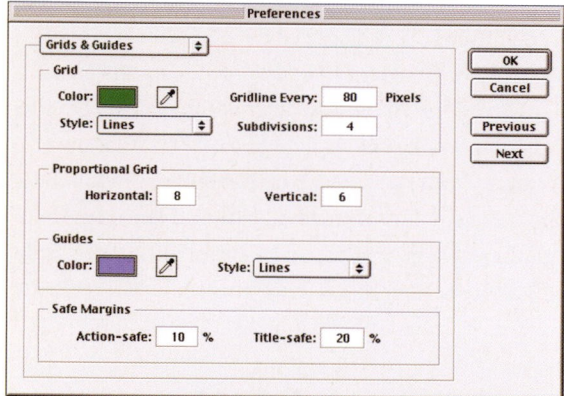

**1** Click on the Next button again to move on to the Grids and Guides panel. If you are an Illustrator user or a Photoshop user you will be familiar with the way these work. After Effects also has rulers to assist with measuring distances within the Composition window which can be accessed in the View menu.

## grid

In the Grid section you can set your grid color, the default color is green but if you were animating a frog jumping across a grass lawn, you may want to change it to another contrasting color! You can also adjust the line spacing and the subdivisions between the lines. The default setting is divisions of 80 pixels with subdivisions of 4. This works well if you are working in frame aspect ratios which are multiples of 80 (e.g. 640 × 480 or 320 × 240) but if you are working with any other formats you may need to adjust these settings. You can also choose whether your grid is displayed using dots, lines or dashed lines.

**1** The grid is activated in the Composition window by going to View > Show Grid.

## proportional grid

After Effects also provides you with a proportional grid to help you with working out perspective and composition in your designs. This differs from the standard grid in that it is proportional, i.e. you tell After Effects how many vertical and horizontal sections you want to split your screen into and it'll work out the correct size for each section. If you resize the comp, the grid would resize along with it. I must say that I find this grid much more useful (and easier to work out!) although the Snap to Grid Alt does not work with the proportional grid.

**2** The Proportional Grid is activated by Alt-clicking on the Title-Action-Safe button in the Composition window.

## guide

Below the Proportional Grid settings are the settings for your guides. Guides can be dragged out from the Rulers when they are visible in the Composition window and are extremely useful for precise positioning of elements. Here you can change the color and the style as with the Grid.

## safe margins

When a picture is broadcast on television it is overscanned, i.e. the picture is broadcast bigger than the visible screen area. This means that when it is viewed on a TV set, the very edges of the picture will be cut off by the edges of the TV screen. This method was originally conceived to avoid distortion of the picture edges which is particularly noticeable on older sets with very convex screens. For this reason safe zones are used by broadcast designers to ensure that essential elements of their designs do not lie outside these specified safe zones.

There are two Safe zones, one for action and another for titles. Any action lying within the Action safe zone (10%) will be guaranteed to be seen on most sets. The Title Safe zone is smaller (20%), this was originally the area which was considered to be the flattest, and therefore least distorted area on the screen, ideal for displaying undistorted text. Aside from this reason, it makes good design sense to place your text within this zone as anything outside this area will be outside the viewer's main focus and will be hard work for them to easily read.

It used to be the case that a designer never had to worry about the very edges of their designs as they would be cut off by the overscan. I would warn against this practice. New flat screen televisions show almost the whole picture and you never know, somebody may want to put your work on DVD, or projection, where the edges would almost certainly show up. So, although anything outside the Action-Safe Zone will probably not be seen, don't depend on it!

The Action Safe and Title Safe zones default settings are pretty much OK to work with if you are working with a traditional 4:3 broadcast. These are pretty much the industry standard safe zones for 4:3 broadcast and work fairly well. Find out more about widescreen safe zones in the Technical.pdf, in the CD > Extras folder.

## label colors

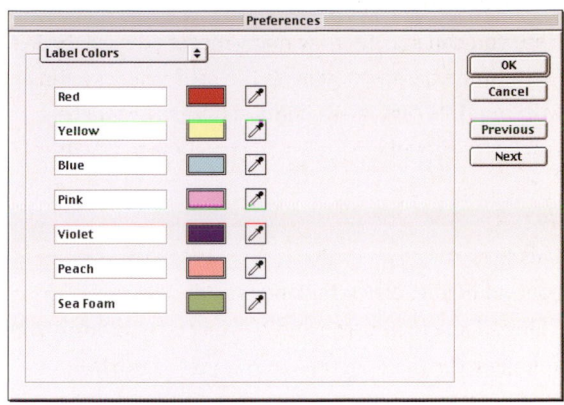

**1** Click on the Next button again to move on to the Label Colors panel.

Another useful feature is After Effects labels. These help to identify pieces of footage in the Timeline, Project window and the Composition Flowchart view. In this dialogue box you can customize the colors that you want to use and label them accordingly. You can also implement Group colors for different types of footage in the Default Labeling section which is in the next Preference Panel; hit the Next button to access it.

## label defaults

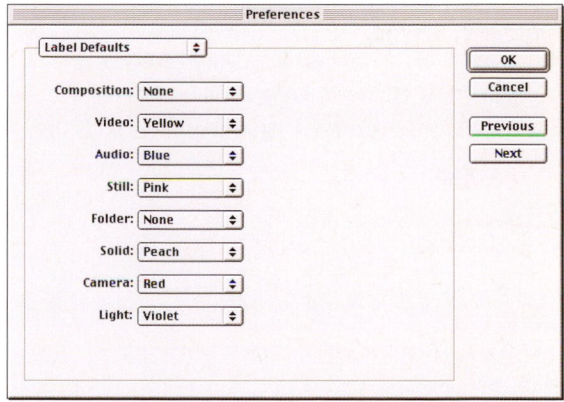

Here you can change the default labeling scheme for the different types of footage you will be working with. I tend to stick with the defaults here.

# cache

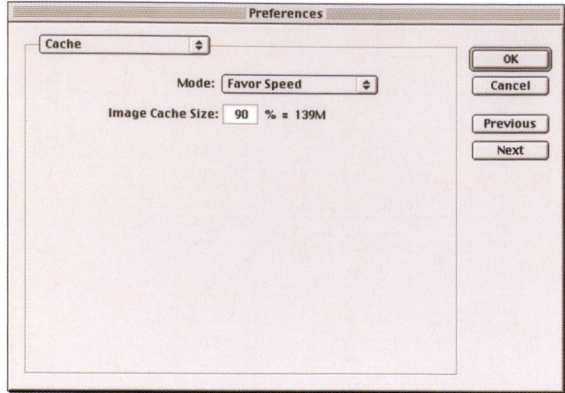

When you preview frames in After Effects the source files and any effects, masks and transformations are rendered together and then stored in and played back from your RAM.

RAM, or Random Access Memory, is much faster than hard disk memory and can play back the rendered frames much faster. The downside is that RAM is only a temporary storage space, as soon as you run short of RAM for a particular operation, the rendered frames will be ditched to make more RAM available. If you make changes to any of the frames which are stored in the RAM, they too will be ditched and then replaced with the newer versions.

There are things that you can do to control the way that After Effects uses RAM to cache images. Unfortunately RAM is managed differently on Mac as it is on Windows so I have listed both methods here.

## mac os cache settings

**1** Open After Effects and then go to Edit > Preferences > Cache. The first thing you'll see is the Mode drop down menu which contains two choices.

### favor memory
is the best choice if you are short of RAM. After Effects will Compact the RAM down as much as it can but be warned, this has the downside of slowing the application down, so only choose this Alt if you are really pushed. If you can possibly afford more RAM that would be a much better solution.

### favor speed
is the best choice if you have plenty of RAM. In this mode After Effects allows the RAM to do its own thing, only Compacting it when absolutely necessary. This is the fastest way to work but uses up the available RAM much quicker.

### image cache size
determines how much of the RAM, allocated to After Effects is being used for caching images. The default setting of 60% should be fine for most situations but if you were desperate to free up some more RAM for your previews then you could adjust this setting. Remember that by altering the value you are decreasing the amount of RAM available for other operations. It is not recommended that you ever push this value past 90%.

## windows cache settings
### maximum memory usage

This sets the maximum amount of RAM to be used in After Effects. Unlike the Mac OS, you can enter values above 100% because virtual memory uses hard-disk space to push the available RAM up to a recommended maximum of 200%.

### Image Cache Size

This works in the same way as the Mac OS Image Cache size, determining how much RAM is available for caching images. The default setting of 60% should be fine for most situations but if you were desperate to free up some more RAM for your previews then you could adjust this setting. Remember that by altering the value you are decreasing the amount of RAM available for other operations. It is not recommended that you ever push this value past 90%.

The Image Cache Size determines how many frames you can play back in your RAM Previews. Increasing the Cache size allows you to play back more frames. If you notice that your RAM Previews are jerky and halt at times during playback (this sometimes happens when After Effects is using virtual memory), then decrease the Cache Size.

When After Effects Compacts the image cache you may notice a pause in operations, this will happen, in the following situations, despite whatever RAM cache settings you have selected.

- When After Effects is preparing for a RAM Preview.
- In between renders in the Render Queue.
- When you go to About Adobe After Effects.

If you notice a pause during any of these operations do not adjust your Cache settings.

## video preview

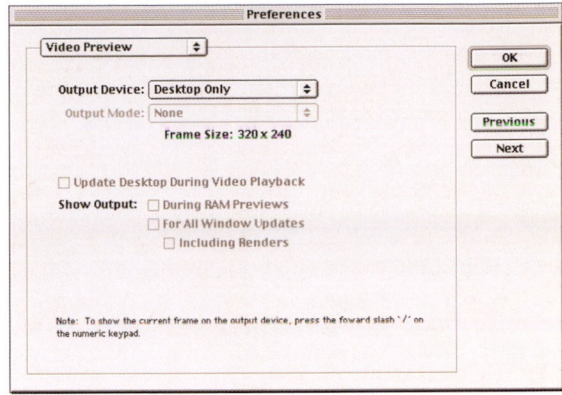

Hit the Next button to jump to the next preference panel. New to Version Five of After Effects is the ability to view your work on an external video monitor. To be able to make use of this you will need to have the monitor connected to a supported video card or a FireWire port on your computer. Once installed you can use the Video Preview preferences to identify the monitor and control the settings. To find out which cards are supported please refer to the Adobe website at: http://www.adobe.com

### output device

Once you have a video monitor attached to your Computer it will appear in this drop down menu. When you select your Output device the Output Mode menu will be highlighted.

The After Effects Video Preview gives you limited control over how images are displayed on your PAL/NTSC monitor. If you want to be able to view your work accurately at the various different aspect ratios you are better using Echo Fire which is a third party plug-in from Synthetic Aperture. As well as offering much more control over the display options, it also includes a RGB system wide broadcast color picker which enables you to choose only broadcast-safe colors for your designs, a very useful feature. Check out the demo version on the CD > Software Demos > Echo Fire folder.

### output mode

The modes listed in this menu will depend on the device you are using to connect the monitor to your Computer. One you have selected an Output Mode, the Frame Size and Frame Rate of the display will be listed below. These settings are not directly related to your Composition settings. With Update Desktop During Video Playback selected you will be able to see the preview displayed on both the Computer screen and the video monitor.

### show output

• With During RAM Previews selected, all RAM Previews will be previewed for you on thevideo monitor.
• When For All Window Updates is selected, the preview on the video monitor will update every time a change is made in any of the After Effects windows.
• Including Renders will show you a preview of each frame as it renders on the video monitor.

## recap

Well, that's about it for the Preferences within After Effects. There are lots of other things you can tinker with throughout the interface which can customize your working environment, we'll cover most of these as we move through the chapters.

Remember to consult the Online Help and the After Effects manual for further information regarding any of the features listed here.

Before moving ahead with the next chapter, here are another few design tips, this time from Birgitta Hosea. I've known Birgitta for a long time, we are very good friends. She is also an animator and designer and is the Animation Course Director at St. Martin's School of Art in London.

• Form follows function: unnecessary ornament is self indulgence.
• A computer does not design. A computer is a tool. Do not allow your work to be defined by the kind of marks that a software program makes.
• Mix software programs, drawings, photographs, scan in collages and objects you have made, experiment.
• Try to enjoy the process of creating the work not just the product at the end.
• Do some life drawing, it can be as theraputic as meditation. Concentrate on drawing and just looking.
• Go to see some art exhibitions and films, make notes of what you liked and didn't like.
• If all that fails my final thing is to clean my entire flat from top to bottom, after a few days of that I get so bored I'm desperate to be creative again!

# chapter five
# importing

## Importing compositions

OK, in this chapter we're going to start by working on an image that's been created in Photoshop. It is important to understand how this image was put together so I've included a tutorial on the CD (Extras > Preparation.pdf) which covers the steps used to produce this image. The tutorial also explains a little bit about channels to help you understand how they work. Please print out the PDF tutorial later, or simply read it on screen to follow the steps.

As you learned in Chapter two, After Effects works with projects and compositions. Do you remember importing individual files and putting them together to make a composition? Well, when you create a layered source image in Photoshop or Illustrator, After Effects can also bring this in as a ready made composition.

**1** Open After Effects. As soon as you open the application a new Project will be created for you. If you accidentally close the project just go to File > New > New Project to open a new one.

**2** Go to File > Import > File to open up the Import File dialog box. From Training > Source Images > Angie Images, click once on the file named, ideas320.psd to select it.

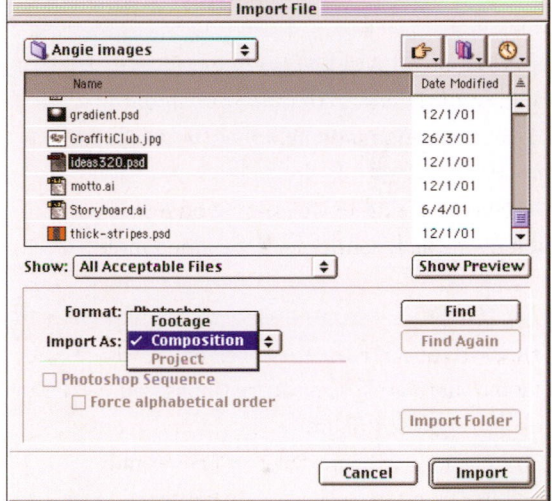

**3** Click on the Import As: drop down menu and choose *Composition*. This will tell After Effects to bring in the Photoshop file as a ready-made Composition with all of the layers, created in Photoshop, retained within the new Composition. Click OK to leave the Import File dialog box.

If you look in the Project window you will see that two things have appeared, a folder and a Composition, both items have the same name have the same name, as the Photoshop file you just imported. After Effects imports all of the layers within a folder and makes up the layers into a Composition for you.

**4** Click the little triangle next to the folder, in the project window, this will open it up and display the contents within. Notice that there are seven new layers and two more Compositions within this folder. These are the layers you created in Photoshop earlier.

**5** Double-click the Bits & Pieces layer to open it up in its own window. Double-clicking a layer in the project window will open it up in its original state. This is a good way of comparing the footage before interpretation by After Effects.

Notice that the layer is smaller than the Composition, it is trimmed to the size that you adjusted it to in Photoshop. If you look at the bottom of the window you will see the four Channel View buttons, colored red, green, blue and white. These buttons allow you to see the individual channels which make up your image, similar to using the Channels palette in Photoshop.

**6** Click the red, green and blue channels on and off to see the three, separate colour channels, each containing an 8-bit grayscale image.

**7** Click on the white button, this shows you the alpha channel for the layer. This is the Layer Mask what I have created in Photoshop, it is imported as an alpha channel, embedded in the layer. Click on the button again to switch the Alpha display off.

So, After Effects retains all of the information about transparency that you set up in Photoshop and keeps all of that information for you in a separate alpha channel. Remember, the black areas represent transparency and the white areas represent opacity.

**8** Close the window for now and go back to the Project window. Click on each layer to see a preview of it in the thumbnail at the top of the project window. Notice that, as you click on each image, you can see information about its dimensions and color depth displayed in the Project window, next to the thumbnail.

**9** Click on the Ideas layer and then click the little triangle, next to the highlighted name at the top of the Project window. A drop down menu will open showing you all the places where this file is used within the project, this is very useful for keeping track of items and finding out whether a footage item is being used in your project.

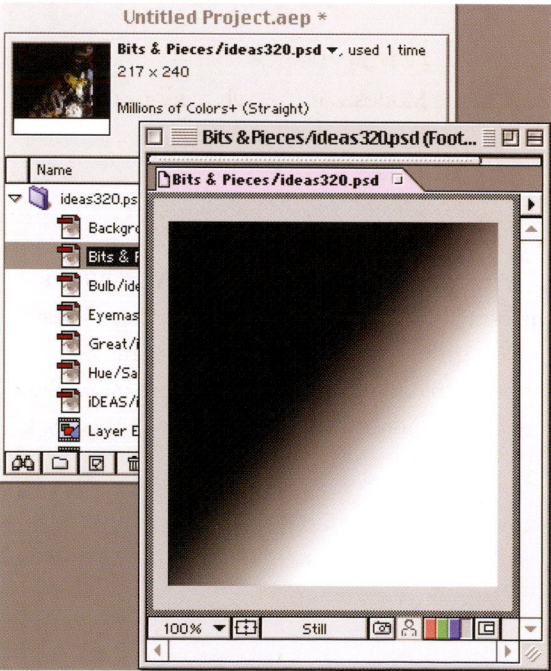

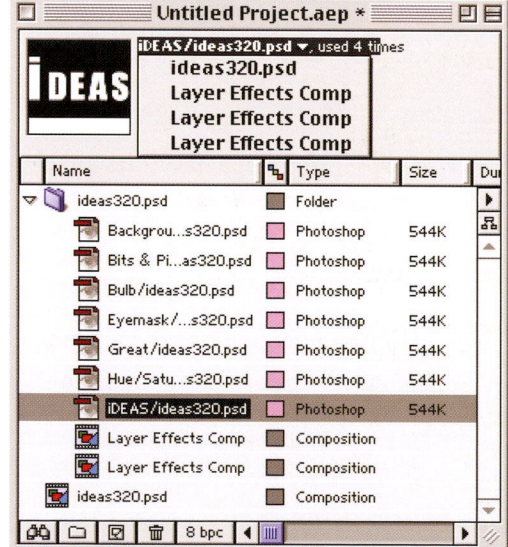

**10** Close the ideas320.psd folder and then double-click on the ideas320.psd Composition, this will open up all of the layers you have just finished looking at in their own ready-made Composition. The items are still there, in the folder if you want to use them individually but After Effects has put them together for you, retaining all of the information about position, transparency, effects etc.

**11** Go to Composition > Composition settings and check that the Frame Rate is set to 15 fps and then click OK.

**12** Go to File > Save as and, in the *Save As* dialog box, navigate to your Creative After Effects folder on the desktop and save the project into the Importing Chapter folder as Ideasb.aep.

**13** Look at the Timeline, notice that After Effects has laid out all the layers from Photoshop in the same order that they appeared in the Photoshop Layers palette. The frontmost layer in the Composition window will be the topmost layer in the Timeline.

**14** As in Photoshop, you can toggle the little Eye icons in the Timeline on and off to view the separate layers. Notice that some of the Eye icons have blackened out centers, this is to indicate that a blending mode has been used on that layer. Try toggling the visibility on and off for each layer. Finish with them all on.

You can move these panels around the Timeline to suit your own preferred way of working. I like to have this panel nearer the layers as there are switches that I use often in this panel.

**15** To move the panel, click and drag the panel heading to the Right till it lies next to the Current-Time Marker.

There are other panels available to you which are not displayed when you are using the default settings.

**16** Context-click on the Parent panel heading and go to Panel > Modes to display the Modes panel.

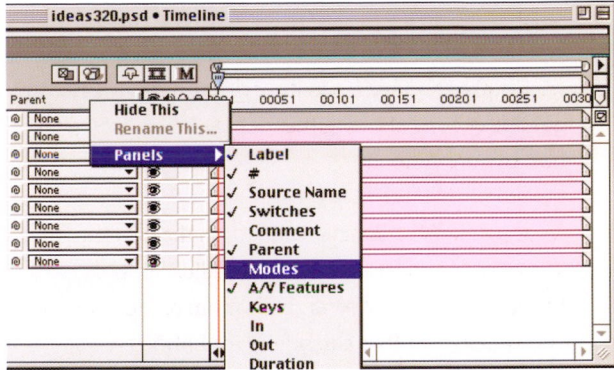

We are rapidly running out of space here in the Timeline. Luckily, you can also hide panels that you are not using to give yourself more space in the Timeline.

**17** Context-click on the Parent panel heading and choose Hide This from the menu to hide the Parent panel. We will not be using this till later.

## layer modes

Look at the Modes panel. Each layer has the same Layer Modes available as are available in Photoshop, in fact there are a couple more modes specifically for moving footage which we'll look at later. The Layer Modes, imported from Photoshop, remain live and can be adjusted in After Effects the same way as they were in Photoshop. These modes are sometimes referred to as Transfer modes or blending modes. To find out more about these layer modes, see the Technical.pdf in the CD > Extras folder.

**1** Click on the Layer Mode drop down menu for the Bulb layer (layer 6), notice that the same layer mode (Exclusion) that was applied to the layer in Photoshop, has been carried over into After Effects. Change the layer's mode to *Normal*. Notice how the Bulb layer now obscures the layers beneath, it is no longer blending with those layers.

**2** Change the Bulb Layers (layer number 6) Layer Mode back to Exclusion.

### adjustment layers

Now look at the Layer Switches column. Notice the switches for layer 5, the Hue/Saturation layer. Notice that there is a circular icon (half white, half black) in the seventh column from the left.

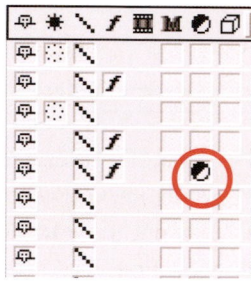

This is the Adjustment Layer switch. Any layer in After Effects can be made into an Adjustment layer by clicking this switch (with the exception of audio files of course!). Adjustment layers can be created inside After Effects but can also be imported directly from Photoshop. You'll learn more about Adjustment Layers as we progress through the following chapters.

**1** Select the Hue/Saturation layer and then hit the E key on the keyboard to open up any effects applied to the layer in the Timeline. Notice how the Hue/Saturation controls have also remained live during their journey here from Photoshop.

**2** Hit Command + Shift + T to open up the Effect Controls window. Alternatively, you can go to Layer > Open Effect Controls or double-click the Hue/Saturation effect name in the Timeline.

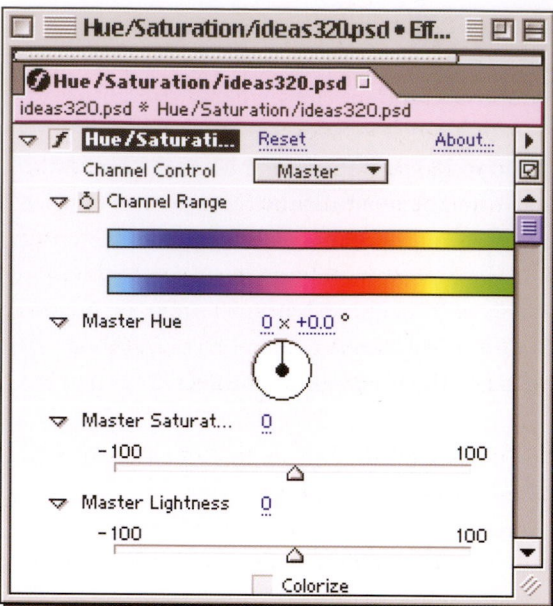

The Effect Controls window will appear on the desktop. Depending on your screen resolution you may need to rearrange your desktop so that you can see all of the open palettes and windows. I normally like to keep my Effect Controls window under the Time Controls palette when limited to working with just one monitor.

**3** If you followed Chapter two, you will have a saved workspace. Go to Window > Workspace > 320 × 240 to readjust your windows to your preferred position.

**4** If you did not follow Chapter two, arrange the windows exactly where you want them and then go to Window > Workspace > Save Workspace. Give your new workspace a name and then click OK to accept it.

If you can afford it, it is much easier to use After Effects with two monitors, one for the Composition window and the other for your other windows and palettes. If not, the ability to save different workspaces for different tasks is a real godsend.

**5** In the Effect Controls window you will see a control wheel under the heading, *Master Hue* (sounds like a character from a Dickens Novel!). Click and drag the black line on the Hue wheel round to 180 degrees, hold down the Shift key to constrain the movement to increments of 45 degrees. In the Composition window, you will see the bulb and the eye turn blue. The layer mask we imported from Photoshop is masking the Adjustment layer so that only those areas will be affected by the Hue/Saturation effect.

**6** Double-click the Hue/Saturation layer to open it up in its own layer window.

After Effects has taken into consideration the matte that you created for this adjustment layer in Photoshop. It has not only imported the file along with all of its information about position, opacity etc. but has also kept the Adjustment Layer live. The controls for the adjustment have exactly the same functionality as the controls in Photoshop.

The difference here is that you can animate the individual effect controls over time. Each property that you see in the Effect Controls window can be individually animated over time, imagine the possibilities, they're endless!

**7** Close the Hue/Saturation Layer Window.

**8** In the Effect Controls window, drag the Saturation slider up to 50, notice that the image dynamically updates over time, dropping the resolution in order to keep up with the speed at which you are dragging.

If you don't want the screen to update whilst you are dragging, you can hold down the Alt key whilst you make the adjustment. Using this shortcut, After Effects will use a wireframe display, only refreshing the screen when you release the slider, this is usually preferred when working with complicated Compositions as it means you do not have to wait for the screen redraw to keep up with your actions.

**9** In the Timeline, click the disclosure triangle next to the Hue/Saturation effect name to open up the effect parameters in there. You will see the same properties that you saw in the Effect Controls window echoed down here in the Timeline. You can control the effects from either or both places, I'll show you how.

**10** Click the little Stopwatch next to the *Channel Range* property name in the Timeline to set a keyframe for that parameter. A keyframe will appear in the Timeline at the position of the Current-Time Marker.

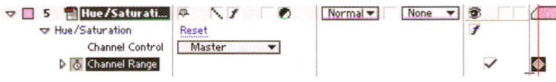

**11** Click again on the Stopwatch or hit the Backspace/Delete key to remove the keyframe.

Creative After Effects

**12** Go back to the Effect Controls window and click on the little Stopwatch next to the property name and a keyframe for that property will appear in the Timeline. Having the ability to set keyframes from the Effect Controls window means you do not have to keep moving down to the Timeline to set keyframes.

**13** Close the Effect properties in the Timeline by clicking the disclosure triangle again and then, with the layer still selected, hit the **U** key on the keyboard, this shortcut will bring only any keyframed properties for the selected layer or layers. It is also referred to as the Uber key.

**14** Hit the O key on the keyboard to move the Current-Time Marker to the Out-point of your selected layer.

**15** Click on the first of the two property values (which currently reads 0) above the Hue dial in the Effect Controls window to open up the Angle Control dialog box. Type in 5 to the Revolutions field and then hit Return.

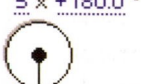

**16** Hit the Home key on your keyboard to move your Current-Time Marker back to the beginning of the Composition and then hit the 0 key, on the number pad, to RAM Preview your changes. The colors will cycle five times through the spectrum during the ten second Composition. If you have a small amount of RAM available to you, holding down the Shift key whilst hitting the 0 key will load every second frame into RAM, allowing you to preview a longer piece of footage.

**17** Go to File > Save as and, in the Save as dialog box, navigate to your Creative After Effects folder on the desktop and save the project into the Importing Chapter folder as ideas01b.aep

# layer effects

As well as importing Image controls, Layer Masks and Adjustment Layers from Photoshop, After Effects will also import any Layer Effects which were applied to your layers in Photoshop.

**1** Open ideas01.aep from Training > Projects > Chapter 05. This is exactly the same as the project you just saved.

**2** Select the Hue/Saturation layer (layer number 5) and then hit the U key again to close your layer.

**3** With the layer still selected, hit Command + the Up Arrow key (on your keyboard) to select the next layer up from the current selection (layer number 4).

**4** Hit the E button to open up any effects that are applied to this layer. You can see that After Effects has also brought in Photoshop's Drop Shadow Layer Effect.

**5** Double-click the effect name, *Photoshop Drop Shadow* in the Timeline to open up the shadow controls in the Effect Controls window. All the properties that were set up in Photoshop are here, ready for you to animate in After Effects.

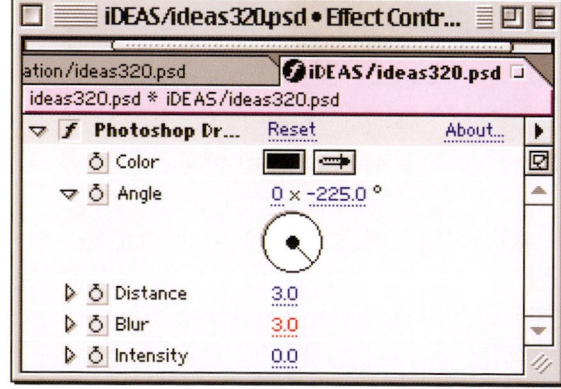

## scrubbable hot text

Since version five, After Effects has had scrubbable hot text fields! What on earth are they?, I hear you cry. Well basically, you can now simply click on almost any value and drag across it to dynamically change that value. I'll show you how it works.

**1** In the Effect Controls window click on the Distance value and scrub (drag) to the left till the value changes to 3. You may find it difficult to be precise, if so, holding down the Command key as you drag will adjust the value in smaller increments.

**2** Repeat this process to change the Blur value to 3. Remember, these were effects which were applied to our file in Photoshop, we are now adjusting them in After Effects, how's that for seamless integration?

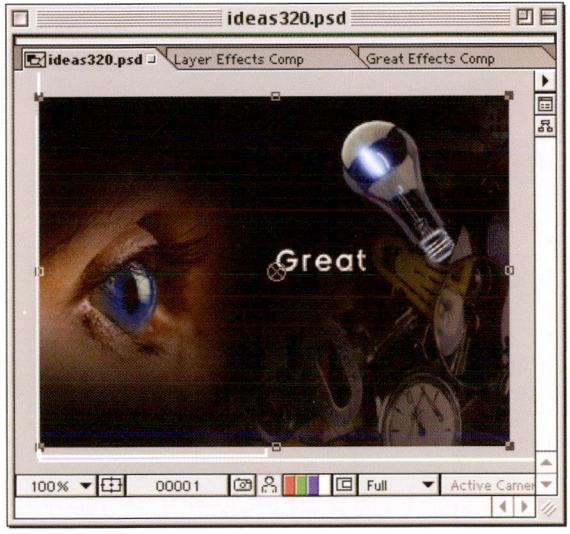

After Effects will now also import (live) any of After Effects' native effects (applied in Premiere 6) when importing a Premiere composition. All settings and keyframes will be imported along with the effects. These effects can then be edited and animated in After Effects.

## copying effect values

You can copy and paste effect, mask and transform property values from one layer to another in After Effects. You can even copy and paste between certain properties, which we'll look at later. You can also copy and paste an effect from one layer on to another.

**1** Hit Command + C to copy the effect values from the current layer.

**2** Hit Command + Up Arrow key twice to move up to the Great layer (which also has a Photoshop Drop Shadow Layer effect applied to it).

**3** Hit Command/Control + V to paste the effect values from one layer to the other.

**4** Close the layer by hitting the E key again.

**5** Go to File > Save as and, in the Save as dialog box, navigate to your Creative After Effects folder on the desktop and save the project into the Importing folder as ideas01c.aep.

One golden rule when doing any sort of design work is to take regular breaks, even when you are working to a tight deadline. It is counter productive to work for long hours without breaks, if you do, you'll become tired and your concentration and speed of thought will suffer. By taking a break you will refresh your senses. Go and take a break.

# seattle evening news

OK, so now we're going to start work on our news titles. If you haven't already read the Briefs chapter, go and do it now, it contains important information about the requirements of this project.

We need a generic project which can be adapted for all the regional news stations. We'll begin by making a title for one of the news regions (Seattle), I'll then show you how to adapt the project for all the other regions.

## sequence layers

**1** Go to File > New > New Project (Command + Alt + N). Then go to File> Import File (Command + I).

**2** In the Import File dialog box, go to Training > Source images > Art Explosion > Select "Seattle news images" and then hit the Import Folder button to import the whole folder of images into your new project.

**3** Open the folder and make the Project window bigger so that you can see the contents within, notice that After Effects brought in all the images as well as the folder which contained them.

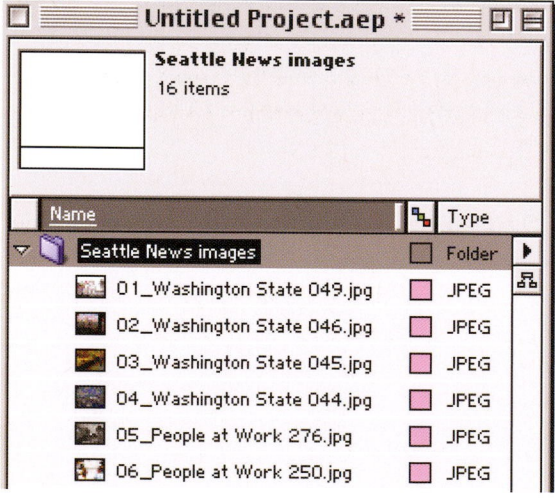

**4** Click on the top-most image and then hit Command + A to select all of the images.

**5** With all the images selected, click and drag them onto the New Composition button at the bottom of the Project window to create a new Composition, containing all of the images. The layers will go into the Composition in the order in which they were selected, numbered from 01 at the top of the Timeline to 16 at the bottom.

**6** Close the Seattle News images folder in the Project window to keep things tidy.

**7** Make the Composition window active and then hit Command + K or go to Composition > Composition Settings. Change the Composition name to 'Sequence Composition', the frame rate to 15 fps and the duration to 480 frames (32 seconds when using a frame rate of 15).

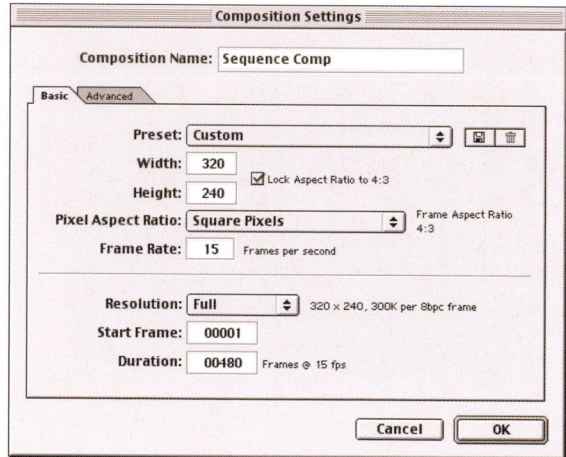

**8** In the Timeline, drag the Navigation slider all the way to the left to maximize your workspace.

**9** Hit Command + G or click on the Timecode display to open the Go To Time dialog box. Enter 17 and click OK to leave the box, notice that the Current-Time Marker has now jumped to the seventeenth (one second and one frame, remember that we are starting frame numbering from 1).

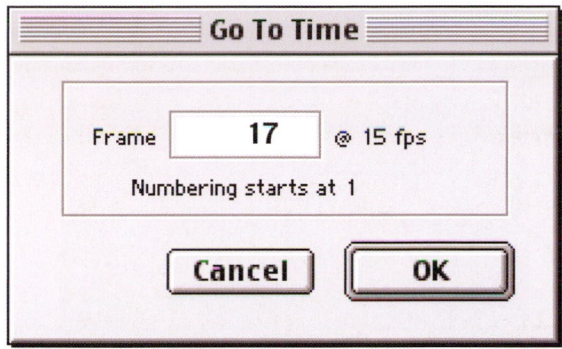

**10** Hit Command + A to make sure all the layers are selected, Hit Alt +] to trim the out-points of all the selected layers to the position of the Current-Time Marker.

**11** Go to Animation > Keyframe Assistant > Sequence Layers. We'll put in a crossfade so that the images fade in and out from each other. Click on the Overlap checkbox and enter a value of 3 for the duration, this will give us a cross-fade which lasts for 3 frames. From the Crossfade drop down menu, choose Front Layer Only. To create a crossfade in After Effects it is usually best to adjust the opacity of the top layer only, if you adjusted the opacity of both layers to 50%, you would be able to see the background color coming through, this is not the effect that we want here.

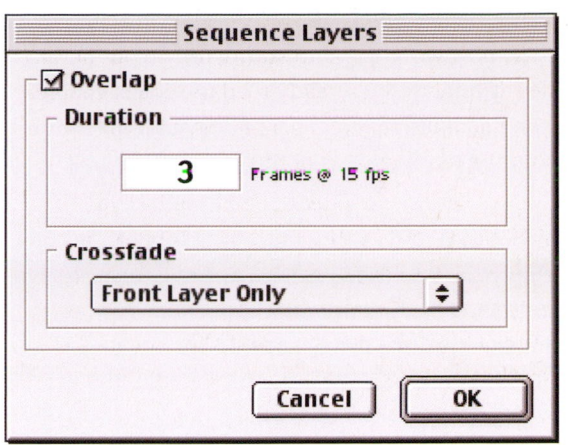

**12** Select all layers and then hit the U key to show all keyframes for selected properties. Notice that After Effects has staggered the layers and keyframed the Opacity of the top layers in order to create the crossfades, saving you a lot of work.

**13** Click OK and then RAM Preview the resulting image sequence.

**14** Move the Current-Time Marker to the beginning of the Composition by hitting the Home key on your keyboard.

After Effects has placed each layer one after the other in a sequence from bottom to top. Note that the sequence will go in whichever order you select the footage. If you had selected the layers in a random order, they would have been staggered in that order. You can experiment with this at the end of this section.

**15** Go to File > Save as and, in the Save as dialog box, navigate to your Creative After Effects folder on the desktop and save the project into the Import folder as SeattleNews01b.aep.

## importing premiere compositions

Although After Effects has some basic editing tools and can be used to edit short sequences, it is not really designed as a fully-fledged editing program. I recommend that you use dedicated editing software such as Adobe Premiere or Apple's Final Cut Pro for capturing footage, putting your sequences together and printing them back out to tape. Both products support both DV and analogue capture and playback with device control and the editing tools provided in these programs will make these jobs a breeze.

I tend to prefer to use Final Cut Pro for most of my editing tasks but Premiere 6 has the edge in terms of integration with After Effects. You can import a Premiere edit directly into an After Effects project, retaining all of the edit decisions you made as well as bringing in markers and transition references.

**1** Open SeattleNews.aep from Training > Projects > Chapter 05. This is an fresh copy of the project you've just saved.

**2** Hit Command + I to go to the Import File dialog box. Select one the file named Edit06.ppj from the Projects folder > Chapter 05, inside the Training folder.

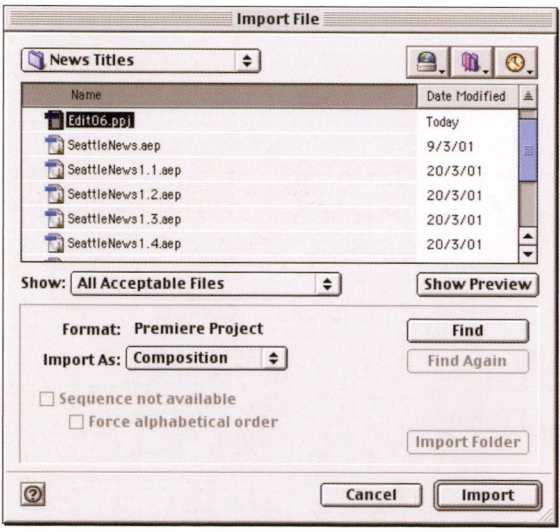

**3** Select *Composition* from the *Import As* drop down menu and then click the Open button to import the Premiere file as a ready-made After Effects Comp.

**4** In the Project window, double-click the Edit06.ppj Composition icon to open up its own Timeline and Composition window.

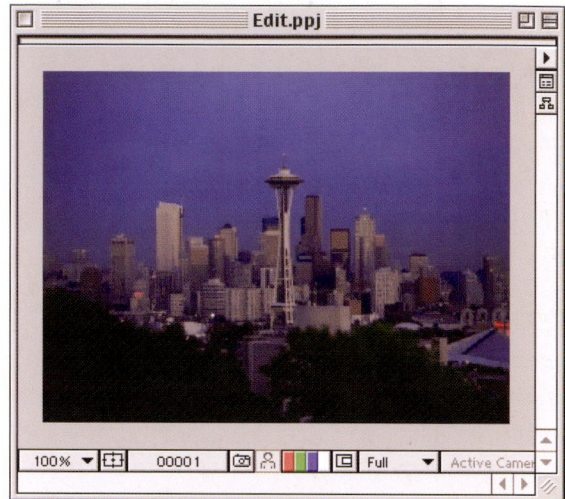

There are two copies of this project on the CD, one was built with Premiere 5.1 (Edit05.ppj) , the other with Premiere 6.0 (Edit06.ppj). If you have a copy of Premiere 5.1 or higher on your system you can open one of these files in Premiere to see the original edit. Notice that the movies have been imported in the order in which they were edited together in Premiere. All In and Out-points are trimmed as they were in Premiere, all markers and labels are also imported. Notice the audio track at the bottom of the Timeline is labeled blue to distinguish it from the yellow-labeled Video tracks. Premiere 6 now includes several After Effects filters. If you apply and set keyframes for these effects in Premiere then they will be brought over live into After Effects too, where you can adjust them and use keyframe assistants on them just as you can with any other keyframes.

**5** Hit Command + K and change the composition Frame Rate to 15 fps and the Duration to 480 frames, click OK to leave the Composition Settings dialog box. RAM Preview the edit.

## replacing footage

This edit consists only of straight cuts but if I had used transitions in my edit, they would have also been represented here in After Effects by red transition marker layers. This serves as a very useful reminder of where the transitions occur, preventing me from adding too much interest to these sections. Notice also that there is an off-line File placeholder where we want our image sequence to appear. The layer consists of standard color bars and was created within Premiere. We'll use a shortcut to replace this placeholder with our pre-prepared footage.

**1** In the Timeline, select the Off-line File placeholder on layer number 7.

**2** Go up to the Project window and select the Sequence Composition that we worked on in the previous section.

**3** Hold down the Alt key and then drag the Composition onto the layer that you wish to replace.

**4** RAM Preview your movie so far.

You can use this method to replace one layer with another layer from within the same project. In this instance we've replaced the layer with a comp. When you drop one Composition into another the process is called Nesting. We will be looking at different methods of nesting Compositions throughout the book, this is just one method.

## slide edit tool

Perhaps you'll have noticed that the views of Seattle at the start and end of the Composition are the wrong way round, the sunrise view should be at the beginning of the Composition, the night view should be at the end. I'll show you how we can change this using some of the editing tools I mentioned earlier.

**1** Select the TC110.mov on layer number and then move the Current-Time Marker over the clip so that you can see its contents displayed in the Composition window.

This section of footage is cut from a time-lapse clip of Seattle, shot from morning, all the way through to night. This is from the Artbeats Time-lapse Cityscapes collection. There are more clips from Artbeats Inc. in the CD > Free Stuff > Footage > Artbeats folder (and in the CD > Training > Source Movies folder) for you to experiment with at the end of this chapter.

Time-lapse photography is very expensive and difficult to set up but you can buy these clips at a very reasonable price from Artbeats. You can then use the clips as often as you like in your own work, it's a great way to source footage which would otherwise be difficult to shoot yourself.

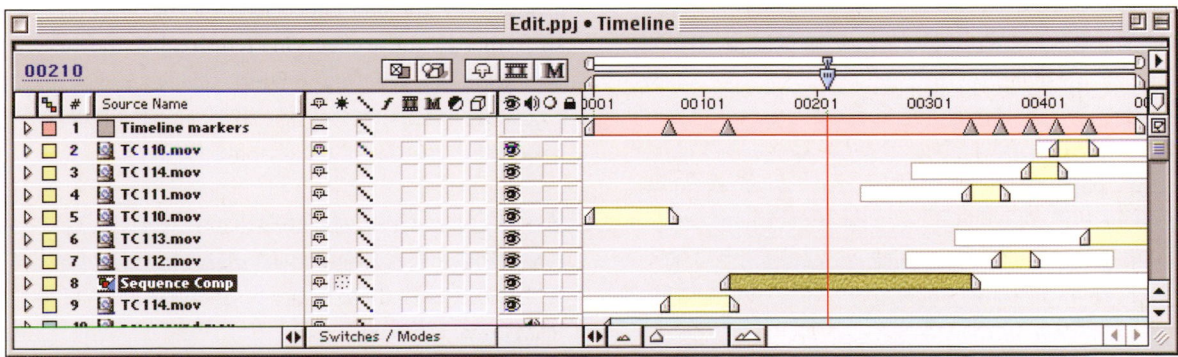

Notice that in this section the sky is light, it is early in the morning. We want this clip to be dark so we need to choose a later section from the same piece of footage. You can see the ghosted sections of available footage underneath the visible, trimmed section of the layer. This tells us that this clip has been trimmed and that there is surplus footage for us to play with. We need to slide the footage that's available along behind the existing edit points.

**2** Place the cursor to the right of the layer's Out-point, the cursor will change to the Slide tool icon, which allows you to slide the surplus footage behind the edit points. Click and drag all the way to the left till you see a blue, evening sky on where it was once a pink, morning one.

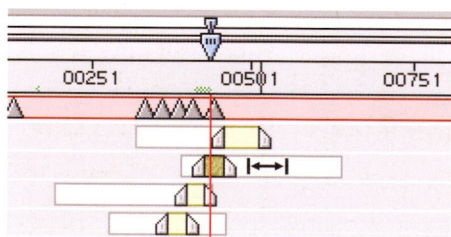

At the beginning of our Composition we want the sky to be morning-pink. This time we'll use another method to adjust the TC110.mov clip on layer 9.

**3** Move the Current-Time Marker over the clip and then double-click the layer name to open it up in its own Layer window. Make sure to position the Layer window so that you can see both it and the Composition window at the same time. You can hit the Tab key to temporarily hide all palettes if need be.

**4** Click on the raised handle in the middle of the yellow bar which represents your trimmed section of the clip. With this handle, you can drag the whole edit along the surplus footage, changing the clip's In and Out-points whilst maintaining the edited clip's length and position in the Timeline.

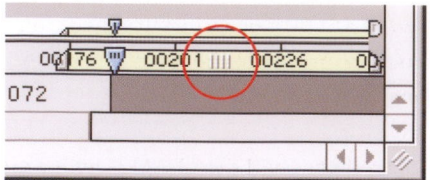

**5** Drag the yellow bar all the way to the left (as in the diagram below) and then close the Layer window.

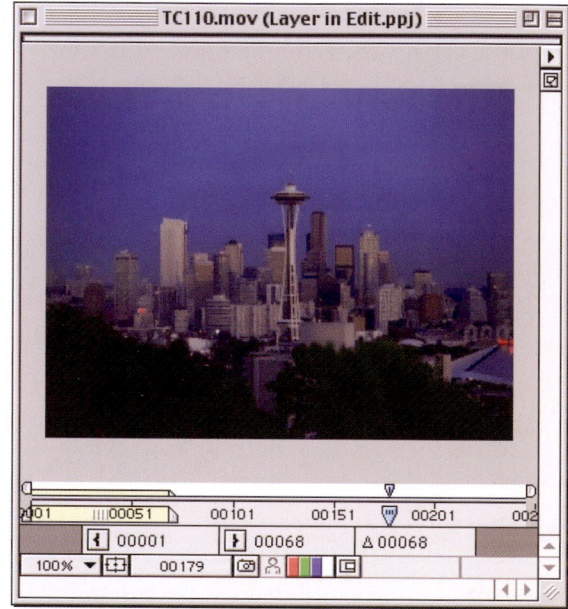

We will use the Sequence Layers Keyframe Assistant again to put crossfades in between all of the movie layers. This time we want to retain the order in which the layers appear in the edit. To do this, we have to select the layers in the same order that we want them to appear in the Timeline.

**6** Click on the first layer in the sequence, Layer number 9, TC110.mov. Now hold down the Shift key and click the top layer, number 2, selecting all the layers in between.

**7** With all of the layers now selected, go to Animation > Keyframe Assistant > Sequence Layers.

**8** Leave the settings on a duration of 3 frames and choose to crossfade the front layer only. Click OK to leave the dialog box.

**9** Close the layers and then RAM Preview your edit. The edits should now happen in time with the music.

**10** Go to File > Save as and, in the Save as dialog box, navigate to your Creative After Effects folder on the desktop and save the project into the Import folder as SeattleNews01c.aep.

OK, let's have a look at how After Effects can import a folder of images as a ready-made image sequence. We'll leave our Seattle News project for now and return to work on it in a later chapter.

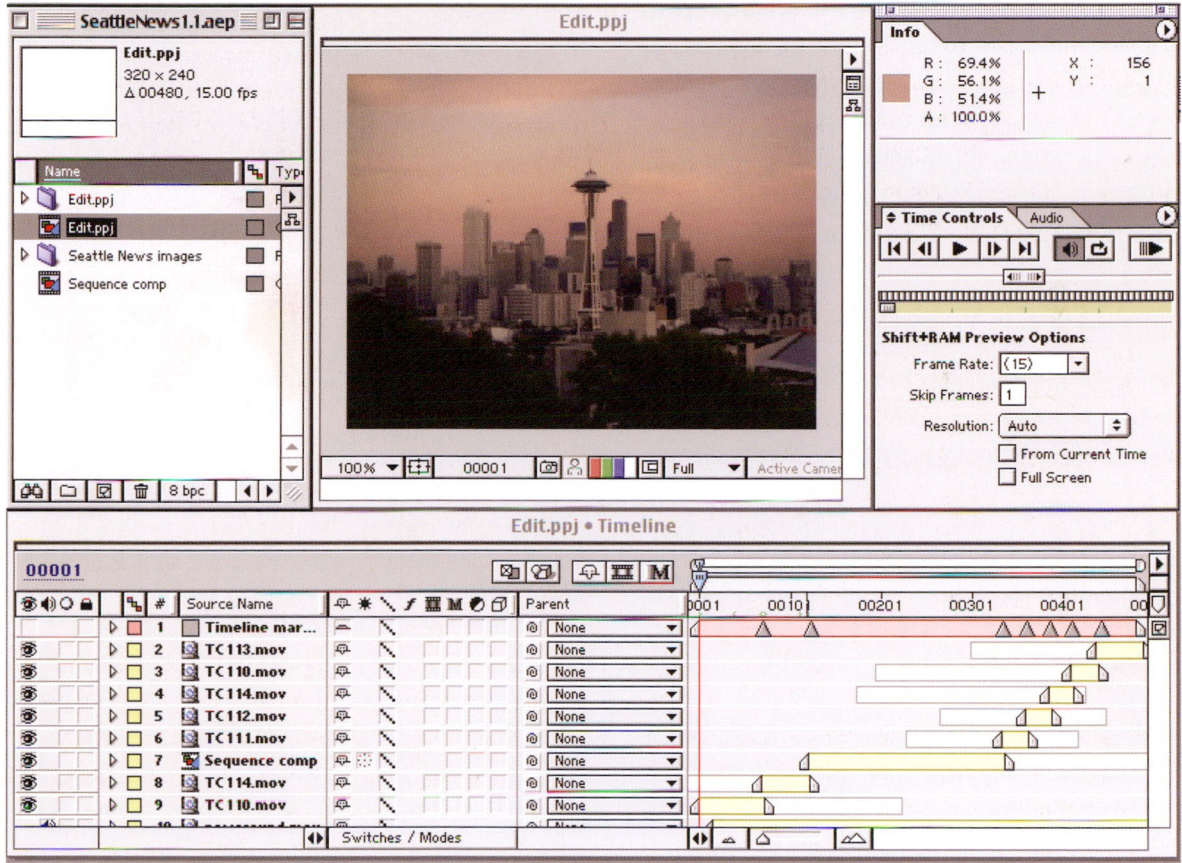

# graffiti club

OK, we're going to start working on our Graffiti Club animation. I want to superimpose the characters in this animation over a fast-paced background with lots of interest and texture. As the program is called 'The Graffiti Club', what better to use than real Graffiti! The first step is to get the images into our project, we could have used the same technique as we used in the previous two lessons but I'm going to show you a new way of creating a sequence from your images.

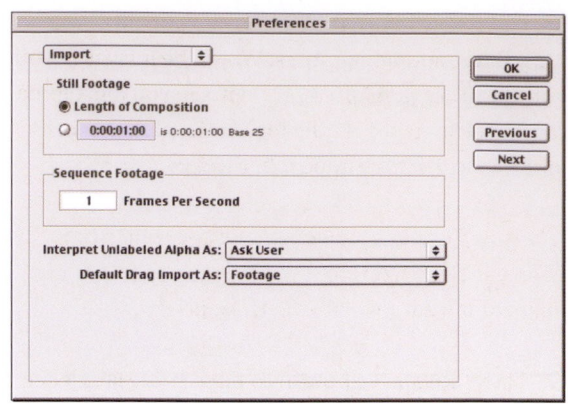

## importing image sequences

A lot of software programs, particularly 3D programs, render out image sequences rather than QuickTime or AVI files. The rendered movie is saved into a folder as a series of still images that can be played back as a movie by any software that supports image sequences.

Many of the proprietary broadcast systems also work with image sequences so it's good to be aware of how to import them into your projects.

The way in which image sequences are imported into After Effects is determined in the Import panel of the Preferences. In here, you can tell After Effects what frame rate Sequence Footage will be imported at.

**1** Create a new project and then go to Edit > Preferences > Import to open the Import panel.

**2** Change the Sequence Footage setting to 1 fps. Normally, you would import an image sequence at the same frame rate as your composition but we want to have one image on screen for every second of our animation. With this setting, After Effects will use one image for every second of our comp.

**3** Hit OK to leave the Preferences dialog box and then hit Command + I to open the Import File dialog box.

**4** Go to Training > Source images > Art Explosion and open the Graffiti Images folder.

**5** Select the first file in the folder and then click on the JPEG Sequence checkbox at the bottom of the Import File dialog box.

This will tell After Effects to bring the footage in as an image sequence. After Effects will bring the files in using alpha-numeric ordering, using the dimensions and bit-depth of the first file you select.

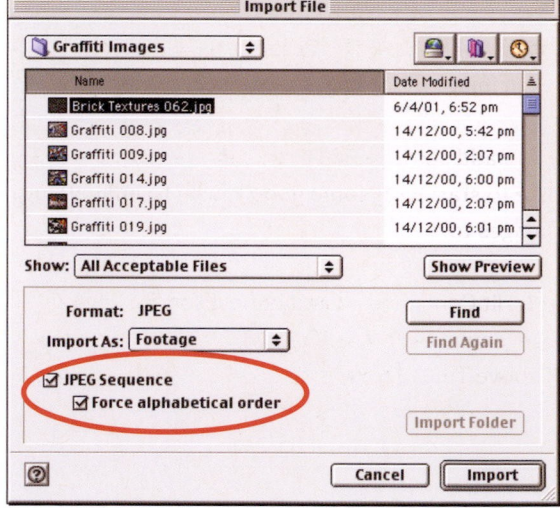

**6** Scroll down the list of JPEGs and you'll see that they have random numbers. When the images in your folder are not numbered sequentially you must force After Effects to import the files in the alphabetical order in which they appear in the window.

Click on the *Force Alphabetical Order* checkbox. Without this selected, After Effects would leave blank frames between non-sequential files.

**7** Click the Import button to import the sequence into your Project.

You can also import image sequences by dragging and dropping the files from their folder, directly into the Project window. If you hold down the Alt key as you drag them, they will be imported as individual files.

**8** Hit Command + N to create a new Composition. Name it Background Sequence, make it 320 × 240, 15 fps and 750 frames long (i.e. fifty seconds).

**9** Select the Graffiti Images sequence in the Project window and hit Command + / to place it into the new Composition. Notice that After Effects names the Image Sequence after the folder which contained the images.

**10** RAM Preview the Composition. Notice that each image stays on screen for exactly one second.

Let's add some music to the animation. I always like to start with some good music to animate my images to.

**11** Hit Command + I and import the file named, Kid_sound.mov from Training > Source sounds > Groove Tunnel folder.

This is a great piece of music for this programme, It was composed and arranged by a very talented guy called Rod Spark of Groove Tunnel (http://www.groovetunnel.com).

Rod has a fully-equipped studio where he produces very high quality original music at very reasonable prices, thoroughly recommended! His details and more samples of his work are in the CD > Free Stuff > Footage > Groove Tunnel folder.

**12** Make sure the Current–Time Marker is at the beginning of your Composition and then place the audio file into the Timeline.

**13** RAM Preview the result. Notice that the images do not match up with the beats of the music. Later, I'm going to show you a couple of easy ways to make this happen.

**14** Go to File > Save as and, in the Save as dialog box, navigate to your Creative After Effects folder on the desktop and save the project into the Import folder as Graffiti01b.aep. We will return to this project later to develop it further.

This technique is great for situations when you simply want a series of images to run with straight cuts in between (obviously, you will not be able to put crossfades in between the images as all the images are combined into one layer in your Comp). It also saves you from having to import lots of image files separately.

# recap

So, in this chapter you've learned a fair bit about some of the import options and some other stuff associated with that:

- Importing Photoshop files as Compositions
- Keeping their Blending Modes intact
- Importing Adjustment layers
- Importing layers with Layer Effects
- the Sequence Layer Keyframe Assistant
- Importing Premiere files as Compositions
- Importing Image Sequences

**15**  Create a new project and import some of the Royalty free clips and images included on the CD. Experiment a bit with the things you've learned in this chapter.

Try building a new Photoshop file to import, with Layer Effects, Blending Modes and Adjustment Layers applied. Try out some different combinations of sequences.

Save any successful ideas into your own Creative After Effects > Import folder and render out any movies you're happy with before moving on to the next section.

Here are a few more tips from another old buddy of mine, Elaine Axten. Elaine is a fine artist and works in lots of media including painting, animation and performance art:

- I think daydreaming and finding time to deliberately do nothing, to transcend the boredom of everyday life to the point of nothingness is the perfect creative pitch.

- I really believe in forgetting about what you are working on for a short period of time – leaving your mind fallow.

- There is a lovely essay on laziness in 'The Grain of the Voice' by Roland Barthes. You can't beat reading stuff like this, its dreamy and inspiring. Bachelard is my big favorite just now, he's the absolute tops.

- Write a design question to yourself before going to sleep and then see what your answer is to it in the morning.

- Go to the gym and get yourself a big endorphin high, it makes you optimistic and buzzy so you can use the next hour or two to think with a most clear and creative mind.

- My other tip is more embarrassing. It involves getting absolutely plastered and forgetting about everything for an evening, and at some point during the next day tapping into a little creative streak (this is a time when you might want more drink – resist this urge and get your ideas down!). I think a strong part of this is  the temporary killing off of the logical part of your mind, so your intuition gets to surface. You might not want to use this as it is the strategy of a reprobate, but it does work!

# chapter six
# masks

## seattle evening news

### multiple masks

OK, so you've seen how After Effects can read transparency information in the form of alpha channels. There are several ways of creating your own areas of transparency in After Effects and one of them is by creating Masks. Masks define which areas of your layer are transparent and which remain opaque, they can be created by using the Mask tools in the Tool Palette. You can also copy and paste any paths from Photoshop, Illustrator or any other application that supports paths.

You can have up to 127 Masks on each layer, you can also animate them. Masks have Modes, which allow you to determine how the Masks interact with each other. You can also use Masks with certain effects which we will look at later. First, let's look at the basics of working with Masks.

**1** If you do not have a project open, open SeattleNews01.aep from the Chapter 06 folder, in Training > Projects.

**2** RAM Preview the Edit.ppj Composition. The comp consists of several movie clips and stills edited in time with the music.

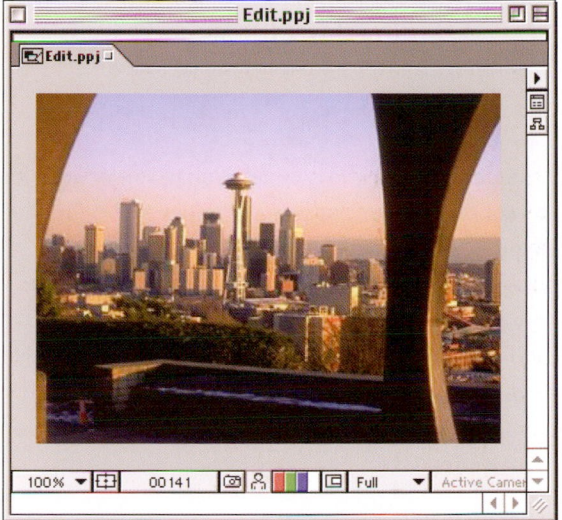

The problem here is that the images are very disparate, the composition contains a mish–mash of images which don't really look as though they belong together. A big part of the problem is the fact that all have been shot using different camera equipment, some clips are DV, some analogue video, others are stills, shot with SLR cameras. Another big problem is with the color of the images. When an artist paints a picture, he/she will choose colors to build the picture with, he/she may do this by instinct but there is still a decision-making process involved.

The trouble with our job is that we are often provided with a lot of source material that we have not shot ourselves, chances are that we were not involved in the decisions about lighting, color schemes etc. It is our job to pull these bits and pieces together into something more unified.

There are several ways of doing this using colors and overlays to give all the individual bits of footage a common thread throughout.

We are going to use multiple masks, layer modes and later, expressions to create an effect layer to place over the Edit.ppj sequence, bringing all the clips together in a delicious design fusion! Let's start by building some new footage.

## solids

There is a popular misconception that you must have some source footage before you start working in After Effects, but this is not true. In After Effects you can create raw footage from scratch by using Solid layers, these are plain, colored layers which can then be animated and transformed by altering properties and applying masks and effects. I quite often work with solids in After Effects, it's a very flexible way of working.

**NB** The one drawback to working with Solids is that they cannot be accessed in the Project window which means that you can't perform certain functions, for example replacing them with files from the finder or changing the file interpretation settings.

**1** Create a new composition, name it Masks Comp and check that the composition size is 384 × 288, slightly bigger than our other comp. The Frame Rate should be 15 fps and Duration should be 480 frames.

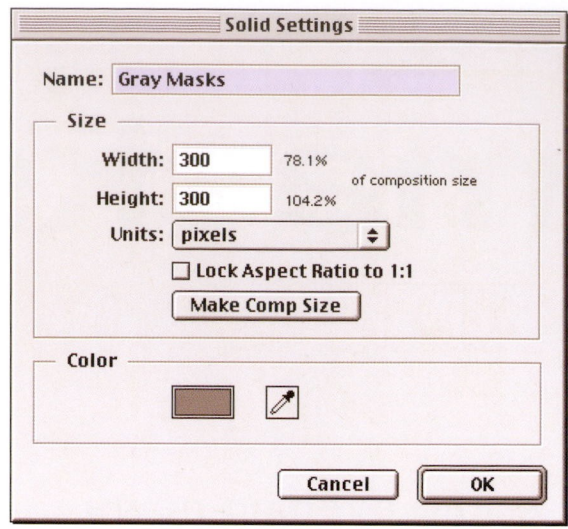

**2** To create a new solid, make sure that the Current-Time Marker is at the beginning of your composition and then go to Layer > New > Solid or hit Command + Y to bring up the Solid Settings dialog box.

**3** In the Solid Settings dialog box, type in *Gray Masks* for the Solid name, change the width and height to 300 pixels (square) and then choose a gray of about 50% for the color. You can do this by eye if you feel confident but if you are unsure, simply enter a value of 70% for each of the RGB channels in the Color picker.

**4** One way of creating different shapes with Solids is to use Masks. Masks alter the alpha channel of your layer. The size and shape of a mask is defined using the Mask Tools in the Tool Palette. These include the Pen tool and the Rectangle and Oval Mask tools. You will be familiar with these tools if you have ever drawn paths in Illustrator or Photoshop.

Creative After Effects

## masking tools

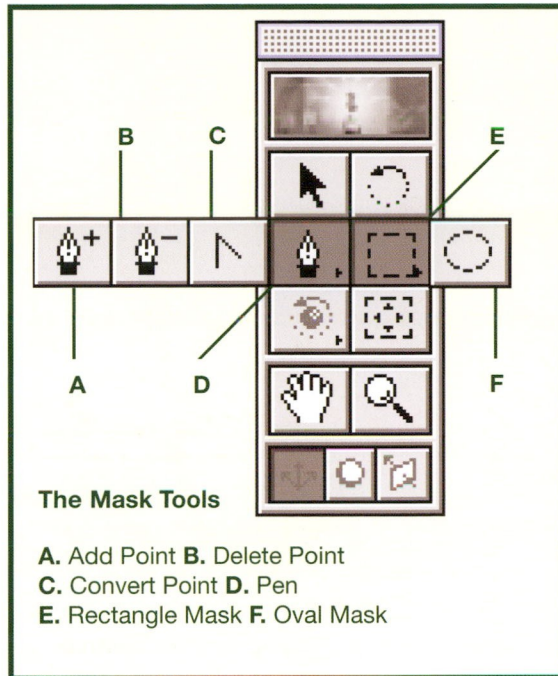

**The Mask Tools**

**A.** Add Point **B.** Delete Point
**C.** Convert Point **D.** Pen
**E.** Rectangle Mask **F.** Oval Mask

Masks are commonly used to isolate (or *mask out*) parts of your image that you either want to be visible or transparent. You define the area by drawing a Bezier path around it. This technique is called *Garbage Matting* and you can find out more about it in the Keying chapter.

Masks can also be used in conjunction with certain filters to create shapes, animations and effects. Here, we will use the Mask modes in conjunction with the Layer modes to create our own custom effect.

There are several ways of drawing Masks, each has its own pros and cons. It is useful to be aware of all of the techniques available to you. I'll show you a few in this exercise and some more in later exercises. We will start by drawing some basic shapes.

**5** The easiest method is to draw your masks directly into the Composition window. To do this, first select the Oval Mask tool from the Tool Palette. The Oval mask tool is situated behind the Rectangular mask tool and can be accessed by clicking and holding on the Rectangular tool till it reveals itself on the pull out strip. A quicker way to access these tools is by using a keyboard shortcut. You can toggle between the Rectangle and Oval Mask tools by repeatedly hitting the Q key on your keyboard.

**6** Double-click the Oval tool in the Tool palette, this will create a default Oval mask exactly the same size of your layer (make sure that Layer Masks are checked in the Composition window wing menu).

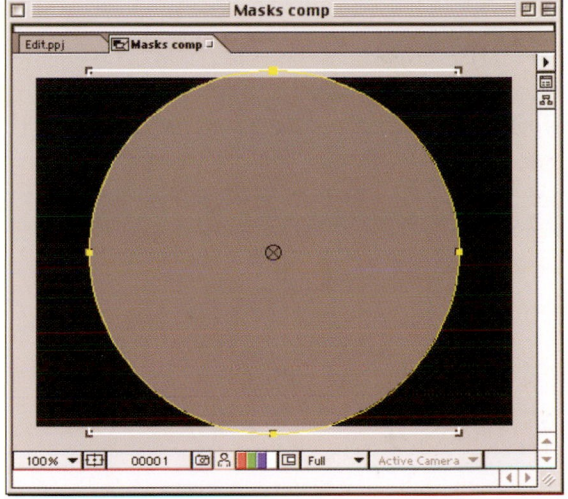

Notice that a default Oval Mask has been created exactly the same size as your Layer. Notice that areas outside the Mask are transparent, areas within the Mask are solid.

If you want to check the transparent areas, you can turn the Checkerboard Background on in the Composition Wing Menu to check the areas of transparency. Switch it off again before continuing with the next section.

## the layer window

Masks can be drawn onto your layer directly in the Composition window or in the Layer window. There may be times when working with multi–layered, complex compositions when drawing masks directly in the Composition window is impractical. In these situations I find it much easier to draw masks in the Layer window for the following reasons;

• The Composition window only shows a layer up to the edges of the composition, the Layer window will show the whole layer.
• Effects and transformations will be rendered on to the layer when viewed in the Composition window, often making it difficult to see exactly what you are doing.
• The Layer window will show you the original file before any Effects and Transformations are applied.

In After Effects Masks are applied before Effects and Transformations so any Masks you add to a layer will be applied to the layer in its original state. I almost always prefer to draw my masks in the Layer window where I can see the complete, original layer.

**7** Double-click the Gray masks layer in the Timeline to open up its layer window. In the Layer window, click anywhere away from the mask to deselect it (Command + Shift + A) and then move the layer window so that you can see both it and the Composition window simultaneously.

**8** Double-click on the Oval Mask tool again to create another Mask the same size as your layer.

**NB** It is important to deselect the first mask before doing this, if you didn't the new mask would replace the selected mask rather than adding a new one.

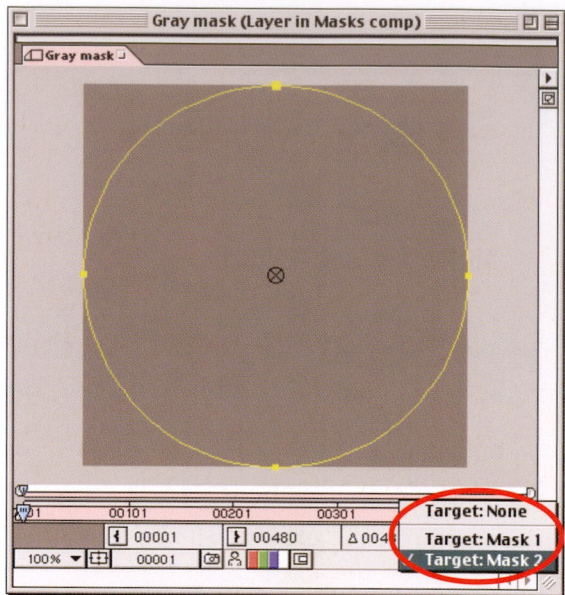

**9** To prove that you have two masks, look in the Target menu at the bottom of the Layer window, this is one place where you can select Masks to make them active. There should be two masks listed in this menu. Make sure that you have the second Mask selected. If you do not have two masks undo your steps and start again, repetition is the best way to learn.

**10** With the new mask still selected, hit Command + T or go to Layer > Mask > Free Transform Points. A bounding box will appear around your mask. This bounding box allows you to move, rotate or reshape your mask using only one tool, the standard Selection Tool.

**11** Make sure that the Info palette is visible and then click on any of the corner handles. Start dragging towards the center of the layer, as you drag, hold down the Command key and the Shift key simultaneously. The Info palette will show you information about the amount of scale you are using, stop dragging when the display reads about 68% of the original scale.

Dragging towards the center of the layer will scale your layer down. Holding the Command key whilst dragging will force the mask to scale around its center point. Holding down the Shift key whilst dragging will constrain the scale so that it scales equally on both the X and Y axes. Your layer window should look similar to the one pictured below.

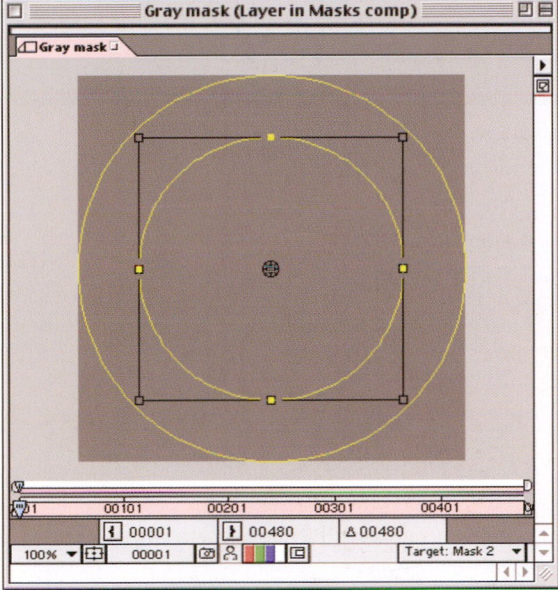

**12** Hit the return key on your keyboard to accept the changes you've made.

To create the final mask we'll copy and paste the last mask we created and then adjust it using the Mask controls in the Timeline.

**13** With the Gray mask layer selected in the Timeline, hit the M key to bring up the Mask Shape properties.

**14** You can select masks by clicking on their names in the Timeline. Try clicking on the masks one at a time and watch as they are selected in both the Layer and Composition windows. When you have finished make sure that you have mask 2 selected.

**15** Hit Command + C or go to Edit > Copy to copy the mask to the clipboard.

As I mentioned in step 8, drawing a new mask (or pasting one) whilst another mask is selected will replace the selected mask. This is a great feature for creating animated masks, allowing you to easily change the shape of a mask by replacing it entirely. However, in this instance we want to add another mask rather than change an existing one. In step 7 we simply deselected the mask before drawing the new one. An alternative method is to lock the masks that you want to keep, preventing you from accidentally replacing them with any new Masks.

**16** Click in the Lock checkboxes for each Mask. These are situated underneath the Padlock icon in the Audio/Video Features panel of the Timeline. These are circled in red in the diagram below.

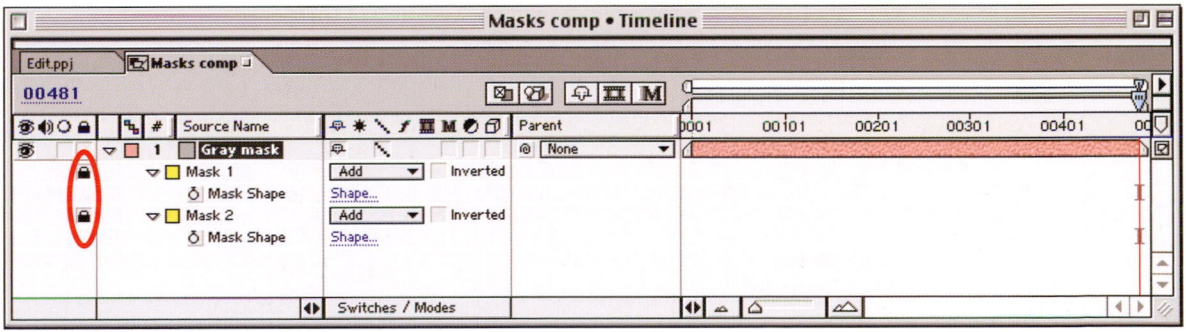

**17** Hit Command + V or go to Edit > Paste to paste a copy of the Mask into the layer.

**18** Select Mask 3 by clicking on it in the Timeline and then hit Command + T to apply the Free Transform bounding box to the mask.

**19** Use the same technique as you used in step 11 to scale the mask down by about 48% and then hit the Return key to accept your changes.

## mask modes

In the Switches panel of the Timeline you'll notice that each mask has a Mask Mode drop down menu where you can choose different ways of combining the masks to make them interact with each other in different ways.

These modes work independently from, but in a very similar way to, Layer modes. Mask Modes can be applied individually to each mask. Each mode will have a different result depending on the content of both the layer it's applied to and the layers above and below it in the Timeline. Any overlapping masks will have their opacities combined, creating the impression of one solid block.

The default mode is *Add*, which will *add* the contents of the mask to the Alpha channel, removing any pixels outside the masked area. The mask modes, like Layer modes cannot be animated over time.

**1** Unlock all masks and then make sure that they are deselected by clicking away from them (if you change the Mask Mode with all masks selected, it will change the mode for all selected layers).

**2** Using the drop down menu, change Mask 2's mode to Subtract. This mode will have the effect of subtracting any pixels within the specified mask from the layer. You can see that Subtract mode does the opposite to Add mode by making the pixels within the mask transparent in the Alpha channel. By combining masks with different modes you can start to create new shapes which would be much more difficult to create with only one mask.

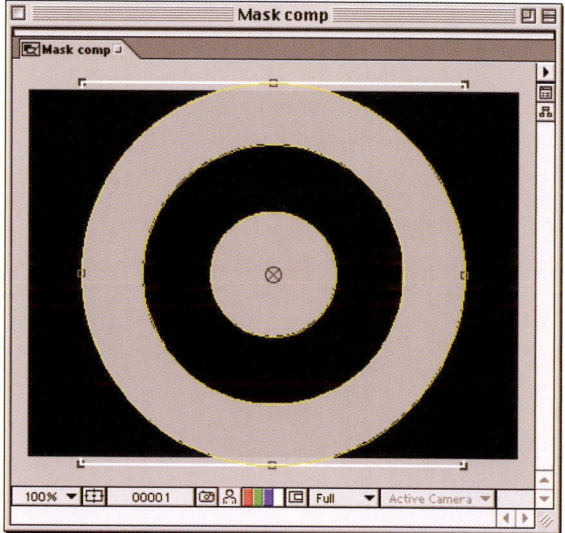

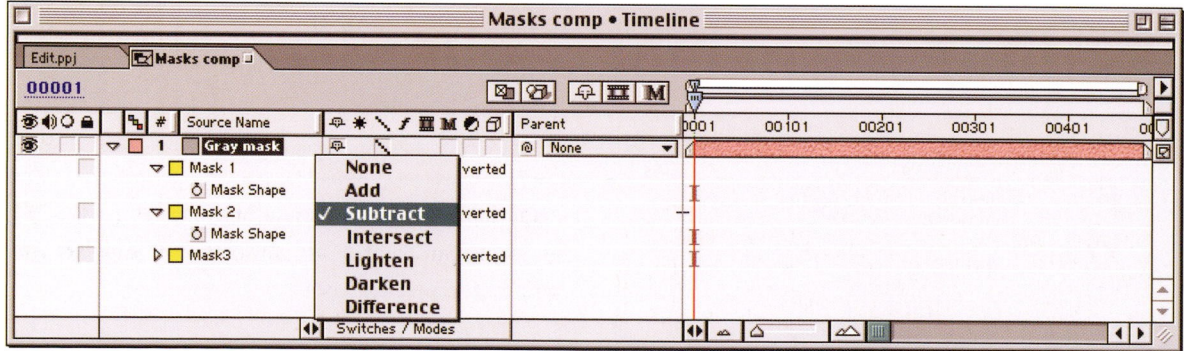

**3** Create another New Solid (Command + Y). This time, name the new layer White Masks. Change the size to 260 pixels square and the color to white.

**4** Go to the Gray Masks Layer window. Select all of the masks (Command + A) and then hit Command + C to copy them to the clipboard.

**5** Double-click the White Masks layer to open up its Layer window. Hit Command + V to paste the masks into the new layer.

**6** Click in the pasteboard area to make the Layer window active and then hit Command + A to select all of the masks. Hit Command + T to bring up the Free Transform mode.

As we discovered earlier, Free Transform allows you to perform different transformations on your masks using one tool. You can use it on specified points of a mask, on the whole mask or, as in this case, on multiple masks.

**7** Move the cursor over one of the corner handles, it will change to a scaling tool. With this tool active, click and drag the corner handle inwards to resize all of the masks. Hold down the Command key whilst dragging to scale around the center point, hold down Shift whilst dragging to maintain the correct aspect ratio. You should resize the masks till they fit snugly inside the Composition window; about 82% of their original size should do it. You can watch the Composition window update as you drag to get a real-time preview of the scaling. You can use the Info palette to get a precise reading, in percentage of how much you are scaling the selection by.

**8** When you are happy with the result, either hit the Return key or double-click inside the bounding box to accept the changes.

**9** In the Timeline, select the White Masks layer and hit the **M** key.

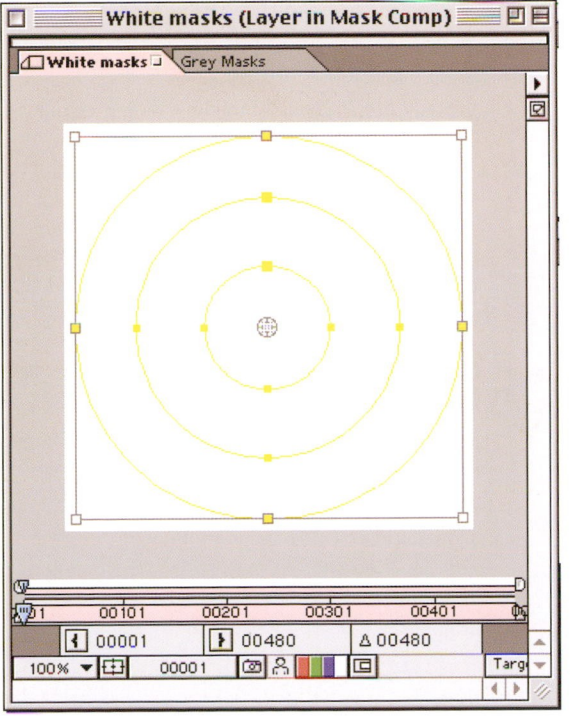

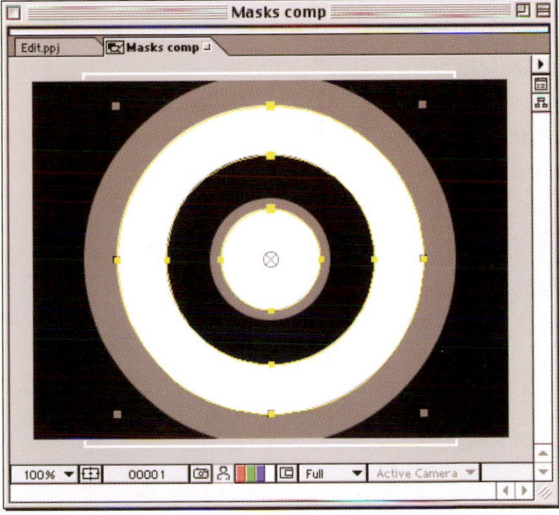

**10** Deselect the masks and then change Mask 2's mode to Subtract. Your comp should look like the one in the picture above.

To make life easier when working with Multiple masks you can change the label color so that they are easier to distinguish. In my example I've chosen primary colors for the white layer (red, yellow and blue) and secondary colors for the gray layer (green, orange and purple). This way, it is easy for me to tell which mask belongs to each layer.

**11** To change the mask's label color, simply click on the Mask's colored label, in the Timeline and choose another color from the color picker. Do this for all of your new masks.

**12** Context-Click on the Switches panel heading in the Timeline to bring up the context-sensitive menu, go to Panels > Modes to bring up the Layer modes panel.

**13** In the Modes panel change both layer's modes to Difference and notice how the layers now react differently with each other. For an explanation of how this mode, and others, work see the Technical.PDF document in the Extras folder on the CD.

**14** Go to File > Save as and, in the Save as dialog box, navigate to your Creative After Effects folder on the desktop and save the project into the Masks folder as SeattleNews02b.aep. We'll return to this project in the next chapter.

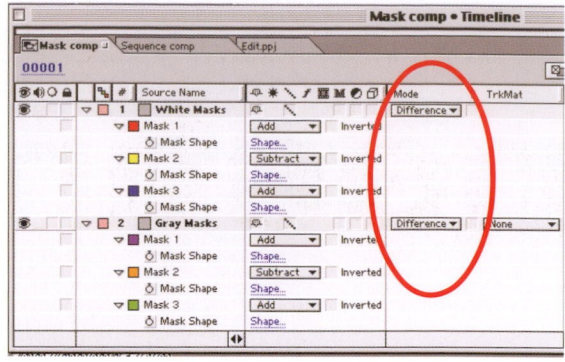

## recap

We will build further on what you have learned in this chapter throughout the book. For now, create a new composition with a couple of New Solids in it, add some Masks to the layers and adjust their Mask Modes to see what effects you can achieve. After the next chapter, you'll be combining some of the bits and pieces you've created from the last few chapters so save anything you do into your Creative After Effects > Masks folder.

Also, check out the website for more tutorials using masks, at;

http://www.angie.abel.co.uk/book.html

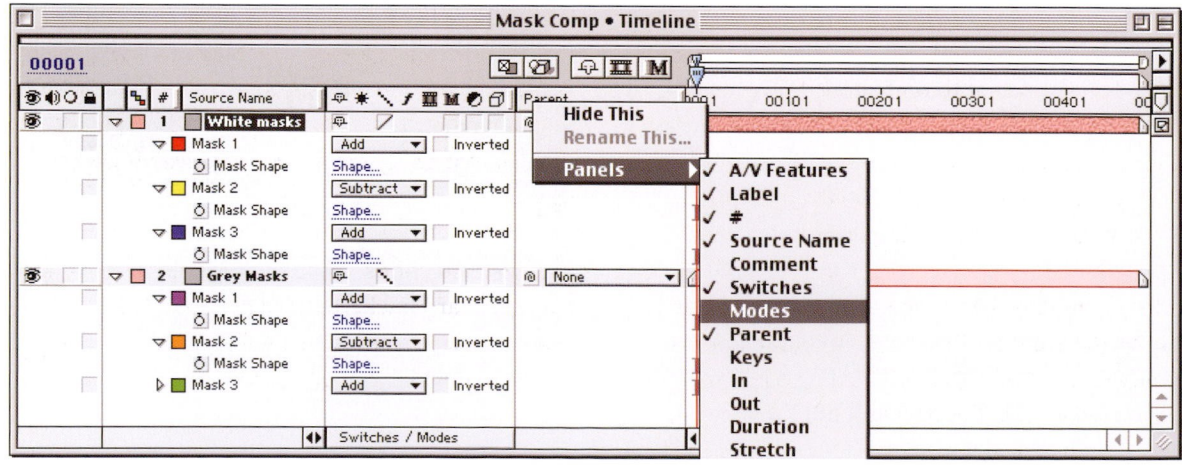

# chapter seven
# nesting

## nesting

As you have seen, you can import multilayered Photoshop files into After Effects as compositions, keeping their alpha (transparency) information intact. Let's have a look at the individual layers to see what information they contain.

**1** Open ideas.02.aep from Training > Projects > Chapter 07. This is the file that we imported into After Effects back in the Import Chapter.

**2** Switch off visibility for all of the layers underneath the Ideas layer by clicking and dragging the cursor over the visibility icons (the little eyes). This is a quick and easy way to toggle visibility on and off for a group of layers.

## changing the background color

The default background color in After Effects is black. It is important to remember, however, that the background in After Effects is not a solid part of your composition but just a background to view your composition against. This is very important to remember when rendering out your movies with embedded alpha channels as the background color will not be visible when rendered. You can change the color at any time so that, for example, if you are working with black text, you can see it contrasted against the background.

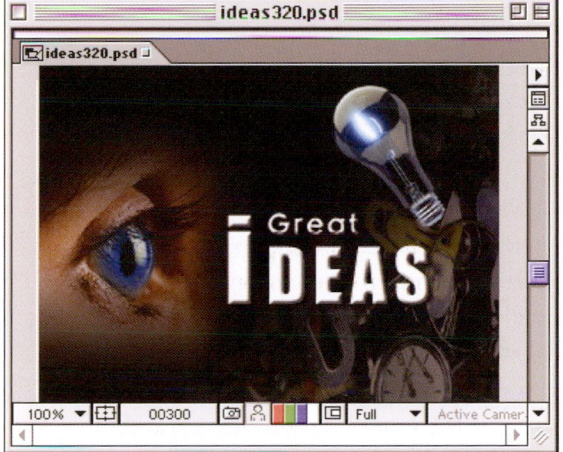

**1** Hit Command + Shift + B or go to Composition > Background Color. The background color dialog box will appear. If you click on the color swatch you can use the default Mac or Windows color pickers to choose a new color. Alternatively, you can click the Eyedropper tool and sample a color from anywhere on the desktop. Choose one of these methods to change the background to a lighter color, I've chosen blue.

You can also choose to view the background as a checkerboard background, à la Photoshop. This makes it easy to see which areas are truly transparent and which are opaque.

**2** Click on the little triangle at the top, right of the Composition window, a drop down menu will appear with a list of choices. Choose Checkerboard Background from the list to see your text against the familiar Photoshop checkerboard.

## renaming layers and comps

**1** Toggle the visibility on and off for layers three and four to see what is contained in each layer. Notice that the shadow is on its own, separate layer and the bevel is on the layer above it. If you look at the icon next to the layer 3 name you will see that it is actually a composition which has been nested within this composition. This is also signified by the color of the layer in the Timeline, it is gray as opposed to pink.

**2** In the Timeline, stretch the Source Name field by clicking and dragging the raised handle on the right edge of the panel heading. Notice that the layer name is Layer Effects Comp, also indicating that this is a nested composition. The Source Name field will, as the name implies, display the name of the source file used for each layer. It can be toggled to show a user-defined Layer Name, this allows you to rename your layers, whilst still keeping track of the original file names.

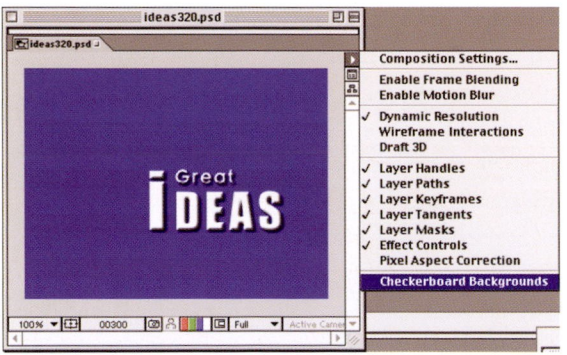

**3** Select layer number 3 (Layer Effects Comp) and then hit the Enter key on your keyboard. Doing this will change the panel heading to Layer Name and will highlight the text so that you can enter a new *Layer Name*.

**4** Type in, 'Ideas Effects Composition' and then hit the Enter key on your keyboard to rename your layer.

**5** Click on the Layer Name panel heading to toggle between Layer Name and Source Name.

This will give your layer a new layer name but will not change the source name of the layer. Notice that there are still two compositions with the same name in the Project window. To change the *Source Name* of a layer, it must be done in the Project window.

**6** Go back to the Project window and open up the folder within it, named, ideas320.psd. Inside this folder you will see all of the layers which were created in Photoshop, plus two compositions, both named *Layer Effects Composition*, one for each of the text layers. These are the same compositions that you can see now in your ideas320.psd composition.

Obviously it can cause confusion when two compositions have the same name, so I'll show you how to change the Source name of one of them.

**7** Select the bottom-most composition and then hit the Enter key on the keyboard. Type in *Great Effects Comp* and then hit the Enter key to accept your changes. Notice that the *Layer name* has also changed in the Timeline.

## opening a nested composition

After Effects allows you to use virtually any image file, sound file or movie file as a layer in a composition. As well as being able to use individual files as layers, you can also use another composition as a layer in your composition. This process is known as nesting. Nesting is a very flexible way of grouping layers together and applying compound effects. In later chapters I will show you how to create your own nested compositions but for now we will look at how, when and why Photoshop automatically nests compositions.

**1** Hold down the Alt key and double-click layer number three (Great Effects Comp). As you do this, the nested Composition will open out in its own tabbed Composition window and Timeline.

You can jump between the two open compositions by clicking the tabs in either the Composition or Timeline, as you do so, the other will update automatically. Notice that the Great Effects Comp consists of three layers.

**2** Making sure you have the Great Effects Comp active, hit Command + A or go to Edit > Select All to select all of the layers for this composition.

**3** Hit the E key to show any effects applied to the layers. You will see that layers one and two both have the same effect applied to them which is called Photoshop Bevel and Emboss.

**4** Stretch out the Layer Name field so that you can see the full name of each layer. Toggle the Layer Name heading back and forth between Source Name and Layer Name.

**5** Look at the Source Name panel and notice that After Effects has created three copies of the same source layer, stacking them on top of each other. The layers have then been renamed, *Ideas Inner Bevel Shadow*, *Ideas Inner Bevel Highlight* and *Ideas*. The top two layers contain the bevel effects and the bottommost layer is the original layer. By doing this, After Effects allows you to control the shadows and highlights of the bevel separately.

**6** Deselect the layers and then select layer number 1, the top layer of the composition.

**7** Double-click the Effect Name, *Photoshop Bevel and Emboss* to open up its tab in the Effect Controls window.

**8** At the bottom of the palette you will see a drop down menu next to the words *Show Bevel*, notice that the menu is set to show *Shadows*. Click on the drop down menu and change it so that it reads *Highlight*. Toggle the menu back and forth so that you can clearly see the difference between the two modes in the Composition window. Make sure that it is set back to Shadow when you have finished looking at the differences.

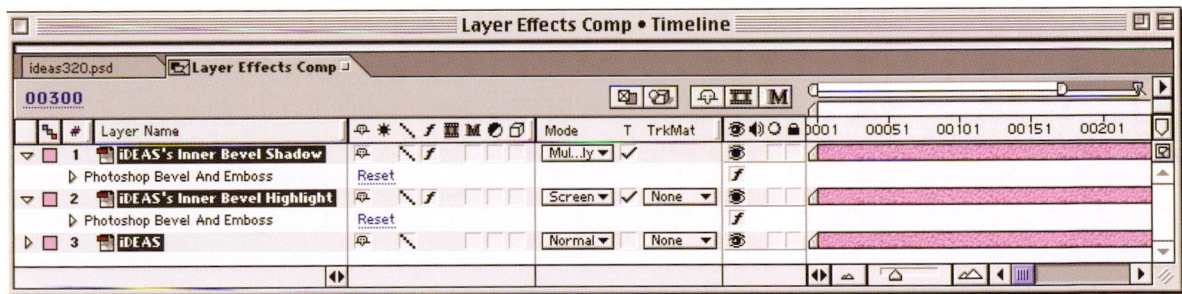

**9** In the Effect Controls window, change the Depth amount to 2 and the Blur amount to 1. Notice the difference that it makes to your layer in the Composition window.

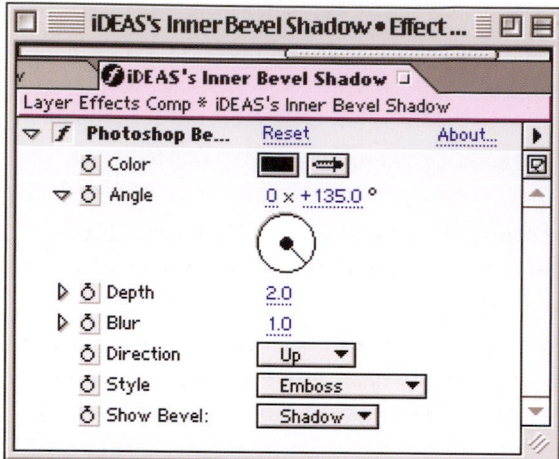

I'm always wary of using too much bevel and shadow on a layer, it can make it look quite tacky if it's over done. Quiet often a slight suggestion of something is far more effective than something that's way over the top.

**10** Select the effect to make it active by clicking the Effect name, either in the Effect Controls window or in the Timeline. When an effect is active, the Effect name will be displayed as white text on a black background both in the Effect Controls window and in the Timeline.

**11** Hit Command + C to copy the effect values. We will use the same settings for the other layer.

**12** Select layer number 2 and then double-click the Effect Name to open up the tab for that layer in the Effect Controls window. Notice that the drop down menu is set for Highlight.

**13** Hit Command + V to paste the effect values from the first layer.

**14** Change the Show Bevel drop down menu back to Highlight again.

By placing the shadows and highlights on separate layers, you have more flexibility and control over how the effect looks. Again, all the effects which we applied in Photoshop have remained live throughout their journey to After Effects. The shadows, highlights and the original layer have been put together in their own separate composition and then brought into this composition as a nested Composition. This means you can make global changes to all layers within the composition.

**15** Click on the iDEAS320.psd tab in either the Composition window or the Timeline, to make it the active composition and then switch off visibility for layer number 4, *iDEA's Drop Shadow.*

## animating nested compositions

Notice that the changes that you made to the shadows and highlights in the Layer Effects Composition have been carried through to the original composition. After Effects updates changes made in nested compositions automatically. We are now going to animate the position of the layer. Because the bevel effects are nested within the layer, they will all move along together.

**1** Switch visibility back on for all of the layers by clicking and dragging across the Eye icons in the Timeline.

**2** Select Layer three, Great Effects Comp and hit the P key to bring up the position values for that layer.

**3** Hit Command + G and, in the Go to Time dialog box type in 31 and then click OK to move the Current-Time Marker to frame 31.

As I mentioned in Chapter One, when creating animations it is quite often much easier to set the end point of the sequence before the start point, especially when animating titles. In this example we will move the text on to the screen by animating its' position and scale values. The text is already where we want it to be once the animation has finished so it is easier to set a keyframe here to lock it in place and then go back to make the changes.

**4** Hit Alt + P to set a keyframe for Position, locking the values at this point in time.

**5** Hit Shift + Alt + S to bringing up the Scale value as well as the Position value and set a Scale keyframe at the same point in time.

**6** Move to frame 16 and then hit Command + Shift + P to bring up the Position dialog box. Enter –10, 148 into the fields and then hit Return.

**7** Click on the Scale value to highlight it, enter a value of 0 and hit Enter to accept the changes.

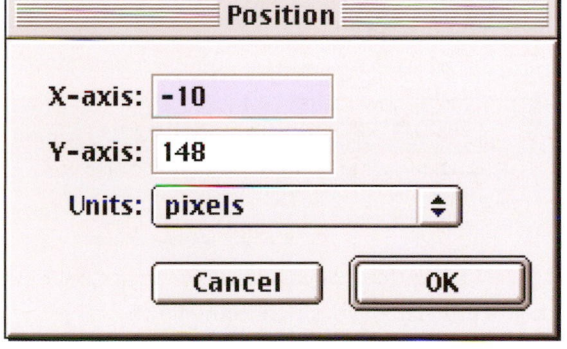

**8** Make sure that visibility is back on for layer number 4 and then RAM Preview the animation. Notice that all layers from the nested Composition move together as one layer but that the shadow is not following the layer. This is because the shadow is on a separate layer from the main text. In order for the shadow to follow the text, it needs to be part of the same nested Composition. This is not a problem as we can simply cut and paste layers from one composition to another.

**9** Select layer 4 and then hit Command + X to cut the layer from the composition to the clipboard.

**10** Click on the Layer Effects Composition tab in the Timeline to make it the active composition and then hit Command + V to paste the shadow layer into the Layer Effects Composition.

**11** When you paste a layer into a composition it will appear as the top layer in the Timeline. Select the layer and drag it down so that it becomes the bottom layer in the composition.

**12** Go back to the Ideas.psd Composition and preview it. Notice that the shadow now follows the text.

You can see how useful Nesting Compositions can be for making global changes to a group of layers. Turn all the layers visibility back on and preview the changes you've made.

We'll return to this file later on in this chapter to develop it a bit further but for now save the project as ideas1.3.aep into your Creative After Effects Nesting folder.

# seattle evening news

## collapsing layers

OK, back to our Seattle News titles, in the last chapter we created a new composition which consisted of a white layer and a gray layer. We added some Masks to the layers to create a sort of target shape.

**1** Open SeattleNews02.aep from the Chapter 07 folder, in Training > Projects.

We now have three separate compositions within this project; the Sequence comp and the Edit.ppj comp which we put together in Import Chapter and the Masks comp, which we built in the Masks Chapter.

When designing for Television, or in fact any medium, the composition of elements on the screen is very important. Good composition will draw the viewer's eye and keep their attention focused on what you want them to see.

In this case we are going to base the design around the center of the screen. This can sometimes have a tendency to make the screen appear quite small and the design too dominating. Later in the book we will be animating the discs in and out from the center. This will bring the diagonals into play a little bit more than with a static image and will carry the viewer's eye around the screen.

Our design problem here is that we need something to break up the circles and accentuate the diagonals. One way of doing this is to divide the screen into quarters. Normally, this would be too rigid a design but remember that the circles will be moving in and out, pulling the design together. This is an example of using two designs which on their own may be too strong but used together can produce something both simple yet visually exciting. We'll start by creating one more masked layer.

**2** Make sure that the Current-Time Marker is back at the beginning of your composition and then create another, white solid (Command + Y). Change its name to Square masks and click the composition size button to make sure that the layer is exactly the same size as the composition.

**3** With the layer selected, click to open the wing menu of the Composition window and make sure that Layer Masks is selected.

With this option selected, you can draw and edit masks directly in the Composition window. This menu (illustrated in the diagram below) allows you to toggle on and off your display settings as well as allowing you access to some of your Composition settings.

**4** Go to View > Show Rulers and then make sure that your info palette is visible.

It is a good habit to get into using rulers, guides and grids to set up your compositions, particularly if you are working with precise geometric shapes as we are about to do here. Guides can be dragged out from the rulers and positioned anywhere within the Composition window.

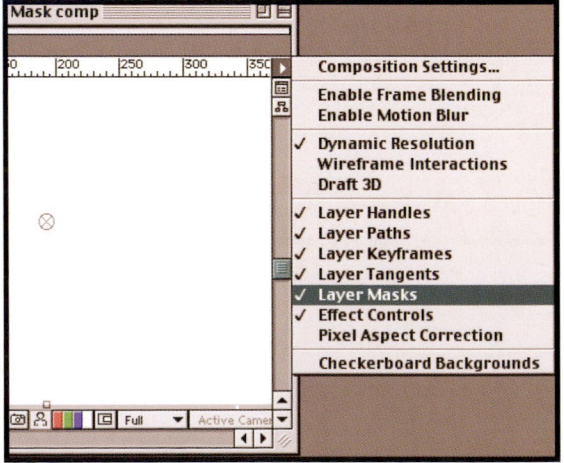

## rulers and guides

You can create custom guides by clicking and dragging on the rulers and then pulling the guides out from the rulers. The Info palette can be used to track the positional values whilst you are dragging the guides.

**1** Drag the horizontal guide from the top ruler, placing it at 144 pixels on the Y axis, so that it crosses the Anchor Point of the layer. Don't worry if you don't get it exactly right the first time, once the guide has been created, it can then be moved simply by clicking and dragging it.

**2** Drag a vertical guide from the left ruler and place it at 192 pixels on the X axis. Your guides should be perfectly central and should meet at the center point of the layer.

**3** Once your guides are in place, go to View > Lock guides to prevent you from accidentally moving them.

**4** Go to the View menu and make sure that the Snap to Guides Option is ticked, this will ensure that any new layers or masks will snap to the guides that you have just created.

**5** Select the Rectangle Mask tool and draw a mask from just outside the top, left corner of the screen to the center point of the layer, you should feel the new mask snap to your guides.

**6** Repeat the last step again, this time drawing from the center to the bottom, right of the composition.

**7** Change the Layer mode to Difference to divide the screen into quarters.

Your composition should now look like the one illustrated on the following page. Difference Mode will subtract the value of the top layer's channel pixels from the bottom layer's channel pixels. This produces similar results to inverting the images color channels, producing an effect comparable to a photographic negative.

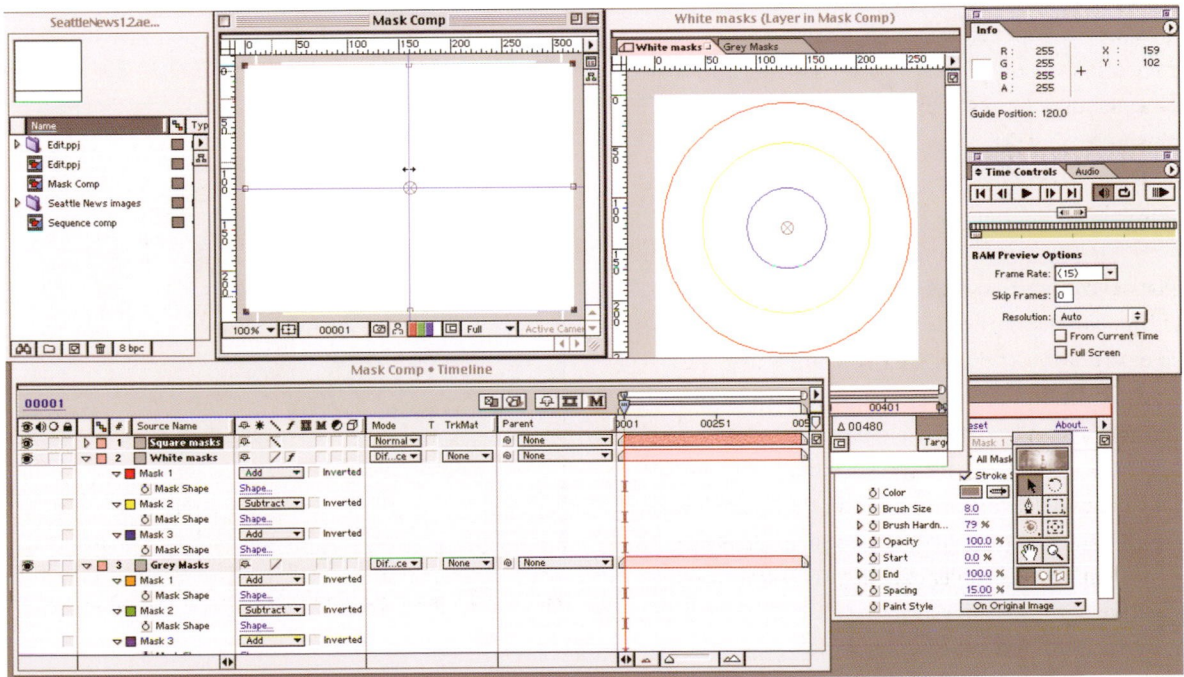

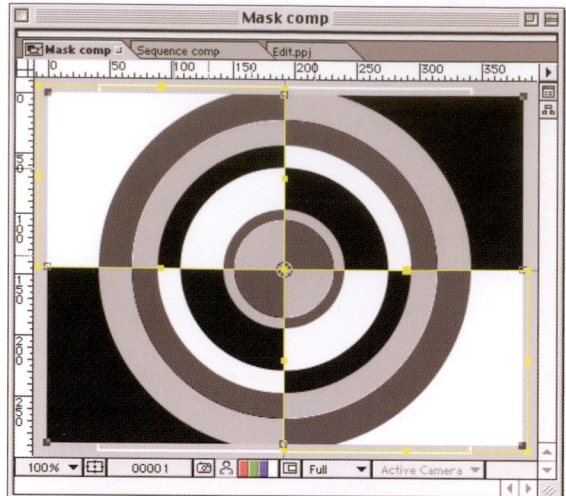

So, by combining Masks, Layer Modes and Effects we have created an interesting geometric image. We will now nest this image into our footage sequence to bring it all together.

As we discussed in Chapter Six, the images in our sequence do not have any common theme to pull them together. We can use the composition we have just created as an overlay and we can then apply color treatments to pull the whole thing together into a cohesive sequence.

**8** Open up your Edit.ppj Composition again and make sure that the Current-Time Marker is at the beginning of your composition.

**9** Go to the Project window and in there, drag the Masks Composition icon directly on to the Edit.ppj Composition icon, this will place it into the Edit.ppj Composition as the top layer.

To enable the Layer modes that we set up in the Masks Composition we have to do what's known as Collapsing the Transformations for this layer. This has the effect of compounding any effects, modes etc. which have already been applied to the layers within the nested composition. You can find out more about this in the After Effects Online Help system.

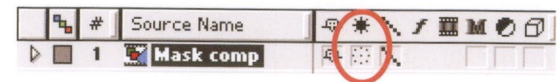

**10** Click on the Collapse Transformations/ Continuously Rasterize layer switch in the Timeline. Now you will see the modes, applied to the layers in the Masks comp.

**11** RAM Preview the composition along with its new layer.

The shapes composited on top of the footage are constant throughout the sequence, giving the piece a common theme throughout. The varying colors of the source footage are still a problem and collapsing the Transformations of a layer will prevent you from being able to apply new Masks and most effects to the layer. But don't worry, I'll show you ways of getting round this problem in the next chapter.

**12** Go to File > Save as and, in the Save as dialog box, navigate to your Creative After Effects folder on the desktop and save the project into the Nesting folder as SeattleNews03b.aep.

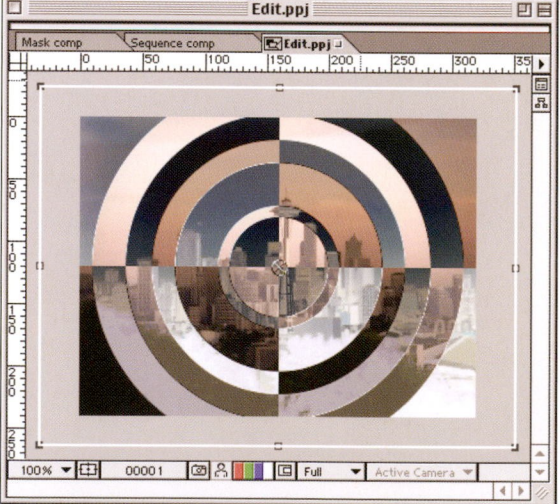

## recap

Well, in this chapter we've covered quite a few topics as well as the basics involved with Nesting. Let's take a look at some of the things you've learned how to do.

- Change the Background Color of your comp
- Rename layers and compositions
- Open nested Comps from a Photoshop  file
- Animate nested Compositions
- How to use Rulers and Guides
- How to Collapse Transformations for a nested Composition.

What I want you to do now is to take the elements that you have created in the last two chapters and put them together. By this point you should have two or three projects to play with, each containing one of the following elements.

- Some sort of sequence, built from the free footage provided on the CD.
- A composition using Masked Solids.
- A storyboard for your planned project.
- You may also have some rendered QuickTime movies which you can include in the following project.

## importing multiple projects

Now I'll show you how to combine these separate elements into one Project.

**1** Create a new Project.

**2** Hit Command + I to open the Import File dialog box.

As well as being able to import various kinds of files and folders into After Effects, you can also import After Effects Projects into one another. This allows you to use elements from other projects in your current one.

**3** Go to Training > Projects > Chapter 07, select the file named SeattleNews1.2.aep and then click OK.

**4** In your Project window you should now have a folder. Open the folder by clicking on its disclosure triangle, you will now see the folders contents, like the one in the following diagram.

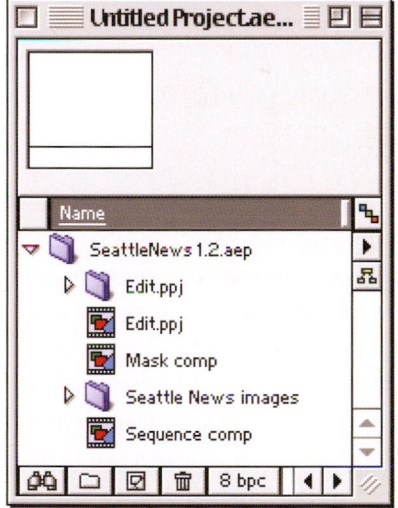

After Effects groups all of the elements from the imported Project into a folder with the same name as the Project, making it easier to manage your files. Notice that all of the comps and source files from the original Project are contained within the folder.

**5** Go to File > Import > Multiple Files (Command + Alt + I).

**6** Go to your Creative After Effects folder and, one by one, select the Projects and QuickTime movies that you want to include in your new project.

**7** Once the files you need are in the Project, save it into your Creative After Effects folder as mission1.aep.

You can choose any comps or QuickTime movies that you have created in the previous chapters, you can also choose from the free footage supplied on the CD. If you have any of your own footage, music, drawings or images that you would like to include, then by all means do.

Once the projects and files are inside After Effects you can open them up and treat them in the same way as any other. Double-click on any of your comps to open up its Composition window and Timeline.

Now, I want you to spend a bit of time on this. You have reached the point where I want you to start developing your project seriously. If necessary, go back and read over The Brief chapter. If any of your compositions or QuickTime movies fit snugly into any one of the briefs then that's probably the best one to go for. If not, then you can use what you've learned so far to make a decision about which brief you want to follow and which techniques you can use to complete your chosen brief.

You will continue learning lots of new things as you progress through the chapters. Your ideas may develop as you learn new techniques or you might even decide to change the whole concept half way through. This really doesn't matter, my main intention is to encourage you to experiment so let yourself and your ideas flourish. As long as you finish the book with one of the briefs completed, I'll be happy!

Remember to keep sketching out and writing down new ideas. Even if you don't use them now, you may work on a job in the future that could present you with a new opportunity to make use of them.

I'm a great believer in doodling! I doodle on the bus, doodle when watching television, doodle on my lunch break, doodle on the telephone or internet. The good thing about doodling is that you usually do it when you are concentrating on something else, the doodling is not your main focus of attention. Because of this, all of your subconscious ideas come out before your ego has had time to stop them.

Just think about how many times your ego has stopped you from proceeding with an idea because it's not 'good enough', any idea is good enough if it's executed well, try not to dismiss anything, give it a go and if it doesn't work, then you've learned something from the experience.

Don't be afraid to make mistakes, I can guarantee you that you'll learn more from your mistakes than from your successes. Learn from them and you'll find the solutions to them.

OK, off you go, by the time you begin the next chapter you should have a basic structure for your finished project. Good luck and enjoy!

# chapter eight
# animation

## history of animation

Before moving ahead with the projects I feel that it is important for you to learn a little more about some of the rules of animation and how we can apply these rules to our work in After Effects, so let's take a break from the projects and concentrate on some keyframing exercises.

Traditional stop-frame animation is created by drawing a series of images which when played back sequentially will give the illusion of a moving image. Traditional animation came into fruition in the early 1900s. It was only ever thought of as a novelty for entertaining children and adults till Walt Disney came along in the 1930s and developed it into the magical art form it is today.

Traditional stop frame animators have collectively had approximately one hundred years to develop their skills and techniques, and have really perfected their art form. As with most forms of art and design, there are rules which are a common thread used in every successful animation.

Computer animation is a lot younger and has not yet developed as far as I believe is possible. The tendency by many computer animators is to use the computer's immense capabilities to copy the physics of the real world.

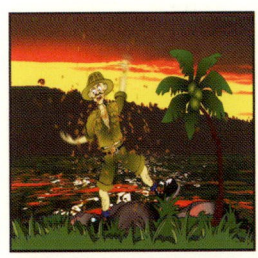
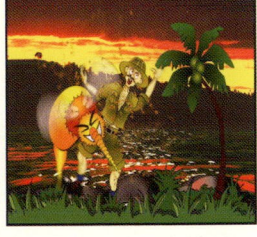
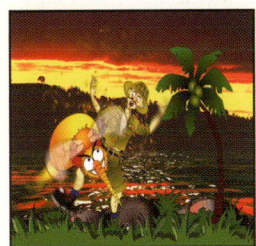

Stills from 'See you, See me – The Inventors' BBC, 1999. I animated the swarm of mosquitos with the Particle Playground and the water with Atomic Power's Psunami.

Whilst this is a good practice to adhere to if you are a special effects artist, it is not so good in animation. In my opinion if something looks too real, it can look dull and uninspiring, you need to exaggerate real life to make it more interesting!

When Disney created Snow White, the animators had real difficulty in developing the human characters, they tried tracing film frames but found that the movements were just too 'real' to be convincing for an animated film. They learned from this that pushing the possibilities of science and nature to extremes would result in a much more dynamic and appealing animation.

Don't get me wrong, I love what computers are capable of and have an immense amount of admiration for the creators of visual effects but I do think that animation is a different skill with different rules. The real skill lies in combining real world visual effects with other-worldly animation. The Disney and Pixar studios have managed this in some of their later films, combining computer-generated effects with traditionally drawn animated frames, I find this concept very exciting.

So, my philosophy for animation is not to mimic the real world too much and to try to adapt the rules developed over the years by traditional animators. Here are a few of the rules and some tips for implementing them in your After Effects work. There are two main types of animation:

## animation rules
### 1 straight ahead animation
This is where the animator draws a series of frames in sequence, one after the other till he or she reaches the end of the animation. This is a very difficult way to animate but is the most experimental approach, allowing the animator to make decisions and change ideas as he/she goes.

### 2 pose to pose animation
This is when the animator draws the main poses in the animation (keyframes), planning the whole story before the animation stage. He/she then fills in all the in-between drawings afterwards. This is the most commonly used approach and one that most of the big animation studios use today. Everything is planned carefully before proceeding with the animation, formulas are followed and risks are minimal.

I use a cross between these two techniques which I like to call straight to pose animation! As you've already experienced, we do indeed use keyframes in After Effects to mark out the key poses within the animations.

You can tell After Effects, I want this object to start here and end there, but you'll find that After Effects does not know, as you do, exactly which path it should take from point A to point B. Therefore I find that a combination of the two techniques works best for me. I'll show you what I mean.

**1** Open the project named Animrule.aep from Training > Projects > Chapter 08. This project consists of several compositions in which I will attempt to explain both the rules of animation and some ways to implement them using the After Effects animation tools.

**2** In the Project window, double-click *Road Composition* to open up its Composition window and Timeline.

In this composition I have two car layers and a road layer. I want to make the cars drive around the roundabout in opposite directions and then leave on the opposite exit road. In traditional animation I would draw the cars start point as my first keyframe and then draw the end point. I would then hand these drawings to my Tweener who would then draw the steps in-between.

Now, as I have already told you, when working in After Effects, you are the Key animator and After Effects is your Tweener. But, the difference between a human Tweener and After Effects is that a human would instinctively know which path the cars should follow to get from point A to point B, After Effects does not. It will animate as the crow flies, in a straight line from point A to point B.

**3** In the Timeline, select both of the car layers and then hit Alt + P to set keyframes for position.

**4** Hit the O key on the keyboard to move to the Out-point of the selected layers.

**5** Now select only the Red Car layer and drag it to the opposite exit road, near the original start position of the Blue Car layer. (Alternatively, you could copy and paste the first Blue Car keyframe into the Red Car layer.)

**6** Select the Blue Car layer and move it to the opposite exit road, near the original start position of the Red Car layer. Notice that two, overlapping, straight motion paths have been drawn between the two points.

**7** RAM Preview the resulting animation. Notice that the layers overlap as they cross the center of the layer.

OK, so that's our pose to pose animation, now what we must do is go in and adjust this to make it work, this is where the straight ahead bit comes in!

**8** Move to frame 76 (which is the middle point of the animation) and select only the Red Car layer.

**9** Drag the Red Car layer to the position that you would expect it to be at this point. See the following diagram if you need help with this.

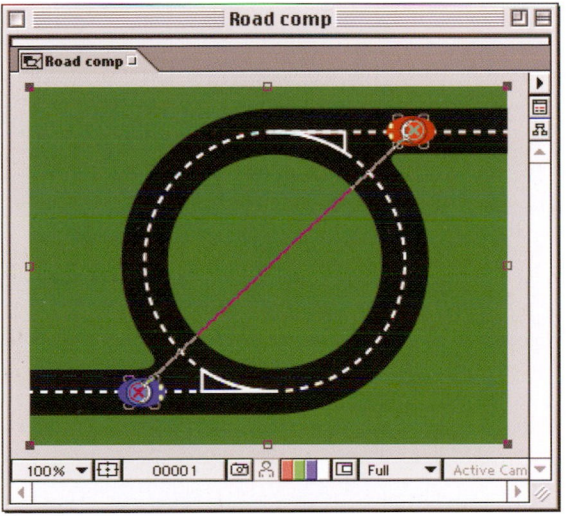

This is where observation of how things work in the real world is important. We take for granted, the fact that we can judge the distance and speed of the cars to decide on their current position but this is something that the computer cannot yet do – reason.

**10** Drag the Blue Car layer to the position you would now expect it to be in. Notice that the paths are now curved. This is because After Effects will, as a default, draw a curved path between points.

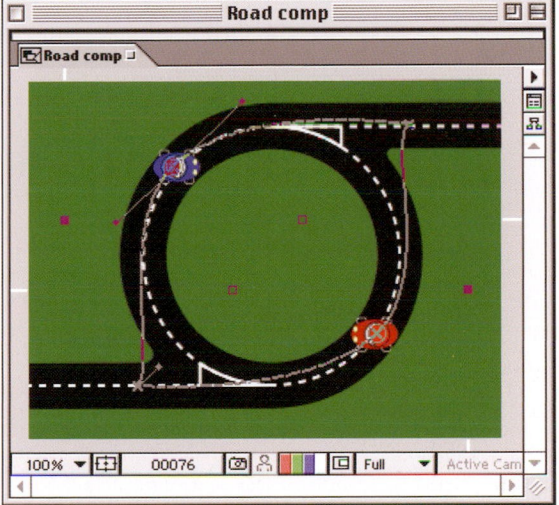

**11** RAM Preview the animation again to see the results of your changes. The cars are now moving more closely along the road but we still need to make more adjustments to the shape of the path so that it fits the road exactly. The aim is to try to do this by using the fewest keyframes possible.

## auto-orientation

The other thing you may have noticed is that the cars remain facing the same direction as they move along the path, they don't turn as they move around the corners. You can make the car change direction automatically as it follows the path by using the Auto-Orient feature.

**1** Select both the Red Car layer and the Blue Car layer simultaneously and then go to Layer > Transform > Auto-Orient (Command + Alt + O).

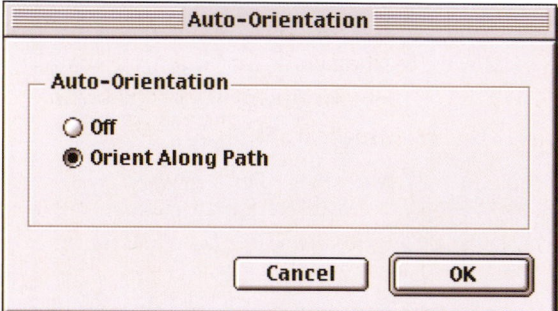

**2** In the Auto-Orientation dialog box, choose Orient Along Path.

**3** Preview the animation to see the results. You'll notice that the cars now align their direction with the path. The only trouble is that the red car is moving backwards, don't worry, it's very easy to correct this.

**4** Select only the Red Car layer and then hit Shift + R key on the keyboard to bring up the Rotation value as well as the Position value.

**5** Highlight the second value for Rotation (which is the value in degrees), type in 180 and hit Enter to rotate the car to face the opposite direction. Doing this will not affect the Auto-Orientation of the layer.

**6** Preview the animation again. All that's left to do now is to adjust the path a little to make the shape more precise.

## adjusting motion paths

I've seen many new users to After Effects try to control the shape of their paths by creating lots of keyframes. There is no need to create any more keyframes for this path, we can control the shape of the path using the existing keyframes and their Bezier handles. These handles work just like the ones that you use in Illustrator to draw your Vector shapes, or the ones you use in Photoshop for drawing paths.

**1** Select the Position keyframes one by one in the Timeline, you will notice that, as you do, they also become selected in the Composition window.

The Composition window is where you can see the spatial positioning of your position keyframes, i.e. their position in space. The Timeline is where you can see their temporal position, i.e. their position in relation to time.

When you view the selected keyframes in the Composition window, you'll see that they have Bezier handles coming out from each side of the keyframe, similar to the one illustrated in the following diagram. These handles allow you to change the direction and amount of curve going into and coming out from the keyframe.

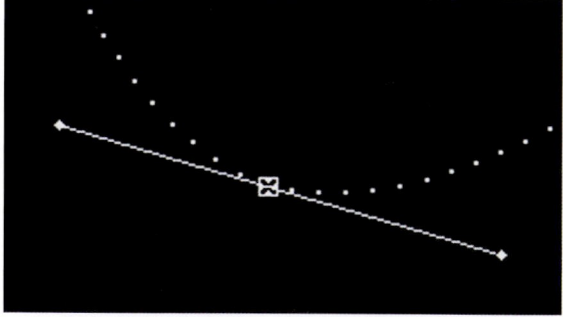

**2** Select the first keyframe for the Red Cars Position value. You can select keyframes either in the Composition window or the Timeline.

**3** Click on the end of the handle and drag it up and out to the left till it is in the same position as the one in the following diagram. Notice that the shape of the curve changes.

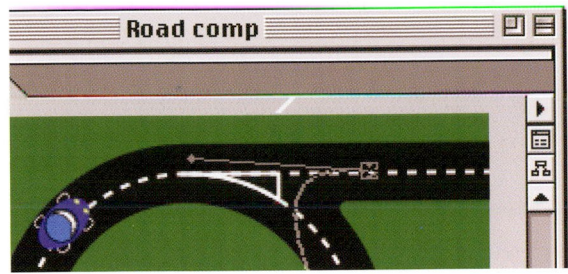

**4** Do the same with the first Blue Car keyframe, this time, dragging it to the right and down, as in the following diagram.

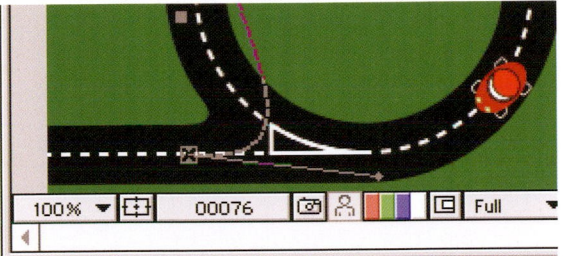

**5** All we need to do now is to adjust the middle keyframes to make the path exactly the right shape.

**6** One by one, select the middle keyframes for the two car layers and adjust them so that the path fits the road. Dragging the handles up and down will change the angle of the curve whilst dragging the handles in and out from the keyframe will change the amount of curve. Use the following diagram as a guide.

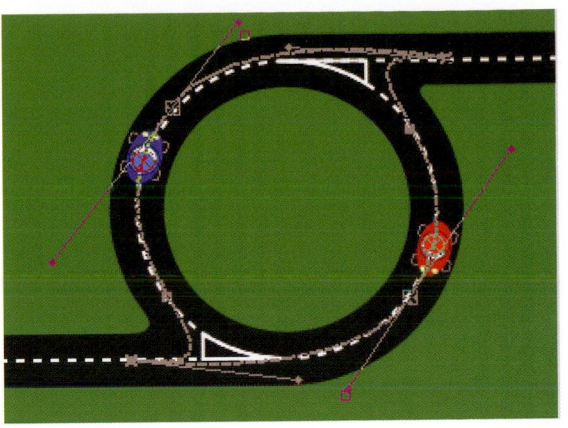

If you don't get it right first time, simply undo your changes and start again till you feel more comfortable with the process, we will be doing more of this in the following lessons.

**7** RAM Preview the animation and notice that the cars are now following the road.

As you can see After Effects will do a good job at animating directly between two defined points, but that manual adjustment of the interpolation by you is often necessary.

**8** Go to File > Save as and, in the Save as dialog box, navigate to your Creative After Effects folder on the desktop and save the project into the Animation Chapter folder as Animrule01b.aep.

## spatial keyframes
### linear

This next exercise is a bit of a classic, it's the good old bouncing ball animation. It's a bit of a cliché I know but I've yet to find a better way of illustrating some of the basic animation rules.

**1** First of all, if you do not have a project open, open Animrule01.aep from Training > Projects > Chapter 08.

**2** Now create a new composition, name it Bouncing Ball Composition with a frame size of 320 × 240, frame rate of 15 fps and duration of 30 frames (2 seconds).

**3** Go to Edit > Preferences > General and check the Default Spatial Interpolation to Linear checkbox. This will force After Effects to use Linear keyframes (resulting in a straight path), rather than the default Auto Bezier keyframes (resulting in a curved path).

I recommend that you work with this preference checked whilst you are learning the software. Once you become comfortable with how Bezier keyframes work, you can change it. The reason I prefer this way of working is that you sometimes get unpredictable results using Bezier keyframes, I think that it is much easier to understand what's happening with Linear keyframes.

**4** In the Project window, select the file named Ball11.eps and hit Command + / to bring it into your Composition.

**5** Scale the layer down to 25% using any of the techniques you have learned in previous lessons.

**6** Move the ball layer up and to the left till it sits just outside the Composition window (position number 1 in the diagram in the next column).

**7** In the Timeline, make sure that the Current-Time Marker is at frame 1 and then set a keyframe for Position by hitting Alt +P.

**8** Move to frame number 8 and then drag the layer down to the bottom of the Composition window, about one quarter of the way into the Composition (position number 2 in the diagram below).

**9** Move to frame number 15 and drag the layer up to the top center of the Composition (position number 3).

**10** At frame number 22, move the layer up to the top again, about three quarters of the way into the Composition (position number 4).

**11** Finally, move to frame number 29 and drag the layer out to the right and to the top of the Composition so that it sits on the pasteboard (position number 5 in the diagram).

If you are not happy with the final position, you can simply click on the individual keyframes in the Composition window and drag them to your preferred position.

**12** Preview the animation, notice that the ball does not look real at all, this is for several reasons which we will now look at.

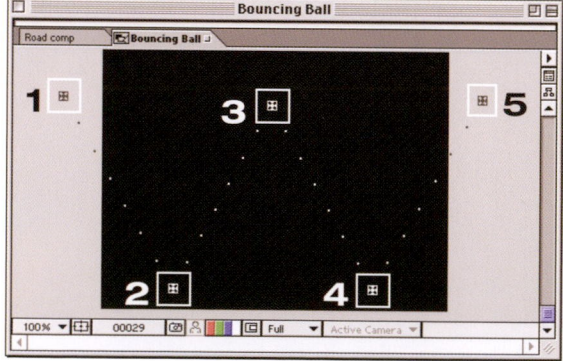

## arc

The shape of the path that the ball follows is also known as its *Arc*. Some things in life follow a straight path, for example a ball dropped from above with no force applied will drop in a straight line because gravity is the only force being applied to it and gravity will always pull in one direction – downwards.

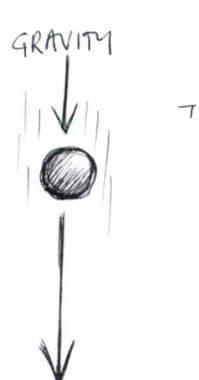

The ball in our animation is being thrown in from the left so it has been given an additional force from the person throwing it, this is a left to right directional force.

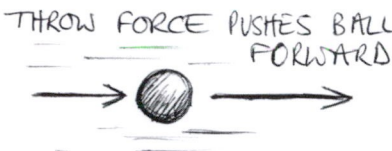

When the two forces are combined, this will produce a curved path because the two forces are acting against each other. The shape of the curve will depend on how strong the throw force is compared to the gravity force which, under normal circumstances, remains constant.

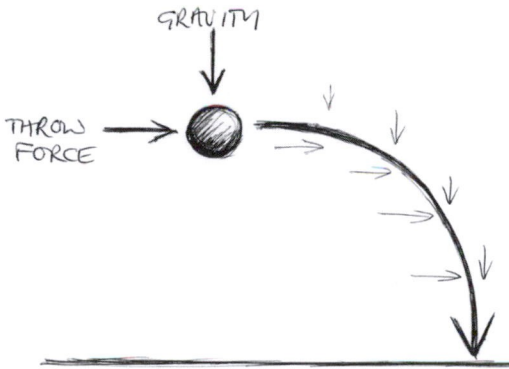

## auto bezier keyframes

Imagine our ball is being thrown quite gently, the gravity pulling down will be slightly stronger than the throw force, this will produce quite a steep curve. Our path is almost straight so let's start by adjusting the curve of our path (or arc).

**1** Select the middle keyframe at the 15 frame mark.

**2** In the Comp window, hold down the Command key and then click once on the keyframe, this will change it into a default Auto Bezier keyframe. This is represented by the two dots at either side of the keyframe which are the handles.

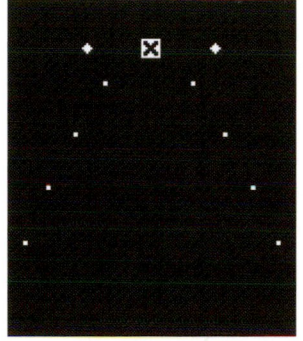

Auto Bezier keyframes are normally the default keyframe type. Their handles (and therefore the curve) always maintain the same *angle* going into and out from the keyframe.

Look at the dots on the lines running between the keyframes, each dot represents one frame of your animation. When the dots are spaced further apart, we know that the layer is moving further on each frame and therefore is moving faster. When the dots are closer together we know the layer has less distance to travel and is moving slower.

Notice how the spacing between the dots changes as we go through the next few steps. OK, now we need this curve to be more pronounced, at the moment it is too pointy (a very scientific term I know!).

**3** Click and drag on the right corner handle and drag to the right a little, as you do, a line will appear joining the handle to the keyframe, as soon as you adjust the angle of an Auto Bezier handle it is converted to a Continuous Bezier keyframe.

**4** Drag each of the handles out till you have an even curve like the one in the following diagram. Notice that the handles going into and out of the curve always form one continuous straight line, meaning that the curve remains smooth and constant.

## continuous bezier keyframes

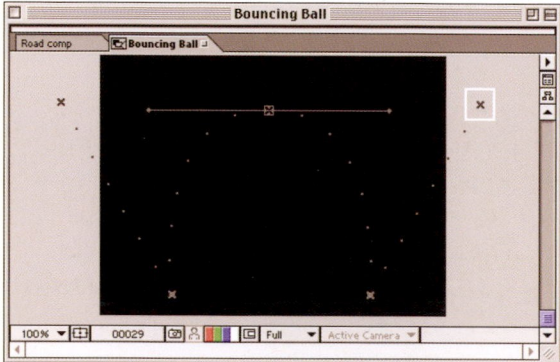

Now we need to create curves on the paths coming into the frame. To do this you need to adjust the curves coming out from the first and into the last keyframes.

**1** Command-click and drag on the first keyframe, pulling the handle to the right till the curve almost touches the middle curve. Command-clicking on a keyframe will interactively convert it to a Continuous Bezier keyframe as you drag.

Notice that the spacing between the dots on the path are becoming slightly wider apart, meaning the layer is now moving faster. Because we are making the layer travel further between the two points, it has to travel faster in order to get to the next keyframe in the same amount of time. A curved line between two points is always longer than a straight line.

As soon as you alter an Auto Bezier keyframe it becomes a Continuous Bezier keyframe. You can see that the handles are now joined to the keyframe by a straight line which, like the Auto Bezier keyframe, will always maintain the same curve *angle*. Whenever you adjust the angle on one side, the other will follow. The difference is that the *amount* of curve can be different on either side of the keyframe.

Notice that this keyframe only has one handle because there is no motion path on the left side of the keyframe.

**2** Repeat this process to drag the last keyframe handle to the left till you have nice curves on either side.

**3** Preview your changes, the movement is slightly more natural but there is one more thing wrong about this spatial path, the ball bounces in and out of the animation at the same height.

When a ball bounces, the object that it bounces against (e.g. the ground) will absorb some of the energy from the ball, the result is that its bounce will be dampened each time it comes into contact with the ground. In other words, the path will gradually get smaller as the ball bounces. The softer the object that it bounces against, the higher the damping force, this means that it will come to a halt quicker after landing on a soft surface than on a hard surface.

**4** In the Comp window, select the middle keyframe and drag it down so that it is almost half way down the Composition window.

**5** Select the last keyframe and drag it down so that it is even lower. Use the following diagram as a reference to guide you.

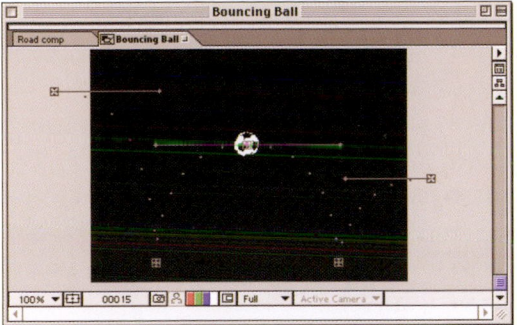

We now have the shape of the path as we want it. It may not be an absolute scientifically accurate projection but it is good enough for our animation. If you want to create an absolutely accurate curve there are physics books listed in the bibliography (http://www.angie.abel.co.uk/book.html) that can help you work the exact angles and curves.

**6** Go to File > Save as and, in the Save as dialog box, navigate to your Creative After Effects folder on the desktop and save the project into the Chapter 03 folder as Animrule02b.aep.

## timing

The next problem with our bouncing ball is the timing. If you preview the animation you'll notice that the speed that the ball travels remains pretty much constant when it travels between the keyframes. This would not happen in the real world, objects accelerate as they fall and decelerate as they rise, this is because of the force of gravity acting on the mass of the object. The amount of acceleration/deceleration depends on the weight of the object.

**1** Close your project and then open Animrule02.aep from Training > Projects > Chapter 08.

**2** In the Timeline, open up the Position value graph by clicking on the disclosure triangle to the left of the property name.

There is a slight change in the timing already because we have altered the shape of the path and, therefore, the distance that the ball has to travel between each pair of keyframes. But notice that the speed remains pretty constant, this is demonstrated by the straight line running between each pair of keyframes. An absolutely straight line means an absolutely constant speed.

It is important that you understand how the value graphs work before continuing with this exercise. Look at the diagram below, of the Position Speed graph. The blue values represent the *range* of the graph, the top value is the *maximum value* displayed, the bottom value is the *minimum value* displayed. This range can be altered but changing these values will not affect your layer, only the display.

The value in black, between the two blue values is the value at the position of the Current-Time Marker, it tells you at what speed the Position is changing. This value and the range values are measured in Pixels Per Second.

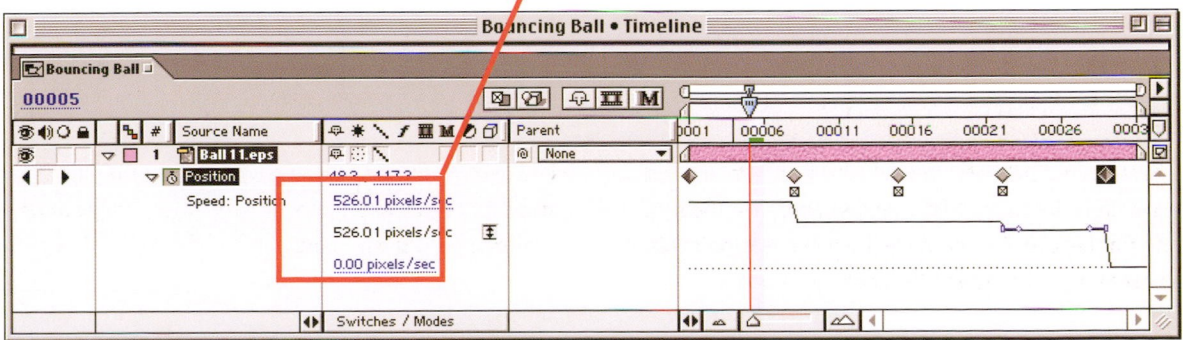

**3** Jump to a position between the first two keyframes and take a reading per second from the Black value. It should read approximately; 526.01 Pixels/Sec. There is a straight line drawn between these two keyframes which tells me that between the first keyframe and the second, the position of the ball is changing at an *even rate* of 526.01 Pixels/Sec.

**NB:** Don't worry if your settings are not exactly the same as mine, there will be slight discrepancies depending on how close your motion path shape is, compared to mine.

**4** Move the Current-Time Marker to the space between keyframes two and three. Again, the line is straight denoting an even speed between the keyframes, the reading tells me that it is an even speed of approximately; 364.58 Pixels/Sec, slower than the speed between the first two keyframes. You can see that it's slower because the line running between the keyframes is lower, in the graph.

**5** Move the Current-Time Marker between keyframes three and four. From the appearance of the graph line joining the two keyframes it would seem that there is no difference in speed. But, if you look at the value, you'll see a reading of 365.46, meaning that the speed going into and out from the middle keyframe is slightly uneven. It is important that this value is even as the ball is in mid-flight and shouldn't suddenly change speed here.

### temporal keyframes
#### roving
In situations like this where the position of your keyframe in the Composition window is fine but the timing is wrong, you can choose to rove your keyframe across time. This will retain the position information associated with the keyframe but will adjust the time at which the keyframe occurs within the animation, enabling After Effects to calculate a smooth, even speed going into and out from the keyframe.

**1** Move the Current-Time Marker so that it's on the middle keyframe. Underneath the keyframe is a little checkbox, this is what locks the keyframe to the time that it was originally created in your sequence.

**2** Click on the little checkbox and watch the speed value as you do . The keyframe icon moves to a new position in the speed graph and it changes to a small circular icon, this is the Roving keyframe icon.

You may also have noticed that the line running through the roving keyframe is immediately levelled, making it the same speed on either side. Also notice that in the Comp window, the dots on the motion path are now evenly spaced between the second and fourth keyframes. All of this indicates that the layer is now moving at a constant speed between these two points.

**3** If you missed any of this, simply undo and redo the last step to see the changes occur.

When you make the keyframe a roving keyframe the position remains the same in the Comp window, (ie. its position in *space* remains the same). Whilst in the Timeline the keyframe jumps to a different point in *time* to ensure that the speed at either side of the keyframe is even/constant.

**4** Preview your animation to see the results of your changes. Roving the keyframe has smoothed out the timing of your animation.

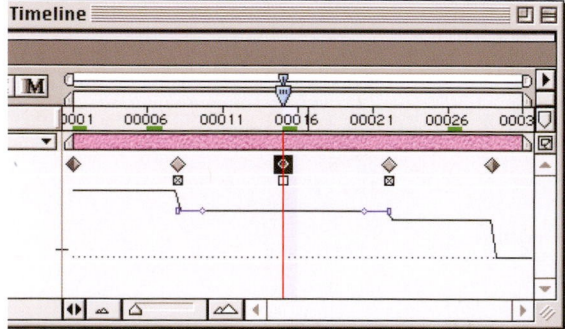

## continuous bezier

As you've discovered there are different types of keyframe. You adjusted the positional curves of your motion path by changing the keyframe type and dragging their handles. You can do a similar thing with the temporal keyframes in the Timeline. First of all, we'll make our graph a bit bigger so that we can see clearly what is happening.

**1** Make the Timeline as wide as you can so that it fills the width of your screen.

**2** Click on the top, blue, maximum value for the graph (which currently reads approximately; 526.01 pixels/sec) and drag to the right till it reads approximately 1000 pixels/sec. The appearance of the graph will change because it now occupies a smaller percentage of the new graph range which lies between 0% (min) and 1000% (max).

**3** Context-click on the Parent panel heading and choose Hide This from the menu to hide the panel from view.

OK, so we determined that the ball should accelerate as it falls and decelerate as it rises. This means we should have curved lines joining the keyframes, rather than straight lines, which tell us that the ball is currently traveling at an even speed.

**4** Place the Current-Time Marker over the first keyframe and select it by clicking once on it. As you do, you'll notice a little blue handle will appear at the same position on the value graph below.

**5** Drag the handle down till it reads approximately 350 pixels/sec. Try to avoid dragging the handle to the left or right.

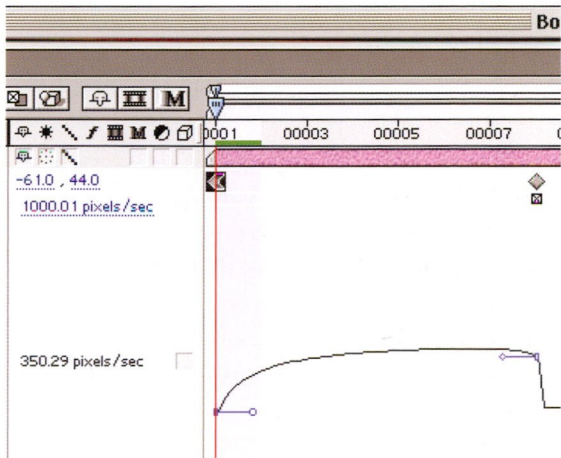

Dragging the handle up or down will affect the value of the keyframe, as the value changes, the line joining the two keyframes will form a curve between the two differing values representing a new uneven speed.

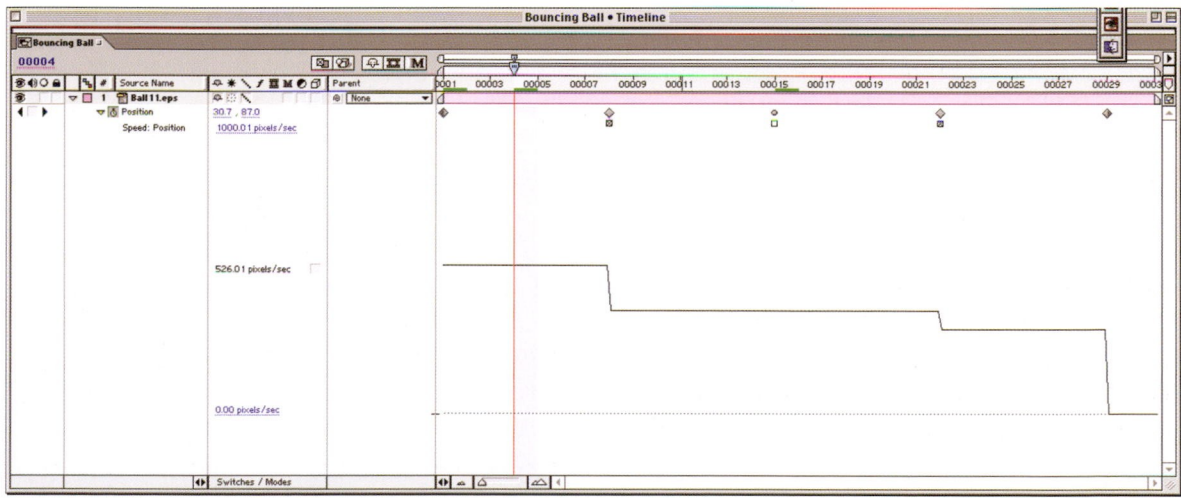

**6** Move the Current-Time Marker along the curve, reading the black, current values as you go, you'll notice that it increases in speed quite rapidly at the beginning, then levels out a bit in the middle before gradually decreasing in speed towards the end.

**7** Preview the animation, OK, it's an improvement but you'll see that the ball needs to have more acceleration, building gradually so that it is moving very fast when it approaches the next keyframe.

We can change how the speed builds by adjusting the *influence* of the curve. The influence determines how quickly the acceleration or deceleration takes place. We've set the speed of the two keyframes at either side of the curve, now we can determine how it graduates from one speed to the next. At the moment it gets slightly faster in the middle of the two keyframes, we want it to get faster as it nears the second keyframe, where the ball will hit the ground.

**8** Click and drag the little blue handle to the right till it is about one third of the way in between the two keyframes. The graph shape will change so that it touches the top of the graph, almost at the second keyframe. Make sure that the top of the curve is not cut off at the top of the graph.

**9** Move to the second keyframe (frame 8 ) and drag the handle in towards the keyframe, notice that it is quite hard to control the velocity by dragging these handles, the only feedback you get is from the curve itself and it's very easy to accidentally move the handle up or down whilst dragging or cut off the tip of the curve. I'll show you an easier way to adjust the velocity settings.

**10** Context-click on the keyframe and choose Keyframe Velocity from the menu. This will open up the Keyframe Velocity dialog box where you can alter the values for speed and velocity.

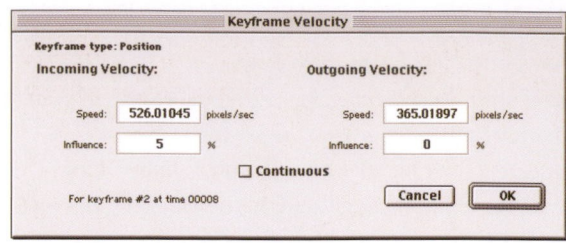

**11** Change the *Incoming Velocity Influence* setting to 5. Doing this will adjust the curve so that the first keyframe value has much more influence on the curve than the last one. The result will be that the ball will accelerate very quickly *into* the second keyframe.

A ball will bounce faster coming out of a bounce than going into it so we need to adjust our outgoing velocity whilst we're in here.

**12** Change the *Outgoing Velocity Speed* setting to 1300 and the *Outgoing Velocity Influence* to 15 and then click OK to leave the dialog box. Notice that your speed graph has changed quite dramatically.

**13** Adjust the graphs maximum value again to approximately 1400 so that you can see the peak of your curve.

Preview your animation and notice how the ball appears to be heavier now, falling to the ground very suddenly.

OK, now we need to adjust the curves between the other keyframes.

**14** move to the fourth keyframe (frame 22) and make it active by clicking once on it.

**15** Drag the little blue handle up and to the left till you have a nice smile-shaped curve like the one in the following diagram. The top point of this curve should be slightly lower than the top point of the first curve as the ball will slow down a little after each bounce.

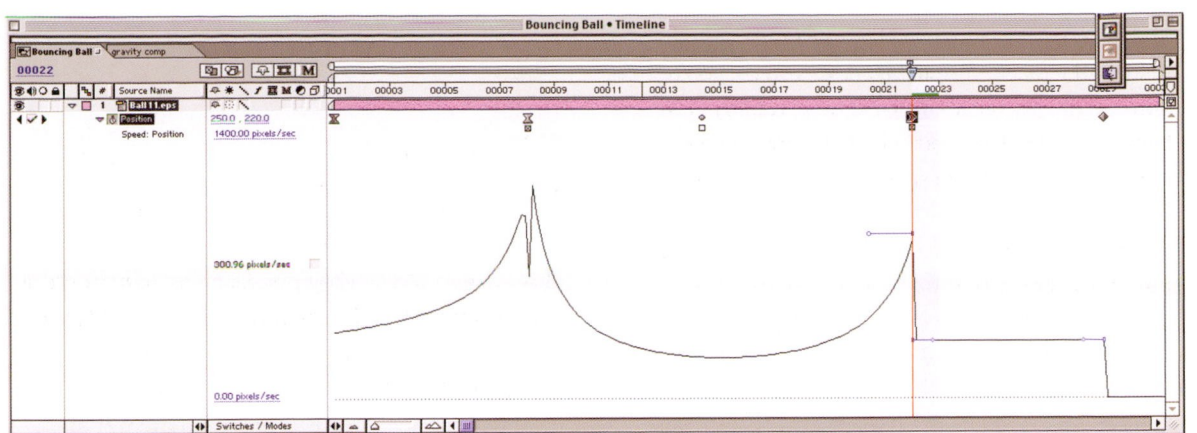

**16** If you have difficulty getting a curve like this, Context-click on the keyframe and enter a value of approximately 860 for the Incoming Speed and 21 for the Incoming Influence. Whilst in the dialog box, enter values of 1000 for the Outgoing Speed and 20 for the Outgoing Influence.

**17** Finally, select the last keyframe and drag the handle till you have another nice, smiley curve like the one in the diagram below. (Incoming Speed 500, Incoming Velocity 30).

**18** Preview your animation, the timing should be much more like a real bouncing ball now, slightly exaggerated for the purposes of this tutorial but you should get an idea of how the graph works.

OK, so to recap, the Timeline is where you adjust the layers movement through *time*. You can adjust the keyframes and the speed graph to determine the rate of change. The keyframes in the Timeline are your *temporal keyframes*.

The Comp window is where you adjust the layers movement through space. You can adjust the keyframes and the curves between them to determine the layers movement in space. The keyframes you see in the Comp window are *spatial keyframes*.

Using these graphs is probably one of the most tricky things that you'll have to deal with when using After Effects but the more practice you get, the more you will start to understand the curves and how they relate to your animations.

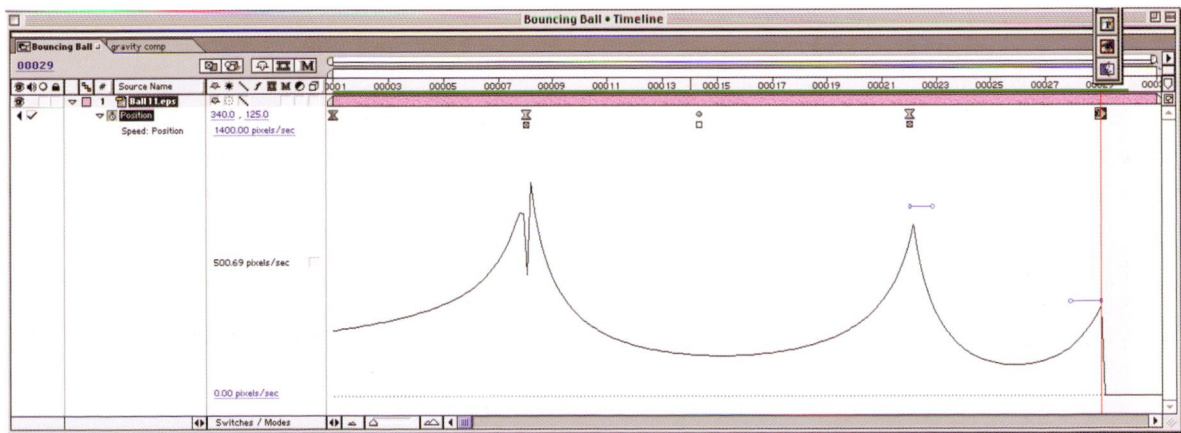

There are a couple of other changes that we can make to this animation to really make it look real. First of all, we'll use the Auto-Orientation feature to make the ball rotate as it is moving through the air.

**19** With the layer selected in the Timeline, go to Layer > Transform > Auto Orient and choose Along Path and then click OK to leave the dialog box.

**20** Go to File > Save as and, in the Save the project into your Creative After Effects > Animation Chapter folder as Animrule03b.aep.

If you want to practice with what you've just learned, start with two or three Position keyframes on a layer. Try to think of some instances where objects move at irregular speeds and do your best to replicate the movement. Don't give up if things get difficult, you'll soon pick it up, it's just like learning to ride a bike.

## squash and stretch

One of the most important rules of animation is the squash and stretch rule. For an object to look convincing it must give a little when external forces are applied to it, such as the ball hitting the ground or being affected by gravity. As a ball hits the ground it will squash as I'm sure you'll know, but did you know that it will also stretch as it falls and rises? The only time the ball is round is at the top of each arc, where resistance is at its least. Obviously a softer ball, for example a beach ball, will squash and stretch a lot whereas a cannonball will hardly squash and stretch at all. You can use squash and stretch techniques to convey an object's density and mass.

We're going to cheat a bit here, to stretch and squash the ball properly we should use a warping tool such as the Production Bundle's Bezier Warp or forge's Freeform these would allow us to squash the ball into exactly the right shape. For this tutorial we'll just use Scale to reshape the ball. We won't get exactly the right shape but it'll be near enough to demonstrate the principles of squash and stretch.

**1** Open Animrule03.aep from Training > Projects > Chapter 08. Close any other open projects. This copy of the project contains the exact coordinates from the previous sections.

**2** With the Current-Time Marker at the beginning of the Composition, select the ball layer and then hit Shift + Alt + S to set a keyframe for Scale and bring up the Scale property alongside the Position property.

**3** Move the Current-Time Marker to the second keyframe at frame 8. At this point the ball would be squashed as its driving force is met by the ground.

It's very important when using the squash and stretch rule that the form of the object always appears to retain the same amount of volume to be believable. In other words, if you squash the object by 50% on the X-axis, you must also stretch it by 50% on the Y-axis. You can pretty much distort it as much as you like, as long as the object appears to contain the same amount of mass. In this case, the ball is currently 25% on each access so we should change these values by the same amount.

## exaggeration

Another great animation rule is the rule of exaggeration. Exaggeration in animation terms is used to emphasizes whatever key idea or feeling you wish to portray. For example, if you produced an animation of a dog smoking a cigarette whilst dancing, you would exaggerate the action which was most relevant to the scene. If the animation was about the joys of dancing (perhaps the cigarette is simply there as a tool to suggest the dog is in a bar somewhere) the dancing would be exaggerated. If, however you wanted to focus on the fact that the dog was smoking (perhaps an anti-smoking advert) you would make him smoke in a very ostentatious way, with his feet making tiny little dancing movements. By exaggerating certain elements you can guide the viewer's eye and give exactly the message that you wish to give.

Taking our bouncing ball as an example, if we scaled this ball by the correct amount the animation would probably look a little weak. Just as we exaggerated the amount of bounce in the timing exercise, we will also exaggerate the amount of squash and stretch. Good use of exaggeration can make an animation come to life, as long as all of the elements are exaggerated to a similar degree.

**4** In the Composition window, click on one of the layers corner handles and re-size the ball, so that it's squashed vertically and stretched horizontally as in the diagram below.

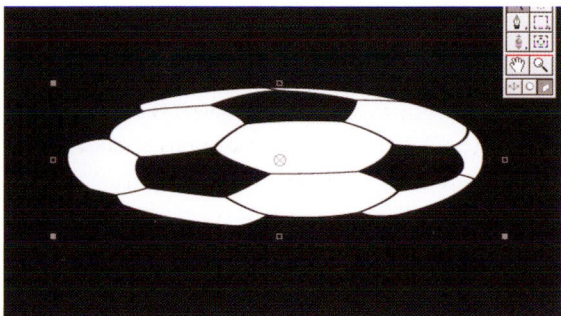

If you look at the scale values in the Timeline, you might be confused, you may have noticed that the values seem to be the wrong way around, the smaller X value appears to be squashing the height of the ball whilst the bigger Y value appears to be stretching the width, surely it should be the other way round? This is happening because we have the layer Auto-Orientated to the path, it is not at it's original rotation.

You have a few options to solve this problem if this happens to you, you could:

• remove the auto-orientation. (but that's too much like giving up!)

• you could reshape the ball in a nested comp before animating it. (this would require a fair amount of planning)

• or you can work around it by adjusting the values by eye, like I have done here. This is a bit of a cheats workaround but, hey, we all have to cheat sometimes to get the job done!

**5** OK, so the Scale value in the Timeline should read; 15, 35. If need be, go to the Timeline and adjust the values till they are exactly right. We have squashed the ball by ten degrees and stretched it by ten degrees, ensuring that the volume remains the same.

**6** Move to frame 22, and, with the second keyframe selected, hit Command + C followed by Command + V to copy and paste the keyframes values into the current frame.

**7** Using the same technique, copy and paste the first keyframe to both Frame 15 and then frame 29.

**8** Move to frame 6 and change the Scale value to 35, 15. This is where the ball will be at its most stretched.

**9** Select the keyframe at frame 6 and hit Command + C to copy it to the clipboard.

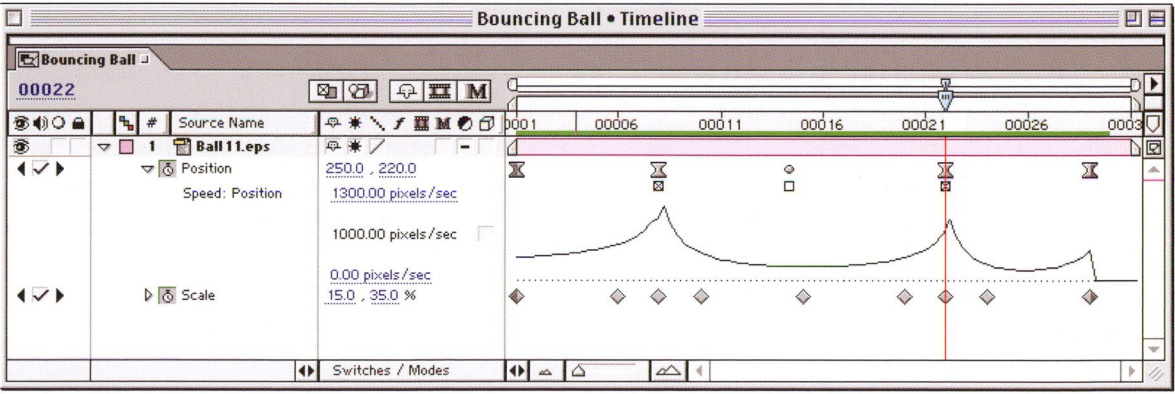

**10** Move the Current-Time Marker to frame 10 and hit Command + V to paste the keyframe there. Repeat this process to paste the keyframe at the following locations; frame 20 and frame 24. These are the points on the path where the ball would be stretched.

**11** Preview the movie. As I said before, a little exaggerated, but I hope it's helped you understand some of the basic animation rules and how to implement them using After Effects animation tools.

**12** Activate the Motion Blur switch for your layer and also enable motion blur for the comp by clicking the Enable Motion Blur button in the Timeline.

**13** Hit Command + K to go to open the Composition Settings, click on the Advanced tab and change the Shutter Angle setting to 20, reducing this setting will reduce the amount of motion blur used in this comp.

**14** Go to File > Save as and, in the Save as dialog box, navigate to your Creative After Effects folder on the desktop and save the project into the Animation chapter folder as Animrule04b.aep.

**15** There is a finished movie in the Project window that you can open up to compare your results with mine. If yours are drastically different, you may have missed some steps. There's also a finished Project named Animrule04.aep in the Training > Projects >Chapter 08 folder. This is my finished project, using all the settings that we have used here.

# more animation rules

So, we've looked at the main types of animation (straight ahead; pose to pose) and how to apply the techniques in After Effects. We've also covered some of the basic rules of animation; timing, arcs, exaggeration and squash and stretch. There are a few more rules that it helps to be familiar with in order to create convincing animation.

**1** Open the project named, Accelerat.aep from Training > Projects > Chapter 08.

This is a ready-made project which I have put together to explain some of the other rules of animation. It's fun to play with text when practicing your animation techniques. If you can put across a feeling or idea using an ordinarily inanimate object, such as a block of text, then you've done a good job. Walt Disney used to have his artists practice animating silhouettes, his belief was that if you can project an idea or emotion with a simple shape, then you have the essence of the action down to a tee. In this example my aim was to portray a feeling of speed. First I'll show you the wrong way!

**2** Open Speedy 1 Composition. Select the Text layer and then hit the U key to bring up any keyframed properties and then RAM Preview the animation.

As you can see I have created two keyframes for the Right Margin value in the Path Text plug-in, making the text move off to the right very quickly. Now, what could possibly be wrong here? I've taken the text and moved it off screen very quickly to give a feeling of speed but the animation is just so lifeless and happens before we even have time to register what's happening.

## staging (setting the scene)

You must remember that the viewer does not have the luxury of knowing what is about to happen in your animations so if something moves very quickly, they may not have time enough to realize what is going on, blink and they'll miss it! This is why it is necessary to set the scene for them. Setting the scene (or staging the animation) involves attracting the viewer's attention and focusing it on a particular subject or area of the screen. It can also set up a mood or feeling that you want the viewer to understand before the main action takes place. Examples of this would be having the subject move suddenly to attract attention or coloring/ lighting your subject in such a way that it stands out from the rest of the scene.

## anticipation

Anticipation can also be used to direct the viewer's attention to part of the screen and is often intermingled with staging. However, there are differences which make it a rule unto itself. Some anticipation occurs naturally, for example, a mouse is about to hit a cat over the head with a mallet. Physically, the mouse would have to pull the mallet back before plunging it down, this is the anticipation moment. By exaggerating this moment you can let the viewer know what is about to happen in the scene.

There are other anticipation tricks which do not always happen in nature but are useful in animation. For example, in the old Road Runner cartoons, when the coyote falls off the cliff, he hangs in the air for a second or two before plummeting to the ground. Without the pause, the viewer would not have time to register his very fast fall to earth.

**3** Open up Speedy 2 Composition and RAM Preview it.

OK, there are a few changes I've made to the animation, let's run through them. Between frames one to twenty-six, I've added a bit of movement to the text using the Jitter settings in Path Text. This is the staging of my animation and serves two purposes, it draws attention to the text and it makes the text appear 'fidgety' as if it is desperate to get moving. So, as well as providing the staging we are also providing motivation.

## motivation

This is when one action clearly shows that another action is about to take place. In this example the Jitter at the start of the animation is like an engine starting up and revving, ready to explode into action.

So, staging, anticipation and motivation have been used here to make the action of the text speeding off more convincing and exciting to the viewer. There's also a fair bit of exaggeration in there for good measure!

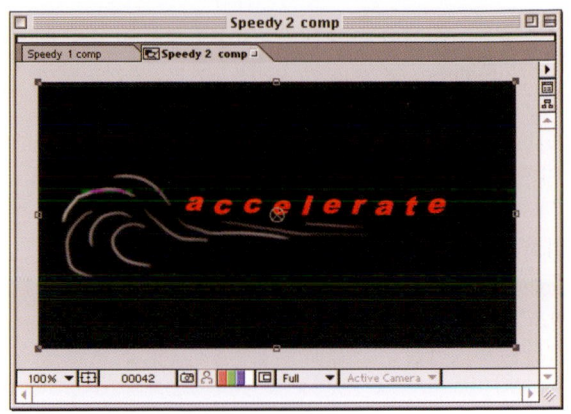

There are another couple of layers beneath the text layer that we are now going to look at. If you have the Production Bundle of After Effects, you can view the animation I have created in Vector Paint. For those of you with the Standard version, I have pre rendered a movie to replace this layer.

**PB** Switch on the visibility for the Smoke layer by hitting the Eye icon in the Timeline or by selecting the layer and then going to Layer > Switches > Video (Command + Shift + Alt + V).

**SV** Switch on the visibility of the Exhaust.mov layer to see a rendered version of the Smoke composition.

**4** RAM Preview the animation again with the Smoke layer switched on.

## secondary action

A secondary action is any type of action which results from the main action. In this example the car zooming off is the *main action*. The *secondary action*, the smoke, emphasizes the speed of the car and illustrates the space left behind after the car has gone. Other secondary actions could be a character's tummy wobbling after they have jumped from a great height or a facial expression of agony after Tom has been hit on the toe by Jerry. One thing to be cautious of is not to make the secondary action more prominent than the main action. I've added a slight blur to my smoke to make it slightly more subtle.

### sound effects

**5** Turn on the audio for the Car.mov layer, which is our sound effects layer. RAM Preview the animation.

Notice how the addition of some good sound effects can really bring the animation to life. If you can make your animation communicate without sound, that's brilliant because you don't want to rely on sound alone to communicate the idea. Animation is primarily a visual form of communication. But, having said all that, a good piece of sound effects work can make all the difference between a great animation and a stunning piece of animation. I advise working closely with a good sound designer. Sound design is a very specialist field and to be really good at it, you need to make it your career. I make up guide sound tracks for my own animations but would always leave the final sound effects and audio mixing to the experts.

### overlap and follow through

Follow through is, again, something that occurs in nature but is often exaggerated in animation. Think of a golfer, taking a swing at a ball, the golf club doesn't stop suddenly when it comes into contact with the ball, it follows through the same path and then gradually settles back down to a halt. This is follow through. You'll also see follow through when you observe a cat flicking its tail. After the cat has flicked its tail a wave of action will follow through to the tip of its tail after the base of its tail has stopped moving.

Overlap is when one action overlaps another. If we look at nature again, very seldom does one action finish completely before another starts. Imagine at breakfast taking a bite of your toast and then having a sip of your tea. You may still be putting the toast back down on your plate with one hand whilst putting the cup to your lips with the other – these are overlapping actions. Your animation will look rigid and unnatural if you don't overlap the actions within it.

**1** Open the Composition named, Text Dangle Composition and RAM Preview it.

This is a very simple example of these two principles. In this animation the text rushes in from the left but does not immediately come to a halt, it goes beyond its stopping point and then eventually comes back to rest at the end point. At the same time, the letter 'g' continues moving after the main action has stopped. It is lighter than the main body of text so takes longer to stop moving, momentum will keep it going for longer. These are both examples of follow-through action and overlapping action combined.

## recap

• We've now covered most of the fundamental rules of animation but there are a few more principles which are worth considering.

• *Balance* is crucial for an animation to be convincing, you must draw your characters in poses which look real and sustainable.

• Balance will change according to the *weight* or *mass* of an object, heavy objects will generally take longer to pick up speed. They will also take longer to stop moving than light objects because more resistance is needed to fight against the heavier weight.

• A good understanding of *rhythm* will help you to work out the timing of your animations.

• A good knowledge of physics and math will certainly help you understand how things work.

• My advice, above everything else, is to get out there and observe how things move and react with their surroundings.

• Life drawing classes are also a very good way of studying form and structure, your local art college will have evening classes you can enrol in.

• Finally, lots of practice is required to be good at anything so if at first you don't succeed, keep trying, eventually you'll get it right if you do.

• Try to think of these rules each time you work, once they become second nature to you, that's when you can start bending and breaking them.

• Velocity, (or speed), is the rate of change of position. Acceleration, (whether negative or positive), is the rate of change of velocity.

# chapter nine
# time

Time, along with motion are the two things that set motion graphic design apart from any other type of design. It is very important that you have a good understanding of how time works in After Effects. We spoke a bit about timing in the animation chapter. You saw how time was represented by a graph which, when manipulated would adjust the timing between keyframes. Now it's time to take a look at how you can play around with time, using certain features, Keyframe Assistants and Effects.

## time remapping

Some of my favorite effects are time-based effects and I reckon that Time Remapping is one of my favorite features in After Effects, you can use it in so many great ways. When you *Enable Time Remapping* for a layer, an extra, animatable property appears in the Timeline. The property which Time Remapping allows you to animate is time itself. You can stretch the time of your layer backwards and forwards at any speed you desire (real time, slow motion or ultra fast). You can also use it for freeze framing your footage.

There are also loads of groovy tricks you can do with Time Remapping, we'll start by having a look at a pre-built project which I'll use to demonstrate some of the basics of Time Remapping. We'll then apply what we've learnt to the projects we've been working on.

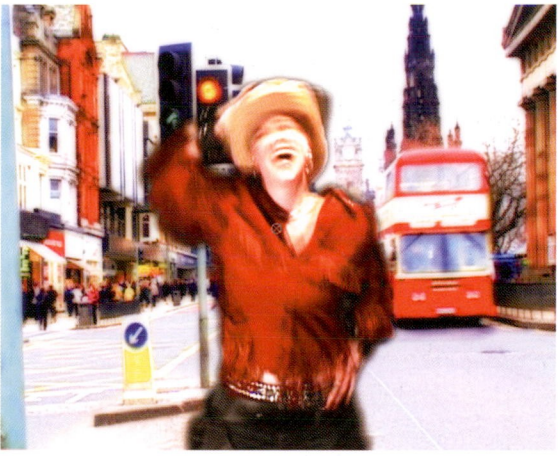

## freezing frames

**1** Go to Training > Projects > Chapter 09 and open the Project named T_remap.aep.

**2** Make sure that the composition named, Comp 1 is open and then RAM Preview it.

This is one of the movies I'm going to be using for the Music video project. It features a certain 'young' lady prancing around like a lunatic! (Yes, it's me!)

**3** Click on the little disclosure triangle next to the Layer Name to open up the layer so that all of its animatable properties are visible.

**4** Select the layer and then go to Layer > Enable Time Remapping (Command + Alt + T).

Notice that a new *Time Remap* Layer Property has appeared in the Timeline with a keyframe already placed at either end of the layer.

**5** Make sure the Current-Time Marker is at the beginning of the Comp and check the Property Value Display, it reads 001.

**6** Move the Current-Time Marker to the 20 frame mark and notice that the value is now 020. When first applied, the Time Remap value will have the same as the current time.

**7** Click the disclosure triangle next to the Property name to open up the Time Remap value graph. You will see a straight diagonal line going from the start keyframe to the end keyframe.

**8** Click on the Time Remap value display and type in the number 1 and then hit Enter to change the value to 1 frame. Notice that the graph has changed to a straight horizontal line between the first and second keyframes. This tells us that the value is remaining the same between these two keyframes. RAM Preview the movie and notice that the movie is standing still for the first 20 frames.

## speeding up footage

What if we wanted to make the movie playback very fast?

**1** You can use Time Remapping to hold frames as stills. Notice also that the movie has to play back faster after the second keyframe because it is having to play back the full 89 frames over the space of 69 frames (89 – 20).

**2** Move to frame 50 and type in 89 (which is the last frame in the layer).

RAM Preview again and notice that the movie now plays very quickly between the second and third keyframes and then remains still between the third and the last (between frame 20 and frame 50, the movie is playing back a total of 89 frames).

## slowing down footage

You can also slow-mo footage using Time Remapping.

**1** Move to end of the layer (frame 89) and change the value to 79, the movie will now play 10 frames worth of footage over the space of 39 frames (between frame 50 and frame 89).

So, to sum up, you can use Time Remapping to animate the time of your movies. You can make them play faster, slower or you can hold them as stills.

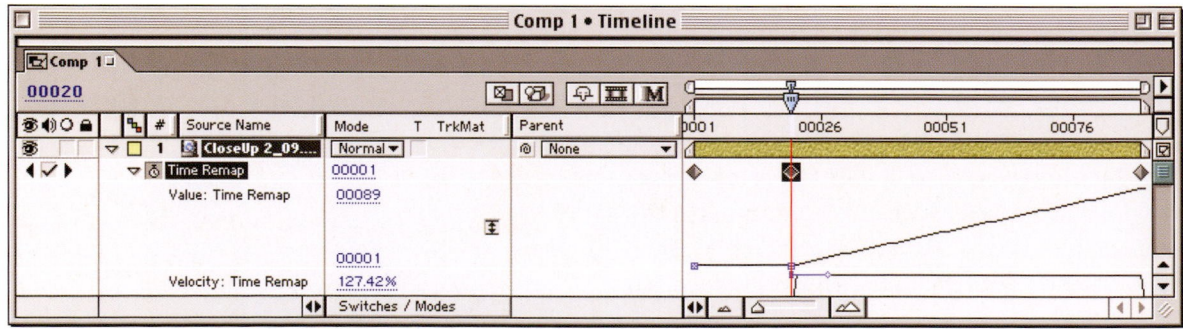

## time remap value graph

The nicest thing about using Time Remapping to alter the speed of your footage (as opposed to simply changing the duration of a clip) is that you can vary the speed over time. You can also tweak the animation using the value graph.

**1** Open up Comp 2 and RAM Preview the movie.

This is one of Liquid ambience, collection courtesy of Artbeats Inc. This is one of the free files on the CD which was kindly donated by Artbeats. This is from a series of great background collections. The movie consists of a thick, flowing liquid. We will use Time Remapping to make this liquid breathe in and out in an eerily regular way.

**2** With the layer selected, double-hit the R key on your keyboard to bring up the Time Remapping property in the Timeline.

**3** Open up the Value Graph, notice that no keyframes have been added as yet.

**4** Select the Pen tool from the tool palette.

As well as being used to draw masks and adjust curves in the Composition window, the Pen tool can also be used to add points to your Value graphs. It's a very quick and easy way to add lots of keyframes for a property without having to move the Current-Time Marker.

If you hold down the Shift key whilst you are drawing, it will ensure that you create Linear keyframes and will prevent you from accidentally creating Bezier keyframes.

**5** Hold down the Shift key and then click on the Value graph at pretty regular intervals. It doesn't have to be exact. See the diagram below for guidance.

**6** Select the standard selection tool (V) from the tool palette and then move back down to the Timeline.

At the moment, no change will have taken place because the keyframes have not been adjusted. We will adjust the values interactively in the Timeline.

You may need to adjust the height of your Value Graph before moving on to the next stage. To do this, place the cursor over the white line at the bottom of the graph till the icon changes to a little, double-headed arrow. Pull the graph down as far as you need to. Remember that you can also use the Navigator to zoom in and out around the Current-Time Marker.

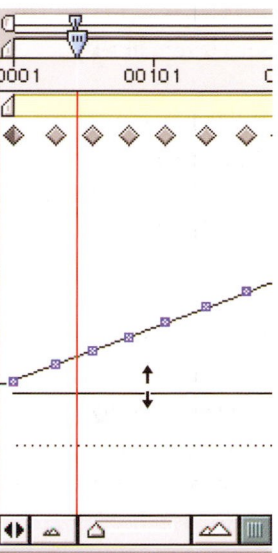

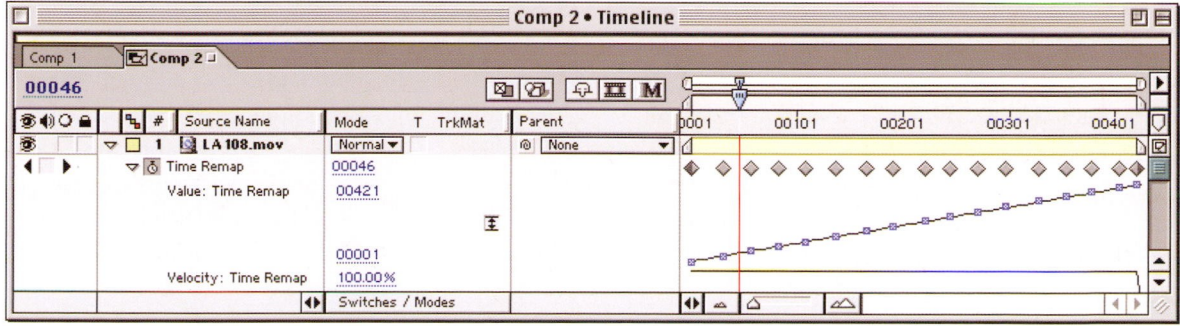

**7** Now, hold your cursor over the points that you have just created and then, one by one, drag every second point up till you have a zig-zag pattern like the one in the diagram below.

**8** RAM Preview the animation, the liquid now appears to breathe in and out. Now we'll smooth out the graph so that the movement is more gradual.

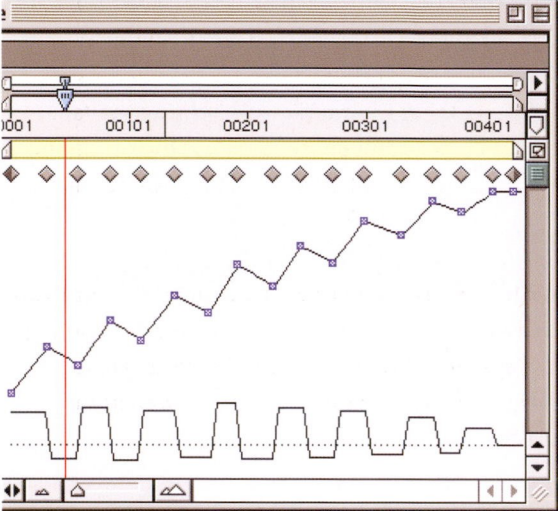

**9** Select all of the keyframes by clicking once on the Time Remap Property Name.

**10** Command-Click on any of the selected keyframes to change them to Auto-Bezier keyframes, notice how the path smooths out to a nice curved shape.

**11** RAM Preview the animation.

OK, so you understand the basics about how Time Remapping works, let's apply what you've learnt to one of our projects.

**12** If you want to, you can save this project into your Creative After Effects > Time Chapter folder for future reference.

# graffiti club

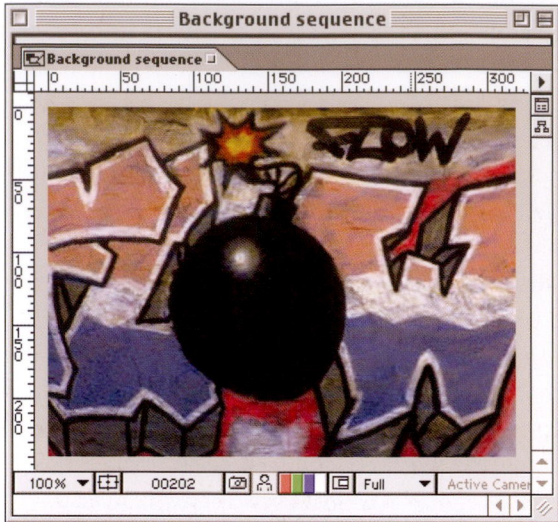

### retiming your edits

**1** Open graffiti.aep from Training > Projects > Chapter 09.

In the Import chapter we imported a series of images as a sequence, we also added a music track to our composition.

**2** RAM Preview the comp to remind yourself of the current state of the Project.

We are going to use Time Remapping to make the images change in time with the music.

**3** Select the Graffiti Composition layer and go to Layer > Enable Time Remapping (Command + Alt + T).

**4** Hit the R key twice in very quick succession to open up the Time Remapping controls and then open up the Time Remapping graph by clicking the disclosure triangle next to the stopwatch.

**5** Select the audio layer and then hit the L key twice in quick succession to bring up the audio waveform. Resize the Timeline if need be.

I'm now going to show you two ways of matching your images in time with the music, one using the Standard version of After Effects, the other using the Production Bundle. If you own the Production Bundle it is still worth going through the first exercise as you may pick up on techniques that you were previously unaware of.

### layer markers (standard version)

Some audio tracks can be so distinct that you can clearly see the beats of the music, if this was the case here you could just draw in your keyframes, with the pen tool at each beat. Unfortunately this audio track contains quite a few sounds, making it difficult to work out the beats visually. This is where After Effects Layer Markers come in handy for marking key points in the audio.

**1** Select the Graffiti Images layer and then make sure the Current-Time Marker is at the beginning of your composition (Home key). Hit the Period key on your number pad to preview the audio.

**2** Listen carefully to the music to determine where you want to mark the beats. You don't want to mark every beat, roughly one beat per second will be plenty. Only choose the main beats as you can always go back and add more markers later. Listen to the music as many times as you need to, till you feel that you know the music well enough to be able to lay down your markers.

Markers can be set at any time, simply by selecting the layer you want to mark and then hitting the * key on the number pad. Using this method, you can even add markers whilst the audio is being previewed. Markers can also be added to a layer by going to Layer > Add Marker.

**3** When you are ready, hit the period key on the number pad to begin previewing your audio and then hit the * (asterisk) key each time you want to add a marker till you reach the end of the audio (make sure that you hit the asterisk key on the number pad, not the one on the main keyboard). There is a bit of a delay before the audio starts so you should have enough time to prepare for the first beat coming in.

Don't worry if you make a few mistakes to begin with, that's only natural. If you do, simply undo the last step and then try again. One undo step will undo all of the markers set during the last preview. Just don't give up! Repeat the process till you get the hang of it. As with most things, it will become easier the more you practice.

**4** Once you've laid down some markers that you are happy with, double-click the layer to open up its Layer window. Make sure that you can see both the Layer window and the Composition window side by side.

**5** See the diagram on the following page for my recommended screen layout. Once you have the layout exactly how you want it, go to
Window > Workspace > Save Workspace
and give your workspace a name.
I've called mine 'Layer window'.

When Time Remapping is enabled for a layer you'll have an extra Timeline, with its own Current-Time Marker, it's situated above the regular Timeline, in your Layer window. You can see it illustrated on the following page.

This is the Time Remapping Timeline and it makes setting Time Remapping keyframes very easy indeed. The Time Remapping Current-Time Marker moves independently from the regular Current-Time Marker and sets keyframes wherever there is a difference between them.

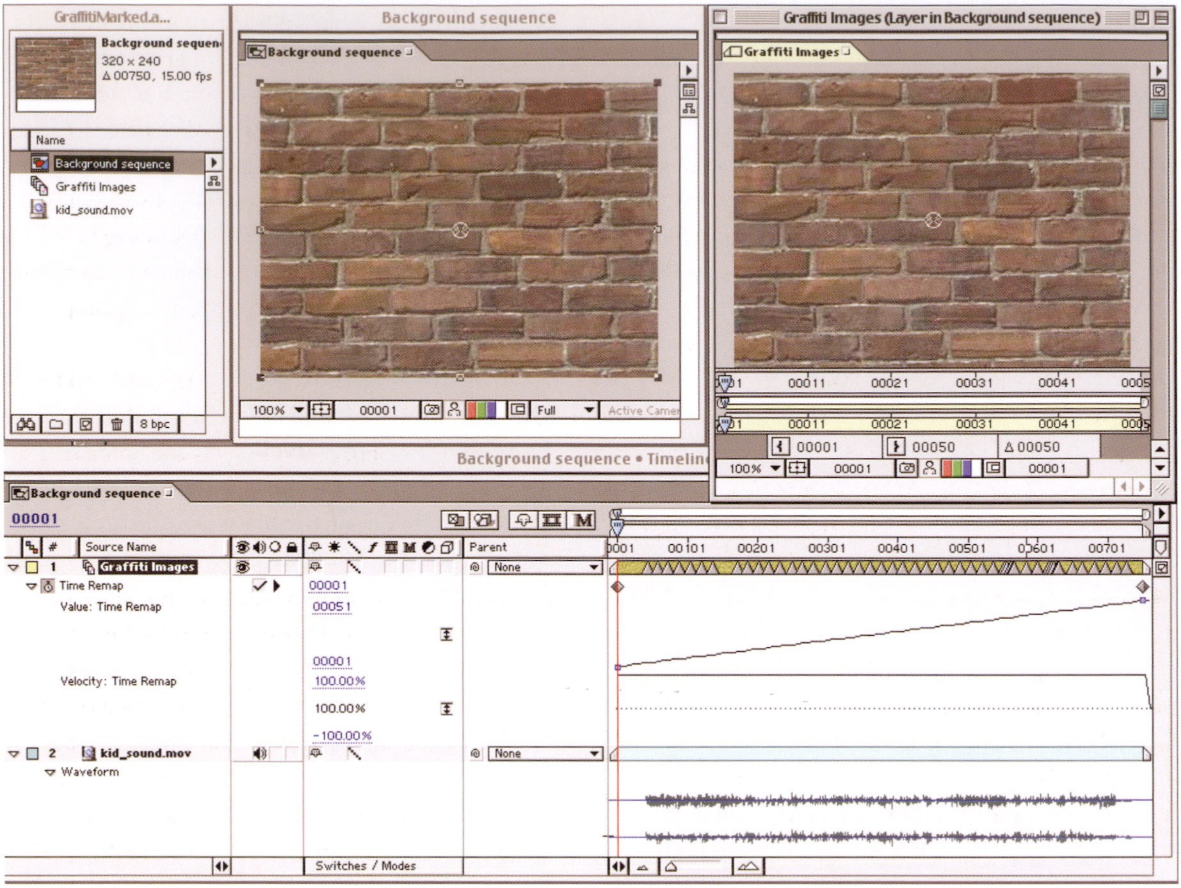

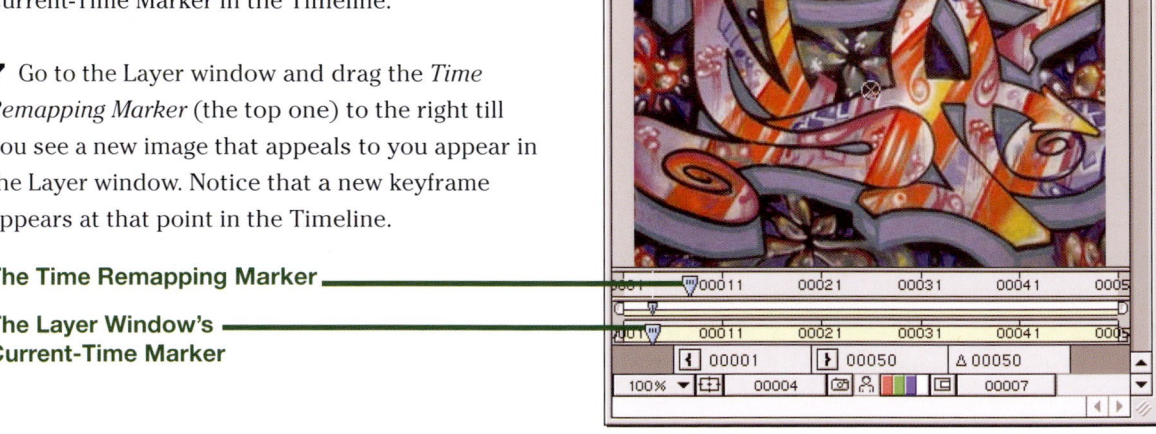

**6** With the Layer window active, use the J and K keys to jump between the Layer Markers till the Current-Time Marker is on the first Layer Marker. You will notice that the Current-Time Marker in the Layer Window moves simultaneously with the Current-Time Marker in the Timeline.

**7** Go to the Layer window and drag the *Time Remapping Marker* (the top one) to the right till you see a new image that appeals to you appear in the Layer window. Notice that a new keyframe appears at that point in the Timeline.

**The Time Remapping Marker**

**The Layer Window's Current-Time Marker**

**8** Jump to the next Layer Marker position and then drag the Time Remapping Marker to the right till you see the next image that appeals to you.

**9** Continue doing this at each marker till you reach frame 538. You can move backwards or forwards to find the image you want, you can also repeat the same image now and then if you wish. Just make sure that the image changes on every marker.

Make sure that you move the Current-Time Marker at each marker to create a new keyframe. If you move to a marker which already has an image you want, create a keyframe at that point by either clicking in the Keyframe checkbox in the Timeline or by slightly moving the Time Remapping Marker to register a change in value.

It is important to have a keyframe at each marker in order to make the images jump in time with the music, to do this we are going to do what's known as Toggle Hold the keyframes so that the changes only occur on the keyframes and no where else, let me explain.

**10** Go to File > Save as and, in the Save as dialog box, navigate to your Creative After Effects > Time Chapter folder. Save the Project as Graffiti01b.aep. We will come back to this project later so make sure that you save it here.

### toggle hold keyframes

When using default keyframes, After Effects interpolates between the keyframes in a linear way. For example, if I was to animate a color from black to white over two seconds, After Effects would go through all the gray tones from one keyframe to the next, showing a gradual change in color over time. Toggle holding a keyframe forces the property to hold on the specified value till another keyframe is met to change the value. In our example, the color would stay at black for two seconds and then suddenly change to white.

Toggle holding a keyframe is very useful in situations where you want a property to switch suddenly from one value to another as opposed to changing linearly (or gradually). For example, if you want to animate lights flashing on and off, or if you want to create some sort of sudden movement. There are a couple of situations where Toggle holding your keyframes can prevent some sticky situations, I'll give you an example.

**1** Open The Project named Toggle_hold.aep from Training > Projects folder. With the 1_Position Composition open, RAM Preview the animation of the square moving from left to right across the bottom of the screen.

Imagine that we want to move the red square to the top of the screen, for it to hold for twenty frames and then for it to move to its final resting place at the right side of the screen. We'll do this the wrong way first to show you what can happen.

**2** Go to two frame 64 (about half way between the two keyframes, this will ensure that the path remains pretty even on both sides) and move the square to the top, center of your composition, holding down the Shift key to constrain the movement to a vertical one.

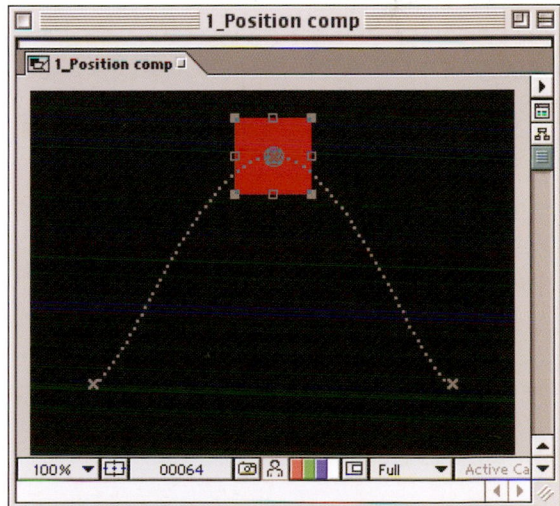

The next logical step would be to move this keyframe ten frames back and then copy and paste another keyframe ten frames (making a total of twenty frames around the center of the curve), so let's try that.

**3** Go to frame 54 which is ten frames back from our current point. Select the middle keyframe and drag it to the left till it meets the Current-Time Marker (holding down the Shift key whilst dragging will snap it to the Marker).

**4** Move the Current-Time Marker to frame 74 (twenty frames ahead).

**5** With the previous keyframe selected, hit Command + C (Edit > Copy) to copy the keyframe followed by Command + V (Edit > Paste) to paste it into the current position of the Current-Time Marker.

**6** RAM Preview the animation, notice that, despite copying and pasting the same values for each keyframe, the object still moves when it is in between the two middle keyframes; it is not holding its position value constant between these two points. The reason for this is that we adjusted the curve after creating the final keyframe. If we had created the keyframes in the order in which they appear, we wouldn't have the same problem. If you zoom in to the center keyframe with the magnifying tool and drag the foremost keyframe up slightly, you will be able to see the curve in the path which causes this phenomenon.

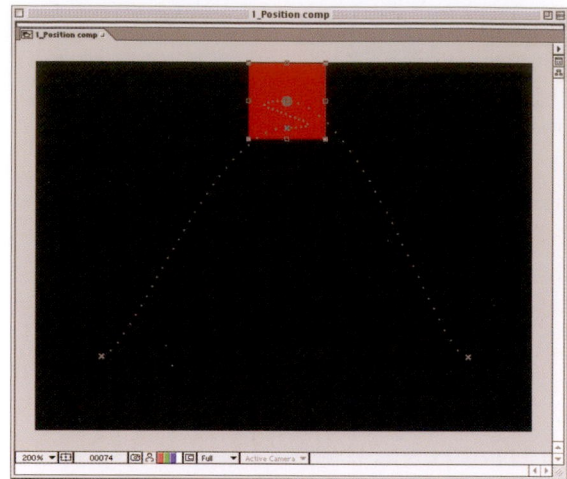

**7** To fix the problem, go to the Timeline and then Context-Click on the second keyframe, choose Toggle Hold Keyframe from the context-sensitive menu.

Notice in the Composition window that the S shaped curve between the two keyframes has disappeared, leaving a gap. Alternatively, you could have Context-clicked on the keyframes in the Composition window to do the same job.

**8** Play the sequence again and notice that we have cured the problem.

Using two non-toggle held keyframes to hold a property static can also lead to problems when rendering out to fields. There's more information about field rendering in CD > Extras > Technical.pdf.

**9** Open up 2_Fields Composition and RAM Preview it. The blue square is jumping up and down between two points. Keyframes which are set one frame apart are being used to prevent the square moving between the key points.

This looks fine at twenty-five frames per second but if you rendered this out using fields (fifty fields per second), you'd see that there is a little hint of the square at the time between the two keyframes. I call this a 'ghost' field. I'll show you how it happens.

**10** Change the frame rate of the composition to 50 fps and move the Current-Time Marker to frame 50 (between the first two keyframes) you will see that there is a single frame, in–between the two keyframes, showing the intermediate position. This would be our 'ghost' frame which would appear when rendering out to fields.

**11** Switch visibility on for Solid 2, which is animated correctly, using Toggle Hold keyframes.

**12** RAM Preview the animation to see the blue 'ghost' square popping up between keyframes.

If you want to, you can save this project into your Creative After Effects > Time Chapter folder for future reference. OK, Let's go back to our Graffiti Project.

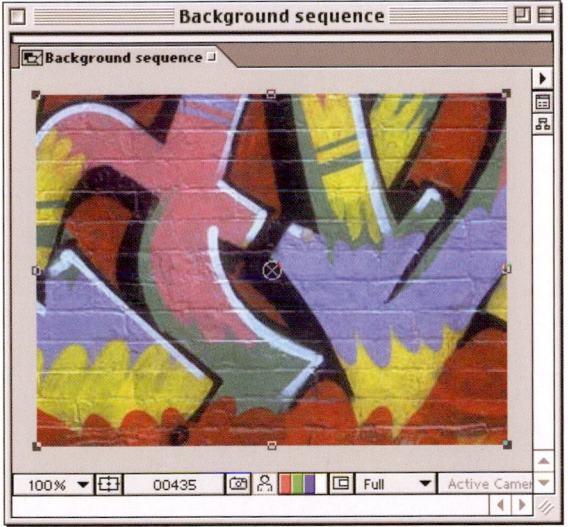

**13** Hit Command + O or go to File > Open Project. Navigate to your Creative After Effects > Chapter Time folder and open the project that you saved in the last section, Graffiti01b.aep.

**14** Select all of the Time Remapping keyframes and then Context-Click on them and choose Toggle Hold Keyframe from the context sensitive menu.

**15** RAM Preview the movie and notice that the cuts now happen in time with the music, with no linear changes in between.

**16** Save the project to your Chapter Time folder.

If you have the Production Bundle version of After Effects you can continue with the following section. If not, simply move ahead to the next section.

## retiming your edits

### motion math (production bundle)

You've seen how easy it is to match frames up with the audio levels of a layer, but what happens if we want the image changing on every single beat of the music? We would need to create hundreds of keyframes, we could do it with the previous method but that would take an awful lot of time and effort. Instead of that I'm going to introduce you to a new, easier way to set your keyframes for what would otherwise be quite complex animation tasks. After Effects Production Bundle comes with its very own scripting interface. Now, if you are anything like me, just the mention of the word scripting will be enough to send you screeching out of the room. When I tell you that the scripting interface is called Motion Math you will probably be sobbing into your handkerchief! Don't despair! Us creative types weren't put on this earth to write scripts and the After Effects team realized this when designing the interface.

The scripting language is relatively easy to learn. Even I have been able to figure out some of the language and have begun customizing existing scripts. But, luckily you don't even have to be able to write the scripts in order to use them.

**1** Close any open projects and then open graffiti.aep again from Training > Projects > Chapter 09.

**2** Select the Graffiti Images layer and go to Layer > Enable Time Remapping (Command + Alt + T).

**3** Open up the Time Remapping controls (RR) and then open up the Time Remapping graph by clicking the disclosure triangle to the left of the property name.

**4** Select the audio layer and then hit the L key twice in quick succession to bring up the audio waveform. Resize the Timeline if need be.

**5** One thing to note when working with the Comp. Audio Motion Math script is that it will not work when the Caps lock key is down so make sure that it is not active.

**6** Context-click on the layer and go to Keyframe Assistant > Motion Math.

Now you should see a dialog box in front of you, this is the point where most people run away with their heads in their hands but I know that you are a better person than that! This dialog box may look quite frightening, with its distinctly programmy-looking text and scary words like; 'Functions' and 'Operators', but I promise you that it's deceptively easy to use. All you need to be able to do in order to use a Motion Math script is read and press buttons, I'll show you how simple it really is.

**7** Click on the Load button and locate the Motion Math scripts folder, which will be inside your After Effects folder, on your hard drive.

There are several pre-written Motion Math scripts in your After Effects folder if you own the Production Bundle version of After Effects. All the scripts we will be using in this exercise are in the Motion Math scripts folder, inside your After Effects folder.

**8** Double-click the file named Cmpaud.mm. The script will now be loaded into the Motion Math window.

Motion Math Script Name
Description of Script function

Instructions for setting up

Program text (scripting language)
Pull-down menus
Pop-up menus

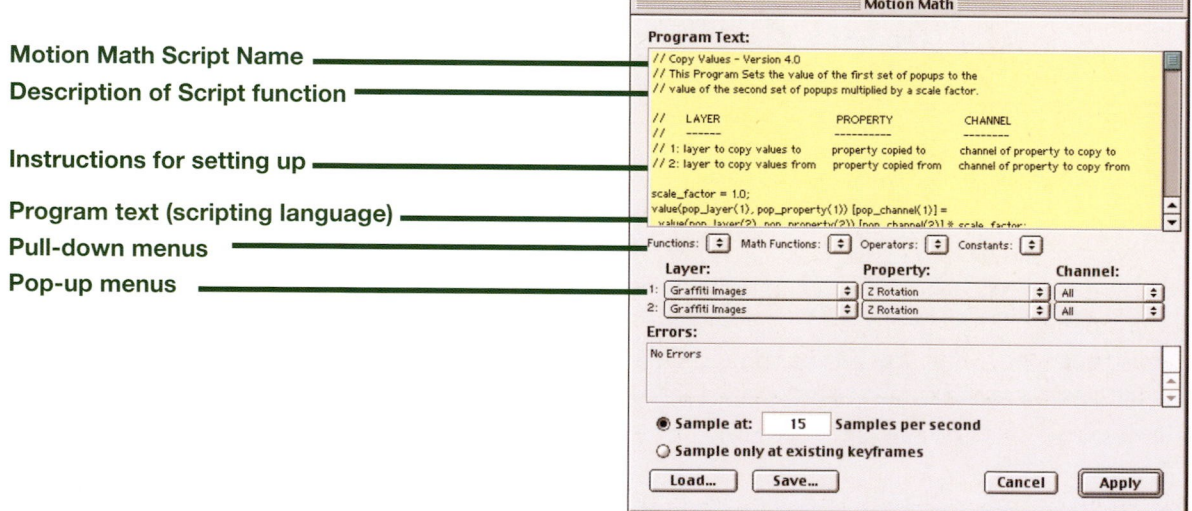

If you look in the Program Text window you will see that the programmers, very kindly, give you plenty of information about what the script does and how you can use it. First of all they tell you the name of the script, in this case it's 'Comp Audio Version 1.2'. This is one of my favorite and, probably slightly overused (by me) scripts, there are so many things that you can do with it. It is a great tool for making *any property* (including Transform properties and most Effect properties) change their value in time with music (or any other sounds).

Underneath the script name is a description of what the it does; 'This Program Sets the value of the first set of popups to the audio level of the comp, scaled to lie within the range [min, max]'. This particular script creates keyframes for a user-defined property based on the audio levels of your composition (scaled to lie within a specified, minimum to maximum range).

Underneath this description you will see instructions on how to set up the pop-up menus for Layer, Property and Channel. It tells you, for pop-up number one, first choose the layer to copy the values into, well in this case we want to copy values into our Graffiti Images layer.

**9** Click on the Pop-up menu number 1 and choose Graffiti Images from the menu.

The script then asks you which property you would like to vary in time with the music. You can choose to apply the script to any layer property. For example, if you wanted to make something move around in time with the music, you would choose to apply the values to the Position or Anchor Point. In this case, we want to adjust the Time Remap value in time with our music.

**10** From the Property pop –up menu (pop - up 1), choose Time Remap.

The next menu allows to choose which channel of the Property you would like to vary. For example, a simple 2D Scale has two channels, the X value and the Y value. If you wanted to animate the Scale property, you could determine whether to animate only the X value, only the Y value, or both simultaneously, just by making your choice in this menu. Time Remap has only one channel because time is a single dimension, so you do not need to alter this menu in this particular case.

You'll notice that there is a second set of pop-up menus beneath the first set. This is because some scripts require that you choose two layers, one to take values from, another to copy values to. In this case we only need to tell the script which layer to affect so the instructions are telling us that this set of pop-ups 'doesn't matter'. In other words, you do not have to change these for this particular script.

Notice that there are also pull-down menus above the pop-ups containing all the Functions, Operators etc. that you may need to write these scripts yourself (if you are that way inclined). The interface acts as a tool for creating the scripts as well as using them. If you have friends who are into programming you can ask them to write scripts for you, using this interface.

Scripts can also be written or edited in any text editing program. We're not going to actually write a script but we are going to edit this script to suit our needs, it is very easy to do, I'll show you how.

**11** Go down to the eighth line of text where you will see two lines; the first starting with the word *max,* the next with the word *min.* This is where you can change the minimum and maximum values you wish to set keyframes for (this is known as the *range*).

The default setting is a maximum of one thousand and a minimum of fifty. The numbers you see here always relate to the particular layer property that you are setting keyframes for. So, for example, if you were setting keyframes for position, these numbers would represent the minimum and maximum values in *pixels*; if we were working with Rotation values, these numbers would represent the values in degrees. We are creating keyframes for the Time Remap value, so in this case, these numbers represent values in seconds.

**12** Our Graffiti Images layer is fifty seconds long, so fifty will be our maximum value. Our minimum value will be zero. This means that After Effects will work on the full range of frames available, between 0 and 50 seconds. If we wanted only to use frames from between frame twenty and frame thirty, we would make our minimum value 20 and our maximum value 30.

This script will essentially automate the process that we used in the Standard version exercise. We will be matching up Time Remapping keyframes with the peaks and troughs of the composition's audio level.

**13** In the line beginning with *max*, select the text which currently reads *1000* and type in 50. In the line beginning with *min*, select the text which currently reads *50* and type in 0.

One important thing to note is that your layer property may never quite reach the minimum and maximum values unless the audio reaches extreme levels e.g. the value will only ever drop to zero if the audio goes completely silent.

**14** Now all you have to do is to hit the Apply button, After Effects will now write hundreds of keyframes for you, mapping the Time Remap value to the audio levels of your Composition, saving you hours of work!

Just have a look at the keyframes and the graph in the Timeline. You would have needed a lot of markers and a lot more time to have accomplished this using the Standard version method. Although both techniques are capable of producing similar results, the Production Bundle method is infinitely easier and is much less time-consuming to use.

There is also a Layer Audio Motion Math script which is useful if you have more than one layer of audio, it allows you to use the levels from a single layer in your comp. For example, if you are making your own music for your animation, save the drum beats as a separate file, then you can put the drums on one layer and the melody on another and have different properties animating to different sounds.

**15** Go to File > Save A Copy and then Navigate to your Creative After Effects folder on the desktop. Save the project into the Chapter time folder as Graffiti01PB.aep.

If you want to experiment more with this script, you can undo the last step and reapply the script, using different minimum and maximum settings.

# MacDonna video

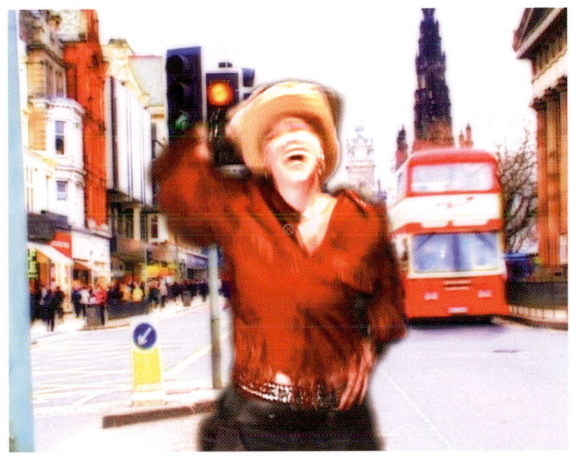

OK, time to introduce another project example. Remember in the project brief chapter I showed you my ideas for the music video? Well, we're going to start on that right here by applying some time based effects to some DV footage. This project example differs from the first two in that we are not going to recreate the whole movie from start to finish, there just wouldn't be enough space on the CD for all the footage. I will, however, show you the most important bits.

## time stretching

Open the movie called MacDonna.mov from the Source Movies > Angie Movies > MacDonna folder and play it, this is the finished movie, it's a pastiche of other music videos. I've always wanted to be a Rock star so I just couldn't let this opportunity go to waste!

As you can see the movie contains lots of edits, time trickery, effects and fast cuts, I put the rough edit together using Final Cut Pro and then rendered a QuickTime movie for After Effects. The whole project was created at full PAL resolution but I have re-rendered parts of it at a smaller resolution for these tutorials.

**1** Create a new Project and then hit Command + I. In the Import File dialog box, navigate to the Training > Source Movies > Angie Movies . MacDonna folder on the desktop and import the file named PrincesSt.mov.

This is footage of my home town, Edinburgh's main shopping street, Prince's Street. I shot this, and the rest of the footage in this project using my trusty Sony PD150 DVCAM camcorder.

**2** Drag the movie file onto the New comp button in the Project window to create a new composition with exactly the same settings as the movie file.

**3** RAM Preview the movie, I had to stand right in the middle of the traffic to get this shot, it was a wee bit scary!

This footage is real time footage of traffic. As I knew that I wanted to speed the footage up, I shot about two or three minutes of it. I'll show you how to alter the timing, and later, how to apply some nice effects to bring it to life even more.

**4** First of all, click the Time Stretch Panels Expand button at the bottom of the Timeline to open up the Time Stretch Panel.

This is where you can alter the speed for the whole duration of a layer. This value cannot be animated.

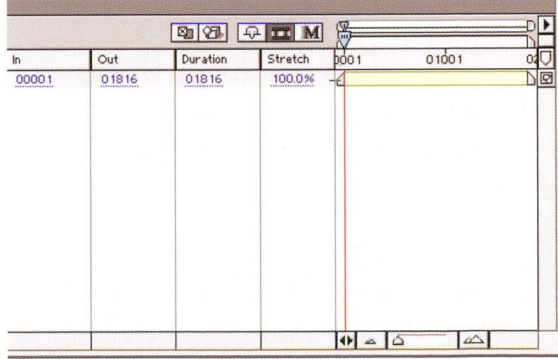

**5** Click on the Stretch value which currently reads 100%, this will bring up the Time Stretch dialog box (clicking on the duration value or the Stretch value will bring up the same dialog box).

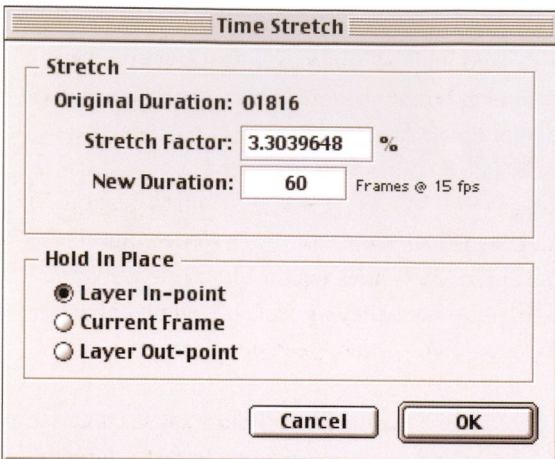

**6** Change the Duration Value to 60 frames. Notice that, as you adjust the duration value, the Percentage value also changes. You can enter a new timing for your layer by adjusting either of these values.

Below the Stretch settings are the Hold in Place settings, these allow you to determine which part of your layer will act as the anchor. With the default Layer In-point selected, the In-point will remain anchored at the beginning of the comp whilst the rest of the layer adjusts itself around it.

**7** Hit OK to leave the dialog box and then RAM Preview the changes so far. We are now playing back two minutes of video footage over the space of four seconds (60 divided by 15).

OK, your comp will now be far too long for your footage so we will have to trim it down a bit.

**8** Close the Time Stretch panel by clicking again on the Expand/collapse button.

**9** With the layer selected, hit the O key on the keyboard to make the Current-Time Marker jump to the Out-point of your layer.

**10** Hit the N key on the keyboard to place the End Handle of your Work Area Marker to the position of the Current-Time Marker.

**Work Area Marker**

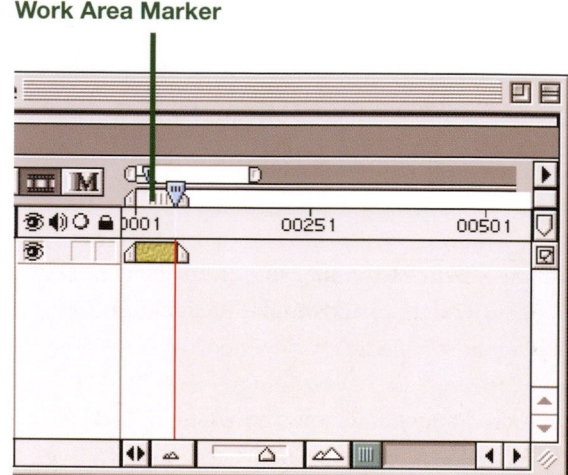

With this area marked After Effects will only preview or render the frames within ignoring any outside the Work area. The B key on the keyboard can be used to set the Beginning Work Area Marker. You can also click and drag these handles.

**11** RAM Preview the comp again, notice that the RAM Preview is only previewing the frames within the Work Area.

As this will be the final length of our footage, we might as well trim the comp to fit our marked Work Area.

**12** Go to Composition > Trim Comp to Work Area to quickly change the comps duration to fit the clip.

## frame blending

OK, so our clip is running nice and quickly now, but it looks a bit jumpy, kind of like a Keystone Cops movie. This is because by speeding up the footage we have removed a considerable amount of intermediate frames, causing people to jump suddenly in and out of shot and cars to appear stuttered in their motion. We can fix this by applying Frame Blending to the layer. I'll explain more.

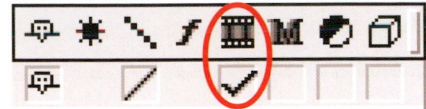

**1** In the Switches panel, click on the checkbox for Frame Blending to activate Frame Blending for the layer.

As well as activating the Frame Blending Switch for the layer, you must also Enable Frame Blending for the whole composition. Frame Blending is very processor intensive and can really slow down your workflow if it is left on whilst you are working. The EnableFrame Blending switch allows you to disable Frame Blending for the comp whilst still having the layer switches activated for the final render.

**2** Either click on the Enable Frame Blending button at the top of the Timeline or click on the Timeline wing menu and choose Enable Frame Blending.

If you RAM Preview the footage now you will notice a slight difference but you will only see the true results of Frame blending on a layer if you preview it in best quality.

**3** Change the Layer Quality switch to Best quality and then RAM Preview it again. Notice that the moving objects now appear to leave a trail or echo behind them as they move. It is a similar effect to using a slow shutter speed on a camera.

When After Effects Frame blends a layer it compares each frame to the last and creates a blend in between them. This is also useful when slowing footage down, creating intermediate frames.

**4** Go back to the project window and create another new composition by dragging the PrincesSt.mov onto the New comp icon.

**5** Open up the time stretch panel in the new comp and this time enter a new Stretch Factor of 200%. By stretching the movie we are effectively slowing it down.

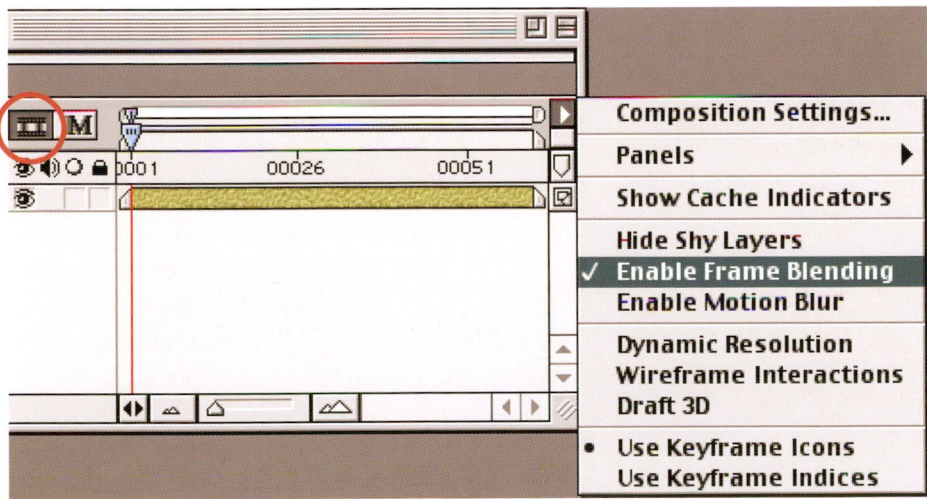

**6** RAM Preview the movie, notice that it is now running slower but that it is not playing back very smoothly. This is because After Effects is having to repeat frames in order to stretch the movie.

**7** Move to frame 15 and then use the Down Arrow key on your keyboard to step through the frames one by one. Notice that After Effects is repeating frames, this means that the movie will appear to have half the frame rate when played back.

**8** Activate Frame Blending for the layer, Enable Frame Blending for the comp and switch the layer Quality switch to Best.

**9** Now step through the frames again, see that After Effects has taken info from both frames and blended them to create intermediate frames.

**10** RAM Preview the footage to see how much smoother the playback now is.

OK, now you've seen what Frame Blending does, you can close the current composition and go back to your original comp, Princes St.mov Comp 1.

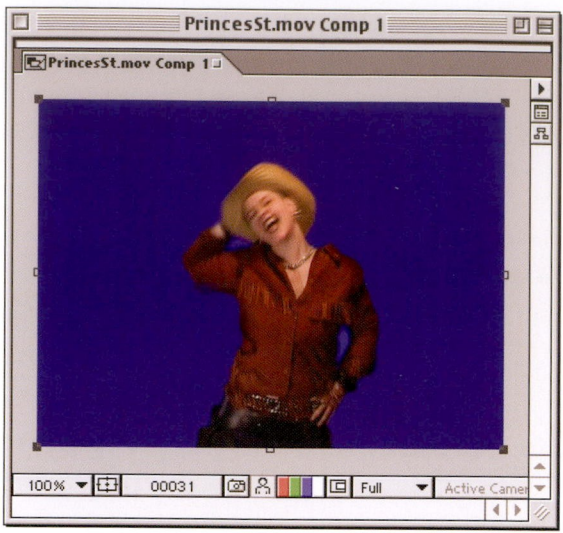

## favorite effects

We'll add some more effects to this in the Effects chapter but for now let's take a look at some of the Time based effects available in After Effects.

**1** Double-click the gray space in the Project window to bring up the Import File dialog box. Navigate to Training > Source Movies > Angie movies > MacDonna folder and choose MeDance.mov.

**2** With the file selected in the Project window, hit Command + / to bring it into the comp.

This is some footage of me showing off in front of my camera (it's a sad existence I know!). I wanted to composite this in front of the Princes Street footage so that it would look like I was dancing in the middle of the street.

In order to fit all of the footage onto the accompanying CD, I have had to compress and resize the movies. Because of this the keying will not be as effective as if we had performed it on a full size, full quality original but it will be good enough to demonstrate the techniques.

We will cover keying in more detail in the Keying chapter so for now, we'll just use a pre-saved Favorite Effect to do the job quickly. The Favorite Effects feature allows you to save your Favorite Effect combinations and settings in a very small file for future use.

**3** Go to Effect > Apply Favorite and navigate to the Training > Favorites folder. If you have the Production bundle of After Effects choose the file named MeDanceKey.ffx. If you have the Standard version, choose StandardKey.ffx.

These are combinations of keying filters which I have set up for this project. The Standard keying tools are not really up to this job, you really need the Production bundle to do good keying work. The standard versions color Key filter does not produce the best results I'm afraid. I'll explain a little bit more about how it works in the Keying chapter. As soon as you apply the Favorite Effect the bluescreen will disappear revealing the background layer beneath. There will still be a slight amount of blue on the Standard version, we'll get rid of that later.

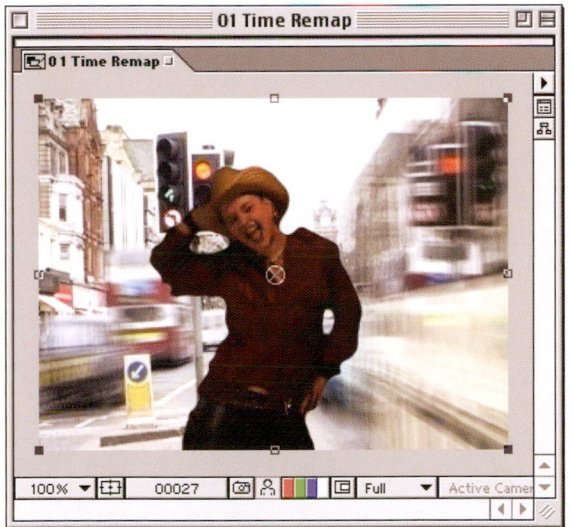

**4** Go to File > Save As and save the project into your Creative After effects folder > Time Chapter as Frameblend.aep.

## improving dancing skills

OK, we're going to use Time Remapping again to make me dance in time with some music.

**1** Hit Command + O and then;

**PB** If you have the Production Bundle version of After Effects, open the Project named MacDonnaPB.aep from Training > Projects > Chapter 09.

**SV** If you have the Standard Version of After Effects, open the Project named MacDonnaStandard.aep from Training > Projects > Chapter 09.

**2** Make sure that 01 Time Remap Comp is active and RAM Preview it. This comp is almost identical to the one that you just saved, the main difference in this one is that I have added some Layer Markers to mark the main beats of the music.

Notice that I am not currently dancing in time with the music, almost but not quite. We'll use the Time Remapping technique that we learnt earlier to make me dance perfectly in time with the music.

**3** Make sure that you can see the Comp window and the Layer window at the same time, you may need to adjust your screen layout to do so.

**4** Select the MeDance.mov layer and then go to Layer > Enable Time Remapping (Command + Alt + T)

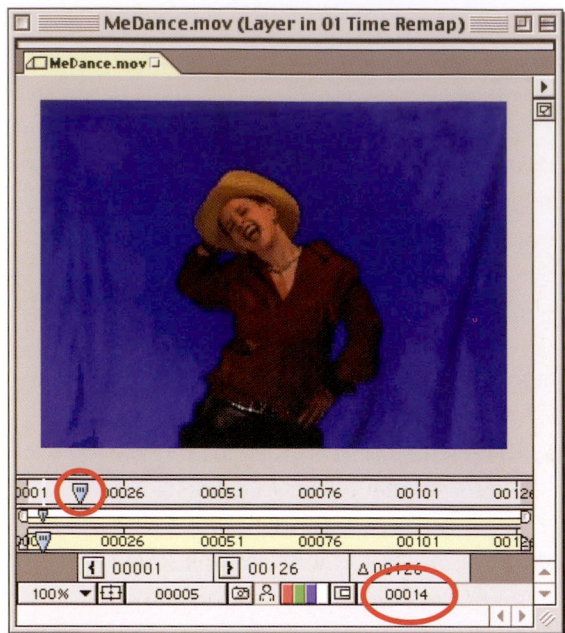

**5** Double hit the R key on the keyboard to bring up the time remap values in the Timeline. Notice that the MeDance.mov is longer than the length of the comp, in fact it is more than double the length of the comp at 126 frames. We will use this extra footage to speed up the dance and time it with the music.

Make the Timeline active and then hit the K key on the keyboard to jump to the first marker. Enabling Time Remapping for a layer automatically creates keyframes at the beginning and end of a layer so there is no need to set your first keyframe manually.

What you want to do here is to look for the main moves of the dance. I move my hips from side to side so just look out for the frame before my hips begin to change direction.

**6** Go to the Layer window and drag the Time Remap Marker (the top one) till you reach the next main move. I chose frame 14.

**7** Hit the K key again to jump to the second marker and move the Time Remap marker till you reach the point where the hips change direction again. I have it as frame 21. Repeat this process to change the Time Remap value at the third marker to 28.

**8** RAM Preview the comp and notice that the music picks up energy after the third marker. Let's make me dance in triple time here to echo the increase in energy.

**9** Move to the fourth marker and move the Time Remap Marker along till I have moved my hips backwards and forwards three times, I have this as frame 49. Do this again at the fifth marker, finishing with a value of 70.

**10** Change the Time Remap values at the next two markers to 86 and 92, respectively. We've slowed the movement down again here to accentuate the bass line coming back in again.

**11** Finally, ignore the penultimate marker and go directly to the end of the comp. Change the Time Remap value to 127.

**12** RAM Preview the results, now I am dancing perfectly in time with the music.

The movement is slightly odd looking but that is the effect that we want to achieve, to make things look a little bit out of the ordinary, playing visual tricks on the viewer.

## practice session

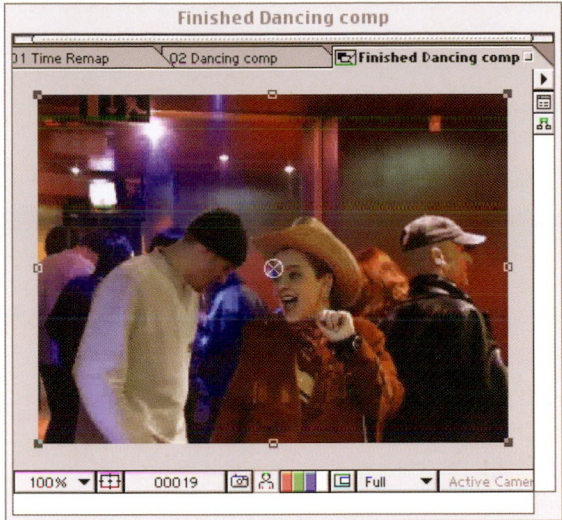

**1** Open 02 Dancing comp from the Project window and preview it, this is more footage shot for another part of the MacDonna video.

My idea here was that I wanted to create the effect of me dancing in real-time whilst all the other people appear to be dancing in fast-forward around me. You'll have seen this effect used a lot on television, particularly in music videos and advertising. It is very easy to reproduce although a little embarrassing to shoot. My friends and I went to a local bar where there was a dancefloor we could use. The idea is to get everyone dancing in real time except for the main character who has to dance as if in slow-motion. Then, when the footage is sped up so that the main character is dancing in real time, the background characters appear to be dancing at break-neck speed. The moment captured on camera was one of the most embarassing moments of my life, the other people in the club were staring at me as if I was mad!

**2** What I want you to do is to use the technique learnt in the last exercise to make my character dance in time with the beats of the music. Use the same technique, I've added some markers for you so all you need to do is to apply Time Remapping to the layer and then line up the moves with the markers.

**3** Once you have finished, RAM Preview the comp and watch as I dance like Ginger Rogers! (Well, not quite!)

I have also saved a finished version of this exercise as it is not the easiest thing to get right first time. You can compare your results with my version.

**4** Open up Finished Dance comp and RAM Preview it to see how I lined up the moves.

**5** RAM Preview your version of the Dance and then go to Composition > Save RAM Preview. Locate your Creative After Effects folder and save the movie into your Time Chapter folder. When you return to your Project window, your RAM Preview movie will be there for you to open and view.

We will add more to this project in later chapters but for now, let's look at some other options we could have taken to make our footage move strangely in time with the music.

**6** Open up 03 Motion Math comp and RAM Preview it. In this composition I used the Comp Audio motion Math Script to animate the Time Remapping values in time with the music. To achieve this result I used exactly the same technique as we used in the Graffiti Club Project.

**7** Open up the 04 Posterize Comp. In this comp, the top layer, MeDancing.mov, has the Posterize Time effect Applied to it with a setting of 2 frames per second (Effect > Time > Posterize Time).

This filter will lock the layer to a specified frame rate. By applying a setting of 2 fps, the movie is only playing back two of its fifteen frames every second of the comp. This filter overrides any effects or masks which are already applied to your layer so you must either apply it before you apply any other effects or apply it to a nested comp.

**8** Select the top layer, MeDancing.mov and then hit Command + Shift + T to bring up its Effect Controls.

**9** Click and drag the Posterize Time effect down to the bottom of the list of effects applied to the layer. Notice that the Keying filters now have no effect on the layer.

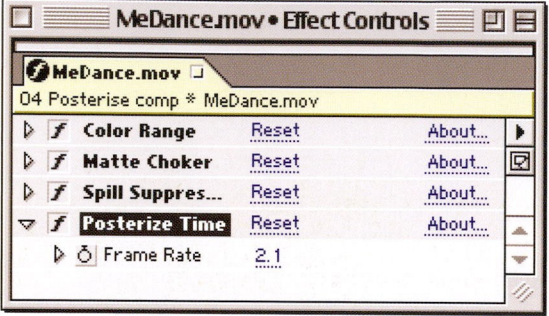

**10** Drag the Posterize Time effect back to the top of the Effect Controls window to return your Keying.

**11** RAM Preview the movie to see the effect that you get from Posterizing the time of a layer.

We will take a look at some other time based effects in the Effects chapter. For now I'd like you to have a bit more practice with the things you've learnt in this chapter.

**12** If you want to you can save a copy of this project into your Creative After Effects > Time Chapter folder as MacDonna02b.aep

## recap

So you can see that time based effects can be used in a really effective way, you can make people better dancers, you can even make characters talk. I've added another Time Remapping example project on the CD > Extras folder, it's called DogTalk.aep and it shows you how to make your animated characters speak any script!

Go and take a break away from the computer for half an hour to clear your mind and to give your eyes a rest. Have a little think about whether you can incorporate any of these ideas into your chosen project. Write down any ideas you may have, sketch down any visual ideas. When you return from your break, start to experiment with your ideas to see if they'll work. Have a look at some adverts and music videos, try to spot where they've used time based effects to good use and then see if you can achieve a similar effect using what you've learned in this chapter.

Remember that you can consult the Online Help system from the Help menu in After Effects if you need more information on any of the things we have covered. If you do not have any definite ideas then read on and then get to work!

OK, let's hear what somebody else has to offer you. Here are some more design tips, courtesy of Vicky Stonebridge, a ceramic designer based in the West Coast of Scotland. Vicky was a contemporary of mine at Edinburgh College of Art between 1982 and 1986. She has a unique outlook on life and has these tips to share with you, I hope they help you with your project.

- The way to produce exiting stuff is to believe in yourself, know that your spin on the thing has got that unique something that no-one else has got. The sum of your knowledge and experience leads to something only you can really use, its your unique contribution, so sit down and use it.
- Create with enthusiasm and a smile on your face and it's sure to be great.
- Don't try to force the creative flow into narrow margins, let it ramble aimlessly at first then once things are flowing, keep in check by re-referring to the original brief, over and over again.

Vicky's website is at: http://www.balnacra.com

# chapter ten
# keying

## keying basics

Keying, also referred to as 'blue-screening' is the process creating a matte, based usually on color or luminance. This matte is then used to define which areas of the shot are to be transparent and which areas are not. Using this technique the subject or subjects can then be isolated from the rest of the shot so that they can then be composited with a different background.

Keying is used extensively in news programs to place the news-reader in front of the program graphics. Keying is also used in weather reports to place the presenter in front of a weather map. In a typical example, the person is filmed against a blue or green screen, the software will then make the blue/green colored parts of the shot transparent, allowing it to be replaced with a new background. Keying is usually based on color, but occasionally on luminance, hue, chroma or by shot comparison.

Blue and green are usually the best colors to use as they offer the most contrast with the majority of flesh tones (unless your subject is a frog of course!). Green is usually the best choice when keying compressed footage, such as DV as it tends to produce less noise, which can make the keying process more difficult.

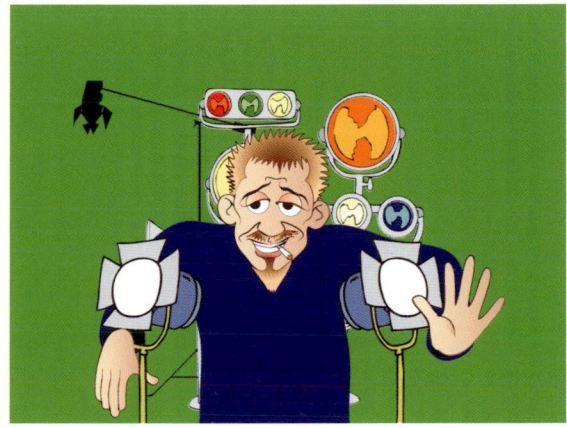

Probably the most important aspect of good keying is preparation, lighting in particular is very important and can be very tricky to set up. The background should be lit evenly with a cold light and the foreground lit with a warm light to accentuate the differences. In most cases the subject must be lit in such a way that they will cast no shadows on to the background, therefore the background needs to be placed far enough behind the subject to allow for the correct lighting angles without a shadow being cast.

It is very important to plan your shots well if you are intending to key out areas of the shot. Always use as little compression as possible on footage intended for keying. Although it is possible to key compressed footage, it is much easier and you will achieve better looking results if you use uncompressed ITUR-601 footage.

Despite rumors to the contrary, it is possible to key DV footage, it is more of a challenge but I've seen it done very successfully. In the following chapter we will even manage to pull a fairly reasonable key from footage that has been compressed once with the DV codec and then again with Cinepak.

Keying is a science unto itself and a whole book could be devoted to it, in fact many are, there are recommendations for some of these books on the website. For now, I will just concentrate on how After Effects deals with keying.

There are two different keying filters in the Standard version of After Effects and a massive eight in the Production Bundle. All have their own strengths and weaknesses.

## standard version keying

In the Standard Version of After Effects there are only two keying tools, the color key and the luma key. Both of these keys are binary keys, the word binary indicates that these keys can create pixels in a choice of two states, either transparent or opaque. These tools cannot create semi-transparent areas like some of the more advanced keying tools. The Standard keying tools are fine for images with well-defined edges and areas of solid color but not for any areas which require semi-transparent pixels. The edges of the key will not be anti-aliased, therefore edge feathering is almost always essential to soften the edge of the Matte. There is a method of pulling keys using the Standard versions *Change Color* filter which produces much better results than the standard color key. There's a project on the CD which demonstrates how to use this method but for now, we'll stick to the Keying menu. Let's take a look at the two Standard Keying filters, we'll start by looking at how they perform when used for their intended purpose, then I'll show you how to use them for some cool and groovy effects!

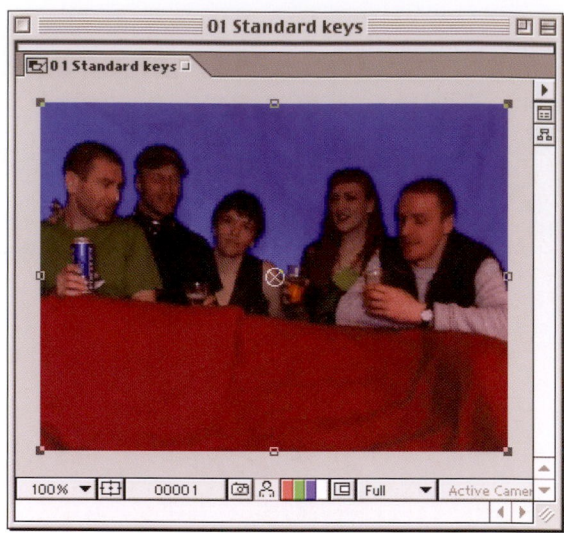

### the color key

**1** Open the project named Keying.aep from the Training > Chapter 10 folder on your desktop.

**2** Make sure that the 01 Standard Keys Comp is open. This comp consists of two layers, a background layer and a foreground layer which has been shot against a Chromatte background.

Whilst at a trade show last year, I was impressed by a product called Chromatte which I saw demonstrated, by a company called Viewercom. Chromatte is a gray material with thousands of tiny glass beads sewn into it which reflect light. You use this in conjunction with a light emitting ring (the Holoset ring for example). The Holoset ring emits blue or green light from around your camera lens, when the light hits the reflective material, it bounces back to the camera giving you a near perfect blue-screen background with very little time and effort. It's a fantastic, extremely portable system which can cope with varying lighting conditions, it even works in candle light! You can find more information about Viewercom and Chromatte on the website. Anyway, I digress, back to the Project.

Now, I'll be the first to admit I am not a professional camera person and I have done very little blue-screening in my time. The lighting equipment I used to shoot this consisted of my old Anglepoise lamp and an overhead tungsten bulb, but the results are pretty good considering how little effort I had to put in. I'm sure that with a little more knowledge, time and patience I could have achieved even better results.

## levels

**3** Let's start by correcting the image, it is very dark and muddy, we'll use the Levels filter to lighten it up. Context-click on the layer and choose Effect > Adjust > Levels.

Levels is my favorite filter for brightening up a dull image. It works in the same way as the Photoshop Levels feature by displaying a histogram (similar to a graph) of the gray levels of your image. This histogram is fairly typical of an image which has been heavily compressed. Notice the staggered appearance of the graph plus the gaps in the white end of the range, the lack of white values is what's causing the image to be so dark. Ideally you want a smooth curve moving from black to white, representing an even range of blacks, whites and grays throughout your image.

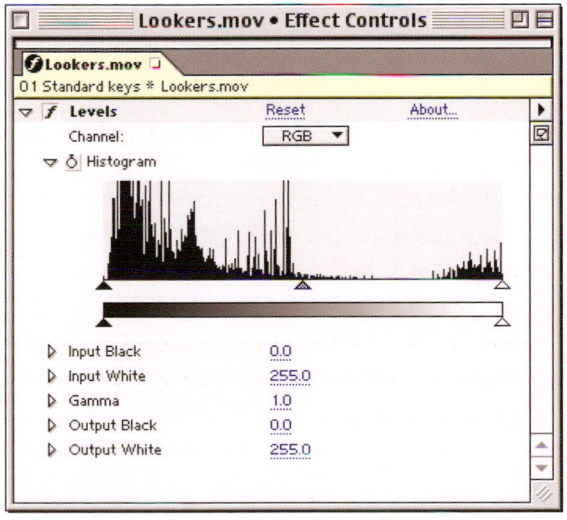

At each end of the Histogram are Input Handles for determining where the black and white levels lie on the Histogram. In the middle is your Gamma slider, this adjusts where the mid gray lies on the histogram. Pulling in the white handle will increase the highlights, pulling in the black handle will increase the shadows.

Underneath the histogram are the Output Levels sliders, these control the output of the tonal range of the image. These sliders can be used to soften the contrast in your images. We need to get rid of the gap in the histogram in order to redistribute the values over a more even range.

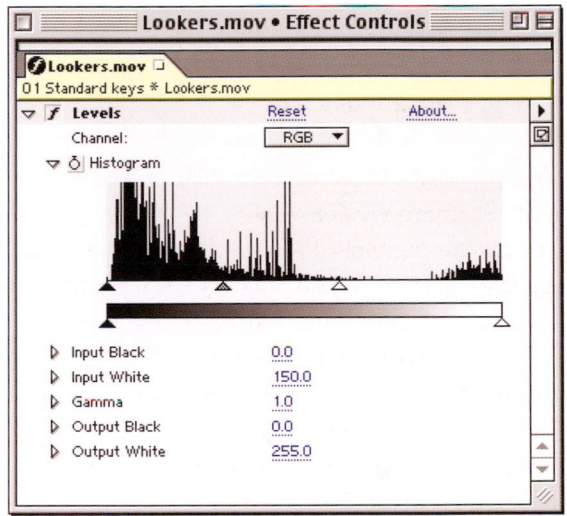

**4** Pull the White Input handle into the center of the histogram. Notice that, when you release the mouse the Input White value changes in the Effect Control panel. Drag the slider in till the Input White reading is about 150. Notice that you now have a lighter, more even image.

**5** Context-Click on the Lookers.mov layer and go to Effect > Keying > Color Key.

**6** In the Effect Controls window, click on the Eyedropper button and then click in the Comp window on the blue background of the image. Try to pick the most abundant blue. Notice that a few pixels have become transparent.

**7** Increase the color tolerance by scrubbing the value to the right in the Effect Controls window till you reach a value of about 110, most of the blue should now disappear, leaving a blue halo around the subjects.

**8** Increase the Edge Thin value to one, this has the effect of trimming the halo all around your key by one pixel. Notice that the edges of this key are quite rough, this is because the Standard keying tools do not anti alias edges.

**9** Switch the layer on to Best quality. Even on best quality the edges are not too great. To get rid of this edge we will have to use a bit of feathering on our key.

**10** Change the Edge Feather value to 1. The edge of the key is now a bit softer but we still have a bit of blue spilling onto the edges of our subjects. If you only have the color key available to you, there are a couple of ways of tidying up those nasty edges a bit more.

### shift channels

**11** Click on each of the Show Color Channel buttons at the bottom of the Composition window and compare the information in each channel, you'll see that most of the blue spill and edge is in the Blue Channel. Notice also that, apart from this, the blue and green channels are quite similar. Switch the Show Channels buttons off when you have finished comparing them.

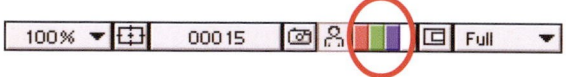

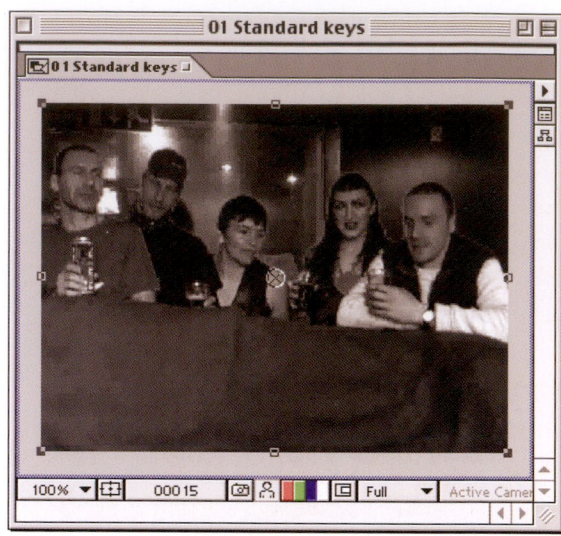

**12** Context-Click the layer again and go to Effect > Channel > Shift Channels. The Shift Channels filter allows you to take information for a specified channel from another channel in the same image.

**13** Change the Take Blue From drop down menu from Blue to Green to take the blue channel information from the green channel. Now, the same grayscale channel information is being used for both the blue and green channels, getting rid of most of the blue spill. This has the added advantage of removing a lot of the noise from an image because most noise information tends to be held in the blue channel.

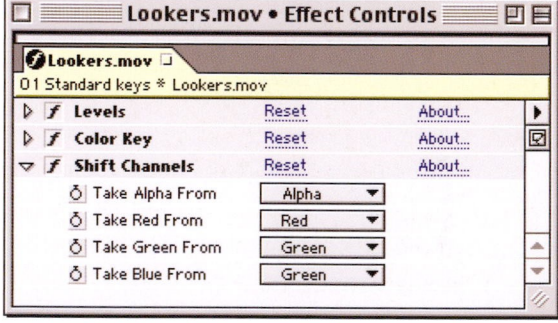

**14** RAM Preview the footage and notice that the can of lager that the man on the left is holding has also been keyed out, I'll show you how to fix this later.

## color key tricks

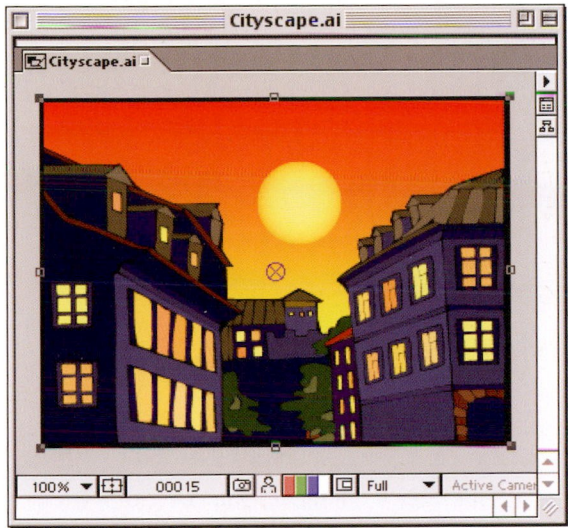

We've seen how the Color Key filter is traditionally used for keying jobs but the focus of this book is on how to use the software *creatively*, so what else can you do with this filter? Well my advice to you is not to dismiss a filter just because it is not particularly good at the job it was designed for; think about what the strengths of this filter are and try to find other ways of using it.

You'll quite often find that a filter has several different uses, take for example the Shift Channels filter. Another great way of using this filter is for creating rich-looking grayscale images. This is achieved by taking each channel's information from the strongest channel in the image, it works much better than merely desaturating an image which can result in a washed out appearance. So, here is another way of using the standard Color Key to good effect. After finishing this chapter, see if you can think of any other ways to use these filters creatively.

**1** Double-click the 02 Color Key Trick Comp to open its Comp window and timeline. This is an image which I have created by customizing an Art Explosion vector file.

**2** Hit the number 1 key on the number pad to select layer one (buildings layer) and go to Effect > Keying > Color Key.

**3** In the Effect Controls window click on the eyedropper and sample the bright yellow color from the center of the sun.

Rather than simply using the Color Key to key out a specific color I will show you how to use it for a simple animation effect. Using only the Color Key we will switch all the lights off and make the sun go down in the town!

**4** Move to frame 15 and set a keyframe for Color Tolerance at zero by clicking on the Stopwatch in the Effect Controls window. Hit the U key on the keyboard to bring up the keyframed property in the Timeline.

**5** Move to frame 201 and change the Color Tolerance value to 125.

**6** Change the edge thin value to 1. If we increased the Color Tolerance any more than this we would begin to lose some of the other colors that we wish to keep. Instead, we've used the Edge Thin control to remove the colored edges by trimming pixels away from the existing Matte.

**7** Put a very slight feather value of 0.4 on there just to soften the edges, this will compensate for the lack of anti-aliasing in the Standard versions keying tools.

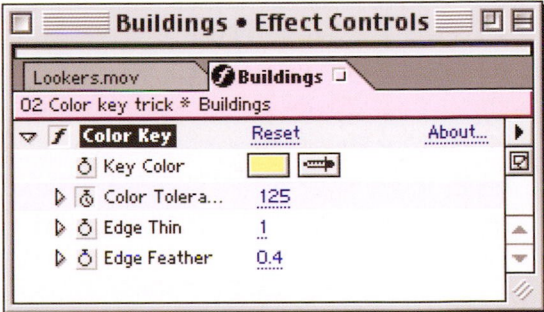

Preview the animation so far. Because the lights at the window are slightly different shades they will switch off at different times depending on the Color Tolerance setting of the key. We'll now use the same technique to create a sunset behind.

**8** Select the Sky layer and then use the J and K keys to jump to frame 15.

**9** Hit Command + Alt + Shift + E to apply the last effect applied, which was the Color Key filter. Because Color Key was the last effect we applied it will also appear at the top of the Effect menu.

**10** Hit Command + Shift + T to make sure your Effect Controls window is showing.

**11** Click on the eyedropper tool and sample the darkest red from the Sky layer.

**12** Change the Edge Feather value to 50 pixels and set a keyframe for that value by clicking on the Edge Feather Stopwatch in the Effect Controls window. Using the same technique set a keyframe for Color Tolerance and then hit the U key to bring up your keyframed properties.

**13** Select the Sun layer and then hit Alt + P to set a keyframe for Position and bring up the property. Follow this by hitting Shift + Alt + S to bring up the Scale properties and set a keyframe for scale.

**14** Hit the K key to jump to the next visible keyframe at frame 201; change color tolerance to 225 and the edge of feather amount to 0.

**15** Whilst still at frame 201, change the Sun's Scale amount to 70% and the position values to 160, 220 to make the sun appear to disappear behind the buildings as the day comes to an end.

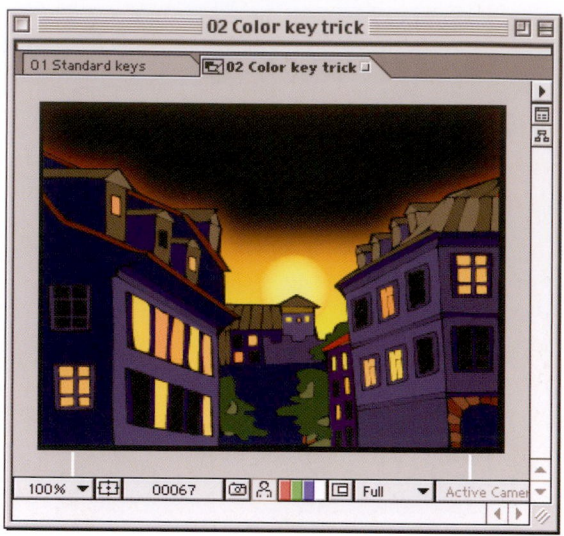

**16** RAM Preview the movie and watch the sun go down and the lights go off in this sleepy little town. If you want to, you can adjust the eases on the keyframes to make the animation a little smoother.

## luma key tricks

The Luma Key works similarly to the Color Key but chooses pixels by their luminance (or brightness); you can choose to key out either the darker shades or the brighter shades.

**1** Open the 03 Luma Key Trick Composition. This is another image that I have taken from the Art Explosion collection and customized for my needs. It is a simple composition, containing a merged Photoshop file. By using the Luma Key filter we will make it appear to contain several different animated elements.

**2** Select the jungle.psd layer and go to Effect > Keying > Luma key.

**3** Change the Key Type drop down menu to Key Out Brighter, the whole image will disappear from view.

The Threshold setting decides on what range of brightness will be worked on. The available luminance values are from 0 to 255. The slider works in opposite directions depending on whether you are keying out darker or lighter shades.

**4** With the Threshold slider at 0, set a keyframe for Threshold at frame 15.

**5** Move to frame 60 and drag the slider all the way up to its maximum value of 255.

**6** Change the Edge Feather value to 1 and RAM Preview your finished movie. The elements in the picture are appearing individually, depending on their luminance values, giving the impression of separate layers being animated.

Nothing fancy but it just shows you how you can set up a very quick and easy animation with a little bit of thought.

*Key Out Similar* or *Dissimilar* are the other alternatives available in the Key Type menu. With these two options you can use the Tolerance slider in conjunction with the threshold slider to determine the range of values you want to work with.

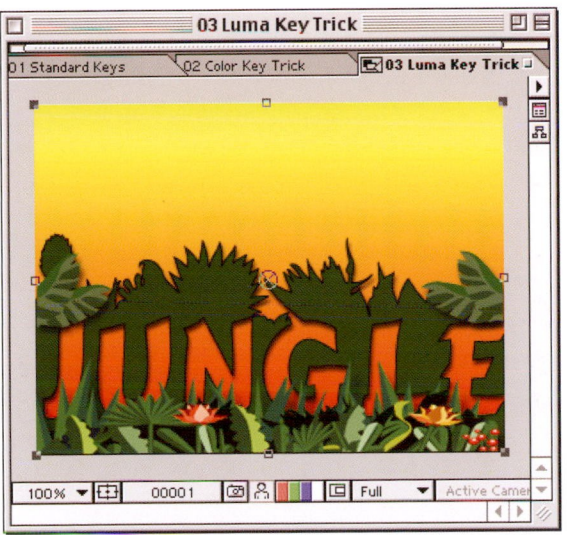

## production bundle keying

First of all I want you to save a copy of your project into the Creative After Effects > Keying Chapter folder as Standardkey.aep.

OK, so now let's take a look at some of the other Keying effects which are available with the Production Bundle version of After Effects. If you are using the Standard version of After Effects you can skip this section and go straight to the next chapter.

### color range

Open the 04 Color Range Key Composition. This is another part of the MacDonna video, from the end of the piece. This section consists of three layers, I wanted to make it look like we were sitting in a nightclub. I couldn't get all of the people that I needed in the shot together at the same time so I had to shoot them separately and then bring them together afterwards. The foreground layer is some sped up footage of me and my friend, BJ. This was shot from a fixed camera (with Holoset ring attached) in my living room against a sheet of Chromatte. This layer has the levels filter applied to it, let's add the Color Range Key to reveal what is behind it.

**1** Context-Click on the top layer and go to Effect > Keying > Color Range. Hit Command + Shift + T to make sure that your Effect Controls window is showing.

The Color Range Keying tool is always a good place to start because it is so versatile. It creates transparency by keying out a user-defined range of colors so is ideal when keying out a multi-colored background or a background that is not evenly lit. As well as working in the RGB color space, it can also work in the Lab or YUV color spaces.

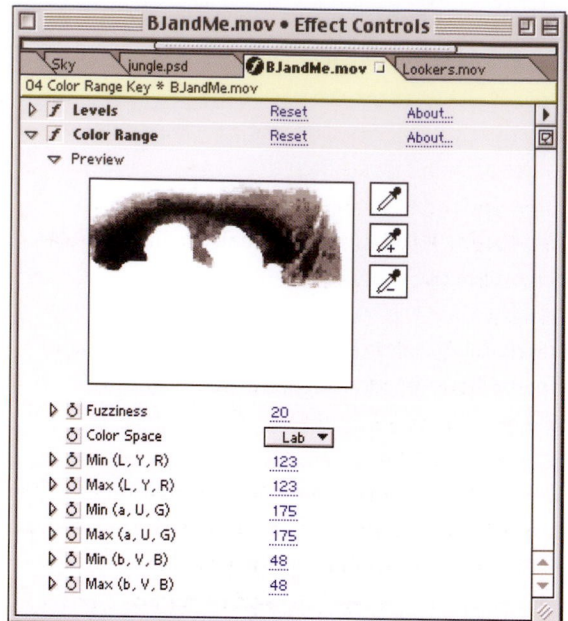

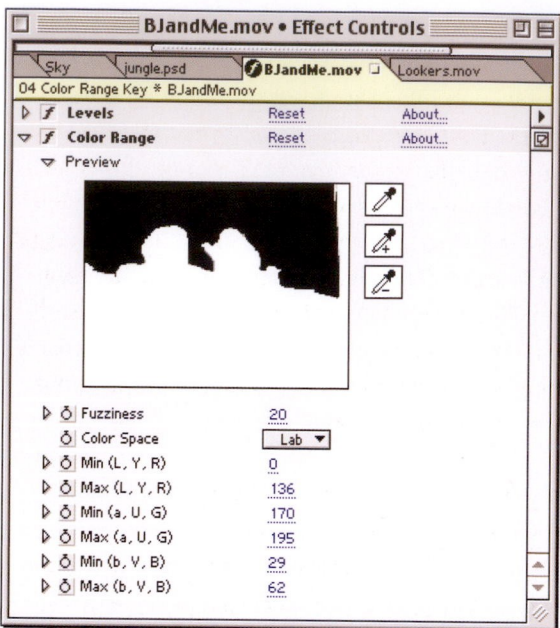

**2** Click on the first Eyedropper tool in the Effect Controls window to select the main color you want to key and then click on the preview pane in the Effect Controls window to select the area where the blue-screen appears.

**3** Once you have selected the main color, click on the next Eyedropper tool which can be used to add more colors to your key.

**4** This time, click and drag the cursor over any other areas you wish to key, as you drag it will remove all the colors that you drag over in the preview pane.

You can then use the sliders below to fine tune the key till you have a nice clean key. Check with the following diagram. All areas that you want to be transparent should be a nice even black, the areas you want to keep should be an even white with no gray areas. Don't worry if there's a slight blue edge on the subject, we can get rid of that with the Simple Choker. This is always the first keying tool that I turn to. It's simple to use and effective in most situations.

## simple choker

When you are keying compressed footage you will quite often get a lot of noise around the edges in your image, for example, where the red couch and the blue background meet. This makes it difficult to get rid of the key colors from these areas, this is where the Matte choker comes in handy!

**1** Context-Click on the layer and go to Effect > Matte Tools > Simple Choker.

**2** The Simple Choker simply removes the edges of your matte by a defined amount of pixels.

**3** Change the Choke Matte value to 3. Notice that you can use the View drop down menu to toggle between your end result and the matte.

**4** There are still slight areas of blue spilling onto our subject, to get rid of these we'll use the Spill Suppressor.

## spill suppressor

The Spill Suppressor is a little life saver, just when you think that you can't get rid of that last bit of blue, it comes to your rescue. It works by removing a specified color from your footage. It works in a very similar way to the Change Color filter which allows you to change a specified color in an image (in fact standard version users can use the Image control > Change Color filter as a substitute for the Spill Suppressor by applying it, choosing the color they wish to remove by Hue and then pulling out the saturation).

**1** Select the Layer and go to Effect > Keying > Spill suppressor. As soon as you apply this filter you will see the blues removed from your image. There is an Eyedropper tool to allow you to specify the exact color you wish to suppress. We don't have to change this as it is almost identical to the color of our background already.

**2** Change the Color Accuracy menu to Best. OK, so we have managed to pull a relatively successful key considering the quality of the footage. Remember this was shot on DVCAM and then compressed with the Cinepak codec.

**3** Use what you've learnt to pull a key on the Lookers layer to reveal the background. Remember that you can copy and paste effects from one layer to another as well as being able to save favorite effects.

Once you have both layers keyed successfully, we'll put some finishing touches onto this composite image.

**4** In the Timeline, select the BJandMe.mov layer and then hit the P key on the keyboard to bring up the Position property.

**5** Scrub on the second Position value (the Y-axis value) till it reads 143.

**6** RAM Preview the movie, notice that the can of lager has also been keyed out as it was blue, I'll show you how to fix this.

## basic vector paint

When you have a hole in your matte you can use the Vector Paint filter to manually paint the hole out of your matte.

**1** Switch off visibility for the BJandME.mov layer and the Dancing.mov layer so that only the Lookers.mov layer is visible.

**2** With the Lookers.mov selected, go to Effect > Paint > Vector Paint. Vector Paint is a new addition to After Effects and has about a million different uses, one of them being to add or remove areas to a matte.

You'll see that some tools appear in the Comp window, we'll take a more careful look at the Vector Paint tools later, for now we'll just use it with its default tools selected.

**3** In the Effect Controls window, change the Composite Paint menu to In Original Alpha Only. At it's default setting, this will tell Vector Paint to add any paint strokes to your existing matte, created by the Color Range Key.

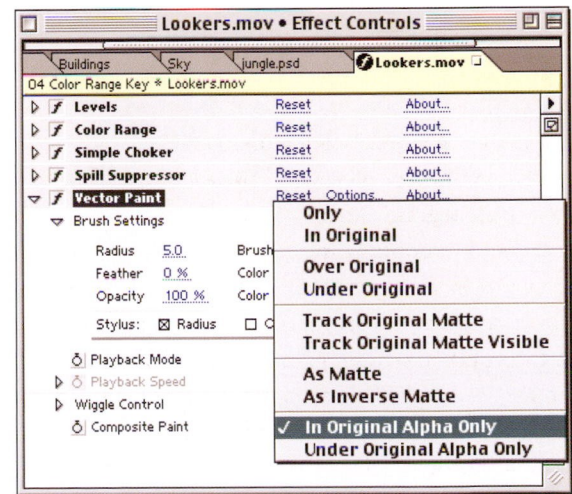

It is very important to keep a couple of things in mind when using Vector Paint;

• Firstly, the effect must be active for it to work, i.e. make sure that the effect is selected in the  Effect Controls window before applying any strokes. When the Effect is active, its name  will be highlighted in the Effect Control Palette.

• If you make a mistake with your strokes, the standard menu Undos will not work to remove them because they are vector based. If you want to undo a stroke at any time you must either hit the Undo button in the Vector Paint interface or select the paint stroke with Vector Paints Selection Tool and then hit backspace to delete it.

**4** With the Vector Paint effect selected in the Effect Controls window, move the cursor over the can of lager and paint over it with the default white paint, use the following diagram as a guide.

**5** When you have finished, RAM Preview the movie, notice that the can disappears in the frame that you painted in but reappears in the rest of the frames.

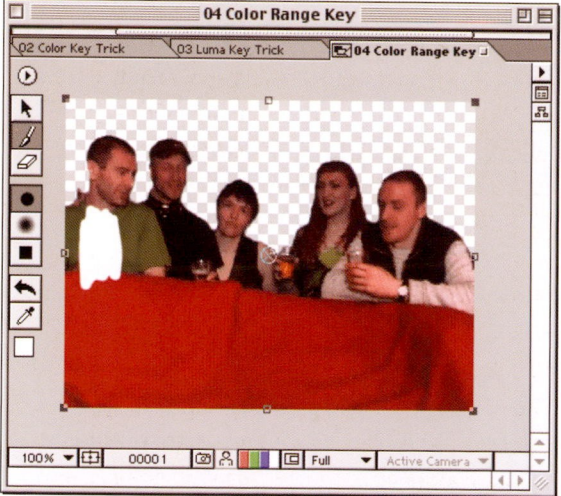

**6** In the Effect Controls window, Change the Playback mode to All Strokes to apply your brush stroke to all frames in your composition.

**7** Switch the other two layers back on and RAM Preview the finished movie.

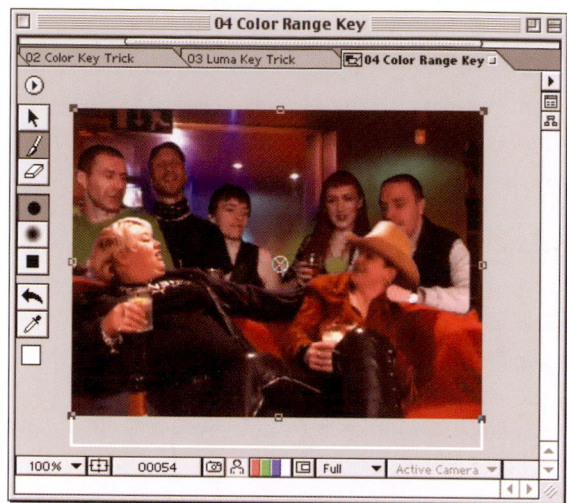

**8** In the next chapter we'll add some more effects to the movie to really bring the whole thing together.

I can't possibly cover all of the keying tools in this book but I just couldn't go without showing you how easy it is to use the formidable Color Difference Key. If you ever need to key out semi transparent materials such as glass, smoke or shadows, then this is the plug-in for you.

**9** Save a copy of this project into your Creative After Effects > Keying Chapter folder as ProBundlekey.aep.

Remember also that you can use several keying tools on top of each other. For example, if you wanted to key out a blue and green background but only had the Standard Color Key filter, you could apply it once to get rid of the blue and then again to get rid of the green.

## color difference key

The Color Difference Key is a very powerful keying tool, particularly in situations where you have to key hair, glass, smoke or any other transparent material. This filter uses old style optical keying to achieve fantastic results. When used with uncompressed footage this keying tool can compete with the best, producing flawless mattes. Unlike the standard bundle's Color Key (and like the Color Range Key), the Color Difference Key anti-alias's the edges of the key, making it appear much smoother on screen. The one set back this filter has is that it is not very intuitive to use, let's have a go at demystifying the Color Difference Key.

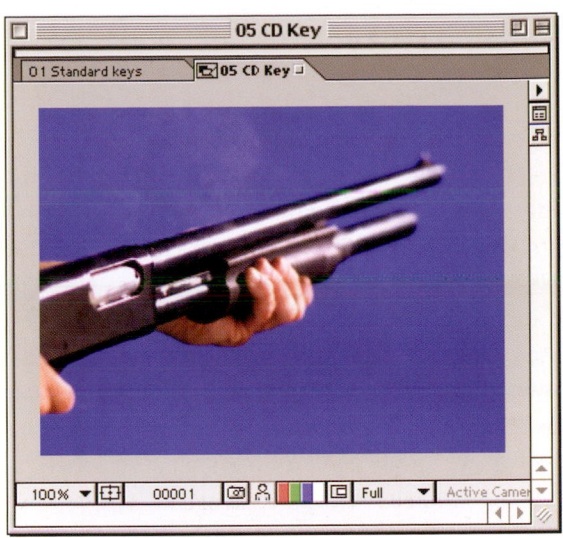

**1** Open the 05 CD Key comp from the Project window and RAM Preview the movie.

This piece of footage is from another one of Artbeats fantastic collections, this one is called Gun Stock and features loads of cool things like bullets being fired into a blue-screen, great for a western movie's opening titles! Check out the Artbeats folders on the CD for more footage like this. OK, we want to key out the background but keep the smoke from the gun.

**2** In the Composition wing menu, make sure that the checkerboard background option is un-checked so that you will be able to see the default background through the key when it's applied.

**3** Hit Command + Shift + B (Composition > Background Color) and change the background color to bright orange, this is the opposite and most contrasting color to our current blue background, this will make it easy to see our key results.

**4** RAM Preview the movie again and notice that the movie is not the best keying source, it has been compressed, using Photo JPEG compression and there is a lot of color spill reflected on to the gun.

I guess that most people reading this book would not have the luxury of using uncompressed footage so, just to show you it can be done and to keep file sizes small, I have also used compressed footage.

Color spill occurs when the color of the background reflects on to the object needing keyed, it is quite difficult to avoid this problem but it can be done with well planned lighting. As you know, there are also ways of removing the spill after keying.

**5** Go to Effect > Keying > Color Difference Key. As soon as you apply this effect you will notice that it works slightly differently from the color key you used earlier, notice how the footage has immediately become semitransparent.

The Color Difference Key works by creating two separate mattes. The first matte is for isolating the background, it determines the transparent areas, by selecting areas *similar* to the background color. The second matte is for isolating the foreground, it determines the transparent areas, by selecting areas *different* from the background color. These two mattes are then brought together to create one, combined, matte.

Having separate control over your background and foreground elements allows you to isolate areas which you want to be semitransparent. Think of it like placing two semitransparent films together, some areas combined would make solid white (opaque), some solid black (transparent) and others would be gray areas between the two (semitransparent). This is yet another instance where you will see the significance of understanding how grayscale images work.

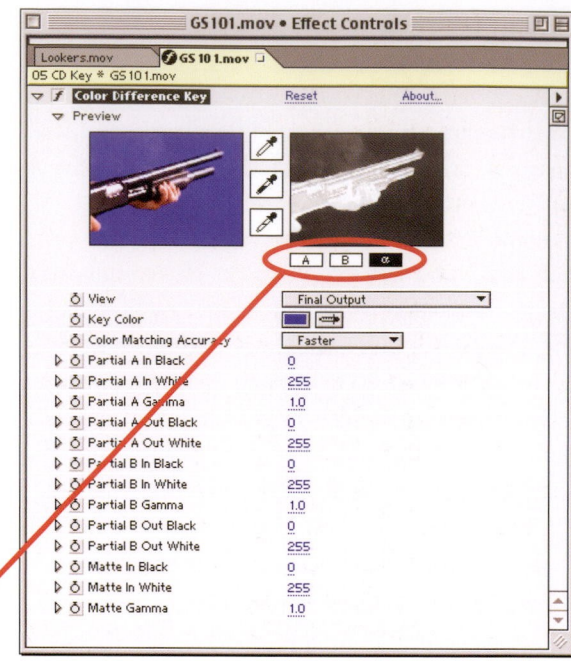

**6** Expand the Effect Controls window so that you can see everything clearly. Notice that there are two preview Windows, one showing the Source image the other showing the selected matte .

Notice the three buttons under the Matte Preview Window (on the right-hand side of the Effect Controls window); A, B and Alpha. By clicking on these buttons you can look at the three separate mattes.

- Partial matte A shows the foreground matte
- Partial matte B shows the background matte
- The combined Matte shows the final alpha channel combining the two A and B mattes.

**7** Look at all three mattes individually by clicking the buttons under the matte preview window. Notice that some areas of the gun will be solid in both partial mattes whilst areas of the smoke are only visible in the foreground matte.

Everyone has a different technique when using this very powerful keying tool. I tend to work on the partial mattes individually before working on the combined matte as this seems to provide me with more subtlety of control, this is just a matter of personal preference.

**8** Select the top Eyedropper tool between the two preview windows and then click to sample the blue background from the left hand Source Preview Window. Doing this determines the key color, you can also do the same job by using the Eyedropper tool next to the Key color swatch.

**9** Select the A matte by clicking on the A button and then click on the middle Eyedropper tool. This tool determines which areas of your image you wish to be black (transparent).

**10** Click once on the blue background at the bottom of the source preview window. Notice that as you click, the *Partial A In Black* value (further down the Effect Controls window) changes. It should now read about 70.

The Eyedropper tool is a good way of quickly sampling the colors. The sliders do exactly the same job but give you more precise control, we will use the sliders to adjust the white values.

**11** Select the B matte and repeat the same process, clicking on the blue background. Remember we want the background to be completely transparent in both partial mattes.

**12** Click on the alpha button to view the partial mattes combined, notice that the gun and hand remain semitransparent (represented by the gray areas). When you look in the Composition window you can see a hint of orange showing through the gun and hand. To make the gun and hand more solid we need to increase the White values in both of the Partial Mattes.

**13** In the Effect Controls window you will see the View drop down menu which now reads *Final Output*. Change this to *[A,B, Matte] Corrected, Final* so that you can preview all three mattes and the final result of your keying in the main Composition window.

**14** Go to the *Partial A In White* value and scrub it till it reads 200. (Remember to hold down the Command key when you scrub for more precision.) Notice the White values increasing in the main Composition window, making the smoke from the gun more visible.

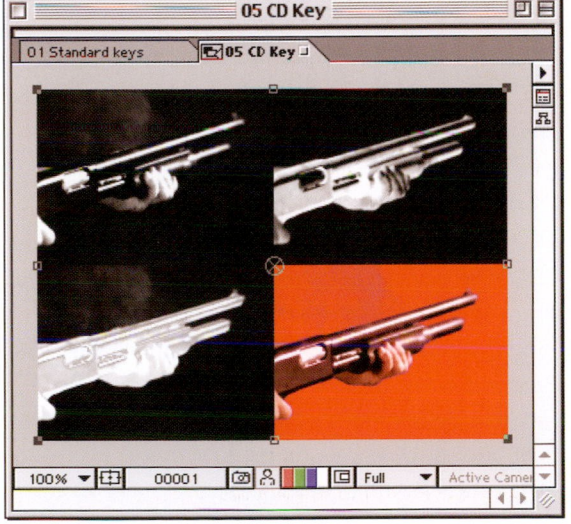

**15** Change the View Menu to *Matte Partial B Corrected*.

**16** Go to the *Partial B in White* value, scrub the value till it reads 200, again notice the increase in White values.

**17** From the view menu choose to view *Final Output*. By making two slight adjustments we have obtained a reasonably good key from this compressed footage. There is still, however a slight, orange tinge to the gun.

**18** Change the view menu to *Matte Corrected* so that you can see the combined Alpha Matte displayed in the Composition window. It is clear to see that there are still gray areas within the gun, remember that any gray areas will be semitransparent, they need to be 100% white to be 100% opaque.

**19** Go to the *Matte In White* value and scrub it to about 195 so that the gun and hand are completely white.

**20** Change your View back to *Final Output* to look at the results, notice that there is still a blue tinge to the smoke and the edges of the matte.

**21** With the layer still selected, go to Effect > Keying > Spill Suppressor, as soon as you apply this effect, the Spill suppressor works by removing the default blue from the image.

**22** The effect uses blue as a default but make sure that you are removing exactly the same shade of blue by clicking on the Color to Suppress Eyedropper and sampling the actual blue from the Color Difference Key's Preview window.

**23** Drag the Suppression slider down to about 80%, we don't want to remove all the blue from the image, the gun steel would naturally have a slight amount of blue in it.

**24** In the project window, open the Footage folder and select the file named, LM113.mov (from Artbeats Life-styles Mixed Cuts collection).

**25** With the Current-Time Marker at the beginning of the comp and then drag the layer onto the Timeline till it's underneath the GS101.mov and then release it.

**26** RAM Preview the composition to see the results. Notice that we have managed to key out the background but still keep the smoke from the gun, amazing!

Notice that there is still a bit of an edge left on the matte. If it weren't for the smoke I could use the Matte Choker to get rid of the dark edge from the matte. However, using the Matte Choker would remove the smoke from the shot. Instead I will use the Bevel Alpha filter to clean up the edge of this matte.

There are third party plug-ins, such as Pinnacle's Puffin Composite Wizzard, Light Wrap, which can sample multiple colors from a background and reflect them onto your Matte to make the keyed image fit in with its new background. I'm afraid we don't have access to that plug-in so we'll use one of my cheat techniques, good old Bevel Alpha! It's not quite as sophisticated but is a good way of achieving similar results.

**27** With the GS101.mov layer selected go to Effect > Perspective > Bevel Alpha. Notice that its default setting actually makes the edge of the matte look worse, but don't despair. We need to change the light angle so that it reflects on the edge we want to get rid of.

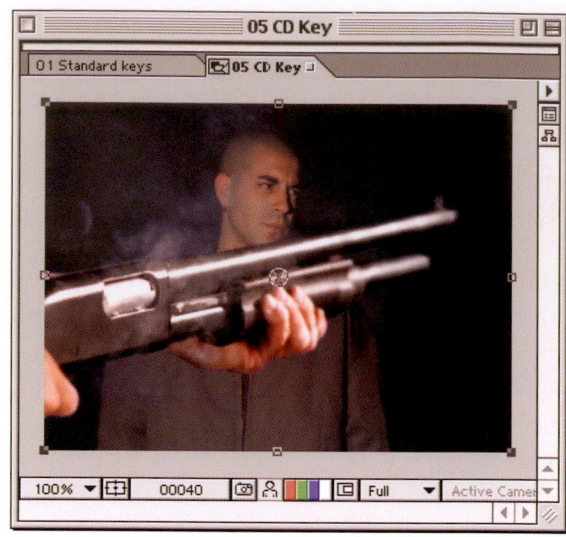

**28** Change the light angle to -90 degrees.

**29** In the Effect Controls window, click on the Eyedropper tool and then sample the color from the gangster's coat to reflect some of the background color on to the edge of your matte. You can do this with any piece of footage you wish to place behind you matte.

**30** Click on the color Swatch and just darken down the color a little. RAM Preview your movie.

So, from a poor keying source, which has been pretty heavily compressed, you can achieve a quite sophisticated level of keying. Imagine the results when working with uncompressed SDI input!!

## recap

OK, so you know all about keying now but did you know that you can also create some pretty nice color treatments by combining multiple copies of a layer using the keying tools and the layer Blending modes. Use some of the free footage on the CD to try out a few ideas before moving onto the next chapter. First of all, save this project into your Creative After Effects > Keying Chapter folder as ProBundlekey.aep

# chapter eleven
# effects

It's taken some time to get to the chapter that I'm sure a lot of you have been itching to get to, the one covering effects! When I teach my two-day 'basics' course on After Effects I always concentrate on teaching everything else first. The reason for this is because you need to have a good, solid understanding about how the software functions before you can make the most of the effects available to you. The other reason is that the effects menu is naturally what most people head straight for when they open up After Effects so I find that most users tend to get to know this menu pretty well without a lot of persuasion.

Obviously I am limited to what I can cover in the pages of this book and there is no way on earth that I could hope to cover every effect available in the Standard and Production Bundle versions of After Effects. So, rather than cover all of the effects sketchily, I decided to cover just a selection of them in a bit more detail. The Adobe After Effects user manual and Online Help system cover what I haven't been able do here. We'll continue to use other effects throughout the remainder of the book, you can also check on the CD for other effect based tutorials.

We'll start by going back to The Graffiti Club project to take it a bit further.

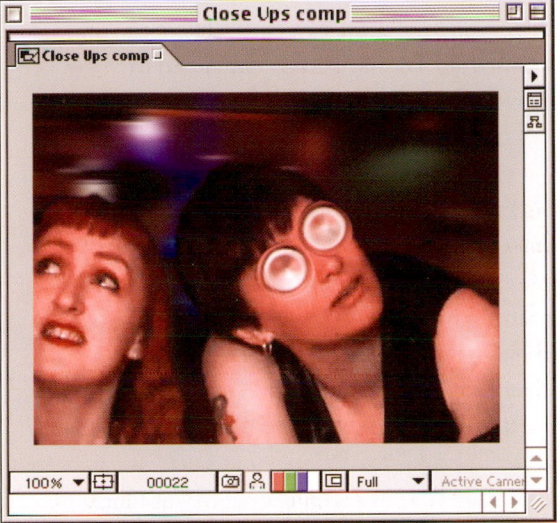

## graffiti club
### color treatment using layer modes

**1** Open Graffiti02PB.aep from Training > Projects > Chapter 11. This was created using the Production Bundle version of After Effects but can be opened with both versions as no Production Bundle filters have been used on it.

**2** RAM Preview the Composition to remind yourself what you have already done in this project. So far, all we have here is a fast moving background consisting of various graffiti images.

This is going to form the background for our main character animation. The imagery and movement is exciting and lively, just as we wanted, but it is too multi-colored and distracting to use for a background. Currently, the images change from one frame to another, there is no common thread such as a color theme to pull them together. We need to introduce an element of design which remains constant throughout, the most obvious and effective element is color. By putting a color treatment over the footage we can bring it all together, making it less visually jarring yet still retaining the same excitement.

Sometimes the best way to apply a color treatment effect to your footage is by not using plug-in effects but by using other layers. Remember that the more filters you use, the slower your comp will become. I always like to encourage my students to first think of ways of achieving certain results without the use of plug-in effects; it's good exercise for the brain and it encourages them to find new ways of working.

The easiest way to bring some structure into the composition and to colorize the image underneath is to superimpose a single layer with some simple, colored, geometric shapes over the animation. This will pull the whole thing together.

**3** Import the file named Thick_stripes.psd from the Training > Source Images > Angie Images folder.

**4** Drag the file into the Background Sequence Composition as its top layer.

**5** Click on the Switches/ Modes panel button to bring up the Modes panel and choose Hard Light from the Layer Mode menu.

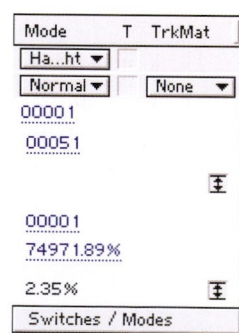

The images will now be composited together, the colors and shapes help to make the background less obtrusive. Dividing the screen into three parts like this will make it appear bigger and take away some of the emphasis from the animated imagery. Using the layer and Layer Modes to colorize the background saves us from having to apply effects to get a similar result.

## RAM Previewing options

Before moving ahead to the effects I want to show you a couple of ways of speeding up your workflow, very important things to know if you are planning to use a lot of effects in your compositions. First of all, make sure that you have as much RAM allocated to After Effects as possible. If you are unsure about how to do this, see the instructions for allocating RAM to applications in your system software's manual or online help system.

**1** RAM Preview your composition. If you find that you don't have enough RAM to preview the whole project, there are a few things you can do to help.

**2** Open up the Time Controls Palette if it is not already open.

**3** Click on the Time controls Palette wing menu and choose *Show RAM Preview Options* from the pull out menu. Doing this will open up some extra options for RAM Previewing your footage.

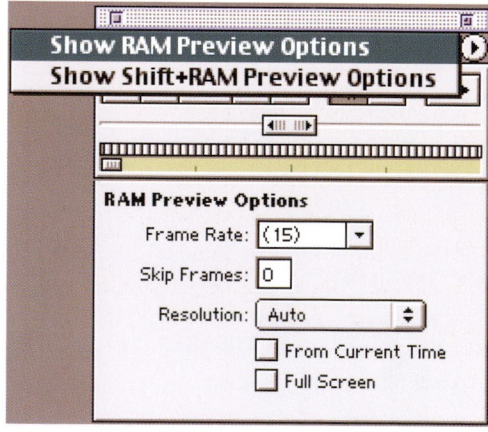

**4** RAM Preview your composition again and watch the display in the RAM Preview palette. You'll notice that After Effects is rendering all 750 frames of your composition. When it plays the frames back to you, it will attempt to play them back at the same rate as your composition, i.e. in real time.

The Frame Rate box tells you how many frames the RAM Preview will attempt to play for every second of your composition.

**5** Highlight the Frame Rate Value and change it to 7.5, which is half the frame rate of your composition. RAM Preview the comp again, you'll notice that After Effects still renders the same amount of frames but will play those frames back at half the speed, taking twice as long to render all of the frames. The images and the audio will play back to you in slow-motion.

**6** Click on the Frame Rate drop down menu and change the Frame Rate back to Auto. This setting will use the current composition's frame rate.

We will leave our RAM Preview at the default setting but will change our Shift + RAM Preview settings. The Shift RAM Preview options allow you to create a new set of preferences for previewing the footage with the Shift key held down. At the default setting, holding down the Shift key whilst activating a RAM Preview will render every second frame of your composition.

By being able to customize these options individually, we have two choices available for the type of RAM Preview we want to use in a given situation. I like to leave the RAM Preview settings at default (rendering every frame in real time) but it's also very handy to use my Shift + RAM Preview for quicker, dirtier previews!

**7** In the Time Controls palette, click on the Wing Menu again and choose *Show Shift + RAM Preview options*. As you can see, we have the same options available as with the RAM Preview options.

**8** Hold down the Shift key and then hit the 0 key on the number pad to activate a Shift + RAM Preview. In the Time Controls palette, notice that After Effects is only loading 375 frames into RAM.

With the *Skip Frame* setting at the default value of 1 After Effects will render the first frame and then skip one frame in between all the others, i.e. it will render every second frame.

**9** Change this setting to 14 and then hold down Shift whilst hitting the 0 key on the keypad to do another Shift + RAM Preview.

**10** If you look in the Time Controls palette whilst the preview plays back you'll notice that After Effects is now playing a total of 50 frames, i.e.. one frame for every second of the composition. It is still playing the footage back to you at the correct speed, it is simply missing out 14 frames out of every 15 frames of your comp.

**11** Change the Skip Frames setting back to 1.

**12** Change the Resolution drop down menu to half, this will drop the pixel resolution making it quicker to process the frames. After Effects will also be able to load twice as many frames into RAM at half resolution.

**13** Click once on the words *Shift + RAM Preview Options* to jump back to the *RAM Preview Options* and change the Skip Frames setting to 14 and then RAM Preview your whole composition once more.

## proxies

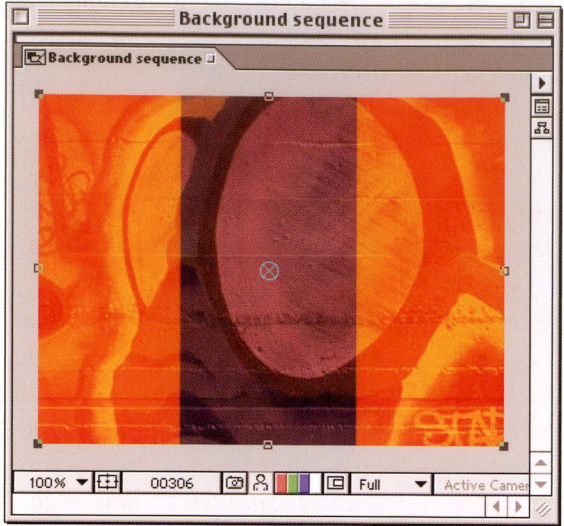

For now, we have finished working on the background. We don't want After Effects to be rendering all of the work we have done up to this point every time we make a change. So, at this point in a project, it's a good idea to render the elements that you know are unlikely to change. One solution would be to render out a movie and replace the layers with the movie but this would make it awkward if you did decide to go back and change anything in the original composition. This is the sort of situation where I prefer to use proxies.

Proxies can be used to substitute any layer or composition in your project. They can be smaller versions, or low resolution versions of your footage (handy when working with very high resolution files) or they can be rendered movies or stills replacing complicated compositions. The purpose of using a proxy is to reduce the amount of processing time needed to preview or render your image. Think of it like a temporary substitute for the original file.

We will use the RAM Preview that we have already built as a proxy for the composition.

**1** Go to Composition > Save RAM Preview.

**2** The *Output Movie To* dialog box will appear, save the file to your Creative After Effects > Effects Chapter folder as Background Sequence RAM.mov and then click OK.

The Render Queue window will now appear and After Effects will render the preview from the RAM directly to your hard disk. Remember that this movie will be rendered using the same settings as you have in your RAM Preview Options.

**3** Once the RAM movie has rendered, close the Render Queue window.

**4** In the Project window, select the Background Sequence Composition.

**5** Go to File > Set Proxy > File or hit Command + Alt + P.

**6** Locate the Background Sequence RAM.mov that you saved into your Creative After Effects > Effects Chapter folder and double-click it to select it as the proxy file for your composition.

You'll now see a black square next to the composition in the Project window, indicating that a proxy is being used in place of the original file. You'll also see that the Background Sequence RAM.mov is now in the Project window, making it easy for you to access it.

**7** Toggle the proxy on and off by clicking the black square on and off, you will notice very little difference between the composition and the proxy whilst the footage is static. Finish with the proxy switched on.

**8** In the Time Controls Palette, change the Skip Frames setting back to 0 and then RAM Preview the composition again.

Notice that it is now much faster to load a full RAM Preview of your composition. When it plays back, you'll see that it is showing only one frame for every second of your composition.

## hue/saturation

Once you have chosen a Proxy file for your layer or composition, you can still make changes to the original, the proxy will remain unchanged but the original layer will update to reflect the changes.

**1** Context-click the Thick-stripes.psd layer in the Timeline and go to Effect > Adjust > Hue Saturation.

**2** In the Effect Controls window, change the Master Hue angle to –90˚. Nothing will appear to change in the Composition window, this is because we are looking at a frame from the proxy file.

**3** In the Project window, click on the black square next to the Background Sequence Composition to switch off the proxy and see the changes to your original layer.

**4** RAM Preview the movie with the new effect applied.

**5** When you have finished looking at the changes you have made, click on the Hue/Saturation name in the Effect Controls window and hit Backspace on your keyboard to delete the effect.

**6** Switch the Proxy back on in the Project window and then save your project to the Creative After Effects > Effects Chapter folder as Graffiti02b.aep. Save over any older version if necessary.

In this case the benefits that we get from using a proxy are minimal but just imagine how much time they can save you when working on more complex, multilayered, effects-laden comps. The fact that they can be turned on and off so easily makes them extremely versatile. The only thing that you must look out for is that you don't forget that your proxy is being used. Many of us have sat in frustration after applying an effect to a layer and not seeing any change, only to realize that a proxy was being used! (Doh!) I have even found myself superimposing another layer (with the word PROXY in big letters), over my composition before rendering it, just to remind myself.

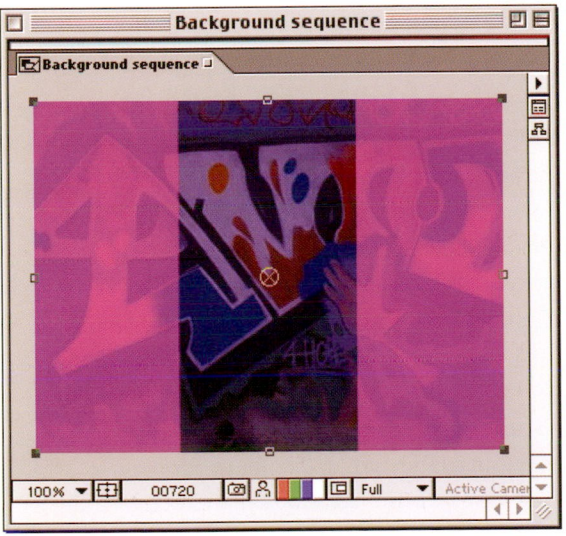

# seattle evening news

OK, let's go back to our Seattle Evening News project. Last time we worked on this was in the Masks chapter where we created a new composition to place over our main edit, let's remind ourselves where we left it.

**1** Open SeattleNews03.aep from the Training > Projects > Chapter 11 folder on your desktop.

**2** RAM Preview the Edit.ppj Composition to remind yourself of the contents of this comp.

We have the same problem here as we did with the Graffiti Club project. The edits are in the right place, we have created some nice, animated, geometric shapes composited over the edit. We now need to use a color treatment on this to bring it all together. This time we will use a plug-in filter to colorize the footage.

## colorama

OK, so we need to give the sequence a uniform color treatment to bring it all together. The easiest way to do this is by using Adjustment layers. Remember, effects applied to Adjustment layers will affect every layer beneath the Adjustment layer so not only will our Masks comp layer be affected by the effect but also all the layers underneath it.

**1** With the Current-Time Marker at the beginning of your comp, Go to Layer > New Adjustment Layer.

**2** Context-Click on the new Adjustment layer and go to Effect > Image Control > Colorama.

Colorama is a great tool. However, like many other filters, I think it is let down by it's default presets. Just look at the following diagram to see what I mean, ouch!

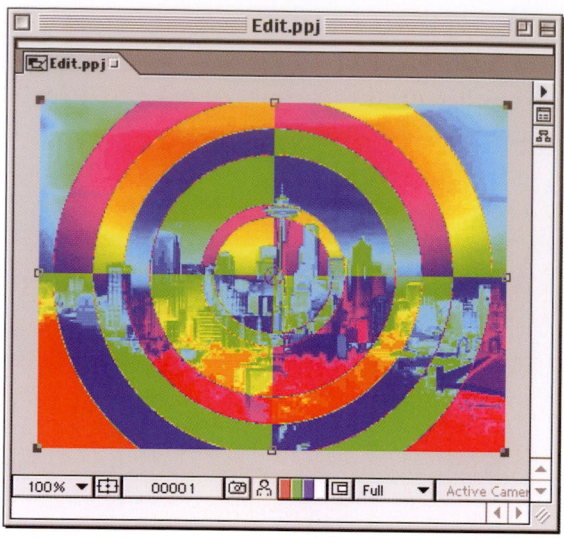

Anyone looking at this for the first time would recoil in horror at the nasty, bright, gaudy colors that greet you when applying the default setting. Don't let this fool you, it is an extremely powerful and useful image control filter and it works by mapping the selected colors that you choose in your Output Cycle onto a grayscale version of the element you choose to affect. The default setting will apply the colors to the whole layer but you can also choose to apply the changes to single channels or other image elements such as Hue, Lightness etc. You can even take these elements from another layer in your comp by using the Input Phase settings.

Colorama was designed and developed by Brian Maffit and the Atomic Power Corporation as a tool for creating Color Cycling animations. You may have seen this type of animation in the 1970s episodes of Top of The Pops or in 70s music videos. You will also be familiar with color cycling if you were, like me, a user of Deluxe Paint. Basically, you choose a range of colors with which to map onto a cycle. You can then animate the cycle so that the colors loop over and over, building as they go. It can be used as a quick and easy way to make animated fire effects.

**3** Open up the Output Cycle settings and you will see a rainbow-colored wheel, this is your Output Cycle, where you can choose the colors you want to make up your image.

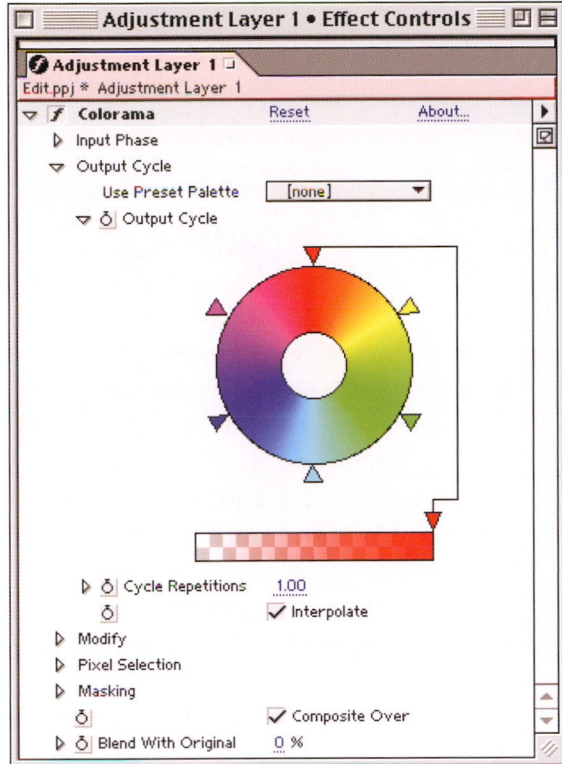

The Output Cycle works similarly to other color wheels, the colors are positioned around the wheel and they interpolate gradually from one to another. Colorama converts your image to a grayscale image and then remaps the Dark areas in your image with the top color selected on the Output Cycle. It then maps all the other shades of gray evenly around the rest of the color wheel, in a clockwise direction, till it reaches pure white, which is back at the top again.

**4** Click on the Preset Palette drop down menu and you will see that there is a list of ready-made presets for you to choose from. These will help you to understand how this plug-in works.

**5** Choose Ramp Green from the Preset palette drop down menu.

This colorama Cycle has only two selected colors, black and green. The two Color Triangles are positioned practically in the same place at the top of the wheel so it appears that there is only one. But the black Color Triangle is actually hiding behind the green one.

**6** Double-click on the green Color Triangle to bring up the Color Picker. Whatever color you choose here will be the color that all the lightest values in your image will be mapped to.

**7** Choose a bright, orange color.
(R = 100%; G = 60%; B = 5%)

**8** Double-click on the very right-hand side of the Color Triangle to bring up the Color Picker for the black color triangle. This is where you will choose the color you wish to map the dark areas of your image to. This is currently set to pure black. Try changing it to a deep, dark brown, almost black but not quite.
(R = 16%; G = 0%; B = 0%)

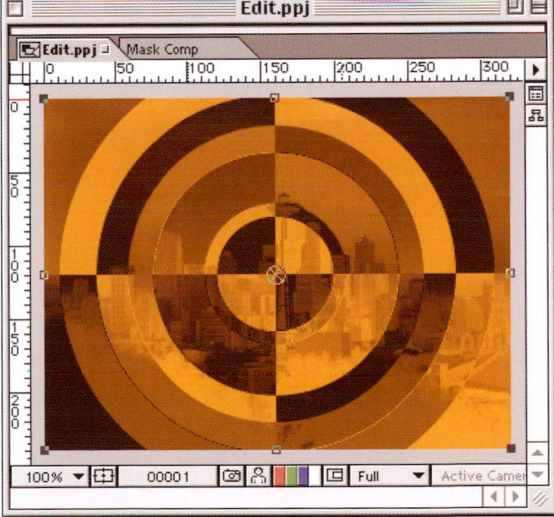

You should be able to see what is happening to your image now. All of the dark areas are now dark brown, all the light areas are bright orange and all the areas in between are interpolated to various shades in between the two colors.

**9** Give your image a more posterized look by un-checking the Interpolate checkbox underneath the Output Cycle. With this unchecked, Colorama jumps from one color to the other rather than changing gradually. This will make it clearer to see what is happening as we go through the next few steps. This posterized effect works really well with bold close-ups of faces. You can experiment with this a bit more at the end of this chapter.

You can add up to 64 new Color Triangles simply by clicking anywhere around the Cycle and choosing a new color.

**10** Position the cursor at the edge of the cycle at about the 3 o'clock position and click once, doing this will bring up the Color Picker. Choose a Deep but bright red (R = 45%; G = 0%; B = 0%) and then hit Enter to leave the Color Picker box.

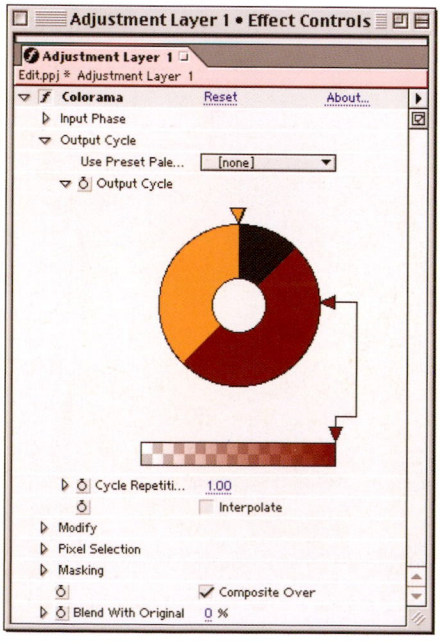

You can also move the Color Triangles easily by dragging them. As with most of the controls in After Effects, holding down the Shift key whilst dragging will constrain the movement to pre-defined increments. In this case it will constrain the movements to increments of 45°.

**11** Click and drag the orange Color Triangle from the 12 o'clock position to the 6 o'clock position. Hold down Shift as you drag to constrain the movement, allowing it to snap into place at the 180° mark.

**12** Double-click the orange Color Triangle to open up the Color Picker again. Change the color to a slightly deeper orange (R = 90%; G = 40%; B = 0%). Click OK to leave the Color Picker box.

You will notice underneath the Output Cycle is a strip. This is the Opacity slider for your colors. Notice that this also has a Color Triangle which is connected to the active Output Cycle Color Triangle by a black line.

**13** Try dragging the opacity triangle all the way to the left to see how it affects the selected color. Notice that the color decreases in opacity as it is dragged to the left. This will allow the original pixels to show through. By placing the triangle half way along the slider you will be blending the original pixels with the new color by 50%. It's nice to be able to adjust the opacity of the colors individually, this feature can even be used for pulling successful keys on footage but we'll leave that for another time!

**14** Once you have finished experimenting with this, drag the slider all the way back to the right again to put the opacity back to 100%.

**15** Click again on the 9 o'clock position of the Output Cycle and this time choose a paler orange from the Color Picker.
(R = 100%; G = 75%; B = 20%)

**16** Click to the left of the top, black Color Triangle (at about five to 12). This time, choose a pale cream color (R = 100%; G = 95%; B = 80%). Click OK to leave the Color Picker.

**17** Hold down the Shift key and drag the new Color Triangle to the right till it snaps against the Black one.

It is clear to see what is happening now. Each color has an equal slice of the pie. Because the lightest and darkest colors are overlapping, they share a segment of pie. This means that there will be half the amount of these colors in the final image, compared to the other three colors which will have an equal distribution in the final image. I find that it helps to set up the color cycle with interpolation switched off so that you can see the distribution of the colors more clearly.

**18** Check the Interpolate checkbox again to blend the colors together gradually.

After Effects gives you the ability to save your own custom Favorite Effects. If you followed the Keying chapter you will already have used this feature. When you've set up an effect or series of effects that you like, and may want to use in a future project, you can save all of the effect settings, including any keyframes as a Favorite Effect. This is a great way to work because the Favorite Effects are very small files which can be easily emailed to other AE workstations and can be applied across platforms. In this case we'll save the Colorama settings that we customized as a Favorite Effect. There are no keyframes in this instance but it is still useful to build up a load of custom settings for your favorite plug-ins.

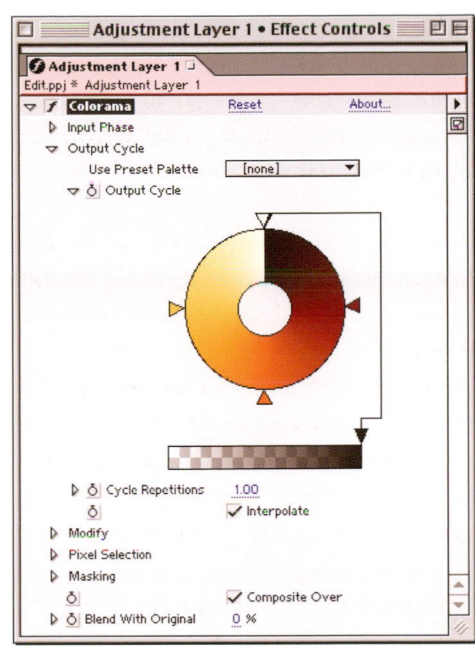

Select the Colorama effect by clicking on its name in the Effect Controls window and then go to Effect > Save Favorite. You can use this Favorite Effect later on another sequence of footage.

**19** Go to File > Save as and, in the Save as dialog box, navigate to your Creative After Effects > Effects Chapter folder on the desktop and save the favorite Effect into there as BurntColorama.ffx.

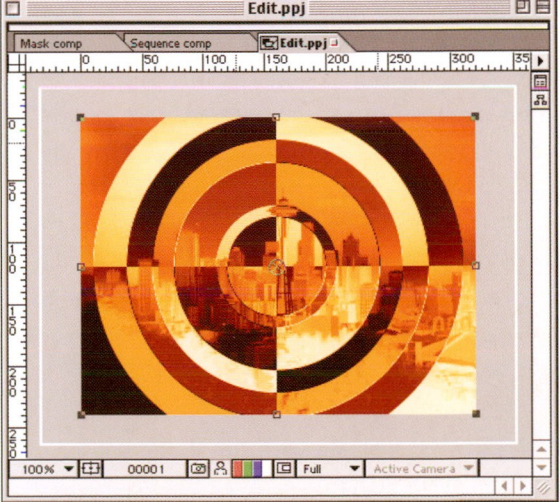

**20** Once you are back inside your After Effects project, go to File > Save As and save your project to your Creative After Effects > Effects Chapter folder as SeattleNews04b.aep.

There are various ways of adjusting the Output Cycle once you have built it:

• Move the color triangles around the Cycle to change the balance of color.
• Command-drag any of the Color Triangles to duplicate them, allowing you to create bigger blocks of color.
• Delete Color Triangles by simply dragging them off the sides of the Palette.
• Create more triangles using the techniques we used in the previous lesson.
• Use the Input phase settings to convert only to a selected channel of your image into grayscale before applying the effect such as Hue, Lightness etc.
• Use the Modify settings to choose only to affect one channel of the final output.

**21** Experiment with some of these techniques on your own project or on a new piece of footage before moving onto the next exercise.

There are also several animatable properties in the Colorama filter. Once you feel comfortable with the parameters, then you can start to experiment by animating their properties. If you need more information on how this filter works, check out the After Effects User Manual, Online Help and the website for tips, tricks and tutorials.

Another of my favorite color control plug-ins at the moment is Color Theory from Toolfarm. It's a digital color wheel which uses formulas based on the RYB color model, which designers have been using for years to work out harmonious color schemes. Check out the demo version in CD > Demos > Toolfarm. OK, back to the MacDonna video.

# MacDonna video

Let's go back to our MacDonna project. If you remember, the last thing we did with this was to play around with some keying effects but cast your mind back to the Time chapter, remember we played around with the timing of our clips to make me dance in time with the music? Well, we're going to work some more on those sections with some more of the After Effects plug-in filters. There are two versions of the Project we are about to work on, each uses it's own keying tools.

**PB** If you have the Production bundle of After Effects then open up MacDonna2PB.aep from the Training > Projects > Chapter 11 folder.

**SV** If you have the Standard version then open up MacDonna2Standard.aep from the Training > Projects > Chapter 11 folder.

**1** RAM Preview the Finished Time Remap composition.

I have provided two versions of the project as I did not want to exclude anyone from the next exercise, however I have to say that I am not as happy with the results of the Standard version. The Production bundle version of this project will look cleaner than the Standard version simply because the keying tools in the Production bundle are far superior. I really recommend upgrading to the Production Bundle version if you want to do a lot of keying. There are also some very good third party plug-in keying tools available such as Pinnacle's Primatte Keyer and the ubiquitous Ultimatte.

We need to work on the background and the foreground of this movie to make it more visually appealing. At the moment the colors are a bit dull and the keyed footage of me dancing looks a little 'cut out' from the rest of the shot. Let's start with the foreground layer.

## echo

The Echo filter is another one of my favorites, it is one of the Time filters and is available in both Standard and Production Bundle versions of After Effects. It creates a visual echo effect by taking information from other frames at either side of the current frame to create the same sort of effect you can get by shooting moving footage with slow shutter speed on your camera. Anything that is moving in your footage will create motion trails as it moves, you can adjust the settings to control how much of this effect you want. It's the sort of effect that is often seen in music videos, it creates a dream-like effect.

**1** Select the MeDance.mov layer and go to Effect > Time > Echo.

The first thing you will notice is that the Echo filter overrides all other filters and mattes, to overcome this problem, you must pre-compose your layer to compound the existing effects.

**2** Hit Command + Z to undo your last step and then, with the layer selected, go to Layer > Pre-compose (Command + Shift + C).

**3** In the pre-compose dialog box, Name the new comp, Dance Pre-comp, select *Move all Attributes into the New Composition*, this will move the layer (along with all of the effects currently applied to it) into a new composition, which will be nested within the Finished Time Remap Comp.

**4** Check the *Open New Composition* checkbox to tell After Effects to open the new comps tab in the Timeline and then click OK to leave the Pre-compose dialog box.

Now that the layer plus all the effects have been pre-composed, you can treat it just like any other movie layer.

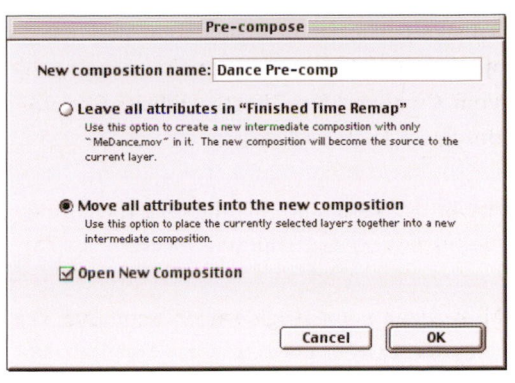

**5** Context-Click on the Dance Comp layer and go to Effect > Echo. Notice that now, the Echo effect no longer overrides the other filters but that nothing appears to have changed in the Comp window. This is because the Echo filters default setting takes information from the previous frames to create the echo. Because there are no previous frames before the first frame, it has nothing to sample from.

**6** Change the echo time setting to 1 and notice that an echo has appeared. Because we have entered a setting of 1, After Effects is taking the echo from the frame 1 second ahead from where we currently are, i.e. Frame 15.

**7** Change the *Number of Echoes* value to 3, we now have three Echoes on our layer, each one will be one second in advance from the last.

**8** RAM Preview the comp to see how this looks. It's a bit too over the top, we can hardly see what is happening.

**9** Change the Echo time value to 0.03 to take the echoes from frames nearer the current frame and RAM Preview the comp again.

We now have a quite nice effect, our movie is creating an echo of itself ahead of the current time. You'll also notice that the image appears to be much brighter, that is because the Echo filter is using an *Add* Echo operator (the same as the Add Layer Mode) to blend the echoes together. The Add operator tends to lighten images.

**SV** If you are using the Standard version of this project, the image may just be a little too bright, you can reduce the brightness by bringing the Decay value down to about 0.5 or 0.6.

**10** RAM Preview the comp to see the results.

OK, I like the effect but I am not happy with the edges of the echoes. We'll use another effect to remedy this problem.

### channel blur

**1** Context-Click on the layer and go to Effect > Blur & Sharpen > Channel Blur.

This filter is designed to blur a single channel of your image, any of the color channels or the alpha channel can be blurred individually using this filter.

**2** In the Effect Controls window, change the Alpha Blurriness value to 15, this will blur the edge of the layers alpha channel, in turn, softening the edges of the echoes.

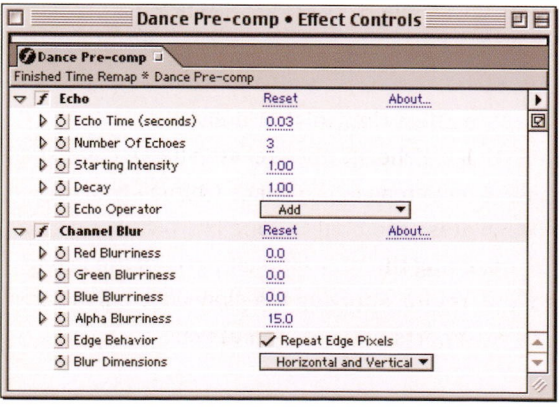

**3** Finally, notice that the bottom edge of the layer is also blurred, which is an undesired effect. Check the *Repeat Edge Pixels Checkbox* to get rid of the blurred edge.

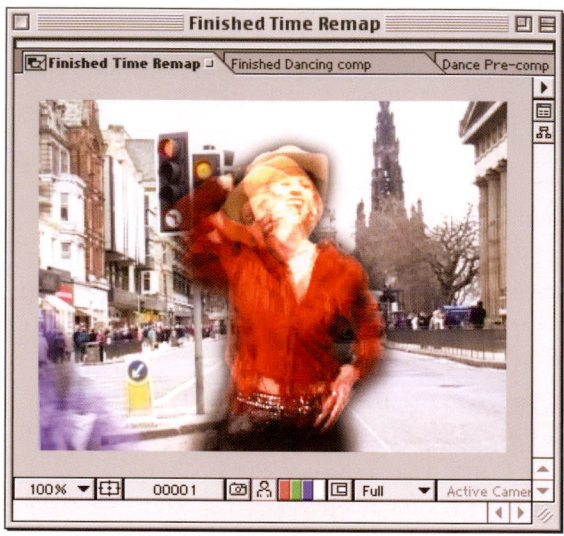

**4** RAM Preview the movie to see the finished result.

**SV** If you are using the Standard version of this project go to Effect > Channel > Remove Color Matting. Click on the *Background color* swatch and choose a bright blue to remove the remaining slight blue edge from the figure before we go on to work on the background layer.

**5** Select the PrincesSt.mov layer and hit Command + D to duplicate the layer, for the effects we are about to use we will need two copies of the same layer.

I'm going to show you two ways of achieving very similar effects, one using the Standard version and another using the Production Bundle filters. In many situations it is possible to achieve the same results with the Standard version as with the Production Bundle, it just takes a little bit more time and imagination. We'll start by using the Pro Bundle filters, I'll then show you how to get a similar effect using only the Standard version.

## production bundle glow

You will only be able to follow this section if you
have the Production bundle of After Effects. If you
are a Standard version user, go directly to the next
section, 'Standard version glow'.

**1** Select the top PrincesSt.mov layer and go to Effect
> Stylize > Glow.

This filter will add a diffuse glow to certain parts of
your image. These areas can be defined by first
selecting the channel that you wish to apply the
glow to (colors or alpha) and then adjusting the
threshold to determine what percentage of area you
wish to apply it to.

Notice that the glow is applied to the brightest parts
of your image, it is accentuating the highlights. This
effect is a bit too much when applied directly to a
layer in this way but what you can do is use a matte
to select the areas you wish to apply it to.

### set matte

**2** Context-Click on the layer and go to Effect >
Channel > Set Matte.

The Set Matte filter allows you to make a matte for
your layer from a wide choice of layer properties,
you can even take the matte from a different layer
altogether.

Effects are applied in the order which they appear
in the Effect Controls window (and, simultaneously
in the Timeline). We want to create the matte first
and then apply the glow only to the areas defined
by the matte. For this reason, the Set Matte filter
needs to be applied before the Glow filter.

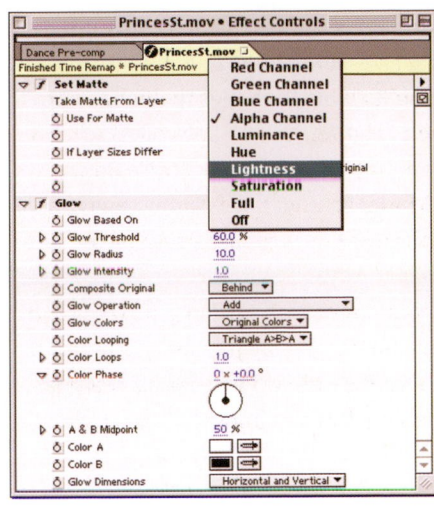

**3** To change the order in which the effects are
applied, simply select the Set Matte effect in the
Effect Controls window (by clicking on its name)
and drag it up, so that it becomes the first effect
listed in the Palette.

**4** Click on the *Use For Matte* menu and choose
Lightness from the list of possible choices. Notice
the choice of other properties available.

**5** To clearly see what effect this is having on your
layer, switch off visibility for the layer beneath it,
layer number 3 and then turn on the Checkerboard Background in the Comp window by
selecting it in the Composition window's
Wing menu.

You'll notice that the image has been made
partially transparent.

**6** In the Effect Controls window, click on the
Invert Matte checkbox to reverse the matte so that
the lightest areas of the image become transparent. What is essentially happening now is that we
are removing the very lightest parts of the image
and, therefore, applying the glow filter only to the
brightest parts of the darker areas.

**7** Switch layer number 3's visibility back on so that you can see the layers composited together. Now we can adjust the glow values to get the effect we desire.

**8** Scrub the Intensity slider up to about 7, notice what effect this is having on your layer. This will do exactly as it says, it will increase or decrease the intensity of the glow.

**9** Scrub the threshold value to determine how much of the area will have the glow applied to it. I find a setting of about 75% works quite well in this instance.

**SV** If you wish to try this technique using the Standard version of this project, the image may just be a little too bright, you can reduce the brightness by bringing the Decay value down to about 0.5 or 0.6.

**10** Finally, change layer number 2's Layer Mode to Hard Light to create a stronger image. The hard light mode tends to increase the contrast in your images, darkening shadows and lightening highlights; it's like shining a bright light on your image to improve its clarity.

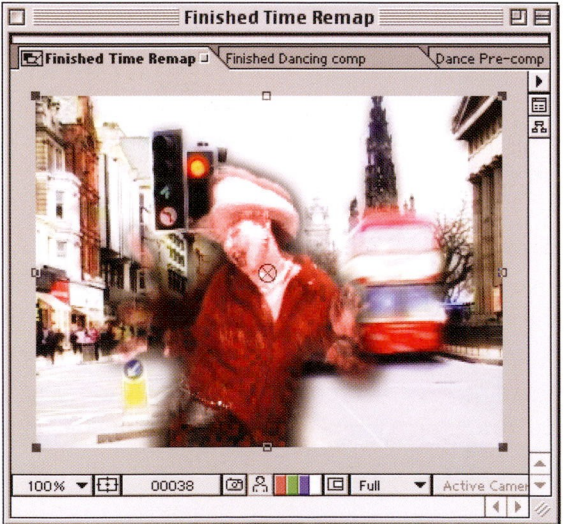

OK, now let's take a look at how you can achieve very similar results using the Standard version.

### standard version glow

**1** Open the finished Dancing Comp so that its Timeline and Comp window are visible and then RAM Preview the composition.

Remember that we re-timed the dancing so that it happened in time with the music? In this exercise we'll add a similar effect to the one used in the Production Bundle Glow exercise, using only Standard version filters. In the Expressions chapter we'll also animate the effect to make it look like the lights are flashing away in the nightclub.

**2** Select the Dancing.mov layer and then hit Command +D to duplicate the layer. Again, we need two versions of our layer to have complete control over this effect. I have already applied a levels filter to the footage to brighten it up a bit.

**3** With the top layer selected, go to Effect > Channel > Set Matte.

**4** Hit Command + Shift + T to bring up the Effect Controls window and choose *Lightness* from the *Use For Matte* drop down menu.

**5** Switch off visibility for the layer below to see the results from this filter. The lighter areas of the image have been made transparent.

**6** Check the Invert Matte button so that it only works on the darker areas of the picture.

**7** Go to Effect > Image Control > Color Balance (HLS). This Image Control filter is for the color correction of images. It allows you to adjust the Hue Lightness and Saturation individually for your layer.

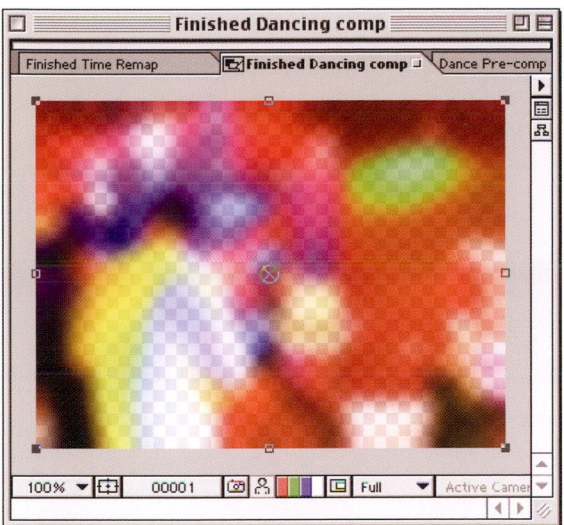

**8** Change the Saturation value to its maximum of 100%. You will notice that there are now some nasty edges where the saturation is making the colors separate, don't worry, we'll get rid of these.

**9** Context-Click on the Layer and go to Effect > Blur & Sharpen > Fast Blur. There are several types of blur available in After Effects, I like this one because it's fast and creates a reasonably good quality blur. For top quality blurs, Gaussian Blur is the best filter to use but it is very slow to render. Try out some of the other blur filters before moving ahead.

My favorite third party blur filter is the Foundry's Tinderbox Blur, it is an incredibly fast Gaussian blur and is of superior quality. It doesn't slow down, even when you increase the radius size. It's amazing. You can find out more about this filter from the Foundry folder in the CD > Software Demos folder.

**10** Click on the Repeat Edge Pixels button to stop the blur affecting the edges of the layer. Your image should now look like the one in the diagram above.

**11** Switch visibility back on for the second Dancing.mov layer.

**12** Change the Layer mode for the top layer to Hard Light, this will bring back some of the contrast to the image.

RAM Preview the finished movie. By using a combination of effects we can achieve very similar results to the Production Bundles Glow filter, just a little more time for experimentation is needed in order to find a way to make it work.

## distortion effects

We're going to take a look at one more part of the MacDonna video in this chapter and that's the end of the sequence where the on-lookers' faces become distorted. There are several distortion effects available in After Effects, let's take a look at some of them.

### split layers

**1** Open Close Ups comp from the project window and RAM Preview the comp. This section of footage fits in at the end of the MacDonna video. The comp consists of two layers, the background layer which is another copy of the Dancing.mov with Levels and Fast Blur applied to it.

**2** Select the Dancing.mov layer and hit the E key on the keyboard to bring up the Effects in the Timeline. Have a look at the settings that have been applied. The levels filter has been used to darken down the image and I've applied a Horizontal Fast Blur to the image to make it seem more distant from the foreground.

**3** Select the CloseUps.mov layer and Hit Command + Shift + T to bring up its Effect Controls window. This has also had some filters applied to it, levels to brighten it up and the Standard color Key tools we used in the Keying chapter.

First of all, we're going to split this movie into parts so that we can apply effects individually to the different sections.

**1** Select the CloseUps.mov layer by hitting the 1 key on your number pad.

**2** Hit Command + G, type in 14 and then Enter to go to Frame 14, this is where the next shot begins.

**3** Hit Command + Shift + D to split the layer at this point in time.

**4** Hit the 2 key on your number pad to select layer 2 and then go to frame 29.

**5** Hit Command + Shift + D again to split the layer.

**6** Repeat the process once more to split the layer again at frame 44. We now have four separate sections of footage to work on.

**7** Switch all of the layers onto Draft quality to speed up your workflow before moving onto the next step.

## standard version

### spherize

We'll start by looking at the Spherize filter. If you have used Photoshop, you'll probably have used the Spherize filter there. The main difference with its equivalent in After Effects is that this one (like most filters) is animatable over time.

**1** Select the top layer in your comp and hit the O key on your keyboard to jump to the Out-point for that layer.

I want to distort the faces to make them look a bit weird and 'trippy'. This is an effect that is quite commonly used in music videos.

There are several ways of doing this. We'll start by looking at the Standard version distortion filters and then we'll take a look at what the Production Bundle has to offer.

**2** With layer 1 selected, go to Effect > Distort > Spherize. Make sure that you can see the Effect Controls in the Effect Controls window, close up any other effects by clicking on the disclosure triangle next to the Effect Name.

**3** In the Composition window you will notice that a little crosshair has appeared in the center of the Comp window, this defines the center of the Sphere effect. You can click on this and drag this control point around directly in the Comp window.

**4** Click and drag the crosshair to position it over the mouth of the person on the left of the screen, notice that the Center of Sphere value in the Effect Controls window changes simultaneously to inform you of the new position value.

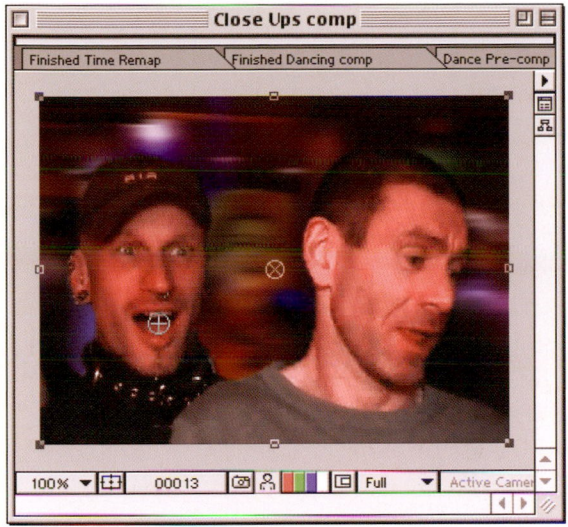

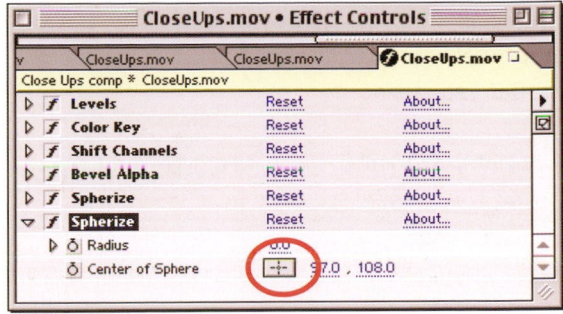

Notice that if you de-select the effect in the Effect Controls window that this crosshair disappears. Any control points or other interface elements associated with an effect are only visible in the Comp window when the effect is actively selected. I've seen this catch a few users out so always remember to make your effects active before adjusting them, just to be sure. Make sure that the effect is active before moving ahead.

**5** Set a keyframe for Radius by clicking on the Radius Stopwatch in the Effect Controls window before moving on to the next step.

**6** Go to Effect > Spherize again. The Spherize effect should be listed at the top of the Effect Controls window now as it was the last effect used.

**7** In the Effect Controls window, click once on the Center of Sphere button. As you do, a cross will appear in the Composition window, move the cursor over the Comp window and position the cross over one of the guys eyes, click the mouse button/ pen to change the center point to this new position.

**8** Hit Command + Shift + Alt + E to apply the last-applied effect to the layer again, now you should have three instances of the Spherize effect applied to the one layer.

**9** Your previewing may be slowing down now so click on the Wireframe Interactions button in the Timeline. This will prevent the Comp window from trying to update every time you move the Current-Time Marker. Instead it will use Wireframe representations of your layer till you release the mouse button when it will redraw the screen at the current display settings.

**10** Remember that you can also drop the resolution menu down to half if things get unbearably slow (as they tend to do when working with multiple effects!).

**11** Click on the Radius Stopwatches to create keyframes for the other two copies of the Spherize effect and then hit the U key on the keyboard to bring up keyframed properties for the selected layer. You should have three keyframes on the layer.

**12** Change the value for the first Spherize Radius value (the mouth) to 50 and the other two Radius values to 30 each.

**13** Hit the I key to jump to the In-point of the layer and change all three Radius values to 0.

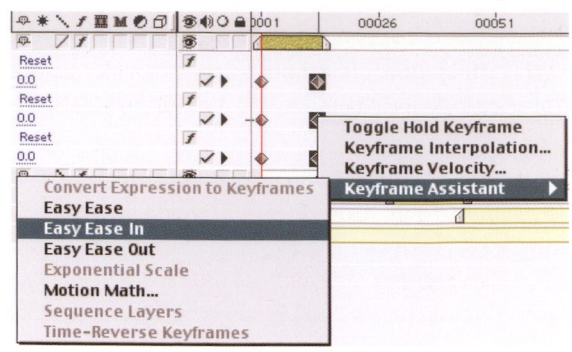

**14** Click and drag a Marquee selection around the last three keyframes and then Context-Click on any of them and go to Keyframe Assistant > Easy Ease In.

**15** Hit the K key followed by the N key to firstly, jump to the out-point of the layer, and secondly, to set that point as the end of you work area.

**16** Switch the layer onto best quality and make sure that you are viewing your comp at full resolution before RAM Previewing the comp so far.

OK, we've got a nice bit of distortion happening there to make the face look more like a weird caricature. Let's do something equally horrible to my other friends!

## smear

**1** Hit the 4 key on the number pad to select layer number 4 and then hit the I key to jump to its In-point.

**2** Go to Effect > Distort > Smear to apply the Smear effect to your layer.

The smear effect allows you to define an area, using the mask tools and then move and distort the pixels within the mask. You can change the rotation, scale and position offset of the pixels within the defined area, smearing the pixels to create the distortions.

**3** Select the Oval Mask Tool (Q) in the Tool Palette and then Double-click on it to create a default oval mask, the size of your comp.

**4** Hit Command + T or go to Layer > Mask > Free Transform Points to place the Free Transform bounding box around your mask.

**5** Place the cursor over the left, middle handle until the cursor changes to a double-headed arrow and then drag the mask handle in to scale the mask down. Repeat this with the handle on the right of the mask, bringing it in till it looks like the one pictured below.

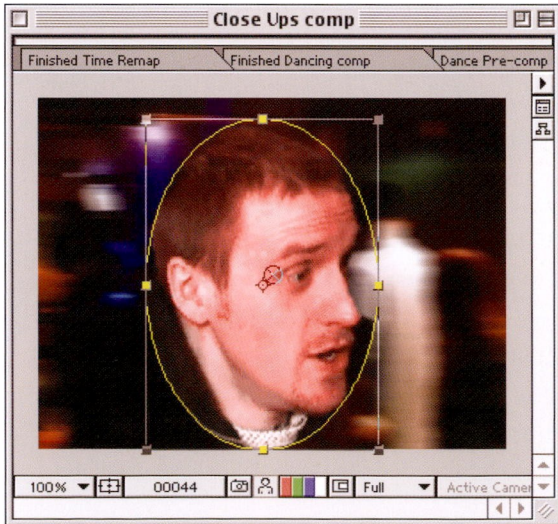

**6** Hit the return key on your keyboard to accept the changes.

**7** Hit the M key on your keyboard to bring up the Mask Shape property and change the Mask Mode to None. We do not want to use the mask to create a matte, we only need the path information for this effect.

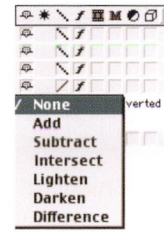

**8** De-select the Mask by clicking on the gray pasteboard in the Comp window or by clicking in the gray area, behind the Mask Name in the Timeline.

This mask will define the area of pixels that we want to distort.

**9** Make sure that the layer is still selected and then select the Rectangle Mask Tool from the Tool palette and then double-click it to create a new Rectangular mask the size of your comp.

**10** This will be the boundary mask for this effect. No pixels from outside this boundary will be affected by the distortion of the effect.

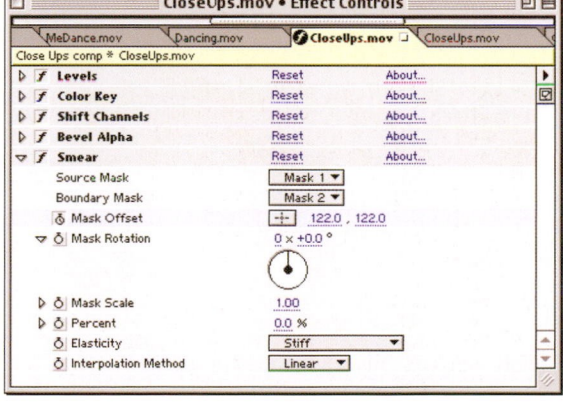

**11** Change the second masks Mask Mode to None. In the Effect Controls window, choose Mask 1 as the Source Mask and Mask 2 as the Boundary Mask.

**12** Click on the Mask Offset stopwatch to set a keyframe for this value. We are going to move his head backwards and forwards in a cartoon-like way as he looks on in horror.

**13** Move the Current-Time Marker to frame 54 and then, back in the Effect Controls window, click on the first Mask Offset Value and change it to 140. Whilst you're there, click on the Stopwatch for the *Percent* value to create a keyframe.

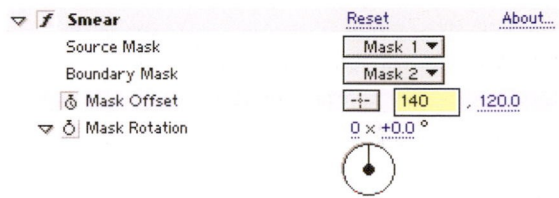

Notice that nothing has changed in your comp, this is because the Percentage value for the effect is set to 0, this value controls the amount of change.

**14** Change the Percent value to 100% and watch as your image distorts.

OK, we are going to do some keyframing now to get the sort of 'boing' movement that we want.

**15** Make the layer active in the Timeline and then hit the U key to bring up your keyframed property. You should already have two keyframes for the Mask Offset.

**16** Move ahead by two frames by hitting the down arrow key on your keyboard twice. Alternatively, use the Frame forward and Frame backward buttons in the Time Controls Palette.

**17** Select the first keyframe and hit Command + G to copy it to the clipboard. Hit Command + V to paste it into the position of the Current-Time Marker.

**18** Move two frames ahead again and then copy and paste the second keyframe into this position. Repeat this process, always copying and pasting the *penultimate (last but one)* keyframe till you reach frame 76.

**19** Bring your work area in around this movie and RAM Preview the comp. His head is moving quickly from side to side, there's one last step to improve this. Earlier we set a keyframe for the Percent value, by bringing this value down over time we can make the movement gradually diminish over time.

**20** Make sure the Current-Time Marker is on frame 76 and then, in the Effect Controls window, bring the Percent value down to 0%.

**21** Finally, select all the keyframes by clicking on the words *Mask Offset* in the Timeline and then Command-click on them to turn them into Auto Bezier keyframes, giving us a smoother interpolation throughout the keyframes.

RAM Preview the finished movie. There is so much more you can do with this filter, I only really have the space to give you tasters of what's available to you. It's up to you to go and experiment with these filters and push them to their limits. Let's take a look at a couple of the Production Bundles Distortion effects. If you are a Standard Version user you can simply read through the following section to get an idea of what's available in the Production bundle version. You can then continue with the next section. If you want to, you can save your project into your Creative After effects > Effects Chapter folder as MacDonna03b.aep.

## production bundle

### bulge

The Production Bundle has some great distortion effects, I only wish I had more space so that I could cover them all in detail. Remember to keep checking the website for new exercises which cover some of the features I haven't been able to cover in the book.

**1** Select layer 2 and hit the I key to jump to its In-point.

**2** Go to Effect > Distort > Bulge. The bulge filter is similar to the Spherize filter but has a lot more control to offer. It also has a bulge Center control point which can be tracked onto a moving image. Which I'll show you how to do in the next chapter.

When the effect is active you can see a circle with four corner handles and a center point, these allow you to interactively adjust the size and position of the bulge.

**3** Click on the center point of the effect and drag it so that it sits over the girl's eye to the right of the picture. Drag the corner handles to resize it so that it looks like the one pictured below.

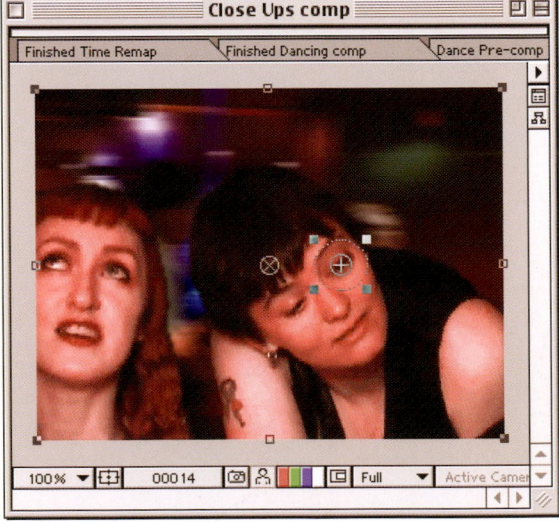

**4** In the Effect Controls window, check the Horizontal and Vertical Radius sizes, they should both be set to about 20.

**5** Change the bulge height setting to its maximum of 4 to create an eye that looks like a fly's eye.

**6** Select the effect in the Effect Controls window and then hit Command + D to duplicate it.

**7** Now, in the Comp window, simply drag the center point of the active effect on to the second eye.

**8** Hit Command + Alt + B to set the work area to your selected layer.

**9** RAM Preview the movie. The girl's head moves during the shot so the effect does not follow the eyes. In the next chapter, I'll show you how to track these effects onto the girl's eyes.

## mesh warp

Now we'll have a look at Mesh Warp. This filter places a mesh over the image which you can then push and pull around to distort the image underneath.

**1** Select layer 3 and then hit the I key to jump to it's In-point and then go to Effect > Distort > Mesh Warp. As soon as you apply the effect you'll see a mesh appear over the layer.

**2** In the Effect Controls window, change the Rows setting to 11, this will adjust the number of rows in the mesh whilst keeping the columns the same size.

**3** Click on the Stopwatch for Grid Values to set a keyframe in the timeline for that value, hit the U key to bring up the value.

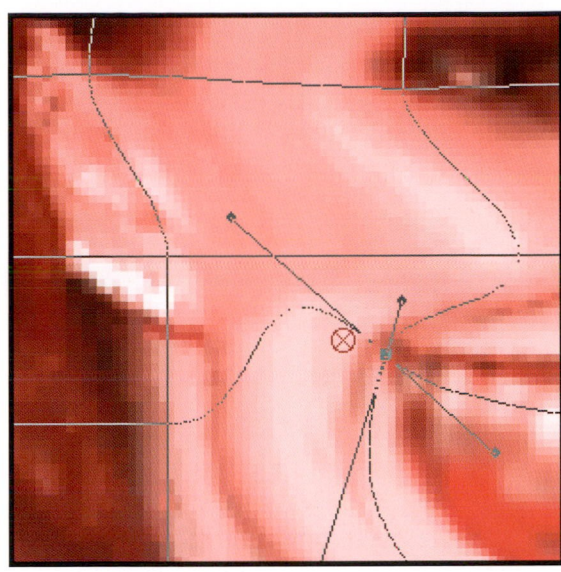

**4** It's much easier to get hold of the points if you zoom into the comp about 400%. You can also drop the resolution of your comp down to about one quarter if necessary.

**5** With the effect selected click once on a point to activate it and then click and drag it to its new location.

**6** After a second or so, the screen will update to show you the distortions on your image, it's like mapping your image onto a rubber sheet and then pulling it around.

**7** You can drag either the center of each point or any of the handles which protrude from the center of each point, these behave in a similar way to the Bezier handles for masks, creating curved shapes between points.

**8** Take time to adjust the mesh till you have a cartoony-looking face like the one in the following diagram.

**9** Move to the Out-point of your layer and then hit the Mesh Warp effect's Reset button in the Effect Controls window to reset the grid to its default setting, the mesh will now animate from our start point back to normal.

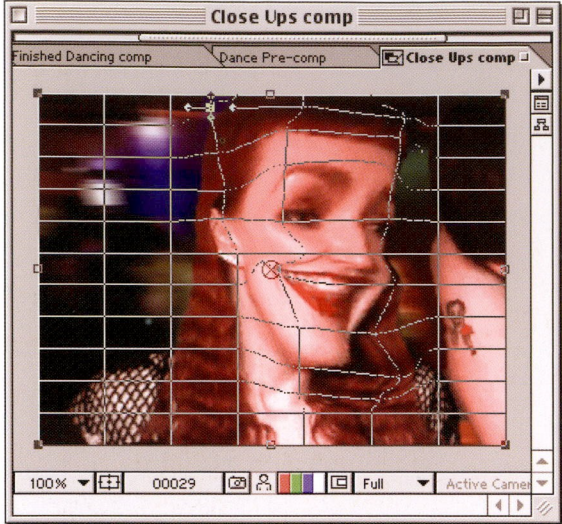

**10** RAM Preview your comp to see the end result. You can continue to play around with these distortion effects but first, please save your project in to your Creative After Effects > Effects chapter folder as MacDonna03b.aep, replacing any existing files.

Well, that is only a very small taster of what is available in the effects menu. Remember, though, that we will be using other effects throughout the book, there are also some extra tutorials in the extras folder on the CD so check in there. I will also be posting tutorials up to the website every now and then so keep checking for new tutorials on: http://www.angie.abel.co.uk

## recap

I want you to take some time to experiment with what you have learned in this chapter. Either start a new project or open the project that you have been working on from the start and experiment with some of the plug-ins in the Effect menu. Remember what you have learned here:

- You can customize effects to get new looks, try not to always use them at their default settings.
- Don't use plug-ins solely for their original intended purpose, bend them a bit to see what else they'll do for you, it's possible to happen upon some interesting combinations.
- Sometimes you need to use a combination of different plug-ins to achieve a look.
- By mixing new combinations of effects together you can come up with so many more creative possibilities, they're endless.
- The order in which you apply effects is very important but the order of effects can be changed at any time.
- There are times when you need to apply effects to nested comps, this compounds any changes made to the original layer and treats it as a new movie.
- Use RAM Previews for Proxies, or drop Resolution when things become slow.

## free plug-ins

In the Free Stuff folder on the CD, you will find some third party plug-ins, donated by some of the best plug-in companies around. These are given to you as a gift from the plug-in companies and mostly consist of single filters from their plug-in collections, please make sure that you install them and experiment with them.

There are also demo versions of some of the complete plug-in collections in the Demos folder, some of these are fully functioning for 30 days, others will be disabled in some way. Please install these to experiment with, they're great fun to play with and it's important that you know what's available in terms of third party plug-ins.

Also contained within these folders are documents containing information about the plug-in companies and instructions on how to install and use these plug-ins. Go on, have some play time, you deserve it!

# chapter twelve
# tracking

After Effects Production Bundle includes very powerful image tracking and stabilizing tools. I felt that it was important to cover these tools, despite the fact that Standard version users would not be able to follow the exercises in this chapter. I still recommend that Standard version users read this chapter as it is useful to understand how this feature works in order for you to decide whether the Production Bundle is something which it would be worthwhile upgrading to for your needs.

We'll start by looking at the Motion Stabilizing tools. These are very easy to use. The first After Effects job that I got, involved stabilizing some footage which had been shot from a moving boat, as you can imagine, the camera work was less than steady. I had never used the Stabilizing tools before but agreed to take on the challenge. Luckily for me the tools fixed the shot in one take on their default settings, we were left with a lovely still shot with no camera wobble to be seen.

## motion stabilizing

The Motion Stabilizer is a powerful tool which is most commonly used to smooth out unwanted motion from footage shot with a hand-held or vehicle-mounted camera. The Motion Stabilizer works by offsetting your layer's position and/or rotation to compensate for the movement of a specified anchor point.

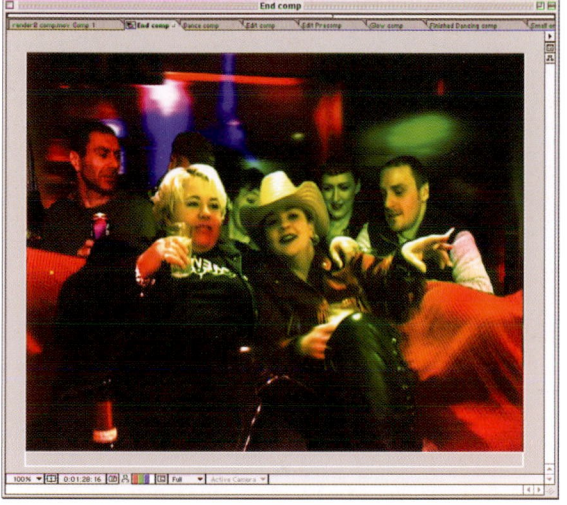

The footage is then finished off by either scaling down the composition, scaling the layer or keying to mask off unwanted areas; we'll take a look at these options later. As you should know by now, there is always more than one use for each of the tools in After Effects, and the Stabilizer is no different. I'm going to show you another use for the Motion Stabilizer, to center a moving object.

**1** Open the Birdtrack.aep project from Training > Projects > Chapter 12 and import the file named BR104.mov from the Training > Source Movies > Artbeats folder. This is one of Artbeats Birds Collection (www.artbeats.com).

**2** Create a new composition by dragging BR104.mov onto the New Composition button in the project window.

**3** Double-click the layer to open up its layer window, this is where you can access the tracking and stabilizing controls.

**4** Click on the Layer windows wing menu and choose Tracker/Stabilizer Controls from the pull out menu.

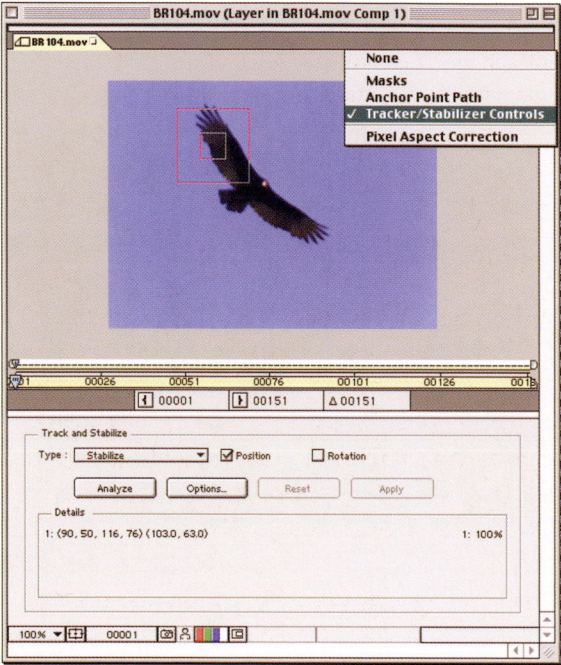

The Motion Stabilizer dialogue box should now open up. You will see a preview of your layer and a Timeline, where you can set in and out the points for the sections you wish to stabilize. You will also see two boxes superimposed over the footage, the inner box is the Feature Region box, this defines the object or part of object you wish to track. It's best to choose an area which contrasts well with the rest of the footage or an area that is brightly colored.

The larger box is the Search Region box, this box defines the area in which After Effects will search for the defined feature region in the following frame. The search region needs to be big enough to accommodate the biggest change in position of the defined *feature region* from one frame to the next, but it's also useful to remember that the bigger the search region, the slower the stabilizing process will be.

**5** In the Motion Stabilizer dialogue box click inside the inner, feature region of box, drag it to the center of the bird. As you drag the Feature Region box, the Search Region box will follow with it.

**6** Resize the Feature Region box so that it is covering the main body of the bird, as in the following diagram.

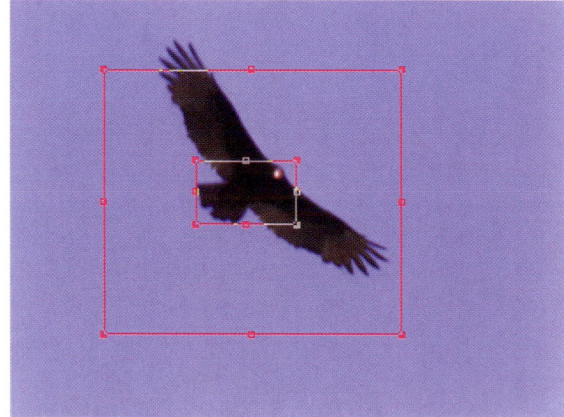

**7** Resize the outer box to accommodate what you think will be the biggest movement between one frame and the next, e.g. if the bird moved suddenly from one side of the image to the other side within the time space of one frame then the Search Region box would have to be big enough to accommodate this movement (i.e. the size of the composition).

**8** Hit the Analyze button to preview the footage. With the default settings the stabilizer tracks the area pretty well till about two thirds into the sequence, and then loses it. Let's take a look at how we can make it more accurate.

**9** Click on the *Options* button. In here you have the various settings which can help you to improve the stabilizer's performance.

**10** Leave the *Time Options* at 15 frames per second. It is usual to track your layer, using the same frame rate as the original footage (although using lower frame rates can produce some interesting results).

If your footage is interlaced there is the option to *Track Fields* for a more accurate track. The *Track in Reverse* option is useful if the feature you wish to track appears half way through your footage.

Checking the Track in Reverse box will tell After Effects to track from the final frame back to the first frame using the Position and Rotation values of the final frame as a reference. Track in Reverse is most useful when the feature you wish to track does not appear in the first frame but appears later in the sequence, making it impossible to define the regions at the In-point.

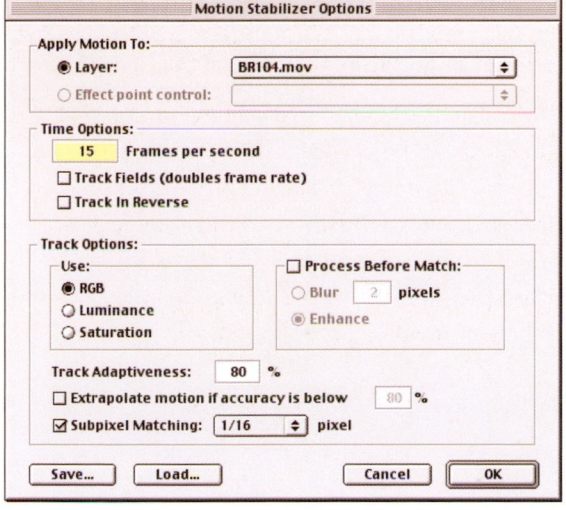

*Track Options* allow you to choose to track using either:
• *RGB*, which will look for differences in the red green and blue channels of the pixels you have selected. This would be ideal if you needed to track a red parrot flying through a blue sky.
• *Luminance* is the best option if the subject you wish to track contains highly contrasting pixels, for example, a black crow flying across a snowy landscape.
• *Saturation* should be chosen when all else fails, this setting can differentiate between different strengths of the same color. This option would be ideal if you wanted to track a bright green frog jumping through dark green grass.

Checking the *Process Before Match* checkbox gives you the choice of either blurring the footage or sharpening the footage (*Enhance*) before Tracking or Stabilizing takes place, to make the subject clearer. You can also specify a Blur amount in pixels for this option. This is useful because a slight blurring can decrease the amount of transient noise in an image thus making the subject easier to track. The processing is only applied for the purpose of Tracking or Stabilizing, it does not affect your original footage on output.

*Track Adaptiveness* determines whether the current frame is compared to its previous frame or to the very first frame of the footage. The default setting of 0% will force After Effects to compare the current frame with the first frame of the footage, this is the fastest setting and works well when your feature region does not change size, shape or color throughout the track. A setting of 100% will compare the current frame to its previous frame, this is much slower but is necessary if your feature region changes color, size or shape during tracking. You can adjust this value anywhere in between to refine your track.

*Extrapolate Motion if Accuracy is Below*, is a bit of a mouthful but describes accurately what this checkbox does. Basically, when you check this box After Effects will guess the speed and direction in which the subject is moving whilst it is not visible. This is extremely useful in situations where the subject moves behind another object in the shot or when the subject passes a background of a similar color to itself.

*Sub-pixel Matching*, well, don't ask me how, but those clever little programmers have managed to split pixels into even smaller units, in this menu you can choose to track in fractions of pixels to increase the accuracy of your track. The smaller the subdivision, the greater the tracking accuracy.

**11** Change the track adaptiveness to 80%, the bird definitely changes shape quite dramatically as it moves around the screen.

**12** Change the Sub-Pixel Matching to one 16th of a pixel to make the track more accurate. Click OK to leave the Motion Stabilizer Options dialogue box.

**13** Move to the point just before the tracking went wrong and then click the Analyze button again to begin tracking the bird.

The bird changes direction (and therefore shape) throughout the sequence, this is why we changed the track adaptiveness to 80% telling After Effects to compare the current frame to the previous one.

Notice that After Effects has now managed to track the bird pretty well. We could adjust this further depending on the amount of accuracy required but this is good enough for our needs right now.

**NB** If your track has not worked as well as mine, it could be that your tracking regions were not set up exactly like mine, if this is the case, move the Current-Time Marker back to frame 1, adjust your tracking regions and start again.

If you are happy with the tracking, hit the apply button to tell After Effects to use the tracking information to stabilize your footage and then close the layer window.

**14** RAM Preview your composition and notice how the Motion Stabilizer works. It moves the layer around the screen to compensate for the movement of the camera, keeping the bird pretty central throughout the shot. After Effects animates the Anchor Point value to record this movement.

**15** Hit the U key on the keyboard to see the keyframes that After Effects has set for you.

You can see that we would have to stretch this layer quite a lot to get rid of the edges, consequently, we would decrease the quality of the footage. Instead, we will use another of After Effects Production Bundle Keying filters to remove the blue-sky and place the bird onto a new Background.

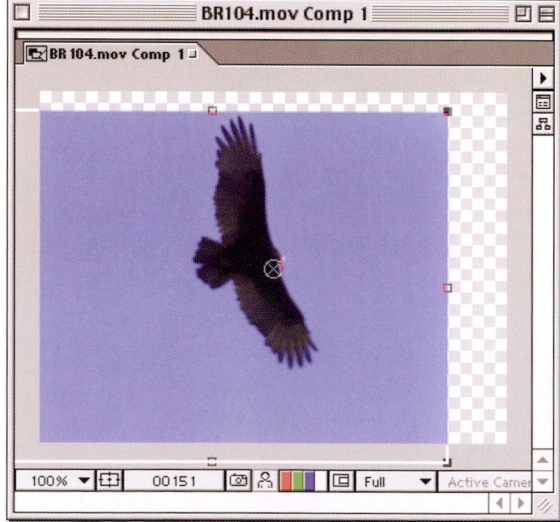

## the linear color key

The Linear Color Key is quite a versatile tool it works by comparing the pixels in your image to a color specified by you. Colors that match are made transparent; colors that don't match are left opaque; areas in between will graduate linearly between 0% and 100% opacity.

**1** With the layer selected go to Effect > Keying > Linear Color key.

At the top of the Effect Controls window, the Linear Color Key has a Source Thumbnail to preview original footage and a Preview Thumbnail for previewing the final key. In between these windows are three eyedropper tools.

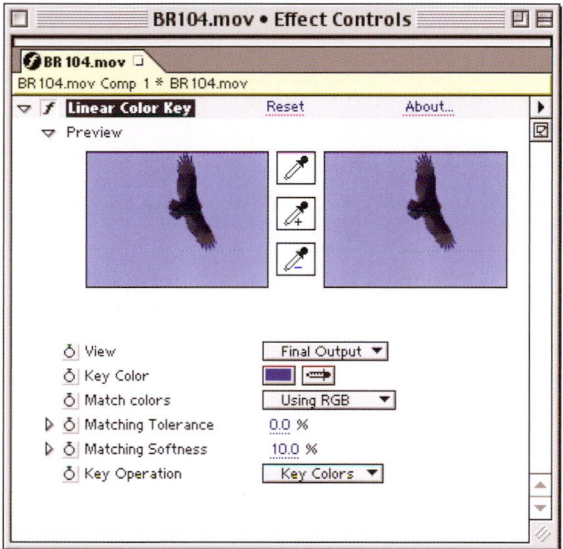

• The top Eyedropper tool is for selecting your Chosen Key Color and does exactly the same job as using the eyedropper tool underneath the preview thumbnails.
• The next Eyedropper is the Plus eyedropper tool, this is used to Add Colors to the key.
• Next is the Minus Eyedropper tool this is used to Remove Colors from the key.

**2** If it is not set already, click on the Wing Menu at the top right of the Composition window and choose Checkerboard Background from the drop down menu.

**3** Click on the top Eyedropper tool.

**4** Make sure that the effect is active and then move the cursor over to the Comp window. Place the cursor over the blue sky and click once to sample the key color.

In this situation there is no need to adjust the *Matching Tolerance* setting as we have a nice, even, blue sky. If the color values varied any more than this you could select a wider range of blues by pushing the *Matching Tolerance* value up a bit.

**5** Change the *Matching Softness* value to 20, this will soften the boundary between keyed colors and non-keyed colors.

**6** Go to Effect > Keying > Spill Suppressor. There is still a slight blue edge on the bird but we will use the Spill Suppressor to get rid of this.

**7** Select the exact shade of blue by clicking on the *Color to Suppress* Eyedropper tool and clicking on the Linear Color Keys *Key Color* swatch.

**8** Finally go to Effect > Perspective > Bevel Alpha. Change the Edge Thickness to 0.6.

We're now going to import another file which we will animate the bird flying over.

**9** In the Project window, double-click the EagleAir.ai Composition to open up its own Composition window and Timeline.

This is a multi-layered Illustrator file which has been imported as a composition.

**10** Select All the layers and then hit Command + U to switch all layers on to best quality and then turn off visibility for all layers except for the Body and Background layers.

## pasting paths as masks

At this point I want us to use some path information that has been copied and pasted into here from Illustrator. If you have a copy of Illustrator or Photoshop, you can easily copy and paste path information from there into After Effects. These paths can be used as masks but can also be used to control certain effects that are available in After Effects. I don't want you to follow the next few steps, these are for information only, so that you can try out the process for yourself later. If you don't have a copy of Illustrator, don't worry, I've pre-saved a mask for you all to use in this exercise. Here's how the mask was brought in.

• I selected the Face layer and hit Command + E or go to Edit > Edit original, this will open the file up for editing in the program from which it originated.
• I then clicked on the face of the Eagle to select the path (if you are using Illustrator version nine you can select the path by clicking on the layers target button in the layers palette).
• I then hit Command + C to copy the path information to the clipboard.
• I then went back to After Effects and selected the Body layer, and then hit Command + V to paste the path into the layer as a mask.
• Finally, I hit Command + A to select all points of the path and then nudged it into position to match it up with the layer.

As a default when you copy and paste path information from Photoshop or Illustrator, After Effects will paste it with its center point aligned with the center point of your layer.

**1** With the body layer selected in the Timeline hit the M key to bring up your Mask Controls. Notice that the Mask Mode menu has been changed to *None*.

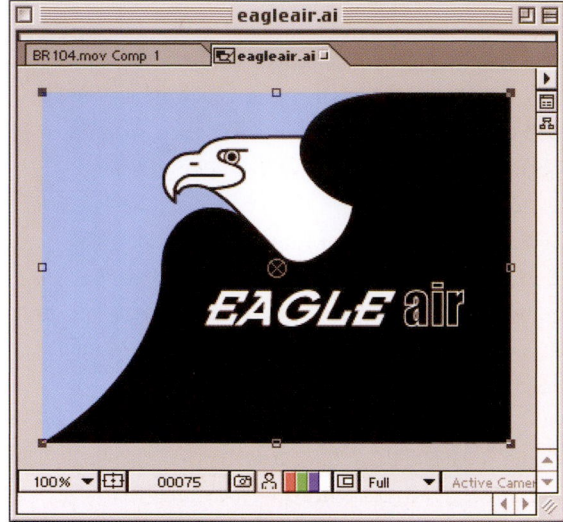

We do not want to use the path information as a Mask, we are going to use the information to control an effect property.

## stroke effect

**1** With the Body layer still selected, go to Effect > Render > Stroke.

The Stroke effect will draw on an outline around a specified Path. By animating the start and end points you can easily give it the appearance of a line being drawn on screen. We need to turn off the Mask display in the Composition window to be able to see our stroke.

**2** Go to the Composition window Wing menu and switch off the mask display by selecting Layer Masks from the list.

**3** From the *Path* menu in the Effect Controls window Choose *Mask 1*. You will now see that a white line (stroke) has been rendered around the selected path. Change the color to black.

**4** Move the Current-Time Marker to frame 30 (two seconds) and create a keyframe for the *Start* value by clicking on the Stopwatch for that value in the Effect Controls window. Change the value to 100%.

**5** Move to frame 75 (five seconds) and scrub the *Start* value all the way down to 0. Preview your work, the line will now be drawn on a screen between two seconds and five seconds.

## fill effect

**1** With the current time marker still at frame 75, go to Effect > Render > Fill. As the name suggests this filter fills a specified path with the color of your choice.

**2** Choose Mask 1 from the drop down menu in the Effect Controls window and change the fill color to White.

**3** Change the Opacity value to 0% and then set a keyframe for Opacity.

**4** Hit Command + G to bring up the Go To Time box and type in +5 to move the Current-Time Marker ahead by five frames.

**5** Change the Opacity value to 100% and then RAM Preview your work so far.

## effect order

Notice also that the black line becomes very thin when the mask is filled. This is because the Fill effect was applied after the Stroke; the fill is lying on top of the stroke. As I mentioned in the Effects chapter earlier, the order in which effects are applied can be changed. Effects are always applied in the order they are seen in the Effect Controls window.

**1** To change the order of effects, select the Stroke effect, by clicking on its name in the Effect Controls window, and then drag it underneath the Fill effect. Doing this will change the order in which the effects are applied, the Stroke will now be applied on top of the fill.

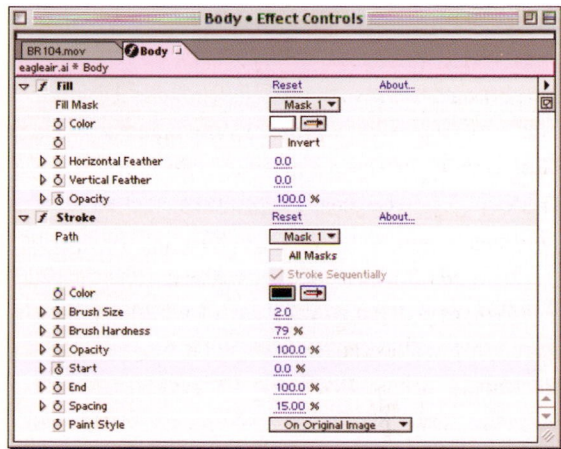

**2** Hit Command/Control-G to open up the Go To Time box type in 90 and hit Enter to move frame 90 (six seconds).

**3** Select Face layer and hit back space to delete it. We no longer need this layer as we have re-created it using the effects.

**4** Turn the other layers visibility back on again and select layers 1, 2 and 3 simultaneously.

## trimming layers

**1** With all three layers selected and the current time marker at frame 90, hit Alt + [ to trim the layers to the position of the Current-Time Marker.

**2** You can also trim the layers by hand. Move to the frame 105 (seven seconds) and click on the gray handle on the left edge of the Air layer. Drag it towards the Current-Time Marker, holding down the Shift key to force it to snap to the Marker.

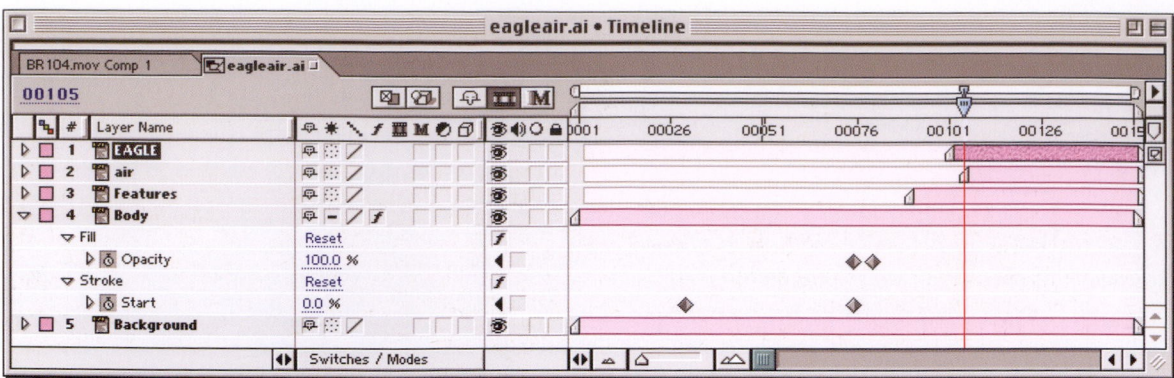

**3** Use either of these techniques to trim the Eagle layer halfway between the Features layer and the Air layer.

**4** RAM Preview your work so far. OK, so it's a pretty basic bit of animation but you can adjust it yourself later to refine it. Meanwhile, let's move onto the next stage. We will make the bird (which we keyed earlier) fly around the path drawing the line as it goes.

## pasting motion paths

**1** Make sure that the Current-Time Marker is at the beginning of your comp by hitting the Home key on the keyboard.

**2** In the Project window click and drag the *BR104.mov Comp 1* Composition in to the Eagle Air Composition by clicking and dragging one icon on to the other.

**3** In the Timeline, double-click the Body layer to bring up its Layer Window.

**4** Click in the Layer Window Wing Menu and choose Masks from the list to display the mask that I copied and pasted from Illustrator.

**5** Hit Command + A to select all of the control points on the mask and then hit Command + C to copy these points to the clipboard. Close the layer window when you have done this.

As well as being able to use path information to control effects, you can also use it to control a layer's position value. A layer's exact position is marked by its Anchor point; when a layer moves around a path the Anchor point will be the part of the layer attached to the path. We want the bird to look as though it is drawing the line on the screen with its beak, therefore we need to move the Anchor point over the head of the bird so that this will be the point which moves along the path.

## adjusting anchor points

There are two ways of adjusting the Anchor point for a layer within After Effects. The method I am about to show you will move the Anchor point and will also adjust the position of the layer to compensate for the adjustment, keeping up the layer in the same position in the Composition window.

**1** Select the BR104.mov Comp 1 layer and then hit the P key on the keyboard to bring up the Position property. Hold down Shift and hit the A key to simultaneously bring up the Anchor point property.

**2** Move to frame 30 and, from the tool palette, select the Pan Behind Tool.

**3** With the Pan Behind Tool selected, click and drag the Anchor Point; move it so that it sits on the head of the bird. Notice, in the Timeline, the values for Anchor point and position have both adjusted to the same value.

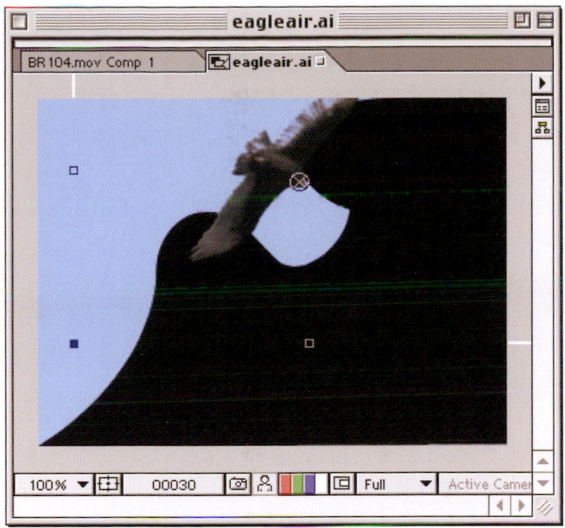

**4** Deselect the layer and then click on the Position property name in the Timeline to make that property active.

**5** Hit Command + V to paste the path information you copied earlier into the position property of the layer.

**6** RAM Preview the result. The bird now flies around the path but there are still a few things wrong with it; the timing is wrong and the bird is flying in the wrong direction. Let's take a look at how we can adjust the path after pasting it in.

**7** Select all of the layers in the Timeline and hit the U key to bring up keyframed properties only. You should now also see the keyframes that you created earlier on the Body layer.

**8** Move to frame 30 and then select all of the position keyframes for the BR104.mov Comp 1 layer by clicking on the Position property name in the Timeline.

**9** With all the keyframes selected, click and drag the keyframes, holding down Shift whilst dragging to snap the first keyframe to the position of the current time Marker.

## time reverse keyframes

The starting position is now correct but as you can see the animation only lasts for two seconds. When you paste path information in to property information the keyframes are automatically roved across time, allowing you to stretch or squash the timing of the keyframes.

**1** To do this deselect all of the keyframes by clicking anywhere away from them and then select the last keyframe which should be diamond-shaped and stretch it to frame 75, notice that all the other keyframes follow.

**2** RAM Preview the movie again. Notice that the bird is flying in the opposite direction from the path.

**3** To change the direction of the bird's flight simply select all the Position keyframes by hitting word Position and go to Animation > Keyframe Assistant > Time Reverse Keyframes.

**4** RAM Preview the animation again. The bird should now pretty much follow the path. Your animation may be slightly different from mine but you can adjust the position of the animation at any time after the Position keyframes have been set.

**5** To adjust the flight path of the bird, you can do so by first making sure that the Current-Time Marker is sitting on a keyframe, you can check this by making sure that the Keyframe Checkbox is ticked.

**6** Select all of the keyframes and nudge the bird into its new position using the Up and Down arrow keys on your keyboard. Because all of the Keyframes are selected, they will all move by the same increment.

**7** Move to frame 105 and create a keyframe by hitting Alt + P, this will lock the bird in position between frames 75 and 105.

**8** To make the bird fly off the screen, move to frame 135 (nine seconds) and adjust your view so that you can see the gray area around your composition. You can do this either by stretching the Composition window or by hitting the Comma key (,) to drop the view size down to 50%.

**9** Click and drag the bird up and to the right off-screen.

**10** Command-Click on the final position keyframe. Click and drag a Bezier handle from the keyframe to turn the straight path, joining the two keyframes, to a curved one.

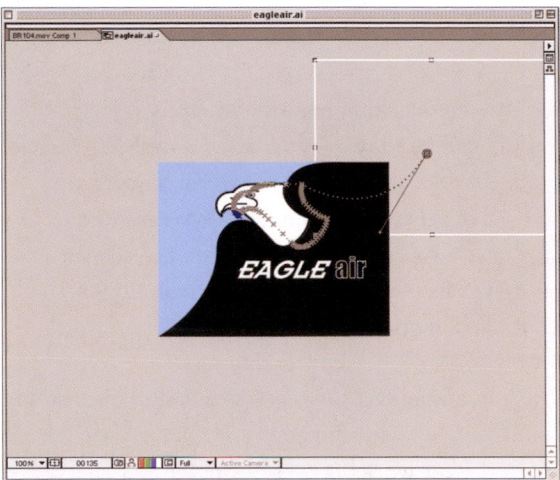

### stylize effect

**1** With the bird still selected go to Effect > Stylize > Find Edges to change the bird from a black one to a white one.

**2** Move to frame 15 and drag the bird layer so that it is in the center of the composition, this will be its start point.

**3** Finally activate motion for the layer and activate the Enable Motion Blur switch for the comp.

**4** RAM Preview your animation, the bird now starts in the center of the comp, flies around the outline of the head and then flies off screen.

OK, so there's a new use for the Motion Stabilizer, you can use it to center an object so that you can animate it along a new motion path.

You've also learned that you can copy and paste paths from Illustrator or Photoshop into Effect properties for a layer.

You can even copy and paste the paths into the Position values for a layer.

Have a go at creating an animation of a logo, all you'll need is an EPS file or Illustrator file containing the logo. Start by copying the main shape from Illustrator and then pasting it into an After Effects layer as a mask. Switch the Mask Mode to None and then apply the Stroke Effect. Animate either the Start or End Point of the Stroke and then, as we say in the UK, Bob's yer uncle! It couldn't be easier.

**5** If you want to, you can save this project into your Creative After Effects > Tracking Chapter folder as Birdtrack02b.aep.

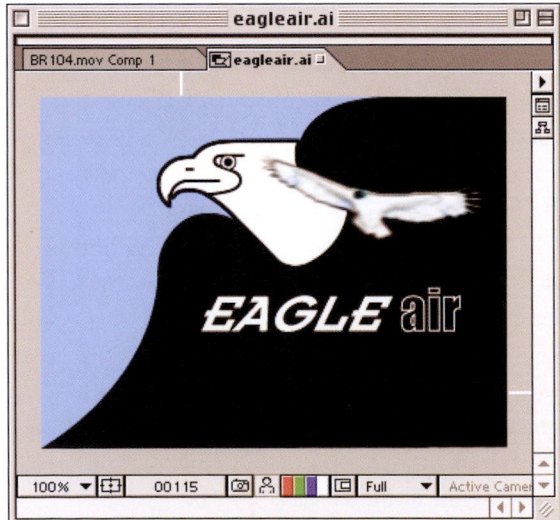

# MacDonna video
## motion tracking

Now let's take a look at Motion Tracking. This is a great technique to learn, once you know the basics you can use it to attach any layer in your composition onto a defined area in another movie layer. For example, you could attach a hat onto somebody's head as they walk through the shot; or attach some flames onto the back of a space rocket, as it flies through the sky. As well as being able to track one layer onto another, you can also track certain effects onto a layer, these include all effects with control points that define the effects position on your layer.

OK, let's go back to our MacDonna video, remember back in the Effects chapter I promised you that I would show you how to track the bulge effect for the eyes onto moving footage?

**1** Open up CloseUps.aep from Training > Projects > Chapter 12.

In this movie, we had applied two bulge effects to the eyes of the girl in the clip, making them look like the eyes of a fly.

**2** RAM Preview the clip to remind yourself of the fact that the effect remained in the same position as the face moved. We need to track the effects onto the eyes of the girl.

**3** Double-click layer (Layer 2) to bring up Layer window. Click on the Wing Menu of the Layer Window and then go to Track/Stabilize.

**4** Choose *Track* from the Track and Stabilize *Type* menu. There are three different types of tracking available to you in this menu. We are going to cover how to perform a basic track but you can also choose to do two types of Corner Pin tracking.

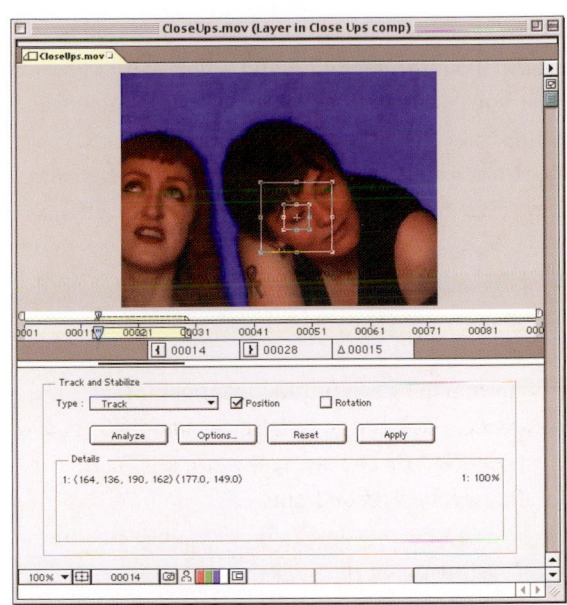

Corner Pin tracking enables you to track multiple points on your layer, allowing you to then attach a layer, in perspective, onto your footage. For example, this would be useful if you wanted to track a new advertising banner on the side of a moving bus. Keep an eye on the website for tutorials on corner pinning.

http://www.angie.abel.co.uk/book.html

The Tracker works in a very similar way to the Stabilizer. You define your regions as before but then instead of centering the region within the comp, After Effects attaches another, user-defined layer to the specified region.

**5** Click to select the inner box which is the Feature Region, position it over the bottom eye as in the picture above. Notice that the other interface elements move with the feature region.

As well as having Feature Region and Search Region boxes the Tracker also has a Track Point (this is the tiny cross in the middle of the boxes). This defines the exact point that the anchor point of the other layer will be attached to.

**6** Hit the *Analyze* button to begin tracking the region. It works very well till the girl opens her eye, the Tracker then loses the track. The reason this happens is that, when the eye opens, the area does not look the same as it did in the first frame. After Effects is still looking for an area exactly like the one defined in the first frame.

**7** Click on the *Options* button. We can make After Effects compare the current frame more to its previous frame than to the first frame of the sequence.

**8** Change the *Track Adaptiveness* value to 80%. Now After Effects will take changes into consideration, if the object changes shape, color or size as it moves, After Effects will recognize the changes and adapt the track to cope with them.

If you look at the *Apply Motion To* section, you'll see that the default applies the motion to another layer in the comp. If we went ahead with this option, the other layer would be attached to our Tracking Point by its anchor point.

**9** We want to track our effect onto the layer so click on the Effect Control Point radio button and then have a look in the menu options available.

As soon as you apply an effect with a control point to your layer, it will appear in this menu, allowing you to choose which effect to track onto your layer. Because we applied the Bulge filter twice, it will appear twice in this menu.

**10** Choose the first *Bulge/Bulge center* from the list and then click OK to leave the Motion Tracker Options box.

**11** Hit the Analyze button again, After Effects now happily tracks the eye throughout the clip. Hit the Apply button to accept the track.

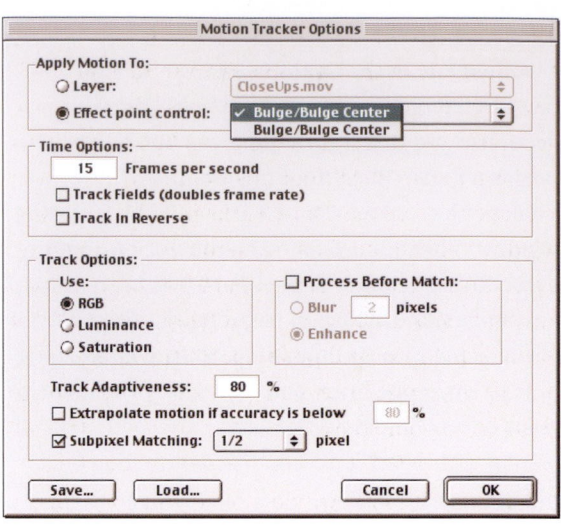

Notice that, in the Comp window, the Bulge effect has jumped onto the bottom eye, both effects are now on this eye. We'll now track the second instance of the Bulge effect onto the other eye.

**12** Move to the first frame of the clip and click once on the main screen to display the region boxes.

**13** Click and drag the Feature Region onto the other eye, the Search Region box and the Track Point will follow.

**14** Hit the Options button again and in the Motion Tracker Options box, change the Apply Motion To menu so that the second Bulge/Bulge Center is selected and then click OK.

**15** Hit the Analyze button to track the eye. The eye should track successfully but, if not, there are a couple of ways of correcting a wayward track.

**16** First you should move to the first frame where the track has gone wrong.

**17** Then, either:

• Adjust any of the Options, Feature Region and/or Search Region to make your track more accurate; and then hit the Analyze button again to perform a new track from this point.

• Move the Current-Time Marker (in the Tracking window) ahead one frame at a time (by using the Down arrow key on the keyboard). At each frame, move the Feature Region, Search Region and Track Point to their desired position. Hit the apply button when you are finished to apply the manual changes to your track.

**18** Close the Layer window once you are happy with your tracking and then RAM Preview the clip you have just finished working on. The effects now follow the eyes wherever they go. You can even adjust the tracking information after you have clicked the Apply button.

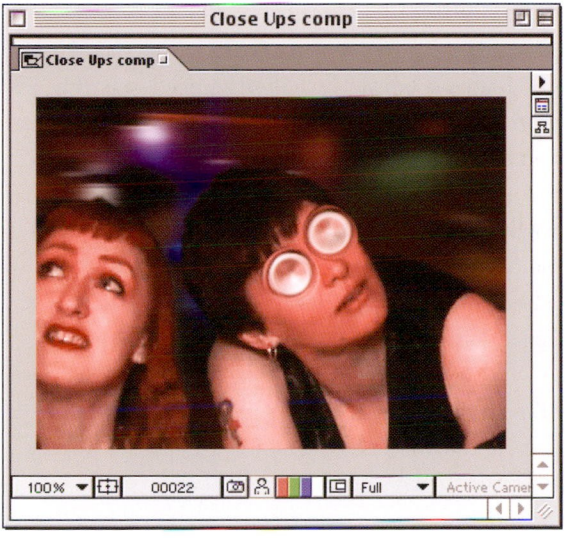

**19** Hit the U key on the keyboard to bring up keyframed properties. Notice that the Tracker has set keyframes for the Bulge Center. These are like any other keyframes, they can be moved, adjusted, copied, pasted, have their interpolation changed, whatever.

**20** If you want to, save this project into your Creative After Effects > Tracking chapter as CloseUps02b.mov.

# recap

OK, so motion stabilizing is great for fixing dodgy camera work and a tracking is generally used to track an object onto moving footage. But as you've seen here, there are also lots of creative ways to use these features. Another nice technique, using motion tracking is for film titles, track the text onto significant elements within the footage to make some pretty interesting animated titles. Try playing around with a few ideas, using these features. Also, keep an eye on the website for further tutorials on perspective motion tracking and various other related subjects.

OK, time for some more design tips. These ones come from one of the many people who I have trained in After Effects. His name is Waleed Al-Temimi and he is a graphic designer at the BBC in London.

In our business we need to answer a brief, to serve a need or solve a problem in the best possible way in the shortest time possible. In television we have a very short time to put across the idea or point, the graphic is on screen for seconds and then it's gone forever, so we need to be very clear and precise, unlike books or magazines which the reader can look at for as long as they want.

It's our experience and knowledge of the capabilities of equipment, supporting staff and time that decides what is achievable on the day. There are days when the story is so difficult to illustrate creatively and innovatively on screen. What we resort to is tried and tested methods or resources at our disposal; such as a library of subjects we have shot previously that covered the same or similar subject. We have shot generic scenes on many themes in the past and have kept the clean versions on tape and labeled accordingly. So, for example, we have generic shots of prisons, education, terrorism, science and many more subjects as well as just 'funky' backgrounds of lights and shadows to use as backings for graphics or film treatment. We also have a variety of props at our disposal to use or we can make them ourselves or buy/hire them from shops or specialist props vendors. They range from playing cards to African masks and spears. You would shoot these and use them as a complimentary part of your design. You can incorporate the text or information needed to be shown into the props themselves adding an element of surprise or fun into the subject.

In other programs or channels they might have a 'house style' which the designers need to stick to. This serves as a 'unifying factor' to the channel or programme (and something to fall back on when you have no time, or a mental block). It's like having a grid on a magazine or book, you know the number of columns, the distances and so on; it's up to you whether you want to stick rigidly to it or to try and break loose from it, it's there as a general guideline and you follow it (or not) as you see fit and appropriate.

When I've designed magazines I would gather all my raw ingredients on screen – the text, the pictures, the headlines – and start to make a composition, mostly by following the grid at first to serve as a basis. Then I would start to break out of it as I go on, I might add different colors, textures, positions of images, shapes of images. Playing with type is a very important aspect in this.

Lots of inspiration comes from looking at other people's work, either in the past or at the present. Magazines, design books and the Internet all give an amazing amount of ideas and inspiration. When you browse the net, you might see a fantastic website and say 'wow! I wish I could do something as good as that'. Or you might see a horrible website and think 'what a piece of rubbish! I can do much better than that'. Both of these realizations can drive you forward.

I find that looking at the world around us is the best inspiration you can have. From the most mundane things to the most extraordinary designs, you can pick ideas, you might look at the way shoes are positioned haphazardly when someone takes them off or the way leaves wilt in the rain on some trees and perk up when the sun shines, or different textures around you from stone to silk, strange shapes made by shadows of building parts or the sound made when your computer boots up. This probably sounds weird but it helps to be weird when you have a mental block.

Some fantastic and valuable information there. To find out more about Waleed and to view his work, visit him at his website on:

http://www.temimi.com

# chapter thirteen
# parenting

## parental hierarchy

This chapter (excluding the Graffiti Club tutorials) was written by Fred Lewis whose biography you can read in the Introduction.

After Effects 5.0 now has a new feature called 'Parental Hierarchy'. Simply put, this new feature allows you to attach one layer to another. When you make this type of attachment, one of the layers is called the *parent* and the other layer is, not surprisingly, called the *child*. When these two layers are attached to each other, we think of the child being attached to the parent, not the other way around because, when the parent is animated, the child moves with it, but when the child is animated, the parent does not move with it.

## basic parenting

To see what I mean by that and get a taste of what parenting is all about (only the animation kind of course!), try the following:

**1** Open After Effects.

**2** Create a new composition of any length and 15 fps, 320 × 240 pixels.

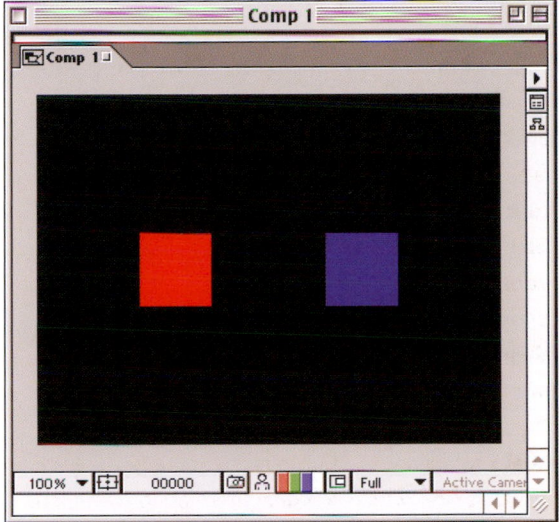

**3** Create two new solids (Command + Y), each 50 × 50 pixels, square. Make one of them Red and name it *Red Parent* and the other one blue, named, *Blue Child*. Naming them makes it easier to keep track of what you are doing.

**4** Place the Red Parent in the left half of the Composition window and the Blue Child in the right half of the Composition window, as shown in the diagram above. (Hold down the Shift key to constrain the movement to a horizontal move only.)

**5** We're now going to Parent the Blue Child to the Red Parent. To do this, click on the Blue Child's *Parent* pop-up menu in the parent panel of the Timeline window (Wing menu > Panels > Parent), and select the Red Parent from the list.

**6** You now have one solid parented to the other. Try moving, rotating and scaling each of the solids one at a time (make sure that you have Wireframe Interactions switched off so that you can see dynamic update in the Comp window).

Notice that when you do anything to the parent (the Red Parent), both the parent and the child are affected. Whatever happens to the parent, the child is brought with it. But when you make changes to the child, only the child is affected. This is how parenting works.

Another thing that happens when you parent one layer to another is that the child's animation be-comes *relative* to the parent's upper-left corner (0, 0). Usually, this means the child's transform values must change when parenting and un-parenting, in order to keep the child in the same place within the composition. To see how this works, try the following.

**7** Rotate the parent layer (Red Parent) to any non-zero rotation value. (Make sure its rotation value in the timeline is not zero.) Then set the child layer's rotation value to zero, in the timeline.

Notice that this immediately rotates the child layer to exactly the same orientation as the parent layer. This will always be the case because child layer's animation values are always *relative* to their parents and a relative value of zero means zero difference between the child and the parent.

**8** Now try setting the child's position values to zero. This aligns the child's position with the parent's upper-left corner. In effect, it positions the child within the composition so that the child's anchor point is exactly on top of the parent's upper-left corner. Again, this is because the child's position values are relative to the parent's upper-left corner.

Why the parent's upper-left corner, you may ask? Why not make the child relative to the parent's anchor point? Very good question. The answer is: When Adobe added parental hierarchy to After Effects, they decided to make child layers be relative to their parent's images rather than their parent's anchor points. And the parent's image, technically speaking, is measured from the upper-left pixel. (It is where the anchor point goes if you zero it.) So, this is where children align to when you zero them.

**9** Try un-parenting the child from the parent. To do this, click on the child's Parent pop-up menu in the Timeline, and choose 'None' from within the pop-up menu. Notice that the child's Position and Rotation values in the Timeline are now no longer set to zero. This is because the child's animation is once again relative to the composition, not the parent.

**10** Undo the last step so that the Red Parent is once again the parent of the Blue Child. Notice that the child's position and rotation values in the Timeline are now once again zero.

By default, this is what happens both when you parent an object and when you un-parent an object. When you parent the object, it stays in the same place in the composition and its transform values become relative to the parent. When you un-parent the object, it stays in the same place in the composi-tion, and its transform values revert back to how they behaved before the object was parented.

You can, however, force the child's values to remain the same when you parent and un-parent, by holding down the Alt key. This causes the child to jump to a new position in the composition when it gets parented or un-parented. This is useful for preserving the child's absolute keyframe values, while changing its parent. To see how this works, try the following.

**11** While holding down the Alt key, un-parent the Blue Child. Because the Blue Child's position values are zero, and you have held the Alt key down to keep them that way, the Blue Child now moves to the upper-left corner of the comp (position zero, within the comp).

**12** Again while holding down the Alt key, re-parent the Blue Child to the Red Parent. The Blue Child's value is still zero, and it pops back into alignment with the parent's upper-left corner.

## hierarchies

OK, that covers the first word in this section heading, *Parental*, but how about that second word, *hierarchy*. The notion of hierarchy comes into play with parenting because of the fact that *any* layer can be a parent, including a layer that is also a child. For an example, try the following.

**1** In the same Comp, Create another new Yellow solid, same size, called *Yellow Grandmother*.

**2** Parent the Red Parent to the Yellow Grandmother by Clicking on the Red Parent's Parent pop-up menu and choose the Yellow Grandmother from within the menu.

**3** Play around with the layers some more by moving, rotating and scaling each of the layers in various ways.

You now have a 3 level hierarchy, with the Yellow Grandmother at the top of the hierarchy, a parent of all the other layers. The Red Parent in the middle of the hierarchy, and the Blue Child at the bottom.

Note that each parent can have an unlimited number of children, but each child can only have one parent. When more than one layer is parented to the same parent, the children are, naturally, called *siblings*.

Also note that, in After Effects, unlike many other programs that have parental hierarchy, the order that the layers are listed in the Timeline window has nothing to do with parental hierarchy. Many popular 3D animation programs also have a parental hierarchy feature. In those programs, the objects are usually listed according to their hierarchy. In After Effects 5.0, there is currently no way to list the objects this way. If you create a project in After Effects that has a complex parental hierarchy, it may help to make a flowchart of the hierarchy on paper. An example of such a flowchart is shown in the following diagram.

### Mechanical Arm Hierarchy

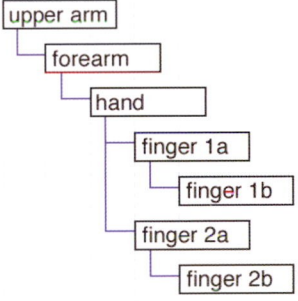

This is a chart of the parental hierarchy of the mechanical arm animation you will create in the next section. In this chart, notice that *finger 1a* and *finger 2a* are siblings. Carrying the analogy even further, *finger 1b* and *finger 2b* can be thought of as cousins.

## uses for parental hierarchy

Parental hierarchy is useful in computer animation in a variety of different ways. The next two sections will each demonstrate one of those ways with a different hands-on example. Then, in the following sections, I'll discuss some of the other uses, as well as more advanced issues with parenting and some pitfalls to watch out for.

## hierarchy of motion

Perhaps the most obvious use for parental hierarchy in animation is to create hierarchical motion. As an example of this kind of use, we'll create and animate a mechanical arm. To see what the completed animation looks like, open and play the QuickTime movie 'Arm.mov' from Training > Projects > Chapter 13.

There are two main tasks involved in creating this animation:
(1) creating the hierarchy, and
(2) creating the keyframes (animating).

The only source file you will need for this whole animation is the Adobe Illustrator file, 'arm.ai', which is in the Training > Source Images folder.

The following 27 steps will set up the hierarchy. When you have completed these, you should have an arm similar to the one pictured at step 27, and you should be ready to animate the arm.

In case you need to skip ahead for any reason, there is a project file called 'arm_animate.aep' on the CD, which will allow you to skip directly to the end of step 27, and start animating straight away. But if you are at all unfamiliar with parenting, you really should follow these steps first, to set up the hierarchy for yourself.

### creating the hierarchy

**1** Open the After Effects project file called 'arm_start.aep'. If you want to, you can save your current project into your Creative After Effects > Parenting Chapter folder as Parent1.aep for later use.

**2** At this point you should already have the *Mechanical arm* comp open. The composition contains a single layer, which is a shape from an Adobe Illustrator file. The shape has a small circle at each end. We want the anchor point of the layer to be on the circle at the larger end of the layer, so that the layer will pivot at that point.

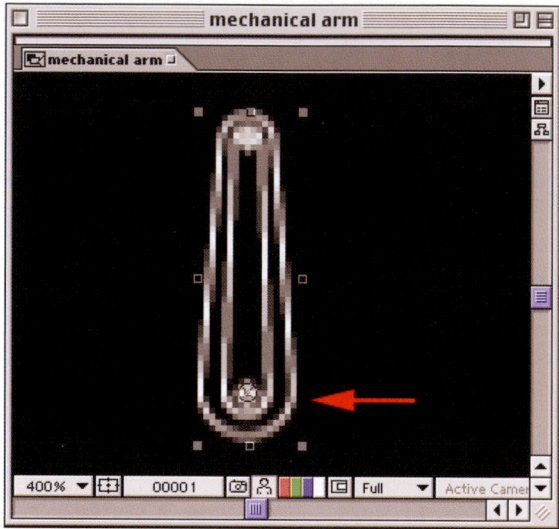

**3** Select the Pan Behind tool from the Tool Palette and drag the layer's anchor point to the middle of the circle at the larger end of the layer (the end closest to the bottom of the screen). This will cause the layer to pivot on its larger circle when rotated. You may need to zoom in a bit to do this.

**4** Next, duplicate the layer (select it and then hit Command + D). Rename the duplicate layer, by hitting Enter on the keyboard and typing in the word, *Hand*.

**5** Set the hand layer's Scale value to 66%.

**6** Choose the Selection tool from the Tool Palette (V) and then, using the Selection tool, drag the Hand layer so that its larger circle (its pivot) lines up with the forearm's smaller circle (as in the following diagram).

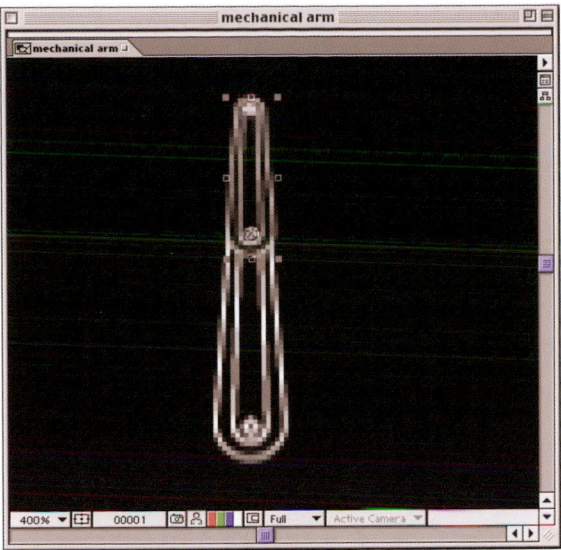

**10** Select the Forearm layer. Set the forearm layer's Scale to 75%. Notice that the hand layer scales down with it in the Composition window.

**11** Drag the Forearm layer so that its larger circle lines up with the Upper arm's smaller circle as in the following image. Notice that the Hand moves with it wherever it goes. The result should look like the one pictured in the following diagram.

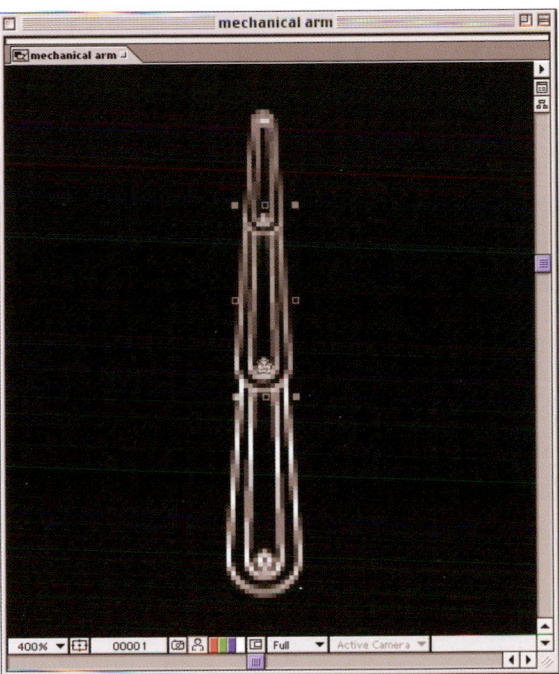

**7** Parent the hand to the forearm by clicking on the hand layer's parent Pickwhip icon (see diagram below) and dragging onto the forearm layer, to choose the forearm layer as the hand's parent.

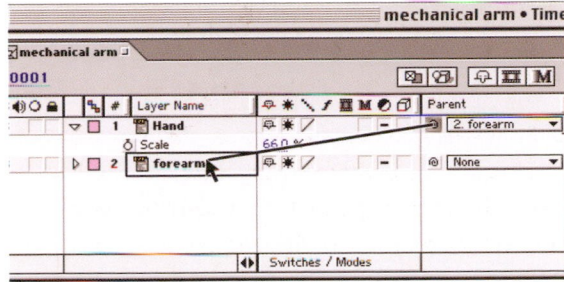

**8** Duplicate the Forearm layer again, this time rename the duplicate layer to *Upper arm*.

**9** In the Timeline window, select the Upper arm layer and then drag it down in the layer list so it is listed after the forearm layer in the Timeline window (this will make it show *behind* the forearm layer in the Composition window). You can also reorder layers by selecting the layer that you want to move, and then holding down Command + Alt whilst hitting the Up and Down arrow keys.

**12** Parent the Forearm to the Upper arm by clicking on the Forearm's parent pop-up menu and selecting the upper arm layer from within the pop-up menu, the upper arm is now the forearm's parent.

**13** Now we'll make the fingers. Duplicate the Hand layer and rename the duplicate layer, *finger 1a*.

**14** Change the Finger1a Scale value to 40%.

**15** Rotate Finger1a by 50°.

**16** Drag Finger1a so that its larger circle lines up with the hand's smaller circle. Use the following diagram as a reference.

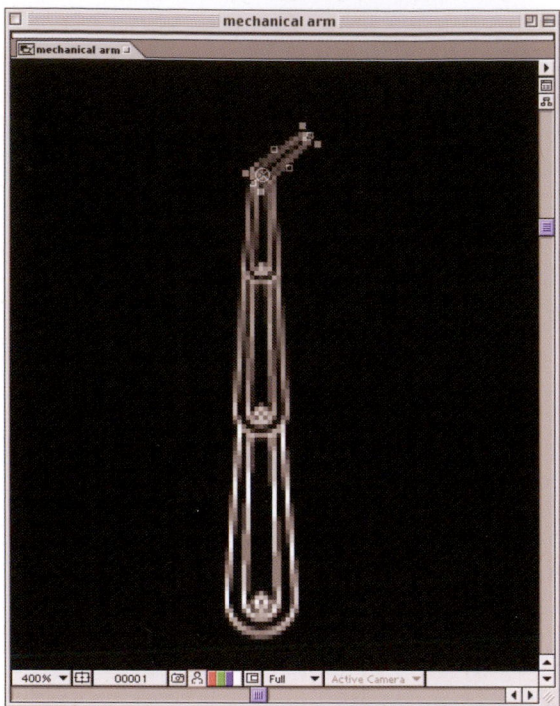

**17** Parent Finger1a to the Hand layer.

**18** Duplicate Finger1a and rename it, Finger1b.

**19** Drag Finger1b so its larger circle lines up with Finger1a's smaller circle.

**20** Parent Finger1b to Finger1a.

**21** Rotate Finger1b to –50°.

**22** Duplicate Finger1a and rename the duplicate to 'finger 2a'.

**23** Duplicate finger 1b and rename the duplicate to 'finger 2b'.

**24** Parent finger 2b to finger 2a.

**25** Rotate finger 2a to –50°.

**26** Rotate finger 2b to +50°.

**27** Select the upper arm layer and drag it downward in the Composition window, to center the entire assembly within the window.

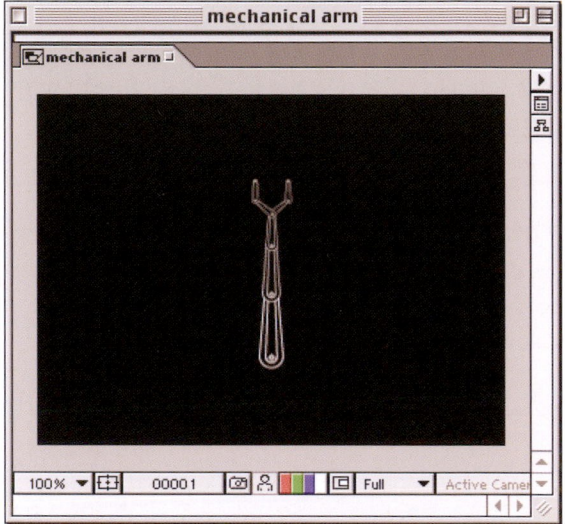

At this point, you should now have something in your Composition window that looks like the diagram above, and your Timeline window should look like the diagram below. The parental hierarchy you have created should match the diagram on page 189.

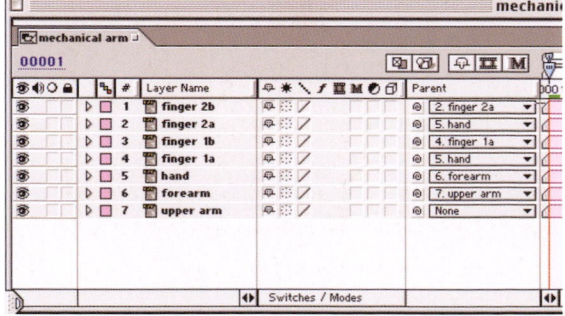

## animation

If you do not have a project open, you can start from this point by loading the project file, *arm_animate.aep*.

The next 8 steps will show you how to create the animation of the arm that we just built. You can view the finished QuickTime movie 'arm.mov' from Training > Projects > Chapter 13. I recommend that you follow all of these steps to create this animation before experimenting on your own. Afterwards, if you wish, you can create your own version of the animation by creating your own rotation keyframes.

**1** Select all of the layers at once (Command + A).

**2** Make sure the Current-Time Marker is at frame 1 and then hit Alt + R key to bring up the Rotation properties and set Rotation keyframes for all selected layers.

**3** Deselect the layers (Command + Shift + A) and then select the Rotation tool (W) from the Tool Palette. In the Composition window, drag the different layers to pose the arm so that it looks like the one in the following diagram.

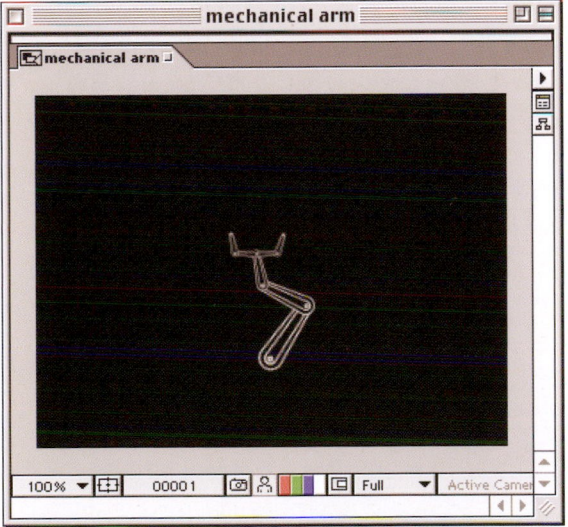

**4** Go to frame 7 and pose the arm to look like this one in the following diagram.

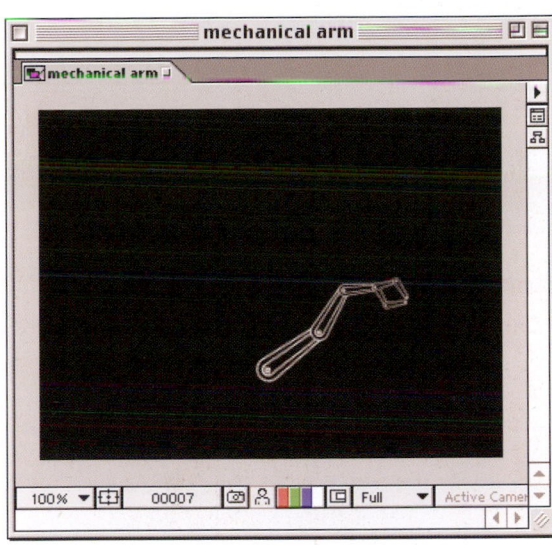

**5** Go to frame 26 and pose the arm to look like this:

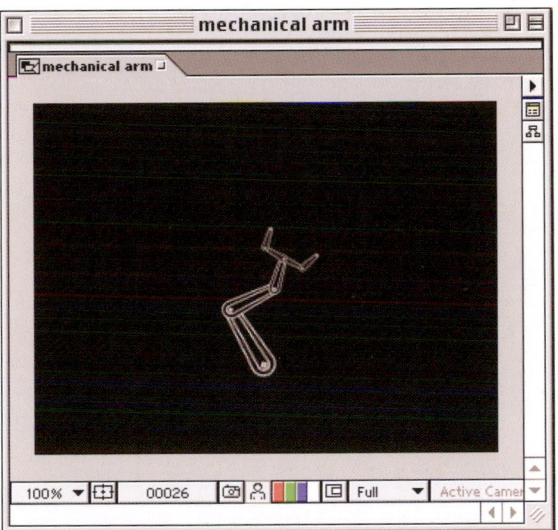

**6** Go to frame 32 and pose the arm to look like the following diagram.

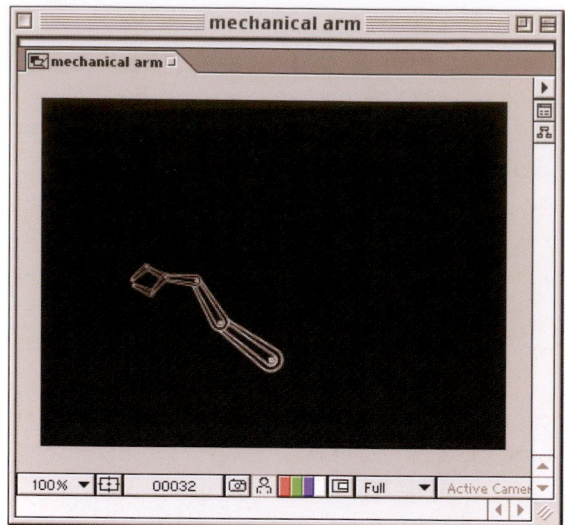

**7** Go to the last frame in the composition and then advance the Current-Time Marker one frame beyond the last frame by pressing the page down key.

**8** One layer at a time, select the Rotation keyframe at frame 1; hit Command + C, followed by Command + V to copy and paste the keyframes to the position of the Current-Time Marker. By creating the final keyframes one frame after the end frame, we will be sure to create a perfect looping animation. RAM Preview the comp to see.

## extra pivot points

In addition to hierarchical motion, demonstrated above, another very important use for Parenting in animation is for the purpose of creating additional pivot points. This allows you to create more complex motion, with objects rotating around more than one pivot at a time, or around different pivot points at different times. Among other things, this is very useful for creating complex camera motion. Let's take a look at an example of this.

**1** Open the project file called *camera_anim_setup.aep*. Choose Don't Save for the previous project

This project file contains two compositions: The mechanical arm animation we did in the last section is in a composition called *Arm Animation*. A separate composition called *Camera Animation* contains a copy of the Arm Animation composition, which has been brought in as a layer, plus a 3D camera, which is already animated.

**2** Make sure that the 'Camera Animation' comp is open. Drag the Current-Time Marker back and forth from the beginning to the end of the composition, to get an idea of what is going on.

Notice that at frame 1 of the composition, the camera's Z position value in the Timeline window is –772.5, and at the end of the composition, frame 124, the camera's Z position value is –357.5. The camera is moving forwards in 3D space, towards the Mechanical Arm animation. So, the Arm Animation appears to grow larger within the view as you drag the Current-Time Marker from beginning to end.

**3** To get a better sense of what the camera is doing, click the 3D View Pop-up menu, at the bottom of the Composition window, and select Custom View 1 from the pop-up menu. Then drag the Current-Time Marker from beginning to end again. (You will find out how to use the After Effects 3D features in the 3D chapter but for now, just follow me and enjoy the ride!)

This is an angled perspective view of the entire scene, with the Arm animation in the distance and the camera (represented by a small box) moving through space towards the Arm.

**4** Try viewing the scene through some of the other view angles in the 3D View Pop-up menu, and drag the Current-Time Marker around again whilst looking through the different views. Each view shows the scene from a different angle, with the camera moving towards the Arm animation.

**5** To look through the camera again, choose Active Camera or Camera 1, from the 3D View Pop-up menu.

## nulls

OK, by now you should have a basic understanding of what is going on in this composition. The camera is moving through 3D space towards the Arm animation. Now we'll use Parental Hierarchy to make this camera move in a more interesting way.

**6** With the Current-Time Marker at frame 1, go to Layer > New > Null Object (Command + Shift + Option + Y).

A new layer called *Null 1* appears in the Timeline window and also appears as a rectangular box with handles in the center of the Comp window. This is a special layer, called a *Null Object* (also sometimes referred to as a *dummy object* or just plain *null* for short). A null object is a special kind of layer that will never show in a final render but has a visible wireframe, so you can select and manipulate it in the Composition window. The main purpose of Null Objects is to act as invisible parents, which is exactly how we're going to use this null object now.

Note that since Null Objects don't render, they can also be used as guides or position markers, to help the animator during complex animations. They can also be used as extra channel holders for use with Expressions, which we'll take a look at in the Expressions Chapter.

**7** Make the null object a 3D layer by clicking on the 3D Layer switch for the Null 1 layer in the Timeline window. Since we're going to use this null with a 3D camera, the null must also be 3D.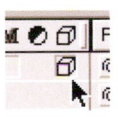

**8** Make sure that the Current-Time Marker is at frame 1 of the composition.

**9** Select Camera 1's parent pickwhip and drag it onto the Null 1 layer, to select Null 1 as the camera's parent.

**10** In the Timeline, select both the Camera 1 and Null 1 layers and hit the R key to open up the Rotation properties. Then click the stopwatches for Null 1's X, Y and Z Rotation channels, and for Camera 1's Z Rotation only. This will create keyframes for these channels at the current frame.

**11** In the Timeline select both Null 1 and Camera 1 at the same time. Then press the U key on your keyboard twice. This will open up all properties which have keyframes. In the Timeline window, you should now see only the X, Y and Z Rotation channels for Null 1 and only the Position and Z Rotation channels for Camera 1.

**12** Make sure you are still at frame 1 in the composition. Then set the following keyframe values:

Null 1, X Rotation   56
Null 1, Y Rotation   −40
Null 1, Z Rotation   0
Camera 1, Z Rotation  −63

**13** Move the Current-Time Marker to the last frame in the composition, frame 124.

**14** Set the following keyframe values:

Null 1, X Rotation   −12
Null 1, Y Rotation   45
Null 1, Z Rotation   10
Camera 1, Z Rotation  44

**15** You have now created a much more interesting camera animation. To see what the new animation looks like through the camera, select Active Camera from the 3D View pop-up menu. Then create a RAM Preview to see the animation.

**16** To see what is really going on, select various other views from the 3D View pop-up menu and drag the Current-Time Marker back and forth whilst looking through these views. You can see the wireframe for the null object and the camera, you can also see that the camera is pivoting on the null object, as the null object rotates. The camera is also rolling on its own Z-axis. Because the null object is located near the center of the Arm animation, the camera move pivots around the Arm animation in an interesting way. This makes a much more interesting camera movement than could be achieved without using a null object.

OK, let's take what we've learnt so far and apply some of it to out Graffiti Club project. We'll use Parenting to link the body parts together of our main characters.

# graffiti club

## character animation

OK, let's go back to our Graffiti Club animation, it's been a while since we've done some work on it. In the Effects chapter we colorized the background and created a Proxy file to speed up previewing, now we're going to get into the exciting stuff, animating the characters. We'll use the same technique as we've just used for the Robot.

I've done a fair bit of character animation using After Effects, mainly cut-out animation, similar to the style Terry Gilliam used in the Monty Python animations and not too dissimilar to South Park's style of animation.

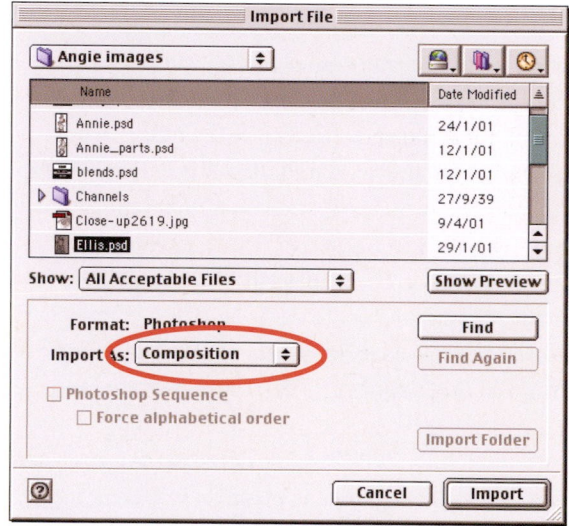

I've always used complex nesting procedures to link the individual parts of my characters together. I would draw them in Illustrator with each part on a separate layer, bring it in as a Comp and then Pre-comp the bits together as needed.

Parenting gets rid of the need for complex nesting hierarchies, I can now link the body parts together in one composition. Needless to say I spend far less money on headache tablets now! I know that it may seem intimidating to those who have never used it before but Parenting really makes life so much simpler.

**1** Open the Project named 'Graffiti02.aep' from Training > Projects > Chapter 13.

**2** Import the file named Ellis.psd as a *Composition* from Training > Source Images > Angie Images (remember to select *Composition* from the *Import as* drop down menu).

**3** In the Project window, double-click the Composition to open its Timeline and Composition windows.

**4** Make sure that the Comp window is active and then hit Command + K to open up the Composition Settings dialog box, change the Duration to 750 frames.

**5** Make the Timeline active and then jump the Current-Time Marker to the end of the comp by hitting the Home key on your keyboard.

**6** Select all of the layers by hitting Command + A and then hit Alt + ] to trim all of the layers out-points to the position of the Current-Time Marker.

**7** Drag a copy of the sound file, Kid_sound.mov from the Project into the Timeline, we will animate the character to this music.

**8** Use the Period key (.) and the Comma key (,) to adjust the magnification of your comp till you are happy with it. Use the Hand tool (H) to move the viewable image around inside the Comp window. Hit the V key to select the selection tool when you are happy.

OK, the first thing that we have to do is to set up our Pivot Points, i. e. the point around which we want our layers to rotate.

**9** Select the Rotation Tool (W) from the Tool Palette and then select the T-shirt layer.

**10** In the Comp window, click and drag on the layer handles to rotate the layer around, the layer currently rotates around its Anchor Point (which lies in the center of the layer).

**11** Undo the Rotation of the layer till you are back to where you started.

**12** Select the Pan Behind Tool (Y) from the Tool Palette. As you learned earlier, the Pan Behind Tool will adjust the Anchor Point without altering the layout you already have in the Composition window.

**13** With the Pan Behind Tool, click and drag the Anchor Point of the T-shirt Layer till it lies in the middle of the characters hips, where you would expect the body to rotate from.

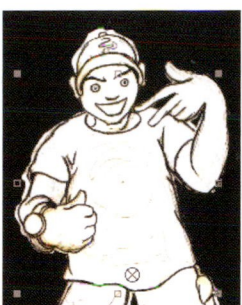

**14** Reselect the Rotation Tool and rotate the layer again. Now it rotates around the correct point.

**15** Undo the rotation and reselect the Selection tool (V) when you have finished.

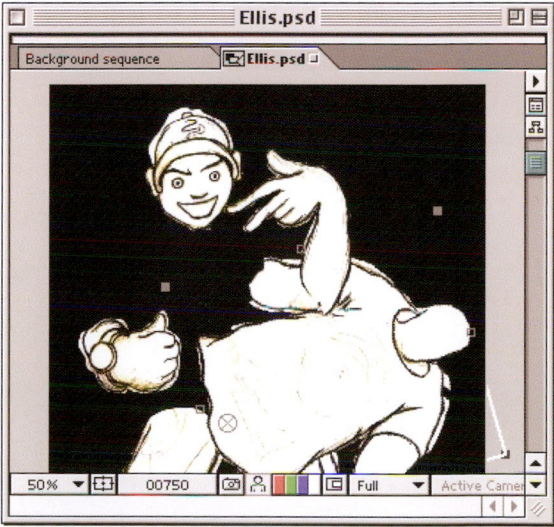

**16** Repeat this process for the Arm layers and the head layer, make sure that you move the Anchor Point to the position you would expect them to rotate from. The arms would rotate around the elbows, the head around the neck. I have circled the appropriate areas in the diagram below, get as close as you can to this as possible.

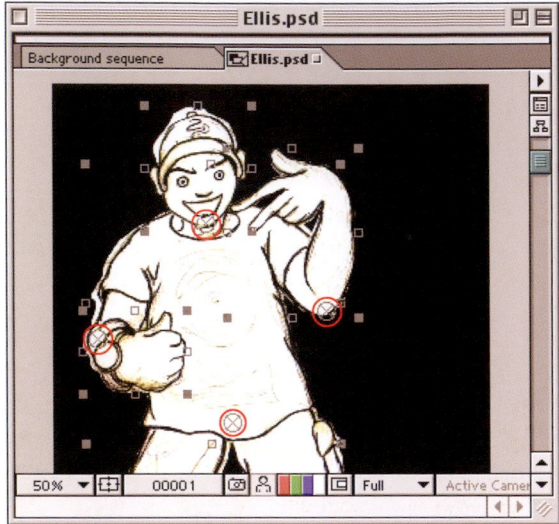

OK, so what we need to do now is to link the limbs and head to the main body of the character. In this case, the legs are staying still so we need to make the T-shirt layer a parent only for the head and arms. Let's start with the arms.

**17** Select the Right Arm layer and then Drag the Pickwhip from there onto the T-shirt layer. Let go of the mouse button/Pen when the T-shirt layer is highlighted and the Parenting menu changes to display the name of the T-shirt layer.

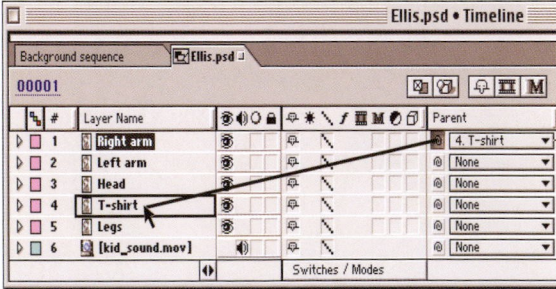

**18** Repeat this process for the Left-arm layer.

**19** Once you have finished setting up the parenting, select the T-shirt layer again and rotate it, now the arms rotate along with the T-shirt when it moves. We also want to Parent the head to the T-shirt but there is a good reason why we are not doing so yet, we want to create some animation on the head before we parent it to the T-shirt layer.

**20** Try rotating the arms and head a little, notice that they rotate independently from the head.

**21** Undo the rotations so that your character is in its original pose.

OK, we're going to start to animate this character now. I want the characters to be dancing in time with the music. We've looked at a couple of methods of making layers move in time with music, we've used Layer Markers to mark beats for use, we've also used a Motion Math Script to automate the process. There is one more method which is fantastic for recording any sort of motion whether it be timed with music or not and that is the Motion Sketch palette.

### basic motion capture

The Motion Sketch palette is available in both Standard and Production Bundle versions of After Effects. It allows you to capture any motion you make with your input device, this can be a Mouse or a Graphics tablet and Pen. I find it much easier to use Motion Sketch with my trusty Wacom tablet rather than a mouse which can be quite cumbersome to move around. If you have never used a graphics tablet before I thoroughly recommend investing in one, they are much easier and more creatively flexible to use than a mouse. They take a little time to adjust to and once you've started using one, you never want to go back.

My tablets of choice are the Wacom Intuos range, you can find information on the CD about Wacom, there are also links to companies on the website who will be able to sell you one of these tablets at a reasonable price.

**1** Using the Motion Sketch palette can take a wee bit of getting used to, so before we move on I want you to save this project to your Creative After Effects folder > Parenting chapter as Graffiti03b.aep.

Remember that you have just saved the project so you can practice the first step till you feel comfortable, if, at any point you get into a muddle with the Motion Sketch palette, simply go to File > Revert at any point to take you back to this stage.

**2** With the Head layer selected, go to Window > Motion Sketch to bring up the Motion Sketch palette.

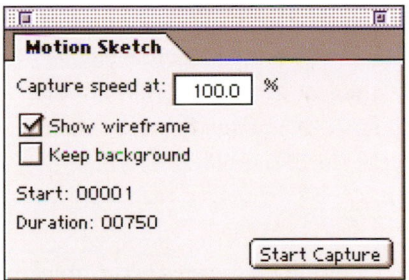

OK, I don't want you to follow these steps yet, just read through the next couple of paragraphs so that you are aware of what the process is.

To use Motion Sketch the first step is to click once on the Start Capture button in the Motion Sketch palette to let it know that you want to capture some motion. With the button clicked, After Effects will not begin to capture the motion until you click again at the point where you wish to begin your animation. As soon as you click the mouse or pen again, anywhere on the screen, After Effects will start to record the motion, it will stop recording when you release the mouse button or lift the pen from the Tablet.

When you do start recording the motion you want to create a fairly small amount of movement, mainly on the X-axis (left to right), where the main beats occur. We will be animating two characters in this comp, we don't want them moving at exactly the same times so remember to leave some gaps for the other character to move. At the Times where the other character will be moving a lot you can make a slight movements from side to side in time with the music.

**3** OK, so first of all, I want you to make sure that the Head layer is selected and then click once on the Start Capture button to activate the Motion Sketch palette.

**4** Move your pen or mouse over the Comp window, taking care not to accidentally click the mouse button or touch the graphics tablet as you do. Position the cursor where you would like to start the motion capture from.

**5** When you are ready, click the mouse button or pen and hold till you hear the music start to play, as soon as you do, start to move the mouse/pen from side to side in time with the music. Don't move it too far, just a little distance from the original point.

You may need a fair bit of practice before getting this absolutely right but don't give up, repetition is the best method for improving your techniques.

**6** Once you are happy with it, drag the Pickwhip from the Parent column of the Head layer onto the T-shirt layer to make the T-shirt the Parent of the Head layer.

The head now moves independently from the T-shirt layer (its parent) yet if you try rotating the T-shirt layer, you'll find that the Head moves with it wherever it goes.

**7** If you are really stuck with this, you can open up my Project, named, Graffiti03.aep from Training > Projects > Chapter 13 and continue with this project from this point on. But keep practicing with this, it's worth learning I promise you.

## make 'em dance!

OK, time to import our second character. To set up the parenting structure for her will be slightly different. I'm going to show you a different technique for each character.

**1** Import the file named, Annie.psd as a *Composition*.

**2** Double-click the new Composition to open it.

**3** Hit the Y key to select Pan behind tool. Select each layer in turn and then move anchor points for each layer where you would imagine the joints to be, the main areas are marked in red in this diagram.

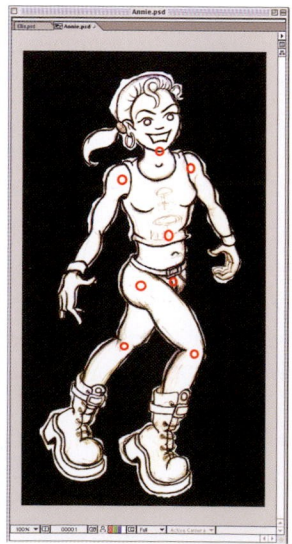

It is now time to set up our parenting structure. It will help you to figure out your parenting structure if you think about the way that the human body works. Your head and arms are linked to your torso, wherever your torso moves, your head and arms always follow.

**4** Click on to the Parent drop down menu for the Head layer and choose Torso from the list of possible choices.

**5** In the Parent column next to the drop down menu for the Left Arm layer click on the Parent Pickwhip icon and drag it onto the torso layer's Layer Name. This does exactly the same as choosing the torso layer from the drop down menu.

**6** Using either of the techniques link the Right Arm layer to the Torso and then the Torso layer to the Belly layer.

**7** Go to the Left Thigh layer's Parent column and choose the Torso layer from the drop down menu.

**8** Go to the left shin menu and choose the Left Thigh layer so that the Shin follows the thigh wherever it goes.

**9** Before you do anything else, save your project as Graffiti04b.aep into you Creative After Effects > Parenting Chapter folder.

OK we are going to leave these character animations for now and learn a little bit more about parenting, we will come back to these in the Expressions chapter where we will animate the linked body parts using Expressions and more parenting.

**10** Have a go at rotating each of the body parts a little bit, just enough to see how the parts link together. *Do not* save the changes.

# other uses for parental hierarchy

Besides creating hierarchical motion (which we covered when we did the Arm animation) and creating additional pivot points (which we covered when we did the camera animation) there are at least a couple of other uses for parental hierarchy. One of them, perhaps the simplest use of all, is simply to use parenting as a method of grouping layers together, as an alternative to precomposing them into a nested composition. There are many cases where this is simply more convenient. Another use for parental hierarchy is controlling axis order, which is covered in the next section.

Warning: The final two sections that follow are on advanced topics. If you feel comfortable with what you've learned so far and are eager for more, please read on. If on the other hand, you feel the need to absorb what you've learned for a while and get used to using parenting in your animations, feel free to hold off on reading the following sections and come back to them later.

## 3D taster

This first section covers a very important method for controlling how layers rotate in 3D space. Now I am aware of the fact that we haven't yet covered the basic 3D features of After Effects but I felt that this section really belonged in the parenting chapter.

If you have no experience with any 3D applications, or have absolutely no understanding about how 3D works in general, then you can come back to this section later, when it is referred to in the 3D chapter. If this is the case, simply continue with the following section, *non-uniform scale problem*.

If you have a basic understanding of 3D, then it is useful to continue with this section as it will give you an clear insight into how After Effects operates rotation in three dimensions.

## controlling rotational axis order

Another use is for Parental Hierarchy is controlling the rotational axis order of 3D layers. For a basic demonstration of what 3D axis order is, open and play the QuickTime movie file, *AxisOrderDemo.mov*. Once you have viewed this movie, keep it open so that you can refer to it now and then throughout this section. To help you understand more, you can also try the following:

**1** Pick up a book and hold it in your hand with the front of the book facing towards you. (Not this book as you will need to keep reading!)

**2** Imagine 3 axes of rotation for the book. Rotating on the book on its X-axis would mean tipping the book in your hand so that either the top or the bottom edge of the book comes towards you. Rotating on the book on its Y-axis would mean twisting the book in your hand so that either the left side or the right edge of the book comes towards you. And rotating on the book on its Z-axis would mean turning the book in your hand like a steering wheel, so that the face of the book continues to point towards you but the book is sideways, with either its left or right edge towards the floor.

**3** Now, to demonstrate what axis order is, try rotating the book in your hand 90 degrees in each of the 3 axes one at a time in the following order: first X, then Y, then Z.

**4** Notice the orientation that the book has ended up in.

**5** Now, reset the book to its original orientation with the front of the book facing towards you again.

**6** This time, rotate the book 90 degrees in each of the 3 axes again but in a different order: first Y, then X, then Z.

**7** Note that the book is now in a different orientation, even though you have rotated it by the exact same amount in each axis as you did before. The reason for this is that the order you rotate the book in each axis makes a huge amount of difference and therefore matters a lot!

In After Effects, when you specify an orientation for a 3D layer using X, Y and Z values, the same issue exists. Depending on what order the rotations are applied, the same set of X, Y and Z rotation values mean a completely different thing. (This is true for both the Orientation channel and After Effects' separate X, Y and Z rotation channels. Either way, After Effects must interpret the 3 values in a particular order.)

The rotational axis order for 3D layers in After Effects is always ZYX. This means that when you enter rotation or orientation values, the Z value is applied to the layer first, then the Y value, then the X value. There are situations where you may need a different axis order for a particular animation. By using extra Null objects as parents, you can control the axis order of any 3D layer.

As an example, here is how to set the axis order of a 3D layer to XYZ.

**1** Open the project file 'Force Axis Order.aep'. This contains a single comp with a single solid in it called 'Layer To Change Order For'. We will change the axis order of this layer to YXZ. This must be done before applying any rotation values to the solid.

**2** Create two null objects, and rename them 'Y' and 'Z' respectively. To rename them, click on each of them one at a time in the Timeline window and press return, then type a new layer name.

**3** Make both null objects 3D layers by clicking their 3D Layer switches in the Timeline window.

**4** Place the null objects in the exact same position (in x, y and z) as the solid. To do this, select the solid's position channel I-beam in the Timeline window and copy it. Then select each of the null's position channel I-beams and paste. See the following diagram for an illustration of the selected I-beam.

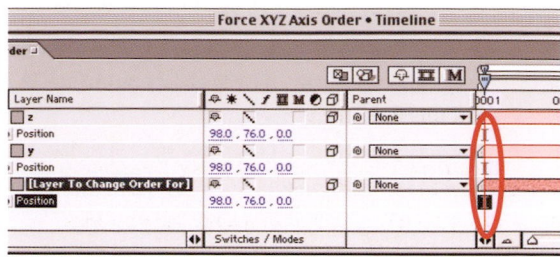

**5** Parent the Y null to the Z null, and parent the solid to the Y null.

**6** When animating, rotate only the Z-axis of the Z null, rotate only the Y-axis of the Y null, and rotate only the X-axis of the solid. Experiment by animating the solid's rotation in this way. Be very careful not to change any other axes besides the Z-axis of the Z null, Y-axis of the Y null, and X-axis of the solid.

Because X is being rotated at the bottom of the parental hierarchy in this case, the effect will be as if X were being applied first. Y being rotated in the middle of the hierarchy will have the same effect as if Y were being applied second, and Z being rotated at the top of the hierarchy will have the same effect as if Z were being applied last. So your effective axis order will be XYZ.

The project file 'AxisOrderExamples.aep' contains examples of this technique already set up for each of the possible axis orders (excluding ZYX since After Effects layers already use ZYX by default).

## non-uniform scale problem

As you saw earlier in this chapter, child layers always animate relative to their parents. When you parent one layer to another, its values become relative to the parent instead of relative to the composition. By default, when you parent an object to another, it stays in the same place in the composition and does not appear to change at the time of parenting. There is one special case, however, where the child will be *forced* to change when it is parented. To see an example of this, do the following:

**1** Open the SkewProblem.aep project from Training > Projects > Chapter 13. Choose *Don't Save* for the previous project.

**2** In the Skew Problem comp, create two solids, a green one and a red one, each 100x100 pixels.

**3** Scale the green solid to 50% in the X-axis but leave it 100% in the Y-axis (non-uniformly scaled).

**4** Rotate the green solid to 45 degrees.

**5** Parent the Red Solid to the green one.

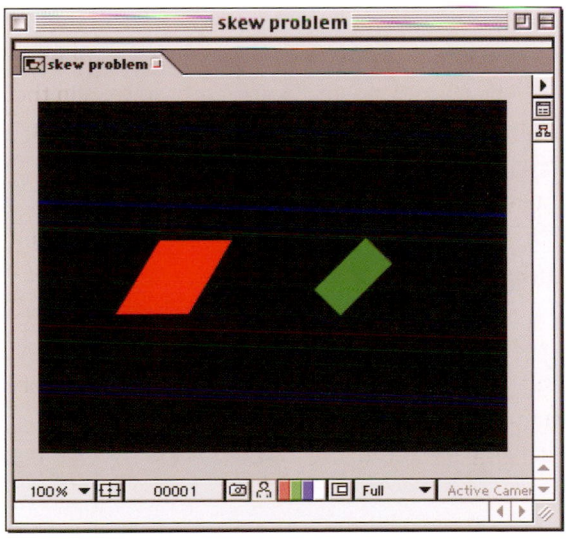

The red solid will suddenly appear skewed. This is because the green solid (parent layer) is non-uniformly scaling at a 45 degree angle compared with the red solid (child) and there is no direct transform that can be applied to the red solid to compensate for non-uniform scaling in this direction (no way to un-scale it at the 45 degree angle it's being scaled by the parent).

There are two different workarounds for this problem. This project contains separate compositions demonstrating the problem and each of the two workarounds; *workaround #1 – precompose* and *workaround #2 – null object.* For now, I'll show you how these two comps were developed. The first workaround is to use nulls to control the rotation.

### solution 1

**1** Undo the last two operations, leaving you with the green solid still non-uniformly scaled but not yet rotated, and the red solid not yet parented to the green solid.

**2** Create a new null object.

**3** Parent the null to the green solid.

**4** Rotate the green solid 45 degrees.

**5** Parent the red solid to the null.

This time, no skewing occurs. That's because the null object was parented to the green solid *before* it was rotated, thus allowing the null to automatically compensate for the non-uniform scaling of the parent with its own equal and opposite non-uniform scaling. To see this, look at the scale values in the Timeline window for both the null and the green solid. The green solid is of course 50% in X and 100% in Y, as you last left it. But the null is now 200% in X and 100% in Y, thus undoing the effects of the non-uniform scaling (because 200% of 50% is 100%). Thus the non-uniform scale has no effect on the red solid.

### solution 2

The second workaround is to pre-compose the scaled parent to a nested composition, moving all attributes to the new composition, before parenting the child to it. This puts the non-uniform scale in the sub-composition, where it cannot affect the child.

**1** Undo the last operation so that the red solid is not yet parented. Then delete the null layer.

**2** Select the green solid layer and go to Layer > Pre-compose to open up the Pre-compose dialog box. Choose to *Move All Attributes into New Composition* and type in *Green Precomp* as the new comps name. Click OK to leave.

**3** Parent the Red solid to the Green Precomp. Once again, no skewing occurs because the non-uniform scale happened in the Precomp so has no bearing on the child.

## recap

Parental Hierarchy is useful to animators in several important ways, including:

- Creating hierarchical motion
- Creating extra pivot points
- Grouping objects together
- Changing axis order.

In combination with Null Objects, Parental Hierarchy can also be useful any time you just need to isolate different components of a complex motion. By using a different null object for each aspect of the same motion, you can easily create and work with much more complex animations than you would otherwise be able to. In short, Parental Hierarchy is a very important tool for animators! I hope this chapter has helped you become familiar with this new tool in After Effects, and its great possibilities. Now take some time to experiment and make your own animations with Parental Hierarchy, and have fun!

Here are some more design tips, this time they're from Amsterdam in Holland where David Keone is a designer for Canto Five Design. See some of his work at: http://www.cantofive.com

- Try to notice how children see things, by watching them. Do you remember when you could see amazing things in your spilled cereal? Or the horror of the weird tree that was thumping on your window in the wind? The spirit of playing is essential to our minds, and many of us forget to take the time to just play. Give yourself 20 minutes to splash paint around on a plate or arrange leaves into patterns on the living room floor. It is no coincidence our greatest inspiration usually comes when we have taken a moment to relax, or do something else. The difficult art is taking the raw ideas that seem obvious to everyone, and putting them together again, and again, and again until you have exhausted every possibility.
- Draw inspiration from everywhere. Keep a box to put those weird shells, and cool bits of fabric in. Scraps of paper with that great idea on it that you just don't have time to think about right now because you have so much work to do. I often raid our child's toyboxes when a deadline is looming, the 99 cent store solved the interface issue for the ToyStory website. You can learn more about marketing from looking at great advertisements for bad products, think movie trailers, music videos, how *did* Bow Wow Wow sell over two million records?
- There are times that you need to just do your thing. Just get started! Everything will work itself out with enough time and effort, but you have to trust yourself to work things through, and give your project all the time and effort it needs to mature. Don't wait! The earlier you have something to work from, the more time you have to revise it and get it right.

# chapter fourteen
# expressions

## what are expressions?

Expressions are one of the most powerful new features in After Effects 5.0; learning how to use them is guaranteed to change the way you use After Effects in the future. This chapter (excluding the Graffiti Club and Seattle Evening News tutorials) was written by Paul Tuersley who's biography you can read in the Introduction. Paul's tutorials use clipart images from Novacorp's Art Explosion collection which you can find out more about on the CD (in the Free Stuff > Art Explosion folder).

An expression is essentially a small script that can be added to a property, allowing you to control its value by linking to and adapting values from other properties. When you consider that After Effects is basically made up of keyframes and values, having a way to link them together opens up lots of possibilities.

There are still certain things that are best done using Motion Math, After Effect's earlier version of scripting (Production Bundle only). For example the cmpaud.mm (Comp Audio) script reads audio levels and converts them into values, while expressions cannot deal with that kind of audio level information. However, in the majority of cases, expressions are much more powerful and far easier to use.

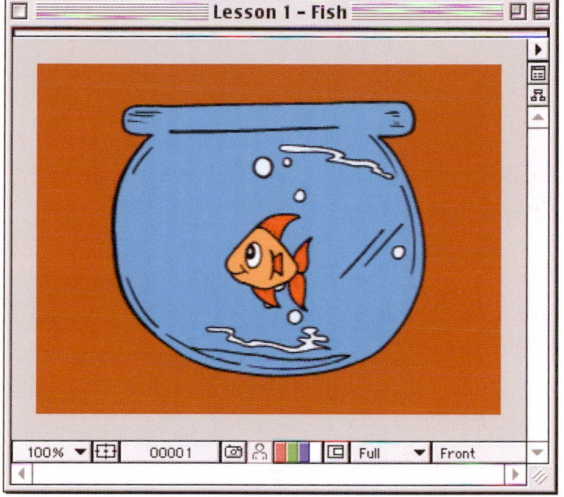

Although expressions are written in Javascript, you shouldn't let that put you off; I myself have no programming experience, but by learning just a little at a time, I've become very comfortable with expressions and find uses for them in almost everything I do.

In the early part of this chapter, we're going to concentrate on the basic rules of the expression language and you may want to go through it a few times. It's important that you understand these rules, as they will form the basis for all of your future expression building.

Creative After Effects

There's quite a bit to learn in this chapter, so find a nice quiet place and plenty of time. Rest assured, after this chapter you'll be well on your way to being an expression guru.

## adding an expression

So, the first step is to learn how to add an expression to a property:

**1** Open the BasicExpStart.aep project from the Training > Projects > Chapter 14 folder.

**2** Open Lesson 1 – Fish and RAM Preview the composition. As you can see, we have a goldfish swimming around inside a bowl, with Opacity keyframes that fade him in and out.

There may be times when you temporarily want to turn off some keyframes, to concentrate on one particular aspect of your animation.

Let's say we want to temporarily turn off the Fish layer's Opacity keyframes, so that we can view the fish's motion more clearly. We can use an expression to override the existing keyframes, while still keeping them safe for later.

**3** Ensure the Fish layer's Opacity property is visible in the Timeline by selecting the Fish layer and hitting the T key.

**4** Click on the word Opacity to highlight the property name.

**5** From the pull-down menu, select Animation > Add Expression.

We see that three little icons are added to the Switches/Modes panel (we'll look at these later), an *equals* (**=**) icon appears next to the stopwatch and an expression text box appears under the keyframes in which the word *opacity* is added automatically.

**6** Click outside of the expression text field, or hit the Enter key on your keyboard's number pad, to activate the expression.

**NB** Don't hit the main Return key on the keyboard by mistake; this won't activate an expression, it will add a new line to it instead.

If you do a RAM Preview now, you'll see that nothing has changed. When an expression is first created, the default expression ensures that the current values (including any keyframes) remain the same.

So the expression *opacity* simply means, 'make me the same as my current Opacity value'.

In other words, it is keeping the opacity the same as it was before.

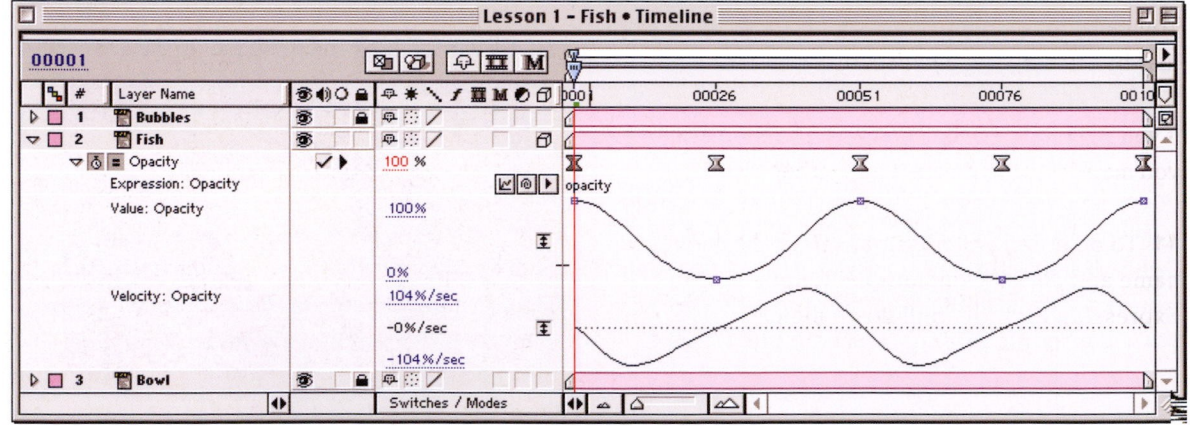

However, in our case we *want* the expression to ignore the current opacity values:

**7** Highlight the current expression text and replace the word *opacity*, so the expression just reads: *100*

**8** Again, activate the expression by clicking outside of the expression text field, or hitting Enter on the number pad of your keyboard.

**9** RAM Preview the animation again. The fish now stays at 100% opacity throughout; the expression is saying, 'ignore the keyframes, just make the expression result equal 100 on every frame'.

Now that the Fish is visible at all times, we get a clearer view of what it's doing and can easily make any adjustments.

To bring back the original fades, we can just switch the expression off. The equals (=) icon next to the stopwatch is the expression's on/off switch.

**10** Move to frame 26 and then click the *equals* (=) icon next to the Opacity stopwatch.

It will become a *does not equal* (≠) icon and the expression is now disabled.

You can turn an expression on or off at any time, just by clicking the *equals* icon.

If you've completely finished with the expression, you may decide to delete it altogether.

**11** To delete the expression, select the property name and choose Animation > Remove Expression from the pull-down menu

# using the pick whip

Although an expression can only control the property (and layer) to which it is applied, it is able to read the values of almost any property, on any layer in the project.

To help us build expressions that read these other values, we have the Pick Whip.

The Pick Whip is the middle of the three icons that appear in the Timeline when an Expression is applied: it works in a similar way to the one in the Parenting panel that we used back in chapter thirteen.

### the pick whip icon

When you drag the expression Pick Whip onto another property, you are basically telling After Effects to write an expression that 'makes *this* property value the same as *that* property value'.

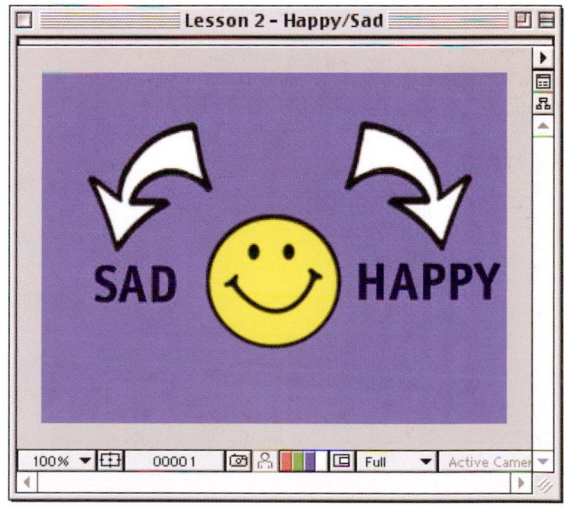

**1** Open Lesson 2 – Happy/Sad. We have a background and two main layers, a Happy Face and a Sad Face.

We're going to use an expression to make the Happy Face layer's Opacity equal to its Rotation. As we rotate the Happy Face layer, it will fade out to reveal the Sad Face layer beneath.

**2** Make sure you can see Happy Face layer's Rotation and Opacity properties. If not, select the Happy Face layer, then press the R key, followed by Shift + T.

This time, we'll use a much quicker way to add an expression.

**3** Hold down the Alt key and click on the Opacity Stopwatch of the Happy Face layer to add an expression (you can also delete expressions in the same way).

**4** Click and drag the Pick Whip (see diagram below) over to the Rotation property and release the mouse when Rotation is highlighted by a black rectangle. Activate the expression by clicking away from the text field, or hitting Enter on the number pad.

The expression should now read: *rotation*

This translates as 'make me (i.e. Opacity) the same as my Rotation value'.

You may have noticed that our face is no longer happy; Happy Face's Opacity now matches the Rotation value of zero, what we're actually seeing is the Sad Face layer underneath.

**5** Select the Rotation tool (W) from the Tools Palette and rotate the Face layer in the Composition window.

Rotate clockwise for happy, anti-clockwise for sad.

Notice that as you rotate between 0 and 100°, Happy Face's Opacity fades between 0 and 100%.

**6** Finish by rotating Happy Face until its value reads 50° (or just enter 50 into Rotation's value box); you will see that the Opacity value has also changed to 50.

## basic arithmetic

We're going to stay with the Happy / Sad Face for the moment as we try to solve his mood swings. It isn't taking much to make him happy or sad; only a small change in rotation is having any effect.

Opacity is now set to equal rotation, but Opacity values only range from 0% to 100%. So, we're only seeing a change in Happy Face's Opacity when the Rotation value moves between 0 and 100 degrees.

We can modify the relationship between these two values by using some basic arithmetic on the end of our expression:

**1** Hightlight the expression text field by clicking on it, and then place the text cursor at the end of the current expression (i.e. after the word *rotation*).

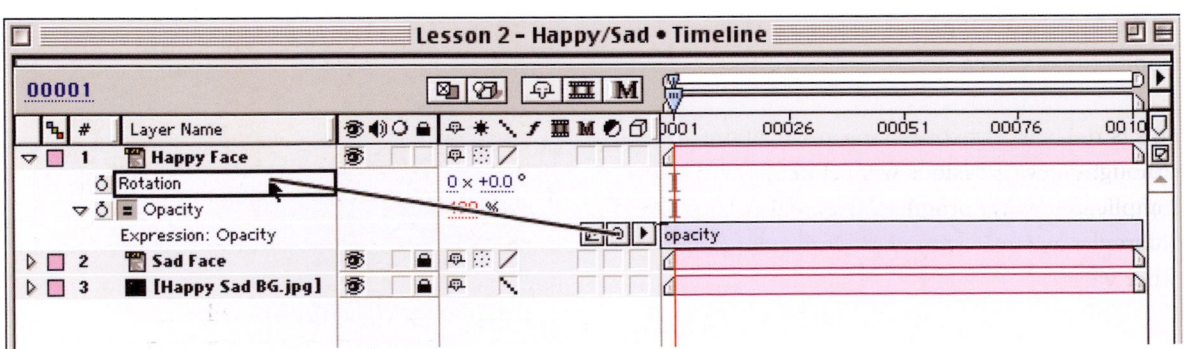

**2** Type */10* (divide by ten) on the end. So the expression now reads: rotation /10

Then activate the expression (click away from the text field or hit Enter on the number pad).

**3** This time, when you rotate the Face layer, you will find it takes many more rotations to fade from the Happy Face to the Sad Face.

Our expression is now saying, 'make me the same as the Rotation value, divided by ten'.

**4** Change the Happy Face layer's Rotation value so it now reads: $0 \times +50°$

You should now find that the Happy Face layer's Opacity is just 5%: the expression is taking the Rotation value of 50 and dividing it by ten.

You can modify values in an expression using any of the four main math symbols:

**+** for addition    **−** for subtraction
**/** for division    **\*** for multiplication

This seems a good time to review what we've looked at so far:

We've seen how to add an expression to a property, how to switch it on and off, and how to permanently delete it.

More importantly, we can use the Pick Whip to read values from other properties, and then modify those values.

This is really what expressions are all about: although the expressions will get longer and more complicated as we progress, they will still just be different ways we've found to read and modify other values.

## pickwhipping other layers

So far, we've only linked an expression to a property on the same layer: but as I've already mentioned, expressions can read the values of properties on any layer.

**1** Open Lesson 3 – Sun & Moon. It's a peaceful suburban scene, just before sunset.

There are three visible layers: the Sun layer is fairly obvious, then the Orange and Blue Ramp (using the Stylise > Ramp effect) layers are the sunset and night-time backgrounds respectively.

We're going to use the Sun layer's Rotation to control the Orange Ramp layer's Opacity; as we rotate the sun away, the orange sunset will fade to reveal the blue night background.

**2** For this, you'll need to be able to see both the Sun's Rotation property, and the Orange Ramp's Opacity (select the Sun and press R, then select Orange Ramp and press T).

**3** Alt-click on Orange Ramp's Opacity stopwatch to add an expression.

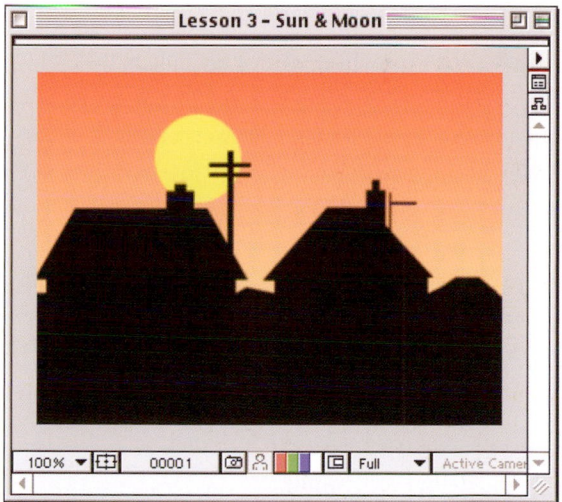

**4** Click and drag the Pick Whip over to the Sun layer's Rotation property, releasing when Rotation is highlighted. Then, activate the expression.

The resulting expression should be:
this_comp.layer("Sun").rotation

**5** Select the Rotation tool (W) from the Tools Palette. Select the Sun layer in the Timeline, and then rotate it *anti-clockwise* in the Composition window.

As the Sun's Rotation value decreases, the Orange Ramp's Opacity value will also decrease, fading out until we're looking at a night-time scene.

Let's look at that expression again:
this_comp.layer("Sun").rotation

Although the expression looks more complicated this time, it's basically saying,
'make me (i.e. Orange Ramp's Opacity) the same value as the Sun layer's Rotation'.

Expressions that read values from their own layer, just need to know which property to read
(i.e. *opacity* or *rotation*).

Expressions that read values from other layers also need to know which layer they are linking to.

It's nothing to worry about. As we've seen, the Pick Whip does most of the hard work for us. But it's still useful to understand how this is written.

An expression describes the location of a layer and property in a similar way to how you might describe the location of a file on your computer.

You might write down the location of a file on your computer as:
Hard Drive / Documents Folder / The File name

Similarly, think of the location of a property in After Effects as:
Composition / Layer / Property

When written as an expression, this would be:
this_comp.layer("layer name").property name

or in our case:
this_comp.layer("Sun").rotation

Notice how each of the three sections are separated by a full stop ( . )

**NB** As we see, expressions refer to other layers by name, so it's a good idea to give each layer a unique name to avoid any problems.

For example, you might find yourself with two layers named *Solid 1* in the same composition,
and an expression such as:
this_comp.layer("Solid 1").rotation

After Effects doesn't know which layer to look at, and in these situations it will always choose the highest of those layers in the Timeline, which isn't necessarily the one you had planned.

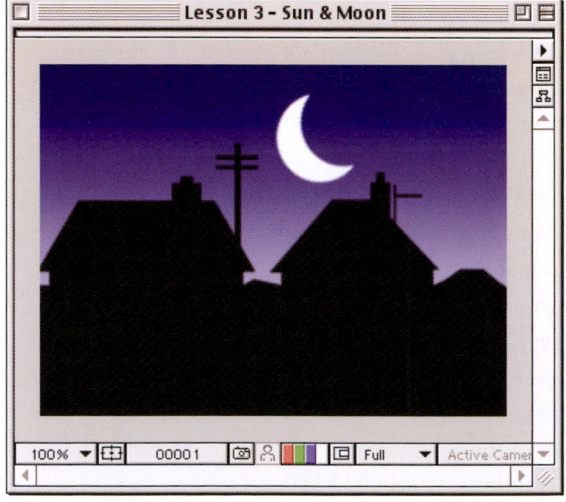

# properties
# and dimensions 1

You may have noticed that so far, we've only been linking between Opacity and Rotation. Opacity and Rotation are examples of properties in After Effects that each contain just one value.

Opacity = a value between 0 and 100%
Rotation = a positive or negative value in degrees

As each consists of just one value, we can call them one-dimensional (or 1D) properties.

Properties such as Position and Scale, are a bit different; they each contain at least two separate values, one for the X-axis (left/right) and one for the Y-axis (up/down).

Position = [X value, Y value]
Scale = [X value, Y value]
These are two-dimensional (2D) properties.

When you start using 3D layers, you'll find that previously 2D properties (like Position and Scale) have gained a third Z value.

Position = [ X value, Y value, Z value ]
Scale = [ X value, Y value, Z value ]
These are three-dimensional (3D) properties.

It's important that you are aware of how many values (or dimensions) a property contains, when you start writing your own expressions.

**NB** Before starting this lesson, make sure that your free Final Effects complete plug-in *Time Blend* is installed. If it's already installed, you can move straight on to the lesson, otherwise, you'll find the plug-in in the *Free Stuff > Media_100_Ice* folder on the CD. Use the instructions provided to install the plug-in and then restart After Effects and this lesson from the original BasicExp.aep project in the Training > Chapter 14 folder.

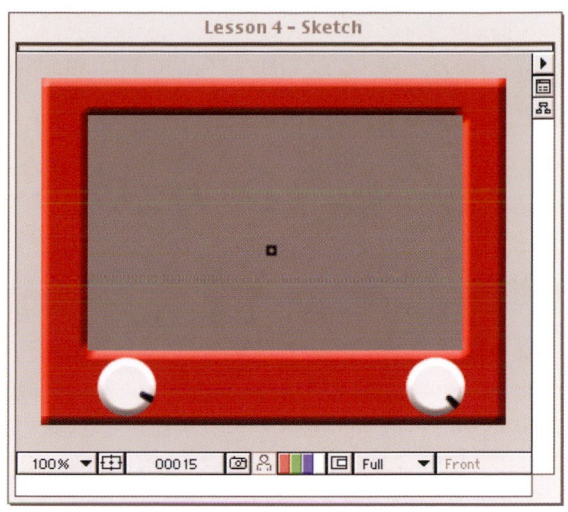

**1** Open Lesson 4 - Sketch and you'll find a new toy to play with. There are three visible layers in the Timeline: a Left Dial, a Right Dial and a Black Dot.

In this lesson, we're going to create an expression that uses Rotation to control Position. Position is a 2D property and requires two values to control it, so we'll need to use two sets of Rotation values.

The Left Dial will provide the Rotation value we need to control the Black Dot's X-axis (left to right motion), while the Right Dial's Rotation will be used to control its Y-axis (up and down motion).

**2** Make sure you can see both the Dial layers' Rotation properties and the Black Dot's Position (if not, select both Dial layers and press R, then select the Black Dot layer and press P).

In Lesson 1, we created a very simple expression for Opacity: we just entered the value 100. Let's try doing the same on Black Dot's Position property:

**3** Alt-click the Black Dot's Position stopwatch to add an expression, replace the word *position* with *100* and then activate the expression.
You should get the following error message:

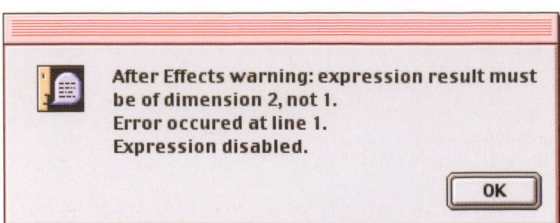

After Effects warning: expression result must be of dimension 2, not 1.
Error occured at line 1.
Expression disabled.

OK

You'll also notice that a couple more things have happened to indicate that the Expression doesn't work:

The *equals* (=) icon will have become a *does not equal* (≠) icon.

A little, yellow warning symbol appears next to the expression icons, telling us that this expression contains an error.

These error messages are nothing to be afraid of, they are actually very useful in helping us work out what's gone wrong. This message is saying that the result of this expression (for Position) must be two values, not one.

For properties that have more than one value (like Position), the correct way to write this expression is: [the X value, the Y value]

We need two values, which must be separated by a comma and placed inside square brackets.

**4** Click the expression text field to highlight the current expression and change it to [150, 100] before activating the expression.

You'll see the Black Dot jump to a new position in the Composition window, proving that the expression works!

Now we know the proper way to write these expressions, let's create the real one.

**5** Click the text field to highlight the expression, then drag the Pick Whip over to the Left Dial's Rotation property, releasing when it is highlighted by a black rectangle. Activate the expression. The result is:
[this_comp.layer("Left Dial").rotation,
this_comp.layer("Left Dial").rotation]

**NB** This expression is written on just one line. There's more room in the Timeline window than in the columns of this book.

It's our longest expression so far, but if we break it down, it's not too hard to see what it means. You should already be familiar with the line:

this_comp.layer("Left Dial").rotation

It simply means, 'make me the same as Left Dial's Rotation value'.

In our new expression that line is repeated twice, it's also separated by a comma and placed inside square brackets: exactly the format that is needed on a 2D property like Position.

**6** Select the Rotation Tool (W) from the Tools Palette and rotate the Left Dial in the Composition window.

As you rotate the Left Dial, the Black Dot moves diagonally in the Composition window; which is obviously wrong.

The expression is applying the value of Left Dial's Rotation to both the X and Y values of Black Dot's Position property. We only want the Left Dial to control the X value, while the Right Dial controls the Y value. We need to make a slight alteration to the expression text.

**7** Replace the second *Left Dial* with *Right Dial*, then activate the expression. It should now read:
[this_comp.layer("Left Dial").rotation,
this_comp.layer("Right Dial").rotation]

**8** Using the Rotation Tool, try rotating the Dials in the Composition window.

You'll see the Position values are matching the Rotation values and that it's only taking a small amount of rotation to move the Black Dot. We'll change this by using some basic arithmetic to divide each of the values by twenty.

**9** Alter the expression one last time, insert /20 (divide by twenty) after each expression value, then activate the expression.

It should now read:
[this_comp.layer("Left Dial").rotation /20, this_comp.layer("Right Dial").rotation /20]

The Black Dot will probably disappear from view. Check in the Timeline and you'll see the Position values are very small; they are now equal to the Rotation values divided by twenty.

**10** To bring the Black Dot back into view, change both of the Dial layer's Rotation values in the Timeline to: 5x +0.0°.

Now, when you rotate the Dials in the Composition window, you'll find they need far more rotation to affect the Black Dot's position.

You've successfully completed this lesson and as a reward, I'm going to show you a little magic. This will only work if the Final Effects plug-in Time Blend is installed on your machine so if you haven't done so already, install it now.

**1** Select Edit > Preferences > Previews from the pull-down and make sure that Dynamic Resolution is turned *off*, then click OK.

**2** Click the Hide Shy Layers button at the top of the Timeline window (see picture) to reveal the hidden layers.

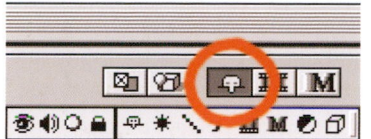

**3** Switch the Sketch Magic layer on (click the layer eyeball) and move the Current-Time Marker to any frame in the composition except the first.

Now try rotating the Dials in the Composition window; if everything has gone to plan, the Black Dot should be leaving trails as it moves around the screen. To clear the screen, move the Current-Time Marker to the first frame of the composition, then away again.

There's nothing to RAM Preview or render out here; this is purely a toy for your amusement.

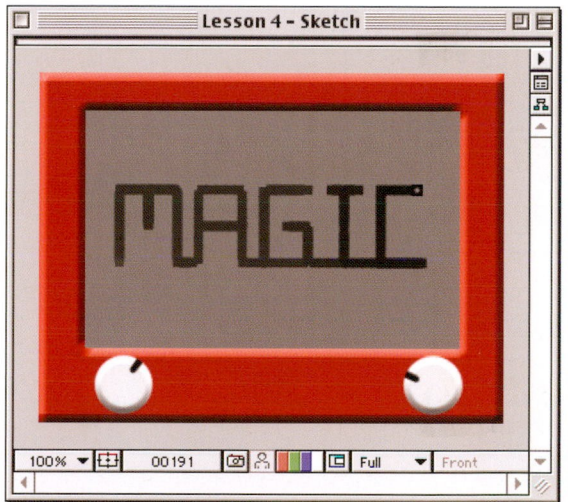

## properties and dimensions 2

**1** Open Lesson 5 – Bee Graph and RAM Preview the composition. You'll see we have an animating Bee layer (created using Motion Sketch) on top of a background. We also have two arrow layers, an Altitude Arrow and a Distance Arrow.

**2** Make sure you can see the Position properties for the Bee and both Arrow layers (if not, select the three layers in the Timeline and hit the P key).

The last lesson showed how to take 1D properties (i.e. Rotation) and apply them to 2D properties (i.e. Position). We take our two separate values and package them up in square brackets, with a comma in the middle.

We only had to do that because we were linking properties of different dimensions. If we were to use an expression to link one layer's Position to another layer's Position, the properties are an exact match (i.e. both are 2D) so the expression will be simpler.

To prove this, let's add an expression to the Distance Arrow layer, linking its Position to the Bee layer's Position.

**3** Alt-click the stopwatch on Distance Arrow's Position property to add an expression, then drag the Pick Whip over to the Bee layer's Position property and release. Activate the expression and do a RAM Preview.

You'll see that the Distance Arrow now matches the position of the Bee layer. The expression is:

this_comp.layer("Bee").position

As I'm sure you already know, this means, 'make me the same as the Bee layer's Position'.

As always, the Pick Whip does a great job making sure the expression is suitable for the properties we choose. That last step was just to prove a point; it has nothing to do with what we are trying to achieve.

Our aim is to try and get each of the Arrow layers to move along their own side of the graph: one will show the Bee's altitude, the other will show its distance from the beehive.

Although we need to link both Arrows to the Bee's Position, Distance Arrow only needs the left/right motion, while the Altitude Arrow only needs the up/down motion.

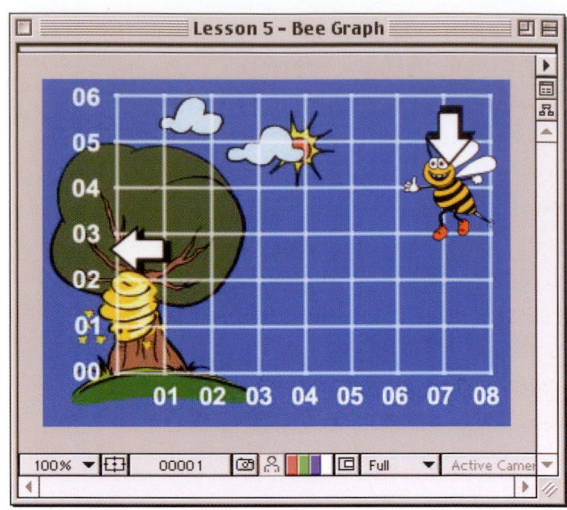

The last lesson showed how to package two separate values into one 2D property (Position), this lesson will show the reverse, i.e. how to pull just one single value out of a 2D property.

**4** Let's turn off that last expression for a while; click the *equals* ( **=** ) icon next to Distance Arrow's stopwatch. It becomes a *does not equal* ( **≠** ) icon and the expression is now disabled.

**5** Scrub one of Distance Arrow's Position values (i.e. 130 or 225) in the Timeline window, watching what happens in the Composition window. Then Undo the last step (hit Command + Z or choose Edit > Undo from the pull-down menus).

**6** Repeat Step 5 with the other Position value. When dragging the first X value (130), you'll see the arrow moves left/right in the Composition window; drag the second Y value (225) and the arrow moves up/down.

We want Distance Arrow to move left and right, in line with the Bee, so we need the X value from the Bee's Position.

But, we don't want the arrow moving up or down, we want to leave the Y value constant at 225. We'll use the Pick Whip to help us, but this time we're building the expression step by step.

Creative After Effects

**7** Highlight the expression text field on the Distance Arrow's Position property, replacing the current expression text with ( [ ), an open square bracket. Don't activate the expression yet.

**8** Now drag the expression Pick Whip over to the actual values, i.e. 279, 75 on the Bee's Position property and select the first of the two values (279), releasing the Pick Whip when the value is highlighted.

The expression should read:
[this_comp.layer("Bee").position[0]
But we're still not finished yet.

**9** Now type in a comma ( , ) at the end of our expression, followed by the number 225 and then the symbol for a closed square bracket ( ] ).
So the expression should now read:
[this_comp.layer("Bee").position[0] , 225 ]

**10** Activate the expression and RAM Preview the result. The Distance Arrow should now be moving left and right in line with the Bee layer's Position. Let's break the expression down:

The expression consists of two values, separated by a comma and inside square brackets, which is the correct way to package two values into a 2D property like Position.

The first value description is:
this_comp.layer("Bee").position[0]
which looks fairly familiar, except for the [0] that we see on the end of it, so what does this mean?

If we want to extract a single value from a 2D property, we have to choose which of those values we want (i.e. the X or the Y).

Curiously, expressions number these individual values starting from zero, so:
X value – [0]
Y value – [1]    And for 3D, Z value – [2]

Back to the full expression, which reads:
[this_comp.layer("Bee").position[0] , 225 ]

The whole expression is saying, 'make *my X value* the same as the X value, on the Position property of the Bee layer, and make *my Y value* a constant value of 225'.

Now all we need to do is add an expression to the Altitude Arrow, linking it up in much the same way.

We don't want Altitude Arrow moving left or right; we want to leave the X value at a constant 50.

We do want the arrow to move up and down so we will need to take the Y value from Bee's Position.

**11** Alt-click the Altitude Arrow's Position stopwatch to add an expression, type an open square bracket ( [  ) followed by the number 50 and finally a comma ( , ) so the expression reads:
[ 50 ,

**12** Now drag the expression Pick Whip over to the second of the Bee's Position values (Y value), releasing the Pick Whip when that value is highlighted.

**13** Finally, add a closed square bracket ( ] ) to the end and activate the expression.

RAM Preview your composition and with a bit of luck, both arrows will now be working correctly, moving along their own side of the graph, marking the Bee's altitude and distance to the hive.

Congratulations, you've now finished this lesson.

By way of a reward, I've already hooked up a more advanced expression, to give you a little taster of what you'll be able to do in the future.

**1** Click the Hide Shy Layers button at the top of the Timeline window to reveal the hidden layer.

**2** Switch the Magic Numbers layer on (click the layer's eyeball) and do a RAM Preview.

You should now see a new set of numbers in the Composition window, that animate to show the exact graph values.

The expressions I've used here are a bit more advanced than anything we've tried so far, so I'd hold off until completing the whole expression chapter, before coming back to figure out how it works. at the end of this chapter, you can also check out the Extras > Expressions folder on the CD; and the book's website at;

http://www.angie.abel.co.uk/book.html

to find some more useful expressions, examples and tutorials.

Although this example is cute and cuddly, it could be turned into some kind of futuristic computer display, with all kinds of values animating on screen. Or it could be used in an educational program to illustrate scientifific information in graph form.

You'll be pleased to hear that we've reached the end of the expression basics section. The things you've learnt in this section are the foundations for all expressions, once you've got to grips with them you'll find things become a lot easier.

For now, I'm going to hand you back to Angie who's going to show you how you can implement some of these expressions within one of your ongoing projects, The Graffiti Club project.

# graffiti club

## using expressions to animate characters

Thanks Paul! Now we're going to return to the Graffiti Project, using what we've learnt to animate one of our main characters. In the Parenting chapter, we linked the body parts and captured some movement for the head using the Motion Sketch palette. Now we'll create some expressions that will animate the other body parts just by using the Head's position values.

**1** Open the Project named, Graffiti04.aep from the Training > Projects > Chapter 14 folder.

**2** Open the Ellis.psd composition. Select the Right Arm layer and hit R view the rotation values. Select the Head layer and hit P to see the Position values. These are the keyframes we created using the Motion Sketch palette. RAM Preview the Elliss.psd comp to remind yourself of what we've done so far.

Remember we concentrated on making most of the Head's movement happen along the X-axis, so this is the best place to take the movement from.

**3** Alt-click the Rotation property stopwatch of the Right Arm layer to add an Expression, then drag the pickwhip on to the first (X) value of the Head layer's Position values (see diagram at the top of the following page).

Activate the expression by clicking outside the text field or hitting Enter on the number pad.
The expression will read:
this_comp.layer("Head").position[0]

With this, we're telling After Effects to make Right Arm's Rotation value the same as Head layer's X Position value (the [0] on the end represents the X value).

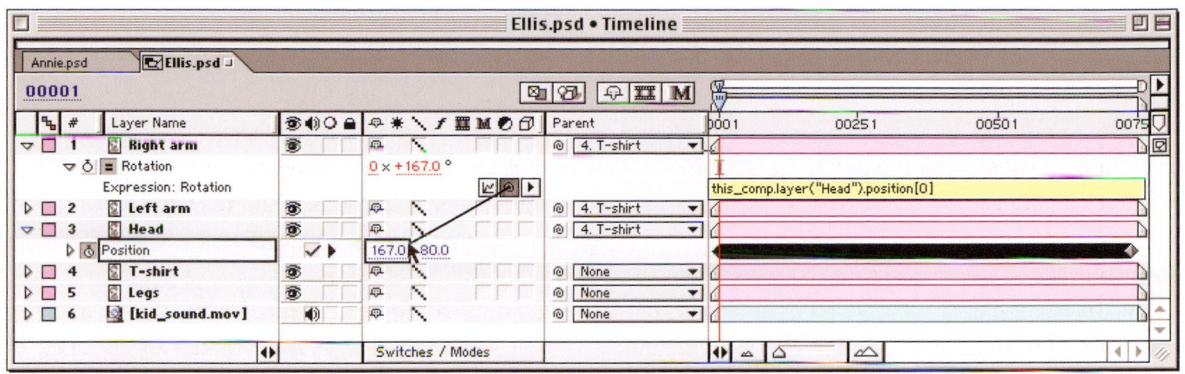

**4** Shift+RAM Preview the composition. The Right Arm is now rotating with the same timing as the Head's X movement, but it's not really moving fast enough.

**5** In the Expression text field, place the cursor after the current expression text and add: *5
so that the expression reads:
this_comp.layer("Head").position[0] *5

We have multiplied the resulting values by five, making the rotation a lot more exaggerated.
The arm is bending back in a most unnatural way, so we just need to nudge all of the rotation a little to compensate.

**6** Place the cursor after the current expression text and add: −150

It should now read:
this_comp.layer("Head").position[0] *5 −150

**7** Activate the expression and RAM Preview the results so far. While the amount of motion stays the same, each of the rotation values throughout the animation will now be 150° less than they were before.

Multiplying and dividing the values causes big changes in the amount of motion, while adding and subtracting will just offset the result by a set amount.

OK, what about if we want the head to scale up and down as it is moving? This would give us a bit of depth, making it appear that the head was jutting forwards and backwards as well as from side to side.

**8** Select the Head layer and hit Shift + S to view the Scale value alongside the Position value.

**9** Alt-click the Scale stopwatch to add an expression, then drag the Pick Whip over to the second Position value (the Y value) on the Head layer.
Activate the expression. It should read:
[position[1], position[1]]

Which means, "make both the X and Y Scale values the same as *this* layer's Y Position value." In this case, there's no need for it to specify the layer name because the Position property is on the same layer as the expression.

Immediately, you'll notice that the Head layer is now far too small for the body. No problem, we'll simply add 25 to the Scale value, right?

**10** OK, try placing the insertion point after the text and typing in;
+ 25
and then hitting the  Enter key. You will get an Error message like the one in the following diagram.

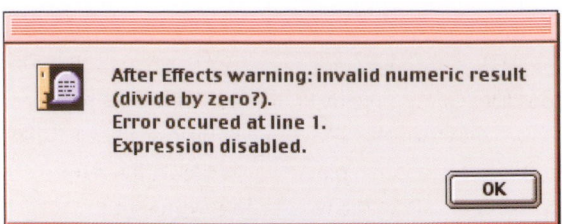

After Effects warning: invalid numeric result (divide by zero?).
Error occured at line 1.
Expression disabled.

OK

This message is telling you that you have an error in the first line of your expression. Why is this? It's always worked up till now? Well, the reason for the error is because the scale property contains two values whilst the four main math symbols(+ − * / ) can only be used to perform arithmetic on single values. After Effects needs separate instructions for each value within the brackets.

**11** Highlight the text field in the Expression and change the line of text so that it reads like this:

[position[1]+25, position[1]+25]

Now the expression is performing the multiplication on each of the X and Y Scale values individually before packaging them back together.

**12** Hit Enter on the number pad and then RAM Preview the comp again. The head is much more of a reasonable size now.

OK, we can take this much further. Let's animate the Left Arm layer, but instead of rotating it we'll scale it up and down, to make it look as if it's punching in and out.

**13** Select the Left Arm layer and hit the S key to view the Scale property.

**14** Alt-click the Scale stopwatch to add an expression, then drag the Pick Whip over to the first Position value (the X value) on the Head layer. You should come up with this expression; [this_comp.layer("Head").position[0], this_comp.layer("Head").position[0]]

The extra *this_comp.layer("Head")* stuff is there because the expression is reading a value from a different layer. But basically it's much like our last expression, saying, 'make both the X and Y Scale values the same as *Head* layer's X Position value'.

**15** Activate the expression and RAM Preview the result.

We can see that the left arm is far too big now; we'll use some more arithmetic to reduce both the scale values by 40.

**16** Adapt the existing expression by placing −40 after each of the values, so the expression reads:

[this_comp.layer("Head").position[0] −40, this_comp.layer("Head").position[0] −40]

Your Timeline should look like the one pictured in the following diagram.

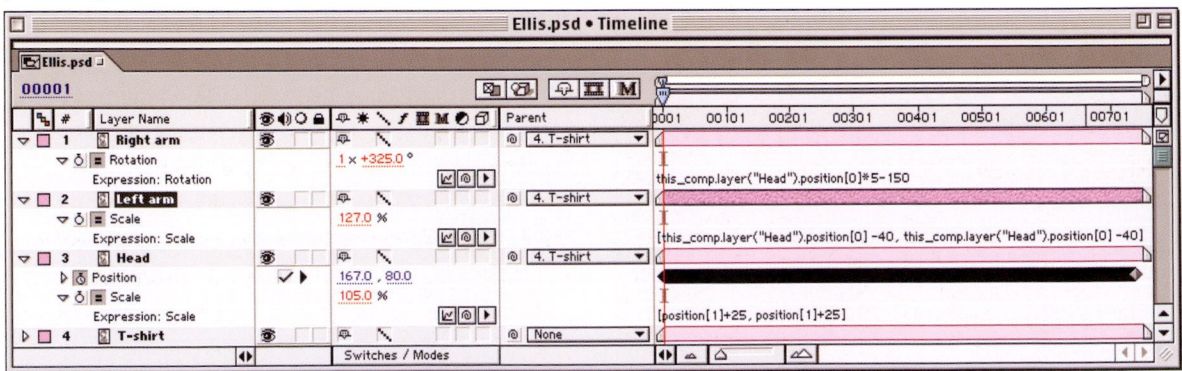

OK, let's animate the T-shirt layer. Remember that we used the T-shirt as a parent for the arms and head, so wherever we move the T-shirt, those layers will follow.

**17** Select the T-shirt layer and press R to see its Rotation property.

**18** Alt-click the Rotation stopwatch to add an expression, then use the Pick Whip to select the X value from the Head layer's Position.

The resulting expression is:
this_comp.layer("Head").position[0]

Activate the expression and you'll see the T-shirt layer's rotation needs to be corrected, it's upside down at the moment.

**19** Adapt the expression by placing –170 after it, so it reads:
this_comp.layer("Head").position[0] –170

**20** Activate the expression and RAM Preview the result. It's looking pretty good. However, I really wanted the T-shirt to rotate in the opposite direction to the Right Arm layer.

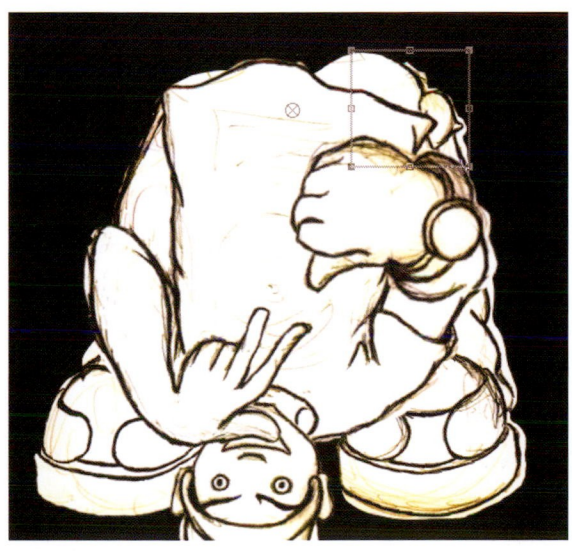

A quick way for us to flip the Rotation values is to multiply them by minus one (i.e. * –1). This will make positive values negative and negative values positive. Now, even though we've done so before, it isn't really a good idea to keep placing one calculation after another to adjust the result of an expression.

for example:
this_comp.layer("Head").position[0] –170 * –1

It's better to break each stage of the process up; this will allow us to perform complex calculations while still keeping the expression relatively simple to understand.

For this expression we're going to use something called a variable. A variable is a character or series of characters which can represent any value in an expression. I'm sure you'll remember your arithmetic classes at school? You would be given equations represented by letters, for example:
x + y = z
You would then work out that:
If: X = 5 and Y = 10, then: Z = 15

This may sound a bit scary, but you've actually been using variables for a while now. As we've seen, the word *rotation* represents whatever the value of the Rotation property is. The word *position* represents two or even three values (depending on whether it's on a 2D or 3D layer).

In the same way, we can take a letter or word and assign values to it; this becomes especially useful as the complexity of our expressions grow.

As this is the Ellis Animation section, I'm going to use the variable *ellis* in the expression.

**21** Place the cursor at the beginning of the current T-shirt layer's Rotation expression and type:
ellis =

**22** As soon as you've done so, drag the Pickwhip onto the Head layer's X Position value.

**23** Type in –170 after the expression so that it reads:

ellis = this_comp.layer("Head").position[0] –170

**24** Now place the cursor at the end of the text and add a semi-colon ( ; ). When you have expressions that are made up of multiple lines, you must end each of those lines with a semi-colon for it to be recognised.

**25** Add a new line to the expression by pressing the main Return key on your keyboard.

You'll see the expression text field automatically expands to show another line.

**26** Now enter *ellis * –1;* on the second line, so that the entire expression reads:

ellis = this_comp.layer("Head").position[0] –170;
ellis * –1;

The first line of the expression is subtracting 170 from the X value of the Head layer's Position and assigning the resulting value to the variable *ellis*.

The second line is then taking that resulting value (now called *ellis*) and multiplying it by minus one.

**27** Activate the expression and RAM Preview to check out the final result. You've now successfully completed this section.

**28** Save the project as Graffiti05b.aep into your Creative After Effects > Expressions chapter folder. We'll return to this project after we've learned some more advanced expressions.

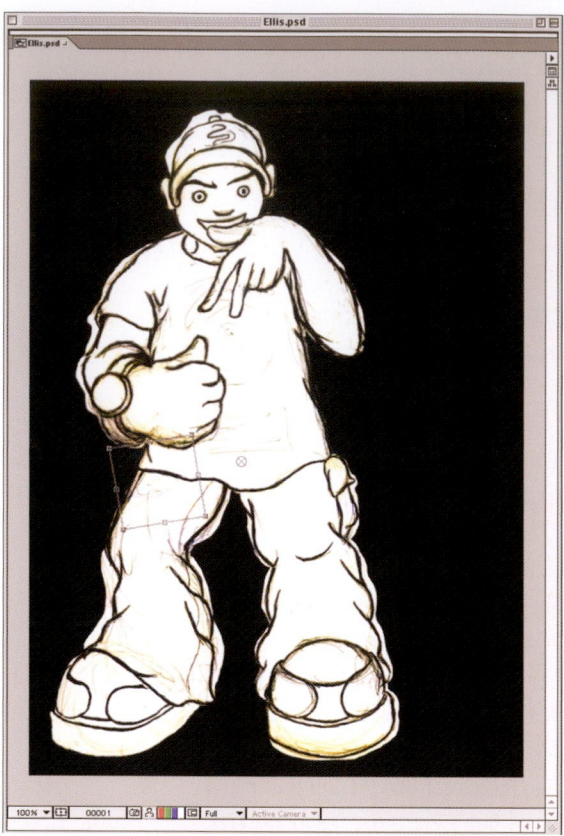

# advanced expressions

Before you go through this section, make sure that you're happy with your understanding of the basic rules of the expression language. Once you are, it's relatively easy to pick up the more advanced stuff.

I'll start by going over some more advanced rules, before moving on to demonstrate what I regard as some of the most useful expression commands.

## lesson 1 – advanced arithmetic

As I explained earlier, properties can contain one or more values. Properties such as Opacity and Rotation are made up of just one value, they are one-dimensional (1D).

Properties like Scale and Position are made up of two or three values (X, Y and sometimes Z too), they are two or three dimensional (2D or 3D).

This distinction becomes important when you try to add, subtract, multiply or divide these values in an expression. We've already seen that we can use the four main math symbols ( + —* / ) to perform arithmetic. As you've seen, this only works when dealing with single values. Performing arithmetic on 2D or 3D properties requires a slightly different approach.

**1** Open the AdvExp.aep project from the Training > Projects > Chapter 14 folder on the CD.

**2** Open the Lesson 1 - Heart and RAM Preview the composition.

**3** Make sure you can see the Scale and Opacity properties (press the S key, followed by Shift + T).

You will see that we have a beating heart shape layer, animated with Scale and Opacity keyframes. Let's say we wanted to increase the opacity of the Heart layer. Rather than having to go through and edit each keyframe, we can use an expression to perform arithmetic on the existing keyframes.

**4** Alt-click the Opacity stopwatch to add an expression and enter the following:
opacity * 2

**5** Activate the expression and RAM Preview to see the result. The existing Opacity keyframes have been multiplied by two, making the heart twice as visible as it was before.

If we also wanted to make the heart layer bigger, you may think we could just do the same thing with the Scale property.

**6** Add an expression to the Scale property and make the expression read:
scale * 2

Activate the expression and you'll get the error: After Effects warning: invalid numeric result.

This is because the Scale property contains two values, while the math symbols can only be used to perform arithmetic on single values. It would work if you used the expression:
[scale[0] * 2, scale[1] * 2]

This expression is performing the multiplication on each of the X and Y Scale values individually before packaging them back together.

**7** There's a far more elegant way of doing this kind of calculation. Replace the current expression on the Scale property with the following:
mul(scale, 2)

Then activate it and RAM Preview the final result. You'll see the expression has now multiplied the existing scale (X and Y) values by two.

The format for doing arithmetic in this way is:
add(1st value, 2nd value)
sub(1st value, 2nd value)

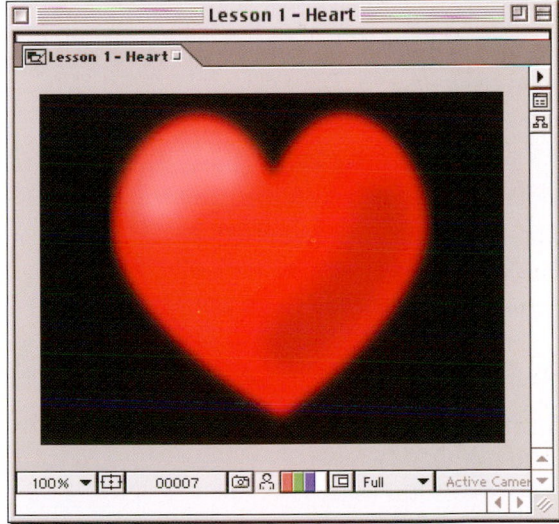

For addition and subtraction, both values can either be 1D, 2D or 3D.

For multiplication and division, the 1st value can be 1D, 2D or 3D, but the 2nd value must be 1D. For example, you can add two 2D values together:

add(position, this_comp.layer("Solid 1").position)

or:

add(scale, [100,200])

But you can't multiply two 2D values, the 2nd value must be a single value. For example:

mul(position, 5)

or

mul(scale, opacity)

This may all seem a bit confusing at first, but it will start to make more sense when you begin experimenting with your own expressions.

## lesson 2 – wiggle

One of my favourite expression commands has to be *wiggle*. You may have already used The Wiggler (Production Bundle only), a floating palette (like Motion Sketch) that randomly varies the values between keyframes. You specify the speed and amount by which it should vary and then After Effects does the rest. It's very easy to do this with an expression.

**1** Open Lesson 2 - Bat Wiggle, you will see we have a picture of a Bat; nothing is animated yet.

**2** Make sure that you can see the Bat's Position property (select the layer and hit P).

**3** Alt-click the Position stopwatch to add an expression, place the cursor at the end of the default expression and type the rest of this line:

position.wiggle(2,200)

Notice the full stop ( . ) between *position* and *wiggle*.

**4** Activate the expression and RAM Preview the result. You'll see that the previously static Bat layer is now moving frantically around the screen. The format that we use to wiggle a property is:

property.wiggle(frequency, amplitude);

Frequency sets the number of times it wiggles per second, amplitude sets the maximum amount by which it will vary (in pixels, degrees or percentage depending on the type of property). In our expression, we're saying, 'take the current Position values and wiggle them twice per second, by up to 200 pixels'.

**NB** The wiggle effect is added to the current property value, including any keyframed values. You can create a motion path with Position keyframes, and then, add an expression to wiggle the layer as it moves along that motion path. Position isn't the only thing we can wiggle either, the expression can be used with any property. Let's try wiggling the Bat layer's Rotation.

**5** Select the Bat layer and press the R key to see its Rotation property.

**6** Add an expression and enter the following:

rotation.wiggle(1, 50)

We're asking it to wiggle the Rotation once every second, by up to 50 degrees.

**7** Activate the expression and RAM Preview the result.

So we've seen that the wiggle command provides us with a very simple way of varying property values. It's easy to adjust the two wiggle values, and we can quickly check the results with a RAM Preview. We're going back to the Position's wiggle next; so let's temporarily switch off the Rotation's wiggle expression.

**8** Click the equals icon (=) next to the Rotation property's Stopwatch to disable the expression.

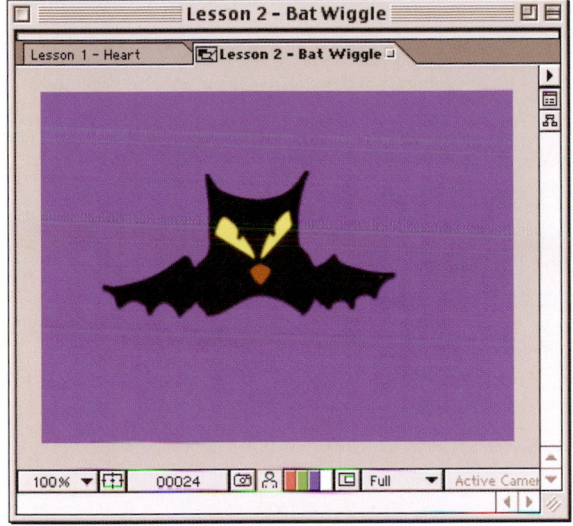

## lesson 3 – variable wiggle

Now we're going to take things a bit further. This is slightly trickier, but there will be rewards later. Let's say that I want to vary the amount of wiggle that is applied. For example, I want the Bat layer's Position to have a small wiggle at the start of the animation, building to a much bigger wiggle at the end. The current expression for Position is:
position.wiggle(2,200)

The second value (200) is the one controlling the amount of wiggle applied, so we need some way to animate that value over time. The solution is to animate the value of a different property, and then get this expression to read that value. We need an expression like:
position.wiggle(2, some other property)

But which property should we animate? We can't change the Bat layer's other main properties (i.e. Scale or Opacty) to get our value, because we'd also then be scaling or fading the layer.

We could quite easily create a new Solid layer and animate its Rotation; then we could turn the layer off (so it isn't visible in the Composition window) and get the expression to read this value.

The same thing can also be done with an effect: we animate a property from an effect applied to the Bat layer, and then get our wiggle expression to read that value. If we turn the effect off, it won't alter the Bat layer in any way, but it will still provide the value we need for our expression.

So let's do it:
**1** Select the Bat layer and press the U key. This will reveal any properties on a layer that contain either a keyframe or an expression.

As you see, I have already applied the effect Color Balance (HLS) to the Bat layer. I've also added a single keyframe to the Hue property and turned the effect off.

**2** Click the small triangle next to the Position stopwatch to see the current expression text:
position.wiggle(2,200)
We're going to replace 200 with the value of the effect's Hue property.

**3** Click the expression text field and hightlight just the 200 using the text cursor.

**4** Drag the Pick Whip over to the Hue property, releasing when the word Hue is highlighted by a black rectangle. Then activate the expression. Your expression (all one line) should read:
position.wiggle(2, effect("Color Balance (HLS)").param("Hue"));

RAM Preview the result and you'll find the layer is no longer moving at all. The amount of wiggle that is being applied is now the same as the Hue value, which is currently zero.

**5** Select the Bat layer and press the F3 key (or Cmd + Shift + T) to bring up the Effect Controls window.

**6** With the Current-Time Marker at frame 1, Rotate the Hue Dial to any value between 0 and 300, then RAM Preview the result. Repeat this step a few times trying out a range of values and you'll see the higher the Hue value, the more the Bat layer will wiggle around. So let's have a look at the new line that the Pick Whip inserted into our expression:

effect("Color Balance (HLS)"). param("Hue")

It's not too hard to work out what this part of the expression means. This line is saying, 'the value of the Hue property (or parameter) on the effect called Color Balance (HLS)'. Remember we talked about the location of a property being described as: Composition / Layer / Property, or:

this_comp.layer("name").property

Well, the location of an effect is described as: Composition / Layer / Effect / Parameter, or:

this_comp.layer("layer name").effect("effect name"). param("parameter name")

Notice that all four sections are separated by a full stop ( . ) As our expression is reading an effect value from it's own layer, the *this_comp.layer("layer name")* portion isn't necessary. This may all sound a bit complicated, but don't forget it's the Pick Whip that does all the hard work, so it's really nothing to worry about. To finish up, we just need to add some keyframes to change the Hue value over time. We'll set the value to 0 at the start of the Timeline and 200 at the end.

**7** Change the keyframed Hue value on the first frame of the Timeline back to zero (0 x +0.0°).

**8** Move to the last frame of the composition and change the value to 200 (so it reads 0 x +200.0°). So you should have just two keyframes, one at the start and one at the end.

**NB** We see Rotation values displayed in the Timeline as revolutions and degrees (0x +200.0°), but it is still just a single value, i.e. an expression reads the value of 1x +200.0° (1 rev + 200 degrees) as being 560 (i.e. 360 + 200).

If you RAM Preview now, you should find that the Bat layer is only wiggling a small amount at the start of the sequence, becoming a much larger wiggle at the end. Now we've got the Position wiggling the way we want, let's turn Rotation's expression back on as we move on to the next stage.

**9** Click the *does not equals* sign(≠) next to the Rotation stopwatch to re-activate the expression.

### lesson 4 – blink

The Bat would look a lot more impressive if its wings flapped as it flew around. I'm going to show you a really quick and easy way of doing just that. One of the more useful Motion Math scripts is the Blink script (blink.mm) which allows you to vary opacity between two values at a constant speed. i.e. you can use it to create 'throbbing' lights. While I don't really know how the script works, I still found that I was able to convert the Motion Math script into an easy-to-use expression. It turns out that it has a lot more uses than just altering opacity values; we're going to use this expression to make the Bat flap its wings. You may have already noticed that the Bat layer we've been working with is in fact a nested composition. Here's the fast way to open a nested composition:

**1** Alt-double-click the Bat's layer name in the current composition. (Alternatively, locate the Bat composition in the Pre-Comps folder in the Project Window and open as you would normally.)

There are three layers in the Bat composition, there's a Body and Left and Right Wing layers. I've used three copies of the same picture, with masks to isolate the different body parts. The Wing layers have their anchor points set in such a way that the wings will rotate correctly around the body. Now we are ready to bring in the Blink expression. There are a several ways in which you can save an expression to use it again later. For example, you could highlight the expression text and copy it into the clipboard, then paste it into a text editing application and save it as a text file.

Later you would open that text file and copy the contents back to the clipboard before pasting it into your new expression. Or, if you have an expression applied to an effect which you then save as a Favorite, the expression will be saved along with all the effects information.

**2** Select the Right Wing layer, then choose Effect > Apply Favorite from the pull-down menu.

**3** Locate the file blink.ffx in the Training > Favorites > Expressions favorites folder and open it.
RAM Preview the composition now and you'll see that the Right Wing is getting lighter then darker in a steady rhythm. The Blink expression was saved as a Favorite effect using Brightness & Contrast.

**4** Select the Right Wing layer and press the U key to view the property that has the expression (Brightness).

**5** Click the small triangle next to the Brightness property's stopwatch and *equals* icon to view the expression text.You will see the line:
high = 100; low = 0; blink_speed = 1;
// enter high + low value and blinks per sec;

This line contains all of the variables you can alter to control the expression; *high* and *low* are values between which you want the property to change, *blink_speed* is how many times it changes each second. The second part of the line is:
// enter high + low value and blinks per sec;
Anything you place on a line after two forward-slashes ( // ) will be ignored by After Effects, so this is simply a way of adding comments to an expression. But this isn't the whole expression.

**6** Click once on the expression text field and the box will automatically resize to show the entire expression.You don't even need to think about what the rest of the expression does. All that matters is that we can use it as a quick way to create our animation.

**7** With all the expression text highlighted, hit Command + C to copy the expression (or select Edit > Copy), then click away from the text field.

**8** Select the Right Wing layer and press R to see the Rotation property.

**9** Alt-click the Rotation stopwatch to add an expression , then press Command + V (or select Edit > Paste) to paste in our blink expression.

**10** Again, click away from the text field or press the Enter key on the number pad to activate the expression, then RAM Preview the result. You'll see the Right Wing is now flapping up and down, rotating between 100 (high) and 0 (low) degrees. We'd better get rid of the Brightness & Contrast effect and expression so the Right Wing doesn't keep flashing:

**11** Select the Right Wing layer and then choose Effect > Remove All from the pull-down menu (or press F3 to view the Effect Controls window and delete the effect from there). Now we need to work out exactly what rotation values we want the Right Wing to move between.

**12** Try using the Rotation Tool (W) to rotate the Right Wing layer in the Composition window, you will get the following message:

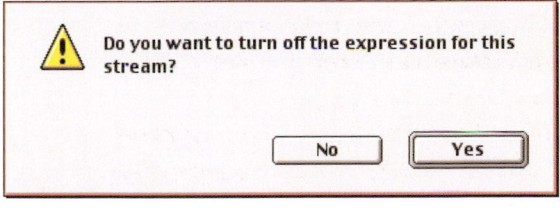

**NB** It isn't possible to change a property when it has an expression which is currently activated, that property is effectively locked at these times.

**13** Select *Yes* from the message window and the expression will now be disabled.

**14** With the Rotation Tool still selected, rotate the Right Wing in the Composition window. Watch the values change in the Timeline (or Info Palette) to help decide which values you want the Wing rotating between. The values I decided on were –30° to 60°. I also want the Wing to flap faster, let's say three times per second.

**15** Click the expression text field to reveal the entire expression, then replace the values in the first line, so it reads:
high = 60;  low = –30;  blink_speed = 3;

**16** Activate the expression and RAM Preview the result. The Right Wing should now be flapping in a suitably bat-like way. As you know, there are no Rotation keyframes on the Right Wing, the flapping motion is created by our expression. If we want some visual feedback in the Timeline window, showing what an expression is doing, we can use the Graph Overlay.

**Graph Overlay Icon**

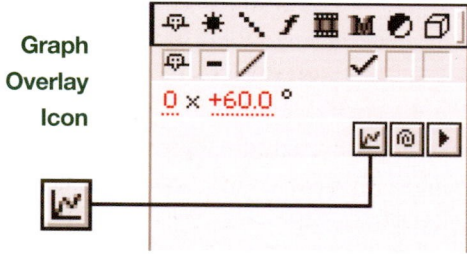

**17** Click the Graph  Overlay icon to the left of the Rotation property's expression. The Value and Velocity Graphs appears in the Timeline, with the result of the expression shown as a red line. If there were any keyframes on the property, the graphs would also have a black line showing the original value and velocity before the expression.

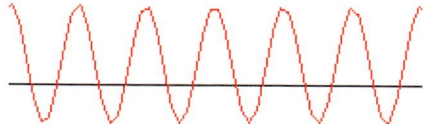

**18** Change *blink_speed* in the expression to a few different values such as 0.5 and 5 (but change it back to 3 before moving on). Notice that the graph updates to show the result of any change to the expression.

**19** Click the Graph Overlay icon once again to switch the graph off. We're nearly there, the Right Wing is flapping well and we can use a trick we learnt earlier to invert the Rotation values and get the Left Wing moving too.

**20** Select the Left Wing layer and press R to view its Rotation property.

**21** Add an expression and drag the Pick Whip over to the Right Wing's Rotation property, then add  * – 1 (multiply by minus one) to the end so it reads:
this_comp.layer("Right Wing").rotation * –1

**22** Activate the expression and RAM Preview the result. Both wings should now be flapping nicely. I've already created some finishing touches for the animation: to make the Body move up and down as the wings flap, I've Parented both Wing layers to the Body and used a blink expression to create a bobbing motion on the Position's Y-axis.

**23** Select the Body layer and press P to view its Position property.

**24** Click the *does not equal* ($\neq$) icon to switch the expression on, then do a RAM Preview. The Bat's animation is now complete. There's no need to try and figure this last bit out right now, save it for after you've completed the chapter. It was created with a slightly more advanced version of the blink expression and you can find a short tutorial about it in the Extras > Expressions folder on the CD.

**25** Open the Lesson 2 - Bat Wiggle composition and RAM Preview the result in combination with the wiggle expressions we created earlier. It's looking pretty good, we just need another Bat: we'll scale it down a bit and place it up and to the left of the current Bat layer.

**26** Select the Bat and hit Command + D to make a duplicate layer.

**27** Select the lower of the two Bat layers in the Timeline window and press S, then Shift + P to see both the Scale and Position properties.

**28** Disable the expression on Position by clicking the *equals* (=) icon, then change the Position value to [80.0, 60.0] and the Scale value to 60.0%.

**29** Turn Position's expression back on by clicking the *equals* (=) icon again, then do a RAM Preview. One last thing, both Bat's are flapping their wings at the same time which isn't very realistic.

**30** In the Timeline window, drag one of the Bat layers to the left, changing its In-point to −1 using the values in the Info Palette to guide you. I've created a background animation for you:

**31** Click the Hide Shy Layers button at the top of the Timeline window to reveal the layer Castle BG, then click its eyeball to turn the layer on.

**32** RAM Preview the finished animation. This just goes to show you that with a little bit of imagination and a bit of patience and practice, you can start to use expressions to create quite convincing animations. Imagine how much longer this would have taken to animate using keyframes.

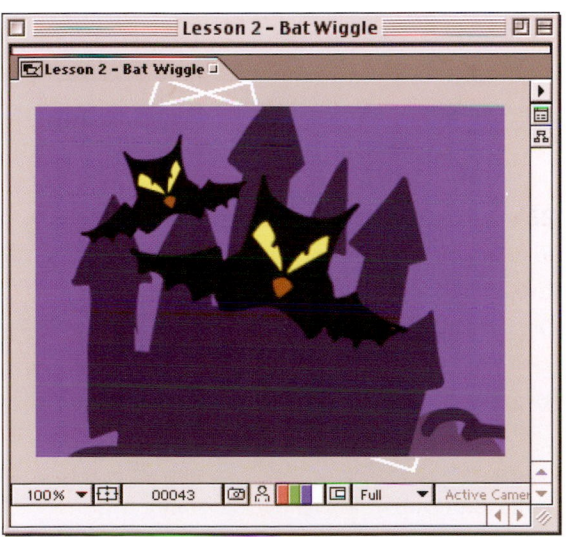

# graffiti club

## advanced motion capture

In the Ellis animation we used the movement of the head to trigger the other parts of the body using expressions. We modified these expressions by adding, subtracting, dividing and multiplying the results. This method works well and is fun to experiment with, but it's based purely upon trial and error. This makes it difficult to predict the results, and to control how the layers affect each other. For our second animated character Annie, we will create a separate composition which we'll use to control the movement of the character. The idea is to create several layers with different movements and then assign these movements to different parts of the body, making the dance more varied and interesting.

The object here is still to animate the character's movement in time with the music, as we did with the Ellis character. After a bit of practice using Motion sketch, you'll be able to give each of the characters different timings, so they appear to be dancing with each other, but using different moves. It may help if you have a look at the first character animation to remind yourself where most of the movement takes place. We'll mostly animate this character at times when the other character is not moving, forcing the viewer to switch concentration between the two characters, rather than focusing on both at the same time. It's good to get the viewer's eye moving around the screen; it creates interest and keeps their attention fixed.

**1** Open Graffiti05aep from the Training > Projects > Chapter 14 folder.

**2** Drag the audio file *Kid_sound.mov* onto the New Comp button at the bottom of the Project window. Hit Command + K and in the Composition Settings window, rename it *Motion Capture Comp*. Make it 100 × 100, 15 fps and 750 frames long.

**3** Hit Command + Shift + B and change your background color to black. Hit Command + Y to create a new solid and call it *X solid*. Make it 20 × 20 pixels and choose a bright red color to contrast it with the black background. We'll use this layer to capture the motion on the X-axis (left to right).

**4** With *X Solid* selected, go to Window > Motion Sketch to open the Motion Sketch palette.

**5** Click the Start Capture button; and then wait until the words, 'Click to begin capture' appear in the Info palette, this means that the audio has been successfully loaded. After Effects will not begin to capture until you click down in the Composition window.

**6** Position the cursor over the middle of the layer and when you're ready, click and hold, waiting for the audio to begin. When the audio starts to play, move the cursor from side to side in time with the music. Try to resist moving the cursor with every beat, leaving some beats for the next capture session.

**7** If you mess up, or just aren't happy with the results, you can Undo the motion capture by hitting Command + Z (or select Edit > Undo Motion Sketch), repeating Step 5 until you are happy with the result.

**8** Create another solid, this time name it *Y solid* and make it a bright blue color. Repeat the Motion Sketch process with this solid, this time creating motion on the Y axis (up and down).

**9** To prepare for the next step, select both the *X solid* and *Y solid* layers and hit the P key to bring up their Position values.

As you know, we can use the Pick Whip to create expressions that read values from other layers in a composition. We can also use the Pick Whip to create expressions that read values from layers in other comps.

In order to do this we need to be able to see both of the Timeline windows simultaneously. After Effects defaults

to using Tabbed Windows. Meaning that any open compositions will appear in the same set of windows, with Tabs along the top of each window (Timeline, Composition and Effect Controls) to let you switch between the different compositions. This is a very useful for people working with only one monitor, helping to keep the limited screen space tidy. Tabbed windows were first introduced in After Effects 4.0. Before then, each composition would have its own Composition and Timeline windows, making the screen quite cluttered if more than one was open at the same time. However, it did have its advantages; for example, it was easier to compare compositions side by side. There are still some users who prefer working the old way with the Tabbed windows preference switched off (in the General preferences window). It is entirely up to you how you prefer to work. Even when Tabbed windows is turned on, you can still pull compositions out of the main windows by dragging them out by their Tabs.

**10** Drag the Motion Capture Comp's tab out from the Timeline and drop it somewhere else on the screen. Resize and position the windows so you can see the Timelines for both the Motion Capture Comp and the Annie.psd Comp. We will be Pick-Whipping from one composition to the other.

**11** Select the Head layer in the Annie.psd comp and hit the R key to view its Rotation property, then Alt-click the Stopwatch to add an expression. We're adding an expression to the Head layer's Rotation property to make Annie's head move from side to side in time with the music.

**12** Drag the Pick Whip over to the Y Solid layer in the Motion Capture Comp's Timeline and select the Position property's Y value (the second value). The resulting expression will be:

comp("Motion Capture comp").layer("Y solid").position[1]

Instead of beginning with *this_comp* our expression begins with *comp("Motion Capture Comp")*.

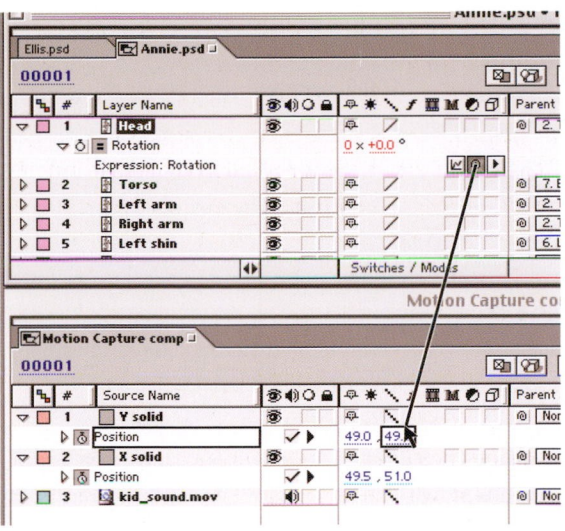

**16** We will also use expressions to add some rotational movement to the arms. Select the Left Arm layer in the Timeline and press R to view its Rotation property.

**17** Alt-click the Stopwatch to add an expression, then drag the Pick Whip over to the X Solid layer in the Motion Capture Comp and select the Position property's X value (the first value). The arm will now rotate with different timings than the head.

**18** Type in – 20 after the current expression text, then activate the expression . This will offset the rotation values by twenty degrees anti-clockwise.

**19** Now select the Right Arm layer and press R to view it's Rotation property. Alt-click the Stopwatch to add an expression, then drag the Pick Whip over to the Left Arm's Rotation property. Place the cursor at the end of the text and add:
* –1
The expression should read:
this_comp.layer("Left arm").rotation * –1

This will multiply the rotation by -1, making the Right Arm rotate the opposite way from, but still with the same timings as the Left arm.

**20** RAM Preview the animation; we now have the head and the arms moving to different beats, so let's continue with the rest of the body.

**21** Close down all the open layers in the Timeline (i.e. hide the properties) except for the Head layer. Select the Belly layer and hit P to bring up the Position property, then add an expression to it.

**22** Drag the Pick Whip over to the Y Solid later in the Motion Capture Comp and select the whole Position property (i.e don't select the individual X or Y values, just highlight the word Position). See the following diagram for details.

As we know, the format for reading a property from the same composition is:
this_comp.layer("layer name").property

The format for reading a property from a different composition is:
comp("comp name").layer("layer name").property

So our expression is saying 'make me the same as the Y Position value (position[1]) on the Y solid layer,
in the Motion Capture Comp'.

**13** Activate the expression and RAM Preview the result. The head is cocked too far to one side, so we'll need to adjust the expression to compensate.

**14** Click the expression text field and place the text cursor after the existing expression, then type in — 50 and activate the expression. It should now read:
comp("Motion Capture comp").layer("Y solid").
position[1] – 50

**15** With the Current-Time Marker at frame 1, drag the audio file *Kid_sound.mov* from the Project Window into the Annie.psd composition and RAM Preview the results so far.

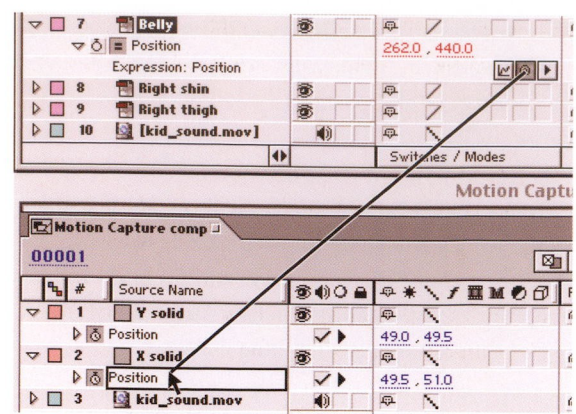

**23** Activate the expression and you'll see that the Belly layer and all the layers that are parented to it, will have disappeared off the top of the Comp window. This is because Belly's Position value now matches that of the Y Solid layer in the Motion Capture Comp.

## null objects and expressions

We'll use a Null object again to control this layer and bring it back down to earth, making it relative to the Y solid layer.

**1** Make sure the Current–Time Marker is at the beginning of your comp and select Layer > New > Null Object from the pull-down menu.

**2** In the Belly layers Parent menu, choose Null 1 to make the null the Belly's Parent. As soon as you choose the Null as the Belly's Parent, the Belly jumps down to almost (but not quite) the right position.

**3** To move the Belly and all parented layers back to their correct position, click the Null Object with the Selection Tool and move it around the Composition window until all layers are back exactly where they should be.

Until now, we've been using expressions to make the various parts of the body move in time to the music. If we just want the other layers to match the current motion, we can simply link the body parts using parenting.

**4** Go to the Left Thigh Parent panel and choose the Torso layer from the drop down menu.

**5** Go to the Left Shin Parent menu and choose the Left Thigh layer. Now the Shin will follow the Thigh and the Thigh will follow the Torso, which in turn follows the Belly wherever it goes.

**6** Preview the animation. The left thigh now follows the torso wherever it moves, making it look like the foot is tapping in time to the music.

**7** Select the Torso layer and add an expression to the Rotation value. Drag the Pick Whip down to the Y Solid layer in the Motion Capture Comp and select the Y Position value.

**8** After the expression, type in:
/4 – 20
to divide the result by four and then subtract 20 degrees.

**9** Activate the expression and then RAM Preview the results and then save the project as Graffiti06b.aep to your Creative After Effects > Expressions Chapter folder.

You could go on and on here linking values (in fact I have in the finished project), the thighs and the shins could have a little bit of Rotation applied, the Belly layer could also have a touch of Rotation applied to it. After this chapter is finished I want you to experiment a bit more with this animation, trying out different combinations of moves to see what you come up with. OK, let's take another look at our Seattle Evening News project.

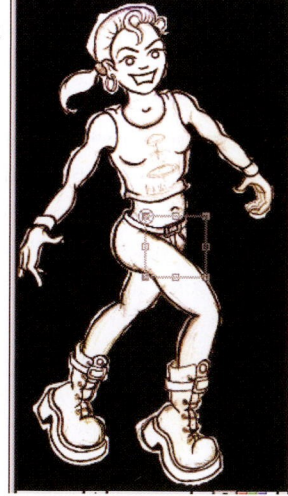

# seattle evening news

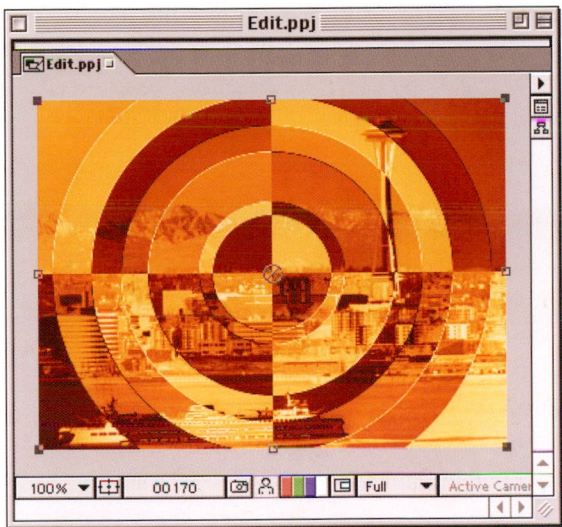

OK, back to our Seattle Evening News titles, we added some effects to bring this piece together. The layers are edited in time with the main beats of the music which is nice but it's a news programme so it needs to be more dynamic, punchy, fast paced and attention-grabbing. The music is a good guide to work to. I like randomness of the noise which conjures up images of radars. I would like my disc's movement to echo the randomness of that sound.

## advanced wiggle

**1** Open SeattleNews04.aep from Training > Projects > Chapter 14. Open the Edit.ppj comp and RAM Preview it to remind yourself of where you are with it.

I want all of the disks to move, and to overlap each other at times, creating different sizes of rings as they pass over each other. To do this I'd normally have to animate the mask layers individually. I could animate the scale property by using keyframes but can you imagine how long it would take to create something truly random?

Instead I'm going to use Expressions. You've learnt quite a bit about them up to now and as you know, you really don't need to be a programming genius to use expressions.

They're relatively easy to use and the more you experiment with them, the more you'll feel comfortable with them.

One great thing about expressions is that they will alter properties on your layers without setting keyframes. This makes it a very flexible way of working; change the expression and the layer will instantly update to show the new result, no need to perform fiddly keyframe editing.

Another is that Expressions are available Production Bundle and Standard users alike, it is a core element of the software unlike Motion Math which is only available to Production Bundle users.

You've learned that expressions can be based upon other layers properties, e.g. you can make one layer change color based on another layer's rotation value. They can also be purely maths based, e.g. you can use expressions to add, subtract, multiply or divide a specified number to your layer's animated property. In this exercise we will use the Wiggle Expression that we learnt about in the Advanced Expressions tutorial to animate the rings moving in and out across each other.

**2** To animate the masks individually, we'll need to go back to the nested Mask Composition. Double-click the Mask Composition icon in the Project window to open up its Timeline and Composition windows.

**3** Select the White Masks layer and press the S key to bring up the Scale values for that layer.

**4** Hold down the Alt key and click on the Scale Stopwatch to add an expression.

**5** Select the White Masks layer and, in the Expression text field place the cursor after the word *scale* and then hit the full stop ( . ) key. Full stops are used to separate the parts which make up an expression.

OK, we're now going to add the wiggle expression command that will apply random scale values to the layer.

The Language Elements menu has a list of commands and properties we can use in 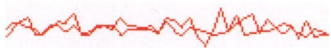 our expressions. Everything you need is in this menu, then it's really just a case of learning the correct order to put them in. I don't use the menu often (preferring to type the expression directly into the text field) but it is useful as a reminder of what is available to you.

**6** Making sure the cursor is still sitting at the end of the current expression, click the Language Elements pull-out menu.

**7** Select Property > wiggle(

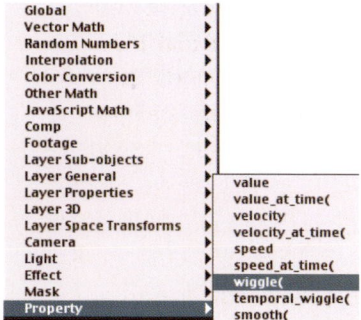

**8** Finish off the expression by placing the cursor at the end of the current expression and typing in: 4, 30)

The whole line should now read: scale.wiggle(4, 30)

The first of the two values (4) is telling After Effects to create a wiggled value four times each second. The second value (30) is setting the maximum amount by which our scale value will change. Then the close bracket ( ] ) ends the expression.

**9** To see what has actually happened, click the Graph Overlay icon to look at a graph of your scale values. You can also RAM Preview your composition to see the circles wiggling about.

Notice that the X and Y properties of the scale are wiggling independently of each other, this may be the desired effect in some circumstances but in this case, we want the same scale on both axes. To achieve this we need to modify the expression slightly.

As we mentioned earlier, you need to think about how many values make up a property, e.g. the Scale property consists of two values, an X and a Y value. The *wiggle* command automatically wiggles each value differently, which is great for things like Position, but not so great for Scale. In order to make the X and Y values behave the same, I need to choose one of the wiggled values (X or Y) and apply it to both of the Scale values.

In this instance we'll use a variable to do the job. To reiterate what we've already covered, a variable is a character or series of characters which can represent any value in an expression.

**10** Place the text cursor before the word *scale* in the expression and type in:
a =
With this you are saying, 'The letter *a* represents my wiggled scale value'.

**11** Place the cursor at the end of your expression and type in a semicolon ( ; ), then hit the main Return key on your keyboard to move to the next line.

We need to write our second line of our expression, telling After Effects to use the same value for both the X and Y axes.

As you know, we can package two values together for a 2D property by placing them within square brackets, separated by a comma, e.g. if we wanted an X value of 10, and a Y value of 20, we would simply type: [10, 20]

Also, our variable (a) now contains the result of the wiggled scale, which consists of two values (X and Y); so our variable is also made up of two values.

We've seen earlier that you can use Position [0] to read just the X value, or Position [1] to read just the Y value from a 2D property. We need to use the same technique to read just one of the values contained in our variable, in this case we will be using the X value, so we'll use [0].

**12** On the second line of the expression, type:
[a[0], a[0]];
then activate the expression.

We are taking the X value from the result of the wiggle ( a[0] ) and applying it to both the X and Y Scale axes by placing it inside square brackets, separated by a comma. Notice the change in the graph display, there appears to be only one red line. That's because the X and Y values are now the same.

**13** RAM Preview the movie again and notice that now the circles are scaling the same amount on each axis. OK, we now need to make the Gray masks move to create that overlapping effect. To do this, we'll set up an expression on the Gray Masks layer by simply typing it directly into the Expression text field.

**14** Close up the White Masks layer's Value Graph, then select the Gray Masks layer and press S to view its Scale property.

**15** Alt-click the Stopwatch to add an expression and type the following two lines:
a = scale.wiggle(1, 100, 4, 0.5);
[a[0],a[0]]
Then, activate the expression.

You'll notice that this time, there are now four numbers in the brackets where there were previously only two, what are they for?

These values refer to the following:
*(frequency, amplitude, no. of times, scale factor)*
The first two numbers still work in the same way:

*Frequency* is the number of wiggles per second, in our case we're asking it to wiggle the Scale once every second.
*Amplitude* is the maximum amount by which it is wiggled, in our case the value is 100.

The second two numbers are optional, and are used to add more detail to the wiggle. Once you have wiggled your layer, you may be happy with the overall timing and movement but feel that it's a bit too smooth and want to roughen it up a bit, this is where the next two numbers come into play.

*No. of times* lets you specify how many times the expression will 're-wiggle' the original wiggle.
*Scale factor* is used to specify how much After Effects will scale your orignal *amplitude* value by between each of the wiggles it applies.

Take our expression:
scale.wiggle(1, 100, 4, 0.5)
it will first wiggle the value by a maximum of 100, then do a second wiggle at 50 (100 * 0.5),
a third at 25 (50 * 0.5)
and a fourth at 12.5 (25 * 0.5),
each one adding another level of detail to the wiggle.

If you still don't understand this, here's a diagram which attempts to explain this in a more visual way.

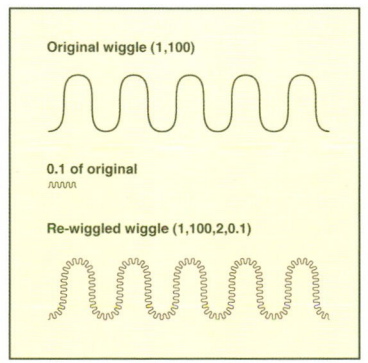

Original wiggle (1,100)

0.1 of original

Re-wiggled wiggle (1,100,2,0.1)

While the diagram is far from accurate, it should give you an idea of how this works.

**16** Open up the Edit.ppj Composition RAM Preview. The changes that you made to your nested comp are updated automatically in the main composition.

We now have some really nice organic looking wiggles going on without concentric circles, really bringing together the whole edit into a more viually exciting sequence. Quite often, adding irregular motion to very regular shapes can create a very pleasing effect.

**17** Save the project into Creative After Effects > Expressions Chapter folder as SeattleNews05b.aep. We'll come back to this project and the Graffiti Club project later.

## recap

So we've reached the end of the Expressions chapter; you should now have a pretty good understanding of the basics of the expression language, which will serve you well as you move on to creating your own expressions.

What we've covered in this chapter is really only the tip of the iceberg in terms of what you can do with expressions. If you're interested in finding out more, there are several resources you can use to further your knowledge.

You'll find a selection of additional tutorials in the CD > Extras > Expressions folder, showing you some more ways you can use expressions. These will also help if you want to go back and figure out how we created some of the more advanced expressions we've been slipping into the projects you've gone through in the chapter.

Remember to also keep an eye on the website at: http//www.angie.abel.co.uk/book.html
Paul and I will be posting new tutorials and examples up there during the coming months.

After Effects' online help is also very useful as a reference tool, providing a complete list of the expression commands that are available to you.

I'd also encourage you to share your expressions with other After Effects' users; one of the best ways of learning how expressions work is to check out as many examples as you can. Taking someone else's expression and modifying it to suit your own needs can be a great time-saver.

It's a really good thing to be able to share your knowledge with others. Whatever you give out, you'll get back one hundredfold, believe me.

Don't make the mistake of feeling that you have to keep all of your new-found knowledge to yourself, otherwise you'll end up limiting yourself and cutting yourself out from a potentially very helpful and sharing community of fellow artists and designers.

Working with other designers on projects is much more fun than being stuck at a desk on your own. Plus, it helps to bounce ideas off other people when going through a creative block, sometimes all you need is a bit of encouragement and to see things from another point of view.

I have found that the most knowledgable and talented designers I have met seem to be the same people who are prepared to share ideas and co-operate with others. Often, the act of hiding ideas and an unwillingness to share are signs of insecurity and lack of confidence, and that's not the reader I know and love!

OK, see if you can develop some more ideas for your own project. Have a good old play around with what you've learned and see what you can come up with. Good luck!

# chapter fifteen
# 3D

This one of the biggest chapters in the book, basically because it is a massive new feature with lots of new interface features and a vast amount of new creative possibilities. I've enlisted the help of two contributors; Maia Sanders who has written the majority of the chapter excluding Paul Tuersley's MacDonna sections and my Graffiti Club tutorials. You can read their biographies in the Introduction.

3D in After Effects consists of a great tool set that allows you to make some interesting and groovy effects. There are essentially two aspects to the 3D functions in After Effects, 3D layers and 3D filters. We will explore some of the cool things they can do, in combination and as stand-alone functions.

## after effects 3D basics

After Effects is not a full 3D application with modelling capabilities, it remains, at heart a 2D image processor with a firm grasp of 3D principles. It has been referred to as '2.5 - D', and also as 'postcards in space', you'll soon see that these are quite accurate descriptions of it's functionality. Although After Effects does not generate the same type of data as a traditional 3D application such as Cinema 4D, 3D Studio Max, Softimage or Maya, it can work with the file's output by these programs in a 3D fashion, utilizing the Z-depth channel (the 3rd dimension) to enhance the appearance of depth in existing 3D scenes. This will be explained later in the section on 3D filters.

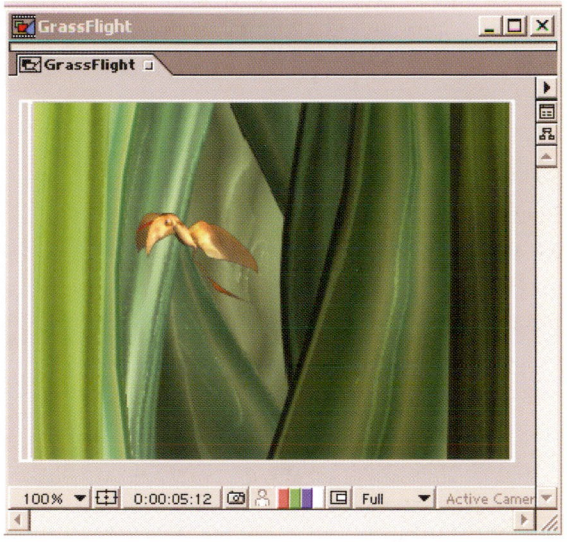

The other way After Effects works in the third dimension is by using its own layers as objects in 3D space, where they can move freely within three dimensions, allowing for some surprising effects. This will be explained in the sections which cover using 3D layers.

Throughout this chapter, you will develop a good understanding of the basic capabilities of 3D in After Effects. Of course, there are a million creative ways to use these tools, and I can't possibly attempt to cover all of them, it's your job to experiment, have fun and find out more tricks after you have completed this chapter!

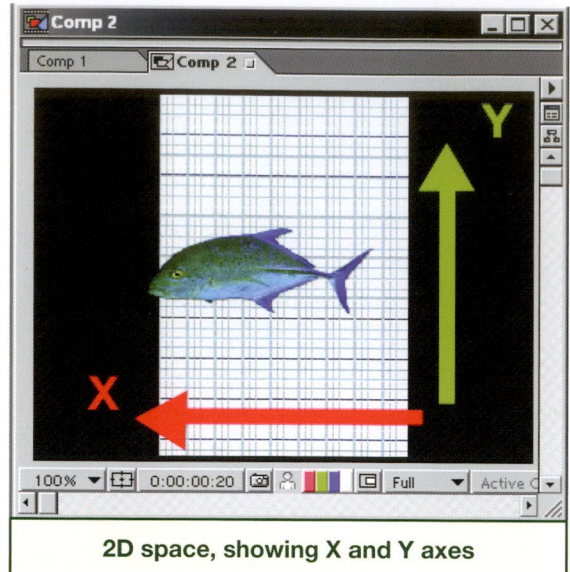

**2D space, showing X and Y axes**

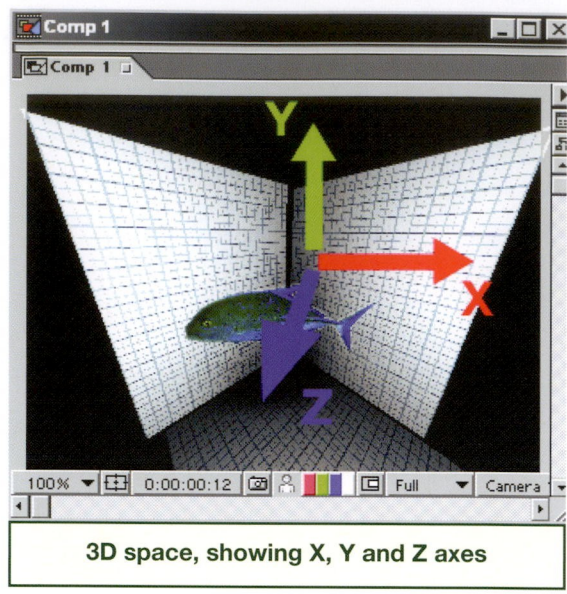

**3D space, showing X, Y and Z axes**

# understanding 3D space

the 3D workspace may sound and look a wee bit intimidating, but it really is nothing more than you see every day in the real world around you. In a regular After Effects composition, you deal with the X-axis (left and right) and the Y-axis (up and down), and all combinations of left-right-up-down. In the After Effects 3D workspace, there is the addition of the Z-axis, which represents in-and-out, back-to-front, near-to far, or, more simply, depth.

# navigating in 3D space

To move around in your 3D space, you can view your scene from many angles. This will help you with precision placement when animating your scene elements.

**1** From Training > Projects > Chapter15.aep, open the 1_Navigation comp. This project will help you understand many of the 3D principles and actions available to you in After Effects.

**2** Double-click on the 1_Navigation comp in the Project Window to open up its Timeline and Composition window.

## 3D View menu

**1** At the lower right of your Comp window, you will see a box that says Active Camera. This is your 3D View menu, where you can chose which view to use while manipulating the layers in your project. Spend a few minutes exploring this 3D set, becoming familiar with the different methods of viewing the scene.

You will notice that the first set of camera angles are orthographic, that is, the views are straight on to the subject with no angles. These views will prove very valuable in precisely placing your objects in relation to each other.

| Front |
|---|
| Left |
| Top |
| Back |
| Right |
| Bottom |

The second set of views, Custom Views, are on-angle 3D views which are different from the Active Camera. These views will also help you with animation and placement.

| Custom View 1 |
|---|
| Custom View 2 |
| Custom View 3 |

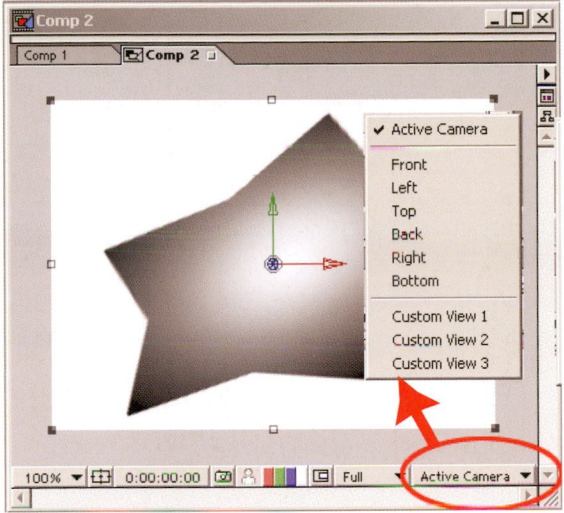

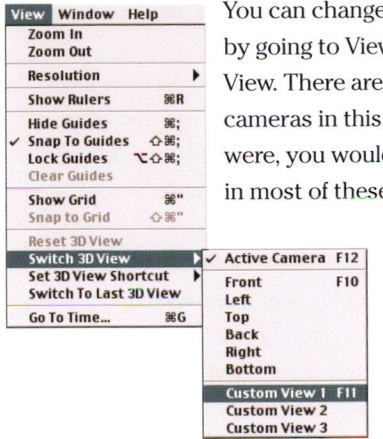

You can change the default view by going to View > Switch 3D View. There are no lights or extra cameras in this scene, if there were, you would see their icons in most of these views, depending on where they are located in relation to the main scene.

**2** Go back to the Active Camera View when you have finished experimenting in with the different views available.

## layer quality

If you are working on a composition with lots of elements or if it is large in size, you might like to use the different Layer Quality modes available. As with any other layer in After Effects, select the layer and go to Layers > Quality to find Draft and Wireframe settings for your layers. You can also use the Quality switches in the Timeline to do the same job. Experiment with these if you are finding that things are beginning to slow down.

## manipulating layers in 3D

You choose whether you want your layer to be 2D or 3D by clicking the 3D switch in the Switches column of the Timeline. Unless you click the 3D layer switch, your layer will still be 2D.

When you make your layer 3D, it no longer follows the rules of the usual After Effects layer hierarchy. With 2D layers, the top layer in the Timeline will be the front-most layer in the Comp window. But when you make a layer 3D, it will override the normal After Effects layer order, the 3D layer nearest the camera will be the front-most in the Comp window, no matter what position it is in the Timeline.

**1** With Training > Projects > Chapter 15.aep opened, double-click on the 2_Animation comp in the Project window.

**2** Change your view to the Custom 1 view, and notice some fish sticking up in a pretty strange way, looking like they are swimming outside the aquarium. Now, look at the other Custom Views, notice that the fish have not moved! This is because they are not on 3D layers yet.

**3** Look at the Timeline window, you will notice a series of boxes to the right of the file names. The 3D layers will have a 3D wireframe cube inside them, the ones with no cube inside are still 2D layers. Go ahead and check the boxes to make all of the layers in the comp 3D. See how the fish are now 3D and are inside the tank with the rest of the fish.

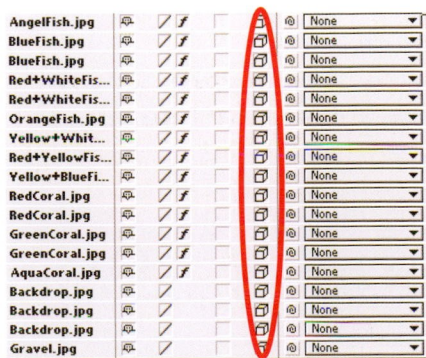

# animating in 3D

The next step we are going to take is to animate some of these fish. Animation in 3D is pretty similar to animating in 2D, the only exception is that you will now have a third dimension, the Z-axis to deal with. This allows for some tricky manipulation and requires a new set of tools.

You may have noticed when you made your layers 3D, that the Tool Palette changed a little, adding some exotic functions to the bottom of the palette, these are the Axis Mode buttons.

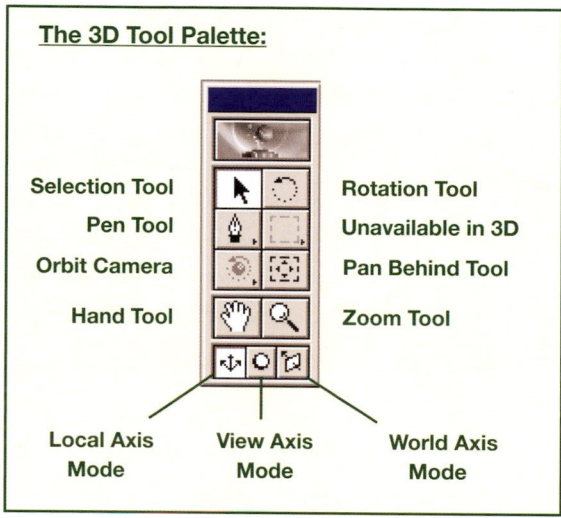

**The 3D Tool Palette:**

Selection Tool
Pen Tool
Orbit Camera
Hand Tool

Rotation Tool
Unavailable in 3D
Pan Behind Tool
Zoom Tool

Local Axis Mode    View Axis Mode    World Axis Mode

• Translation (changing the Position value) is almost the same as before and is performed using the Selection Tool. The only difference now is that as well as being able to move in the X dimension and the Y dimension, you can also move in the Z dimension.
• The Rotation Tool now allows you to Rotate your layer in all three dimensions.
• The Pen Tool, Pan Behind Tool, Hand Tool and Zoom tool behave in pretty much the same way as they do in 2D.

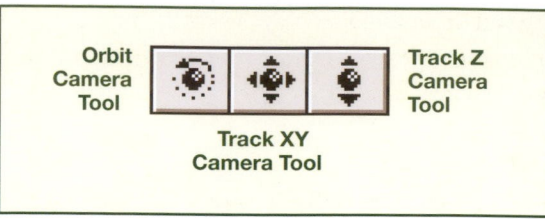

Orbit Camera Tool    Track Z Camera Tool

Track XY Camera Tool

There are three camera tools available under the Orbit tool. You can use these tools to adjust your views when in any of the Custom Views, Orthographic Views or any of your new camera views (with the exception of the default 3D camera which cannot be adjusted). You cannot use these tools in Active Camera view until you create a new camera layer, when you do, using these tools will affect the active camera.

• The *Orbit Camera Tool* will rotate the current view around the point of interest.
• The *Track XY Camera Tool* will adjust the view horizontally and vertically.
• The *Track Z Camera Tool* will adjust the view along the Z depth (moving in and out).

By using these tools in any of the orthographic or custom views, you will not affect the position of your layers or camera, only your view of the scene will change. If you are having trouble seeing something clearly while in one of these views, the Orbit Camera Tool can be used to rotate your scene, the Track XY Camera Tool can move your view along the X and Y axes, and the Track Z Camera Tool can be used to move nearer or further from your scene. Other important buttons are the Axis Mode buttons:

• Local Axis Mode will allow you to rotate around the central axes of your object.
• World Axis Mode will allow you to rotate around the geometric center of your 3D scene.
• View Axis Mode allows you to rotate aroundthe geometric center of your scene as it is currently being viewed.

These three Axis Modes allow for very fine tuning in your animation when working in the different views.

We will be working solely in Local Axis mode during this chapter. Now it's time to experiment with some animation in three dimensions.

## translation

It is very common, in the majority of 3D applications, to refer to the movement of a layer's Position as its *Translation*. Let's take a look at how to control a 3D layer's translation (or movement) in 3D space.

**1** You should still have the Chapter 15.aep open. If not, reopen it from Training > Projects > Chapter 15. Open the 2_Animation comp and make sure that all of the layers are 3D layers. Also make sure that you are in Active Camera view mode.

**2** Now, a fish tank isn't very much fun to watch if all the fish do is sit there without moving, so open the AngelFish.jpg layer, which appears in the top slot of the Timeline window, and then hit Alt + P key to bring up the Position property and set the first Position keyframe at frame 1.

**3** Move the time slider to frame 60, and select your layer. As soon as you do so, you'll see three colored arrows appearing from the center of the layer, these are called the axes.

Each arrow controls a corresponding axis, they are color-coded in the following way;
• The red arrow represents the X axis, dragging with this selected will move your layer left to right.
• The green arrow represents the Y axis, dragging with this selected will move your layer up and down.
• The blue arrow represents the Z axis, dragging with this selected will move your layer in and out of the screen.

When you place the cursor over one of the arrows on the axes, a little X, Y, or Z symbol appears next to the pointer, telling you which axis is active. I find it quite easy to remember which color represents which axis by thinking, 'RGB equals XYZ'.

**4** Click on the red, or X-axis, arrow, and move the AngelFish.jpg layer to the center of the screen, until the Position property values, displayed in the Timeline, read: 160, 37, 0. Notice that you can only move the layer on the X-axis.

If you are having a hard time seeing what is going on while working in your scene, remember that you can switch to any of the Custom Views, use the Camera manipulation tools to extend your view.

**5** Now move the cursor over the blue arrow (Z value) and drag downwards to push the layer back towards the rear of the fish tank. You should see the layer appear to get smaller as it moves away from the active camera. Your Position Property values in the Timeline should now read 160, 37, 170.

**6** At frame 90, click on the main axes to move the Angel Fish layer towards the front of the tank, and farther to the right (−60, 30, −40).

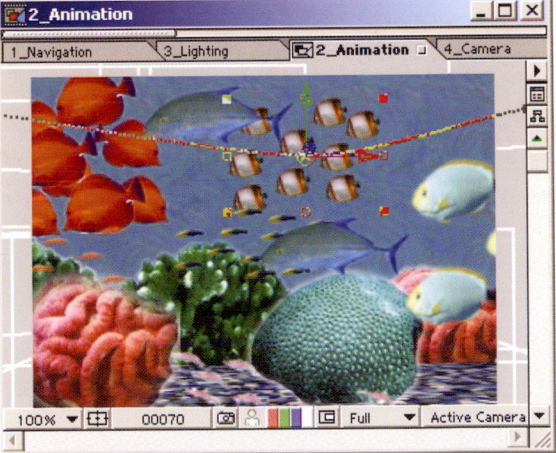

**7** Go back to the beginning and add some similar animation to the OrangeFish.jpg layer using the same techniques. Make the fish swim in the opposite direction to the Angel Fish layer. Your coordinates for the Position property values should now read:
frame 0: 5, 30, 100;
frame 60: 140, 140, −40;
frame 149: 400, 100, 0.

**8** Switch to an alternate view of your scene, either custom 1 or 2. With the Layers selected, you should see motion paths that arc in two different directions. RAM Preview your animation.

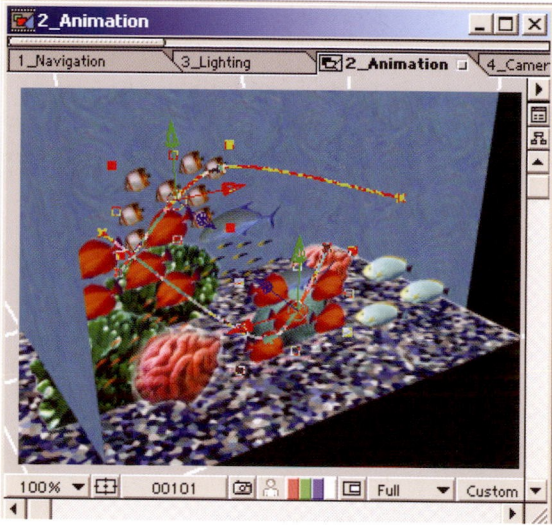

## rotation

Fish and most other objects usually turn to face in the direction they are moving. I'm now going to show you a couple of ways of adding a little rotation to your school of little fishes so that they are always facing in the correct direction.

**1** With the Current-Time Marker at the beginning of the comp, select the OrangeFish.jpg layer and then hit Shift + R key on the keyboard to bring up the Rotation values, alongside the Position values. Notice that there are four options available; Orientation, X Rotation, Y Rotation and Z Rotation.

There are two ways of manually adjusting the rotation of a layer in 3D;

• Orientation works by animating the layer along the shortest path possible to get from one rotational position to the next, there is no control over the separate axes but this produces a natural type of motion in most situations. When you animate Orientation, one keyframe is set for all three axes. This is the default orientation used when you rotate layers directly in the comp window.

• XYZ rotation is the other option. This provides you with three separate controls for each axis, allowing you to control each axis independently, this gives you more control over the angle of your rotations but can sometimes produce strange looking results if not used with knowledge and understanding of the basic principles. There is more information about rotational axis order (and how to understand and control it) in the Parenting section. When using XYZ rotation you must set keyframes for each axis individually. To animate the X, Y and Z axis individually in the Comp window, you must hold down the Alt key whilst dragging.

For now we will use the orientation method on the AngelFish.jpg layer to animate its Rotation value.

**2** Be sure that you are in local axis mode by clicking an the Local Axis Mode button in the Tools palette. This will allow the fish layer to rotate around its own center, rather than the center of the scene or view. Change your View Mode to Top and select the Rotation Tool from the Tool Palette.

**3** With the AngelFish.jpg layer selected, grab the green (Y-axis) arrow. Notice the tiny Y icon that indicates you will be rotating around the Y-axis.

**4** Go to Frame 1 and then turn the layer so it appears that the fish are heading towards the back of the tank at a shallow angle, your Orientation Properties should read about: 0, 58, 0. Set a keyframe for Orientation by clicking the Orientation stopwatch in the Timeline.

**5** At frame 60, when the fish reaches the point nearest the back of the aquarium, turn the layer so that it's parallel to the background layer. At this point, your Orientation Properties should read 0, 0, 0, and the layer should be exactly parallel to the plane of the scene.

**6** At frame 90, turn the fish to face into the direction that the path is heading once more (approximately 307 degrees).

**7** RAM Preview the comp so far and then relax and enjoy the peaceful sight of a tropical aquarium, ahhh!

**8** Play around with the other fish layers, animate their position, and rotation values in 3D space. Remember, the corals at the bottom of the fish tank are also on 3D layers, so see if you can make fish swim in amongst them.

# lighting

One of the coolest things that After Effects 3D can do is its 3D lighting. The rules for 3D lighting are similar across all areas of 3D simulation, so a brief explanation of these rules will help you understand the principles involved.

## the four light types

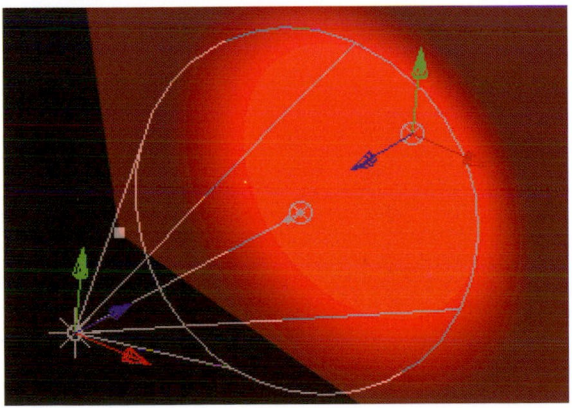

## ambient

Ambient light is a soft, even, overall scene lighting with little or no shadow casting power of its own. It is also sometimes known as *scene lighting, diffuse lighting*, or *default lighting*. This light type is useful for brightening a scene without adding shadows or hotspots, but is not very atmospheric. Ambient lighting has no real equivalent in the natural world, unlike the other three types of light commonly used in 3D space.

## parallel

Parallel light is a shadow casting light, emerging from one direction only. Imagine an infinitely tall and wide plane, emitting light at a ninety-degree angle to its surface. Parallel light is also commonly referred to as *directional light*. This light type is useful for broad illumination from a single angle with shadows cast, for a gentle or strong wash of light across a scene with no spread, and for a soft fill of light for a dark corner. Parallel light can be found in the real world, during what photographers and cinematographers call 'the magic hour', the half hour after sunrise and before sunset, when the sun is close to the horizon and it's rays are nearly parallel to the earth. It can be found in the movie and photographer's studio, and in cities and stadiums, as a giant wall of light bulbs. The photographer's flashbulb also has the effect of a parallel light if sufficiently powerful.

## point

Point light is light evenly emitted from a single point of origin. It is a soft, shadow casting light that illuminates only what is in its path. It is easy to use, as the light casts shadows, but has no hard edges itself. It is useful for all lighting setups, providing an even illumination in an area whose size is determined by the distance the point light is from its subject. The sun is the ultimate point light, casting evenly in all directions unless something blocks its way. Our human adaptation of the point light is the incandescent light bulb.

## spot

A spot light is, well, a spot-light. A light focused by a cone, the closer it is to the surface it is illuminating, the smaller and more intense the light becomes. This is the most dramatic, and possibly the most versatile of the light types, as the parameters are so varied for its use. The spot light cone can be adjusted for angle and softness as well as brightness, shadow and color attributes. Spot lights are a dramatic and often overused light type, so be sure you need the spotlight instead of automatically reaching for it every time.

## using multiple lights

When lighting a scene, the use of multiple lights allows for greater flexibility and control in the look of the scene. Individual light attributes can be keyframed, just by opening the light layer as you would any other layer and adjusting the attributes. We will explore three different lighting setups, just to get you started.

## light options window

We'll start off with a neutral, classic three-point setup, useful in lots of situations. Next on our list will be a dark, mysterious film-noir type setup, great for arty shots and for creating suspense. Finally we'll go for a camp, and exciting, party atmosphere.

> **Here are examples of all four types of light, used within the same scene**

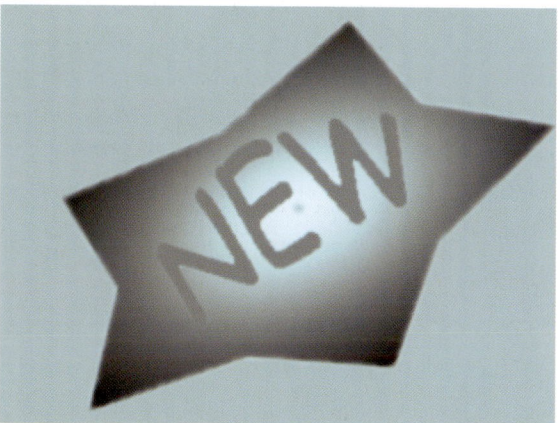

**Ambient**

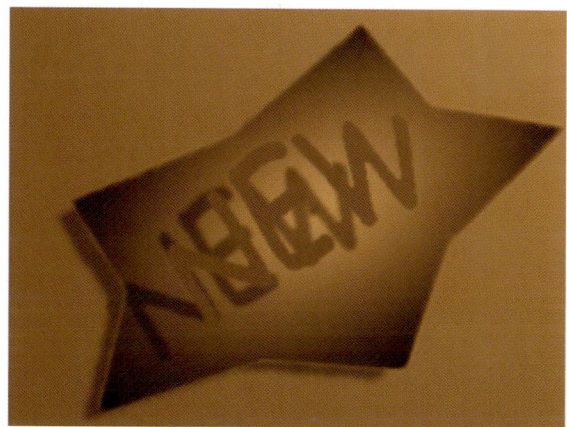

**Point**

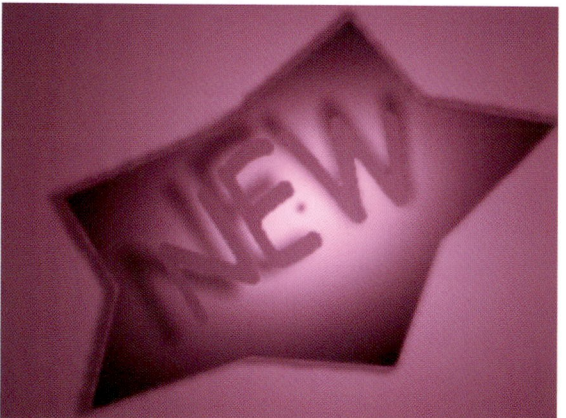

**parallel**

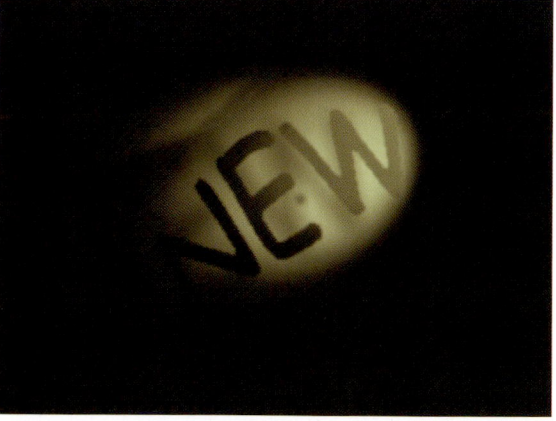

**Spot**

## lighting scheme one – basic

First, you will set the key light, the brightest and usually warmest light in the scene. This light also indicates the light direction or source, this is vitally important to remember when continuity between scenes is a consideration.

**1** Still in the Chapter 15.aep project, open the 3a_Lighting comp. You should see three, 3D layers in the Timeline. Solo each layer on and off to check the contents of each layer.

**2** Go to Layer > New > Light. In the light options palette, name the new light, 'Point Light 1', set the light type to point light; set the intensity to 90% and change the color to a pale, buttery yellow. Turn on the Cast Shadows option, set shadow darkness to 30%, and set shadow diffusion to 10 pixels. Click OK to create your light. The layers now have a nice depth to them, coming from the shadows cast by the light.

**3** In the Timeline, click on the Wireframe interactions button, this will speed up your previews whilst changes are being made.

**4** In the Comp window, select the Point Light icon and then use the axis arrows to move it to the upper left of the scene, exactly the same as moving a 3D layer.

Next, we'll set the fill light, the subordinate light that softens harsh shadows and fills out the chromatic range of the lighting scheme. This light is usually cooler than the key light, and often is used to give a clue as to the color of the general environment of the scene being lit.

**5** In the Layer menu, make another new light (Command + Shift + Alt + L). In the light options palette, set the light type to point light and name it Point Light 2. Set the intensity to 30%, and the color to a cool, pale violet. Turn on cast shadows and set shadow darkness to 20%, and shadow diffusion to 5 pixels. Click OK to create the new light.

**6** In the Comp window, using the axes, pull the new point light icon to the lower right of the scene. Notice how the addition of this light really improves the scene, making it look more natural and balancing the color.

Finally, you will make a bounce light, to simulate the reflection from the photographer's scrim. A *scrim* is a reflective sheet used to add a general wash of light to the scene, providing that little bit of extra sparkle and illumination. In this case, you will use a neutral, cool tone to mimic the look of daylight lighting.

**7** Make a new light and in the light settings dialog, change the Light name to 'Bounce Light' set the light type to parallel. Set the color to a cool pale blue-gray. Set the intensity to 30%, and turn shadows off. It's a good idea to get into the habit of naming your lights so that you can easily see what job they're doing by looking at them in the Timeline.

In the Comp window you will notice that this light has a slightly different icon to the others, it has a Point of Interest attached to it (the wheel-shaped icon at the end of the line which extends from the light icon).
This is because it is a directional light. The Point of Interest is like the target for the light, wherever it lies is the place that the light will point towards.

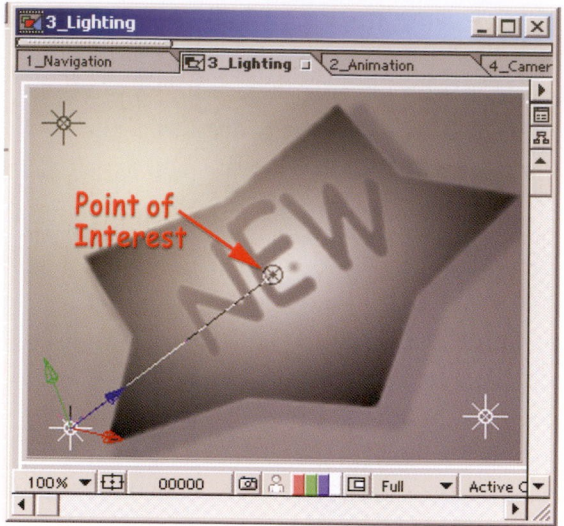

**8**  Command-Click on the X arrow and then Y arrow to move the light icon to the bottom-left of the screen.

If we had moved the light without simultaneously holding down the Command key, the Point of Interest would have moved along with the light. Holding down the Command key whilst dragging will move the light whilst maintaining the Point of Interest's current position.

## lighting scheme two – shadow casting

In this exercise, we'll make a screen for our light to shine through, casting mysterious venetian blind type shadows on your scene. This technique is adapted from theatre and film lighting, where the lighting technician will put a cutout of the off-stage, shadow-casting element. It's very common to use silhouettes of tree branches, for example, to give the set an outdoors feeling.

**1**  Double-click the 3b_Lighting comp in the project window to open it up. This is exactly the same as the comp we started with in the first lighting setup, with the addition of a VenetianBlinds.psd layer. Turn on visibility for the Venetian Blinds layer to see what's what.

**2**  Make the VenetianBlinds.psd layer 3D by clicking the 3D Layer checkbox in the Timeline, its position will now change in relation to the other layers.

**3**  With the blinds layer selected, hit the A key on the keyboard twice in very quick succession to open the material attributes for the Blinds layer, turn on the casts shadows option by clicking once on the word *Off*, to ensure the layer will cast shadows onto other layers.

**4**  Switch to Custom View 1 and move the Blinds.psd layer to the front of the scene, and off to the right side. Use the Camera Z Track Tool to adjust your view if need be, doing this will not affect the Active camera view when in any of the Custom or orthographic views. Check that the Position properties read 350, 120, –80.

**5**  Use the rotation tool to rotate the layer by about 90 degrees around the Y-axis so the light coming through the window can rake across the scene at an oblique angle. Press R to open the Orientation Properties. Your Orientation properties should read 0, 90, 0.

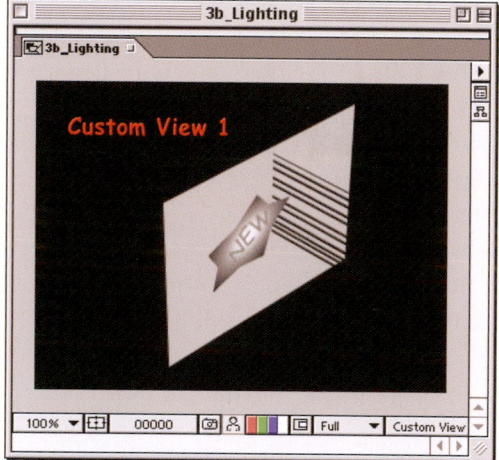

**6**  Check your progress in the Active Camera View. Notice that you Active view has not changed, despite using the Camera Track tool.

**7**  It is important that you cannot see the Blinds layer in the Active View.

**8**  Switch back to Custom View 1 when you have finished and then make sure that the Blinds.psd layer is selected.

**9** Go to Effect > Channel > Set Matte and choose Blinds.psd from the Take Matte From drop down menu. For the Use For Matte option, select lightness. This should have the effect of making the black areas transparent, leaving only the white areas.

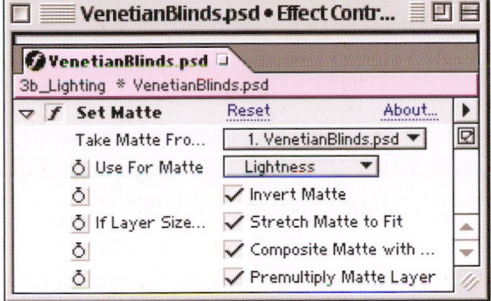

**10** Click on the Invert matte checkbox to reverse the effect so that only the black areas are showing.

Now, we'll make a street light to shine through the window, telling us that we are deep inside the concrete jungle, at midnight, waiting for a mysterious femme fatale to walk in the door! Can't wait, can you?

**11** Go to Layer > New > Light and then set the Light Type to Spot. Name the light, *Street light*, set the Intensity to 110% and make sure that the color is pure white.

**12** Check the Cast Shadows checkbox. Set the Shadow Darkness to 100%, and the Shadow Diffusion to 15 pixels, and click OK to make the light.

**13** Make sure that you have the selection tool (V) selected and then with the Light layer selected, press P to open Position properties. Command-Drag the Spotlight icon to the far right of the scene, *behind* the Blinds.psd layer. You may want to change your views to help you position the light. Try using the orthographic views, for example, go to Top view when you want to position the light on the X-axis and Z-axis, swap to Right view to move it on the Y-axis (remember to always hold down the Command key whilst dragging to prevent you from moving the Point of Interest).

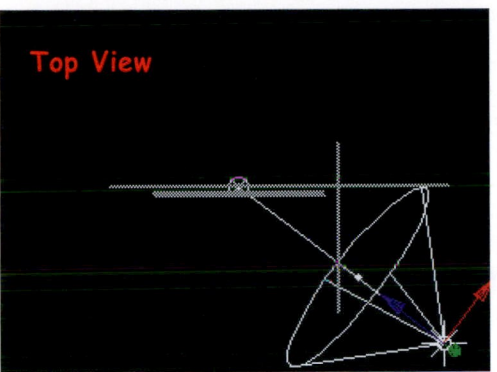

**14** Keep referring back to the Active View to check the results of the changes. The final coordinates of the new Spotlight should be about 550, 230, –300, the Point of Interest should remain at or near the center of the scene. You should now see the shadow casting across the surface of the scene.

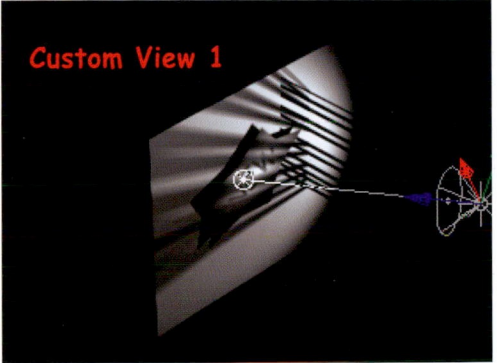

**15** Go back to Active Camera view, feel the oppression! Finally, we'll make a fill light to soften the 'near' edge of the scene and give a greater feeling of depth.

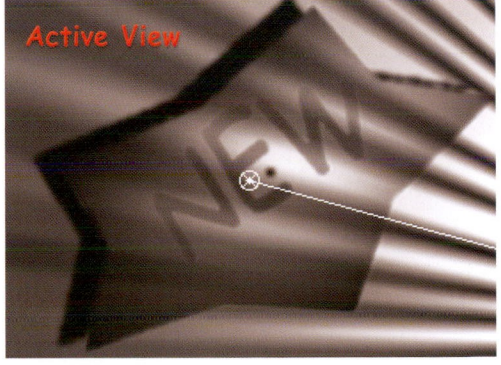

**16** Make a new light. Set type to point, with an intensity of 85%. Set the color to bright, foggy blue and turn off shadows, and click OK to create the light. In the Active Camera view, move it to the lower left of the screen, or around 70, 190, –115.

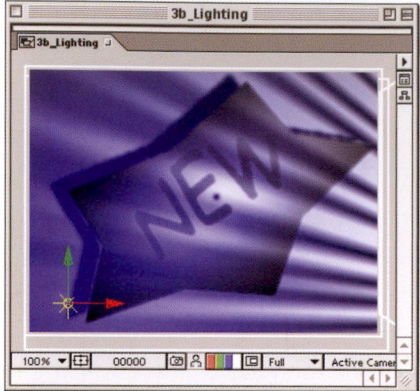

### extra credit

Try making a new blinds layer using the Effects > Transitions > Venetian Blinds filter. This way you can make the blinds move as the light shines through them. Remember that you must pre-compose the Venetian Blinds layer with all the effects compounded into a new comp before trying to shine a light through it, otherwise, After Effects will try to shine the light through the layer before the transition has been applied. You must also make the Pre-comp into a 3D layer for this to work.

If you are feeling very ambitious, later you can try making an animated mask to provide atmospheric effects, using the free Tinderbox Caustics filter for water effects or the free Boris Continuum Fire filter to create fire effects (both of these filters can be found on the CD in the Free Stuff > Plugins folder, install them now if you haven't already done so).

## the 3D camera

Understanding cameras can be a lifelong career for some people, but the basics are fairly simple to get to grips with. After Effects provides a number of excellent presets in the camera menu, but some knowledge of basic camera functions will help you on your way.

In this set of exercises, you should imagine that you are making a cartoon western. Your director gives you a script with the only direction in this scene reading: 'we open on a small church in the shadow of the mountains'. To make the director happy, you want to present a small range of options, so, we will take three different approaches to filming the scene, animating three different aspects of the After Effects Camera.

### technique 1 – aperture change

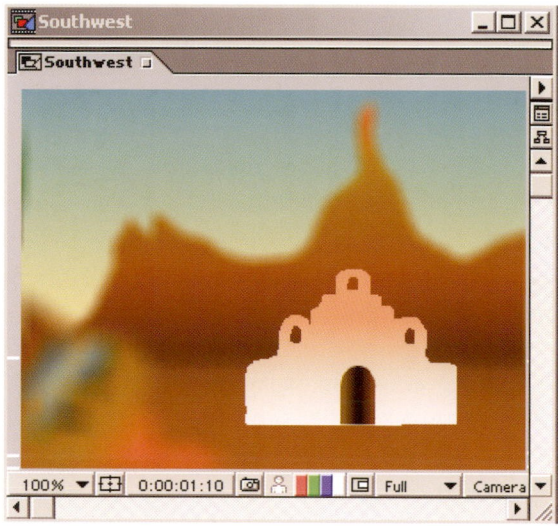

This approach isolates the church by gradually blurring out its surroundings and leaving it in focus. This is achieved through changing the aperture of the camera, which mimics the real world effect of a narrowing focal plane.

**1** Open the 4_Camera Apeture comp from the Project Window.

**2** Go to Layer > New > Camera. In the Camera Settings window, use the preset 15 mm. This is a nice neutral setting for this scene. Also, enable Depth of field by checking inside its box. Click OK to leave the Camera Settings window and then notice that the view in the Comp window has changed.

**3** Change to Custom View 1, and notice where the camera is in relation to the scene. Using the Blue arrow (Z), drag the camera back till the Z coordinate reads –170. Notice that the Point of Interest is moving with the camera.

This is a nice way to reposition layers but is not always the best way to animate your cameras, due to the fact that you cannot get any feedback for your Active Camera View at the same time as moving the camera in the Custom Views.

**4** You can also move the camera along the Z-axis by using the Track Z Camera tool when in Active View. Go back to Active View and then select the Track Z camera tool.

**5** Select the Camera layer and then hit the P key so that you can see the Position values displayed in the Timeline.

**6** In the Comp window, click and drag downwards with the Track Z tool till the Z position reading is about -214.

**7** If you find this difficult, you can also type the new coordinates directly into the Position values, displayed in the Timeline. The coordinates for this should be 160, 120, –214. Close up the Property value when you have finished.

**8** Set the Current-Time Marker to frame 1 and then, in the Timeline window, open the camera options menu by twirling down the little disclosure triangle to the left of the Camera layer, and then clicking on the Options disclosure triangle.

**9** Set the Aperture value to 0, and set a keyframe by clicking on the stopwatch. Now, this aperture is impossible in the real world, but in After Effects land, it works just great.

**10** Move the Current-Time Marker to the end of your layer (hit the O key to move to selected layers Out-point and change the aperture value to 60).

**11** Make a RAM Preview, and then go to Composition > Save RAM Preview. Save the RAM Preview movie to your Creative After Effects > 3D Chapter folder for later comparison with the other camera moves.

## technique 2 – push in

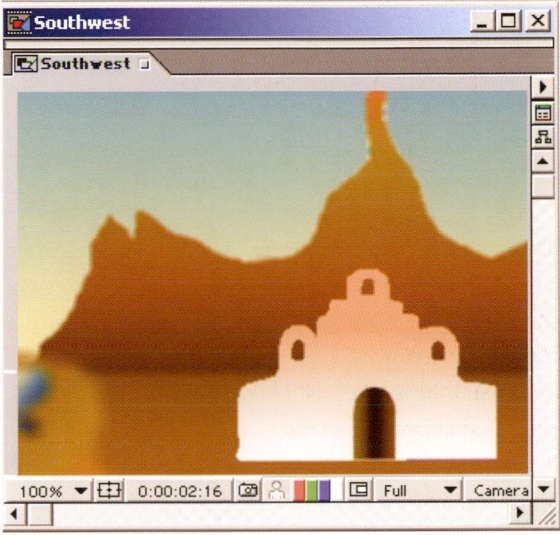

This approach uses the motion of the camera to move past the foreground until the church is large in frame and in focus. We will be animating both the camera and its point of interest here, to simulate a moving camera with a fixed focus.

To better explain, imagine if you are at a wedding, with an inexpensive, disposable camera. You want to take a picture of the bride, who is in front of the wedding cake, and you also want a picture of the cake. In order to do this, you stand in front of the bride, snap a picture, and then move past the bride to snap a picture of the cake. In the first picture, the cake may be in the picture you took of the bride, but it will be out of focus and lower in the picture frame, thereby taking a subordinate role to that of the bride.

In the second picture, you may see part of the bride's dress, but it will be out of focus and cut off by the picture plane, thereby taking a subordinate role to the cake.

**1** Open the 4_Camera Push comp from the Project window.

**2** With the Current-Time Marker at frame 1, hit Command + Shift + Option + C to create a new camera. Choose the 15 mm preset from the Presets menu and enable Depth of Field by checking in the Enable Depth of Field checkbox. Make sure that the *Lock to Zoom* checkbox is unchecked (this enables you to set precise attributes for aperture, focal length and distance). Set the Aperture to 10.0 pixels, Focal Length to 50, and Focus Distance to 100 pixels.

**3** With the Current-Time Marker still at frame 1, open the camera's Transform values by clicking on the disclosure triangle to the right of the camera layer in the timeline. Make sure that the layer is selected before moving on to the next step.

**4** Change to Custom View 1, Hold down the Command key and then drag the Blue axis arrow until the Position value reads 160, 120, –214. Notice that as you drag this axis, that the Point of Interest Z value stays at 0, if we hadn't held down the Command key whilst dragging, it would have moved along with the camera as it did in the apeture camera exercise.

**5** Set keyframes for the Point of Interest and the Position properties by clicking on the stopwatch icons.

**6** Move the Current-Time Marker to frame 44, and in Custom View 1, use the individual axis arrows to move the camera until the Position values read 184, 154, –184. Don't hold down the Command key this time, allow the Point of Interest to move with the camera. The Point of Interest properties should now read 184, 154, 30.

**7** Return to the Active Camera View and then RAM Preview your comp. Save the RAM Preview to your Creative After Effects > 3D chapter folder for later comparison.

## technique 3 – rack focus

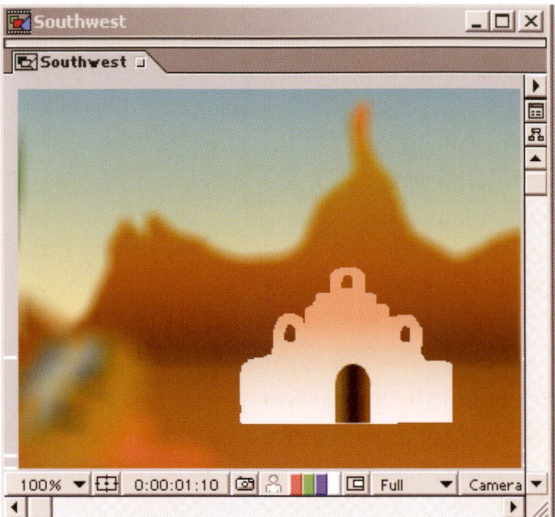

This approach uses a shallow depth of field, and changes, or 'racks' focus from the extreme foreground to the object of interest. This will allow you to change the focal length without moving your camera, which is vital for this technique. Usually, the focal plane travels with the lens of the camera, and as a camera zooms, it actually moves its lens, along with the focal plane. What we will be doing here is leaving the lens stationary, and changing only the focus. To better explain, imagine that you are on holiday (vacation), taking a picture of your sister, who's standing in front of the Taj Mahal. You focus the camera on your sister, and then take a photograph. The resulting photograph will show a clear, in-focus sister and a blurred Taj Mahal. Then you twist the focus ring on your camera, so you can focus on the Taj Mahal, and you take another photograph. The result here will be a blurred sister and a clear, in-focus Taj Mahal. Now, imagine animating between these two images. This type of focus shift is called a rack or a pull focus. Your eyes do this all the time, they can focus on something near then focus on something far, without you really noticing.

This is an unobtrusive camera move (because the camera does not actually 'move'). It's used far more often in the movies and on TV than you probably realize, watch out for it.

**1** Open the 4_Camera Rack comp from the Project window.

**2** Make sure that you are at frame 1 and then create a new Camera using either of the methods we used earlier.

**3** In the Camera settings window, make sure that the Lock To Zoom option is unchecked, this will enable the camera to change its focus without changing any of the other settings. You'll also need to make sure that Depth of Field is enabled to achieve the desired effect (this will create a nice blurring around the extremities of the shot). Do this by checking inside the Enable Depth of Field checkbox. Finally, set the camera to preset 15 mm, and set the aperture to 30.0 pixels before clicking OK to leave the Camera Settings box.

**4** Open the Camera layer's Position properties by selecting the Camera layer and hitting the P key on the keyboard. Change the coordinates to 160, 120, –214. Close the Position property after altering the values. You should now be able to see the whole scene.

**5** Still at frame 1, open up the Camera Options by clicking on the disclosure triangle to the left of the Camera layer and then clicking on the Options disclosure triangle. Set the Focus Distance to 90 pixels and watch the Comp window as the Mission house becomes more blurred and the lizard becomes focused. Set a keyframe by clicking the stopwatch icon.

**6** Move the time slider to frame 44 and change the Focus Distance to 140 pixels. Now you'll see that the focus has swapped, the lizard is now blurred and the mission is in focus. This effect is a classic for guiding the viewer's attention from the foreground to the background (or vice versa).

**7** Be sure you are in Active Camera. Make a RAM Preview. Now turn your back, walk six paces, and REACH FOR THE SKY!!! This is a classic camera trick from American cinema.

**8** Save your RAM Preview and then compare all three RAM Previews to see the different methods for isolating parts of your shot.

# pro bundle – 3D Channel effects

This is a production bundle only section, Standard Version users are advised to read through the steps as you may pick up ideas from it. You can continue following the tutorials in the Putting It All Together section.

After Effects Production Bundle has a set of filters that can act on 3D or z-depth information that renders with certain file types from true 3D applications. Most 3D modelling and animation programs will output some sort of file containing depth information. In the following exercise, you will be using RLA files output from Alias/Wavefront Maya.

The 3D filter effects can be used in conjunction with regular 2D filters, in a variety of cool ways, but first, you need to see how they work in isolation.

We'll be using them on their own to produce two effects that, while possible to reproduce with full 3D rendering applications, can often be faster and more flexible to produce in post-production.

We'll be experimenting with three of the effects available, 3D fog, depth of field, and 3D depth matte.

## 3D depth matte

**1** Open 5_Effects 1 comp from the Project window. RAM Preview the composition to see what's already been done.

Basically, we have six layers, the top and bottom layers have been switched off so that you can only see the layers in between them. OK, so in between the top and bottom layers we have four copies of the same piece of footage, this is a 3D animation of a humming bird which was rendered out from Alias/Wavefront Maya as an RLA sequence. This is a sequence of images with extra information pertaining to the depth information. We want to do a couple of things here. The bird is currently flying repeatedly from right to left, so first of all we'll make the bird change direction each time it passes the screen.

**2** Select layers 2 and 4 (Command-select them to select non-contiguous items) and then hit the S key to bring up the Scale values for these two layers.

**3** Context-click on the scale value of either of the two layers and choose *Edit Value*.

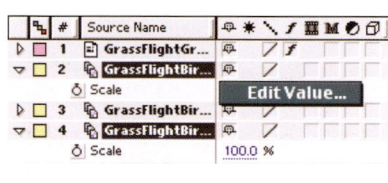

**4** In the Scale dialog box, change the Preserve menu to None and then change the Width to −100, this will have the effect of reversing the direction in which the bird moves. RAM Preview the movie to see the result, the bird now flies forwards then backwards across the screen.

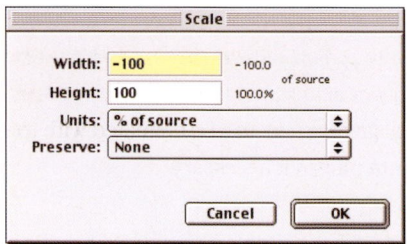

**5** Switch on the background layer (layer 6), this is a single RLA file, rendered also from Maya. The still image also contains depth information. RAM Preview the comp again, what we are going to do is to use the depth information in this file to make the bird fly in and out from the layers of foliage.

**6** Switch visibility off for the background layer and then switch the top layer on (layer 1). This is an exact replica of the background layer. We are going to use this layer to mask out the areas where the bird would be behind the grass. At the moment you cannot see the bird at all, the grass is obscuring it.

**7** Context-click on the top GrassFlightGrass.rla layer (Layer 1) and then go to Effect > 3D channel > Depth Matte. This filter can read the Z-depth information contained in this RLA file and create a matte based upon that information. In other words, it can separate your image into chunks along the Z depth, it'll be easier to show you what I mean.

**8** In the Effect Controls window, Context-click on the Depth Value and go to Edit Value, this will take you to the Slider Control dialog box where you can adjust the range of the slider.

**9** Change the minimum Slider Range value to 0 and the maximum value to 1 and then click OK. With this RLA file, the range of depth lies between the values of 0 and 1. We don't want our values to go any further than these points, if we use the slider with these extremes set, we cannot accidentally go too high or too low.

**10** Make sure to switch off the Wireframe Interactions button in the Timeline (or use the Timeline's wing menu to switch it off).

**11** Now, back in the Effect Controls window, *slowly* drag the Depth slider all the way to the right. Notice that as you get past the 0.5 mark, that the grass layers disappear one at a time. The grass layers were positioned at different Z depths in Maya, even though this appears to be a 2D image, After Effects is reading the original depth information and removing the layers one by one, depending on their position in 3D space. Mind boggling but true!

How is this useful? Well, we can use this top layer to mask out the bird when we want it to be moving behind the grass, I'll show you what I mean.

**12** Move to frame 16 and then change the Depth slider to 0.55. You should now see the bird peeking out from behind the foliage.

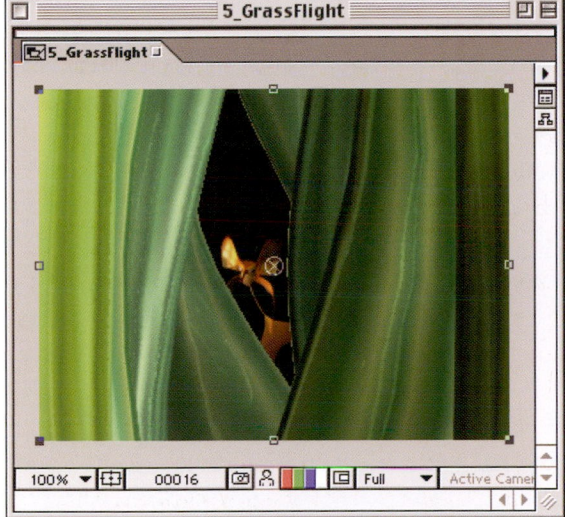

**13** Now switch on the background layer. You can see that the identical copy, placed behind the bird, fills in the spaces, matted out in the top layer. Preview the footage to see the bird moving behind the grass.

OK, we can take this a step further by animating the depth value so that it looks as though the bird is moving forwards through the foliage.

**14** Move back to frame 1 and then set a keyframe for the depth value.

**15** Move to the beginning of the second bird layer (layer3). Switch off visibility for the background layer again so that it is easier to see what you are about to do.

**16** Select the top layer again and then, in the Effect Controls window, drag the slider till the next set of grass blades disappear from view (approx. 75).

**17** Repeat this at the In-points of the next two bird layers. Set the following values for the Depth of the top layer: Frame 60 – 0.85; Frame 90 – 0.95.

**18** OK, if you preview the animation, you'll see that the values change gradually from one depth to another, we want the depth to suddenly change each time the bird changes direction. To do this we must Toggle Hold the keyframes so that they hold on the current value till the next keyframe is encountered. Remember we used this type of keyframe back in the Animation chapter?

**19** Select the top layer and hit the U key to bring up the keyframed values for that layer.

**20** Select all of the depth keyframes (hit the Property name in the Timeline) and then got to Animation > Toggle Hold Keyframe (Command + Alt + H).

**21** Preview the animation to see the bird fly through the blades of grass. Now we'll make the bird get bigger as it approaches the screen to increase the realism.

**22** Select the first three bird layers, one by one, and resize them so that they have the following Scale values: Layer2: –50, 50; Layer 3: 70;
Layer 4: –90, 90; Layer 5: 100.

Switch the background layer back on and preview the comp. Notice how the blocking out of certain areas in the top layer causes the illusion of depth when the bird layers are sandwiched between that and another copy of the layer. This layer could also be animated with the same Depth Matte plug-in if necessary.

### 3D depth fog

We're going to start by adding some spooky, fog to the scene to make it more swamp-like. We'll then add a rack focus to emphasize the depth and bring the whole thing together.

**1** Open 7_Waterbirds comp, this is a short RLA sequence animation of two birds feeding in a lagoon.

**2** Context-click on the waterbirds layer and go to Effect > 3D Channel > 3D Fog.

**3** In the Effect Controls window, set the Start Depth to 0.98, End Depth to 0.90, Opacity to 95, and Scattering to 75. Change the Fog color to a pale, yellowish-green color, we want to make this look like a gassy swampland. Set keyframes at frame 1 for: Fog Start Depth and Fog End Depth.

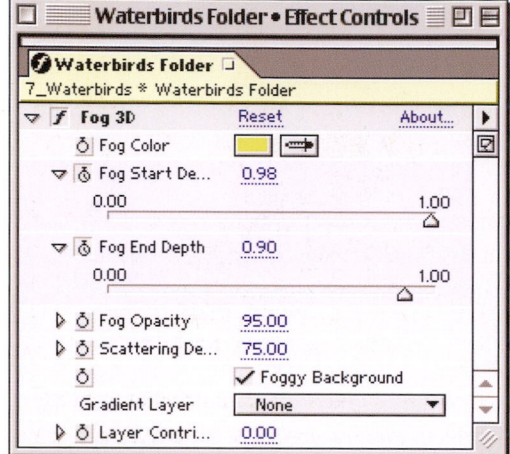

**4** Move to the last frame (40) and change the Fog Start Depth to 1 and the Fog End Depth to 0.5. Preview the movie to see the fog rolling away across the swamp.

## depth of field

Now, we're going to use the Depth of Field filter to create a similar effect to the one we created earlier in the Camera Rack Focus tutorial.

**1** Select the Waterbirds layer and hit the E key on the keyboard to bring up any effects applied to the layer. Notice that the Depth of Field filter has been applied to the layer.

**2** Double-click on the effect name in the Timeline to bring up the Effect Controls window. In the Effect Controls window, activate the effect by clicking in the little checkbox beside the layer name.

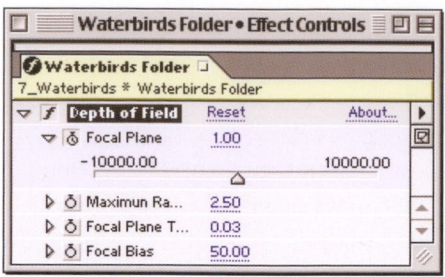

The Focal Plane value has already been set to 1, as I said earlier, this seems to be the magic number as far as Maya RLA files are concerned. The Focal Plane value determines the position in 3D space (or Z value) which will be in focus.

I've also preset the Maximum Radius value (which determines how blurred the rest of the image will be) and the Focal Plane thickness value (which determines how deep the focused area will be).

**3** Move to the end of the layer and then slowly drag the Focal Plane slider all the way down to 0.92. Notice that the focal area (the area which is in focus) shifts from the foreground bird to the background bird.

**4** Experiment with the settings for both filters. Try animating the Fog Color so that it mutates as it crosses the swamp. You could also animate the Ramp effect on the background layer to create unusual sky effects.

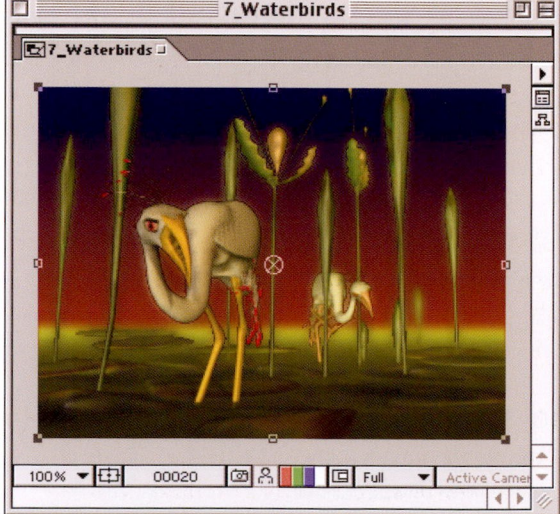

# graffiti club

OK, so you've learned some of the basics of how 3D works in After Effects. Let's see how we can apply some of the techniques to a working project. Let's go back to our Graffiti Project, the last thing we did to this project was to animate our main characters using Expressions. Here, we'll use some very basic 3D animation to add some more movement to our characters. So far we have created three main compositions, one for each character and another for the background. It is good to get into the habit of creating separate compositions for each of the elements within your final movie. It keeps things tidy and manageable whilst making it easier to mix and match elements to try out different combinations.

**1** Open Graffiti06.aep from Training > Projects > Chapter 15 folder. Save your previous project to your Creative After Effects > 3D chapter folder as Chapter15b.aep.

**2** Create a new composition, name it *Titles comp* and make its frame size 320 × 240, 15 fps for the frame rate and 750 frames for the duration (50 seconds).

**3** In the project window, Command-Select Annie.psd comp, Ellis.psd comp and Background Sequence comp. Hit Command + / to bring them into the new Composition.

**4** Deselect all layers by hitting Command + Shift + A or by clicking anywhere in the gray area underneath the layers and then drag the Background Sequence layer down so that it is beneath the two character layers.

**5** Turn the audio off for all of the layers except the Background sequence layer and then select the top two main character layers and hit the S key to solo their scale values.

**6** Highlight the scale value for either of the two layers and type in 25. Because both layers are selected when you change the value, both layers will scale down to 25% of their original size.

**7** Bring up the Position values (P) for both layers and then scrub the X values (the first value) to position the two characters at either side of the Composition window. Use the following diagram as a reference.

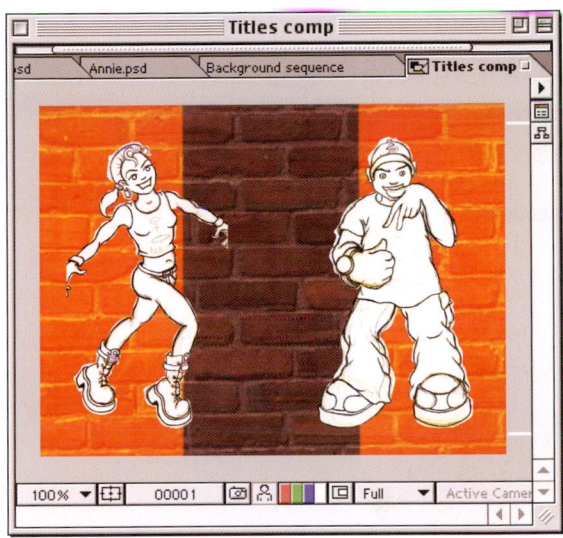

**8** RAM Preview the layers and notice that there are times in the animation where the Annie character gets cropped off at the edges. The reason for this is that the original composition in which it was animated was not wide enough to accommodate the movement of the limbs. This is a common mistake to make when starting out in After Effects but luckily it is just as easy to correct this sort of problem as it is to create it.

**9** Open up Annie.psd comp and hit Command + K to open up the Composition Settings box. Deselect the lock Aspect Ratio checkbox and then change the Width setting to 680, then click OK.

**10** Go back to the Titles Comp and preview the animation, the problem should now be gone.

**NB** Another way you could have solved this problem is by activating the Collapse Transformations switches for the two character layers. This has the effect of ignoring the boundaries of the original composition. The only drawback is that we would not have then been able to use any effects or layer modes on the layers.

As you have learned in this chapter, you can now make your After Effects layers 3D. This means that as well as having X (right to left) and Y (up and down) dimensions, you layer can also have a Z (in and out) dimension .

When a 2D layer is changed to a 3D layer, it still remains a rectangular flat plane (hence the 'Post-cards in space analogy), the difference with a 3D layer is that it can now be scaled rotated and moved within three dimensions. 3D is implemented on a layer by layer basis. This means you can make all the of the layers in your Composition 3 D or choose to have a mixture of 2 D and 3 D Layers within the same composition.

We are going to animate our layers in 3D space and animate a camera in 3D space so that you can see what the differences are between using each method.

**11** Save your project into the Creative After Effects > 3D Chapter folder as Graffiti06b.aep.

We are going to time some camera moves to markers in the comp. To save time and to make sure that we are all at the same point, I have pre-saved a version of this project with the markers already attached. After you have completed this chapter, you can come back to the project you have just saved, and lay down your own markers wherever you want them. For now, though, we'll open my pre-saved project.

## animating the camera

**1** Open up the Project named Graffiti06a.aep from the Training > Projects > Chapter 15 folder.

This project is exactly the same as the one you have just saved except for one thing. There is a new camera layer in the comp with some markers attached to it.

**2** Hit the Period key on the number pad to preview the audio of the comp. Watch the Current-Time Marker as it passes the markers and take note of the points that I have marked. These will be where our camera moves will take place.

The two properties that we will be animating are Point of Interest (think of this as the camera's target) and the Zoom property.

**3** Click on the disclosure triangle next to the Camera name to open up its properties and then open up both the Transform properties and the options properties for the camera.

**4** Use the K key to jump to the first marker on the Camera layer and then click on the Stopwatches for Point of Interest and Zoom to create keyframes for those values.

**5** Hit the U key on the keyboard to show only keyframed properties for the camera layer.

**6** Jump to the next visible marker (frame 169) by hitting the K key again.

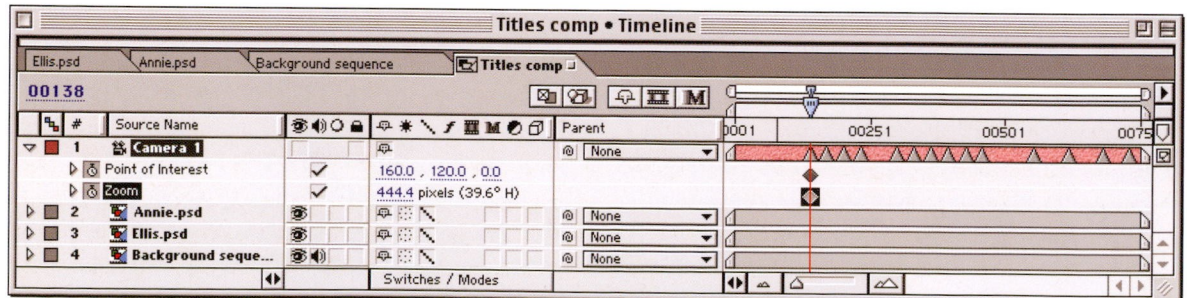

**7** Before we can use the Camera on our layers, we need to make the layers 3D, otherwise the camera will have no effect on them.

**8** Click on the 3D switch for each of the character layers to make them 3D layers.

**9** Scrub the Point of Interest X value (the first value) to the left till it reads around about 70 and the Annie character is in the center of the Comp window.

**10** Scrub the zoom value to the right till it reads around about 1000. This will zoom the camera into the Annie character, making her appear bigger in the Comp window.

**11** Jump to the next marker (200 frames), using the K key again.

**12** Select the previous two keyframes from the frame 200 mark and then hit Command + C to copy them to the clipboard, than hit Command + V to paste them into the position of the Current-Time Marker.

**13** Jump to the marker at frame 234 and then copy and paste the first two keyframes into that position.

**14** Hit the N key on the keyboard to bring the End Work Area Marker into the Current-Time Marker and then Shift + RAM Preview your work so far.

**15** Annie is now being 'zoomed into' by the camera. Notice that the background layer is not affected by the zoom and remains filling the screen throughout the camera zoom.

**16** Move to the fifth marker at frame 299, set two identical keyframes to the last two by checking the keyframe checkboxes in the Timeline for both Point of Interest and Zoom values.

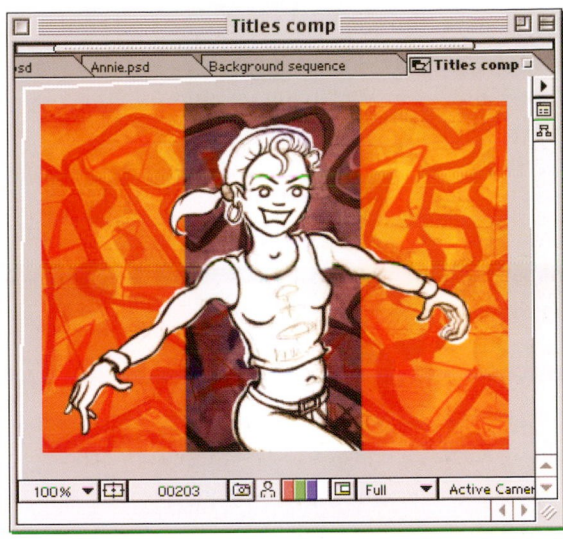

**17** Jump to the next marker at frame 330 by hitting the K key and change the camera's Point of Interest and Zoom values to zoom into the Ellis character.

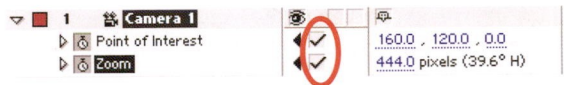

**18** Jump to the next marker at frame 362, and create identical keyframes by clicking in the keyframe checkboxes again.

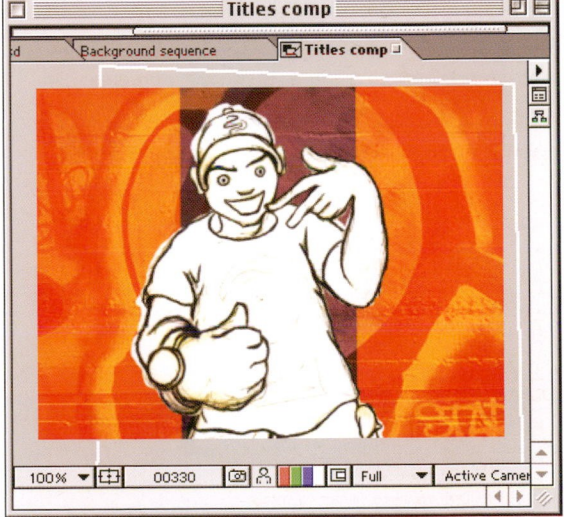

**19** Jump to the marker at frame 395 and copy and paste the first keyframes for Zoom and Point of Interest into the position of the Current-Time Marker.

**20** Finally, select all of the keyframes by dragging a selection marquee around them. Command-click on any of them to change them into Auto Bezier keyframes, this will smooth out the zoom, making more fluid keyframes.

**21** Switch off visibility for the background layer and then change your view to Top view, in the View Modes menu. You will see your two layers from the top.

**22** Hit the C key repeatedly till you have the Track Z Camera tool selected in the Tool Palette and then make sure that you have the Camera layer selected. Move the Current-Time Marker back to frame 1.

**23** Click with the Track Z tool, in the Comp window and drag downwards to adjust the view of your scene in the Comp window. Drag it down repeatedly till your view looks like mine in the following diagram.

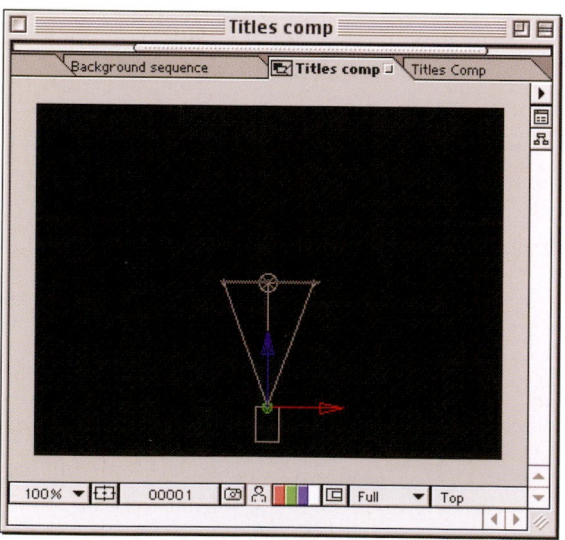

**24** Move to the first marker and then hit the spacebar to preview the camera zooming into the layers.

**25** Later, you can try adjusting the velocity of the camera keyframes to get some really nice, natural looking zooms.

**26** Go back to the Active Camera View, switch on the Background layer and RAM Preview the comp.

## animating the 3D layers

OK, so we've created quite a simple 3D camera move on the 3D layers. This time, we'll leave the camera where it is and, instead, animate the layers towards the camera.

**1** Move to the marker at frame 553 and select the Ellis.psd layer. Hit Alt + P to set a keyframe for Rotation and to bring up its value in the Timeline.

**2** Move to frame 574 and then type in the following values for the Ellis.psd layers Position; 200, 180, –288.

**3** Select the Annie.psd layer and then jump to the next marker at frame 617. Set a keyframe for the Position value at this point.

**4** Move to frame 637 and change the Position property values to: 134, 186, –280.

**5** Jump back to frame 533 and then go to Custom view 1 in the View modes menu, in the Comp window.

**6** Use the Track Z tool again to pull out from the scene a little till you can see the main characters and the camera (represented by a little box). Hit the Spacebar again to preview the layers moving towards the camera.

**7** Try previewing the scene through some of the other Custom views before returning to the Active Camera View.

**8** Move to frame 660, select the Camera layer and then hit Alt + P key to bring up the Camera Position values and set a keyframe for Camera Position.

**9** Jump to the next marker by hitting the K key and then change the Z Position value to –279. The camera will now have moved in front of our two main characters, they are now positioned behind the camera. In the next stage, we'll add some titles to this section.

**10** Ease the keyframes if you want to before RAM Previewing the complete, finished animation.

**11** Save your project as Graffiti07.aep to the Creative After Effects > Chapter 15 folder.

OK, so now we are about ready to add some titles to this project but we'll leave that till the Type chapter. Let's take a look at another section of the MacDonna video. Open and play the MacDonna.mov again, pay particular attention to the section of footage just before the club scene, where I am in a night-time street scene, this was built entirely from 3D layers!

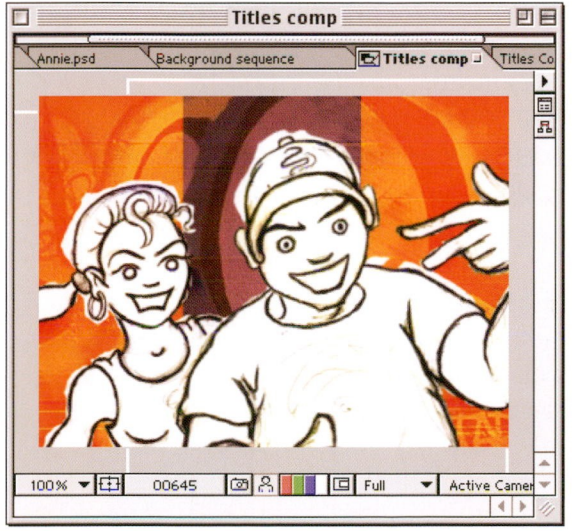

# MacDonna video

OK, now we're going to use some of what we've learned about 3D to create a piece of footage for our MacDonna project. The idea is to replicate the effect of driving through a city at night, with car lights and various other stuff streaking past the camera. To do this, we're actually going to recreate a little 3D city street scene, and then fly the camera through it as if it were attached to the bonnet of a car.

### building a 3D city

Firstly, we need to create a four-sided block which is going to be our skyscraper.

**1** Open the project 3DCityStart.aep from the Training > Chapter 15 folder.

You will see that I've already created some pre-comps containing the elements we will be using in this section. If you have a look in the Building Side comp, you will see that I've used a combination of the Venetian Blinds and Block Dissolve effects to create one side of our skyscraper. The handy thing about the way I've got this set up is that you can vary the number of lights on in the building by altering the Transition Completion property on the Block Dissolve effect.

**2** Drag the Building Side composition onto the New Composition icon at the bottom of the project window, select Composition > Composition Settings (Command +K) and rename the new comp 'Skyscraper Comp'.

**3** Set the Building Side layer to Best Quality and make sure you're viewing the composition at Full resolution.

I'm going to suggest you do all of the work in this particular project with layers set to Best Quality and the compositions set to Full Resolution. It simply won't look very good if you're viewing in Draft Quality or at lower resolutions.

However, I would suggest that you use Dynamic Resolution to speed things up a bit while you're moving elements around in the compositions.

**4** Select Edit > Preferences > Previews from the pull down menu, turn Dynamic Resolution on, and set the Degradation Limit to 1/2. Then hit OK to exit the Preferences window.

**5** Make the Building Side layer a 3D layer by switching on its 3D button.

We're basically going to construct the skyscraper block by creating three more copies of the Building Side layer, which we will then move around and rotate to form the four sides.

**5** To get a better view of what's going on in the composition, use the 3D view menu at the bottom right of the Composition window, or go to View > Switch 3D View and switch from Active Camera to Custom View 1.

**7** Duplicate the Building Side layer by selecting the layer in the Timeline and hitting Command + D, or by going to Edit > Duplicate.

**8** Now would be a good time to rename the layers, to avoid confusion later on. Select one of the layers and press the Enter key, then rename it 'Front'. Select the other layer and in the same way rename it 'Back'.

Now we need to move the Back layer backwards in Z-space to make the skyscraper's back. The original Building Side comp is 200 pixels wide, so this is the amount we should move the layer backwards.

**9** Select the Back layer, hit the P key to bring up the Position property, and enter 200 into the Z value, so the layer's position should read [100, 300, 200].

OK, we have the front and back, now it's time to create one of the sides.

**10** Duplicate the original Front layer (Command + D), and rename the duplicate 'Left'.

**11** Select the Left layer and hit the R key to bring up the Rotation properties.

You'll see we have the two different types of rotation controls, an all-in-one Orientation property as well as individual controls for X, Y and Z rotation. In truth, it doesn't make any difference which set of controls we use for this exercise, but I'm going to suggest we stick with the individual controls.

**12** We want to rotate the Left layer through 90 degrees around the Y-axis, so simply type in 90 for the Y rotation property (it should read; 0 x +90.0).

As the layer's anchor point is in the middle of the layer, it has ended up intersecting the original 'Front' layer; we will need to move the layer both left (on the X-axis) and backwards (on the Z-axis) to position it in the right place. We know the layer's width is 200 pixels, so to position it correctly we will need to move it 100 pixels to the left and 100 pixels backwards.

**13** Hit the P key to bring up the Left layer's Position property. To move the layer to the left on the X-axis, select the first position value and change it from 100 to 0. To move the layer backwards on the Z-axis, select the third position value and change it from 0 to 100 so the Left layer's Position should now be [0, 300, 100].

Now we have the left side of the skyscraper, the quickest way to create the right side would be to duplicate the Left layer and move it to the right along the X-axis.

**14** Duplicate the Left layer and rename the newly created layer Right.

**15** Hit the P key to view the position property and change the first (X-axis) value from 0 to 200. So the Right layer's Position will be [200, 300, 100].

So now we have our finished skyscraper. You could argue of course that it doesn't have a roof; but we're going to be driving past in a car, not flying past in a helicopter, so it really isn't necessary.

**16** Select the Camera Orbit tool from the Tool Palette, and then drag around in the Composition window to see that we do indeed have a reasonably convincing skyscraper.

**17** We've done all we need to do in the Skyscraper Comp so close it before moving on.

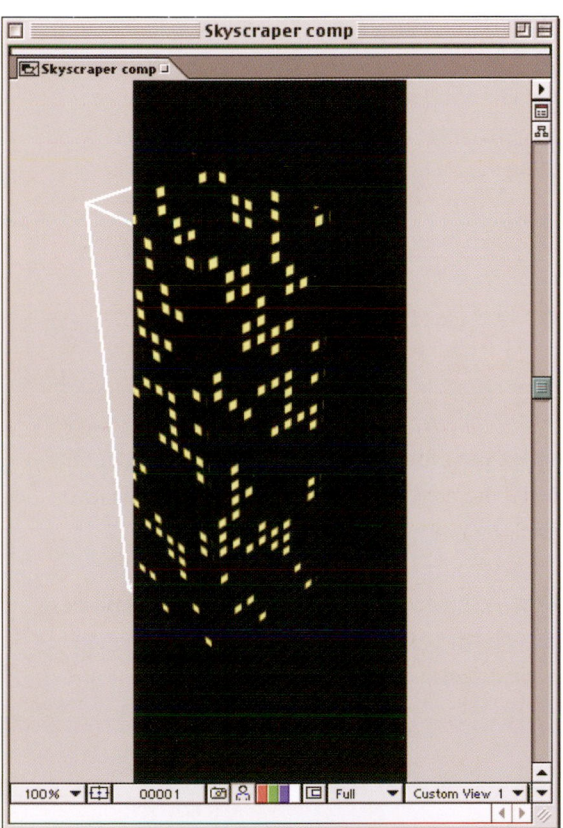

### adding skyscrapers to our city

Now we have all the elements we need to create the city landscape: cars (well, black solids with white and red spots on them), a lamp-post (a masked solid) and our 3D skyscraper.

**1** Open the composition named City Comp.

You will see that I've already created a couple of solid layers, one called Ground, another called Road. Eventually we will be turning these layers off as they aren't intended for the final render; these layers are simply there to help us place the different elements inside our 3D scene.

So firstly we are going to place our skyscrapers alongside the road.

**2** Let's switch to a custom camera view to get a clearer view of what we're doing. In this case, let's select Custom View 2.

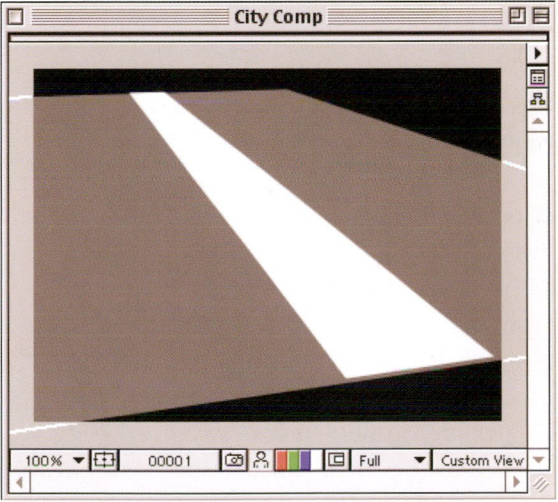

**3** Making sure the Current-Time Marker is on frame 1, drag the Skyscraper Comp into the Timeline Window of our City Comp. Dragging into the left part of the Timeline Window (i.e. the part containing the Layer Name, Switches and A/V Features panels) will ensure the Skyscraper Comp layer is placed at the same frame as the current time.

It makes no difference whether this layer is placed above or below the Road and Ground layers in terms of their layer order in the Timeline window. 3D layers are sorted according to their position in 3D space, unlike 2D layer's which are sorted by their order in the Timeline window.

**4** Switch the Skyscraper layer to Best Quality and turn on both the Collapse Transformations and 3D buttons.

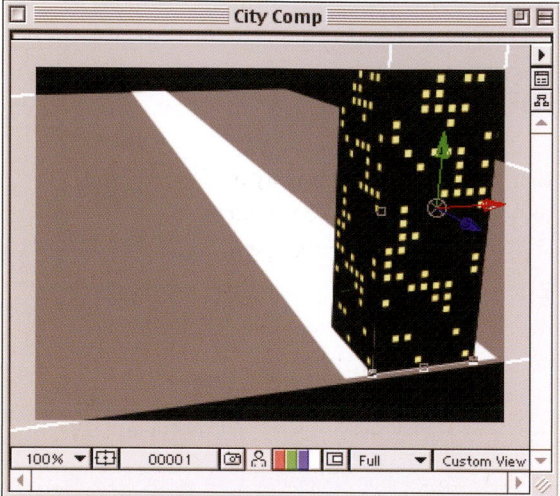

One of the nicest things about After Effect's 3D environment is the way that collapsing a nested composition works. When you collapse a nested composition that contains 3D elements, those elements will retain their 3D geometry in the new composition. This means that you can set up complex 3D scenes in one composition before combining them together in another and flying a camera through them, all still in glorious 3D.

Something to bear in mind is the fact that when you collapse a layer in this way, any cameras or lights contained in the nested composition will be ignored, it will be the cameras and lights that are contained in the current composition that are use to move through and illuminate the 3D scene.

As you can see, at the moment the skyscraper is sitting in the middle of the road; let's reposition it further back and to the left-hand side.

**5** Hit the P key to view the Skyscraper's Position property. We won't be moving the layer using numerical entries, but it'll be helpful if you can approximately place the elements at the same positions as I have.

As the Skyscraper layer is now a 3D layer, it has the red, green and blue axes arrows which are used to position things in 3D space.

**6** Ensure the standard Selection Tool is selected in the Tools Palette (V), then move the cursor over the red arrow part of the layer axes (the cursor should now have an X next to it, identifying the axis).

**7** Drag the red arrow to the left, moving the skyscraper to the left of the road, until the layer's X position (the first value) reads approximately –200. If you hold down the Shift key whilst you're dragging, this will increase the amount the layer moves by a factor of ten.

**8** Select the blue arrow (Z-axis) and drag the skyscraper further back in the comp, so that the Z position (the third value) is about 400.

**9** We're now going to duplicate the Skyscraper layer to create another skyscraper further back in the scene. Duplicate the layer by hitting Command + D. Then Shift-drag the blue arrow until this layer position reads about 2000 on a Z-axis.

Now we'll duplicate both of these layers and drag them to the right-hand side of the road, quickly creating even more skyscrapers.

**10** Select both Skyscraper layers and then hit Command + D. With both of the newly created layers still selected, Shift-drag one of the layer's red arrows to the right until both skyscrapers are sitting a similar distance from the road on the right-hand side. For me, the X position values read about 530.

We also want to move these skyscrapers (the ones on the right of the road) backwards a bit, so that we're staggering their layout.

**11** To get a clearer view of what we're about to do use the 3D view menu to switch from Custom View 2 to Top View.

**12** Make sure that both of the Skyscraper layers on the right side of the road are still selected, then Shift-drag one of the layers by its blue arrow to move both layer's higher in the Composition window (i.e. further back along the Z-axis). Basically, we're trying to make it so the lower of these skyscraper layers is halfway between the two skyscrapers on the left of the road. The Z-values for these two layers should now be around 2850 and 1250. Watch the Info palette whilst dragging to see a display of the coordinates of the layer you are moving.

**13** Switch back to the previous view (Custom View 2) to see the result, by pressing the Escape key.

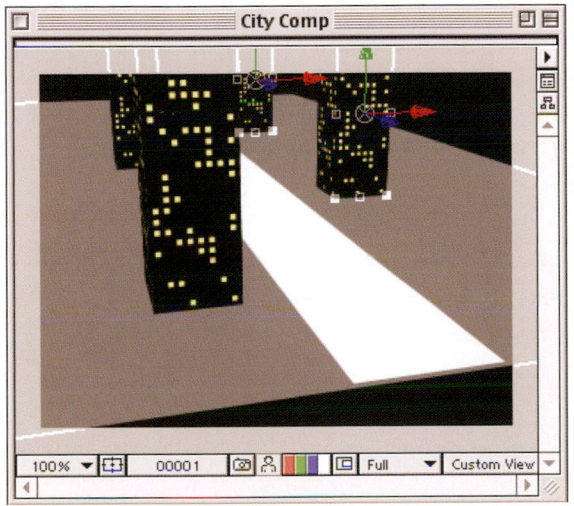

You can use the Escape key at any time to switch between the current and previous 3D view. This can come in very handy when you just want to switch to another view to check something, or to make a slight alteration before quickly switching back to your main view.

### adding lamp-posts to our city

Now we're going to place a few lamp-posts along the sides of our road.

**1** In the same way we did with the original Skyscraper layer, drag the Lamp-post composition into our City Comp's Timeline window.

**2** Switch the Lamp-post layer to Best Quality. The layer is currently a 2D layer, so switch on the Lamp-post layer's 3D button to make it a part of our 3D scene.

**NB** Do not Collapse the layer as we did with the Skyscraper layer. Collapsing a layer causes it to inherit its 2D or 3D properties from the nested composition from which it originated.

In the case of the Lamp-post, the layer within the nested composition is a 2D layer, whereas, if you remember, the layers in our skyscraper were all 3D layers.

So collapsing the Lamp-post would switch it back to being a 2D layer, regardless of whether the 3D switch is turned on in the current composition.

This may seem a little confusing at first, but I wouldn't worry about it too much right now. However, when experimenting in the future, it's certainly something to bear in mind if things don't seem to be working in exactly the way you intended.

OK, now it looks like the lamp-post is pretty well placed in our 3D scene, but in the world of 3D, things are not always as they appear . . .

**3** Use the 3D view menu to switch to the Front view and you'll see that the lamp-post is actually floating in the air above our road.

To make it easier to reposition the lamp-post, let's change our composition's background color.

**4** Select Composition > Background Color (or hit Command + Shift + B ) and make the background color white.

**5** Using both the green and red arrows, reposition the lamp-post so that it sits on the same level as and to the right of the road layer. Its position should now be about 375, 340, 0.

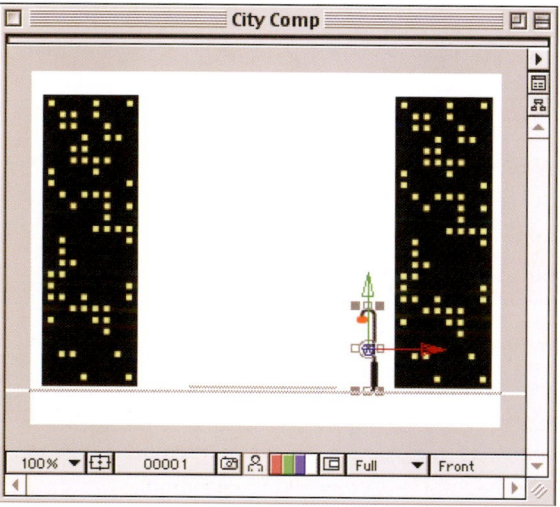

Now we've positioned the lamp-post correctly on both the X-axis and Y-axis, we need to do the same on the Z-axis.

**6** Use the 3D view menu to switch to the Left view, then Shift-drag the Lamp-post layer's blue arrow, until the lamp-post is positioned directly in the middle of the right-most skyscraper. So the lamp-post's position should now be about 375, 340, 510.

**7** Duplicate the Lamp-post layer (Command + Shift + D) and once again, Shift-drag the blue arrow until this second lamp-post is in the middle of the next skyscraper along on the left.

**8** Repeat the last step twice more, until you have four lamp-posts, one in the middle of each skyscraper.

**9** Switch back to Custom View 2 to check on how the scene is looking.

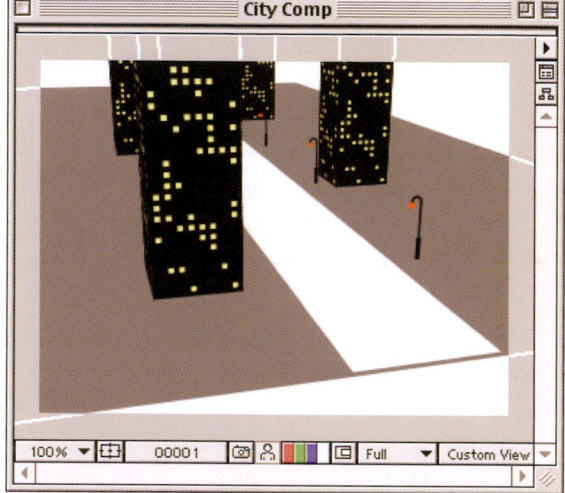

At the moment we only have lamp-posts along the right side of the road. We're now going to duplicate all four lamp-posts, drag the duplicates to the other side of the road and flip them, creating a mirrored set of lamp-posts on the left side of the road.

**10** Use the 3D view menu to switch back to the Front view.

**11** Select all four layers by selecting the top Lamp-post layer in the Timeline window, then Shift-selecting the lowest of those four layers.

**12** Hit Command- D to create duplicates of all four layers, then use the red arrow to drag those layers to a similar position on the left side of the road. The X position value for these new layers should now be about –55.

**13** With the four layers still selected, hit the S key to view the layer's scale properties.

The Lamp-post layer's are all currently at 100% scale. In order to flip them, we need to change only the X scale value so that it becomes –100%.

**14** Context-click on one of the selected layer's scale values and select Edit Value.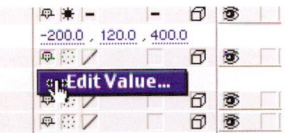

**15** We only want to change the Width (or X scale) value, so we need to switch the Preserve menu from *Current Aspect Ratio (XYZ)* to *None*. Then change the *Width* value from 100% to –100%. Hit OK to exit the Scale 3D window.

This has now flipped the four lamp-posts on the left side of the road, giving us our perfect mirror image.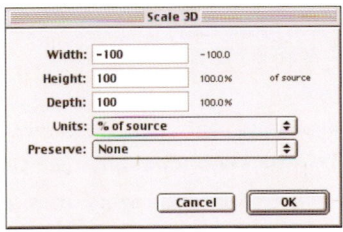

**16** Press the Escape key to switch back to Custom View 2.

**17** Select the Camera Orbit Tool from the Tool Palette. Do this by hitting the C key repeatedly till it is selected. The first time you hit C, it will select the currently active Camera Tool in the Tools Palette, subsequently hitting C will cycle through the three tools (Orbit, Track XY and Track Z).

**18** Drag around in the Composition window using the Orbit Tool to give yourself a better view of all the elements that now exist in your 3D scene.

Whenever you are in any of the orthographic 3D views (for example, Front, Left etc.), and including the three Custom Views, you can quite freely use any of the Orbit, Track XY and Track Z tools to move around your 3D scene, in order to see your elements more clearly. Doing so will in no way affect the final outcome of your animation, which will be determined by whatever is shown in the Active Camera view. These other views are purely there to aid you in the construction of your scenes.

### adding a car to the scene

Now we just need to add a car moving along the road before we can add a camera and animate our 'drive' along the street.

**1** Start by dragging the Car Front composition into the Timeline window in the same way that we've done before, switch the layer to Best Quality and turn on its 3D button.

**2** Switch to the Front 3D view, and then make sure that you have the Selection Toll (V) selected. In the same way we did with the Lamp-post, reposition the Car Front layer so that it sits on the right side of the road. Its position value should be about 240, 395, 0.0.

Of course, depending on what part of the world you're in, you may want to have the car driving along the other side of the road, but you can always fix that later.

**3** The current position of the Car Front layer will be fine for the end point in our animation, so move to frame 200 (by hitting Command + G and entering 200 into the Go To Time window).

**4** Hit Alt + P to view the position property (if you haven't already), and simultaneously add a keyframe.

**5** Now we need to set the start point of the car's motion. Move back to the first frame in the Timeline, then switch to the Top 3D view.

**6** Shift-drag the Car Front layer's blue arrow and drag the layer up the screen until it's roughly level with the back-most lamp-post layer. The position value should be about 240, 395, 3000.

**7** Switch back to Custom View 2, and step through the Timeline to confirm that the car is traveling along the street towards us.

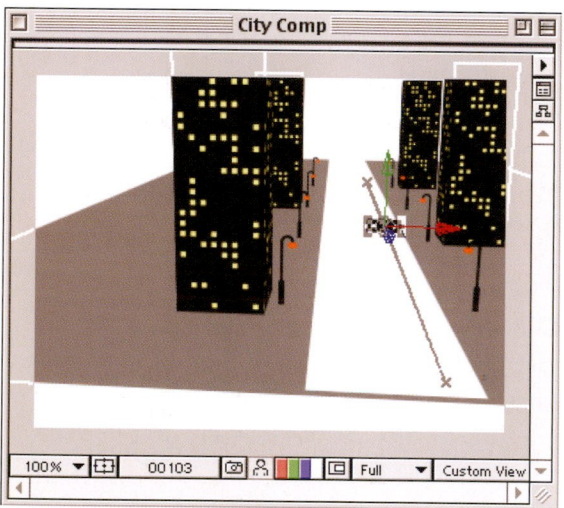

### creating and animating the camera

The effect we're trying to achieve is that we (and therefore the camera) are a car, traveling along the road on the left-hand side, with the animated car passing us by on the right. So we're going to create a camera, position it correctly on the left side of the road and then animate it down the street, right past the final skyscrapers and lamp-posts.

**1** Move the Current Time Marker back to the first frame in the Timeline, then select Layer > New > Camera from the pull down menu.

**2** Select 50 mm from the Preset menu at the top of the Camera Settings window, ensure that Enable Depth of Field is turned off, then click OK.

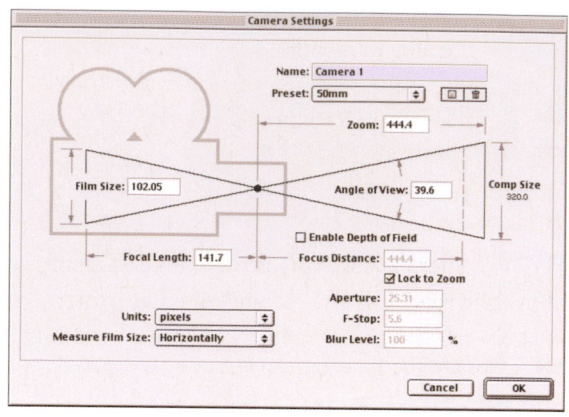

There are various different ways of animating cameras in After Effects; in this project we'll be using what I regard to be the simplest.

**3** With the Camera layer selected, choose Layer > Transform > Auto Orient, from the pull down menu.

The Auto-Orientation window will appear, containing three options: Off, Orient Along Path and Orient Towards Point of Interest.

By default, After Effects cameras always Orient Towards their Point of Interest. Cameras not only have a Position property, they also have a Point of Interest property. While Point of Interest is another positional property, rather than specifying where the camera is in 3D space, the Point of Interest specifies the point in 3D space that the camera is looking at, think of it as the camera's target.

As we are only interested in having the camera looking directly forwards, it is a lot easier to turn the Point of Interest off. This means that we don't have to worry about animating the Point of Interest as well (we could still rotate the camera if we wanted to, by using the camera's rotational properties).

**4** Select Off from the list of choices available in the Auto-Orient window.

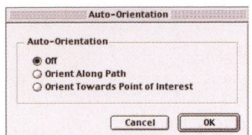

Now we're going to position the camera correctly, so that it sits on the road, at about the same level as if it we're attached to the bonnet of a car.

**5** Switch the 3D view to Front.

**6** The camera is currently floating in the air, way above the road. Use the red and green arrows to drag the camera down and to the left, so it's sitting in a suitable place on the left side of the road. The cameras position should be about 100, 395, –444.

**7** Click the Stopwatch on the camera's Position property to add a new keyframe (or hit Alt + P) .

**8** Go To frame 200 in the Timeline, then switch the 3D view to Active Camera.

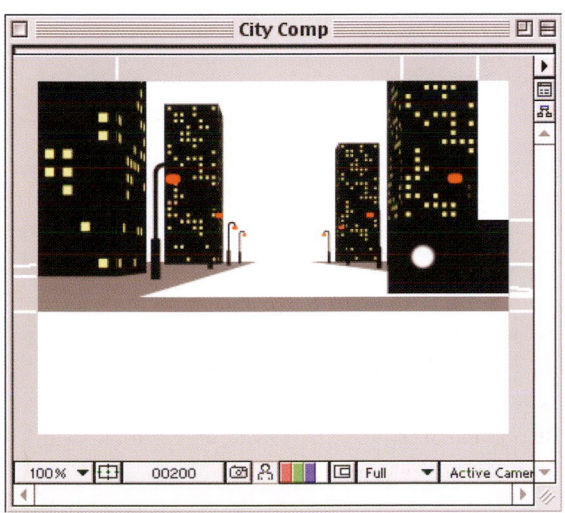

**9** Select the Track Z tool from the camera controls in the Tools Palette.

**10** Holding down the Shift key, drag to the right in the Composition window, moving the camera down the road until the last lamp-post and skyscraper moves out of sight off the edge of the composition.

Your position value should be about 100, 395, 2600. Now we'll turn our guide layers off, and return the Background color to black.

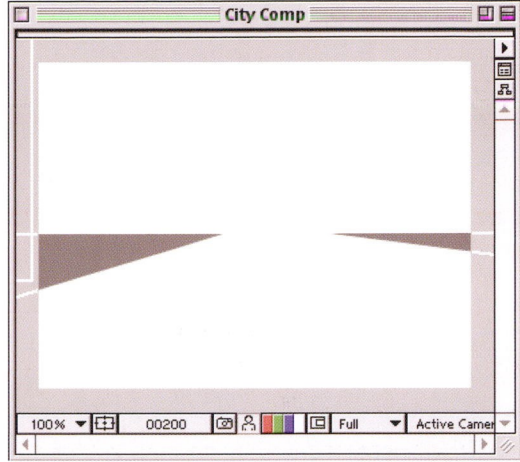

**11** In the Timeline, click on the visibility icons for both the Road and Ground layers to turn them off.

**12** Select Composition > Background Color (or Command + Shift + B) and change the background color back to pure black.

**13** Make sure that the composition is set to Full resolution, then select Composition > Preview > RAM Preview (or press 0 on the numeric pad) to playback the result.

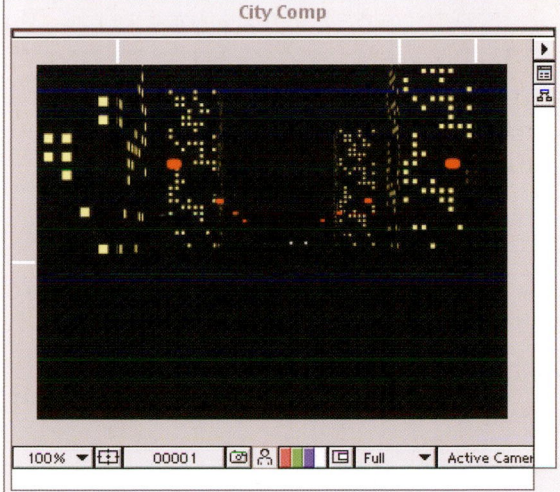

## intersecting layers and the advanced 3D renderer

You may have noticed something strange happening to the skyscrapers during the RAM Preview playback. It appears as if the sides of the skyscrapers are flicking on and off at certain points during the animation.

While this may look like some kind of bug in After Effects, it's actually caused by a limitation in the way After Effects renders its 3D scenes.

**1** Select Composition > Composition Settings from the pull down menu (or hit Command + K) to bring up the Composition Settings window, and click on the Advanced tab at the top of the window. You will see that the Rendering Plug-in is currently set to 'Standard 3D'.

Standard 3D is the default plug-in used to render 3D scenes within After Effects. Unfortunately, the one limitation with this renderer is that it is unable to render intersecting layers. You may remember that when we created the four walls of the sky-scraper, we built it so that the layers joined up to each other exactly on the four corners of the skyscraper. Just having layers that line up in this way is enough for these layers to be considered as intersecting, and this is the reason we are seeing problems in our animation.

There are two different ways of solving this problem:

Solution 1 – The After Effects team have created a second plug-in renderer called the Advanced 3D renderer. You may already have this plug-in loaded into your copy of After Effects, in which case all you need to do is click on the Rendering Plug-in menu in the Composition Settings window and select Advanced 3D from the choices available.

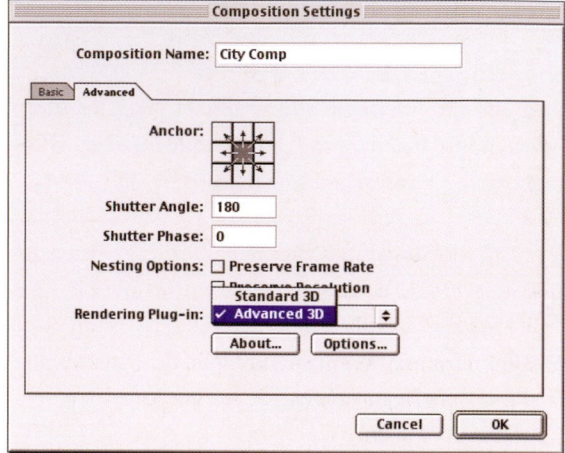

If you don't yet have this plug-in loaded into your copy of After Effects, you can go to the Adobe website (http://www.adobe.com) and download it from the After Effects download section; you can then follow the instructions given with the download to place it into the After Effect's plug-in folder. If you do this, you'll need to save your project into your Creative After Effects > 3D Chapter folder and then restart After Effects. You can then open your project and select Advanced 3D in the City Comp's Composition Settings window as explained above.

Solution 2 – Our problem is caused by the fact that the four layers that make up our skyscraper are touching each other on the corners; so another way to solve this problem is to make sure the layers aren't quite touching. Only follow the next step if you do not have the Advanced 3D renderer.

**1** Open up the Skyscraper Comp and adjust the position values of the Front and Back layer's to [100, 300, –1] and [100, 300, 201] respectively. This will pull the layer's just far enough apart to stop any of the layers from touching each other, meaning that you can continue using the default Standard 3D renderer as before.

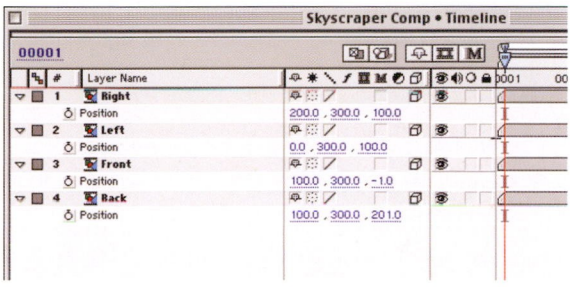

## extending our 3D city

One problem with the scene that we've created is that the street simply isn't long enough for us to create this animation of speeding down a city street at night. I'm going to show you a really quick way to extend our 3D scene.

**1** From the Project window, drag the City Comp onto the New Comp icon at the bottom of the project window. This will take our City Comp and place it, as a layer, into a new composition of the same size and frame rate as our City Comp.

**2** Hit Command-K to bring up the Composition Settings window, and rename the new composition, 'City Comp 2'.

**3** Set the layer to Best Quality, then turn on both the 3D layer and Collapse buttons (all using the switches in the Timeline window 's Switches panel).

You will notice that the view changes when you turn on the Collapse button. The reason for this, as I explained earlier, is that collapsing a nested composition that contains 3D layers causes it to re-inherit those 3D properties from the nested composition.

In other words, collapsing the layer causes it to change from what is essentially just a two dimensional piece of footage, into something that retains all the 3D geometry from the previous composition.

As I also mentioned, doing this will mean that any cameras or lights contained in the nested composition will be ignored, so we'll need to go and grab a copy of our camera from the City comp.

**4** Open the City Comp, deselect all by hitting F2 (to make sure no keyframes are still highlighted), then select the Camera layer and copy it by hitting Command + C.

**5** Move back to City Comp 2 and paste the camera layer into it by hitting Command + V.

You'll see that the resulting view in City Comp 2's Composition window is now identical to that of the original City Comp, with the camera move doing exactly the same thing as it did before. The difference is that now it is the camera in our City Comp 2 that is controlling the camera move, the camera in our original City Comp is being totally ignored.

Now this is where the magic happens. In the same way as we did when creating multiple copies of the skyscraper, we're going to use the collapsed layer behavior to our advantage by duplicating the entire 3D city scene, and then placing the duplicate version of the scene further into the distance. We'll be doubling the length of the street that we're moving our camera along in just a few easy steps.

**6** Make sure that you have the City Comp layer selected and then hit Command + D to duplicate the layer.

**7** Hit the P key to view the Position property, then change the value of one of the City Comp layers to 160, 120, 3000. This will move the layer further away from us on the Z-axis.

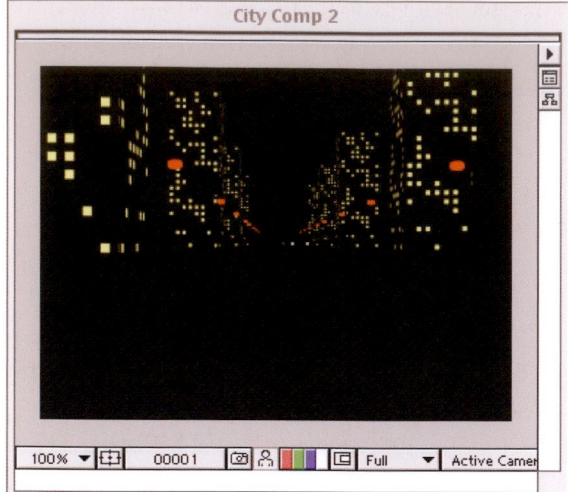

The city scene now extends twice as far as it previously did into the distance. However, our camera move currently finishes on frame 200, so we're going to have to change it so the camera keeps going beyond our last keyframe.

Here's a really useful tip for doing this in such a way as to ensure the second part of the move runs at the same speed as the first part. This method works well in any situation where you would want to extend a move (or scale, rotation etc.) while keeping the rate of change constant.

**8** Select the Camera layer and press the P key to view its Position property.

**9** Click the triangle to the left of the Position property to flip open the speed graph.

We should have two keyframes, one on the first frame of the timeline, and another on frame 200. The Z position value on frame 1 should be –444, and on frame 200 it should be 2600. From this we know that if we want the camera to carry on moving through to frame 500, the Z value that we'll need on frame 500 will be considerably higher than 2600.

**10** Move the Current-Time Marker to the end of the timeline, frame 500.

**11** Alter the Camera's Z position value by Shift-scrubbing the value in the Timeline towards the right. Watching the levels on the position's speed graph, keep dragging the value until the line on the right of the speed graph matches up with the line on the left.

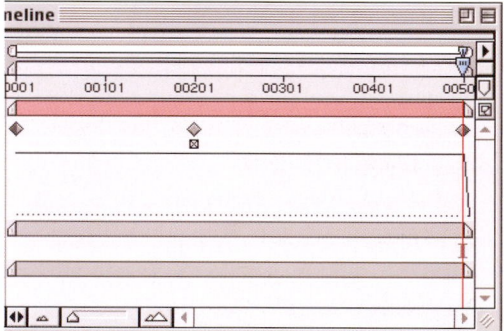

The final Z Position value on the last keyframe should be about 7190. We've used the speed graph to ensure the camera's speed between the second and third keyframes matches the speed between the first and second keyframes.

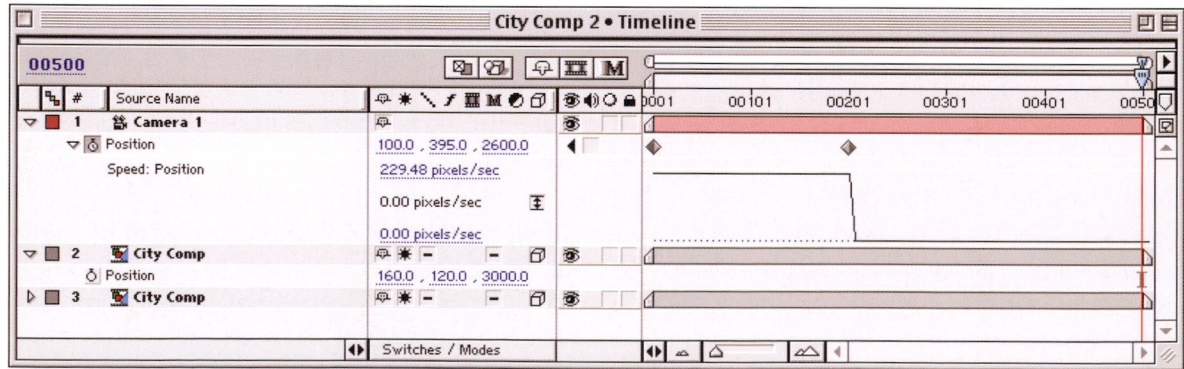

One more thing to remember; if you solved the intersecting layers problem by switching to the Advanced 3D renderer, you will also need to go into the Composition Settings window of the current City Comp 2 and make sure that Advanced 3D is also selected in this composition. The job of rendering the 3D geometry is now being handled by this composition.

## adding bounce to the camera

As this street scene is vaguely inspired by a recent trip to New York, I can't resist adding an effect to try to recreate the bouncy nature of a car ride along one of the city's pot-holed roads. For this we're going to use the 'wiggle' expression that we learned in the expression chapter.

**1** Still in City Comp 2, add an expression to the Position property of the Camera layer (Alt + click the Position stopwatch) and type the following expression:

```
bump = position.wiggle(1,20);
[position[0], bump[1], position[2]];
```

I only want to make the camera bounce up and down (on the Y-axis), so the first line of the expression is telling After Effects to 'wiggle' the keyframed camera, once every second, by up to 20 pixels, and to apply the result to the variable 'bump'. Then, the second line of the expression is telling After Effects to take the X and Z position values from the original camera move, but to take the Y position value from the result of the wiggle command.

With that one simple expression, we now have a fairly authentic, bouncy, New York car ride. RAM Preview the comp to see the results.

## viewing the scene in 3D wireframe

I've suggested that you work in this project at Full resolution, but unless you're working on a particularly fast machine, things will be taking quite a while to RAM Preview by now. I'm going to show you a method of quickly switching the whole 3D scene into wireframe mode, which will significantly speed up our ability to preview motion in the scene.

**NB** At the time of going to press, this method will only work with the Standard 3D plug-in so make sure your Comp Settings > Advanced > Rendering plug-in is set to Standard 3D before moving ahead.

**1** Select Edit > Preferences > General from the pull down menu and ensure the *Switches Affect Nested Comps* option is turned on, then hit OK to exit the preferences window.

**2** In the City Comp 2 composition, turn off the Collapse button on both of the City Comp layers.

**3** Select both of the City Comp layers and choose Layer > Quality > Wireframe from the pull down menu.

**4** Turn the Collapse button back on for both layers.

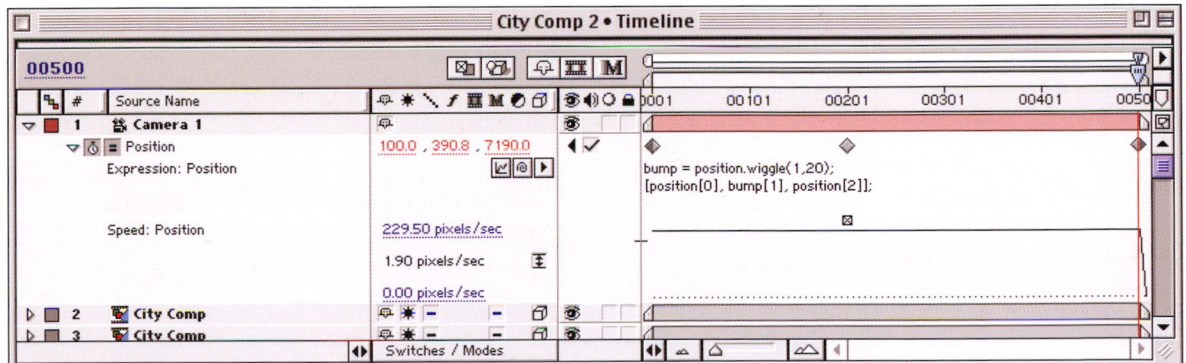

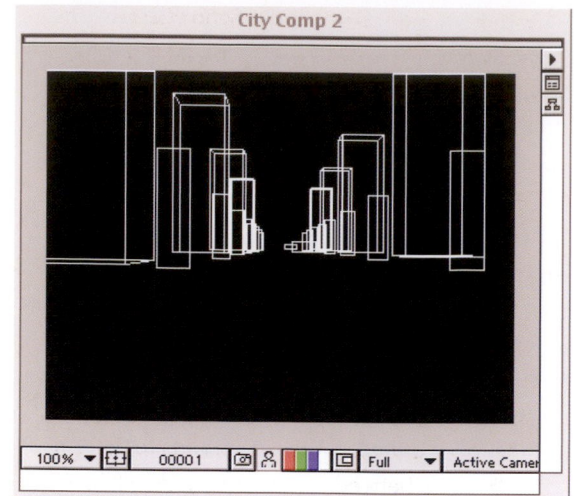

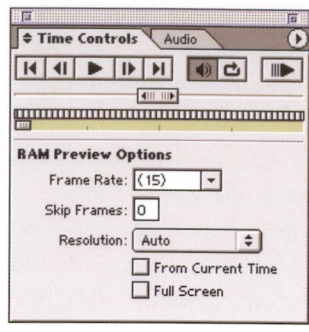

After temporarily switching off the collapsed nature of the layers, we've switched them to wireframe; at this point, After Affects has gone back through the nested compositions, switching all of the layers to wireframe mode. Then, when we re-collapse the layers, they regain their original 3D geometry, but are now displaying it in wireframe.

This technique can come in very handy if things start to slow down while working in 3D.

**5** Do a RAM Preview to see the results of the bouncing camera in City Comp 2.

As you may have noticed, we're not exactly speeding our way down the street. This is actually by design; the plan is to render out the final movie, then import that movie back into After Effects and speed it up by Time Stretching the footage when we eventually use it in the MacDonna music video.

In order to view the RAM Preview at a slightly more realistic speed, we can use the RAM Preview options in the Time Controls palette.

**6** If the Time Controls palette isn't visible on screen, select Window > Time Controls from the pull down menu (or press Command + 3).

**7** If you can't see the RAM Preview options at the bottom of the Time Controls palette, select Show RAM Preview options from the wing menu (a circle with a triangle in it) at the top right of the Time Controls palette.

**NB:** Make sure it is the RAM Preview Options that is being displayed, not the Shift RAM Preview Options.

At the moment, the Frame Rate is probably displayed as (15). The brackets around the frame rate indicate that the RAM Preview is set to playback at whatever frame rate the composition is set to. This is chosen by selecting 'Auto' from the frame rate menu in the Time Controls palette and is what After Effects uses as its default.

However, it's entirely possible to get After Effects to playback the frames it holds in its RAM Preview at a much higher frame rate; this doesn't affect the frame rate of the original composition in anyway, it just gives us the option to play our RAM Preview back quicker (or slower) if we so desire.

**8** Choose 60 from the Frame Rate menu in the Time Controls palette.

**9** Now do a RAM Preview of our City Comp 2.

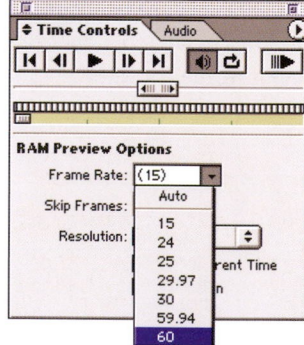

This is the equivalent of playing back our animation at four times the original speed.

Before moving on to the final stage of our project, let's switch from displaying our scene in wireframe, back to viewing it normally at best quality.

**10** Turn off the Collapse button on both of the City Comp layers.

**11** Switch both of the City Comp layers back to Best Quality mode and turn the Collapse button back on for both of the layers. If you have the 3D renderer installed, you can switch your Comp settings > Advanced > Rendering Plug-in back to Advanced 3D.

## adding speed trails to our scene

OK, we're finally coming to the end of this project. All we need to do now is to add trails to our animation to recreate the look of the lights streaking past our camera. For this, we're going to be using the Echo effect.

**1** From the Project window, drag City Comp 2 onto the New Comp icon at the bottom of the project window.

**2** Hit Command-K to bring up the Composition Settings window and rename the composition 'Echo Comp'.

**3** Switch the City Comp 2 layer to Best Quality.

**4** Select Effect > Time > Echo to add the Echo effect to the layer. The Echo effect works by sampling a number of different points in time from our animation, and then blending them together to produce a trail or 'Echo' type effect, perfect for what we're trying to achieve here.

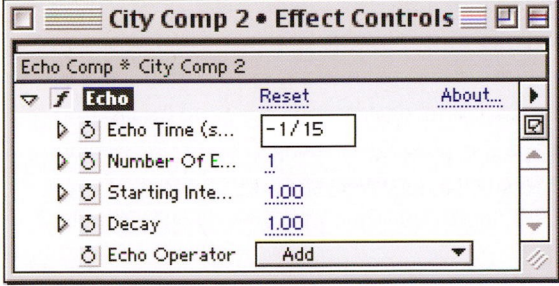

The first two properties in the Echo effect are the most important; Echo Time (seconds) is used to specify the time difference between each point in time being sampled, Number of Echoes controls (as it suggests) the number of points in time that are sampled.

**5** For Echo Time (seconds) enter, all in one line –1 / 15 into the value box.

Now this may seem a little strange, minus one divided by fifteen, what's that all about then? Well, Echo Time requires a value in seconds to determine the difference between each point in time being sampled; as the frame rate of our composition is 15 frames per second, a value of one (second) divided by fifteen (frames) is the exact duration of each frame in our composition.

After Effects will always try to hold on to as many previously rendered frames as it can during a render or a RAM Preview, and as the Echo effect is sampling a number of frames and then blending them together, the most efficient way to use the Echo effect is to have it sampling frames that are already stored in After Effects' memory.

The reason we want the value to be a negative value, is that this tells the Echo to sample the frames earlier than the current time, so the effect will be a trail of what's already happened. A positive value would mean the trails would be later than the current time, so we would see trails from a point in time that hasn't even happened yet.

Don't worry if you don't entirely understand the reasoning behind this. A simple rule is to always try to use a value that is, for example:

minus one divided by the frame rate
minus one divided by half the frame rate
minus one divided by twice the frame rate

This way, you'll be able to have quite a large Number Of Echoes, without causing you horrendously long render times.

**6** For Number Of Echoes, enter a value of 20.

**7** We can leave Starting Intensity at its default of 1.00, but we'll change the Decay value to 0.90, meaning that the trails will slowly fade out the further back they are.

**8** Finally, switch the Echo Operator to Screen; this controls the way the effect blends each of our 20 sampled points in time together and Screen seems to give the nicest effect in this case.

So, now it's time to RAM Preview the end results. If you've still got you're RAM Preview Options set to play back at 60 fps, you'll be able to see a fairly close approximation of how we've used this footage in the MacDonna sequence. Open up the MacDonna.mov again to see where this has been used in that project.

Just remember to switch the RAM Preview Frame Rate option back to Auto once you've finished, as this can easily get missed later, and you'll start wondering why all your animation appears to be playing back far too fast.

**9** Save your project into the Creative After effects > 3D chapter folder as 3DCity01b.aep.

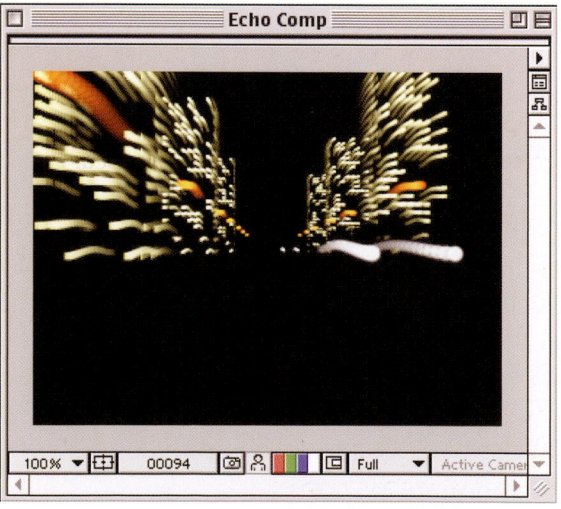

## recap

Thanks to Paul Tuersley for the imaginative use of the new 3D compositing features of After Effects 5.0.

And there we have it, a reasonably convincing night-time scene of driving through a city at night. Hopefully, you'll be inspired to go back into the City Comp and add many more details; you'll probably want to add a few more cars traveling towards the camera, possibly a few cars moving along in front of the camera on our side of the road (using the Car Back composition for this).

After that, there's no end to how much detail you could add to the scene; neon signs, traffic lights, Walk/Don't Walk signs etc. all of which can be animated in their nested compositions (so that the traffic lights change color, the neon signs flash etc.) to really bring your city scene to life.

You could create duplicates of the City Comp, each of which are a little different, then mix and match them in City Comp 2 to vary the layout of the city. You could even put streets in that cross our main central street, then switch the Auto-Orient option on the camera to Orient Along Path before sending the camera down side streets. Maybe you'll even add a Helicopter landing pad to the roof of the skyscraper and send the camera off into the air, flying through our city scene. The possibilities are endless!

On the CD, I've included some Illustrator files of some classic street signs for you to use when developing this project further. You can find these in the Free Stuff > Art Explosion folder. Art Explosion is an excellent resource for symbols, signs et cetera, as well as textures and general images. I thoroughly recommend it, it's a great reference resource and has saved me an enormous amount of time and money over the years that I have been using it. The latest version comes with 750,000 images for you to use in your work, as well as fonts, software and other goodies.

# chapter sixteen
# Type

In this chapter we are going to take a look at a couple of different ways that you can create some interesting text effects for your finished projects. Understanding the rules of typography is a very important part of the graphic designer's job, we'll discuss some of these rules in the following pages.

As this is the last chapter of the book, we will also be putting the finishing touches to our projects and rendering them out as finished QuickTime movies. Let's start with our Seattle Evening News project.

## seattle evening news

The only thing to be done to this Project now is to add some titles so in preparation for this I want to create a new Composition which will contain all of the work that we have done so far. It is always good practice to keep your Compositions organized and manageable. Once a Composition is finished and I am happy with it I usually want to treat it as one layer in a new comp. This helps me keep things tidy as well as making it easier to apply global changes to the composition.

**1** If you do not have a project open, open SeattleNews05.aep from the Training > Projects > Chapter 16.

**2** In the Project window, drag the Edit.ppj Composition icon onto the New Composition button.

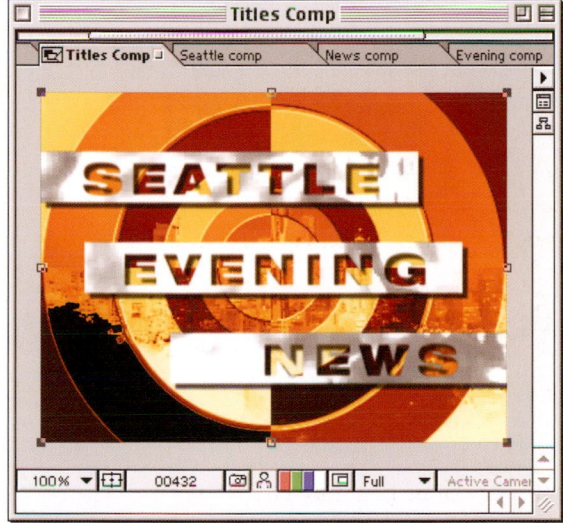

**3** Hit Command + K and, in the Composition Settings box, change the Composition Name to Titles Comp and then click OK to leave the box. This project is now ready for the Titles to be added.

## track mattes

We are going to create what is commonly referred to as a Track Matte. What we are going to be doing is, basically, punching a whole in one layer, using a grayscale image from another layer as a sort of stencil. Using this technique, the grayscale image can be taken form another layers Alpha channel or from its luminance value.

OK, so here we have a background that we're happy with, now we need to build in the actual titles.

**4** Create a new Solid (Command + Y). Call it *Seattle* and make it white with a width of 260 pixels and a height of 35 pixels.

**5** Duplicate this layer by going to Edit > Duplicate (Command + D).

**6** There are times when the easiest way to create a new layer is to duplicate it. At these times you will need to rename the layer to distinguish it from the original. Select the layer and then hit the Return key on the keyboard; this will make the layer name active. Whilst the layer name is active, type in Seattle text and then hit the Return key again to accept the changes. You can also rename layers in the Project window using the same method.

## basic text

A lot of people who I have trained have had the understanding that it was better to create their type in Photoshop than directly in After Effects. I must say that I strongly disagree with this. There are some great type tools in After Effects, let's start by taking a look at the good old Basic Text plug-in.

**1** Context-click on the Seattle text layer and choose Effect > Text > Basic Text from the menu.

**2** In the Basic Text dialog box type in the word SEATTLE (in uppercase) and choose a nice, clean typeface. In my example I chose *Eurostile T Black Extended* but you will be limited to the fonts that you have installed on your system. Helvetica Bold or Arial Black will be fine for now so choose one of these if you don't have the Eurostile font, I will give details for all three fonts where applicable.

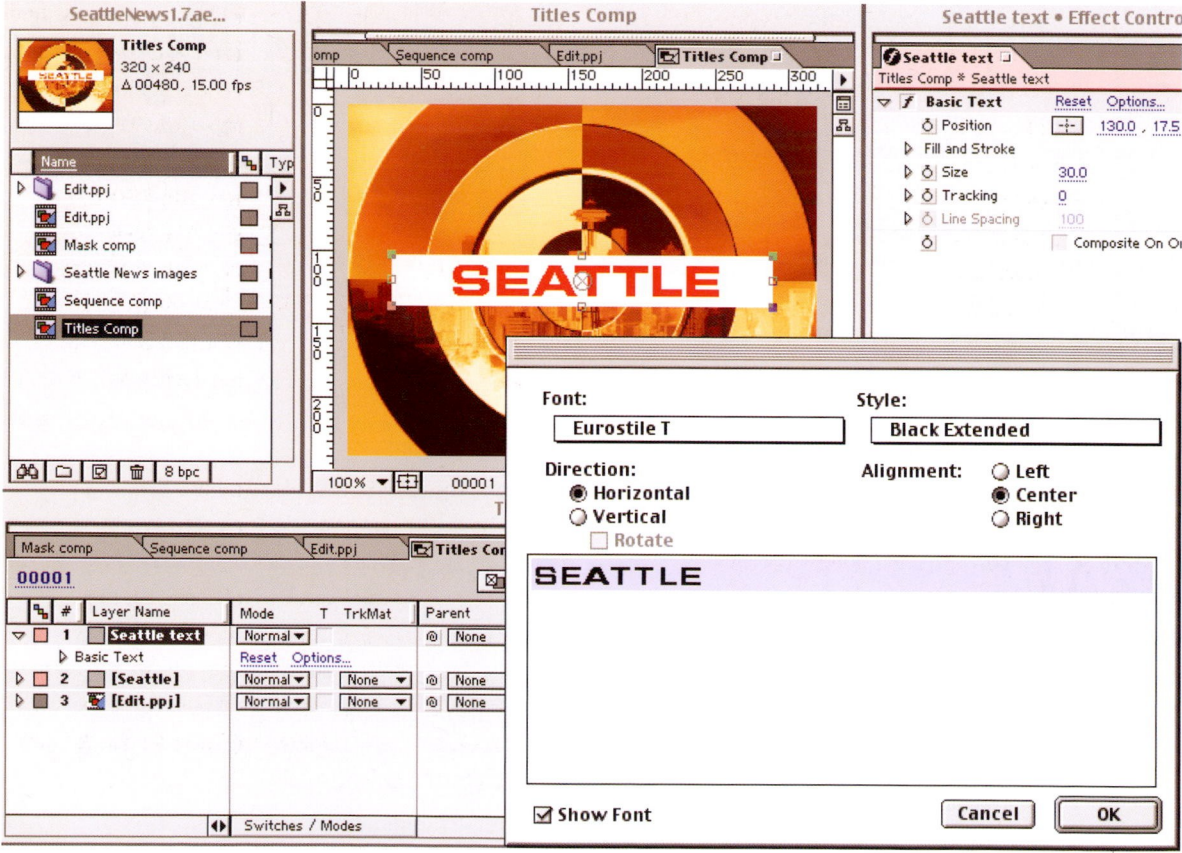

Basic Text is exactly what it says it is; it's a great, basic, text plug-in. I try to create my text directly in After Effects wherever possible; the reasons for this include;

• The text within After Effects is vector based and therefore resolution independent. As long as you use the Effect controls within the text plug-in, you can resize and reshape it without losing quality.

**NB** It is important to note, however, that using the Transform properties (or certain effects which will greatly alter the size of the text) to alter the size or shape of this text will result in quality loss, if you intend to use these Transformations on the text, you should use Illustrator to create the text. Illustrator text can be continuously rasterized so that it will lose no quality when resized. For more information on this subject, see the Technical.pdf in CD > Extras.

• I can easily update any text at any time within the program. If, in a case like this, I need to repurpose the project for Another job, it's very easy to just go straight in and change the text immediately. We'll have a look at how to do that later.
• The text plug-ins in After Effects have animatable parameters, so I can see immediately how well a certain typeface will read when it's moving and make design decisions on the spot. Again, we'll look at this in a bit more detail later.

I'm a great fan of the old school fonts; Helvetica and Gill Sans are two of my favorites, they are well designed and will work flexibly in lots of different situations. It pays to get acquainted with these fonts before you start using some of the more unusual, modern fonts. If you can accumulate a good understanding of the old faithfuls then you won't go wrong; most of the decent new fonts are based on the same basic shapes as these old classics anyway. Once again that old adage raises its head 'You have to learn the rules first in order to have fun breaking them'.

There are two main types of fonts, and Serif and Sans Serif (also referred to as simply 'Sans'). Serif fonts have little tails on the letterforms to maximize the readability. These fonts are generally easier to read and are used in magazines and books for the body text. The font used in the body text of this book is a Serif font called Cheltenham. Times is the most commonly used Serif font.

Sans Serif (meaning 'without Serif') fonts don't have the tails that Serif fonts have and are generally simpler in shape. These fonts tend to be used a lot for headings, headlines, posters and of course TV titles. They are generally cleaner to use than serif fonts for TV design. Sometimes serif fonts tails can create problems with interlacing if the letterforms are too small on screen. The headings in this book are all Helvetica Neue which is a sans serif font.

There aren't many situations where I would advocate the use of upper case throughout a design, words are generally harder to read in upper case and it's usually a bit too 'in your face' for my liking. However, this is a news program so this is one of the few occasions where upper case letters will work. Headlines and notices are often written in upper case so people are used to seeing this bolshy, attention-grabbing typography in these contexts. It will also serve to reinforce the 'Newsy' feel of the titles. We'll give the text a little more tracking than we would if we were using mixed case, this will make it more legible.

**3** Go to the Effect Controls window:
If you have chosen Arial Black as your typeface, change the font size to 32 and the Tracking value to 8. If you have chosen Helvetica bold, change the Tracking value to 2 or 3. If you have chosen *Eurostile T Black Extended*, then change the size to 30 and the tracking to 0. This is an extended version of the font (meaning stretched horizontally) so you can get away with no extra tracking at all.

When working with text on screen it is always important to give text a little more tracking than you would normally do for, say, printed graphics. The reason for this is because screens emmit light and the light tends to bleed at the edges of the letterforms making the text appear slightly bolder and more tightly tracked. This is most noticeable when using light colored text on a dark colored background or when foreground and background colors clash but is worth considering in all typographical situations.

We have the text pretty much how we want it but I really want to have the background showing through the text, like a stencil. To do this we are going to use what is known in After Effects as a Track Matte. The Track Matte mode allows you to use one layer to punch a hole in another layer, similar to the way a stencil works.

**4** Solo the Seattle Text layer by clicking on the layers Solo button (or select the layer and go to Layer > Switches > Solo). This will turn off any other layers, leaving only the Seattle text layer visible.

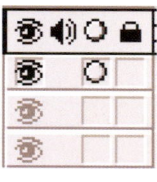

**5** Click on the Show Only Alpha button at the bottom of the Composition window to see only the Alpha Channel of the composition displayed in the Composition window. Notice that the layer has a transparent background.

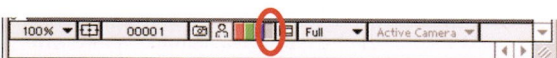

Basic Text always defaults to this state which is my preferred way of working. This way, it is easy to apply shadows, bevels and other effects to the text independent of its background layer. If you wanted to Composite the text directly onto the layer it is applied to, you can check the Composite on Original checkbox to do exactly that but you will lose the ability to easily add other effects to the text without also affecting the original layer.

**6** Click on the Composite on Original checkbox in the Effect Controls window and notice how the alpha channel now extends to the edges of the original layer.

**7** Turn off the Show Only Alpha button to see all channels again and then uncheck the Composite on Original checkbox.

So, the Alpha Channel of this layer is the same shape as the text and it is this Alpha information that we can use as a stencil to punch a hole through our other Seattle layer in our comp. I will show you how easy it is to use Alpha information from one layer to affect another layer.

**8** Click on the Solo button for the Seattle layer so that you have that and the Seattle text layer visible.

**9** Make sure that your Modes panel is visible, if not, Context-click on any of the other panel headings and choose Panels > Modes.

**10** On the right side of the Modes panel you will see the Track Matte (Trkmat) menus. Click on the Track Matte menu for layer 2, Seattle and choose *Alpha Matte "Seattle Text"* from the menu.

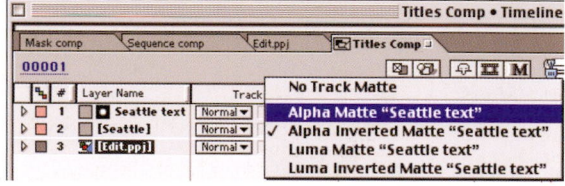

At a first glance, all that appears to have happened is that the text has turned white, this is not the case, the red text layer is being used to cut out the same shape in the layer beneath it which happens to be white.

To set up a Track matte you need to put the layer which you want to be the 'stencil' above the layer which you want to have 'punched out'. You will notice that layer 1 has no track matte menu, this is because there is no layer above it to take a matte from.

**11** To make it easier to see the text, make sure that the Checkerboard Background is turned off by going to the Comp window's wing menu and making sure that it is un-ticked in the menu.

**12** Look in the Layer Name panel and you will see that a new icon has appeared next to the layer name of the Seattle Text layer; this indicates that this layer is being used for a Track Matte. If you then look at the Video switch for that layer, you'll notice that visibility for the layer is turned off.

**13** Go back to the Track Matte menu and choose Alpha Inverted Matte "Seattle Text". This will invert the Alpha channel before applying it to the layer, reversing the effect; we now have the text 'punched out' of the layer, allowing us to see through it.

**14** Turn off the Solo switch for the Seattle layer to see the text Composited over our background.

**15** Go to File > Save as and, in the Save as dialog box, navigate to your Creative After Effects > Type Chapter folder and save the project as SeattleNews06b.aep. There's a backup of this project named, SeattleNews06.aep in Training > Projects > Chapter 16, if you should need it.

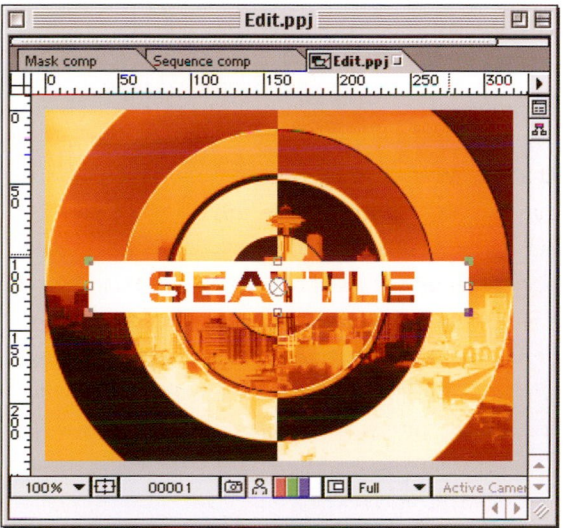

## pre-composing

OK, so we have a background layer which is a nested Composition. Above this are our two other layers which together form a Track Matte. Currently, the two layers behave independently from each other; we need to make these layers behave as one unit by pre-composing them into one layer.

**1** Select the top layer, Seattle Text and move it slightly to the right. Because you are moving the original text layer, the Alpha channel is also moving.

**2** Hit Command + Z to undo the last step and then select the second layer, Seattle; move it slightly to the left. Notice that the layer is moving without the Alpha Channel.

As with many things in After Effects, there is more than one way of grouping these layers together to be moved as one unit, I'm going to show you how to do it by Pre-Composing. If you've followed this book through from the beginning you will be familiar with the process of Nesting one Composition inside another. To recap, Nesting is when you take one Composition (a) and place it inside another (b);
(a) then becomes a single layer within (b) which can then be treated like any other layer. This is a very good way to work as you can apply masks, effects and transformations to the whole Composition and yet still have the ability to go back and edit the original layers.

Nesting calls for careful planning of your projects. You need to think in advance about which elements will be best grouped together and which are better left as individual layers. In my opinion this is a good practice to follow as it forces you to plan your projects well and to think about how they will work before you actually execute them. However, there are situations when you think 'Oh dear! I should have put those two layers together in a separate Composition and then nested it into this one'. Situations like this are classic examples of when you should use Pre-Composing.

Pre-Composing is like Nesting backwards in time. The two layers which you thought should have been put together in a separate Composition can be selected and grouped together to make exactly that, a separate Composition which can be accessed in the Project window like any other Composition.
The layers will then appear as one layer in your current Composition, allowing you to make the global changes you need to make.

**3** Hit Command + Z again to undo the last step and then select both layers, (Seattle Text & Seattle) either by Shift-clicking or by dragging a marquee around them.

**4** Go to Layer > Pre-Compose (Command + Shift + C). In the Pre-Compose dialog box type in 'Seattle Comp' as the name of your new Composition. Choose to *Move all attributes into the new composition.*

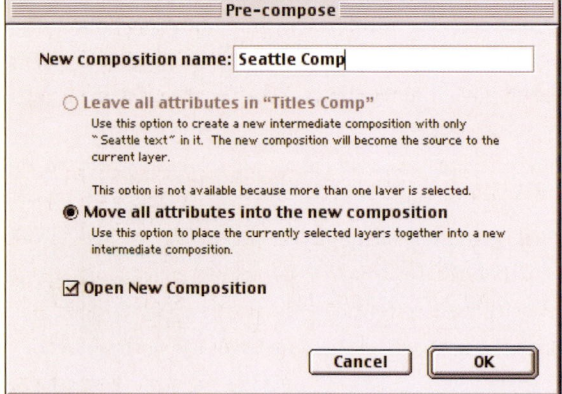

**5** Click the checkbox to Open New Composition. With this checked, After Effects will automatically open the new Composition with its own Timeline and Composition window (without this selected, you would have to double-click on the new Comp icon in the Project Window to open it).

**6** Watch your Composition change as you click OK to leave the dialog box. The original two layers have been replaced by a single layer.

This new layer is your new Comp. If you look in the Project window you will also see a new Composition icon in there, named, Seattle Comp.

**7** There is one other thing that you will notice has changed. Select the new layer in the Timeline and then look in the Composition window; notice that the new comps layer handles are right at the edge of the Comp. This is because when you pre-Compose, the new Composition will have exactly the same Composition Settings as the Composition you were in when you chose to Pre-Compose.

**8** If you want to watch these changes occur again, simply keep undoing the last step and then redoing it (Command + Z followed by Command + Shift + Z) till you have understood what is going on.

**9** When you have finished looking at the changes make sure that you are at the same stage as in the following diagram, with two layers: the Seattle Composition layer and the Edit.ppj layer.

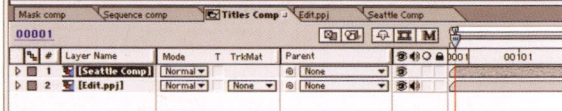

**10** Select the Seattle Composition layer in the Timeline. You can do this by clicking the corresponding number keys on the keypad. Hit the 1 key to select layer number 1.

**11** In the Composition window, click and drag the new layer around, notice that both layers now move together.

Pre-Comping (as it is commonly referred to) should only be used in situations where no other solution can be found. In my opinion it is not good practice to jump into a project without an idea, roughly of where it is going. You will learn much more if you plan ahead, pre-planned nesting is much easier to manage than a project full of Pre-Compositions with confusing structures.

However pre-comping is an extremely handy and flexible way of working; to be able to work backwards as well as forwards means that it is never too late to make changes to your designs.

The program that these titles are being designed for is called 'Seattle Evening News' so we need to create the other two words. Does that mean we have to go through the same procedure to create this twice more? Of course not, After Effects allows you to copy, paste and duplicate Compositions; we can then go back in time to change the text, I'll show you how it's done.

Now, you may think that the thing to do would be to duplicate the layer in the Timeline, wrong! By duplicating the layer in the Timeline you would simply be making another copy of the same *Composition*. In this case, any changes made to the layers in the Timeline would make the layers different from *each other* but the source Composition would remain the same. We want to adjust the settings of the source Composition which held the Basic Text effect. In order to do this we have to make duplicates of the original Composition in the *Project window* and then bring them into our Titles Composition as new layers.

**12** With the Seattle Composition layer selected in the Project window, hit Command + D or go to Edit > Duplicate to make an exact copy of your layer. Do it again to make another copy. You should now have three copies of the

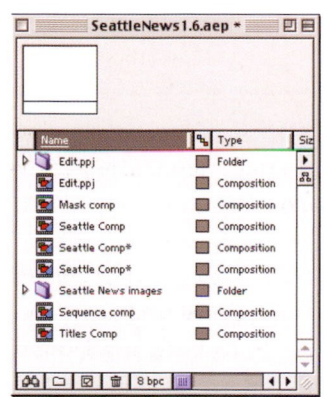

same Composition in the Project window. The two copies will each have an asterisk beside their names to distinguish them from the originals.

**13** With the one of the new comps selected in the Project window, hit the Return key on your keyboard and type in 'Evening Comp' and then hit Return again to accept the changes. Repeat this process to rename the third duplicate Comp, 'News Comp'.

**14** In the Project window, select the Evening Comp and then hold down the Command key and click on the News Comp. Holding down Command whilst selecting will allow you to select non-contiguous items from a list. Remember that the items will be placed into the Timeline in the order in which you select them in the Project window.

**15** Drag the two items down to the Timeline; as you drag items up and down over the layers in the Timeline, you will notice a thick black line moving between the other layers. This line is to show you where the items will be placed when dropped. Make sure that the black line is between the two layers (Seattle Comp and Background [Edit.ppj] comp) and then drop them into place. Don't worry if you don't get it right first time, you can always undo and then try again.

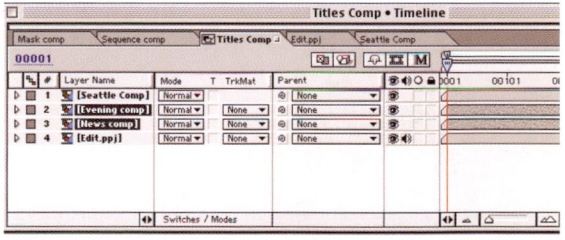

**16** Hold down the Alt key and double-click the Evening Composition layer in the Timeline window to open up its own Timeline and Composition windows. The layer will still have the word 'Seattle' in it but we can easily change that.

**17** Select the Seattle Text layer and then hit the E key on the keyboard to bring up any Effects applied to the layer.

**18** Hit the word *Options* in the Modes panel to bring up your Basic Text options and then type in the word 'EVENING' in upper case. Click OK to close the Effect Options box when you have finished. The layer will update to show the new text.

**19** In the Project window, double-click the News Composition to open it up.

**20** Repeat steps 17 to 19 with this Composition so that the text reads 'NEWS'.

**21** Go back to the Titles Composition and look at the layers individually by toggling on and off their visibility using either the video button or the solo button, whichever you prefer.

### mixing 2D and 3D

OK, so now we have three layers, one for each word in our titles, Seattle Evening News. We now need to animate the titles coming into our screen in a dynamic way. There are literally hundreds of ways of animating text in After Effects. As you will see in later exercises, you can make your characters dance, change color, distort and even morph – you can practically make them sing! In this example the television program is of a quite serious nature so we don't really want to go too over the top with the design, best to keep it simple.

We could animate the text moving in from the sides but I think that a left to right movement would detract from the rings moving in and out of the screen. This movement suggest depth even though it is just a purely 2D project. I would like to keep that feeling of depth by moving the text through 3D space, moving towards the camera from different 3D directions. I could fake this move by animating Scale and Anchor point simultaneously but why bother when I can choose to make any layer I like a 3D layer?

After Effects allows you to toggle the 3D-ness of a layer on and off as it suits you. This is a revolutionary way of working, I can leave my 2D layer as it is but animate the text layers in 3D. This concept may take a bit of getting used to for both 2D and 3D designers. To be able to mix 2D and 3D in the same space is quite a new concept but one that is infinitely flexible and intuitive once you get the hang of it (which you will do, believe me).

We are going to animate these titles coming in from 3D space and settling in their end positions; we want them to move in time with the drum beats at the end of the sequence, the easiest way to time this correctly is with the use of markers.

**1** Go to Edit > Preferences > Preview and check that your Audio Preview duration is set to at least 32 seconds.

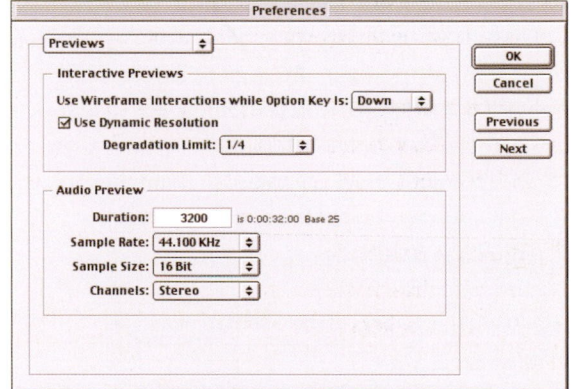

**2** Move the Current-Time Marker to the 300 frame mark and then hit the Period (Full Stop) key on the number pad of your keyboard to preview the audio from this point onwards.

Pay particularly close attention to the drum crashes at the end of the piece, this is where we will bring in the Titles. It will help you enormously if you get to know the audio very well before you attempt to lay down the markers so listen to the section a few times till you feel that you know it really well.

**3** Select the top layer of the Composition; this will be the layer which the markers will be applied to. I always find it easiest to mark the top layer of the Composition, this way the markers are always visible at the top of the Timeline.

**4** When you are ready I want you to hit the period key again to preview the audio but this time I want you to hit the Asterisk (*) key on the numberpad at the point of each drum crash.

I make it five main drum crashes at the end so when you finish you should have five markers on your layer. If not, just undo the last step and try again; keep repeating the steps till you have successfully laid down five layer markers in time with the drums. (I have markers at 389, 393, 399, 406 and 413 frame marks) We will use the last three markers to time the three words with, the other two markers will be useful guides for our timing. You can also add markers by going to Layer > Add Marker.

**5** Use the J and K keys on your keyboard to jump between the visible markers till you are settled on the fifth marker (approximately 413 frames).

**6** Adjust the Navigator at the bottom of the Timeline (by dragging it to the right) so that you can see all of the markers more clearly.

**7** Make sure the Switches panel is visible (Context-click on the panels and choose Switches) and then activate 3D layer switches for each of the three text layers, they are now 3D layers. You will notice that there are now three values representing each of their Position properties, one for each dimension: X, Y, and Z.

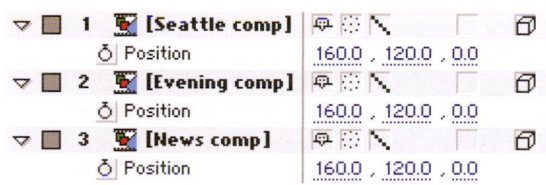

**8** Click and scrub on the Seattle Comp layers Y value (the second value) in the Switches panel of the Timeline till it reads 58.

**9** Do the same with the News layers Y value till it reads 182. By doing this you have evenly spaced out the text so that both top and bottom lines of text anchor points are exactly sixty-two pixels away from the center line.

**10** Switch on the Title safe guides by hitting the Title-Action Safe button at the bottom/left of the Composition window. For any text to be easily readable on screen it should always fit inside the Title-Safe guide which is the inner rectangle shown on screen.

**11** Scrub the X values of both the Seattle layer and the News layer till the edges of the text lie up against the Title-Safe guides on either side of the screen. Use the following illustration for guidance.

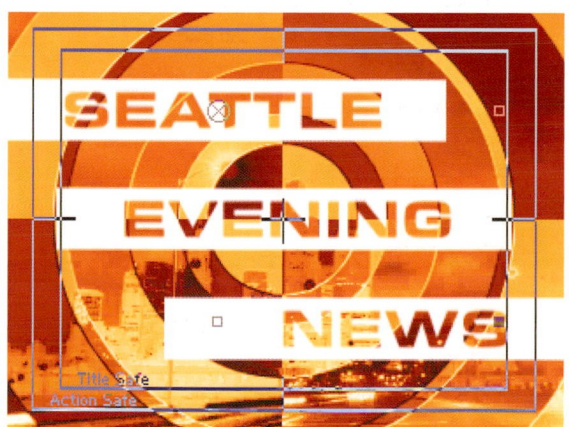

At this point we want all of our layers to have settled in their final positions, therefore this is the best point to begin animating from.

**12** In the Timeline select the three text layers and then hit Alt + P key on the keyboard to bring up the Position property and simultaneously set keyframes for all three layers.

Remember that this will be the end point of this animation, we want the words to come to rest, one by one, on the last three beats, we must stagger these three keyframes. The News layer should come to rest last so we'll leave it on this, the final marker.

**13** Holding down the Shift key, click and drag the Evening Comps Position keyframe so that it snaps to the penultimate marker (frame 406).

**14** Do the same with the Seattle Composition layer's keyframe so that it snaps to the third marker (frame 399). Now that we have set up the end positions, let's set our starting positions.

**15** Move to the first marker and then click and scrub the Z value (the third value) of the Seattle Comp layer till it moves beyond the camera and the value reads –334.0. By doing this we are moving the layer on the Z-axis so that it moves behind the position of the camera.

**16** Still on the first marker, change the Evening Comp layers Z value to 16500.0, you may find it easier to type this value in rather than scrub it. If you do want to scrub the value, holding down the Shift key whilst scrubbing will scrub between larger increments. A layer has to move a long distance before it becomes invisible to the eye. We have to move this layer 16500 pixels in front of our camera before it disappears.

**17** Move to the fourth marker scrub the News Comp layers Z Position value to –334.0, this will move the layer out to the same Z-depth as the Seattle layer. Notice that they move in very different directions. This is because the camera is bang in the middle of all of these layers so the layers will orient themselves around the center point of the camera.

**18** Finally, Shift-select the last Position keyframes of each of the layers so that they are all selected. Context click on any of them and choose Keyframe Assistant > Easy Ease In from the menu to ease the motion on the way into the keyframe.

**19** Use the Navigator to zoom out again so that you can see the whole timeline. Move the Current-Time Marker so that it sits on the first marker and then hit the B key on the keyboard. This will move the Beginning point of the Work Area to the Current-Time Marker.

**20** Jump to the last marker and hit the N key on the keyboard, this will move the End point of the Work Area to the Current-Time Marker.

Remember the RAM Preview will run for the length of the current work area; by moving the beginning and end of the work area you can define the length of your previews.

**21** Hit the 0 key on the number pad of your keyboard to RAM Preview your new titles. If you need to speed up your preview building you can turn off visibility for the Edit.ppj layer whilst previewing; but remember to turn it back on before saving the project.

**22** Go to File > Save as and, in the Save as dialog box, navigate to your Creative After Effects > Type Chapter folder on the desktop and save the project into the folder as SeattleNews07b.aep. There's a backup of this file in Training > Projects > Chapter 16. Later in this chapter, we will put some finishing touches to the text before rendering out our finished animation as a QuickTime movie. Firstly, let's return to our Graffiti Club titles.

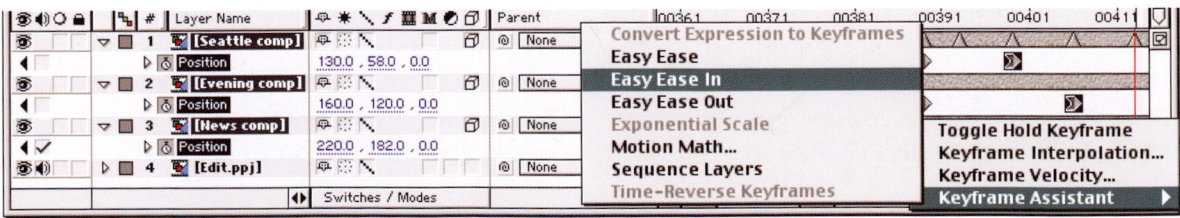

# graffiti club

## path text

First, I'm going to show a bit about the Path Text plug-in, which is available both in the Standard and Pro Bundle versions of After Effects. Path Text has to be one of my favorite After Effects plug-ins, it's because of this filter that I prefer to create my text directly within After effects, it's just so versatile and easy to use. Its main purpose is for animating text along a Bezier path but also included in the plug-in are a wide range of animatable values which can give you amazing typographic control over your text.

**1** Before you start, please make sure that you have installed all of the free fonts which were provided to you on the CD. If you haven't already installed them, please close After Effects, install the fonts on to your system and then restart your machine.

**2** Open Graffiti07.aep from Training > Projects > Chapter 16.

Here we have our Graffiti Club movie which we last worked on in the 3D chapter. All that's left to do in this project is to add some titles and captions to it. Later we'll use Vector Paint (PB) or Path Text (Standard) to create the actual title of the show. First of all, we'll work on some captions.

These captions will be very important as they will tell the viewer what sort of subjects will be covered in the show, the animation sets the mood of the show, the captions are there simply to add information. The words are not intended to be read in sequence but are intended as subliminal keywords which may or may not be noticed immediately. The show is broadcast weekly so the viewers may pick up on different keywords each time they tune in to the show.

**3** Hit Command + Y to create a new solid. Make it the same size as your comp, and any color. Name it Text crawl.

**4** Context-click on the layer and go to Effect > Text > Path Text. As soon as you apply this filter you will be greeted with the following dialog box.

**5** Type in the words that you see illustrated in the diagram below, placing four spaces between each word. These are some of the keywords representing subjects covered in the show.

**6** Choose `Cherry Coke` as the font. This font was kindly contributed by Jonathan Edwards at Future Fonts (find out more about Future Fonts in CD > Free Stuff). I chose this font because it has a hand drawn appearance which goes well with our Graffiti theme, it also looks quite modern because of its angular shapes and the chunkiness of the letterforms. Click OK to leave the box.

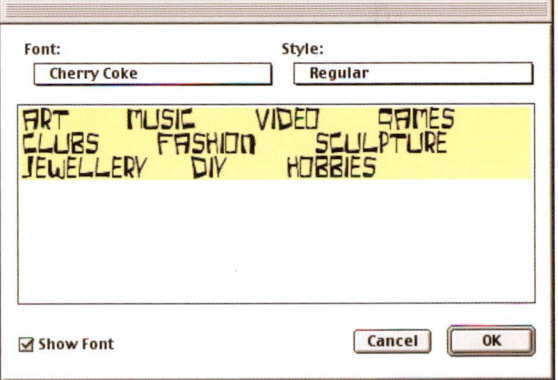

**7** In the timeline, hit the Solo button so that you can see only the Text Crawl layer and click the Quality switch once to see your layer in best, anti-aliased quality.

When the effect is selected in the Effect Controls window, you'll see four control points joined to a path which the text is sitting upon. See the following diagram which illustrates these points.

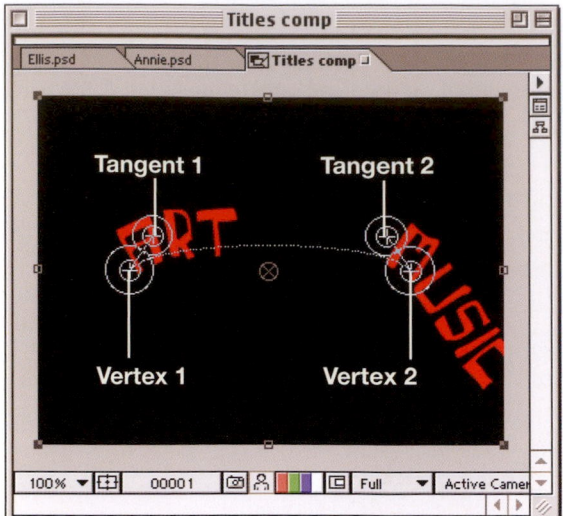

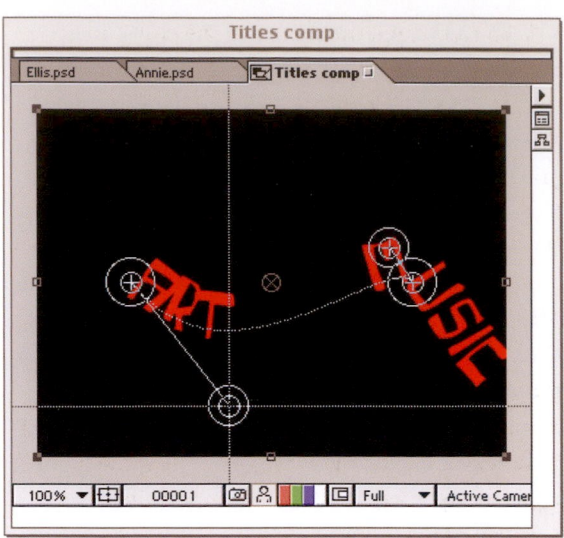

**8** Open the Effect Controls window (Command + Shift + T) and then open up the Path Options > Control Points by twirling down the little triangles beside the property names.

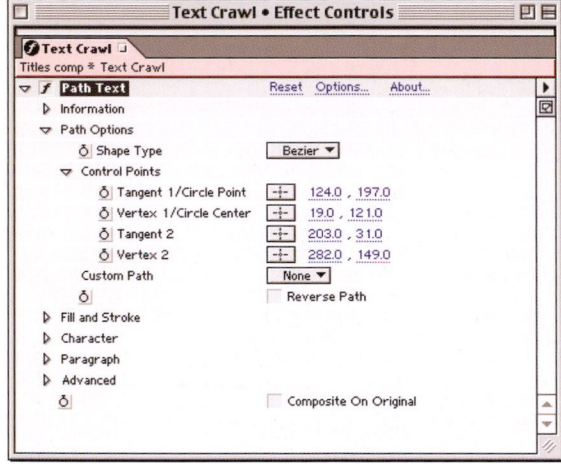

In here you will see four crosshair boxes, each representing one of the four control points seen in the Comp window.

**9** Click on the first crosshair box and then move over to the Comp window. You'll see a large cross over your layer, the center of this cross represents the position of the Tangent1/Circle Point.

**10** Move the Cross to the bottom-center of your screen and then click once with your mouse/pen to apply the new position to the control point. Your layer should look similar to the one pictured above.

You can also click and drag the control points around, interactively in the main Comp window.

**11** In the Comp window, click on Tangent 2 and drag it to the top-center of the comp. Notice that you can see the text change as you drag, giving you immediate feedback.

**12** One by One, click and drag Vertex 1 out to the left-center and Vertex 2 to the right-center of your composition.

This is the default curved path which you can use to create simple curved shapes with in Path Text. Look at the Shape Type menu which is also situated in the Path Options section.

**13** Choose *Circle* from the Shape Type menu. Notice that the text is now wrapped around a circle. The center point of the circle defaults to the position of Vertex 1.

**14** To reposition the center of the circle in the center of your comp, Type in 160, 120 as the new Vertex 1/ Circle Center position. The text now follows the circular path but is too big to fit readably onto the path. When using a circular path, the text will wrap around the path repeatedly, overlapping as it goes.

**15** Open up the Character section in the Effect Controls window, here you will see a set of typographic controls for your text. Change the Size setting to 10 by scrubbing the value (holding down Shift whilst you scrub will move in increments of 10, holding down Command will move in increments of .1) .

**16** Check the reverse Path checkbox to see your text wrapped around the inside of the circle. Uncheck it again after you have seen what it does.

**17** Open up the Paragraph section and scrub the Left Margin value to the right, till it reads 770. Notice the text is moving around the path (in the Comp window) as you drag. This is the value you would animate to move the text along the path when it's anchored on the Left margin.

**18** Go back to the Shape Type menu and choose *Loop* from the list, your text has disappeared! Don't worry I'll show you where it's hiding.

**19** Drag the Left margin slider back to 0, the text will come in from the left and then move around the path. Drag the slider into –250 to make the text begin to move off to the right after 'looping the loop'.

**20** Change the Shape Type menu to *Line* and then change the Left margin value to 0. You should now see your text on a horizontal line. Drag Vertex 1 to the left till it is about 20 pixels from the edge of the screen.

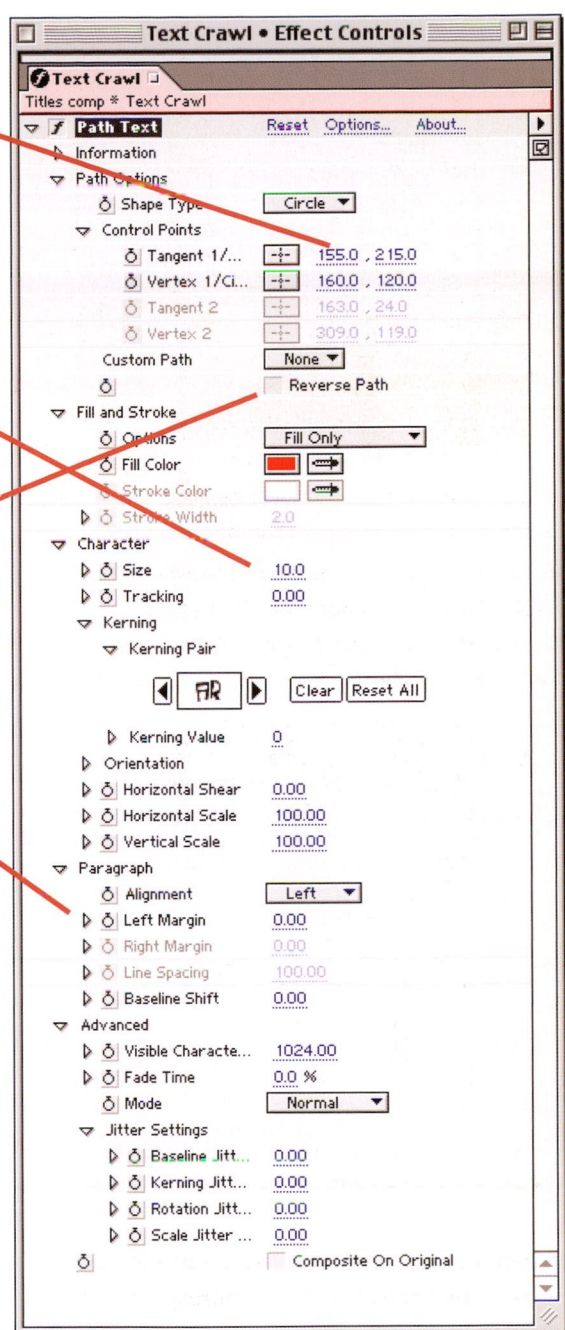

**21** Scrub the Size value up to about 24, notice that the text scales from the Left. The scaling depends on the Alignment setting.

**22** Change the Alignment menu to Right, notice that we now see the words at the end of our list.

**23** Try scaling the text up and down now, notice that the text is now scaling from the right side of the path. The text will be anchored based on its alignment setting. Notice now that the Left Margin value has been dimmed and has been replaced by a Right Margin value.

**24** Change the Alignment to Center and then scrub the Size value up and down. Notice that now the text is scaling in and out from the center of the comp. When you have Center alignment selected you have both Left and Right Margin values available.

**25** Finish with your Size value at 30 and your Alignment set to Left.

**26** In the Character section change the Tracking value to 4. Tracking (sometimes referred to as letter spacing) is a traditional typographic term. Increasing the Tracking value will increase the spaces between all of the letters by the same amount.

As I mentioned earlier in this chapter, it's important to give your text a little more tracking than you would use for, say, a print document, due to the bleeding effect that is caused by the light emitting from the TV screen. It's particularly important when using capital letters as the typographer designed the font (including the spacing) to be used in mixed case. When using all caps, the text tends to appear a little too tight and needs some extra space to breathe.

As well as Tracking, Path Text also has some fairly useful kerning controls. Kerning is another typographic term used to describe the spacing between pairs of letters. This control allows you to adjust the space between individual letter pairs.

To use the Kerning controls you first have to select the pair of letters which you want to adjust the space between.

**27** Open up the Kerning part of the Character section. First of all look at the Kerning Pair controls. You have a little preview box which shows you the letter pair currently selected. There are two black arrow buttons at either side of this box, these allow you to jump between letter pairs.

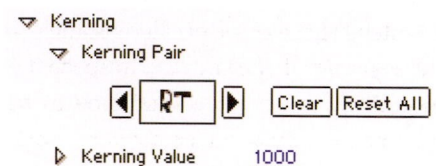

**28** Click on the right arrow button once to jump the next letter pair which is RT.

**29** Now scrub the Kerning Value to approximately 1000. Notice that the spacing only changes between the two letters selected in the Kerning Pair selection box. Once you have understood what changes have occurred, change the value to −100.

Normally, I would go through the text, checking that all the Kerning pairs had the correct amount of spacing between them. It can be tricky for a beginner to know exactly how much spacing to use between the letters but it helps if you can be aware of what's known as the 'typographic color' of your text. This term refers to the density of your text as a unit.

To become an accomplished typographer you need to start thinking of letterforms as shapes rather than text, each letter is an individual shape, when these letters are combined into words, they create new shapes, the words are combined to make sentences and then sentences become paragraphs. The combination of the type and the space around it will form a pattern, the key to good typography is to make sure that the amount of space compared to the amount of solid text is pretty even.

As a test, pick up a good magazine and have a look at some text blocks through half-closed eyes. If the typography is good, you should see an even spread of gray throughout the text. If, however you do the same with a cheap newspaper, you'll probably see big chunks of white space amongst the paragraphs, making the text look uneven and causing it to be more difficult to read.

The most common cause of bad typography is the use of Justified Alignment, this is when the text is forced to extend to the edges of columns, the computer makes a guess at the best way to space the letters to fit the space. As you should know by now, computers are great tools but are not very good at making design decisions, that's your job, it takes a trained eye to know what's needed.

You can learn a lot about typography by observing text very carefully in every-day life, it's all around you. Notice the fonts used for different purposes (e.g. billboards, magazines, shop signs, graffiti, TV, film, web etc.) Pay attention to the spacing and colors, try to start seeing letters, words and phrases as shapes.

When I was studying at art college I found tracing letterforms by hand an extremely useful exercise. We used what's known as a *Grant projector* to enlarge letters from magazines, we then traced the letters and created individual designs around each of the letters of the alphabet. This is a great way of getting to know the shapes, why not try it, using a photocopier to enlarge the text. Hand drawn text has a lovely raw quality that's hard to achieve using a computer, it's also very therapeutic.

**30**   OK, we can't spend too much time on kerning our text here, so let's take a look at a few more Path Text feature. In the Effect Controls window, go up to the *Fill and Stroke* section and open it up. Click on the *Fill* color swatch and change it to a deep blue color. Change the *Options* menu to *Stroke over Fill* to apply the default white, 2 pixel stroke on top of the fill.

**31**   Move over to the Comp window. Earlier we moved the control points individually by clicking and dragging them to their new locations. You can also move all the control points simultaneously by dragging the outer circles around the control points.

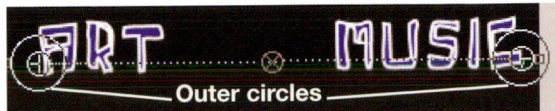
— Outer circles —

**32**   Click on the Title Safe button in the Comp window to see your safe zones and then drag either of the outer circles down to the bottom of the screen, holding down the Shift key as you drag to constrain the movement to a vertical one only.

We are going to animate the text moving along the bottom of the screen, this is known as a *text crawl*. OK, so now we need to animate the text moving along the path.

**33**   Go back to the Paragraph section in the Effect Controls window and Shift + scrub the Left Margin value till it reads 320, the text will disappear off to the right. In the Timeline, move to the first marker and set a keyframe for this value by clicking the little stopwatch beside the value name.

**34**   Click on the Timeline to make it active and then use the K key to jump between markers till you reach the eleventh marker at frame 553. Shift + scrub the Left Margin value till it reads –2250. This will move the text all the way off screen to the left.

**35**   Whilst still at frame 553, and with the layer still selected, hit Alt + ] to trim the layer to the Current - Time Marker. There is no point having the layer extend any further than this as the text crawl is now finished.

**36**   Switch off the Solo button so that you can see all of the layers again and then RAM Preview the comp to view the results. The text now crawls across the screen.

**37** In the Modes panel of the Timeline, change the Text Crawl layers Layer Mode to Difference so that it creates some nice, contrasting colors to the background.

**38** OK, a basic text crawl is a bit dull so we'll have a look at some of the Advanced settings in here. In the Effect Controls window, open up the Advanced section and have a look at what's available to you.

**39** Open up the Jitter settings section. Most of the values in Path Text are animated by setting keyframes, just like any other value but these values are slightly different. These values will animate automatically as soon as you set their value higher than 0, these are known as *procedural* values, presumably because they go through a procedure automatically.

**40** Change the Baseline jitter setting to 50 and then preview some of the comp, notice that the Baseline value (which is another value that you can adjust in the Paragraph section) is now animating randomly as it moves along the path, we didn't even have to set any keyframes!

**41** Change the Baseline Jitter value to 10 and then change the Rotation and Scale Jitter values to 100. Preview a section of the comp and notice the letters are now scaling and rotating randomly,

**42** Change these values to 10 after you've seen the results and then, making sure that the layer is still selected, hit Command + Alt + B to make the work area the same size as the selected layer.

**43** RAM Preview this section of your animation.

**44** Deselect the layer and hit Command + Alt + B again to stretch the work area back to the size of the comp.

**45** Save your project as Graffiti08b.aep to your Creative After Effects > Type chapter folder.

OK, so you've seen how the Path Text plug-in is fantastic for (excuse the pun) giving your characters character! There are so many more things that I'd like to show you regarding this plug-in but I just don't have the space here to go into it in too much detail. I will, however, be posting new Path Text tutorials on the website every now and then so keep a look out for new Path Text techniques coming your way very soon!

**46** Now, I want you to open the project named Graffiti09.aep from the Training > Projects > Chapter 16 folder.

**47** Have a look at this project, I have added a few things here. Firstly, I have applied an open path to the Crawl layer. Go to the wing menu and make sure that the Layer Masks option is checked so that you can see the mask displayed in the Comp window with the layer selected. You can use an open or closed path as a shape for this filter by either drawing a mask directly onto your layer or by copying and pasting it into the layer. You would then turn the Mask Mode to *None* and then selecting the mask in the Custom Path menu in the Effect Controls window. Remember that as well as animating the Path Text values, you can animated the mask itself.

**48** Look at the Title layer, here I have animated the Visible Characters value to make the letters appear individually. Check out the Effect Controls windows for each effect to see how they work.

**49** OK, now I want you to use any of these techniques to create a similar end title to the one I have created here. You should be comfortable enough now to go it alone. Open up Graffiti08.aep from Training > Projects > Chapter 16 and create a new Titles layer. Try playing around with some Path Text effect combinations to come up with some funky text ideas. When you have finished creating your titles, save the project into your Creative After Effects > Type Chapter folder as Graffiti09.aep.

## advanced vector paint (pro bundle)

The following exercise is a fairly advanced Production Bundle exercise and uses the Vector Paint filter that we used back in the Keying chapter. As well as the Production Bundle version of After Effects, you will also need sticky tape, a printer and a graphic tablet to be able to complete the exercise. I realize that these are very specific equipment requirements and may exclude several readers from being able to complete this section but I really felt that this technique was important to pass on to you. If you don't have a Graphic tablet already, then it is really worthwhile considering the purchase of a tablet, it will really add a new dimension to your work processes.

If you are a Standard version user or do not have the necessary equipment listed below, you can jump to the next section, *rendering your movie-part one* to find out how to render out the movie that you completed in the last section.

At the time of publication, the tablet features supported by Vector Paint were Wacom and Creation Station tablets' pressure-stylus and erase functions. I have used a Wacom Intuos A4 graphic tablet for this exercise and the instructions given are specific to this particular tablet. If you have any other supported tablet, you will still be able to follow the exercise but you may have to experiment with settings to achieve the same result as me. I have endeavoured to explain the steps in as much general detail as I can. Although I cannot guarantee that it will work using any unsupported tablets, you are welcome to try it out. Please let us know if it works by posting the results on the website at:
http://www.angie.abel.co.uk/book.html

**1** I have provided you with a printable template of the text we are going to use for these titles, I simply drew the text by hand and then scanned it into the computer. Print out the file named GraffitiClub.jpg which is in the Graffiti Club folder inside Training > Source Images > Angie Images.

Before moving on, use the graphic tablet's control panel to make sure that your tablet is set to *Pen mode* (or equivalent); this exercise will not work in Mouse mode. Whilst in the control panel, please make sure that the *Display* option is set to *All* (or equivalent) and its *Aspect* is set to *Proportional* (or equivalent). If you have problems accessing your control panel, please see your tablet's manual for details.

The screen resolution I have used for this exercise is $1024 \times 576$. If you have a lower screen resolution you may need to adjust the size of your Comp window and the position of your template to suit.

**2** Open Graffiti08.aep from the Training > Projects > Chapter 16 folder.

**3** Create a New Composition; name it *Vector Paint*; make it; $320 \times 240$; Full resolution: 15 fps; Duration of 150 frames (10 seconds).

**4** Hit Command + Y to create a New Solid. Name the solid *Outline Layer*; make it white and click the Comp Size button to make it $320 \times 240$.

**5** Context-click the Outline Layer and chose Effect > Paint > Vector Paint from the menu.

**6** Hit Alt + . (Period/full stop) till your Magnification is 200%.

**7** In Effect Controls window; change the Paint Color to black; the Radius amount to 15 and the feather amount to 3. These settings will produce a reasonably sharp-edged, thin, black line.

**8** Change the Playback mode to Animate Strokes.

**9** Place the printed image on your tablet.

If you want, you can place the image under the clear plastic overlay on the tablet but I prefer to place images intended for tracing on top of this overlay.

The reason for this is that I find it easier to control the pens movement on a paper surface, I find that it tends to slip on the shiny plastic surface. You may need to trim the paper to make it fit in the available space, depending on the size of your tablet.

OK, the idea here is to move the paper around the tablet till it is in the correct position (so that the edges of the text fit within the Comp window).

**10** If you hold your pen above the surface without actually touching the surface, you will be able to see the pen icon on screen. Make sure that you don't touch the surface with the pen otherwise you may inadvertently start to draw before you are ready. With the paper placed on or under the surface, check on screen that the edges of the text lie within the center of your Comp window. If they don't simply move the sheet of paper around till you have the image centered in the Comp window.

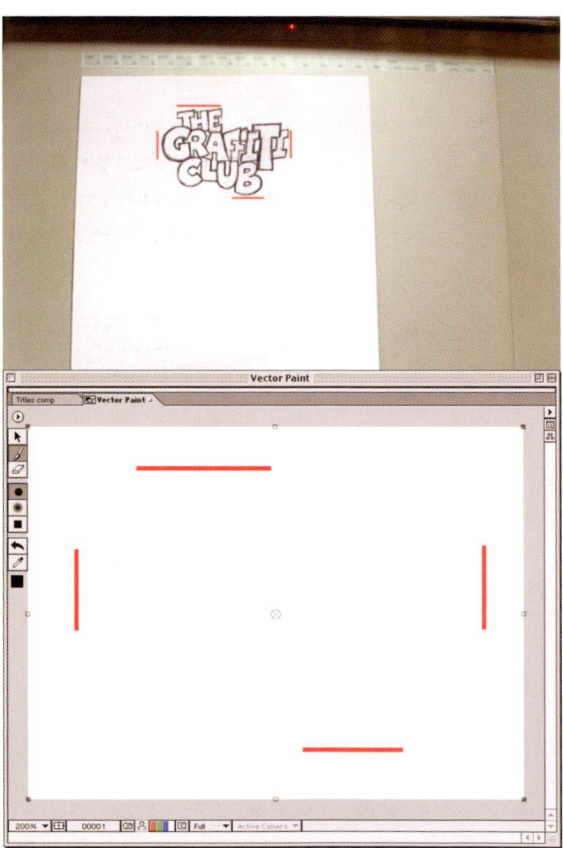

Make sure that the cursor is inside the comp at all times. You can also tinker around with the Magnification settings if it makes it easier for you to get it right. Use the previous diagrams as guides, notice that the red lines on the graphic tablet should correspond with the red lines in the Comp window.

Once you have the correct position, you need to make sure to keep the image in position. It is vitally Important that you must not move the paper or the Comp window once the correct positions are set because the corresponding points on the computer screen and the tablet need to match up at all times.

**11** If you have chosen to draw on top of the plastic overlay, simply drop the overlay carefully over the image to hold it in place. If, like me, you have decided to draw directly on to the paper you will need to attach the paper to the tablet in the correct position using sticky tape.

OK, so you saw briefly how Vector Paint works in the Keying chapter. Normally, if you were to set the Current-Time Marker at two seconds; draw a stroke; lift the pen and then draw another stroke, both strokes would be painted on at the two-second mark, Vector Paint would draw them back simultaneously. You can change the way that Vector Paint works by using the Shift-Record settings; these allow you to draw a series of strokes, one after the other and have Vector Paint record and then play them back to you exactly as you drew them, one after the other. It will also play them back at exactly the same speed that you drew them; it's sort of like Motion Sketch for painting.

**12** Option-click on the Work Area Bar to make sure that it is extended out to its full comp length.

**13** Make sure that the Vector Paint effect is active by clicking on its name in the Effect Controls window so that it is highlighted.

You can tell when the effect is active because you will see the Vector Paint tools displayed in the Comp window. Vector paint will not work without the effect selected so if you ever have a situation where the tools have disappeared from the Comp window, simply click on the effect name in the Effect Controls window to re-activate the effect.

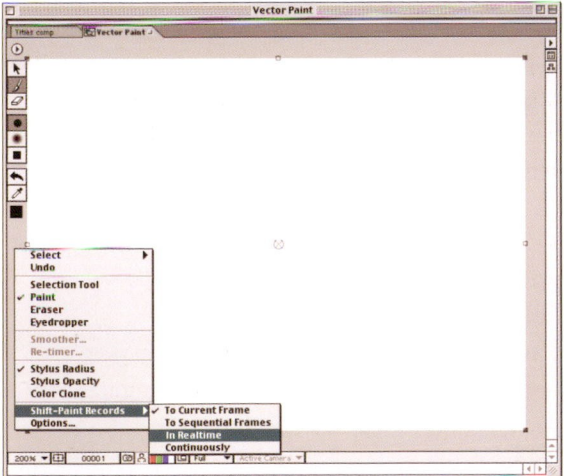

**14**  With the effect active, Context-click on Comp window to bring up the Vector Paint sub-menu. Choose Shift-Paint Records > In Real Time. This will tell Vector Paint to record the strokes in real time.

The Shift key needs to be held down throughout the recording process for the Shift-Record option to work (hence the name Shift-Record!). The problem I have with this is that I prefer to have both hands free whilst drawing. Good balance is important when using pens and brushes; it's common for most people to lean on the paper with their other arm to help them to keep a steady hand whilst drawing.

**15**  First, make sure the Current-Time Marker is at the beginning of your Composition. We want Vector Paint to start playing back the stroke from the position of the Current-Time Marker.

**16**  OK, so here's my solution, this is a highly technical procedure so beware! Take some sticky tape (about a 5 cm strip should do it) and tape down the Shift key on your keyboard so that it is held down for the whole duration of the recording; told you it was tricky!

**17**  You are now ready to trace over the printed image. Now, put yourself in the shoes of a graffiti artist; you're probably drawing quite quickly to avoid being caught so don't draw absolutely perfect lines. We want some grittiness here so go over each line two or three times before moving onto the next; as if you were drawing this freehand. The text does, however, need to be legible so don't go too far over the edges of the lines. You can look at the screen every now and then to make sure you are doing OK but don't pause for too long because we are recording it in real time. Having said that the odd little pause here and their will add to the realism, perhaps the graffiti artist was looking round to check the police weren't on their way?

**18**  When you have finished tracing over your image you should still see the result of your sketching on the screen, you can quickly touch up any areas that need it but make sure that you are quick about it.

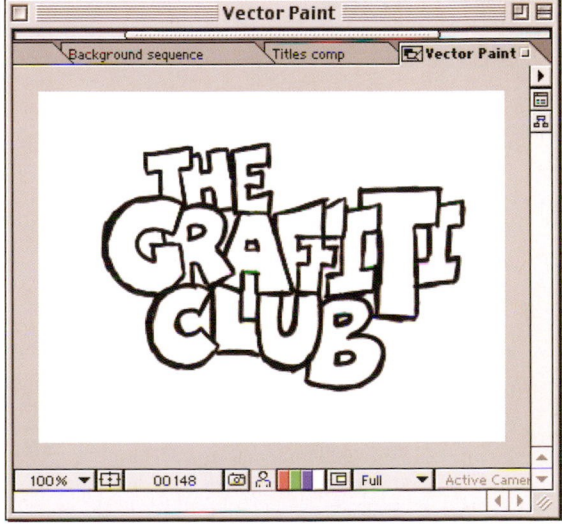

**19** Once you have finished, remove the sticky tape from the Shift key and your image will disappear! Don't worry it's not gone for good; hit the RAM Preview button and wonder in amazement as Vector Paint plays back your very own strokes in real time!

You'll probably notice that because your comp is only ten seconds long and that you more than likely took a lot longer than that to trace the text, that you have run out of time. You've probably only seen the T drawn on screen before the end of the Comp is reached. Don't worry, you can easily change most of the settings after drawing your text. Vector Paint will still store all of the stroke information from your drawing.

**20** Change the Playback Speed value to 60 and then RAM Preview the Comp again, it should now play back over approximately 4 or 5 seconds, depending on how long it took for you to draw it in the first place. Feel free to adjust this value till your animation happens over four seconds. My tracing session lasted about 4 minutes originally, by changing my setting to 60, I have made the animation happen over four seconds.

**21** If you are not happy with your first attempt you can simply delete the strokes you have made and follow the next step. If you are happy with your strokes just move on to step 24, if not, then follow the next few steps.

**22** To delete all strokes you first need to make sure that the Vector Paint effect is selected and active in the Effect Controls window; it has to be active before you move on to the next step.

**23** Make the Comp window active and then hit Command + A to select all of the strokes; you should now see that the strokes are highlighted in the Comp window; hit backspace or the delete key to delete them and then start again from step 15.

It may take a few attempts before you feel completely comfortable with the process but don't despair it'll become second nature after a short while. Because the strokes are vector based, they can be selected, adjusted or deleted quite easily.

**24** When you are happy with your animation we'll move on to the next step which is to create a fill for the outlines.

**25** Make sure that the Current-Time Marker is at the beginning of your comp and then bring in the ThickStripes.psd image. Place the image in the Timeline as the bottom-most layer. We'll use this as a temporary background to help us visualize the final effect.

**26** Select the Outline layer and, in the Effect Controls window, change the Playback mode to *All Strokes* so we can see outline throughout the whole comp. This way, we can use the existing lines as our template, we will no longer have to use the paper template on the tablet.

**27** In the Effect Controls window, change the Composite Paint mode to *Only* and then RAM Preview the comp again. Now you should see the complete title composited onto the thick stripes throughout the comp, no animation should be taking place at this point.

**28** Create another New Solid with the same settings as before, name this on, Fill layer.

**29** Apply Vector Paint to this layer and change the Composite Paint mode to *Only* so that you can see the other two layers.

**30** Select the Fill layer again and make sure that the Vector Paint effect is active again by clicking on the effect name in the Effect Controls window. Also make sure that the Brush tool is selected in the Comp window.

**31** Move the cursor over the letter T, in the word 'The'. You can change the brush settings interactively in the Comp window by using modifier keys. Hold down the Command key and then click and drag the cursor to change the brush size interactively. In the Effect Controls window, check that the brush size is at about 8. There are lots more keyboard shortcuts for the Vector Paint tool listed in the After Effects manual and also in the Online Help. Please have a look through these after finishing this exercise.

**32** In the Effect Controls window, change the Brush Type to *Air* by clicking once on the Brush Type name.

**33** Change the Playback mode to Animate Strokes.

**34** With the effect active, Context-click on Comp window to bring up the Vector Paint sub-menu. Choose Shift-Paint Records > In Real Time. This will tell Vector Paint to record the strokes in real time.

**35** Stick down the Shift key with some sticky tape again.

**36** Paint in fill quite roughly, Vector Paint takes advantage of the pressure sensitive nature of your tablet, its default setting is to vary the width of the stroke according to pressure so remember to use the pen lightly for thin strokes, pressing harder when you want thick lines.

**37** Remove the sticky tape, change the Playback Speed till the fill happens in time with the outline. I have a setting of 37 on mine, it generally doesn't take as long to do the fill as it does to do the outline.

RAM Preview the comp. Notice that the outline is no longer animating and that it is lying under the fill layer.

**38** Select the outline layer and drag it up to the top of the Timeline. Whilst it is still selected, change the Outline layer's Playback mode to Animate Strokes and RAM Preview again.

OK, it's looking pretty good now but I didn't want to use white for the fill, this is no problem, because the strokes are vectors, we can select them and change their attributes after drawing them. Brush size, feather and color can all be changed after the strokes have been applied, making this tool incredibly flexible.

**39** Move to frame 60 and then make sure that the Effect is active in the Effect Controls window. Activate the Comp window by clicking on its title bar.

**40** Hit Command + A to select all of the strokes for this layer and then move back to the Effect Controls window. Choose a new color for the Fill, I've chosen a nice turquoise-blue which contrasts nicely with the orange. All selected strokes will change to the new color.

**41** RAM Preview the comp again to see your finished text animation.

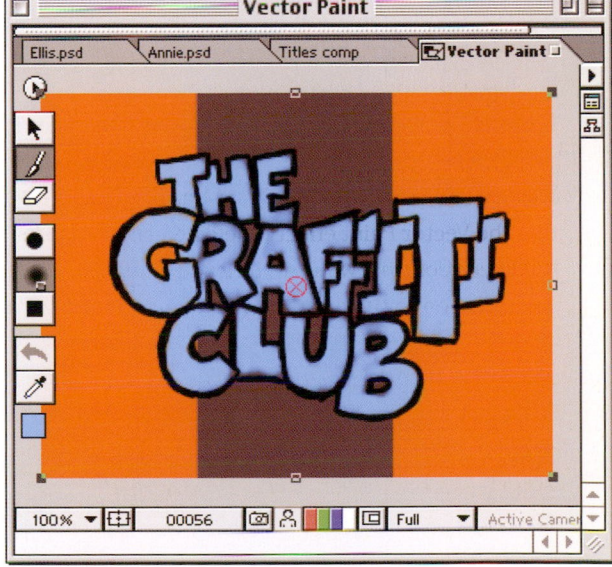

OK, so now we have the animated strokes happening just how we wanted, the next step is to composite this animation into the Titles comp.

**42** Select the ThickStripes.psd layer and then hit Backspace to delete it. We no longer need this layer, it was only used as a guide.

**43** Go back to the Titles comp again and go to frame 675. Drag the Vector Paint comp into the Titles comp as its top layer. RAM Preview the animation in its new home. The animation looks OK but is a bit flat, when you paint on brickwork or any other rough surface, the texture will show through, distorting the paintwork and creating depth in shadowy areas. We will use displacement maps and layer modes to give our paint a nice rough surface.

**44** Go back to the Vector Paint comp and make sure that the Current-Time Marker is at the beginning of your comp.

## displacement map

The Displacement Map effect will displace pixels by a user defined amount, based on the color values of any chosen layer in your comp. By displacing the pixels in this way you can make it appear as if the texture and movement of one layer is being applied to another. I'll show you what I mean.

**1** First of all we need to bring in a layer to use as our Displacement Map, the brick texture layer from our Background Sequence.

**2** Hit Command + I and import the file named BrickTextures062.jpg from the Training > Source Images > Art Explosion > Graffiti Images folder.

**3** Drag it into your Vector Paint comp as the bottom layer.

**4** Go to Layer > New > Adjustment Layer. Context click on the Adjustment Layer and go to Effect > Distort > Displacement Map. You must always apply the Displacement Map filter to the layer which you want to apply the distortion to. In this case, we want to apply the effect to both the Outline layer and the Fill layer, the Adjustment layer will work nicely for this, meaning that I only have to apply the filter once.

**5** In the Effect Controls window, select the Brick Texture062.jpg layer as the Displacement Map layer. This is the layer that you wish to take the distortion from. Notice that the graffiti text is immediately distorted, it's a little over the top so we'll use the controls to calm it down a little.

**6** Underneath this you will see another two drop down menus for choosing the value used for the distortion. Choose Luminance for both Horizontal and Vertical values.

**7** Change the Max Horizontal Displacement to 3 and the Max Vertical Displacement to –3.

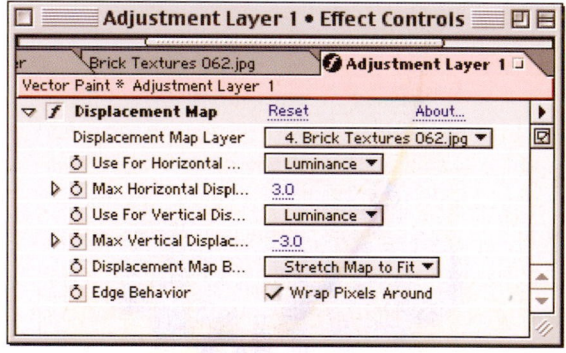

OK, the text is now distorted as if it has been painted upon a rough surface but it is still a flat, even color. If it were on a real brick wall, the shadows created by the dents and grooves in the brick would show through the paint as well as the wall. We'll use some blending modes to recreate this effect.

**8** Drag the Brick Textures062.jpg layer up to the top of the Timeline so that it covers the other layers and is no longer affected by the Adjustment layer.

**9** In the Modes Panel, click in the Preserve Underlying Transparency checkbox. Notice that, as you do, the layer is trimmed to fit exactly around the solid areas of the layers below it in the Timeline. With this checked, all areas of transparency underneath this layer will be preserved. This layer will only be opaque in areas which are sitting over other opaque areas below.

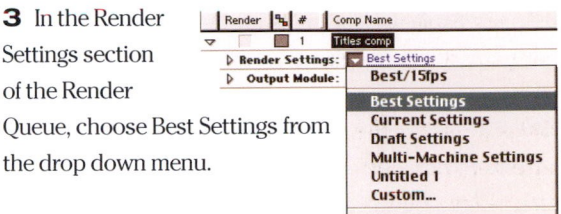

**10** Change the Layer mode to Hard Light to blend the layers together, allowing the brick texture to show through the paint.

**11** In order to just brighten the image up a little bit more, select the Fill layer and then hit Command + D to duplicate it. Drag it to the top of the Timeline and change it's Layer Mode to Color Burn.

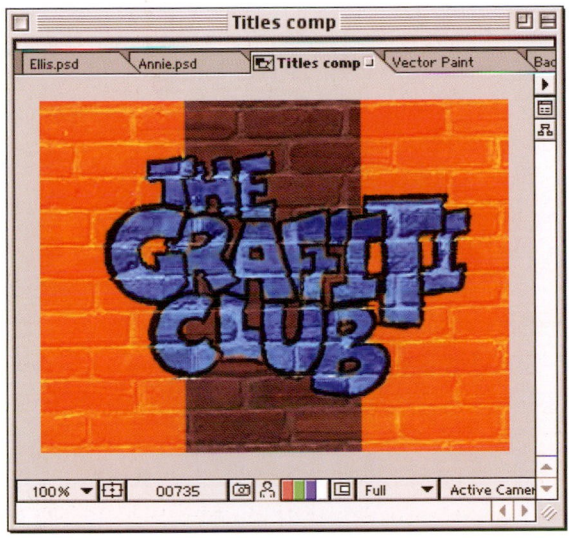

**12** Go back to the Titles comp and preview your finished comp.

## rendering your movie – part one

**1** Save your project into your Creative After Effects > Type Chapter folder as Graffiti10.aep.

So, we've now completed this project, it's finally finished so we can render it out as a finished movie. You saw in the first chapter how to render out a movie using the Make Movie command in the main menu, this allowed us to have access to the Render Queue window. You can also use the *Add to Render Queue* command in the Composition menu to do the same job.

**2** With the Timeline or Comp window active, go to Composition > Add to Render Queue.

**3** In the Render Settings section of the Render Queue, choose Best Settings from the drop down menu.

**4** Move to the Output Module section and click on the word 'Lossless' to bring up the Output module Settings window. Check the *Import Into Project When Done* checkbox.

**5** Check the *Audio Output* checkbox and change the audio settings to 22.050khz; 16 bit; Mono. Click OK to leave.

**6** Under *Output To:* click on the words *Not Yet Specified*, and in the *Output Movie To* dialog box, name your movie, Graffiti.mov and save it into your Creative After Effects folder.

**7** Click on the Render button to render your finished movie to the hard disk. Remember that you can open up the *Current Render Details* to watch the movies progress.

**8** When the movie has finished rendering, go back to the Project window where a copy of the rendered movie will be. Double-click the movie and play it back before moving on to the next section.

# seattle evening news – adding texture

OK, time to put the finishing touches to our Seattle Evening News project. It's always a good idea to get the movement of your animation right before moving on to the next stage which is adding texture and shadow. Texture and shadow will give the text layers more depth and definition but will also take longer to render, hence the fact that we leave these finishing touches till the last possible moment.

In a real life project I would probably have experimented with these textures before I reached this stage (actually, I did!). Don't forget that a lot of experimentation is carried out before you see the final design that somebody has executed. Many people seem to think that great designs are arrived at in moments of sheer inspiration on the part of the designer; one flick of a button and there it is, the perfect design. It really doesn't work that way I'm afraid. For every one good design idea, there have probably been scores trashed in despair before reaching that moment of (almost!) satisfaction. The point I am trying to make is that you must try out as many ideas as you can to arrive at the best solution.

After trying out different techniques on these layers of text I decided that a cold but sophisticated chrome-like finish would work well in contrast with the warm-colored background. There are several ways of creating a chrome finish in After Effects.

**1** Open SeattleNews06.aep from the Training > Projects > Chapter 16 folder.

Make sure that you have the Titles comp open in front of you; notice that there are three layers above the background layer, we need to give the same treatment to all three layers. This is another example of when Pre-Composing comes in very handy; it would be much easier to apply changes to all three layers as a unit rather than applying individual effects to each layer.

**2** Select the top three layers in the Timeline (Seattle Composition; Evening Composition & News Composition) and then hit Command + Shift + C or go to Layer > Pre-Compose.

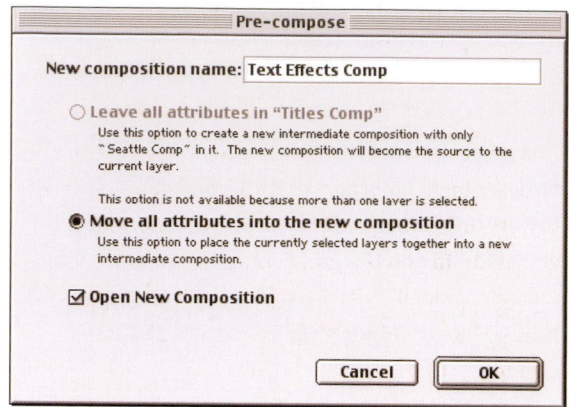

**3** In the Pre-Compose dialog box change the New Composition Name to Text Effects Comp; check that Open New Composition is checked and then click OK.

Again, your layers are grouped together in to a new Composition, which now appears as a single layer within your currently active Composition.

**4** Click on the Text Effects Composition tab at the top of the Timeline to make it the active comp and then make sure that the Current-Time Marker is at the beginning of your Composition by hitting the Home key on your keyboard.

**5** Hit Command + I or go to File > Import > File. In the Import File dialog box, hit the Find button and then type in LA138 and hit OK, After Effects should find the appropriate file on your hard disk for you. (If not, the file is in Training > Projects > Source Movies > Artbeats).

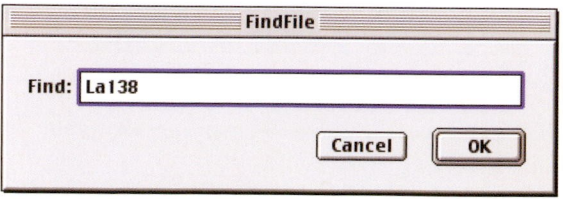

**6** In the Project window, select LA138.mov and then hit Command + / to bring the file into your Composition as the top layer.

**7** RAM Preview the movie file; we are going to use this footage of water to give our text a moving chrome texture.

This piece of royalty-free footage comes from Artbeats Inc. and is part of the Liquid Ambience set. Royalty- free footage like this is a real time-saver when working on the job. Footage companies like Artbeats specialize in supplying you with high-quality footage which would otherwise be very hard to get hold of.

It would be possible to re-create this sort of effect by using a solid layer with Fractal Noise and Caustics applied but using royalty-free textures and backgrounds can free you up to concentrate on the more crucial aspects of the design like animation and typography.

You'll notice that the layer is too short to stretch the whole length of the Composition. This isn't a problem, we can time-stretch the layer and add frame blending to it to increase the amount of time we have. Doing this will have the effect of slowing the footage down but, luckily this suits the effect I want to achieve in this instance. At the moment the water is moving to fast so slowing it down will work well.

**8** Click on the Expand/Collapse Duration 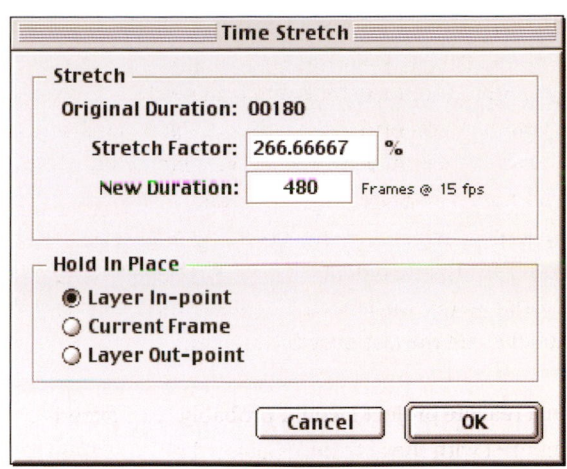 Panel button at the bottom/center of the Timeline; this will open up all the controls needed for numerically adjusting the In-point, Out-point, Duration and Time Stretch for your layer.

**9** Click on the Duration value to bring up the Time Stretch dialog box and, in the Duration field, type in 480 (the length of our Composition). Make sure that you have the Hold In Place set to Layer In-point, this will ensure that the layer is stretched from the beginning of your Composition to the end. Click OK to leave the box.

**10** Close up the Time Stretch panel by clicking the Open/Collapse button again.

**11** RAM Preview the Composition again; notice that the movie is playing back quite jittery. A movie only has so many frames so when you Time Stretch a movie After Effects has to repeat frames to fill in the gaps. To overcome this problem After Effects can perform what's known as Frame Blending on your layer. Frame Blending is a process where After Effects creates new intermediate frames to blend between the existing ones. It does this by taking the two frames at either side of the current frame and creating a blend between them by combining half of each frame.

**12** In the Switches panel, click on the Frame Blending switch to tell After Effects that you want it to perform Frame Blending for this layer. When using Frame Blending you also need to enable frame blending for the whole Composition.

**13** Frame Blending will not take place till you enable it for the whole Composition, to do this you need to activate the Enable Frame Blending Composition switch.

**14** Click the Enable Frame Blending switch at the top of the Timeline and then RAM Preview the results; you will now see that the movie plays back in a much smoother way.

To make this movie look more like chrome we need to get rid of the color from it. The easiest way would be to reduce the saturation for the layer but this tends to deaden the image, making it flat and lifeless. Remember that all RGB images consist of three separate grayscale images; a Red channel; Green channel and a Blue channel. If you look at the three channels of most images you'll find that one contains more of the contrast information than the others.

**15** Click on the Channel buttons at the bottom of the Composition window one by one to see the different channels displayed. Notice that the Blue channel contains significantly more contrast than the others, it would make a very good chrome texture for our text. In the Effects menu we have a Channel menu which is dedicated to helping you play around with the channel information within your images. There are some fantastic tools in here for creating some great effects; it's a menu that is often overlooked but contains an awful lot of power. We'll look at one of those effects now, the Shift Channels filter.

**16** Context-click on LA138.mov in the Timeline and go to Effect > Channel > Shift Channels.

This filter allows you to swap around the Channels of an image or movie. At its default setting, it will take the layers Alpha information from the Alpha channel within your image; Red will be taken from the Red channel; Blue from the Blue channel and Green from the Green channel. In other words, it will not change anything unless you adjust the settings.

Each of the Channels has a drop down menu where you can choose to take any channel's information from another channel within the same image. In other words if we take all of our channel's information from the Blue channel we should end up with an image containing only information from the original Blue channel.

**17** In the Effect Controls window, click on the Take Red From menu and choose Blue from the menu. Repeat this for the Take Green From menu.

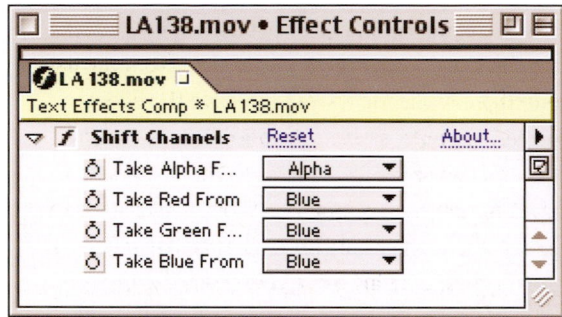

**18** You should now have an image, which looks exactly like the Blue channel of the original layer. If you click on the Display Channel buttons at the bottom of the Composition window again, you will see that all three color channels now look the same.

**19** So, how do we apply this texture to our text layers? That's easy. Move to frame 428, toggle the visibility on and off for the LA138.mov so that you can see all of the layers in their final position. Finish with the LA138.mov visible.

**20** In the Modes panel click in the checkbox underneath the Preserve Underlying Transparency switch. This switch will show the current 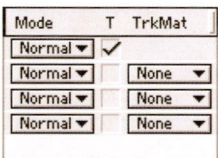 layer only where there are solid areas of Alpha information underneath. In other words, the selected layer will not show in areas which are currently transparent, *preserving the transparency* in those areas.

**21** Click back on the Titles Comp tab so that you can see how the changes affect the finished article. The text layers are far too dark and dull as they are so we need to lighten the colors without losing the contrast which will give us a chrome look.

**22** Once you've Compared the Compositions click back on the Text Effects Composition tab to make that the active Composition. One way to make the text look more metallic is to use a blending mode.

**23** In the modes panel, click on the Mode menu for the LA138.mov and choose Hard Light from the list. Hard light applied to a layer will have the effect of increasing contrast and saturation in the underlying layer, this gives a similar effect to shining a powerful light through the layer onto the layer below. Because the layer below is white, this will increase the very bright areas, creating more contrast but will also soften the midtones.

**24** With the Layer selected, hit the T key to bring up the LA138.mov layers Opacity property. This is looking more metallic now but is still too dark; we'll decrease the transparency of the layer to lessen its effect on the layer below it.

**25** Scrub the Opacity value down to about 75%. You can keep toggling back and forwards between the two comps to Compare your results as you go.

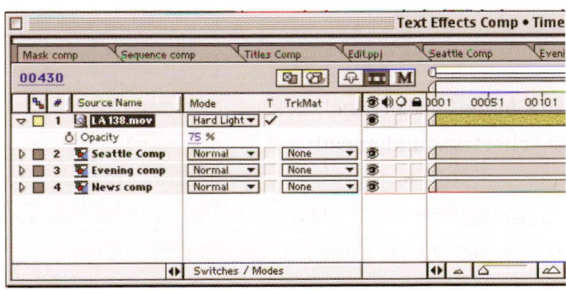

**26** The other way you can change the brightness and contrast of the layer is to use the Brightness & Contrast effect.

This is the same as the equivalent Photoshop filter of the same name with the difference that it can be animated over time. The brightness and contrast of an image can be adjusted separately using this filter.

**27** With the layer still selected, go to Effect > Adjust > Brightness & Contrast. Change the Brightness setting to 20.

**28** Click back on the Titles Composition to see what the text now looks like; in my opinion there is not enough definition on the text layers, they look too flat and have no real depth. We'll use the Drop Shadow Effect to make it look as though the layers have depth and definition.

**29** Context-click on the Text Effects layer in the Titles Composition's Timeline and go to Effect > Perspective > Drop Shadow. In the Effect Controls window change the Opacity to 75%.

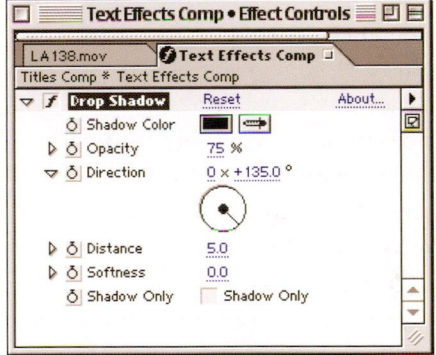

# rendering your movie – part two

**1** Reset your work area so that it covers the whole comp and then go to Composition > Add to Render Queue (Command + Shift + /). This time, we'll render out two different versions of the same movie. When a project is finished, I usually render out a copy of the movie at the best quality with no compression, this way I have a perfect copy of the movie that I can reformat at any time and for any use, simply by running it through Media Cleaner Pro (http://www.media100.com) or running it again through After Effects.

## output templates

When I deliver my final movies to my clients, I usually provide them with a totally uncompressed version for their archives. Because most of my movies are pretty short, I can usually fit them uncompressed onto a CD which is a great, cheap and easy way for me to deliver my material. The client can then reformat the movie for any purpose required. Alternatively, I can format the movie for any editing system by simply installing the required codec onto my system and rendering out from After Effects using the appropriate settings.

**2** In the Render Queue window, choose Best Settings from the Render Settings drop down menu.

**3** In the Output Module drop down menu, choose Make Template. After Effects allows you to set up templates for your most commonly used settings.

**4** In the Output Module Templates dialog box, type in None as the new template name. We'll set up a template for using no compression on output.

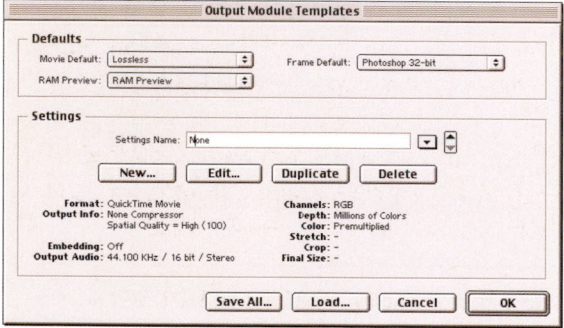

**5** Hit the Edit button to bring up the Output Module Settings dialog box which you will already be familiar with. At the top of the window, check the Import Into Project When Done checkbox.

**6** In the Audio Output section, check the Audio Output checkbox to enable the output of audio from your comp. Make sure that the settings are at 44.100KHz; 16 bit; Stereo.

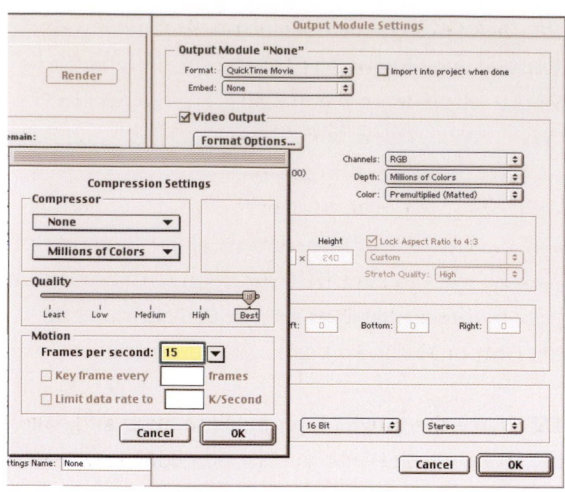

**7** Click on the format options button to open up the Compression settings dialog box and change the compressor to None. With this setting, After Effects will use no compression at all on your movies. Click OK to leave the compression Settings dialog box and then click OK again, in the Output Module Settings, to go back to your Output module Templates dialog box.

**8** In the Defaults section at the top, click on the Movie Default drop down menu and choose None from the list, this will ensure that the settings that you have just determined will be the default settings used when rendering out a movie from After Effects. Notice that there are separate settings for Frame output and RAM Previews.

**9** Finally, to save the settings as a file which can then be transferred to other systems or simply kept as a backup, hit the Save All button at the bottom of the Output Module Templates box.

**10** Save the Output Module Template as None.aom into your Creative After Effects folder. I normally save all of my Templates into an After Effects Render Templates folder on my hard drive. You can also build and save custom templates for your render settings, it's a great time saver if there are specific settings that you use time and time again.

**11** Click OK to leave the Output Module Templates dialog box and then look in the Output Module drop down menu again, notice that the None option is now at the top of the list.

We've chosen our movie settings, now we need to name our movie and determine where on our hard disk we want to save it. In the Output To section, click on the words, Not Yet Specified to open up the Output Movie To box.

**12** Name the movie, UncompNews.mov and save it into your Creative After Effects folder. It will help you enormously if you stick to the same naming convention for all movies of the same type. I always prefix my uncompressed movies with 'Uncomp', this way, it's easy to group them together when performing searches.

### rendering multiple items

In here, you can set up several items to render in sequence, hence the name Render Queue window. You can select multiple comps in the Project window and send them to the Render Queue as we did before or you can duplicate the items directly in the render queue.

**13** Select the *Titles Comp* item in the Render Queue by clicking on its name. Hit Command + D to duplicate the item.

**14** Click on the Render Settings drop down menu and choose Custom from the list.

**15** In the Render Settings box, change the Resolution setting to Half and then in the *Use This Frame Rate* box, type in 10. Here, we are going to output a low-res movie to email to our client for approval. The Render Settings box is also where you would set up your interlacing options when outputting for TV or video. Notice the Field Render section where you can choose the correct field order for your footage.

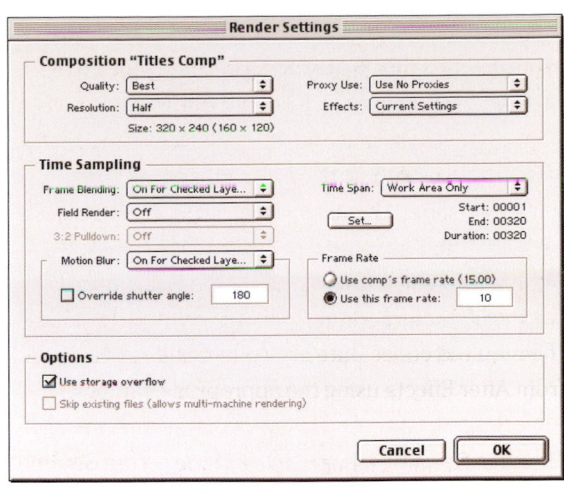

**16** In the Output Module section, click on the word None to open up the Output Module Settings box.

**17** Click on the Format Options button and, in the Compression Settings box, change the Compressor to Sorenson. Change the Quality slider to Medium and then click OK to leave.

**18** Click on the Audio Output checkbox, then change the drop down menus to 11.025 KHz; 8 Bit; Mono. Dropping the quality of the audio and video settings will greatly reduce the file sizes.

**19** Click on the *Output To* option, which reads, *Not Yet Specified* and save your movie into your Creative After Effects folder as LowResNews.mov.

When you Duplicate a Render Queue item like this After Effects will render two separate movies. There is another option for situations when you want to render out two versions of the same movie, with different output formats. You can do this by adding a new Output module to the movie, this allows you to render out multiple output formats simultaneously, saving you time when rendering.

**20** With the second Item in the queue still selected, go to Composition > Add Output Module. A new Output module will appear under the first one.

**21** Click on the word, None, beside the Output Module drop down menu to open the Output Module Settings box.

**22** Change the Format options so that you are using the Cinepak codec at Medium Quality. Change the Audio settings to 22.050 KHz, 16 bit; Mono. Click OK to leave.

**23** Now that you have set up your Render Queue, simply press down the Caps Lock key to lock the display in the Comp window and then hit the Render button to begin rendering your finished movies.

**24** If you open up the current Render Details whilst the second queue item is rendering, you will see that After Effects is rendering two movies simultaneously. Well, to be precise, it's rendering the movie once and then compressing and writing it to disk twice! This method is extremely useful for comparing the results of the different codecs on a piece of footage.

**25** Compare the three movies for file size versus quality and then save your finished project as SeattleNews07b.aep into your Creative After Effects > Type Chapter folder.

This project could easily be updated with new footage by simply replacing the Edit.ppj comp layer with a new Premiere edit containing footage of other cities. The text is also easily updated by clicking on the Basic Text Options and replacing the words. You could even save the Basic Text plug-in as a favorite effect for use in another project.

**26** Have a go at redeveloping this into a news program for your own area. You can use any footage found on the CD or you can add your own.

## recap

OK, so you should have completed all of the tutorials in this book, it's now time for you to take what you've learned and develop your own project to a finished state.

By this time you should have built up a fair amount of work. In your Creative After Effects folder there should be a whole host of projects and movies that you can use in your finished project, some of you may have even started developing these into a finished piece already, if so, keep up the good work.

There are also loads more bits and pieces for you to look at on the CD. The Extras folder contains technical information, more tutorials and projects for you to experiment with. The Free stuff folder contains lots of free plug-ins, kindly donated by the plug-in companies, have a play around with them to see what you can come up with. There's also a demos folder which contains demo versions of some great applications and plug-ins that I simply couldn't live without, see what you think of them. Also in here is the Free Footage folder, which, together with the three Source folders (Movies, Images and Sounds) provides you with stacks of inspiring raw materials for you to go wild with!

You should also check on the website regularly at;

http//www.angie.abel.co.uk/book.html

Paul and I will be updating this website with new tutorials, information and revisions on a regular basis. There are also links in here to other useful sites and mailing lists, where you can post questions and opinions to some of the most experienced After Effects users on the planet.

I'd like to finish by thanking you for buying this book and following these tutorials, I hope you've found them useful and informative and hope that you get as much pleasure from using After Effects as I have done over the years. Happy keyframing!

# Index

Creative After Effects